Kubernetes

Kubernetes
in Action

MARKO LUKŠA

MANNING

SHELTER ISLAND

For online information and ordering of this and other Manning books, please visit www.manning.com. The publisher offers discounts on this book when ordered in quantity. For more information, please contact

    Special Sales Department
    Manning Publications Co.
    20 Baldwin Road
    PO Box 761
    Shelter Island, NY 11964
    Email: orders@manning.com

Manning Publications Co.
20 Baldwin Road
PO Box 761
Shelter Island, NY 11964

Development editor: Elesha Hyde
Review editor: Aleksandar Dragosavljević
Technical development editor: Jeanne Boyarsky
Project editor: Kevin Sullivan
Copyeditor: Katie Petito
Proofreader: Melody Dolab
Technical proofreader: Antonio Magnaghi
Illustrator: Chuck Larson
Typesetter: Dennis Dalinnik
Cover designer: Marija Tudor

ISBN: 9781617293726
Printed in the United States of America
5 6 7 8 9 10 – SP – 22 21 20 19 18

To my parents,
who have always put their children's needs above their own

brief contents

contents

preface

After working at Red Hat for a few years, in late 2014 I was assigned to a newly-established team called Cloud Enablement. Our task was to bring the company's range of middleware products to the OpenShift Container Platform, which was then being developed on top of Kubernetes. At that time, Kubernetes was still in its infancy—version 1.0 hadn't even been released yet.

Our team had to get to know the ins and outs of Kubernetes quickly to set a proper direction for our software and take advantage of everything Kubernetes had to offer. When faced with a problem, it was hard for us to tell if we were doing things wrong or merely hitting one of the early Kubernetes bugs.

Both Kubernetes and my understanding of it have come a long way since then. When I first started using it, most people hadn't even heard of Kubernetes. Now, virtually every software engineer knows about it, and it has become one of the fastest-growing and most-widely-adopted ways of running applications in both the cloud and on-premises datacenters.

In my first month of dealing with Kubernetes, I wrote a two-part blog post about how to run a JBoss WildFly application server cluster in OpenShift/Kubernetes. At the time, I never could have imagined that a simple blog post would ultimately lead the people at Manning to contact me about whether I would like to write a book about Kubernetes. Of course, I couldn't say no to such an offer, even though I was sure they'd approached other people as well and would ultimately pick someone else.

And yet, here we are. After more than a year and a half of writing and researching, the book is done. It's been an awesome journey. Writing a book about a technology is absolutely the best way to get to know it in much greater detail than you'd learn as just a user. As my knowledge of Kubernetes has expanded during the process and Kubernetes itself has evolved, I've constantly gone back to previous chapters I've written and added additional information. I'm a perfectionist, so I'll never really be absolutely satisfied with the book, but I'm happy to hear that a lot of readers of the Manning Early Access Program (MEAP) have found it to be a great guide to Kubernetes.

My aim is to get the reader to understand the technology itself and teach them how to use the tooling to effectively and efficiently develop and deploy apps to Kubernetes clusters. In the book, I don't put much emphasis on how to actually set up and maintain a proper highly available Kubernetes cluster, but the last part should give readers a very solid understanding of what such a cluster consists of and should allow them to easily comprehend additional resources that deal with this subject.

I hope you'll enjoy reading it, and that it teaches you how to get the most out of the awesome system that is Kubernetes.

acknowledgments

Before I started writing this book, I had no clue how many people would be involved in bringing it from a rough manuscript to a published piece of work. This means there are a lot of people to thank.

First, I'd like to thank Erin Twohey for approaching me about writing this book, and Michael Stephens from Manning, who had full confidence in my ability to write it from day one. His words of encouragement early on really motivated me and kept me motivated throughout the last year and a half.

I would also like to thank my initial development editor Andrew Warren, who helped me get my first chapter out the door, and Elesha Hyde, who took over from Andrew and worked with me all the way to the last chapter. Thank you for bearing with me, even though I'm a difficult person to deal with, as I tend to drop off the radar fairly regularly.

I would also like to thank Jeanne Boyarsky, who was the first reviewer to read and comment on my chapters while I was writing them. Jeanne and Elesha were instrumental in making the book as nice as it hopefully is. Without their comments, the book could never have received such good reviews from external reviewers and readers.

I'd like to thank my technical proofreader, Antonio Magnaghi, and of course all my external reviewers: Al Krinker, Alessandro Campeis, Alexander Myltsev, Csaba Sari, David DiMaria, Elias Rangel, Erisk Zelenka, Fabrizio Cucci, Jared Duncan, Keith Donaldson, Michael Bright, Paolo Antinori, Peter Perlepes, and Tiklu Ganguly. Their positive comments kept me going at times when I worried my writing was utterly awful and completely useless. On the other hand, their constructive criticism helped improve sections that I'd quickly thrown together without enough effort. Thank you for pointing out the hard-to-understand sections and suggesting ways of improving the book. Also, thank you for asking the right questions, which made me realize I was wrong about two or three things in the initial versions of the manuscript.

I also need to thank readers who bought the early version of the book through Manning's MEAP program and voiced their comments in the online forum or reached out to me directly—especially Vimal Kansal, Paolo Patierno, and Roland Huß, who noticed quite a few inconsistencies and other mistakes. And I would like to thank everyone at Manning who has been involved in getting this book published. Before I finish, I also need to thank my colleague and high school friend Aleš Justin, who brought me to Red Hat, and my wonderful colleagues from the Cloud Enablement team. If I hadn't been at Red Hat or in the team, I wouldn't have been the one to write this book.

Lastly, I would like to thank my wife and my son, who were way too understanding and supportive over the last 18 months, while I was locked in my office instead of spending time with them.

Thank you all!

about this book

Kubernetes in Action aims to make you a proficient user of Kubernetes. It teaches you virtually all the concepts you need to understand to effectively develop and run applications in a Kubernetes environment.

Before diving into Kubernetes, the book gives an overview of container technologies like Docker, including how to build containers, so that even readers who haven't used these technologies before can get up and running. It then slowly guides you through most of what you need to know about Kubernetes—from basic concepts to things hidden below the surface.

Who should read this book

The book focuses primarily on application developers, but it also provides an overview of managing applications from the operational perspective. It's meant for anyone interested in running and managing containerized applications on more than just a single server.

Both beginner and advanced software engineers who want to learn about container technologies and orchestrating multiple related containers at scale will gain the expertise necessary to develop, containerize, and run their applications in a Kubernetes environment.

No previous exposure to either container technologies or Kubernetes is required. The book explains the subject matter in a progressively detailed manner, and doesn't use any application source code that would be too hard for non-expert developers to understand.

Readers, however, should have at least a basic knowledge of programming, computer networking, and running basic commands in Linux, and an understanding of well-known computer protocols like HTTP.

How this book is organized: a roadmap

This book has three parts that cover 18 chapters.

Part 1 gives a short introduction to Docker and Kubernetes, how to set up a Kubernetes cluster, and how to run a simple application in it. It contains two chapters:

- Chapter 1 explains what Kubernetes is, how it came to be, and how it helps to solve today's problems of managing applications at scale.
- Chapter 2 is a hands-on tutorial on how to build a container image and run it in a Kubernetes cluster. It also explains how to run a local single-node Kubernetes cluster and a proper multi-node cluster in the cloud.

Part 2 introduces the key concepts you must understand to run applications in Kubernetes. The chapters are as follows:

- Chapter 3 introduces the fundamental building block in Kubernetes—the pod—and explains how to organize pods and other Kubernetes objects through labels.
- Chapter 4 teaches you how Kubernetes keeps applications healthy by automatically restarting containers. It also shows how to properly run managed pods, horizontally scale them, make them resistant to failures of cluster nodes, and run them at a predefined time in the future or periodically.
- Chapter 5 shows how pods can expose the service they provide to clients running both inside and outside the cluster. It also shows how pods running in the cluster can discover and access services, regardless of whether they live in or out of the cluster.
- Chapter 6 explains how multiple containers running in the same pod can share files and how you can manage persistent storage and make it accessible to pods.
- Chapter 7 shows how to pass configuration data and sensitive information like credentials to apps running inside pods.
- Chapter 8 describes how applications can get information about the Kubernetes environment they're running in and how they can talk to Kubernetes to alter the state of the cluster.
- Chapter 9 introduces the concept of a Deployment and explains the proper way of running and updating applications in a Kubernetes environment.
- Chapter 10 introduces a dedicated way of running stateful applications, which usually require a stable identity and state.

Part 3 dives deep into the internals of a Kubernetes cluster, introduces some additional concepts, and reviews everything you've learned in the first two parts from a higher perspective. This is the last group of chapters:

- Chapter 11 goes beneath the surface of Kubernetes and explains all the components that make up a Kubernetes cluster and what each of them does. It also explains how pods communicate through the network and how services perform load balancing across multiple pods.

- Chapter 12 explains how to secure your Kubernetes API server, and by extension the cluster, using authentication and authorization.
- Chapter 13 teaches you how pods can access the node's resources and how a cluster administrator can prevent pods from doing that.
- Chapter 14 dives into constraining the computational resources each application is allowed to consume, configuring the applications' Quality of Service guarantees, and monitoring the resource usage of individual applications. It also teaches you how to prevent users from consuming too many resources.
- Chapter 15 discusses how Kubernetes can be configured to automatically scale the number of running replicas of your application, and how it can also increase the size of your cluster when your current number of cluster nodes can't accept any additional applications.
- Chapter 16 shows how to ensure pods are scheduled only to certain nodes or how to prevent them from being scheduled to others. It also shows how to make sure pods are scheduled together or how to prevent that from happening.
- Chapter 17 teaches you how you should develop your applications to make them good citizens of your cluster. It also gives you a few pointers on how to set up your development and testing workflows to reduce friction during development.
- Chapter 18 shows you how you can extend Kubernetes with your own custom objects and how others have done it and created enterprise-class application platforms.

As you progress through these chapters, you'll not only learn about the individual Kubernetes building blocks, but also progressively improve your knowledge of using the kubectl command-line tool.

About the code

While this book doesn't contain a lot of actual source code, it does contain a lot of manifests of Kubernetes resources in YAML format and shell commands along with their outputs. All of this is formatted in a `fixed-width font like this` to separate it from ordinary text.

Shell commands are mostly **in bold**, to clearly separate them from their output, but sometimes only the most important parts of the command or parts of the command's output are in bold for emphasis. In most cases, the command output has been reformatted to make it fit into the limited space in the book. Also, because the Kubernetes CLI tool `kubectl` is constantly evolving, newer versions may print out more information than what's shown in the book. Don't be confused if they don't match exactly.

Listings sometimes include a line-continuation marker (➡) to show that a line of text wraps to the next line. They also include annotations, which highlight and explain the most important parts.

Within text paragraphs, some very common elements such as Pod, Replication-Controller, ReplicaSet, DaemonSet, and so forth are set in regular font to avoid over-proliferation of code font and help readability. In some places, "Pod" is capitalized to refer to the Pod resource, and lowercased to refer to the actual group of running containers.

All the samples in the book have been tested with Kubernetes version 1.8 running in Google Kubernetes Engine and in a local cluster run with Minikube. The complete source code and YAML manifests can be found at https://github.com/luksa/kubernetes-in-action or downloaded from the publisher's website at www.manning.com/books/kubernetes-in-action.

Book forum

Purchase of *Kubernetes in Action* includes free access to a private web forum run by Manning Publications where you can make comments about the book, ask technical questions, and receive help from the author and from other users. To access the forum, go to https://forums.manning.com/forums/kubernetes-in-action. You can also learn more about Manning's forums and the rules of conduct at https://forums.manning.com/forums/about.

Manning's commitment to our readers is to provide a venue where a meaningful dialogue between individual readers and between readers and the author can take place. It is not a commitment to any specific amount of participation on the part of the author, whose contribution to the forum remains voluntary (and unpaid). We suggest you try asking the author some challenging questions lest his interest stray! The forum and the archives of previous discussions will be accessible from the publisher's website as long as the book is in print.

Other online resources

You can find a wide range of additional Kubernetes resources at the following locations:

- The Kubernetes website at https://kubernetes.io
- The Kubernetes Blog, which regularly posts interesting info (http://blog.kubernetes.io)
- The Kubernetes community's Slack channel at http://slack.k8s.io
- The Kubernetes and Cloud Native Computing Foundation's YouTube channels:
  - https://www.youtube.com/channel/UCZ2bu0qutTOM0tHYa_jkIwg
  - https://www.youtube.com/channel/UCvqbFHwN-nwalWPjPUKpvTA

To gain a deeper understanding of individual topics or even to help contribute to Kubernetes, you can also check out any of the Kubernetes Special Interest Groups (SIGs) at https://github.com/kubernetes/kubernetes/wiki/Special-Interest-Groups-(SIGs).

And, finally, as Kubernetes is open source, there's a wealth of information available in the Kubernetes source code itself. You'll find it at https://github.com/kubernetes/kubernetes and related repositories.

about the author

Marko Lukša is a software engineer with more than 20 years of professional experience developing everything from simple web applications to full ERP systems, frameworks, and middleware software. He took his first steps in programming back in 1985, at the age of six, on a second-hand ZX Spectrum computer his father had bought for him. In primary school, he was the national champion in the Logo programming competition and attended summer coding camps, where he learned to program in Pascal. Since then, he has developed software in a wide range of programming languages.

In high school, he started building dynamic websites when the web was still relatively young. He then moved on to developing software for the healthcare and telecommunications industries at a local company, while studying computer science at the University of Ljubljana, Slovenia. Eventually, he ended up working for Red Hat, initially developing an open source implementation of the Google App Engine API, which utilized Red Hat's JBoss middleware products underneath. He also worked in or contributed to projects like CDI/Weld, Infinispan/JBoss Data-Grid, and others.

Since late 2014, he has been part of Red Hat's Cloud Enablement team, where his responsibilities include staying up-to-date on new developments in Kubernetes and related technologies and ensuring the company's middleware software utilizes the features of Kubernetes and OpenShift to their full potential.

about the cover illustration

The figure on the cover of *Kubernetes in Action* is a "Member of the Divan," the Turkish Council of State or governing body. The illustration is taken from a collection of costumes of the Ottoman Empire published on January 1, 1802, by William Miller of Old Bond Street, London. The title page is missing from the collection and we have been unable to track it down to date. The book's table of contents identifies the figures in both English and French, and each illustration bears the names of two artists who worked on it, both of whom would no doubt be surprised to find their art gracing the front cover of a computer programming book ... 200 years later.

The collection was purchased by a Manning editor at an antiquarian flea market in the "Garage" on West 26th Street in Manhattan. The seller was an American based in Ankara, Turkey, and the transaction took place just as he was packing up his stand for the day. The Manning editor didn't have on his person the substantial amount of cash that was required for the purchase, and a credit card and check were both politely turned down. With the seller flying back to Ankara that evening, the situation was getting hopeless. What was the solution? It turned out to be nothing more than an old-fashioned verbal agreement sealed with a handshake. The seller proposed that the money be transferred to him by wire, and the editor walked out with the bank information on a piece of paper and the portfolio of images under his arm. Needless to say, we transferred the funds the next day, and we remain grateful and impressed by this unknown person's trust in one of us. It recalls something that might have happened a long time ago. We at Manning celebrate the inventiveness, the initiative, and, yes, the fun of the computer business with book covers based on the rich diversity of regional life of two centuries ago, brought back to life by the pictures from this collection.

Introducing Kubernetes

This chapter covers

- Understanding how software development and deployment has changed over recent years
- Isolating applications and reducing environment differences using containers
- Understanding how containers and Docker are used by Kubernetes
- Making developers' and sysadmins' jobs easier with Kubernetes

Years ago, most software applications were big monoliths, running either as a single process or as a small number of processes spread across a handful of servers. These legacy systems are still widespread today. They have slow release cycles and are updated relatively infrequently. At the end of every release cycle, developers package up the whole system and hand it over to the ops team, who then deploys and monitors it. In case of hardware failures, the ops team manually migrates it to the remaining healthy servers.

Today, these big monolithic legacy applications are slowly being broken down into smaller, independently running components called microservices. Because microservices are decoupled from each other, they can be developed, deployed, updated, and scaled individually. This enables you to change components quickly and as often as necessary to keep up with today's rapidly changing business requirements.

But with bigger numbers of deployable components and increasingly larger data-centers, it becomes increasingly difficult to configure, manage, and keep the whole system running smoothly. It's much harder to figure out where to put each of those components to achieve high resource utilization and thereby keep the hardware costs down. Doing all this manually is hard work. We need automation, which includes automatic scheduling of those components to our servers, automatic configuration, supervision, and failure-handling. This is where Kubernetes comes in.

Kubernetes enables developers to deploy their applications themselves and as often as they want, without requiring any assistance from the operations (ops) team. But Kubernetes doesn't benefit only developers. It also helps the ops team by automat-ically monitoring and rescheduling those apps in the event of a hardware failure. The focus for system administrators (sysadmins) shifts from supervising individual apps to mostly supervising and managing Kubernetes and the rest of the infrastructure, while Kubernetes itself takes care of the apps.

> **NOTE** *Kubernetes* is Greek for pilot or helmsman (the person holding the ship's steering wheel). People pronounce Kubernetes in a few different ways. Many pronounce it as *Koo-ber-nay-tace*, while others pronounce it more like *Koo-ber-netties*. No matter which form you use, people will understand what you mean.

Kubernetes abstracts away the hardware infrastructure and exposes your whole data-center as a single enormous computational resource. It allows you to deploy and run your software components without having to know about the actual servers under-neath. When deploying a multi-component application through Kubernetes, it selects a server for each component, deploys it, and enables it to easily find and communi-cate with all the other components of your application.

This makes Kubernetes great for most on-premises datacenters, but where it starts to shine is when it's used in the largest datacenters, such as the ones built and oper-ated by cloud providers. Kubernetes allows them to offer developers a simple platform for deploying and running any type of application, while not requiring the cloud pro-vider's own sysadmins to know anything about the tens of thousands of apps running on their hardware.

With more and more big companies accepting the Kubernetes model as the best way to run apps, it's becoming the standard way of running distributed apps both in the cloud, as well as on local on-premises infrastructure.

1.1 *Understanding the need for a system like Kubernetes*

Before you start getting to know Kubernetes in detail, let's take a quick look at how the development and deployment of applications has changed in recent years. This change is both a consequence of splitting big monolithic apps into smaller microservices and of the changes in the infrastructure that runs those apps. Understanding these changes will help you better see the benefits of using Kubernetes and container technologies such as Docker.

1.1.1 *Moving from monolithic apps to microservices*

Monolithic applications consist of components that are all tightly coupled together and have to be developed, deployed, and managed as one entity, because they all run as a single OS process. Changes to one part of the application require a redeployment of the whole application, and over time the lack of hard boundaries between the parts results in the increase of complexity and consequential deterioration of the quality of the whole system because of the unconstrained growth of inter-dependencies between these parts.

Running a monolithic application usually requires a small number of powerful servers that can provide enough resources for running the application. To deal with increasing loads on the system, you then either have to vertically scale the servers (also known as scaling up) by adding more CPUs, memory, and other server components, or scale the whole system horizontally, by setting up additional servers and running multiple copies (or replicas) of an application (scaling out). While scaling up usually doesn't require any changes to the app, it gets expensive relatively quickly and in practice always has an upper limit. Scaling out, on the other hand, is relatively cheap hardware-wise, but may require big changes in the application code and isn't always possible—certain parts of an application are extremely hard or next to impossible to scale horizontally (relational databases, for example). If any part of a monolithic application isn't scalable, the whole application becomes unscalable, unless you can split up the monolith somehow.

SPLITTING APPS INTO MICROSERVICES

These and other problems have forced us to start splitting complex monolithic applications into smaller independently deployable components called microservices. Each microservice runs as an independent process (see figure 1.1) and communicates with other microservices through simple, well-defined interfaces (APIs).

Monolithic application   Microservices-based application

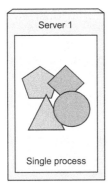
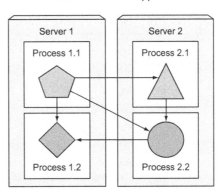

Figure 1.1 Components inside a monolithic application vs. standalone microservices

Microservices communicate through synchronous protocols such as HTTP, over which they usually expose RESTful (REpresentational State Transfer) APIs, or through asynchronous protocols such as AMQP (Advanced Message Queueing Protocol). These protocols are simple, well understood by most developers, and not tied to any specific programming language. Each microservice can be written in the language that's most appropriate for implementing that specific microservice.

Because each microservice is a standalone process with a relatively static external API, it's possible to develop and deploy each microservice separately. A change to one of them doesn't require changes or redeployment of any other service, provided that the API doesn't change or changes only in a backward-compatible way.

SCALING MICROSERVICES

Scaling microservices, unlike monolithic systems, where you need to scale the system as a whole, is done on a per-service basis, which means you have the option of scaling only those services that require more resources, while leaving others at their original scale. Figure 1.2 shows an example. Certain components are replicated and run as multiple processes deployed on different servers, while others run as a single application process. When a monolithic application can't be scaled out because one of its parts is unscalable, splitting the app into microservices allows you to horizontally scale the parts that allow scaling out, and scale the parts that don't, vertically instead of horizontally.

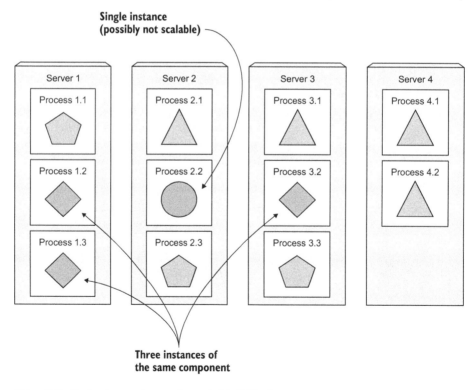

Figure 1.2   Each microservice can be scaled individually.

DEPLOYING MICROSERVICES

As always, microservices also have drawbacks. When your system consists of only a small number of deployable components, managing those components is easy. It's trivial to decide where to deploy each component, because there aren't that many choices. When the number of those components increases, deployment-related decisions become increasingly difficult because not only does the number of deployment combinations increase, but the number of inter-dependencies between the components increases by an even greater factor.

Microservices perform their work together as a team, so they need to find and talk to each other. When deploying them, someone or something needs to configure all of them properly to enable them to work together as a single system. With increasing numbers of microservices, this becomes tedious and error-prone, especially when you consider what the ops/sysadmin teams need to do when a server fails.

Microservices also bring other problems, such as making it hard to debug and trace execution calls, because they span multiple processes and machines. Luckily, these problems are now being addressed with distributed tracing systems such as Zipkin.

UNDERSTANDING THE DIVERGENCE OF ENVIRONMENT REQUIREMENTS

As I've already mentioned, components in a microservices architecture aren't only deployed independently, but are also developed that way. Because of their independence and the fact that it's common to have separate teams developing each component, nothing impedes each team from using different libraries and replacing them whenever the need arises. The divergence of dependencies between application components, like the one shown in figure 1.3, where applications require different versions of the same libraries, is inevitable.

Server running a monolithic app   Server running multiple apps

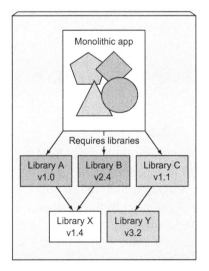 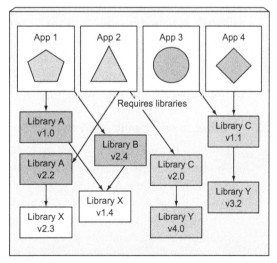

Figure 1.3   Multiple applications running on the same host may have conflicting dependencies.

Deploying dynamically linked applications that require different versions of shared libraries, and/or require other environment specifics, can quickly become a nightmare for the ops team who deploys and manages them on production servers. The bigger the number of components you need to deploy on the same host, the harder it will be to manage all their dependencies to satisfy all their requirements.

1.1.2 *Providing a consistent environment to applications*

Regardless of how many individual components you're developing and deploying, one of the biggest problems that developers and operations teams always have to deal with is the differences in the environments they run their apps in. Not only is there a huge difference between development and production environments, differences even exist between individual production machines. Another unavoidable fact is that the environment of a single production machine will change over time.

These differences range from hardware to the operating system to the libraries that are available on each machine. Production environments are managed by the operations team, while developers often take care of their development laptops on their own. The difference is how much these two groups of people know about system administration, and this understandably leads to relatively big differences between those two systems, not to mention that system administrators give much more emphasis on keeping the system up to date with the latest security patches, while a lot of developers don't care about that as much.

Also, production systems can run applications from multiple developers or development teams, which isn't necessarily true for developers' computers. A production system must provide the proper environment to all applications it hosts, even though they may require different, even conflicting, versions of libraries.

To reduce the number of problems that only show up in production, it would be ideal if applications could run in the exact same environment during development and in production so they have the exact same operating system, libraries, system configuration, networking environment, and everything else. You also don't want this environment to change too much over time, if at all. Also, if possible, you want the ability to add applications to the same server without affecting any of the existing applications on that server.

1.1.3 *Moving to continuous delivery: DevOps and NoOps*

In the last few years, we've also seen a shift in the whole application development process and how applications are taken care of in production. In the past, the development team's job was to create the application and hand it off to the operations team, who then deployed it, tended to it, and kept it running. But now, organizations are realizing it's better to have the same team that develops the application also take part in deploying it and taking care of it over its whole lifetime. This means the developer, QA, and operations teams now need to collaborate throughout the whole process. This practice is called DevOps.

UNDERSTANDING THE BENEFITS

Having the developers more involved in running the application in production leads to them having a better understanding of both the users' needs and issues and the problems faced by the ops team while maintaining the app. Application developers are now also much more inclined to give users the app earlier and then use their feedback to steer further development of the app.

To release newer versions of applications more often, you need to streamline the deployment process. Ideally, you want developers to deploy the applications themselves without having to wait for the ops people. But deploying an application often requires an understanding of the underlying infrastructure and the organization of the hardware in the datacenter. Developers don't always know those details and, most of the time, don't even want to know about them.

LETTING DEVELOPERS AND SYSADMINS DO WHAT THEY DO BEST

Even though developers and system administrators both work toward achieving the same goal of running a successful software application as a service to its customers, they have different individual goals and motivating factors. Developers love creating new features and improving the user experience. They don't normally want to be the ones making sure that the underlying operating system is up to date with all the security patches and things like that. They prefer to leave that up to the system administrators.

The ops team is in charge of the production deployments and the hardware infrastructure they run on. They care about system security, utilization, and other aspects that aren't a high priority for developers. The ops people don't want to deal with the implicit interdependencies of all the application components and don't want to think about how changes to either the underlying operating system or the infrastructure can affect the operation of the application as a whole, but they must.

Ideally, you want the developers to deploy applications themselves without knowing anything about the hardware infrastructure and without dealing with the ops team. This is referred to as *NoOps*. Obviously, you still need someone to take care of the hardware infrastructure, but ideally, without having to deal with peculiarities of each application running on it.

As you'll see, Kubernetes enables us to achieve all of this. By abstracting away the actual hardware and exposing it as a single platform for deploying and running apps, it allows developers to configure and deploy their applications without any help from the sysadmins and allows the sysadmins to focus on keeping the underlying infrastructure up and running, while not having to know anything about the actual applications running on top of it.

1.2 *Introducing container technologies*

In section 1.1 I presented a non-comprehensive list of problems facing today's development and ops teams. While you have many ways of dealing with them, this book will focus on how they're solved with Kubernetes.

Kubernetes uses Linux container technologies to provide isolation of running applications, so before we dig into Kubernetes itself, you need to become familiar with the basics of containers to understand what Kubernetes does itself, and what it offloads to container technologies like *Docker* or *rkt* (pronounced "rock-it").

1.2.1   *Understanding what containers are*

In section 1.1.1 we saw how different software components running on the same machine will require different, possibly conflicting, versions of dependent libraries or have other different environment requirements in general.

When an application is composed of only smaller numbers of large components, it's completely acceptable to give a dedicated Virtual Machine (VM) to each component and isolate their environments by providing each of them with their own operating system instance. But when these components start getting smaller and their numbers start to grow, you can't give each of them their own VM if you don't want to waste hardware resources and keep your hardware costs down. But it's not only about wasting hardware resources. Because each VM usually needs to be configured and managed individually, rising numbers of VMs also lead to wasting human resources, because they increase the system administrators' workload considerably.

ISOLATING COMPONENTS WITH LINUX CONTAINER TECHNOLOGIES

Instead of using virtual machines to isolate the environments of each microservice (or software processes in general), developers are turning to Linux container technologies. They allow you to run multiple services on the same host machine, while not only exposing a different environment to each of them, but also isolating them from each other, similarly to VMs, but with much less overhead.

A process running in a container runs inside the host's operating system, like all the other processes (unlike VMs, where processes run in separate operating systems). But the process in the container is still isolated from other processes. To the process itself, it looks like it's the only one running on the machine and in its operating system.

COMPARING VIRTUAL MACHINES TO CONTAINERS

Compared to VMs, containers are much more lightweight, which allows you to run higher numbers of software components on the same hardware, mainly because each VM needs to run its own set of system processes, which requires additional compute resources in addition to those consumed by the component's own process. A container, on the other hand, is nothing more than a single isolated process running in the host OS, consuming only the resources that the app consumes and without the overhead of any additional processes.

Because of the overhead of VMs, you often end up grouping multiple applications into each VM because you don't have enough resources to dedicate a whole VM to each app. When using containers, you can (and should) have one container for each application, as shown in figure 1.4. The end-result is that you can fit many more applications on the same bare-metal machine.

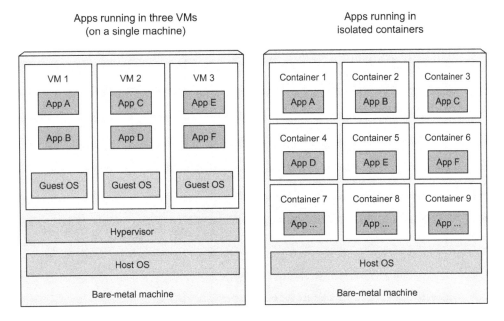

Figure 1.4   Using VMs to isolate groups of applications vs. isolating individual apps with containers

When you run three VMs on a host, you have three completely separate operating systems running on and sharing the same bare-metal hardware. Underneath those VMs is the host's OS and a hypervisor, which divides the physical hardware resources into smaller sets of virtual resources that can be used by the operating system inside each VM. Applications running inside those VMs perform system calls to the guest OS' kernel in the VM, and the kernel then performs x86 instructions on the host's physical CPU through the hypervisor.

NOTE Two types of hypervisors exist. Type 1 hypervisors don't use a host OS, while Type 2 do.

Containers, on the other hand, all perform system calls on the exact same kernel running in the host OS. This single kernel is the only one performing x86 instructions on the host's CPU. The CPU doesn't need to do any kind of virtualization the way it does with VMs (see figure 1.5).

The main benefit of virtual machines is the full isolation they provide, because each VM runs its own Linux kernel, while containers all call out to the same kernel, which can clearly pose a security risk. If you have a limited amount of hardware resources, VMs may only be an option when you have a small number of processes that

Apps running in multiple VMs

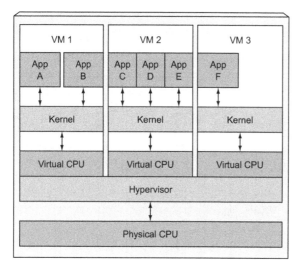

Apps running in isolated containers

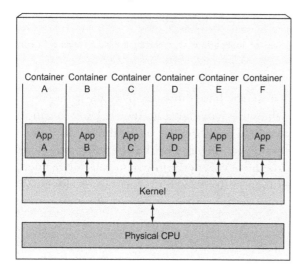

Figure 1.5   The difference between how apps in VMs use the CPU vs. how they use them in containers

you want to isolate. To run greater numbers of isolated processes on the same machine, containers are a much better choice because of their low overhead. Remember, each VM runs its own set of system services, while containers don't, because they all run in the same OS. That also means that to run a container, nothing needs to be booted up, as is the case in VMs. A process run in a container starts up immediately.

INTRODUCING THE MECHANISMS THAT MAKE CONTAINER ISOLATION POSSIBLE

By this point, you're probably wondering how exactly containers can isolate processes if they're running on the same operating system. Two mechanisms make this possible. The first one, *Linux Namespaces*, makes sure each process sees its own personal view of the system (files, processes, network interfaces, hostname, and so on). The second one is *Linux Control Groups (cgroups)*, which limit the amount of resources the process can consume (CPU, memory, network bandwidth, and so on).

ISOLATING PROCESSES WITH LINUX NAMESPACES

By default, each Linux system initially has one single namespace. All system resources, such as filesystems, process IDs, user IDs, network interfaces, and others, belong to the single namespace. But you can create additional namespaces and organize resources across them. When running a process, you run it inside one of those namespaces. The process will only see resources that are inside the same namespace. Well, multiple kinds of namespaces exist, so a process doesn't belong to one namespace, but to one namespace of each kind.

The following kinds of namespaces exist:

- Mount (mnt)
- Process ID (pid)
- Network (net)
- Inter-process communication (ipc)
- UTS
- User ID (user)

Each namespace kind is used to isolate a certain group of resources. For example, the UTS namespace determines what hostname and domain name the process running inside that namespace sees. By assigning two different UTS namespaces to a pair of processes, you can make them see different local hostnames. In other words, to the two processes, it will appear as though they are running on two different machines (at least as far as the hostname is concerned).

Likewise, what Network namespace a process belongs to determines which network interfaces the application running inside the process sees. Each network interface belongs to exactly one namespace, but can be moved from one namespace to another. Each container uses its own Network namespace, and therefore each container sees its own set of network interfaces.

This should give you a basic idea of how namespaces are used to isolate applications running in containers from each other.

LIMITING RESOURCES AVAILABLE TO A PROCESS

The other half of container isolation deals with limiting the amount of system resources a container can consume. This is achieved with cgroups, a Linux kernel feature that limits the resource usage of a process (or a group of processes). A process can't use more than the configured amount of CPU, memory, network bandwidth, and so on. This way, processes cannot hog resources reserved for other processes, which is similar to when each process runs on a separate machine.

1.2.2   *Introducing the Docker container platform*

While container technologies have been around for a long time, they've become more widely known with the rise of the Docker container platform. Docker was the first container system that made containers easily portable across different machines. It simplified the process of packaging up not only the application but also all its libraries and other dependencies, even the whole OS file system, into a simple, portable package that can be used to provision the application to any other machine running Docker.

When you run an application packaged with Docker, it sees the exact filesystem contents that you've bundled with it. It sees the same files whether it's running on your development machine or a production machine, even if it the production server is running a completely different Linux OS. The application won't see anything from the server it's running on, so it doesn't matter if the server has a completely different set of installed libraries compared to your development machine.

For example, if you've packaged up your application with the files of the whole Red Hat Enterprise Linux (RHEL) operating system, the application will believe it's running inside RHEL, both when you run it on your development computer that runs Fedora and when you run it on a server running Debian or some other Linux distribution. Only the kernel may be different.

This is similar to creating a VM image by installing an operating system into a VM, installing the app inside it, and then distributing the whole VM image around and running it. Docker achieves the same effect, but instead of using VMs to achieve app isolation, it uses Linux container technologies mentioned in the previous section to provide (almost) the same level of isolation that VMs do. Instead of using big monolithic VM images, it uses container images, which are usually smaller.

A big difference between Docker-based container images and VM images is that container images are composed of layers, which can be shared and reused across multiple images. This means only certain layers of an image need to be downloaded if the other layers were already downloaded previously when running a different container image that also contains the same layers.

UNDERSTANDING DOCKER CONCEPTS

Docker is a platform for packaging, distributing, and running applications. As we've already stated, it allows you to package your application together with its whole environment. This can be either a few libraries that the app requires or even all the files that are usually available on the filesystem of an installed operating system. Docker makes it possible to transfer this package to a central repository from which it can then be transferred to any computer running Docker and executed there (for the most part, but not always, as we'll soon explain).

Three main concepts in Docker comprise this scenario:

- *Images*—A Docker-based container image is something you package your application and its environment into. It contains the filesystem that will be available to the application and other metadata, such as the path to the executable that should be executed when the image is run.
- *Registries*—A Docker Registry is a repository that stores your Docker images and facilitates easy sharing of those images between different people and computers. When you build your image, you can either run it on the computer you've built it on, or you can *push* (upload) the image to a registry and then *pull* (download) it on another computer and run it there. Certain registries are public, allowing anyone to pull images from it, while others are private, only accessible to certain people or machines.
- *Containers*—A Docker-based container is a regular Linux container created from a Docker-based container image. A running container is a process running on the host running Docker, but it's completely isolated from both the host and all other processes running on it. The process is also resource-constrained, meaning it can only access and use the amount of resources (CPU, RAM, and so on) that are allocated to it.

BUILDING, DISTRIBUTING, AND RUNNING A DOCKER IMAGE

Figure 1.6 shows all three concepts and how they relate to each other. The developer first builds an image and then pushes it to a registry. The image is thus available to anyone who can access the registry. They can then pull the image to any other machine running Docker and run the image. Docker creates an isolated container based on the image and runs the binary executable specified as part of the image.

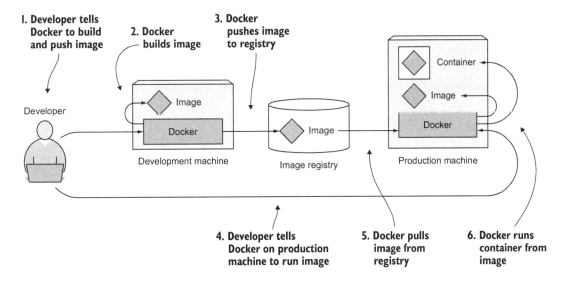

Figure 1.6   Docker images, registries, and containers

COMPARING VIRTUAL MACHINES AND DOCKER CONTAINERS

I've explained how Linux containers are generally like virtual machines, but much more lightweight. Now let's look at how Docker containers specifically compare to virtual machines (and how Docker images compare to VM images). Figure 1.7 again shows the same six applications running both in VMs and as Docker containers.

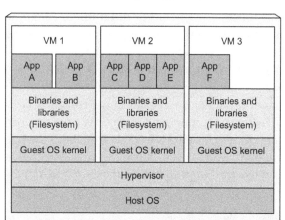

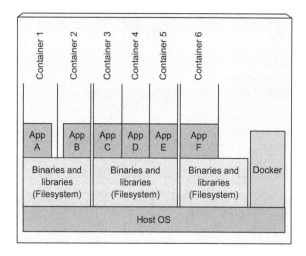

Figure 1.7   Running six apps on three VMs vs. running them in Docker containers

You'll notice that apps A and B have access to the same binaries and libraries both when running in a VM and when running as two separate containers. In the VM, this is obvious, because both apps see the same filesystem (that of the VM). But we said that each container has its own isolated filesystem. How can both app A and app B share the same files?

UNDERSTANDING IMAGE LAYERS

I've already said that Docker images are composed of layers. Different images can contain the exact same layers because every Docker image is built on top of another image and two different images can both use the same parent image as their base. This speeds up the distribution of images across the network, because layers that have already been transferred as part of the first image don't need to be transferred again when transferring the other image.

But layers don't only make distribution more efficient, they also help reduce the storage footprint of images. Each layer is only stored once. Two containers created from two images based on the same base layers can therefore read the same files, but if one of them writes over those files, the other one doesn't see those changes. Therefore, even if they share files, they're still isolated from each other. This works because container image layers are read-only. When a container is run, a new writable layer is created on top of the layers in the image. When the process in the container writes to a file located in one of the underlying layers, a copy of the whole file is created in the top-most layer and the process writes to the copy.

UNDERSTANDING THE PORTABILITY LIMITATIONS OF CONTAINER IMAGES

In theory, a container image can be run on any Linux machine running Docker, but one small caveat exists—one related to the fact that all containers running on a host use the host's Linux kernel. If a containerized application requires a specific kernel version, it may not work on every machine. If a machine runs a different version of the Linux kernel or doesn't have the same kernel modules available, the app can't run on it.

While containers are much more lightweight compared to VMs, they impose certain constraints on the apps running inside them. VMs have no such constraints, because each VM runs its own kernel.

And it's not only about the kernel. It should also be clear that a containerized app built for a specific hardware architecture can only run on other machines that have the same architecture. You can't containerize an application built for the x86 architecture and expect it to run on an ARM-based machine because it also runs Docker. You still need a VM for that.

1.2.3 *Introducing rkt—an alternative to Docker*

Docker was the first container platform that made containers mainstream. I hope I've made it clear that Docker itself doesn't provide process isolation. The actual isolation of containers is done at the Linux kernel level using kernel features such as Linux Namespaces and cgroups. Docker only makes it easy to use those features.

After the success of Docker, the Open Container Initiative (OCI) was born to create open industry standards around container formats and runtime. Docker is part of that initiative, as is *rkt* (pronounced "rock-it"), which is another Linux container engine.

Like Docker, rkt is a platform for running containers. It puts a strong emphasis on security, composability, and conforming to open standards. It uses the OCI container image format and can even run regular Docker container images.

This book focuses on using Docker as the container runtime for Kubernetes, because it was initially the only one supported by Kubernetes. Recently, Kubernetes has also started supporting rkt, as well as others, as the container runtime.

The reason I mention rkt at this point is so you don't make the mistake of thinking Kubernetes is a container orchestration system made specifically for Docker-based containers. In fact, over the course of this book, you'll realize that the essence of Kubernetes isn't orchestrating containers. It's much more. Containers happen to be the best way to run apps on different cluster nodes. With that in mind, let's finally dive into the core of what this book is all about—Kubernetes.

1.3   Introducing Kubernetes

We've already shown that as the number of deployable application components in your system grows, it becomes harder to manage them all. Google was probably the first company that realized it needed a much better way of deploying and managing their software components and their infrastructure to scale globally. It's one of only a few companies in the world that runs hundreds of thousands of servers and has had to deal with managing deployments on such a massive scale. This has forced them to develop solutions for making the development and deployment of thousands of software components manageable and cost-efficient.

1.3.1   Understanding its origins

Through the years, Google developed an internal system called *Borg* (and later a new system called *Omega*), that helped both application developers and system administrators manage those thousands of applications and services. In addition to simplifying the development and management, it also helped them achieve a much higher utilization of their infrastructure, which is important when your organization is that large. When you run hundreds of thousands of machines, even tiny improvements in utilization mean savings in the millions of dollars, so the incentives for developing such a system are clear.

After having kept Borg and Omega secret for a whole decade, in 2014 Google introduced Kubernetes, an open-source system based on the experience gained through Borg, Omega, and other internal Google systems.

1.3.2   Looking at Kubernetes from the top of a mountain

Kubernetes is a software system that allows you to easily deploy and manage containerized applications on top of it. It relies on the features of Linux containers to run heterogeneous applications without having to know any internal details of these applications and without having to manually deploy these applications on each host. Because these apps run in containers, they don't affect other apps running on the same server, which is critical when you run applications for completely different organizations on the same hardware. This is of paramount importance for cloud providers, because they strive for the best possible utilization of their hardware while still having to maintain complete isolation of hosted applications.

Kubernetes enables you to run your software applications on thousands of computer nodes as if all those nodes were a single, enormous computer. It abstracts away the underlying infrastructure and, by doing so, simplifies development, deployment, and management for both development and the operations teams.

Deploying applications through Kubernetes is always the same, whether your cluster contains only a couple of nodes or thousands of them. The size of the cluster makes no difference at all. Additional cluster nodes simply represent an additional amount of resources available to deployed apps.

UNDERSTANDING THE CORE OF WHAT KUBERNETES DOES

Figure 1.8 shows the simplest possible view of a Kubernetes system. The system is composed of a master node and any number of worker nodes. When the developer submits a list of apps to the master, Kubernetes deploys them to the cluster of worker nodes. What node a component lands on doesn't (and shouldn't) matter—neither to the developer nor to the system administrator.

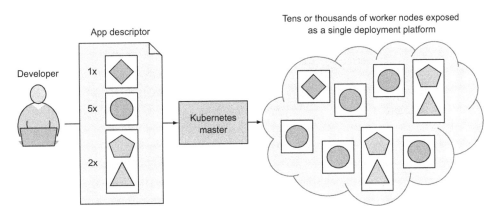

Figure 1.8 Kubernetes exposes the whole datacenter as a single deployment platform.

The developer can specify that certain apps must run together and Kubernetes will deploy them on the same worker node. Others will be spread around the cluster, but they can talk to each other in the same way, regardless of where they're deployed.

HELPING DEVELOPERS FOCUS ON THE CORE APP FEATURES

Kubernetes can be thought of as an operating system for the cluster. It relieves application developers from having to implement certain infrastructure-related services into their apps; instead they rely on Kubernetes to provide these services. This includes things such as service discovery, scaling, load-balancing, self-healing, and even leader election. Application developers can therefore focus on implementing the actual features of the applications and not waste time figuring out how to integrate them with the infrastructure.

HELPING OPS TEAMS ACHIEVE BETTER RESOURCE UTILIZATION
Kubernetes will run your containerized app somewhere in the cluster, provide information to its components on how to find each other, and keep all of them running. Because your application doesn't care which node it's running on, Kubernetes can relocate the app at any time, and by mixing and matching apps, achieve far better resource utilization than is possible with manual scheduling.

1.3.3 *Understanding the architecture of a Kubernetes cluster*

We've seen a bird's-eye view of Kubernetes' architecture. Now let's take a closer look at what a Kubernetes cluster is composed of. At the hardware level, a Kubernetes cluster is composed of many nodes, which can be split into two types:

- The *master* node, which hosts the *Kubernetes Control Plane* that controls and manages the whole Kubernetes system
- Worker *nodes* that run the actual applications you deploy

Figure 1.9 shows the components running on these two sets of nodes. I'll explain them next.

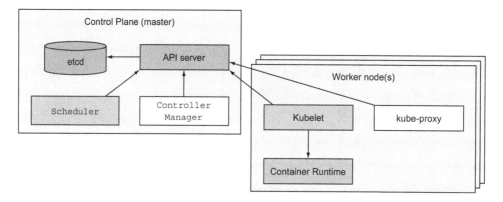

Figure 1.9   The components that make up a Kubernetes cluster

THE CONTROL PLANE
The Control Plane is what controls the cluster and makes it function. It consists of multiple components that can run on a single master node or be split across multiple nodes and replicated to ensure high availability. These components are

- The *Kubernetes API Server*, which you and the other Control Plane components communicate with

- The *Scheduler*, which schedules your apps (assigns a worker node to each deployable component of your application)
- The *Controller Manager*, which performs cluster-level functions, such as replicating components, keeping track of worker nodes, handling node failures, and so on
- *etcd*, a reliable distributed data store that persistently stores the cluster configuration.

The components of the Control Plane hold and control the state of the cluster, but they don't run your applications. This is done by the (worker) nodes.

THE NODES

The worker nodes are the machines that run your containerized applications. The task of running, monitoring, and providing services to your applications is done by the following components:

- Docker, rkt, or another *container runtime*, which runs your containers
- The *Kubelet*, which talks to the API server and manages containers on its node
- The *Kubernetes Service Proxy (kube-proxy)*, which load-balances network traffic between application components

We'll explain all these components in detail in chapter 11. I'm not a fan of explaining how things work before first explaining *what* something does and teaching people to use it. It's like learning to drive a car. You don't want to know what's under the hood. You first want to learn how to drive it from point A to point B. Only after you learn how to do that do you become interested in how a car makes that possible. After all, knowing what's under the hood may someday help you get the car moving again after it breaks down and leaves you stranded at the side of the road.

1.3.4 *Running an application in Kubernetes*

To run an application in Kubernetes, you first need to package it up into one or more container images, push those images to an image registry, and then post a description of your app to the Kubernetes API server.

The description includes information such as the container image or images that contain your application components, how those components are related to each other, and which ones need to be run co-located (together on the same node) and which don't. For each component, you can also specify how many copies (or *replicas*) you want to run. Additionally, the description also includes which of those components provide a service to either internal or external clients and should be exposed through a single IP address and made discoverable to the other components.

UNDERSTANDING HOW THE DESCRIPTION RESULTS IN A RUNNING CONTAINER

When the API server processes your app's description, the Scheduler schedules the specified groups of containers onto the available worker nodes based on computational resources required by each group and the unallocated resources on each node at that moment. The Kubelet on those nodes then instructs the Container Runtime (Docker, for example) to pull the required container images and run the containers.

Examine figure 1.10 to gain a better understanding of how applications are deployed in Kubernetes. The app descriptor lists four containers, grouped into three sets (these sets are called *pods*; we'll explain what they are in chapter 3). The first two pods each contain only a single container, whereas the last one contains two. That means both containers need to run co-located and shouldn't be isolated from each other. Next to each pod, you also see a number representing the number of replicas of each pod that need to run in parallel. After submitting the descriptor to Kubernetes, it will schedule the specified number of replicas of each pod to the available worker nodes. The Kubelets on the nodes will then tell Docker to pull the container images from the image registry and run the containers.

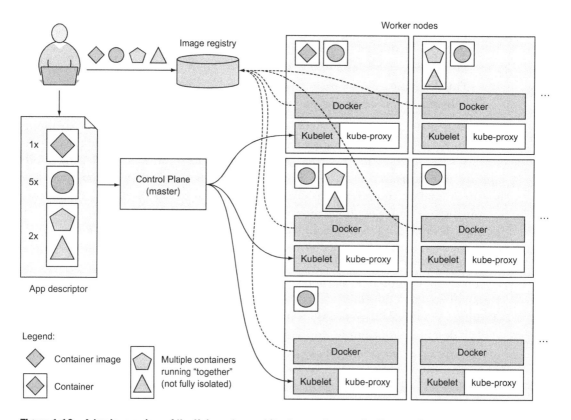

Figure 1.10   A basic overview of the Kubernetes architecture and an application running on top of it

KEEPING THE CONTAINERS RUNNING

Once the application is running, Kubernetes continuously makes sure that the deployed state of the application always matches the description you provided. For example, if you specify that you always want five instances of a web server running, Kubernetes will always keep exactly five instances running. If one of those instances stops working properly, like when its process crashes or when it stops responding, Kubernetes will restart it automatically.

Similarly, if a whole worker node dies or becomes inaccessible, Kubernetes will select new nodes for all the containers that were running on the node and run them on the newly selected nodes.

SCALING THE NUMBER OF COPIES

While the application is running, you can decide you want to increase or decrease the number of copies, and Kubernetes will spin up additional ones or stop the excess ones, respectively. You can even leave the job of deciding the optimal number of copies to Kubernetes. It can automatically keep adjusting the number, based on real-time metrics, such as CPU load, memory consumption, queries per second, or any other metric your app exposes.

HITTING A MOVING TARGET

We've said that Kubernetes may need to move your containers around the cluster. This can occur when the node they were running on has failed or because they were evicted from a node to make room for other containers. If the container is providing a service to external clients or other containers running in the cluster, how can they use the container properly if it's constantly moving around the cluster? And how can clients connect to containers providing a service when those containers are replicated and spread across the whole cluster?

To allow clients to easily find containers that provide a specific service, you can tell Kubernetes which containers provide the same service and Kubernetes will expose all of them at a single static IP address and expose that address to all applications running in the cluster. This is done through environment variables, but clients can also look up the service IP through good old DNS. The kube-proxy will make sure connections to the service are load balanced across all the containers that provide the service. The IP address of the service stays constant, so clients can always connect to its containers, even when they're moved around the cluster.

1.3.5　*Understanding the benefits of using Kubernetes*

If you have Kubernetes deployed on all your servers, the ops team doesn't need to deal with deploying your apps anymore. Because a containerized application already contains all it needs to run, the system administrators don't need to install anything to deploy and run the app. On any node where Kubernetes is deployed, Kubernetes can run the app immediately without any help from the sysadmins.

SIMPLIFYING APPLICATION DEPLOYMENT

Because Kubernetes exposes all its worker nodes as a single deployment platform, application developers can start deploying applications on their own and don't need to know anything about the servers that make up the cluster.

In essence, all the nodes are now a single bunch of computational resources that are waiting for applications to consume them. A developer doesn't usually care what kind of server the application is running on, as long as the server can provide the application with adequate system resources.

Certain cases do exist where the developer does care what kind of hardware the application should run on. If the nodes are heterogeneous, you'll find cases when you want certain apps to run on nodes with certain capabilities and run other apps on others. For example, one of your apps may require being run on a system with SSDs instead of HDDs, while other apps run fine on HDDs. In such cases, you obviously want to ensure that particular app is always scheduled to a node with an SSD.

Without using Kubernetes, the sysadmin would select one specific node that has an SSD and deploy the app there. But when using Kubernetes, instead of selecting a specific node where your app should be run, it's more appropriate to tell Kubernetes to only choose among nodes with an SSD. You'll learn how to do that in chapter 3.

ACHIEVING BETTER UTILIZATION OF HARDWARE

By setting up Kubernetes on your servers and using it to run your apps instead of running them manually, you've decoupled your app from the infrastructure. When you tell Kubernetes to run your application, you're letting it choose the most appropriate node to run your application on based on the description of the application's resource requirements and the available resources on each node.

By using containers and not tying the app down to a specific node in your cluster, you're allowing the app to freely move around the cluster at any time, so the different app components running on the cluster can be mixed and matched to be packed tightly onto the cluster nodes. This ensures the node's hardware resources are utilized as best as possible.

The ability to move applications around the cluster at any time allows Kubernetes to utilize the infrastructure much better than what you can achieve manually. Humans aren't good at finding optimal combinations, especially when the number of all possible options is huge, such as when you have many application components and many server nodes they can be deployed on. Computers can obviously perform this work much better and faster than humans.

HEALTH CHECKING AND SELF-HEALING

Having a system that allows moving an application across the cluster at any time is also valuable in the event of server failures. As your cluster size increases, you'll deal with failing computer components ever more frequently.

Kubernetes monitors your app components and the nodes they run on and automatically reschedules them to other nodes in the event of a node failure. This frees the ops team from having to migrate app components manually and allows the team to immediately focus on fixing the node itself and returning it to the pool of available hardware resources instead of focusing on relocating the app.

If your infrastructure has enough spare resources to allow normal system operation even without the failed node, the ops team doesn't even need to react to the failure immediately, such as at 3 a.m. They can sleep tight and deal with the failed node during regular work hours.

AUTOMATIC SCALING

Using Kubernetes to manage your deployed applications also means the ops team doesn't need to constantly monitor the load of individual applications to react to sudden load spikes. As previously mentioned, Kubernetes can be told to monitor the resources used by each application and to keep adjusting the number of running instances of each application.

If Kubernetes is running on cloud infrastructure, where adding additional nodes is as easy as requesting them through the cloud provider's API, Kubernetes can even automatically scale the whole cluster size up or down based on the needs of the deployed applications.

SIMPLIFYING APPLICATION DEVELOPMENT

The features described in the previous section mostly benefit the operations team. But what about the developers? Does Kubernetes bring anything to their table? It definitely does.

If you turn back to the fact that apps run in the same environment both during development and in production, this has a big effect on when bugs are discovered. We all agree the sooner you discover a bug, the easier it is to fix it, and fixing it requires less work. It's the developers who do the fixing, so this means less work for them.

Then there's the fact that developers don't need to implement features that they would usually implement. This includes discovery of services and/or peers in a clustered application. Kubernetes does this instead of the app. Usually, the app only needs to look up certain environment variables or perform a DNS lookup. If that's not enough, the application can query the Kubernetes API server directly to get that and/or other information. Querying the Kubernetes API server like that can even save developers from having to implement complicated mechanisms such as leader election.

As a final example of what Kubernetes brings to the table, you also need to consider the increase in confidence developers will feel knowing that when a new version of their app is going to be rolled out, Kubernetes can automatically detect if the new version is bad and stop its rollout immediately. This increase in confidence usually accelerates the continuous delivery of apps, which benefits the whole organization.

1.4 *Summary*

In this introductory chapter, you've seen how applications have changed in recent years and how they can now be harder to deploy and manage. We've introduced Kubernetes and shown how it, together with Docker and other container platforms, helps deploy and manage applications and the infrastructure they run on. You've learned that

- Monolithic apps are easier to deploy, but harder to maintain over time and sometimes impossible to scale.

- Microservices-based application architectures allow easier development of each component, but are harder to deploy and configure to work as a single system.
- Linux containers provide much the same benefits as virtual machines, but are far more lightweight and allow for much better hardware utilization.
- Docker improved on existing Linux container technologies by allowing easier and faster provisioning of containerized apps together with their OS environments.
- Kubernetes exposes the whole datacenter as a single computational resource for running applications.
- Developers can deploy apps through Kubernetes without assistance from sysadmins.
- Sysadmins can sleep better by having Kubernetes deal with failed nodes automatically.

In the next chapter, you'll get your hands dirty by building an app and running it in Docker and then in Kubernetes.

First steps with Docker and Kubernetes

This chapter covers

- Creating, running, and sharing a container image with Docker
- Running a single-node Kubernetes cluster locally
- Setting up a Kubernetes cluster on Google Kubernetes Engine
- Setting up and using the `kubectl` command-line client
- Deploying an app on Kubernetes and scaling it horizontally

Before you start learning about Kubernetes concepts in detail, let's see how to create a simple application, package it into a container image, and run it in a managed Kubernetes cluster (in Google Kubernetes Engine) or in a local single-node cluster. This should give you a slightly better overview of the whole Kubernetes system and will make it easier to follow the next few chapters, where we'll go over the basic building blocks and concepts in Kubernetes.

2.1 Creating, running, and sharing a container image

As you've already learned in the previous chapter, running applications in Kubernetes requires them to be packaged into container images. We'll do a basic introduction to using Docker in case you haven't used it yet. In the next few sections you'll

1 Install Docker and run your first "Hello world" container
2 Create a trivial Node.js app that you'll later deploy in Kubernetes
3 Package the app into a container image so you can then run it as an isolated container
4 Run a container based on the image
5 Push the image to Docker Hub so that anyone anywhere can run it

2.1.1 Installing Docker and running a Hello World container

First, you'll need to install Docker on your Linux machine. If you don't use Linux, you'll need to start a Linux virtual machine (VM) and run Docker inside that VM. If you're using a Mac or Windows and install Docker per instructions, Docker will set up a VM for you and run the Docker daemon inside that VM. The Docker client executable will be available on your host OS, and will communicate with the daemon inside the VM.

To install Docker, follow the instructions at http://docs.docker.com/engine/ installation/ for your specific operating system. After completing the installation, you can use the Docker client executable to run various Docker commands. For example, you could try pulling and running an existing image from Docker Hub, the public Docker registry, which contains ready-to-use container images for many well-known software packages. One of them is the `busybox` image, which you'll use to run a simple `echo "Hello world"` command.

RUNNING A HELLO WORLD CONTAINER

If you're unfamiliar with busybox, it's a single executable that combines many of the standard UNIX command-line tools, such as `echo`, `ls`, `gzip`, and so on. Instead of the busybox image, you could also use any other full-fledged OS container image such as Fedora, Ubuntu, or other similar images, as long as it includes the `echo` executable.

How do you run the `busybox` image? You don't need to download or install anything. Use the `docker run` command and specify what image to download and run and (optionally) what command to execute, as shown in the following listing.

> Listing 2.1   Running a Hello world container with Docker

```
$ docker run busybox echo "Hello world"
Unable to find image 'busybox:latest' locally
latest: Pulling from docker.io/busybox
9a163e0b8d13: Pull complete
fef924a0204a: Pull complete
Digest: sha256:97473e34e311e6c1b3f61f2a721d038d1e5eef17d98d1353a513007cf46ca6bd
Status: Downloaded newer image for docker.io/busybox:latest
Hello world
```

This doesn't look that impressive, but when you consider that the whole "app" was downloaded and executed with a single command, without you having to install that app or anything else, you'll agree it's awesome. In your case, the app was a single executable (busybox), but it might as well have been an incredibly complex app with many dependencies. The whole process of setting up and running the app would have been exactly the same. What's also important is that the app was executed inside a container, completely isolated from all the other processes running on your machine.

UNDERSTANDING WHAT HAPPENS BEHIND THE SCENES

Figure 2.1 shows exactly what happened when you performed the docker run command. First, Docker checked to see if the busybox:latest image was already present on your local machine. It wasn't, so Docker pulled it from the Docker Hub registry at http://docker.io. After the image was downloaded to your machine, Docker created a container from that image and ran the command inside it. The echo command printed the text to STDOUT and then the process terminated and the container stopped.

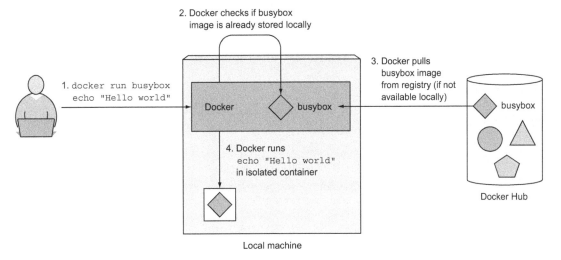

Figure 2.1   Running echo "Hello world" in a container based on the busybox container image

RUNNING OTHER IMAGES

Running other existing container images is much the same as how you ran the busybox image. In fact, it's often even simpler, because you usually don't need to specify what command to execute, the way you did in the example (echo "Hello world"). The command that should be executed is usually baked into the image itself, but you can override it if you want. After searching or browsing through the publicly available images on http://hub.docker.com or another public registry, you tell Docker to run the image like this:

```
$ docker run <image>
```

VERSIONING CONTAINER IMAGES

All software packages get updated, so more than a single version of a package usually exists. Docker supports having multiple versions or variants of the same image under the same name. Each variant must have a unique tag. When referring to images without explicitly specifying the tag, Docker will assume you're referring to the so-called *latest* tag. To run a different version of the image, you may specify the tag along with the image name like this:

```
$ docker run <image>:<tag>
```

2.1.2 Creating a trivial Node.js app

Now that you have a working Docker setup, you're going to create an app. You'll build a trivial Node.js web application and package it into a container image. The application will accept HTTP requests and respond with the hostname of the machine it's running in. This way, you'll see that an app running inside a container sees its own hostname and not that of the host machine, even though it's running on the host like any other process. This will be useful later, when you deploy the app on Kubernetes and scale it out (scale it horizontally; that is, run multiple instances of the app). You'll see your HTTP requests hitting different instances of the app.

Your app will consist of a single file called app.js with the contents shown in the following listing.

Listing 2.2 A simple Node.js app: app.js

```
const http = require('http');
const os = require('os');

console.log("Kubia server starting...");

var handler = function(request, response) {
  console.log("Received request from " + request.connection.remoteAddress);
  response.writeHead(200);
  response.end("You've hit " + os.hostname() + "\n");
};

var www = http.createServer(handler);
www.listen(8080);
```

It should be clear what this code does. It starts up an HTTP server on port 8080. The server responds with an HTTP response status code 200 OK and the text "You've hit <hostname>" to every request. The request handler also logs the client's IP address to the standard output, which you'll need later.

> **NOTE** The returned hostname is the server's actual hostname, not the one the client sends in the HTTP request's Host header.

You could now download and install Node.js and test your app directly, but this isn't necessary, because you'll use Docker to package the app into a container image and enable it to be run anywhere without having to download or install anything (except Docker, which does need to be installed on the machine you want to run the image on).

2.1.3   Creating a Dockerfile for the image

To package your app into an image, you first need to create a file called Dockerfile, which will contain a list of instructions that Docker will perform when building the image. The Dockerfile needs to be in the same directory as the app.js file and should contain the commands shown in the following listing.

> **Listing 2.3   A Dockerfile for building a container image for your app**

```
FROM node:7
ADD app.js /app.js
ENTRYPOINT ["node", "app.js"]
```

The `FROM` line defines the container image you'll use as a starting point (the base image you're building on top of). In your case, you're using the `node` container image, tag 7. In the second line, you're adding your app.js file from your local directory into the root directory in the image, under the same name (app.js). Finally, in the third line, you're defining what command should be executed when somebody runs the image. In your case, the command is `node app.js`.

> **Choosing a base image**
>
> You may wonder why we chose this specific image as your base. Because your app is a Node.js app, you need your image to contain the `node` binary executable to run the app. You could have used any image that contains that binary, or you could have even used a Linux distro base image such as `fedora` or `ubuntu` and installed Node.js into the container at image build time. But because the `node` image is made specifically for running Node.js apps, and includes everything you need to run your app, you'll use that as the base image.

2.1.4   Building the container image

Now that you have your Dockerfile and the app.js file, you have everything you need to build your image. To build it, run the following Docker command:

```
$ docker build -t kubia .
```

Figure 2.2 shows what happens during the build process. You're telling Docker to build an image called `kubia` based on the contents of the current directory (note the dot at the end of the build command). Docker will look for the Dockerfile in the directory and build the image based on the instructions in the file.

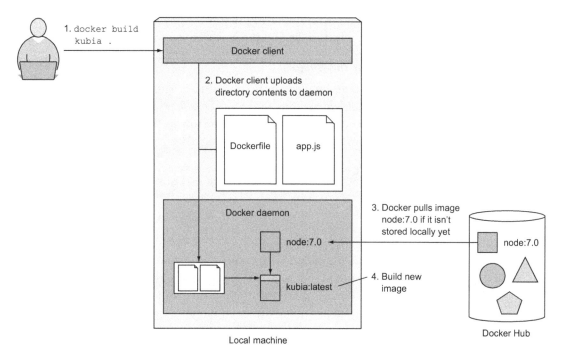

Figure 2.2   **Building a new container image from a Dockerfile**

UNDERSTANDING HOW AN IMAGE IS BUILT

The build process isn't performed by the Docker client. Instead, the contents of the whole directory are uploaded to the Docker daemon and the image is built there. The client and daemon don't need to be on the same machine at all. If you're using Docker on a non-Linux OS, the client is on your host OS, but the daemon runs inside a VM. Because all the files in the build directory are uploaded to the daemon, if it contains many large files and the daemon isn't running locally, the upload may take longer.

> **TIP** Don't include any unnecessary files in the build directory, because they'll slow down the build process—especially when the Docker daemon is on a remote machine.

During the build process, Docker will first pull the base image (node:7) from the public image repository (Docker Hub), unless the image has already been pulled and is stored on your machine.

UNDERSTANDING IMAGE LAYERS

An image isn't a single, big, binary blob, but is composed of multiple layers, which you may have already noticed when running the busybox example (there were multiple Pull complete lines—one for each layer). Different images may share several layers, which makes storing and transferring images much more efficient. For example, if you create multiple images based on the same base image (such as node:7 in the example), all the layers comprising the base image will be stored only once. Also, when pulling an image, Docker will download each layer individually. Several layers may already be stored on your machine, so Docker will only download those that aren't.

You may think that each Dockerfile creates only a single new layer, but that's not the case. When building an image, a new layer is created for each individual command in the Dockerfile. During the build of your image, after pulling all the layers of the base image, Docker will create a new layer on top of them and add the app.js file into it. Then it will create yet another layer that will specify the command that should be executed when the image is run. This last layer will then be tagged as kubia:latest. This is shown in figure 2.3, which also shows how a different image called other:latest would use the same layers of the Node.js image as your own image does.

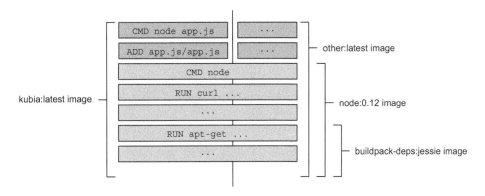

Figure 2.3 Container images are composed of layers that can be shared among different images.

When the build process completes, you have a new image stored locally. You can see it by telling Docker to list all locally stored images, as shown in the following listing.

Listing 2.4 Listing locally stored images

```
$ docker images
REPOSITORY    TAG      IMAGE ID        CREATED         VIRTUAL SIZE
kubia         latest   d30ecc7419e7    1 minute ago    637.1 MB
...
```

COMPARING BUILDING IMAGES WITH A DOCKERFILE VS. MANUALLY
Dockerfiles are the usual way of building container images with Docker, but you could also build the image manually by running a container from an existing image, executing commands in the container, exiting the container, and committing the final state as a new image. This is exactly what happens when you build from a Dockerfile, but it's performed automatically and is repeatable, which allows you to make changes to

the Dockerfile and rebuild the image any time, without having to manually retype all the commands again.

2.1.5 *Running the container image*

You can now run your image with the following command:

```
$ docker run --name kubia-container -p 8080:8080 -d kubia
```

This tells Docker to run a new container called `kubia-container` from the `kubia` image. The container will be detached from the console (`-d` flag), which means it will run in the background. Port 8080 on the local machine will be mapped to port 8080 inside the container (`-p 8080:8080` option), so you can access the app through http://localhost:8080.

If you're not running the Docker daemon on your local machine (if you're using a Mac or Windows, the daemon is running inside a VM), you'll need to use the hostname or IP of the VM running the daemon instead of localhost. You can look it up through the `DOCKER_HOST` environment variable.

ACCESSING YOUR APP

Now try to access your application at http://localhost:8080 (be sure to replace localhost with the hostname or IP of the Docker host if necessary):

```
$ curl localhost:8080
You've hit 44d76963e8e1
```

That's the response from your app. Your tiny application is now running inside a container, isolated from everything else. As you can see, it's returning 44d76963e8e1 as its hostname, and not the actual hostname of your host machine. The hexadecimal number is the ID of the Docker container.

LISTING ALL RUNNING CONTAINERS

Let's list all running containers in the following listing, so you can examine the list (I've edited the output to make it more readable—imagine the last two lines as the continuation of the first two).

> **Listing 2.5 Listing running containers**

```
$ docker ps
CONTAINER ID   IMAGE          COMMAND             CREATED         ...
44d76963e8e1   kubia:latest   "/bin/sh -c 'node ap  6 minutes ago   ...

...   STATUS           PORTS                 NAMES
...   Up 6 minutes     0.0.0.0:8080->8080/tcp   kubia-container
```

A single container is running. For each container, Docker prints out its ID and name, the image used to run the container, and the command that's executing inside the container.

GETTING ADDITIONAL INFORMATION ABOUT A CONTAINER

The docker ps command only shows the most basic information about the containers. To see additional information, you can use docker inspect:

```
$ docker inspect kubia-container
```

Docker will print out a long JSON containing low-level information about the container.

2.1.6 *Exploring the inside of a running container*

What if you want to see what the environment is like inside the container? Because multiple processes can run inside the same container, you can always run an additional process in it to see what's inside. You can even run a shell, provided that the shell's binary executable is available in the image.

RUNNING A SHELL INSIDE AN EXISTING CONTAINER

The Node.js image on which you've based your image contains the bash shell, so you can run the shell inside the container like this:

```
$ docker exec -it kubia-container bash
```

This will run bash inside the existing kubia-container container. The bash process will have the same Linux namespaces as the main container process. This allows you to explore the container from within and see how Node.js and your app see the system when running inside the container. The -it option is shorthand for two options:

- -i, which makes sure STDIN is kept open. You need this for entering commands into the shell.
- -t, which allocates a pseudo terminal (TTY).

You need both if you want the use the shell like you're used to. (If you leave out the first one, you can't type any commands, and if you leave out the second one, the command prompt won't be displayed and some commands will complain about the TERM variable not being set.)

EXPLORING THE CONTAINER FROM WITHIN

Let's see how to use the shell in the following listing to see the processes running in the container.

> **Listing 2.6 Listing processes from inside a container**

```
root@44d76963e8e1:/# ps aux
USER   PID %CPU %MEM    VSZ    RSS TTY STAT START TIME COMMAND
root     1  0.0  0.1 676380 16504 ?   Sl  12:31 0:00 node app.js
root    10  0.0  0.0  20216  1924 ?   Ss  12:31 0:00 bash
root    19  0.0  0.0  17492  1136 ?   R+  12:38 0:00 ps aux
```

You see only three processes. You don't see any other processes from the host OS.

UNDERSTANDING THAT PROCESSES IN A CONTAINER RUN IN THE HOST OPERATING SYSTEM

If you now open another terminal and list the processes on the host OS itself, you will, among all other host processes, also see the processes running in the container, as shown in listing 2.7.

> **NOTE** If you're using a Mac or Windows, you'll need to log into the VM where the Docker daemon is running to see these processes.

Listing 2.7   A container's processes run in the host OS

```
$ ps aux | grep app.js
USER   PID %CPU %MEM    VSZ   RSS TTY STAT START TIME COMMAND
root   382  0.0  0.1 676380 16504 ?   Sl  12:31 0:00 node app.js
```

This proves that processes running in the container are running in the host OS. If you have a keen eye, you may have noticed that the processes have different IDs inside the container vs. on the host. The container is using its own PID Linux namespace and has a completely isolated process tree, with its own sequence of numbers.

THE CONTAINER'S FILESYSTEM IS ALSO ISOLATED

Like having an isolated process tree, each container also has an isolated filesystem. Listing the contents of the root directory inside the container will only show the files in the container and will include all the files that are in the image plus any files that are created while the container is running (log files and similar), as shown in the following listing.

Listing 2.8   A container has its own complete filesystem

```
root@44d76963e8e1:/# ls /
app.js boot etc  lib    media opt   root  sbin sys usr
bin    dev  home lib64  mnt   proc  run   srv  tmp var
```

It contains the app.js file and other system directories that are part of the node:7 base image you're using. To exit the container, you exit the shell by running the exit command and you'll be returned to your host machine (like logging out of an ssh session, for example).

> **TIP** Entering a running container like this is useful when debugging an app running in a container. When something's wrong, the first thing you'll want to explore is the actual state of the system your application sees. Keep in mind that an application will not only see its own unique filesystem, but also processes, users, hostname, and network interfaces.

2.1.7   *Stopping and removing a container*

To stop your app, you tell Docker to stop the kubia-container container:

```
$ docker stop kubia-container
```

This will stop the main process running in the container and consequently stop the container, because no other processes are running inside the container. The container itself still exists and you can see it with `docker ps -a`. The -a option prints out all the containers, those running and those that have been stopped. To truly remove a container, you need to remove it with the `docker rm` command:

```
$ docker rm kubia-container
```

This deletes the container. All its contents are removed and it can't be started again.

2.1.8 *Pushing the image to an image registry*

The image you've built has so far only been available on your local machine. To allow you to run it on any other machine, you need to push the image to an external image registry. For the sake of simplicity, you won't set up a private image registry and will instead push the image to Docker Hub (http://hub.docker.com), which is one of the publicly available registries. Other widely used such registries are Quay.io and the Google Container Registry.

Before you do that, you need to re-tag your image according to Docker Hub's rules. Docker Hub will allow you to push an image if the image's repository name starts with your Docker Hub ID. You create your Docker Hub ID by registering at http://hub.docker.com. I'll use my own ID (`luksa`) in the following examples. Please change every occurrence with your own ID.

TAGGING AN IMAGE UNDER AN ADDITIONAL TAG

Once you know your ID, you're ready to rename your image, currently tagged as `kubia`, to `luksa/kubia` (replace `luksa` with your own Docker Hub ID):

```
$ docker tag kubia luksa/kubia
```

This doesn't rename the tag; it creates an additional tag for the same image. You can confirm this by listing the images stored on your system with the `docker images` command, as shown in the following listing.

Listing 2.9 A container image can have multiple tags

```
$ docker images | head
REPOSITORY        TAG      IMAGE ID        CREATED            VIRTUAL SIZE
luksa/kubia       latest   d30ecc7419e7    About an hour ago  654.5 MB
kubia             latest   d30ecc7419e7    About an hour ago  654.5 MB
docker.io/node    7.0      04c0ca2a8dad    2 days ago         654.5 MB
...
```

As you can see, both `kubia` and `luksa/kubia` point to the same image ID, so they're in fact one single image with two tags.

PUSHING THE IMAGE TO DOCKER HUB

Before you can push the image to Docker Hub, you need to log in under your user ID with the `docker login` command. Once you're logged in, you can finally push the `yourid/kubia` image to Docker Hub like this:

```
$ docker push luksa/kubia
```

RUNNING THE IMAGE ON A DIFFERENT MACHINE

After the push to Docker Hub is complete, the image will be available to everyone. You can now run the image on any machine running Docker by executing the following command:

```
$ docker run -p 8080:8080 -d luksa/kubia
```

It doesn't get much simpler than that. And the best thing about this is that your application will have the exact same environment every time and everywhere it's run. If it ran fine on your machine, it should run as well on every other Linux machine. No need to worry about whether the host machine has Node.js installed or not. In fact, even if it does, your app won't use it, because it will use the one installed inside the image.

2.2   *Setting up a Kubernetes cluster*

Now that you have your app packaged inside a container image and made available through Docker Hub, you can deploy it in a Kubernetes cluster instead of running it in Docker directly. But first, you need to set up the cluster itself.

Setting up a full-fledged, multi-node Kubernetes cluster isn't a simple task, especially if you're not well-versed in Linux and networking administration. A proper Kubernetes install spans multiple physical or virtual machines and requires the networking to be set up properly, so that all the containers running inside the Kubernetes cluster can connect to each other through the same flat networking space.

A long list of methods exists for installing a Kubernetes cluster. These methods are described in detail in the documentation at http://kubernetes.io. We're not going to list all of them here, because the list keeps evolving, but Kubernetes can be run on your local development machine, your own organization's cluster of machines, on cloud providers providing virtual machines (Google Compute Engine, Amazon EC2, Microsoft Azure, and so on), or by using a managed Kubernetes cluster such as Google Kubernetes Engine (previously known as Google Container Engine).

In this chapter, we'll cover two simple options for getting your hands on a running Kubernetes cluster. You'll see how to run a single-node Kubernetes cluster on your local machine and how to get access to a hosted cluster running on Google Kubernetes Engine (GKE).

A third option, which covers installing a cluster with the `kubeadm` tool, is explained in appendix B. The instructions there show you how to set up a three-node Kubernetes cluster using virtual machines, but I suggest you try it only after reading the first 11 chapters of the book.

Another option is to install Kubernetes on Amazon's AWS (Amazon Web Services). For this, you can look at the kops tool, which is built on top of kubeadm mentioned in the previous paragraph, and is available at http://github.com/kubernetes/kops. It helps you deploy production-grade, highly available Kubernetes clusters on AWS and will eventually support other platforms as well (Google Kubernetes Engine, VMware, vSphere, and so on).

2.2.1 Running a local single-node Kubernetes cluster with Minikube

The simplest and quickest path to a fully functioning Kubernetes cluster is by using Minikube. Minikube is a tool that sets up a single-node cluster that's great for both testing Kubernetes and developing apps locally.

Although we can't show certain Kubernetes features related to managing apps on multiple nodes, the single-node cluster should be enough for exploring most topics discussed in this book.

INSTALLING MINIKUBE

Minikube is a single binary that needs to be downloaded and put onto your path. It's available for OSX, Linux, and Windows. To install it, the best place to start is to go to the Minikube repository on GitHub (http://github.com/kubernetes/minikube) and follow the instructions there.

For example, on OSX and Linux, Minikube can be downloaded and set up with a single command. For OSX, this is what the command looks like:

```
$ curl -Lo minikube https://storage.googleapis.com/minikube/releases/
    v0.23.0/minikube-darwin-amd64 && chmod +x minikube && sudo mv minikube
    /usr/local/bin/
```

On Linux, you download a different release (replace "darwin" with "linux" in the URL). On Windows, you can download the file manually, rename it to minikube.exe, and put it onto your path. Minikube runs Kubernetes inside a VM run through either VirtualBox or KVM, so you also need to install one of them before you can start the Minikube cluster.

STARTING A KUBERNETES CLUSTER WITH MINIKUBE

Once you have Minikube installed locally, you can immediately start up the Kubernetes cluster with the command in the following listing.

> **Listing 2.10 Starting a Minikube virtual machine**

```
$ minikube start
Starting local Kubernetes cluster...
Starting VM...
SSH-ing files into VM...
...
Kubectl is now configured to use the cluster.
```

Starting the cluster takes more than a minute, so don't interrupt the command before it completes.

INSTALLING THE KUBERNETES CLIENT (KUBECTL)

To interact with Kubernetes, you also need the kubectl CLI client. Again, all you need to do is download it and put it on your path. The latest stable release for OSX, for example, can be downloaded and installed with the following command:

```
$ curl -LO https://storage.googleapis.com/kubernetes-release/release
    /$(curl -s https://storage.googleapis.com/kubernetes-release/release
    /stable.txt)/bin/darwin/amd64/kubectl
    && chmod +x kubectl
    && sudo mv kubectl /usr/local/bin/
```

To download kubectl for Linux, replace darwin in the URL with linux. For Windows, replace it with windows and add .exe at the end.

> **NOTE** If you'll be using multiple Kubernetes clusters (for example, both Minikube and GKE), refer to appendix A for information on how to set up and switch between different kubectl contexts.

CHECKING TO SEE THE CLUSTER IS UP AND KUBECTL CAN TALK TO IT

To verify your cluster is working, you can use the kubectl cluster-info command shown in the following listing.

Listing 2.11 Displaying cluster information

```
$ kubectl cluster-info
Kubernetes master is running at https://192.168.99.100:8443
KubeDNS is running at https://192.168.99.100:8443/api/v1/proxy/...
kubernetes-dashboard is running at https://192.168.99.100:8443/api/v1/...
```

This shows the cluster is up. It shows the URLs of the various Kubernetes components, including the API server and the web console.

> **TIP** You can run minikube ssh to log into the Minikube VM and explore it from the inside. For example, you may want to see what processes are running on the node.

2.2.2 *Using a hosted Kubernetes cluster with Google Kubernetes Engine*

If you want to explore a full-fledged multi-node Kubernetes cluster instead, you can use a managed Google Kubernetes Engine (GKE) cluster. This way, you don't need to manually set up all the cluster nodes and networking, which is usually too much for someone making their first steps with Kubernetes. Using a managed solution such as GKE makes sure you don't end up with a misconfigured, non-working, or partially working cluster.

SETTING UP A GOOGLE CLOUD PROJECT AND DOWNLOADING THE NECESSARY CLIENT BINARIES

Before you can set up a new Kubernetes cluster, you need to set up your GKE environment. Because the process may change, I'm not listing the exact instructions here. To get started, please follow the instructions at https://cloud.google.com/container-engine/docs/before-you-begin.

Roughly, the whole procedure includes

1 Signing up for a Google account, in the unlikely case you don't have one already.
2 Creating a project in the Google Cloud Platform Console.
3 Enabling billing. This does require your credit card info, but Google provides a 12-month free trial. And they're nice enough to not start charging automatically after the free trial is over.)
4 Enabling the Kubernetes Engine API.
5 Downloading and installing Google Cloud SDK. (This includes the *gcloud* command-line tool, which you'll need to create a Kubernetes cluster.)
6 Installing the kubectl command-line tool with gcloud components install kubectl.

NOTE Certain operations (the one in step 2, for example) may take a few minutes to complete, so relax and grab a coffee in the meantime.

CREATING A KUBERNETES CLUSTER WITH THREE NODES

After completing the installation, you can create a Kubernetes cluster with three worker nodes using the command shown in the following listing.

Listing 2.12 Creating a three-node cluster in GKE

```
$ gcloud container clusters create kubia --num-nodes 3
➥ --machine-type f1-micro
Creating cluster kubia...done.
Created [https://container.googleapis.com/v1/projects/kubia1-
    1227/zones/europe-west1-d/clusters/kubia].
kubeconfig entry generated for kubia.
NAME    ZONE    MST_VER MASTER_IP     TYPE      NODE_VER NUM_NODES STATUS
kubia   eu w1d 1.5.3    104.155.92.30 f1-micro 1.5.3     3         RUNNING
```

You should now have a running Kubernetes cluster with three worker nodes as shown in figure 2.4. You're using three nodes to help better demonstrate features that apply to multiple nodes. You can use a smaller number of nodes, if you want.

GETTING AN OVERVIEW OF YOUR CLUSTER

To give you a basic idea of what your cluster looks like and how to interact with it, see figure 2.4. Each node runs Docker, the Kubelet and the kube-proxy. You'll interact with the cluster through the kubectl command line client, which issues REST requests to the Kubernetes API server running on the master node.

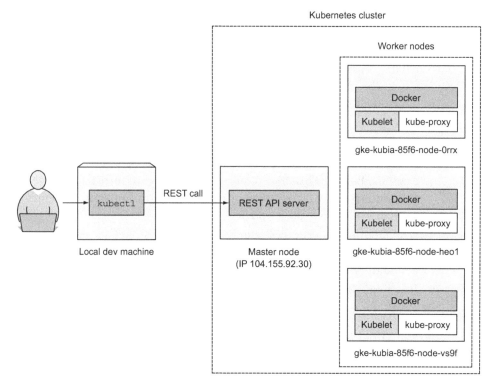

Figure 2.4 How you're interacting with your three-node Kubernetes cluster

CHECKING IF THE CLUSTER IS UP BY LISTING CLUSTER NODES

You'll use the kubectl command now to list all the nodes in your cluster, as shown in the following listing.

Listing 2.13 Listing cluster nodes with kubectl

```
$ kubectl get nodes
NAME                        STATUS   AGE   VERSION
gke-kubia-85f6-node-0rrx    Ready    1m    v1.5.3
gke-kubia-85f6-node-heo1    Ready    1m    v1.5.3
gke-kubia-85f6-node-vs9f    Ready    1m    v1.5.3
```

The kubectl get command can list all kinds of Kubernetes objects. You'll use it constantly, but it usually shows only the most basic information for the listed objects.

> **TIP** You can log into one of the nodes with gcloud compute ssh <node-name> to explore what's running on the node.

RETRIEVING ADDITIONAL DETAILS OF AN OBJECT

To see more detailed information about an object, you can use the kubectl describe command, which shows much more:

```
$ kubectl describe node gke-kubia-85f6-node-0rrx
```

I'm omitting the actual output of the describe command, because it's fairly wide and would be completely unreadable here in the book. The output shows the node's status, its CPU and memory data, system information, containers running on the node, and much more.

In the previous kubectl describe example, you specified the name of the node explicitly, but you could also have performed a simple kubectl describe node without typing the node's name and it would print out a detailed description of all the nodes.

> **TIP** Running the describe and get commands without specifying the name of the object comes in handy when only one object of a given type exists, so you don't waste time typing or copy/pasting the object's name.

While we're talking about reducing keystrokes, let me give you additional advice on how to make working with kubectl much easier, before we move on to running your first app in Kubernetes.

2.2.3   *Setting up an alias and command-line completion for kubectl*

You'll use kubectl often. You'll soon realize that having to type the full command every time is a real pain. Before you continue, take a minute to make your life easier by setting up an alias and tab completion for kubectl.

CREATING AN ALIAS

Throughout the book, I'll always be using the full name of the kubectl executable, but you may want to add a short alias such as k, so you won't have to type kubectl every time. If you haven't used aliases yet, here's how you define one. Add the following line to your ~/.bashrc or equivalent file:

```
alias k=kubectl
```

> **NOTE** You may already have the k executable if you used gcloud to set up the cluster.

CONFIGURING TAB COMPLETION FOR KUBECTL

Even with a short alias such as k, you'll still need to type way more than you'd like. Luckily, the kubectl command can also output shell completion code for both the bash and zsh shell. It doesn't enable tab completion of only command names, but also of the actual object names. For example, instead of having to write the whole node name in the previous example, all you'd need to type is

```
$ kubectl desc<TAB> no<TAB> gke-ku<TAB>
```

To enable tab completion in bash, you'll first need to install a package called `bash-completion` and then run the following command (you'll probably also want to add it to `~/.bashrc` or equivalent):

```
$ source <(kubectl completion bash)
```

But there's one caveat. When you run the preceding command, tab completion will only work when you use the full `kubectl` name (it won't work when you use the `k` alias). To fix this, you need to transform the output of the `kubectl completion` command a bit:

```
$ source <(kubectl completion bash | sed s/kubectl/k/g)
```

> **NOTE** Unfortunately, as I'm writing this, shell completion doesn't work for aliases on MacOS. You'll have to use the full `kubectl` command name if you want completion to work.

Now you're all set to start interacting with your cluster without having to type too much. You can finally run your first app on Kubernetes.

2.3   *Running your first app on Kubernetes*

Because this may be your first time, you'll use the simplest possible way of running an app on Kubernetes. Usually, you'd prepare a JSON or YAML manifest, containing a description of all the components you want to deploy, but because we haven't talked about the types of components you can create in Kubernetes yet, you'll use a simple one-line command to get something running.

2.3.1   *Deploying your Node.js app*

The simplest way to deploy your app is to use the `kubectl run` command, which will create all the necessary components without having to deal with JSON or YAML. This way, we don't need to dive into the structure of each object yet. Try to run the image you created and pushed to Docker Hub earlier. Here's how to run it in Kubernetes:

```
$ kubectl run kubia --image=luksa/kubia --port=8080 --generator=run/v1
replicationcontroller "kubia" created
```

The `--image=luksa/kubia` part obviously specifies the container image you want to run, and the `--port=8080` option tells Kubernetes that your app is listening on port 8080. The last flag (`--generator`) does require an explanation, though. Usually, you won't use it, but you're using it here so Kubernetes creates a *ReplicationController* instead of a *Deployment*. You'll learn what ReplicationControllers are later in the chapter, but we won't talk about Deployments until chapter 9. That's why I don't want `kubectl` to create a Deployment yet.

As the previous command's output shows, a ReplicationController called kubia has been created. As already mentioned, we'll see what that is later in the chapter. For now, let's start from the bottom and focus on the container you created (you can assume a container has been created, because you specified a container image in the run command).

INTRODUCING PODS

You may be wondering if you can see your container in a list showing all the running containers. Maybe something such as kubectl get containers? Well, that's not exactly how Kubernetes works. It doesn't deal with individual containers directly. Instead, it uses the concept of multiple co-located containers. This group of containers is called a Pod.

A pod is a group of one or more tightly related containers that will always run together on the same worker node and in the same Linux namespace(s). Each pod is like a separate logical machine with its own IP, hostname, processes, and so on, running a single application. The application can be a single process, running in a single container, or it can be a main application process and additional supporting processes, each running in its own container. All the containers in a pod will appear to be running on the same logical machine, whereas containers in other pods, even if they're running on the same worker node, will appear to be running on a different one.

To better understand the relationship between containers, pods, and nodes, examine figure 2.5. As you can see, each pod has its own IP and contains one or more containers, each running an application process. Pods are spread out across different worker nodes.

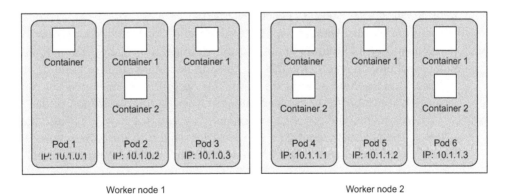

Figure 2.5 The relationship between containers, pods, and physical worker nodes

LISTING PODS

Because you can't list individual containers, since they're not standalone Kubernetes objects, can you list pods instead? Yes, you can. Let's see how to tell kubectl to list pods in the following listing.

Listing 2.14   Listing pods

```
$ kubectl get pods
NAME          READY      STATUS      RESTARTS    AGE
kubia-4jfyf   0/1        Pending     0           1m
```

This is your pod. Its status is still `Pending` and the pod's single container is shown as not ready yet (this is what the `0/1` in the `READY` column means). The reason why the pod isn't running yet is because the worker node the pod has been assigned to is downloading the container image before it can run it. When the download is finished, the pod's container will be created and then the pod will transition to the `Running` state, as shown in the following listing.

Listing 2.15   Listing pods again to see if the pod's status has changed

```
$ kubectl get pods
NAME          READY      STATUS      RESTARTS    AGE
kubia-4jfyf   1/1        Running     0           5m
```

To see more information about the pod, you can also use the `kubectl describe` pod command, like you did earlier for one of the worker nodes. If the pod stays stuck in the Pending status, it might be that Kubernetes can't pull the image from the registry. If you're using your own image, make sure it's marked as public on Docker Hub. To make sure the image can be pulled successfully, try pulling the image manually with the `docker pull` command on another machine.

UNDERSTANDING WHAT HAPPENED BEHIND THE SCENES

To help you visualize what transpired, look at figure 2.6. It shows both steps you had to perform to get a container image running inside Kubernetes. First, you built the image and pushed it to Docker Hub. This was necessary because building the image on your local machine only makes it available on your local machine, but you needed to make it accessible to the Docker daemons running on your worker nodes.

When you ran the `kubectl` command, it created a new ReplicationController object in the cluster by sending a REST HTTP request to the Kubernetes API server. The ReplicationController then created a new pod, which was then scheduled to one of the worker nodes by the Scheduler. The Kubelet on that node saw that the pod was scheduled to it and instructed Docker to pull the specified image from the registry because the image wasn't available locally. After downloading the image, Docker created and ran the container.

The other two nodes are displayed to show context. They didn't play any role in the process, because the pod wasn't scheduled to them.

> **DEFINITION**   The term scheduling means assigning the pod to a node. The pod is run immediately, not at a time in the future as the term might lead you to believe.

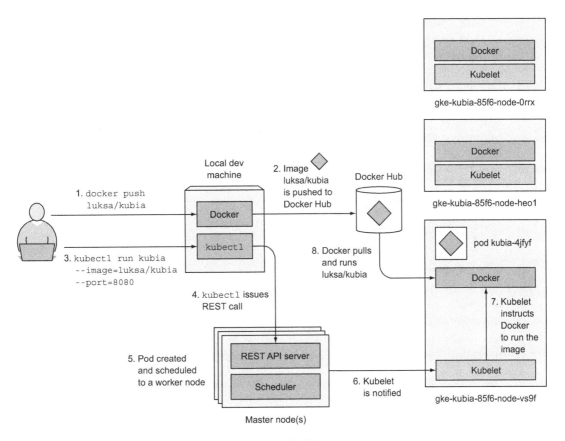

Figure 2.6 Running the `luksa/kubia` **container image in Kubernetes**

2.3.2 *Accessing your web application*

With your pod running, how do you access it? We mentioned that each pod gets its own IP address, but this address is internal to the cluster and isn't accessible from outside of it. To make the pod accessible from the outside, you'll expose it through a Service object. You'll create a special service of type LoadBalancer, because if you create a regular service (a ClusterIP service), like the pod, it would also only be accessible from inside the cluster. By creating a LoadBalancer-type service, an external load balancer will be created and you can connect to the pod through the load balancer's public IP.

CREATING A SERVICE OBJECT

To create the service, you'll tell Kubernetes to expose the ReplicationController you created earlier:

```
$ kubectl expose rc kubia --type=LoadBalancer --name kubia-http
service "kubia-http" exposed
```

NOTE We're using the abbreviation `rc` instead of `replicationcontroller`. Most resource types have an abbreviation like this so you don't have to type the full name (for example, `po` for `pods`, `svc` for `services`, and so on).

LISTING SERVICES

The `expose` command's output mentions a service called `kubia-http`. Services are objects like Pods and Nodes, so you can see the newly created Service object by running the `kubectl get services` command, as shown in the following listing.

Listing 2.16 Listing Services

```
$ kubectl get services
NAME            CLUSTER-IP      EXTERNAL-IP    PORT(S)          AGE
kubernetes      10.3.240.1      <none>         443/TCP          34m
kubia-http      10.3.246.185    <pending>      8080:31348/TCP   4s
```

The list shows two services. Ignore the `kubernetes` service for now and take a close look at the `kubia-http` service you created. It doesn't have an external IP address yet, because it takes time for the load balancer to be created by the cloud infrastructure Kubernetes is running on. Once the load balancer is up, the external IP address of the service should be displayed. Let's wait a while and list the services again, as shown in the following listing.

Listing 2.17 Listing services again to see if an external IP has been assigned

```
$ kubectl get svc
NAME            CLUSTER-IP      EXTERNAL-IP     PORT(S)          AGE
kubernetes      10.3.240.1      <none>          443/TCP          35m
kubia-http      10.3.246.185    104.155.74.57   8080:31348/TCP   1m
```

Aha, there's the external IP. Your application is now accessible at http://104.155.74 .57:8080 from anywhere in the world.

NOTE Minikube doesn't support `LoadBalancer` services, so the service will never get an external IP. But you can access the service anyway through its external port. How to do that is described in the next section's tip.

ACCESSING YOUR SERVICE THROUGH ITS EXTERNAL IP

You can now send requests to your pod through the service's external IP and port:

```
$ curl 104.155.74.57:8080
You've hit kubia-4jfyf
```

Woohoo! Your app is now running somewhere in your three-node Kubernetes cluster (or a single-node cluster if you're using Minikube). If you don't count the steps required to set up the whole cluster, all it took was two simple commands to get your app running and to make it accessible to users across the world.

TIP When using Minikube, you can get the IP and port through which you can access the service by running `minikube service kubia-http`.

If you look closely, you'll see that the app is reporting the name of the pod as its hostname. As already mentioned, each pod behaves like a separate independent machine with its own IP address and hostname. Even though the application is running in the worker node's operating system, to the app it appears as though it's running on a separate machine dedicated to the app itself—no other processes are running alongside it.

2.3.3 *The logical parts of your system*

Until now, I've mostly explained the actual physical components of your system. You have three worker nodes, which are VMs running Docker and the Kubelet, and you have a master node that controls the whole system. Honestly, we don't know if a single master node is hosting all the individual components of the Kubernetes Control Plane or if they're split across multiple nodes. It doesn't really matter, because you're only interacting with the API server, which is accessible at a single endpoint.

Besides this physical view of the system, there's also a separate, logical view of it. I've already mentioned Pods, ReplicationControllers, and Services. All of them will be explained in the next few chapters, but let's quickly look at how they fit together and what roles they play in your little setup.

UNDERSTANDING HOW THE REPLICATIONCONTROLLER, THE POD, AND THE SERVICE FIT TOGETHER

As I've already explained, you're not creating and working with containers directly. Instead, the basic building block in Kubernetes is the pod. But, you didn't really create any pods either, at least not directly. By running the `kubectl run` command you created a ReplicationController, and this ReplicationController is what created the actual Pod object. To make that pod accessible from outside the cluster, you told Kubernetes to expose all the pods managed by that ReplicationController as a single Service. A rough picture of all three elements is presented in figure 2.7.

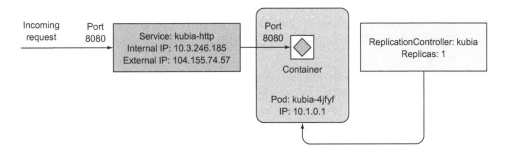

Figure 2.7   Your system consists of a ReplicationController, a Pod, and a Service.

UNDERSTANDING THE POD AND ITS CONTAINER

The main and most important component in your system is the pod. It contains only a single container, but generally a pod can contain as many containers as you want. Inside the container is your Node.js process, which is bound to port 8080 and is waiting for HTTP requests. The pod has its own unique private IP address and hostname.

UNDERSTANDING THE ROLE OF THE REPLICATIONCONTROLLER

The next component is the `kubia` ReplicationController. It makes sure there's always exactly one instance of your pod running. Generally, ReplicationControllers are used to replicate pods (that is, create multiple copies of a pod) and keep them running. In your case, you didn't specify how many pod replicas you want, so the Replication-Controller created a single one. If your pod were to disappear for any reason, the ReplicationController would create a new pod to replace the missing one.

UNDERSTANDING WHY YOU NEED A SERVICE

The third component of your system is the `kubia-http` service. To understand why you need services, you need to learn a key detail about pods. They're ephemeral. A pod may disappear at any time—because the node it's running on has failed, because someone deleted the pod, or because the pod was evicted from an otherwise healthy node. When any of those occurs, a missing pod is replaced with a new one by the ReplicationController, as described previously. This new pod gets a different IP address from the pod it's replacing. This is where services come in—to solve the problem of ever-changing pod IP addresses, as well as exposing multiple pods at a single constant IP and port pair.

When a service is created, it gets a static IP, which never changes during the lifetime of the service. Instead of connecting to pods directly, clients should connect to the service through its constant IP address. The service makes sure one of the pods receives the connection, regardless of where the pod is currently running (and what its IP address is).

Services represent a static location for a group of one or more pods that all provide the same service. Requests coming to the IP and port of the service will be forwarded to the IP and port of one of the pods belonging to the service at that moment.

2.3.4 *Horizontally scaling the application*

You now have a running application, monitored and kept running by a Replication-Controller and exposed to the world through a service. Now let's make additional magic happen.

One of the main benefits of using Kubernetes is the simplicity with which you can scale your deployments. Let's see how easy it is to scale up the number of pods. You'll increase the number of running instances to three.

Your pod is managed by a ReplicationController. Let's see it with the `kubectl get` command:

```
$ kubectl get replicationcontrollers
NAME        DESIRED     CURRENT     AGE
kubia       1           1           17m
```

Listing all the resource types with kubectl get

You've been using the same basic `kubectl get` command to list things in your cluster. You've used this command to list Node, Pod, Service and ReplicationController objects. You can get a list of all the possible object types by invoking `kubectl get` without specifying the type. You can then use those types with various `kubectl` commands such as `get`, `describe`, and so on. The list also shows the abbreviations I mentioned earlier.

The list shows a single ReplicationController called `kubia`. The DESIRED column shows the number of pod replicas you want the ReplicationController to keep, whereas the CURRENT column shows the actual number of pods currently running. In your case, you wanted to have a single replica of the pod running, and exactly one replica is currently running.

INCREASING THE DESIRED REPLICA COUNT

To scale up the number of replicas of your pod, you need to change the desired replica count on the ReplicationController like this:

```
$ kubectl scale rc kubia --replicas=3
replicationcontroller "kubia" scaled
```

You've now told Kubernetes to make sure three instances of your pod are always running. Notice that you didn't instruct Kubernetes what action to take. You didn't tell it to add two more pods. You only set the new desired number of instances and let Kubernetes determine what actions it needs to take to achieve the requested state.

This is one of the most fundamental Kubernetes principles. Instead of telling Kubernetes exactly what actions it should perform, you're only declaratively changing the desired state of the system and letting Kubernetes examine the current actual state and reconcile it with the desired state. This is true across all of Kubernetes.

SEEING THE RESULTS OF THE SCALE-OUT

Back to your replica count increase. Let's list the ReplicationControllers again to see the updated replica count:

```
$ kubectl get rc
NAME        DESIRED     CURRENT     READY     AGE
kubia       3           3           2         17m
```

Because the actual number of pods has already been increased to three (as evident from the CURRENT column), listing all the pods should now show three pods instead of one:

```
$ kubectl get pods
NAME            READY     STATUS      RESTARTS     AGE
kubia-hczji     1/1       Running     0            7s
kubia-iq9y6     0/1       Pending     0            7s
kubia-4jfyf     1/1       Running     0            18m
```

As you can see, three pods exist instead of one. Two are already running, one is still pending, but should be ready in a few moments, as soon as the container image is downloaded and the container is started.

As you can see, scaling an application is incredibly simple. Once your app is running in production and a need to scale the app arises, you can add additional instances with a single command without having to install and run additional copies manually.

Keep in mind that the app itself needs to support being scaled horizontally. Kubernetes doesn't magically make your app scalable; it only makes it trivial to scale the app up or down.

SEEING REQUESTS HIT ALL THREE PODS WHEN HITTING THE SERVICE

Because you now have multiple instances of your app running, let's see what happens if you hit the service URL again. Will you always hit the same app instance or not?

```
$ curl 104.155.74.57:8080
You've hit kubia-hczji
$ curl 104.155.74.57:8080
You've hit kubia-iq9y6
$ curl 104.155.74.57:8080
You've hit kubia-iq9y6
$ curl 104.155.74.57:8080
You've hit kubia-4jfyf
```

Requests are hitting different pods randomly. This is what services in Kubernetes do when more than one pod instance backs them. They act as a load balancer standing in front of multiple pods. When there's only one pod, services provide a static address for the single pod. Whether a service is backed by a single pod or a group of pods, those pods come and go as they're moved around the cluster, which means their IP addresses change, but the service is always there at the same address. This makes it easy for clients to connect to the pods, regardless of how many exist and how often they change location.

VISUALIZING THE NEW STATE OF YOUR SYSTEM

Let's visualize your system again to see what's changed from before. Figure 2.8 shows the new state of your system. You still have a single service and a single ReplicationController, but you now have three instances of your pod, all managed by the ReplicationController. The service no longer sends all requests to a single pod, but spreads them across all three pods as shown in the experiment with `curl` in the previous section.

As an exercise, you can now try spinning up additional instances by increasing the ReplicationController's replica count even further and then scaling back down.

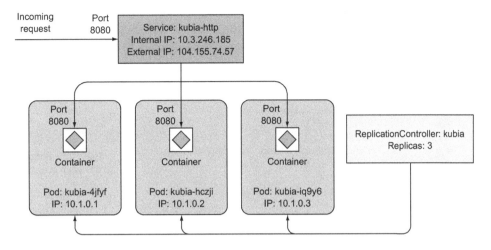

Figure 2.8   Three instances of a pod managed by the same ReplicationController and exposed through a single service IP and port.

2.3.5   *Examining what nodes your app is running on*

You may be wondering what nodes your pods have been scheduled to. In the Kubernetes world, what node a pod is running on isn't that important, as long as it gets scheduled to a node that can provide the CPU and memory the pod needs to run properly.

Regardless of the node they're scheduled to, all the apps running inside containers have the same type of OS environment. Each pod has its own IP and can talk to any other pod, regardless of whether that other pod is also running on the same node or on a different one. Each pod is provided with the requested amount of computational resources, so whether those resources are provided by one node or another doesn't make any difference.

DISPLAYING THE POD IP AND THE POD'S NODE WHEN LISTING PODS

If you've been paying close attention, you probably noticed that the kubectl get pods command doesn't even show any information about the nodes the pods are scheduled to. This is because it's usually not an important piece of information.

But you can request additional columns to display using the -o wide option. When listing pods, this option shows the pod's IP and the node the pod is running on:

```
$ kubectl get pods -o wide
NAME          READY   STATUS    RESTARTS   AGE   IP         NODE
kubia-hczji   1/1     Running   0          7s    10.1.0.2   gke-kubia-85...
```

INSPECTING OTHER DETAILS OF A POD WITH KUBECTL DESCRIBE

You can also see the node by using the kubectl describe command, which shows many other details of the pod, as shown in the following listing.

Listing 2.18   Describing a pod with kubectl describe

```
$ kubectl describe pod kubia-hczji
Name:         kubia-hczji
Namespace:    default
Node:         gke-kubia-85f6-node-vs9f/10.132.0.3        ◁─┐  Here's the node the pod
Start Time:   Fri, 29 Apr 2016 14:12:33 +0200              │  has been scheduled to.
Labels:       run=kubia
Status:       Running
IP:           10.1.0.2
Controllers:  ReplicationController/kubia
Containers:   ...
Conditions:
  Type        Status
  Ready       True
Volumes: ...
Events: ...
```

This shows, among other things, the node the pod has been scheduled to, the time when it was started, the image(s) it's running, and other useful information.

2.3.6   Introducing the Kubernetes dashboard

Before we wrap up this initial hands-on chapter, let's look at another way of exploring your Kubernetes cluster.

Up to now, you've only been using the kubectl command-line tool. If you're more into graphical web user interfaces, you'll be glad to hear that Kubernetes also comes with a nice (but still evolving) web dashboard.

The dashboard allows you to list all the Pods, ReplicationControllers, Services, and other objects deployed in your cluster, as well as to create, modify, and delete them. Figure 2.9 shows the dashboard.

Although you won't use the dashboard in this book, you can open it up any time to quickly see a graphical view of what's deployed in your cluster after you create or modify objects through kubectl.

ACCESSING THE DASHBOARD WHEN RUNNING KUBERNETES IN GKE

If you're using Google Kubernetes Engine, you can find out the URL of the dashboard through the kubectl cluster-info command, which we already introduced:

```
$ kubectl cluster-info | grep dashboard
kubernetes-dashboard is running at https://104.155.108.191/api/v1/proxy/
➥ namespaces/kube-system/services/kubernetes-dashboard
```

Figure 2.9 Screenshot of the Kubernetes web-based dashboard

If you open this URL in a browser, you're presented with a username and password prompt. You'll find the username and password by running the following command:

```
$ gcloud container clusters describe kubia | grep -E "(username|password):"
  password: 32nENgreEJ632A12
  username: admin
```

The username and password
for the dashboard

ACCESSING THE DASHBOARD WHEN USING MINIKUBE

To open the dashboard in your browser when using Minikube to run your Kubernetes cluster, run the following command:

```
$ minikube dashboard
```

The dashboard will open in your default browser. Unlike with GKE, you won't need to enter any credentials to access it.

2.4   *Summary*

Hopefully, this initial hands-on chapter has shown you that Kubernetes isn't a complicated platform to use, and you're ready to learn in depth about all the things it can provide. After reading this chapter, you should now know how to

- Pull and run any publicly available container image
- Package your apps into container images and make them available to anyone by pushing the images to a remote image registry

- Enter a running container and inspect its environment
- Set up a multi-node Kubernetes cluster on Google Kubernetes Engine
- Configure an alias and tab completion for the `kubectl` command-line tool
- List and inspect Nodes, Pods, Services, and ReplicationControllers in a Kubernetes cluster
- Run a container in Kubernetes and make it accessible from outside the cluster
- Have a basic sense of how Pods, ReplicationControllers, and Services relate to one another
- Scale an app horizontally by changing the ReplicationController's replica count
- Access the web-based Kubernetes dashboard on both Minikube and GKE

Pods: running containers in Kubernetes

This chapter covers

- Creating, running, and stopping pods
- Organizing pods and other resources with labels
- Performing an operation on all pods with a specific label
- Using namespaces to split pods into non-overlapping groups
- Scheduling pods onto specific types of worker nodes

The previous chapter should have given you a rough picture of the basic components you create in Kubernetes and at least an outline of what they do. Now, we'll start reviewing all types of Kubernetes objects (or *resources*) in greater detail, so you'll understand when, how, and why to use each of them. We'll start with pods, because they're the central, most important, concept in Kubernetes. Everything else either manages, exposes, or is used by pods.

3.1   Introducing pods

You've already learned that a pod is a co-located group of containers and represents the basic building block in Kubernetes. Instead of deploying containers individually, you always deploy and operate on a pod of containers. We're not implying that a pod always includes more than one container—it's common for pods to contain only a single container. The key thing about pods is that when a pod does contain multiple containers, all of them are always run on a single worker node—it never spans multiple worker nodes, as shown in figure 3.1.

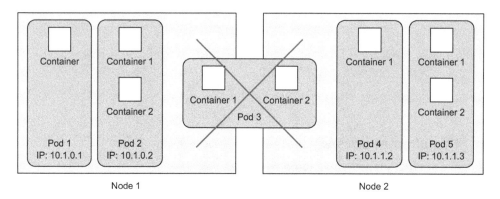

Figure 3.1   **All containers of a pod run on the same node. A pod never spans two nodes.**

3.1.1   Understanding why we need pods

But why do we even need pods? Why can't we use containers directly? Why would we even need to run multiple containers together? Can't we put all our processes into a single container? We'll answer those questions now.

UNDERSTANDING WHY MULTIPLE CONTAINERS ARE BETTER THAN ONE CONTAINER RUNNING MULTIPLE PROCESSES

Imagine an app consisting of multiple processes that either communicate through *IPC* (Inter-Process Communication) or through locally stored files, which requires them to run on the same machine. Because in Kubernetes you always run processes in containers and each container is much like an isolated machine, you may think it makes sense to run multiple processes in a single container, but you shouldn't do that.

Containers are designed to run only a single process per container (unless the process itself spawns child processes). If you run multiple unrelated processes in a single container, it is your responsibility to keep all those processes running, manage their logs, and so on. For example, you'd have to include a mechanism for automatically restarting individual processes if they crash. Also, all those processes would log to the same standard output, so you'd have a hard time figuring out what process logged what.

Therefore, you need to run each process in its own container. That's how Docker and Kubernetes are meant to be used.

3.1.2 *Understanding pods*

Because you're not supposed to group multiple processes into a single container, it's obvious you need another higher-level construct that will allow you to bind containers together and manage them as a single unit. This is the reasoning behind pods.

A pod of containers allows you to run closely related processes together and provide them with (almost) the same environment as if they were all running in a single container, while keeping them somewhat isolated. This way, you get the best of both worlds. You can take advantage of all the features containers provide, while at the same time giving the processes the illusion of running together.

UNDERSTANDING THE PARTIAL ISOLATION BETWEEN CONTAINERS OF THE SAME POD

In the previous chapter, you learned that containers are completely isolated from each other, but now you see that you want to isolate groups of containers instead of individual ones. You want containers inside each group to share certain resources, although not all, so that they're not fully isolated. Kubernetes achieves this by configuring Docker to have all containers of a pod share the same set of Linux namespaces instead of each container having its own set.

Because all containers of a pod run under the same Network and UTS namespaces (we're talking about Linux namespaces here), they all share the same hostname and network interfaces. Similarly, all containers of a pod run under the same IPC namespace and can communicate through IPC. In the latest Kubernetes and Docker versions, they can also share the same PID namespace, but that feature isn't enabled by default.

> **NOTE** When containers of the same pod use separate PID namespaces, you only see the container's own processes when running ps aux in the container.

But when it comes to the filesystem, things are a little different. Because most of the container's filesystem comes from the container image, by default, the filesystem of each container is fully isolated from other containers. However, it's possible to have them share file directories using a Kubernetes concept called a *Volume*, which we'll talk about in chapter 6.

UNDERSTANDING HOW CONTAINERS SHARE THE SAME IP AND PORT SPACE

One thing to stress here is that because containers in a pod run in the same Network namespace, they share the same IP address and port space. This means processes running in containers of the same pod need to take care not to bind to the same port numbers or they'll run into port conflicts. But this only concerns containers in the same pod. Containers of different pods can never run into port conflicts, because each pod has a separate port space. All the containers in a pod also have the same loopback network interface, so a container can communicate with other containers in the same pod through localhost.

INTRODUCING THE FLAT INTER-POD NETWORK

All pods in a Kubernetes cluster reside in a single flat, shared, network-address space (shown in figure 3.2), which means every pod can access every other pod at the other pod's IP address. No *NAT* (Network Address Translation) gateways exist between them. When two pods send network packets between each other, they'll each see the actual IP address of the other as the source IP in the packet.

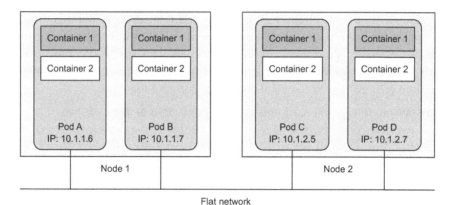

Figure 3.2   Each pod gets a routable IP address and all other pods see the pod under that IP address.

Consequently, communication between pods is always simple. It doesn't matter if two pods are scheduled onto a single or onto different worker nodes; in both cases the containers inside those pods can communicate with each other across the flat NAT-less network, much like computers on a local area network (LAN), regardless of the actual inter-node network topology. Like a computer on a LAN, each pod gets its own IP address and is accessible from all other pods through this network established specifically for pods. This is usually achieved through an additional software-defined network layered on top of the actual network.

To sum up what's been covered in this section: pods are logical hosts and behave much like physical hosts or VMs in the non-container world. Processes running in the same pod are like processes running on the same physical or virtual machine, except that each process is encapsulated in a container.

3.1.3   *Organizing containers across pods properly*

You should think of pods as separate machines, but where each one hosts only a certain app. Unlike the old days, when we used to cram all sorts of apps onto the same host, we don't do that with pods. Because pods are relatively lightweight, you can have as many as you need without incurring almost any overhead. Instead of stuffing everything into a single pod, you should organize apps into multiple pods, where each one contains only tightly related components or processes.

Having said that, do you think a multi-tier application consisting of a frontend application server and a backend database should be configured as a single pod or as two pods?

SPLITTING MULTI-TIER APPS INTO MULTIPLE PODS

Although nothing is stopping you from running both the frontend server and the database in a single pod with two containers, it isn't the most appropriate way. We've said that all containers of the same pod always run co-located, but do the web server and the database really need to run on the same machine? The answer is obviously no, so you don't want to put them into a single pod. But is it wrong to do so regardless? In a way, it is.

If both the frontend and backend are in the same pod, then both will always be run on the same machine. If you have a two-node Kubernetes cluster and only this single pod, you'll only be using a single worker node and not taking advantage of the computational resources (CPU and memory) you have at your disposal on the second node. Splitting the pod into two would allow Kubernetes to schedule the frontend to one node and the backend to the other node, thereby improving the utilization of your infrastructure.

SPLITTING INTO MULTIPLE PODS TO ENABLE INDIVIDUAL SCALING

Another reason why you shouldn't put them both into a single pod is scaling. A pod is also the basic unit of scaling. Kubernetes can't horizontally scale individual containers; instead, it scales whole pods. If your pod consists of a frontend and a backend container, when you scale up the number of instances of the pod to, let's say, two, you end up with two frontend containers and two backend containers.

Usually, frontend components have completely different scaling requirements than the backends, so we tend to scale them individually. Not to mention the fact that backends such as databases are usually much harder to scale compared to (stateless) frontend web servers. If you need to scale a container individually, this is a clear indication that it needs to be deployed in a separate pod.

UNDERSTANDING WHEN TO USE MULTIPLE CONTAINERS IN A POD

The main reason to put multiple containers into a single pod is when the application consists of one main process and one or more complementary processes, as shown in figure 3.3.

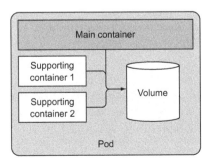

Figure 3.3 Pods should contain tightly coupled containers, usually a main container and containers that support the main one.

For example, the main container in a pod could be a web server that serves files from a certain file directory, while an additional container (a sidecar container) periodically downloads content from an external source and stores it in the web server's directory. In chapter 6 you'll see that you need to use a Kubernetes Volume that you mount into both containers.

Other examples of sidecar containers include log rotators and collectors, data processors, communication adapters, and others.

DECIDING WHEN TO USE MULTIPLE CONTAINERS IN A POD

To recap how containers should be grouped into pods—when deciding whether to put two containers into a single pod or into two separate pods, you always need to ask yourself the following questions:

- Do they need to be run together or can they run on different hosts?
- Do they represent a single whole or are they independent components?
- Must they be scaled together or individually?

Basically, you should always gravitate toward running containers in separate pods, unless a specific reason requires them to be part of the same pod. Figure 3.4 will help you memorize this.

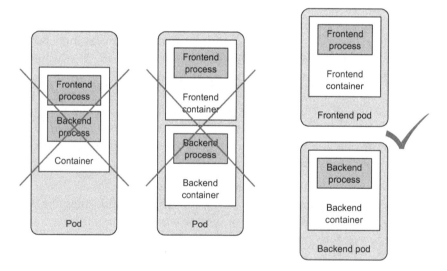

Figure 3.4   A container shouldn't run multiple processes. A pod shouldn't contain multiple containers if they don't need to run on the same machine.

Although pods can contain multiple containers, to keep things simple for now, you'll only be dealing with single-container pods in this chapter. You'll see how multiple containers are used in the same pod later, in chapter 6.

3.2   *Creating pods from YAML or JSON descriptors*

Pods and other Kubernetes resources are usually created by posting a JSON or YAML manifest to the Kubernetes REST API endpoint. Also, you can use other, simpler ways of creating resources, such as the `kubectl run` command you used in the previous chapter, but they usually only allow you to configure a limited set of properties, not all. Additionally, defining all your Kubernetes objects from YAML files makes it possible to store them in a version control system, with all the benefits it brings.

To configure all aspects of each type of resource, you'll need to know and understand the Kubernetes API object definitions. You'll get to know most of them as you learn about each resource type throughout this book. We won't explain every single property, so you should also refer to the Kubernetes API reference documentation at http://kubernetes.io/docs/reference/ when creating objects.

3.2.1   *Examining a YAML descriptor of an existing pod*

You already have some existing pods you created in the previous chapter, so let's look at what a YAML definition for one of those pods looks like. You'll use the `kubectl get` command with the `-o yaml` option to get the whole YAML definition of the pod, as shown in the following listing.

> **Listing 3.1   Full YAML of a deployed pod**

```
$ kubectl get po kubia-zxzij -o yaml
apiVersion: v1                                 ◁────  Kubernetes API version used
                                                      in this YAML descriptor
kind: Pod                                      ◁────  Type of Kubernetes
metadata:                                             object/resource
  annotations:
    kubernetes.io/created-by: ...
  creationTimestamp: 2016-03-18T12:37:50Z
  generateName: kubia-
  labels:
    run: kubia                                        Pod metadata (name,
  name: kubia-zxzij                                   labels, annotations,
  namespace: default                                  and so on)
  resourceVersion: "294"
  selfLink: /api/v1/namespaces/default/pods/kubia-zxzij
  uid: 3a564dc0-ed06-11e5-ba3b-42010af00004
spec:
  containers:
  - image: luksa/kubia
    imagePullPolicy: IfNotPresent
    name: kubia                                       Pod specification/
    ports:                                            contents (list of
    - containerPort: 8080                             pod's containers,
      protocol: TCP                                   volumes, and so on)
    resources:
      requests:
        cpu: 100m
```

```
        terminationMessagePath: /dev/termination-log
        volumeMounts:
        - mountPath: /var/run/secrets/k8s.io/servacc
          name: default-token-kvcqa
          readOnly: true
    dnsPolicy: ClusterFirst
    nodeName: gke-kubia-e8fe08b8-node-txje
    restartPolicy: Always
    serviceAccount: default
    serviceAccountName: default
    terminationGracePeriodSeconds: 30
    volumes:
    - name: default-token-kvcqa
      secret:
        secretName: default-token-kvcqa
  status:
    conditions:
    - lastProbeTime: null
      lastTransitionTime: null
      status: "True"
      type: Ready
    containerStatuses:
    - containerID: docker://f0276994322d247ba...
      image: luksa/kubia
      imageID: docker://4c325bcc6b40c110226b89fe...
      lastState: {}
      name: kubia
      ready: true
      restartCount: 0
      state:
        running:
          startedAt: 2016-03-18T12:46:05Z
    hostIP: 10.132.0.4
    phase: Running
    podIP: 10.0.2.3
    startTime: 2016-03-18T12:44:32Z
```

Pod specification/ contents (list of pod's containers, volumes, and so on)

Detailed status of the pod and its containers

I know this looks complicated, but it becomes simple once you understand the basics and know how to distinguish between the important parts and the minor details. Also, you can take comfort in the fact that when creating a new pod, the YAML you need to write is much shorter, as you'll see later.

INTRODUCING THE MAIN PARTS OF A POD DEFINITION

The pod definition consists of a few parts. First, there's the Kubernetes API version used in the YAML and the type of resource the YAML is describing. Then, three important sections are found in almost all Kubernetes resources:

- *Metadata* includes the name, namespace, labels, and other information about the pod.
- *Spec* contains the actual description of the pod's contents, such as the pod's containers, volumes, and other data.

- *Status* contains the current information about the running pod, such as what condition the pod is in, the description and status of each container, and the pod's internal IP and other basic info.

Listing 3.1 showed a full description of a running pod, including its status. The `status` part contains read-only runtime data that shows the state of the resource at a given moment. When creating a new pod, you never need to provide the `status` part.

The three parts described previously show the typical structure of a Kubernetes API object. As you'll see throughout the book, all other objects have the same anatomy. This makes understanding new objects relatively easy.

Going through all the individual properties in the previous YAML doesn't make much sense, so, instead, let's see what the most basic YAML for creating a pod looks like.

3.2.2 *Creating a simple YAML descriptor for a pod*

You're going to create a file called kubia-manual.yaml (you can create it in any directory you want), or download the book's code archive, where you'll find the file inside the Chapter03 directory. The following listing shows the entire contents of the file.

Listing 3.2   A basic pod manifest: kubia-manual.yaml

```
apiVersion: v1        ◁      Descriptor conforms to version v1 of Kubernetes API
kind: Pod             ◁      You're describing a pod.
metadata:
  name: kubia-manual  ◁      The name of the pod
spec:
  containers:
  - image: luksa/kubia  ◁    Container image to create the container from
    name: kubia          ◁    Name of the container
    ports:
    - containerPort: 8080  ◁  The port the app is listening on
      protocol: TCP
```

I'm sure you'll agree this is much simpler than the definition in listing 3.1. Let's examine this descriptor in detail. It conforms to the `v1` version of the Kubernetes API. The type of resource you're describing is a `pod`, with the name `kubia-manual`. The pod consists of a single container based on the `luksa/kubia` image. You've also given a name to the container and indicated that it's listening on port `8080`.

SPECIFYING CONTAINER PORTS

Specifying ports in the pod definition is purely informational. Omitting them has no effect on whether clients can connect to the pod through the port or not. If the container is accepting connections through a port bound to the 0.0.0.0 address, other pods can always connect to it, even if the port isn't listed in the pod spec explicitly. But it makes sense to define the ports explicitly so that everyone using your cluster can quickly see what ports each pod exposes. Explicitly defining ports also allows you to assign a name to each port, which can come in handy, as you'll see later in the book.

Using kubectl explain to discover possible API object fields

When preparing a manifest, you can either turn to the Kubernetes reference documentation at http://kubernetes.io/docs/api to see which attributes are supported by each API object, or you can use the `kubectl explain` command.

For example, when creating a pod manifest from scratch, you can start by asking `kubectl` to explain pods:

```
$ kubectl explain pods
DESCRIPTION:
Pod is a collection of containers that can run on a host. This resource
          is created by clients and scheduled onto hosts.

FIELDS:
   kind        <string>
     Kind is a string value representing the REST resource this object
     represents...

   metadata <Object>
     Standard object's metadata...

   spec        <Object>
     Specification of the desired behavior of the pod...

   status     <Object>
     Most recently observed status of the pod. This data may not be up to
     date...
```

Kubectl prints out the explanation of the object and lists the attributes the object can contain. You can then drill deeper to find out more about each attribute. For example, you can examine the `spec` attribute like this:

```
$ kubectl explain pod.spec
RESOURCE: spec <Object>

DESCRIPTION:
    Specification of the desired behavior of the pod...
    podSpec is a description of a pod.

FIELDS:
   hostPID    <boolean>
     Use the host's pid namespace. Optional: Default to false.

   ...

   volumes    <[]Object>
     List of volumes that can be mounted by containers belonging to the
     pod.
```

```
Containers <[]Object> -required-
   List of containers belonging to the pod. Containers cannot currently
   Be added or removed. There must be at least one container in a pod.
   Cannot be updated. More info:
   http://releases.k8s.io/release-1.4/docs/user-guide/containers.md
```

3.2.3 *Using kubectl create to create the pod*

To create the pod from your YAML file, use the `kubectl create` command:

```
$ kubectl create -f kubia-manual.yaml
pod "kubia-manual" created
```

The `kubectl create -f` command is used for creating any resource (not only pods) from a YAML or JSON file.

RETRIEVING THE WHOLE DEFINITION OF A RUNNING POD

After creating the pod, you can ask Kubernetes for the full YAML of the pod. You'll see it's similar to the YAML you saw earlier. You'll learn about the additional fields appearing in the returned definition in the next sections. Go ahead and use the following command to see the full descriptor of the pod:

```
$ kubectl get po kubia-manual -o yaml
```

If you're more into JSON, you can also tell `kubectl` to return JSON instead of YAML like this (this works even if you used YAML to create the pod):

```
$ kubectl get po kubia-manual -o json
```

SEEING YOUR NEWLY CREATED POD IN THE LIST OF PODS

Your pod has been created, but how do you know if it's running? Let's list pods to see their statuses:

```
$ kubectl get pods
NAME           READY   STATUS    RESTARTS   AGE
kubia-manual   1/1     Running   0          32s
kubia-zxzij    1/1     Running   0          1d
```

There's your `kubia-manual` pod. Its status shows that it's running. If you're like me, you'll probably want to confirm that's true by talking to the pod. You'll do that in a minute. First, you'll look at the app's log to check for any errors.

3.2.4 *Viewing application logs*

Your little Node.js application logs to the process's standard output. Containerized applications usually log to the standard output and standard error stream instead of writing their logs to files. This is to allow users to view logs of different applications in a simple, standard way.

The container runtime (Docker in your case) redirects those streams to files and allows you to get the container's log by running

```
$ docker logs <container id>
```

You could use ssh to log into the node where your pod is running and retrieve its logs with docker logs, but Kubernetes provides an easier way.

RETRIEVING A POD'S LOG WITH KUBECTL LOGS

To see your pod's log (more precisely, the container's log) you run the following command on your local machine (no need to ssh anywhere):

```
$ kubectl logs kubia-manual
Kubia server starting...
```

You haven't sent any web requests to your Node.js app, so the log only shows a single log statement about the server starting up. As you can see, retrieving logs of an application running in Kubernetes is incredibly simple if the pod only contains a single container.

> **NOTE** Container logs are automatically rotated daily and every time the log file reaches 10MB in size. The kubectl logs command only shows the log entries from the last rotation.

SPECIFYING THE CONTAINER NAME WHEN GETTING LOGS OF A MULTI-CONTAINER POD

If your pod includes multiple containers, you have to explicitly specify the container name by including the -c <container name> option when running kubectl logs. In your kubia-manual pod, you set the container's name to kubia, so if additional containers exist in the pod, you'd have to get its logs like this:

```
$ kubectl logs kubia-manual -c kubia
Kubia server starting...
```

Note that you can only retrieve container logs of pods that are still in existence. When a pod is deleted, its logs are also deleted. To make a pod's logs available even after the pod is deleted, you need to set up centralized, cluster-wide logging, which stores all the logs into a central store. Chapter 17 explains how centralized logging works.

3.2.5   *Sending requests to the pod*

The pod is now running—at least that's what kubectl get and your app's log say. But how do you see it in action? In the previous chapter, you used the kubectl expose command to create a service to gain access to the pod externally. You're not going to do that now, because a whole chapter is dedicated to services, and you have other ways of connecting to a pod for testing and debugging purposes. One of them is through *port forwarding*.

FORWARDING A LOCAL NETWORK PORT TO A PORT IN THE POD

When you want to talk to a specific pod without going through a service (for debugging or other reasons), Kubernetes allows you to configure port forwarding to the pod. This is done through the `kubectl port-forward` command. The following command will forward your machine's local port 8888 to port 8080 of your kubia-manual pod:

```
$ kubectl port-forward kubia-manual 8888:8080
... Forwarding from 127.0.0.1:8888 -> 8080
... Forwarding from [::1]:8888 -> 8080
```

The port forwarder is running and you can now connect to your pod through the local port.

CONNECTING TO THE POD THROUGH THE PORT FORWARDER

In a different terminal, you can now use `curl` to send an HTTP request to your pod through the `kubectl port-forward` proxy running on `localhost:8888`:

```
$ curl localhost:8888
You've hit kubia-manual
```

Figure 3.5 shows an overly simplified view of what happens when you send the request. In reality, a couple of additional components sit between the `kubectl` process and the pod, but they aren't relevant right now.

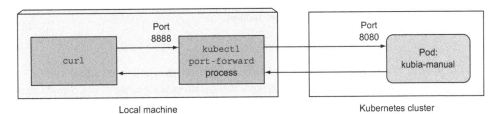

Figure 3.5 A simplified view of what happens when you use `curl` with `kubectl port-forward`

Using port forwarding like this is an effective way to test an individual pod. You'll learn about other similar methods throughout the book.

3.3 *Organizing pods with labels*

At this point, you have two pods running in your cluster. When deploying actual applications, most users will end up running many more pods. As the number of pods increases, the need for categorizing them into subsets becomes more and more evident.

For example, with microservices architectures, the number of deployed microservices can easily exceed 20 or more. Those components will probably be replicated (multiple copies of the same component will be deployed) and multiple versions or releases (stable, beta, canary, and so on) will run concurrently. This can lead to hundreds of pods in the system. Without a mechanism for organizing them, you end up with a big, incomprehensible mess, such as the one shown in figure 3.6. The figure shows pods of multiple microservices, with several running multiple replicas, and others running different releases of the same microservice.

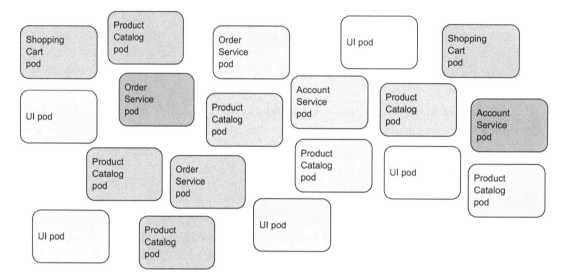

Figure 3.6   Uncategorized pods in a microservices architecture

It's evident you need a way of organizing them into smaller groups based on arbitrary criteria, so every developer and system administrator dealing with your system can easily see which pod is which. And you'll want to operate on every pod belonging to a certain group with a single action instead of having to perform the action for each pod individually.

Organizing pods and all other Kubernetes objects is done through *labels*.

3.3.1 *Introducing labels*

Labels are a simple, yet incredibly powerful, Kubernetes feature for organizing not only pods, but all other Kubernetes resources. A label is an arbitrary key-value pair you attach to a resource, which is then utilized when selecting resources using *label selectors* (resources are filtered based on whether they include the label specified in the selector). A resource can have more than one label, as long as the keys of those labels are unique within that resource. You usually attach labels to resources when you create them, but you can also add additional labels or even modify the values of existing labels later without having to recreate the resource.

Let's turn back to the microservices example from figure 3.6. By adding labels to those pods, you get a much-better-organized system that everyone can easily make sense of. Each pod is labeled with two labels:

- *app*, which specifies which app, component, or microservice the pod belongs to.
- *rel*, which shows whether the application running in the pod is a stable, beta, or a canary release.

DEFINITION A canary release is when you deploy a new version of an application next to the stable version, and only let a small fraction of users hit the new version to see how it behaves before rolling it out to all users. This prevents bad releases from being exposed to too many users.

By adding these two labels, you've essentially organized your pods into two dimensions (horizontally by app and vertically by release), as shown in figure 3.7.

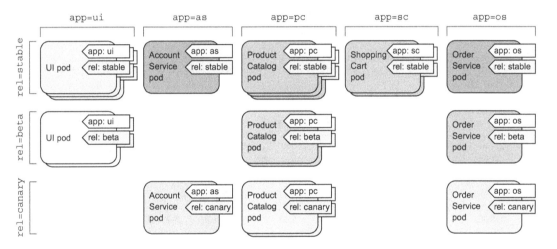

Figure 3.7   Organizing pods in a microservices architecture with pod labels

Every developer or ops person with access to your cluster can now easily see the system's structure and where each pod fits in by looking at the pod's labels.

3.3.2   *Specifying labels when creating a pod*

Now, you'll see labels in action by creating a new pod with two labels. Create a new file called kubia-manual-with-labels.yaml with the contents of the following listing.

> **Listing 3.3   A pod with labels: kubia-manual-with-labels.yaml**

```
apiVersion: v1
kind: Pod
metadata:
  name: kubia-manual-v2
```

```
labels:
  creation_method: manual
  env: prod
spec:
  containers:
  - image: luksa/kubia
    name: kubia
    ports:
    - containerPort: 8080
      protocol: TCP
```

| **Two labels are attached to the pod.**

You've included the labels creation_method=manual and env=prod in the metadata
.labels section. You'll create this pod now:

```
$ kubectl create -f kubia-manual-with-labels.yaml
pod "kubia-manual-v2" created
```

The kubectl get pods command doesn't list any labels by default, but you can see
them by using the --show-labels switch:

```
$ kubectl get po --show-labels
NAME            READY   STATUS    RESTARTS   AGE LABELS
kubia-manual    1/1     Running   0          16m <none>
kubia-manual-v2 1/1     Running   0          2m  creat_method=manual,env=prod
kubia-zxzij     1/1     Running   0          1d  run=kubia
```

Instead of listing all labels, if you're only interested in certain labels, you can specify
them with the -L switch and have each displayed in its own column. List pods again
and show the columns for the two labels you've attached to your kubia-manual-v2 pod:

```
$ kubectl get po -L creation_method,env
NAME            READY   STATUS    RESTARTS   AGE   CREATION_METHOD   ENV
kubia-manual    1/1     Running   0          16m   <none>            <none>
kubia-manual-v2 1/1     Running   0          2m    manual            prod
kubia-zxzij     1/1     Running   0          1d    <none>            <none>
```

3.3.3   *Modifying labels of existing pods*

Labels can also be added to and modified on existing pods. Because the kubia-manual pod was also created manually, let's add the creation_method=manual label to it:

```
$ kubectl label po kubia-manual creation_method=manual
pod "kubia-manual" labeled
```

Now, let's also change the env=prod label to env=debug on the kubia-manual-v2 pod,
to see how existing labels can be changed.

> **NOTE**   You need to use the --overwrite option when changing existing labels.

```
$ kubectl label po kubia-manual-v2 env=debug --overwrite
pod "kubia-manual-v2" labeled
```

List the pods again to see the updated labels:

```
$ kubectl get po -L creation_method,env
NAME            READY   STATUS    RESTARTS   AGE   CREATION_METHOD   ENV
kubia-manual    1/1     Running   0          16m   manual            <none>
kubia-manual-v2 1/1     Running   0          2m    manual            debug
kubia-zxzij     1/1     Running   0          1d    <none>            <none>
```

As you can see, attaching labels to resources is trivial, and so is changing them on existing resources. It may not be evident right now, but this is an incredibly powerful feature, as you'll see in the next chapter. But first, let's see what you can do with these labels, in addition to displaying them when listing pods.

3.4 *Listing subsets of pods through label selectors*

Attaching labels to resources so you can see the labels next to each resource when listing them isn't that interesting. But labels go hand in hand with *label selectors*. Label selectors allow you to select a subset of pods tagged with certain labels and perform an operation on those pods. A label selector is a criterion, which filters resources based on whether they include a certain label with a certain value.

A label selector can select resources based on whether the resource

- Contains (or doesn't contain) a label with a certain key
- Contains a label with a certain key and value
- Contains a label with a certain key, but with a value not equal to the one you specify

3.4.1 *Listing pods using a label selector*

Let's use label selectors on the pods you've created so far. To see all pods you created manually (you labeled them with `creation_method=manual`), do the following:

```
$ kubectl get po -l creation_method=manual
NAME            READY   STATUS    RESTARTS   AGE
kubia-manual    1/1     Running   0          51m
kubia-manual-v2 1/1     Running   0          37m
```

To list all pods that include the env label, whatever its value is:

```
$ kubectl get po -l env
NAME            READY   STATUS    RESTARTS   AGE
kubia-manual-v2 1/1     Running   0          37m
```

And those that don't have the env label:

```
$ kubectl get po -l '!env'
NAME            READY   STATUS    RESTARTS   AGE
kubia-manual    1/1     Running   0          51m
kubia-zxzij     1/1     Running   0          10d
```

NOTE   Make sure to use single quotes around !env, so the bash shell doesn't evaluate the exclamation mark.

Similarly, you could also match pods with the following label selectors:

- `creation_method!=manual` to select pods with the `creation_method` label with any value other than `manual`
- `env in (prod,devel)` to select pods with the `env` label set to either `prod` or `devel`
- `env notin (prod,devel)` to select pods with the `env` label set to any value other than `prod` or `devel`

Turning back to the pods in the microservices-oriented architecture example, you could select all pods that are part of the product catalog microservice by using the `app=pc` label selector (shown in the following figure).

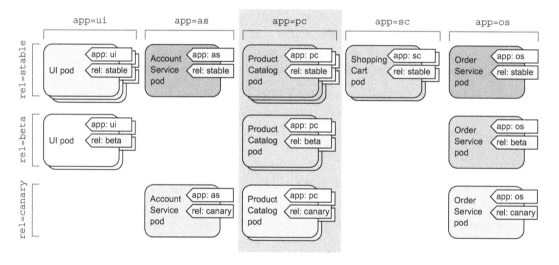

Figure 3.8   Selecting the product catalog microservice pods using the "app=pc" label selector

3.4.2   Using multiple conditions in a label selector

A selector can also include multiple comma-separated criteria. Resources need to match all of them to match the selector. If, for example, you want to select only pods running the beta release of the product catalog microservice, you'd use the following selector: `app=pc,rel=beta` (visualized in figure 3.9).

Label selectors aren't useful only for listing pods, but also for performing actions on a subset of all pods. For example, later in the chapter, you'll see how to use label selectors to delete multiple pods at once. But label selectors aren't used only by `kubectl`. They're also used internally, as you'll see next.

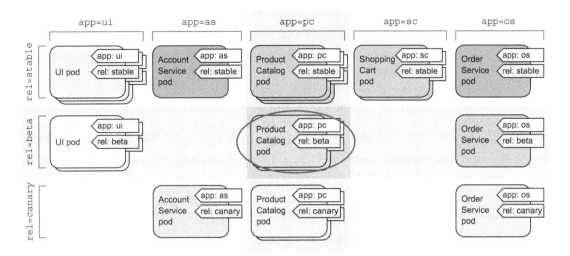

Figure 3.9 Selecting pods with multiple label selectors

3.5   *Using labels and selectors to constrain pod scheduling*

All the pods you've created so far have been scheduled pretty much randomly across your worker nodes. As I've mentioned in the previous chapter, this is the proper way of working in a Kubernetes cluster. Because Kubernetes exposes all the nodes in the cluster as a single, large deployment platform, it shouldn't matter to you what node a pod is scheduled to. Because each pod gets the exact amount of computational resources it requests (CPU, memory, and so on) and its accessibility from other pods isn't at all affected by the node the pod is scheduled to, usually there shouldn't be any need for you to tell Kubernetes exactly where to schedule your pods.

Certain cases exist, however, where you'll want to have at least a little say in where a pod should be scheduled. A good example is when your hardware infrastructure isn't homogenous. If part of your worker nodes have spinning hard drives, whereas others have SSDs, you may want to schedule certain pods to one group of nodes and the rest to the other. Another example is when you need to schedule pods performing intensive GPU-based computation only to nodes that provide the required GPU acceleration.

You never want to say specifically what node a pod should be scheduled to, because that would couple the application to the infrastructure, whereas the whole idea of Kubernetes is hiding the actual infrastructure from the apps that run on it. But if you want to have a say in where a pod should be scheduled, instead of specifying an exact node, you should describe the node requirements and then let Kubernetes select a node that matches those requirements. This can be done through node labels and node label selectors.

3.5.1 Using labels for categorizing worker nodes

As you learned earlier, pods aren't the only Kubernetes resource type that you can attach a label to. Labels can be attached to any Kubernetes object, including nodes. Usually, when the ops team adds a new node to the cluster, they'll categorize the node by attaching labels specifying the type of hardware the node provides or anything else that may come in handy when scheduling pods.

Let's imagine one of the nodes in your cluster contains a GPU meant to be used for general-purpose GPU computing. You want to add a label to the node showing this feature. You're going to add the label gpu=true to one of your nodes (pick one out of the list returned by kubectl get nodes):

```
$ kubectl label node gke-kubia-85f6-node-0rrx gpu=true
node "gke-kubia-85f6-node-0rrx" labeled
```

Now you can use a label selector when listing the nodes, like you did before with pods. List only nodes that include the label gpu=true:

```
$ kubectl get nodes -l gpu=true
NAME                        STATUS AGE
gke-kubia-85f6-node-0rrx    Ready  1d
```

As expected, only one node has this label. You can also try listing all the nodes and tell kubectl to display an additional column showing the values of each node's gpu label (kubectl get nodes -L gpu).

3.5.2 Scheduling pods to specific nodes

Now imagine you want to deploy a new pod that needs a GPU to perform its work. To ask the scheduler to only choose among the nodes that provide a GPU, you'll add a node selector to the pod's YAML. Create a file called kubia-gpu.yaml with the following listing's contents and then use kubectl create -f kubia-gpu.yaml to create the pod.

> **Listing 3.4 Using a label selector to schedule a pod to a specific node: kubia-gpu.yaml**

```
apiVersion: v1
kind: Pod
metadata:
  name: kubia-gpu
spec:
  nodeSelector:          nodeSelector tells Kubernetes
    gpu: "true"          to deploy this pod only to
  containers:            nodes containing the
  - image: luksa/kubia   gpu=true label.
    name: kubia
```

You've added a `nodeSelector` field under the `spec` section. When you create the pod, the scheduler will only choose among the nodes that contain the `gpu=true` label (which is only a single node in your case).

3.5.3 Scheduling to one specific node

Similarly, you could also schedule a pod to an exact node, because each node also has a unique label with the key `kubernetes.io/hostname` and value set to the actual hostname of the node. But setting the `nodeSelector` to a specific node by the hostname label may lead to the pod being unschedulable if the node is offline. You shouldn't think in terms of individual nodes. Always think about logical groups of nodes that satisfy certain criteria specified through label selectors.

This was a quick demonstration of how labels and label selectors work and how they can be used to influence the operation of Kubernetes. The importance and usefulness of label selectors will become even more evident when we talk about Replication-Controllers and Services in the next two chapters.

> **NOTE** Additional ways of influencing which node a pod is scheduled to are covered in chapter 16.

3.6 Annotating pods

In addition to labels, pods and other objects can also contain *annotations*. Annotations are also key-value pairs, so in essence, they're similar to labels, but they aren't meant to hold identifying information. They can't be used to group objects the way labels can. While objects can be selected through label selectors, there's no such thing as an annotation selector.

On the other hand, annotations can hold much larger pieces of information and are primarily meant to be used by tools. Certain annotations are automatically added to objects by Kubernetes, but others are added by users manually.

Annotations are also commonly used when introducing new features to Kubernetes. Usually, alpha and beta versions of new features don't introduce any new fields to API objects. Annotations are used instead of fields, and then once the required API changes have become clear and been agreed upon by the Kubernetes developers, new fields are introduced and the related annotations deprecated.

A great use of annotations is adding descriptions for each pod or other API object, so that everyone using the cluster can quickly look up information about each individual object. For example, an annotation used to specify the name of the person who created the object can make collaboration between everyone working on the cluster much easier.

3.6.1 Looking up an object's annotations

Let's see an example of an annotation that Kubernetes added automatically to the pod you created in the previous chapter. To see the annotations, you'll need to request the full YAML of the pod or use the `kubectl describe` command. You'll use the first option in the following listing.

Listing 3.5   A pod's annotations

```
$ kubectl get po kubia-zxzij -o yaml
apiVersion: v1
kind: Pod
metadata:
  annotations:
    kubernetes.io/created-by: |
      {"kind":"SerializedReference", "apiVersion":"v1",
      "reference":{"kind":"ReplicationController", "namespace":"default", ...
```

Without going into too many details, as you can see, the `kubernetes.io/created-by` annotation holds JSON data about the object that created the pod. That's not something you'd want to put into a label. Labels should be short, whereas annotations can contain relatively large blobs of data (up to 256 KB in total).

> **NOTE** The `kubernetes.io/created-by` annotations was deprecated in version 1.8 and will be removed in 1.9, so you will no longer see it in the YAML.

3.6.2   *Adding and modifying annotations*

Annotations can obviously be added to pods at creation time, the same way labels can. They can also be added to or modified on existing pods later. The simplest way to add an annotation to an existing object is through the `kubectl annotate` command.

You'll try adding an annotation to your `kubia-manual` pod now:

```
$ kubectl annotate pod kubia-manual mycompany.com/someannotation="foo bar"
pod "kubia-manual" annotated
```

You added the annotation `mycompany.com/someannotation` with the value `foo bar`. It's a good idea to use this format for annotation keys to prevent key collisions. When different tools or libraries add annotations to objects, they may accidentally override each other's annotations if they don't use unique prefixes like you did here.

You can use `kubectl describe` to see the annotation you added:

```
$ kubectl describe pod kubia-manual
...
Annotations:     mycompany.com/someannotation=foo bar
...
```

3.7   *Using namespaces to group resources*

Let's turn back to labels for a moment. We've seen how they organize pods and other objects into groups. Because each object can have multiple labels, those groups of objects can overlap. Plus, when working with the cluster (through `kubectl` for example), if you don't explicitly specify a label selector, you'll always see all objects.

But what about times when you want to split objects into separate, non-overlapping groups? You may want to only operate inside one group at a time. For this and other reasons, Kubernetes also groups objects into namespaces. These aren't the Linux namespaces we talked about in chapter 2, which are used to isolate processes from each other. Kubernetes namespaces provide a scope for objects names. Instead of having all your resources in one single namespace, you can split them into multiple namespaces, which also allows you to use the same resource names multiple times (across different namespaces).

3.7.1 Understanding the need for namespaces

Using multiple namespaces allows you to split complex systems with numerous components into smaller distinct groups. They can also be used for separating resources in a multi-tenant environment, splitting up resources into production, development, and QA environments, or in any other way you may need. Resource names only need to be unique within a namespace. Two different namespaces can contain resources of the same name. But, while most types of resources are namespaced, a few aren't. One of them is the Node resource, which is global and not tied to a single namespace. You'll learn about other cluster-level resources in later chapters.

Let's see how to use namespaces now.

3.7.2 Discovering other namespaces and their pods

First, let's list all namespaces in your cluster:

```
$ kubectl get ns
NAME           LABELS     STATUS     AGE
default        <none>     Active     1h
kube-public    <none>     Active     1h
kube-system    <none>     Active     1h
```

Up to this point, you've operated only in the `default` namespace. When listing resources with the `kubectl get` command, you've never specified the namespace explicitly, so `kubectl` always defaulted to the `default` namespace, showing you only the objects in that namespace. But as you can see from the list, the `kube-public` and the `kube-system` namespaces also exist. Let's look at the pods that belong to the `kube-system` namespace, by telling `kubectl` to list pods in that namespace only:

```
$ kubectl get po --namespace kube-system
NAME                                 READY     STATUS     RESTARTS     AGE
fluentd-cloud-kubia-e8fe-node-txje   1/1       Running    0            1h
heapster-v11-fz1ge                   1/1       Running    0            1h
kube-dns-v9-p8a4t                    0/4       Pending    0            1h
kube-ui-v4-kdlai                     1/1       Running    0            1h
l7-lb-controller-v0.5.2-bue96        2/2       Running    92           1h
```

TIP You can also use `-n` instead of `--namespace`.

You'll learn about these pods later in the book (don't worry if the pods shown here don't match the ones on your system exactly). It's clear from the name of the namespace that these are resources related to the Kubernetes system itself. By having them in this separate namespace, it keeps everything nicely organized. If they were all in the default namespace, mixed in with the resources you create yourself, you'd have a hard time seeing what belongs where, and you might inadvertently delete system resources.

Namespaces enable you to separate resources that don't belong together into non-overlapping groups. If several users or groups of users are using the same Kubernetes cluster, and they each manage their own distinct set of resources, they should each use their own namespace. This way, they don't need to take any special care not to inadvertently modify or delete the other users' resources and don't need to concern themselves with name conflicts, because namespaces provide a scope for resource names, as has already been mentioned.

Besides isolating resources, namespaces are also used for allowing only certain users access to particular resources and even for limiting the amount of computational resources available to individual users. You'll learn about this in chapters 12 through 14.

3.7.3   *Creating a namespace*

A namespace is a Kubernetes resource like any other, so you can create it by posting a YAML file to the Kubernetes API server. Let's see how to do this now.

CREATING A NAMESPACE FROM A YAML FILE

First, create a custom-namespace.yaml file with the following listing's contents (you'll find the file in the book's code archive).

> **Listing 3.6   A YAML definition of a namespace: custom-namespace.yaml**

```
apiVersion: v1
kind: Namespace          This says you're
metadata:                defining a namespace.
  name: custom-namespace    This is the name
                            of the namespace.
```

Now, use kubectl to post the file to the Kubernetes API server:

```
$ kubectl create -f custom-namespace.yaml
namespace "custom-namespace" created
```

CREATING A NAMESPACE WITH KUBECTL CREATE NAMESPACE

Although writing a file like the previous one isn't a big deal, it's still a hassle. Luckily, you can also create namespaces with the dedicated kubectl create namespace command, which is quicker than writing a YAML file. By having you create a YAML manifest for the namespace, I wanted to reinforce the idea that everything in Kubernetes has a corresponding API object that you can create, read, update, and delete by posting a YAML manifest to the API server.

You could have created the namespace like this:

```
$ kubectl create namespace custom-namespace
namespace "custom-namespace" created
```

> **NOTE** Although most objects' names must conform to the naming conventions specified in RFC 1035 (Domain names), which means they may contain only letters, digits, dashes, and dots, namespaces (and a few others) aren't allowed to contain dots.

3.7.4 *Managing objects in other namespaces*

To create resources in the namespace you've created, either add a namespace: custom-namespace entry to the metadata section, or specify the namespace when creating the resource with the kubectl create command:

```
$ kubectl create -f kubia-manual.yaml -n custom-namespace
pod "kubia-manual" created
```

You now have two pods with the same name (kubia-manual). One is in the default namespace, and the other is in your custom-namespace.

When listing, describing, modifying, or deleting objects in other namespaces, you need to pass the --namespace (or -n) flag to kubectl. If you don't specify the namespace, kubectl performs the action in the default namespace configured in the current kubectl context. The current context's namespace and the current context itself can be changed through kubectl config commands. To learn more about managing kubectl contexts, refer to appendix A.

> **TIP** To quickly switch to a different namespace, you can set up the following alias: alias kcd='kubectl config set-context $(kubectl config current-context) --namespace '. You can then switch between namespaces using kcd some-namespace.

3.7.5 *Understanding the isolation provided by namespaces*

To wrap up this section about namespaces, let me explain what namespaces don't provide—at least not out of the box. Although namespaces allow you to isolate objects into distinct groups, which allows you to operate only on those belonging to the specified namespace, they don't provide any kind of isolation of running objects.

For example, you may think that when different users deploy pods across different namespaces, those pods are isolated from each other and can't communicate, but that's not necessarily the case. Whether namespaces provide network isolation depends on which networking solution is deployed with Kubernetes. When the solution doesn't provide inter-namespace network isolation, if a pod in namespace foo knows the IP address of a pod in namespace `bar`, there is nothing preventing it from sending traffic, such as HTTP requests, to the other pod.

3.8 *Stopping and removing pods*

You've created a number of pods, which should all still be running. You have four pods running in the `default` namespace and one pod in `custom-namespace`. You're going to stop all of them now, because you don't need them anymore.

3.8.1 *Deleting a pod by name*

First, delete the `kubia-gpu` pod by name:

```
$ kubectl delete po kubia-gpu
pod "kubia-gpu" deleted
```

By deleting a pod, you're instructing Kubernetes to terminate all the containers that are part of that pod. Kubernetes sends a `SIGTERM` signal to the process and waits a certain number of seconds (30 by default) for it to shut down gracefully. If it doesn't shut down in time, the process is then killed through `SIGKILL`. To make sure your processes are always shut down gracefully, they need to handle the `SIGTERM` signal properly.

> **TIP** You can also delete more than one pod by specifying multiple, space-separated names (for example, `kubectl delete po pod1 pod2`).

3.8.2 *Deleting pods using label selectors*

Instead of specifying each pod to delete by name, you'll now use what you've learned about label selectors to stop both the `kubia-manual` and the `kubia-manual-v2` pod. Both pods include the `creation_method=manual` label, so you can delete them by using a label selector:

```
$ kubectl delete po -l creation_method=manual
pod "kubia-manual" deleted
pod "kubia-manual-v2" deleted
```

In the earlier microservices example, where you had tens (or possibly hundreds) of pods, you could, for instance, delete all canary pods at once by specifying the `rel=canary` label selector (visualized in figure 3.10):

```
$ kubectl delete po -l rel=canary
```

3.8.3 *Deleting pods by deleting the whole namespace*

Okay, back to your real pods. What about the pod in the `custom-namespace`? You no longer need either the pods in that namespace, or the namespace itself. You can

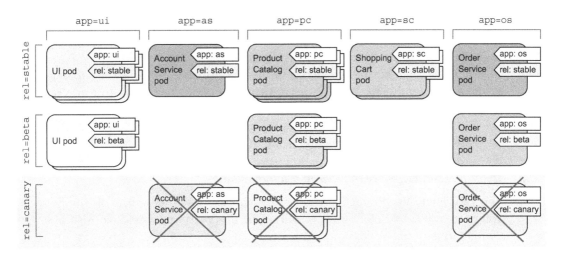

Figure 3.10   Selecting and deleting all canary pods through the `rel=canary` label selector

delete the whole namespace (the pods will be deleted along with the namespace auto-matically), using the following command:

```
$ kubectl delete ns custom-namespace
namespace "custom-namespace" deleted
```

3.8.4   Deleting all pods in a namespace, while keeping the namespace

You've now cleaned up almost everything. But what about the pod you created with the `kubectl run` command in chapter 2? That one is still running:

```
$ kubectl get pods
NAME          READY   STATUS    RESTARTS   AGE
kubia-zxzij   1/1     Running   0          1d
```

This time, instead of deleting the specific pod, tell Kubernetes to delete all pods in the current namespace by using the `--all` option:

```
$ kubectl delete po --all
pod "kubia-zxzij" deleted
```

Now, double check that no pods were left running:

```
$ kubectl get pods
NAME          READY   STATUS        RESTARTS   AGE
kubia-09as0   1/1     Running       0          1d
kubia-zxzij   1/1     Terminating   0          1d
```

Wait, what!?! The kubia-zxzij pod is terminating, but a new pod called kubia-09as0, which wasn't there before, has appeared. No matter how many times you delete all pods, a new pod called *kubia-something* will emerge.

You may remember you created your first pod with the kubectl run command. In chapter 2, I mentioned that this doesn't create a pod directly, but instead creates a ReplicationController, which then creates the pod. As soon as you delete a pod created by the ReplicationController, it immediately creates a new one. To delete the pod, you also need to delete the ReplicationController.

3.8.5 *Deleting (almost) all resources in a namespace*

You can delete the ReplicationController and the pods, as well as all the Services you've created, by deleting all resources in the current namespace with a single command:

```
$ kubectl delete all --all
pod "kubia-09as0" deleted
replicationcontroller "kubia" deleted
service "kubernetes" deleted
service "kubia-http" deleted
```

The first all in the command specifies that you're deleting resources of all types, and the --all option specifies that you're deleting all resource instances instead of specifying them by name (you already used this option when you ran the previous delete command).

> **NOTE** Deleting everything with the all keyword doesn't delete absolutely everything. Certain resources (like Secrets, which we'll introduce in chapter 7) are preserved and need to be deleted explicitly.

As it deletes resources, kubectl will print the name of every resource it deletes. In the list, you should see the kubia ReplicationController and the kubia-http Service you created in chapter 2.

> **NOTE** The kubectl delete all --all command also deletes the kubernetes Service, but it should be recreated automatically in a few moments.

3.9 *Summary*

After reading this chapter, you should now have a decent knowledge of the central building block in Kubernetes. Every other concept you'll learn about in the next few chapters is directly related to pods.

In this chapter, you've learned

- How to decide whether certain containers should be grouped together in a pod or not.

- Pods can run multiple processes and are similar to physical hosts in the non-container world.
- YAML or JSON descriptors can be written and used to create pods and then examined to see the specification of a pod and its current state.
- Labels and label selectors should be used to organize pods and easily perform operations on multiple pods at once.
- You can use node labels and selectors to schedule pods only to nodes that have certain features.
- Annotations allow attaching larger blobs of data to pods either by people or tools and libraries.
- Namespaces can be used to allow different teams to use the same cluster as though they were using separate Kubernetes clusters.
- How to use the `kubectl explain` command to quickly look up the information on any Kubernetes resource.

In the next chapter, you'll learn about ReplicationControllers and other resources that manage pods.

Replication and other controllers: deploying managed pods

This chapter covers

- Keeping pods healthy
- Running multiple instances of the same pod
- Automatically rescheduling pods after a node fails
- Scaling pods horizontally
- Running system-level pods on each cluster node
- Running batch jobs
- Scheduling jobs to run periodically or once in the future

As you've learned so far, pods represent the basic deployable unit in Kubernetes. You know how to create, supervise, and manage them manually. But in real-world use cases, you want your deployments to stay up and running automatically and remain healthy without any manual intervention. To do this, you almost never create pods directly. Instead, you create other types of resources, such as Replication-Controllers or Deployments, which then create and manage the actual pods.

When you create unmanaged pods (such as the ones you created in the previous chapter), a cluster node is selected to run the pod and then its containers are run on that node. In this chapter, you'll learn that Kubernetes then monitors those containers and automatically restarts them if they fail. But if the whole node fails, the pods on the node are lost and will not be replaced with new ones, unless those pods are managed by the previously mentioned ReplicationControllers or similar. In this chapter, you'll learn how Kubernetes checks if a container is still alive and restarts it if it isn't. You'll also learn how to run managed pods—both those that run indefinitely and those that perform a single task and then stop.

4.1 Keeping pods healthy

One of the main benefits of using Kubernetes is the ability to give it a list of containers and let it keep those containers running somewhere in the cluster. You do this by creating a Pod resource and letting Kubernetes pick a worker node for it and run the pod's containers on that node. But what if one of those containers dies? What if all containers of a pod die?

As soon as a pod is scheduled to a node, the Kubelet on that node will run its containers and, from then on, keep them running as long as the pod exists. If the container's main process crashes, the Kubelet will restart the container. If your application has a bug that causes it to crash every once in a while, Kubernetes will restart it automatically, so even without doing anything special in the app itself, running the app in Kubernetes automatically gives it the ability to heal itself.

But sometimes apps stop working without their process crashing. For example, a Java app with a memory leak will start throwing OutOfMemoryErrors, but the JVM process will keep running. It would be great to have a way for an app to signal to Kubernetes that it's no longer functioning properly and have Kubernetes restart it.

We've said that a container that crashes is restarted automatically, so maybe you're thinking you could catch these types of errors in the app and exit the process when they occur. You can certainly do that, but it still doesn't solve all your problems.

For example, what about those situations when your app stops responding because it falls into an infinite loop or a deadlock? To make sure applications are restarted in such cases, you must check an application's health from the outside and not depend on the app doing it internally.

4.1.1 Introducing liveness probes

Kubernetes can check if a container is still alive through *liveness probes*. You can specify a liveness probe for each container in the pod's specification. Kubernetes will periodically execute the probe and restart the container if the probe fails.

> **NOTE** Kubernetes also supports *readiness probes*, which we'll learn about in the next chapter. Be sure not to confuse the two. They're used for two different things.

Kubernetes can probe a container using one of the three mechanisms:

- An *HTTP GET* probe performs an HTTP GET request on the container's IP address, a port and path you specify. If the probe receives a response, and the response code doesn't represent an error (in other words, if the HTTP response code is 2xx or 3xx), the probe is considered successful. If the server returns an error response code or if it doesn't respond at all, the probe is considered a failure and the container will be restarted as a result.

- A *TCP Socket* probe tries to open a TCP connection to the specified port of the container. If the connection is established successfully, the probe is successful. Otherwise, the container is restarted.
- An *Exec* probe executes an arbitrary command inside the container and checks the command's exit status code. If the status code is 0, the probe is successful. All other codes are considered failures.

4.1.2   Creating an HTTP-based liveness probe

Let's see how to add a liveness probe to your Node.js app. Because it's a web app, it makes sense to add a liveness probe that will check whether its web server is serving requests. But because this particular Node.js app is too simple to ever fail, you'll need to make the app fail artificially.

To properly demo liveness probes, you'll modify the app slightly and make it return a 500 Internal Server Error HTTP status code for each request after the fifth one—your app will handle the first five client requests properly and then return an error on every subsequent request. Thanks to the liveness probe, it should be restarted when that happens, allowing it to properly handle client requests again.

You can find the code of the new app in the book's code archive (in the folder Chapter04/kubia-unhealthy). I've pushed the container image to Docker Hub, so you don't need to build it yourself.

You'll create a new pod that includes an HTTP GET liveness probe. The following listing shows the YAML for the pod.

Listing 4.1   Adding a liveness probe to a pod: kubia-liveness-probe.yaml

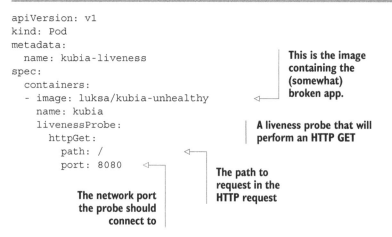

```
apiVersion: v1
kind: Pod
metadata:
  name: kubia-liveness
spec:
  containers:
  - image: luksa/kubia-unhealthy          This is the image
    name: kubia                            containing the
    livenessProbe:                         (somewhat)
      httpGet:                             broken app.
        path: /
        port: 8080
```

A liveness probe that will
perform an HTTP GET

The path to
request in the
HTTP request

The network port
the probe should
connect to

The pod descriptor defines an `httpGet` liveness probe, which tells Kubernetes to periodically perform HTTP GET requests on path / on port `8080` to determine if the container is still healthy. These requests start as soon as the container is run.

After five such requests (or actual client requests), your app starts returning HTTP status code 500, which Kubernetes will treat as a probe failure, and will thus restart the container.

4.1.3 Seeing a liveness probe in action

To see what the liveness probe does, try creating the pod now. After about a minute and a half, the container will be restarted. You can see that by running `kubectl get`:

```
$ kubectl get po kubia-liveness
NAME             READY      STATUS      RESTARTS    AGE
kubia-liveness   1/1        Running     1           2m
```

The `RESTARTS` column shows that the pod's container has been restarted once (if you wait another minute and a half, it gets restarted again, and then the cycle continues indefinitely).

> ### Obtaining the application log of a crashed container
> In the previous chapter, you learned how to print the application's log with `kubectl logs`. If your container is restarted, the `kubectl logs` command will show the log of the current container.
>
> When you want to figure out why the previous container terminated, you'll want to see those logs instead of the current container's logs. This can be done by using the `--previous` option:
>
> ```
> $ kubectl logs mypod --previous
> ```

You can see why the container had to be restarted by looking at what `kubectl describe` prints out, as shown in the following listing.

Listing 4.2 A pod's description after its container is restarted

```
$ kubectl describe po kubia-liveness
Name:           kubia-liveness
...
Containers:
  kubia:
    Container ID:     docker://480986f8
    Image:            luksa/kubia-unhealthy
    Image ID:         docker://sha256:2b208508
    Port:
    State:            Running                              The container is
      Started:        Sun, 14 May 2017 11:41:40 +0200      currently running.
```

```
Last State:          Terminated                                  The previous
    Reason:          Error                                       container terminated
    Exit Code:       137                                         with an error and
    Started:         Mon, 01 Jan 0001 00:00:00 +0000            exited with code 137.
    Finished:        Sun, 14 May 2017 11:41:38 +0200
  Ready:             True
  Restart Count:     1                                          ◁─┐  The container
  Liveness:          http-get http://:8080/ delay=0s timeout=1s     has been
                     period=10s #success=1 #failure=3               restarted once.
  ...
Events:
... Killing container with id docker://95246981:pod "kubia-liveness ..."
    container "kubia" is unhealthy, it will be killed and re-created.
```

You can see that the container is currently running, but it previously terminated because of an error. The exit code was 137, which has a special meaning—it denotes that the process was terminated by an external signal. The number 137 is a sum of two numbers: 128+x, where x is the signal number sent to the process that caused it to terminate. In the example, x equals 9, which is the number of the SIGKILL signal, meaning the process was killed forcibly.

The events listed at the bottom show why the container was killed—Kubernetes detected the container was unhealthy, so it killed and re-created it.

NOTE   When a container is killed, a completely new container is created—it's not the same container being restarted again.

4.1.4   *Configuring additional properties of the liveness probe*

You may have noticed that kubectl describe also displays additional information about the liveness probe:

```
Liveness: http-get http://:8080/ delay=0s timeout=1s period=10s #success=1
          ⤷ #failure=3
```

Beside the liveness probe options you specified explicitly, you can also see additional properties, such as delay, timeout, period, and so on. The delay=0s part shows that the probing begins immediately after the container is started. The timeout is set to only 1 second, so the container must return a response in 1 second or the probe is counted as failed. The container is probed every 10 seconds (period=10s) and the container is restarted after the probe fails three consecutive times (#failure=3).

These additional parameters can be customized when defining the probe. For example, to set the initial delay, add the initialDelaySeconds property to the liveness probe as shown in the following listing.

Listing 4.3   A liveness probe with an initial delay: kubia-liveness-probe-initial-delay.yaml

```
livenessProbe:
  httpGet:
    path: /
```

```
        port: 8080
        initialDelaySeconds: 15
```
◁─┤ **Kubernetes will wait 15 seconds
before executing the first probe.**

If you don't set the initial delay, the prober will start probing the container as soon as it starts, which usually leads to the probe failing, because the app isn't ready to start receiving requests. If the number of failures exceeds the failure threshold, the container is restarted before it's even able to start responding to requests properly.

> **TIP** Always remember to set an initial delay to account for your app's startup time.

I've seen this on many occasions and users were confused why their container was being restarted. But if they'd used `kubectl describe`, they'd have seen that the container terminated with exit code 137 or 143, telling them that the pod was terminated externally. Additionally, the listing of the pod's events would show that the container was killed because of a failed liveness probe. If you see this happening at pod startup, it's because you failed to set `initialDelaySeconds` appropriately.

> **NOTE** Exit code 137 signals that the process was killed by an external signal (exit code is 128 + 9 (SIGKILL). Likewise, exit code 143 corresponds to 128 + 15 (SIGTERM).

4.1.5 *Creating effective liveness probes*

For pods running in production, you should always define a liveness probe. Without one, Kubernetes has no way of knowing whether your app is still alive or not. As long as the process is still running, Kubernetes will consider the container to be healthy.

WHAT A LIVENESS PROBE SHOULD CHECK

Your simplistic liveness probe simply checks if the server is responding. While this may seem overly simple, even a liveness probe like this does wonders, because it causes the container to be restarted if the web server running within the container stops responding to HTTP requests. Compared to having no liveness probe, this is a major improvement, and may be sufficient in most cases.

But for a better liveness check, you'd configure the probe to perform requests on a specific URL path (/health, for example) and have the app perform an internal status check of all the vital components running inside the app to ensure none of them has died or is unresponsive.

> **TIP** Make sure the /health HTTP endpoint doesn't require authentication; otherwise the probe will always fail, causing your container to be restarted indefinitely.

Be sure to check only the internals of the app and nothing influenced by an external factor. For example, a frontend web server's liveness probe shouldn't return a failure when the server can't connect to the backend database. If the underlying cause is in the database itself, restarting the web server container will not fix the problem.

Because the liveness probe will fail again, you'll end up with the container restarting repeatedly until the database becomes accessible again.

KEEPING PROBES LIGHT

Liveness probes shouldn't use too many computational resources and shouldn't take too long to complete. By default, the probes are executed relatively often and are only allowed one second to complete. Having a probe that does heavy lifting can slow down your container considerably. Later in the book, you'll also learn about how to limit CPU time available to a container. The probe's CPU time is counted in the container's CPU time quota, so having a heavyweight liveness probe will reduce the CPU time available to the main application processes.

> **TIP** If you're running a Java app in your container, be sure to use an HTTP GET liveness probe instead of an Exec probe, where you spin up a whole new JVM to get the liveness information. The same goes for any JVM-based or similar applications, whose start-up procedure requires considerable computational resources.

DON'T BOTHER IMPLEMENTING RETRY LOOPS IN YOUR PROBES

You've already seen that the failure threshold for the probe is configurable and usually the probe must fail multiple times before the container is killed. But even if you set the failure threshold to 1, Kubernetes will retry the probe several times before considering it a single failed attempt. Therefore, implementing your own retry loop into the probe is wasted effort.

LIVENESS PROBE WRAP-UP

You now understand that Kubernetes keeps your containers running by restarting them if they crash or if their liveness probes fail. This job is performed by the Kubelet on the node hosting the pod—the Kubernetes Control Plane components running on the master(s) have no part in this process.

But if the node itself crashes, it's the Control Plane that must create replacements for all the pods that went down with the node. It doesn't do that for pods that you create directly. Those pods aren't managed by anything except by the Kubelet, but because the Kubelet runs on the node itself, it can't do anything if the node fails.

To make sure your app is restarted on another node, you need to have the pod managed by a ReplicationController or similar mechanism, which we'll discuss in the rest of this chapter.

4.2   *Introducing ReplicationControllers*

A ReplicationController is a Kubernetes resource that ensures its pods are always kept running. If the pod disappears for any reason, such as in the event of a node disappearing from the cluster or because the pod was evicted from the node, the ReplicationController notices the missing pod and creates a replacement pod.

Figure 4.1 shows what happens when a node goes down and takes two pods with it. Pod A was created directly and is therefore an unmanaged pod, while pod B is managed

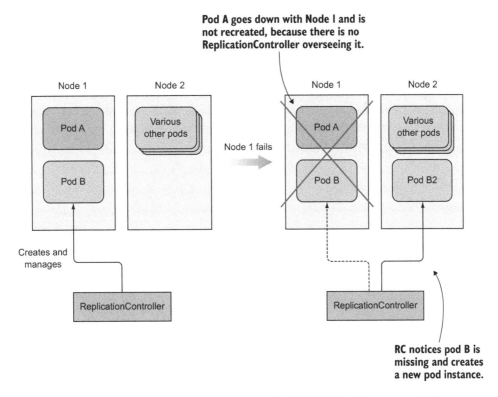

Figure 4.1 When a node fails, only pods backed by a ReplicationController are recreated.

by a ReplicationController. After the node fails, the ReplicationController creates a new pod (pod B2) to replace the missing pod B, whereas pod A is lost completely—nothing will ever recreate it.

The ReplicationController in the figure manages only a single pod, but Replication-Controllers, in general, are meant to create and manage multiple copies (replicas) of a pod. That's where ReplicationControllers got their name from.

4.2.1 The operation of a ReplicationController

A ReplicationController constantly monitors the list of running pods and makes sure the actual number of pods of a "type" always matches the desired number. If too few such pods are running, it creates new replicas from a pod template. If too many such pods are running, it removes the excess replicas.

You might be wondering how there can be more than the desired number of replicas. This can happen for a few reasons:

- Someone creates a pod of the same type manually.
- Someone changes an existing pod's "type."
- Someone decreases the desired number of pods, and so on.

I've used the term pod "type" a few times. But no such thing exists. Replication-Controllers don't operate on pod types, but on sets of pods that match a certain label selector (you learned about them in the previous chapter).

INTRODUCING THE CONTROLLER'S RECONCILIATION LOOP

A ReplicationController's job is to make sure that an exact number of pods always matches its label selector. If it doesn't, the ReplicationController takes the appropriate action to reconcile the actual with the desired number. The operation of a Replication-Controller is shown in figure 4.2.

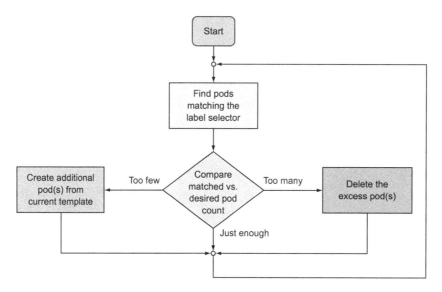

Figure 4.2   A ReplicationController's reconciliation loop

UNDERSTANDING THE THREE PARTS OF A REPLICATIONCONTROLLER

A ReplicationController has three essential parts (also shown in figure 4.3):

- A *label selector*, which determines what pods are in the ReplicationController's scope
- A *replica count*, which specifies the desired number of pods that should be running
- A *pod template*, which is used when creating new pod replicas

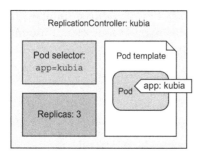

Figure 4.3   The three key parts of a ReplicationController (pod selector, replica count, and pod template)

A ReplicationController's replica count, the label selector, and even the pod template can all be modified at any time, but only changes to the replica count affect existing pods.

UNDERSTANDING THE EFFECT OF CHANGING THE CONTROLLER'S LABEL SELECTOR OR POD TEMPLATE

Changes to the label selector and the pod template have no effect on existing pods. Changing the label selector makes the existing pods fall out of the scope of the ReplicationController, so the controller stops caring about them. ReplicationControllers also don't care about the actual "contents" of its pods (the container images, environment variables, and other things) after they create the pod. The template therefore only affects new pods created by this ReplicationController. You can think of it as a cookie cutter for cutting out new pods.

UNDERSTANDING THE BENEFITS OF USING A REPLICATIONCONTROLLER

Like many things in Kubernetes, a ReplicationController, although an incredibly simple concept, provides or enables the following powerful features:

- It makes sure a pod (or multiple pod replicas) is always running by starting a new pod when an existing one goes missing.
- When a cluster node fails, it creates replacement replicas for all the pods that were running on the failed node (those that were under the ReplicationController's control).
- It enables easy horizontal scaling of pods—both manual and automatic (see horizontal pod auto-scaling in chapter 15).

NOTE A pod instance is never relocated to another node. Instead, the ReplicationController creates a completely new pod instance that has no relation to the instance it's replacing.

4.2.2 *Creating a ReplicationController*

Let's look at how to create a ReplicationController and then see how it keeps your pods running. Like pods and other Kubernetes resources, you create a ReplicationController by posting a JSON or YAML descriptor to the Kubernetes API server.

You're going to create a YAML file called kubia-rc.yaml for your ReplicationController, as shown in the following listing.

Listing 4.4 A YAML definition of a ReplicationController: kubia-rc.yaml

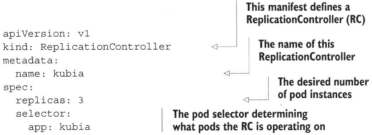

```
apiVersion: v1
kind: ReplicationController        ◁──  The name of this
metadata:                                ReplicationController
  name: kubia                      ◁──
spec:
  replicas: 3                      ◁──  The desired number
  selector:                              of pod instances
    app: kubia
```

This manifest defines a
ReplicationController (RC)

The pod selector determining
what pods the RC is operating on

```
template:
  metadata:
    labels:
      app: kubia
  spec:
    containers:
    - name: kubia
      image: luksa/kubia
      ports:
      - containerPort: 8080
```

The pod template for creating new pods

When you post the file to the API server, Kubernetes creates a new Replication-Controller named `kubia`, which makes sure three pod instances always match the label selector `app=kubia`. When there aren't enough pods, new pods will be created from the provided pod template. The contents of the template are almost identical to the pod definition you created in the previous chapter.

The pod labels in the template must obviously match the label selector of the ReplicationController; otherwise the controller would create new pods indefinitely, because spinning up a new pod wouldn't bring the actual replica count any closer to the desired number of replicas. To prevent such scenarios, the API server verifies the ReplicationController definition and will not accept it if it's misconfigured.

Not specifying the selector at all is also an option. In that case, it will be configured automatically from the labels in the pod template.

> **TIP** Don't specify a pod selector when defining a ReplicationController. Let Kubernetes extract it from the pod template. This will keep your YAML shorter and simpler.

To create the ReplicationController, use the `kubectl create` command, which you already know:

```
$ kubectl create -f kubia-rc.yaml
replicationcontroller "kubia" created
```

As soon as the ReplicationController is created, it goes to work. Let's see what it does.

4.2.3   *Seeing the ReplicationController in action*

Because no pods exist with the `app=kubia` label, the ReplicationController should spin up three new pods from the pod template. List the pods to see if the Replication-Controller has done what it's supposed to:

```
$ kubectl get pods
NAME          READY     STATUS              RESTARTS   AGE
kubia-53thy   0/1       ContainerCreating   0          2s
kubia-k0xz6   0/1       ContainerCreating   0          2s
kubia-q3vkg   0/1       ContainerCreating   0          2s
```

Indeed, it has! You wanted three pods, and it created three pods. It's now managing those three pods. Next you'll mess with them a little to see how the Replication-Controller responds.

SEEING THE REPLICATIONCONTROLLER RESPOND TO A DELETED POD

First, you'll delete one of the pods manually to see how the ReplicationController spins up a new one immediately, bringing the number of matching pods back to three:

```
$ kubectl delete pod kubia-53thy
pod "kubia-53thy" deleted
```

Listing the pods again shows four of them, because the one you deleted is terminating, and a new pod has already been created:

```
$ kubectl get pods
NAME          READY    STATUS              RESTARTS    AGE
kubia-53thy   1/1      Terminating         0           3m
kubia-oini2   0/1      ContainerCreating   0           2s
kubia-k0xz6   1/1      Running             0           3m
kubia-q3vkg   1/1      Running             0           3m
```

The ReplicationController has done its job again. It's a nice little helper, isn't it?

GETTING INFORMATION ABOUT A REPLICATIONCONTROLLER

Now, let's see what information the `kubectl get` command shows for Replication-Controllers:

```
$ kubectl get rc
NAME    DESIRED    CURRENT    READY    AGE
kubia   3          3          2        3m
```

NOTE We're using `rc` as a shorthand for `replicationcontroller`.

You see three columns showing the desired number of pods, the actual number of pods, and how many of them are ready (you'll learn what that means in the next chapter, when we talk about readiness probes).

You can see additional information about your ReplicationController with the `kubectl describe` command, as shown in the following listing.

> **Listing 4.5 Displaying details of a ReplicationController with** `kubectl describe`

```
$ kubectl describe rc kubia
Name:          kubia
Namespace:     default
Selector:      app=kubia
Labels:        app=kubia
Annotations:   <none>
Replicas:      3 current / 3 desired
Pods Status:   4 Running / 0 Waiting / 0 Succeeded / 0 Failed
Pod Template:
  Labels:      app=kubia
  Containers:  ...
```

The actual vs. the desired number of pod instances

Number of pod instances per pod status

```
Volumes:          <none>
Events:
From                     Type      Reason           Message
----                     -------   ------           -------
replication-controller   Normal    SuccessfulCreate Created pod: kubia-53thy
replication-controller   Normal    SuccessfulCreate Created pod: kubia-k0xz6
replication-controller   Normal    SuccessfulCreate Created pod: kubia-q3vkg
replication-controller   Normal    SuccessfulCreate Created pod: kubia-oini2
```

The events related to this ReplicationController

The current number of replicas matches the desired number, because the controller has already created a new pod. It shows four running pods because a pod that's terminating is still considered running, although it isn't counted in the current replica count.

The list of events at the bottom shows the actions taken by the Replication-Controller—it has created four pods so far.

UNDERSTANDING EXACTLY WHAT CAUSED THE CONTROLLER TO CREATE A NEW POD

The controller is responding to the deletion of a pod by creating a new replacement pod (see figure 4.4). Well, technically, it isn't responding to the deletion itself, but the resulting state—the inadequate number of pods.

While a ReplicationController is immediately notified about a pod being deleted (the API server allows clients to watch for changes to resources and resource lists), that's not what causes it to create a replacement pod. The notification triggers the controller to check the actual number of pods and take appropriate action.

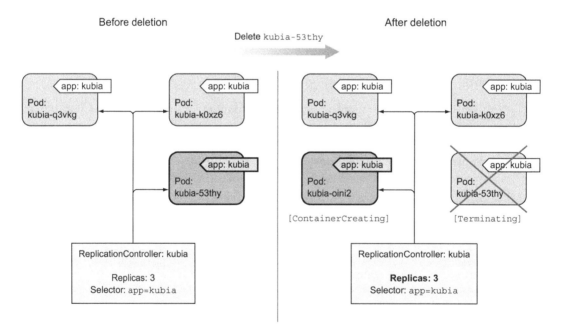

Figure 4.4   If a pod disappears, the ReplicationController sees too few pods and creates a new replacement pod.

RESPONDING TO A NODE FAILURE

Seeing the ReplicationController respond to the manual deletion of a pod isn't too interesting, so let's look at a better example. If you're using Google Kubernetes Engine to run these examples, you have a three-node Kubernetes cluster. You're going to disconnect one of the nodes from the network to simulate a node failure.

> **NOTE** If you're using Minikube, you can't do this exercise, because you only have one node that acts both as a master and a worker node.

If a node fails in the non-Kubernetes world, the ops team would need to migrate the applications running on that node to other machines manually. Kubernetes, on the other hand, does that automatically. Soon after the ReplicationController detects that its pods are down, it will spin up new pods to replace them.

Let's see this in action. You need to ssh into one of the nodes with the `gcloud compute ssh` command and then shut down its network interface with `sudo ifconfig eth0 down`, as shown in the following listing.

> **NOTE** Choose a node that runs at least one of your pods by listing pods with the `-o wide` option.

Listing 4.6   Simulating a node failure by shutting down its network interface
---

```
$ gcloud compute ssh gke-kubia-default-pool-b46381f1-zwko
Enter passphrase for key '/home/luksa/.ssh/google_compute_engine':

Welcome to Kubernetes v1.6.4!
...

luksa@gke-kubia-default-pool-b46381f1-zwko ~ $ sudo ifconfig eth0 down
```

When you shut down the network interface, the ssh session will stop responding, so you need to open up another terminal or hard-exit from the ssh session. In the new terminal you can list the nodes to see if Kubernetes has detected that the node is down. This takes a minute or so. Then, the node's status is shown as `NotReady`:

```
$ kubectl get node
NAME                                    STATUS     AGE
gke-kubia-default-pool-b46381f1-opc5    Ready      5h
gke-kubia-default-pool-b46381f1-s8gj    Ready      5h
gke-kubia-default-pool-b46381f1-zwko    NotReady   5h
```

Node isn't ready, because it's disconnected from the network

If you list the pods now, you'll still see the same three pods as before, because Kubernetes waits a while before rescheduling pods (in case the node is unreachable because of a temporary network glitch or because the Kubelet is restarting). If the node stays unreachable for several minutes, the status of the pods that were scheduled to that node changes to `Unknown`. At that point, the ReplicationController will immediately spin up a new pod. You can see this by listing the pods again:

```
$ kubectl get pods
NAME          READY    STATUS     RESTARTS    AGE
kubia-oini2   1/1      Running    0           10m
kubia-k0xz6   1/1      Running    0           10m
kubia-q3vkg   1/1      Unknown    0           10m
kubia-dmdck   1/1      Running    0           5s
```

This pod's status is unknown, because its node is unreachable.

This pod was created five seconds ago.

Looking at the age of the pods, you see that the `kubia-dmdck` pod is new. You again have three pod instances running, which means the ReplicationController has again done its job of bringing the actual state of the system to the desired state.

The same thing happens if a node fails (either breaks down or becomes unreachable). No immediate human intervention is necessary. The system heals itself automatically.

To bring the node back, you need to reset it with the following command:

```
$ gcloud compute instances reset gke-kubia-default-pool-b46381f1-zwko
```

When the node boots up again, its status should return to `Ready`, and the pod whose status was `Unknown` will be deleted.

4.2.4   *Moving pods in and out of the scope of a ReplicationController*

Pods created by a ReplicationController aren't tied to the ReplicationController in any way. At any moment, a ReplicationController manages pods that match its label selector. By changing a pod's labels, it can be removed from or added to the scope of a ReplicationController. It can even be moved from one ReplicationController to another.

> **TIP** Although a pod isn't tied to a ReplicationController, the pod does reference it in the `metadata.ownerReferences` field, which you can use to easily find which ReplicationController a pod belongs to.

If you change a pod's labels so they no longer match a ReplicationController's label selector, the pod becomes like any other manually created pod. It's no longer managed by anything. If the node running the pod fails, the pod is obviously not rescheduled. But keep in mind that when you changed the pod's labels, the replication controller noticed one pod was missing and spun up a new pod to replace it.

Let's try this with your pods. Because your ReplicationController manages pods that have the `app=kubia` label, you need to either remove this label or change its value to move the pod out of the ReplicationController's scope. Adding another label will have no effect, because the ReplicationController doesn't care if the pod has any additional labels. It only cares whether the pod has all the labels referenced in the label selector.

ADDING LABELS TO PODS MANAGED BY A REPLICATIONCONTROLLER

Let's confirm that a ReplicationController doesn't care if you add additional labels to its managed pods:

```
$ kubectl label pod kubia-dmdck type=special
pod "kubia-dmdck" labeled

$ kubectl get pods --show-labels
NAME          READY  STATUS    RESTARTS  AGE   LABELS
kubia-oini2   1/1    Running   0         11m   app=kubia
kubia-k0xz6   1/1    Running   0         11m   app=kubia
kubia-dmdck   1/1    Running   0         1m    app=kubia,type=special
```

You've added the type=special label to one of the pods. Listing all pods again shows the same three pods as before, because no change occurred as far as the Replication-Controller is concerned.

CHANGING THE LABELS OF A MANAGED POD

Now, you'll change the app=kubia label to something else. This will make the pod no longer match the ReplicationController's label selector, leaving it to only match two pods. The ReplicationController should therefore start a new pod to bring the number back to three:

```
$ kubectl label pod kubia-dmdck app=foo --overwrite
pod "kubia-dmdck" labeled
```

The --overwrite argument is necessary; otherwise kubectl will only print out a warning and won't change the label, to prevent you from inadvertently changing an existing label's value when your intent is to add a new one.

Listing all the pods again should now show four pods:

Newly created pod that replaces the pod you removed from the scope of the ReplicationController

```
$ kubectl get pods -L app
NAME          READY  STATUS             RESTARTS  AGE  APP
kubia-2qneh   0/1    ContainerCreating  0         2s   kubia    <-----------
kubia-oini2   1/1    Running            0         20m  kubia
kubia-k0xz6   1/1    Running            0         20m  kubia
kubia-dmdck   1/1    Running            0         10m  foo      <-- Pod no longer
                                                                    managed by the
                                                                    ReplicationController
```

NOTE You're using the -L app option to display the app label in a column.

There, you now have four pods altogether: one that isn't managed by your Replication-Controller and three that are. Among them is the newly created pod.

Figure 4.5 illustrates what happened when you changed the pod's labels so they no longer matched the ReplicationController's pod selector. You can see your three pods and your ReplicationController. After you change the pod's label from app=kubia to app=foo, the ReplicationController no longer cares about the pod. Because the controller's replica count is set to 3 and only two pods match the label selector, the

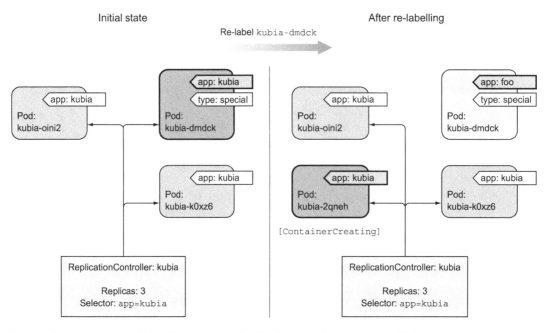

Figure 4.5   Removing a pod from the scope of a ReplicationController by changing its labels

ReplicationController spins up pod kubia-2qneh to bring the number back up to three. Pod kubia-dmdck is now completely independent and will keep running until you delete it manually (you can do that now, because you don't need it anymore).

REMOVING PODS FROM CONTROLLERS IN PRACTICE

Removing a pod from the scope of the ReplicationController comes in handy when you want to perform actions on a specific pod. For example, you might have a bug that causes your pod to start behaving badly after a specific amount of time or a specific event. If you know a pod is malfunctioning, you can take it out of the Replication-Controller's scope, let the controller replace it with a new one, and then debug or play with the pod in any way you want. Once you're done, you delete the pod.

CHANGING THE REPLICATIONCONTROLLER'S LABEL SELECTOR

As an exercise to see if you fully understand ReplicationControllers, what do you think would happen if instead of changing the labels of a pod, you modified the ReplicationController's label selector?

If your answer is that it would make all the pods fall out of the scope of the ReplicationController, which would result in it creating three new pods, you're absolutely right. And it shows that you understand how ReplicationControllers work.

Kubernetes does allow you to change a ReplicationController's label selector, but that's not the case for the other resources that are covered in the second half of this chapter and which are also used for managing pods. You'll never change a controller's label selector, but you'll regularly change its pod template. Let's take a look at that.

4.2.5   *Changing the pod template*

A ReplicationController's pod template can be modified at any time. Changing the pod template is like replacing a cookie cutter with another one. It will only affect the cookies you cut out afterward and will have no effect on the ones you've already cut (see figure 4.6). To modify the old pods, you'd need to delete them and let the Replication-Controller replace them with new ones based on the new template.

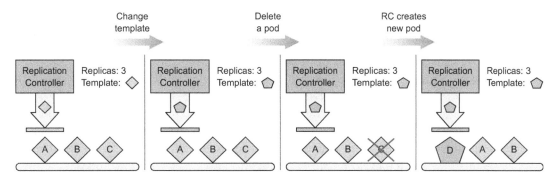

Figure 4.6   Changing a ReplicationController's pod template only affects pods created afterward and has no effect on existing pods.

As an exercise, you can try editing the ReplicationController and adding a label to the pod template. You can edit the ReplicationController with the following command:

```
$ kubectl edit rc kubia
```

This will open the ReplicationController's YAML definition in your default text editor. Find the pod template section and add an additional label to the metadata. After you save your changes and exit the editor, kubectl will update the ReplicationController and print the following message:

```
replicationcontroller "kubia" edited
```

You can now list pods and their labels again and confirm that they haven't changed. But if you delete the pods and wait for their replacements to be created, you'll see the new label.

Editing a ReplicationController like this to change the container image in the pod template, deleting the existing pods, and letting them be replaced with new ones from the new template could be used for upgrading pods, but you'll learn a better way of doing that in chapter 9.

Configuring kubectl edit to use a different text editor

You can tell `kubectl` to use a text editor of your choice by setting the `KUBE_EDITOR` environment variable. For example, if you'd like to use `nano` for editing Kubernetes resources, execute the following command (or put it into your `~/.bashrc` or an equivalent file):

```
export KUBE_EDITOR="/usr/bin/nano"
```

If the `KUBE_EDITOR` environment variable isn't set, `kubectl edit` falls back to using the default editor, usually configured through the `EDITOR` environment variable.

4.2.6 *Horizontally scaling pods*

You've seen how ReplicationControllers make sure a specific number of pod instances is always running. Because it's incredibly simple to change the desired number of replicas, this also means scaling pods horizontally is trivial.

Scaling the number of pods up or down is as easy as changing the value of the replicas field in the ReplicationController resource. After the change, the ReplicationController will either see too many pods exist (when scaling down) and delete part of them, or see too few of them (when scaling up) and create additional pods.

SCALING UP A REPLICATIONCONTROLLER

Your ReplicationController has been keeping three instances of your pod running. You're going to scale that number up to 10 now. As you may remember, you've already scaled a ReplicationController in chapter 2. You could use the same command as before:

```
$ kubectl scale rc kubia --replicas=10
```

But you'll do it differently this time.

SCALING A REPLICATIONCONTROLLER BY EDITING ITS DEFINITION

Instead of using the `kubectl scale` command, you're going to scale it in a declarative way by editing the ReplicationController's definition:

```
$ kubectl edit rc kubia
```

When the text editor opens, find the `spec.replicas` field and change its value to `10`, as shown in the following listing.

Listing 4.7 **Editing the RC in a text editor by running** `kubectl edit`

```
# Please edit the object below. Lines beginning with a '#' will be ignored,
# and an empty file will abort the edit. If an error occurs while saving
# this file will be reopened with the relevant failures.
apiVersion: v1
kind: ReplicationController
```

```
metadata:
  ...
spec:
  replicas: 3          ⊲—|  Change the number 3
  selector:                 to number 10 in
    app: kubia              this line.
  ...
```

When you save the file and close the editor, the ReplicationController is updated and it immediately scales the number of pods to 10:

```
$ kubectl get rc
NAME      DESIRED   CURRENT   READY   AGE
kubia     10        10        4       21m
```

There you go. If the `kubectl scale` command makes it look as though you're telling Kubernetes exactly what to do, it's now much clearer that you're making a declarative change to the desired state of the ReplicationController and not telling Kubernetes to do something.

SCALING DOWN WITH THE KUBECTL SCALE COMMAND

Now scale back down to 3. You can use the `kubectl scale` command:

```
$ kubectl scale rc kubia --replicas=3
```

All this command does is modify the `spec.replicas` field of the ReplicationController's definition—like when you changed it through `kubectl edit`.

UNDERSTANDING THE DECLARATIVE APPROACH TO SCALING

Horizontally scaling pods in Kubernetes is a matter of stating your desire: "I want to have *x* number of instances running." You're not telling Kubernetes what or how to do it. You're just specifying the desired state.

This declarative approach makes interacting with a Kubernetes cluster easy. Imagine if you had to manually determine the current number of running instances and then explicitly tell Kubernetes how many additional instances to run. That's more work and is much more error-prone. Changing a simple number is much easier, and in chapter 15, you'll learn that even that can be done by Kubernetes itself if you enable horizontal pod auto-scaling.

4.2.7 *Deleting a ReplicationController*

When you delete a ReplicationController through `kubectl delete`, the pods are also deleted. But because pods created by a ReplicationController aren't an integral part of the ReplicationController, and are only managed by it, you can delete only the ReplicationController and leave the pods running, as shown in figure 4.7.

This may be useful when you initially have a set of pods managed by a Replication-Controller, and then decide to replace the ReplicationController with a ReplicaSet, for example (you'll learn about them next.). You can do this without affecting the

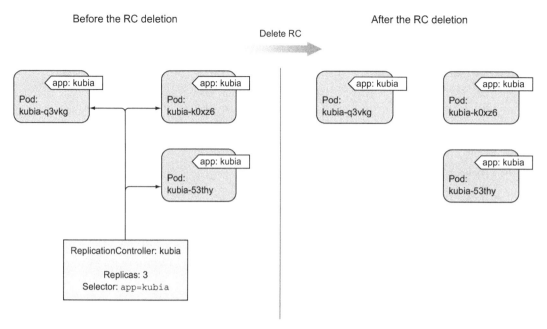

Figure 4.7   **Deleting a replication controller with `--cascade=false` leaves pods unmanaged.**

pods and keep them running without interruption while you replace the Replication-Controller that manages them.

When deleting a ReplicationController with `kubectl delete`, you can keep its pods running by passing the `--cascade=false` option to the command. Try that now:

```
$ kubectl delete rc kubia --cascade=false
replicationcontroller "kubia" deleted
```

You've deleted the ReplicationController so the pods are on their own. They are no longer managed. But you can always create a new ReplicationController with the proper label selector and make them managed again.

4.3   *Using ReplicaSets instead of ReplicationControllers*

Initially, ReplicationControllers were the only Kubernetes component for replicating pods and rescheduling them when nodes failed. Later, a similar resource called a ReplicaSet was introduced. It's a new generation of ReplicationController and replaces it completely (ReplicationControllers will eventually be deprecated).

You could have started this chapter by creating a ReplicaSet instead of a Replication-Controller, but I felt it would be a good idea to start with what was initially available in Kubernetes. Plus, you'll still see ReplicationControllers used in the wild, so it's good for you to know about them. That said, you should always create ReplicaSets instead of ReplicationControllers from now on. They're almost identical, so you shouldn't have any trouble using them instead.

You usually won't create them directly, but instead have them created automatically when you create the higher-level Deployment resource, which you'll learn about in chapter 9. In any case, you should understand ReplicaSets, so let's see how they differ from ReplicationControllers.

4.3.1 Comparing a ReplicaSet to a ReplicationController

A ReplicaSet behaves exactly like a ReplicationController, but it has more expressive pod selectors. Whereas a ReplicationController's label selector only allows matching pods that include a certain label, a ReplicaSet's selector also allows matching pods that lack a certain label or pods that include a certain label key, regardless of its value.

Also, for example, a single ReplicationController can't match pods with the label env=production and those with the label env=devel at the same time. It can only match either pods with the env=production label or pods with the env=devel label. But a single ReplicaSet can match both sets of pods and treat them as a single group.

Similarly, a ReplicationController can't match pods based merely on the presence of a label key, regardless of its value, whereas a ReplicaSet can. For example, a Replica-Set can match all pods that include a label with the key env, whatever its actual value is (you can think of it as env=*).

4.3.2 Defining a ReplicaSet

You're going to create a ReplicaSet now to see how the orphaned pods that were created by your ReplicationController and then abandoned earlier can now be adopted by a ReplicaSet. First, you'll rewrite your ReplicationController into a ReplicaSet by creating a new file called kubia-replicaset.yaml with the contents in the following listing.

> **Listing 4.8 A YAML definition of a ReplicaSet: kubia-replicaset.yaml**

```
apiVersion: apps/v1beta2      ReplicaSets aren't part of the v1
kind: ReplicaSet              API, but belong to the apps API
metadata:                     group and version v1beta2.
  name: kubia
spec:
  replicas: 3                 You're using the simpler matchLabels
  selector:                   selector here, which is much like a
    matchLabels:              ReplicationController's selector.
      app: kubia
  template:
    metadata:
      labels:                 The template is
        app: kubia            the same as in the
    spec:                     ReplicationController.
      containers:
      - name: kubia
        image: luksa/kubia
```

The first thing to note is that ReplicaSets aren't part of the v1 API, so you need to ensure you specify the proper apiVersion when creating the resource. You're creating a resource of type ReplicaSet which has much the same contents as the Replication-Controller you created earlier.

The only difference is in the selector. Instead of listing labels the pods need to have directly under the selector property, you're specifying them under selector .matchLabels. This is the simpler (and less expressive) way of defining label selectors in a ReplicaSet. Later, you'll look at the more expressive option, as well.

> **About the API version attribute**
> This is your first opportunity to see that the apiVersion property specifies two things:
>
> - The API group (which is apps in this case)
> - The actual API version (v1beta2)
>
> You'll see throughout the book that certain Kubernetes resources are in what's called the core API group, which doesn't need to be specified in the apiVersion field (you just specify the version—for example, you've been using apiVersion: v1 when defining Pod resources). Other resources, which were introduced in later Kubernetes versions, are categorized into several API groups. Look at the inside of the book's covers to see all resources and their respective API groups.

Because you still have three pods matching the app=kubia selector running from earlier, creating this ReplicaSet will not cause any new pods to be created. The ReplicaSet will take those existing three pods under its wing.

4.3.3 Creating and examining a ReplicaSet

Create the ReplicaSet from the YAML file with the kubectl create command. After that, you can examine the ReplicaSet with kubectl get and kubectl describe:

```
$ kubectl get rs
NAME      DESIRED   CURRENT   READY     AGE
kubia     3         3         3         3s
```

> **TIP**   Use rs shorthand, which stands for replicaset.

```
$ kubectl describe rs
Name:           kubia
Namespace:      default
Selector:       app=kubia
Labels:         app=kubia
Annotations:    <none>
Replicas:       3 current / 3 desired
Pods Status:    3 Running / 0 Waiting / 0 Succeeded / 0 Failed
Pod Template:
  Labels:       app=kubia
```

```
   Containers:     ...
   Volumes:        <none>
Events:            <none>
```

As you can see, the ReplicaSet isn't any different from a ReplicationController. It's showing it has three replicas matching the selector. If you list all the pods, you'll see they're still the same three pods you had before. The ReplicaSet didn't create any new ones.

4.3.4   *Using the ReplicaSet's more expressive label selectors*

The main improvements of ReplicaSets over ReplicationControllers are their more expressive label selectors. You intentionally used the simpler `matchLabels` selector in the first ReplicaSet example to see that ReplicaSets are no different from Replication-Controllers. Now, you'll rewrite the selector to use the more powerful `matchExpressions` property, as shown in the following listing.

> **Listing 4.9   A `matchExpressions` selector: kubia-replicaset-matchexpressions.yaml**

```
selector:                         This selector requires the pod to
  matchExpressions:               contain a label with the "app" key.
    - key: app
      operator: In                The label's value
      values:                     must be "kubia".
        - kubia
```

> **NOTE**   Only the selector is shown. You'll find the whole ReplicaSet definition in the book's code archive.

You can add additional expressions to the selector. As in the example, each expression must contain a `key`, an `operator`, and possibly (depending on the operator) a list of `values`. You'll see four valid operators:

- `In`—Label's value must match one of the specified `values`.
- `NotIn`—Label's value must not match any of the specified `values`.
- `Exists`—Pod must include a label with the specified key (the value isn't important). When using this operator, you shouldn't specify the `values` field.
- `DoesNotExist`—Pod must not include a label with the specified key. The `values` property must not be specified.

If you specify multiple expressions, all those expressions must evaluate to true for the selector to match a pod. If you specify both `matchLabels` and `matchExpressions`, all the labels must match and all the expressions must evaluate to true for the pod to match the selector.

4.3.5   *Wrapping up ReplicaSets*

This was a quick introduction to ReplicaSets as an alternative to ReplicationControllers. Remember, always use them instead of ReplicationControllers, but you may still find ReplicationControllers in other people's deployments.

Now, delete the ReplicaSet to clean up your cluster a little. You can delete the ReplicaSet the same way you'd delete a ReplicationController:

```
$ kubectl delete rs kubia
replicaset "kubia" deleted
```

Deleting the ReplicaSet should delete all the pods. List the pods to confirm that's the case.

4.4   *Running exactly one pod on each node with DaemonSets*

Both ReplicationControllers and ReplicaSets are used for running a specific number of pods deployed anywhere in the Kubernetes cluster. But certain cases exist when you want a pod to run on each and every node in the cluster (and each node needs to run exactly one instance of the pod, as shown in figure 4.8).

Those cases include infrastructure-related pods that perform system-level operations. For example, you'll want to run a log collector and a resource monitor on every node. Another good example is Kubernetes' own kube-proxy process, which needs to run on all nodes to make services work.

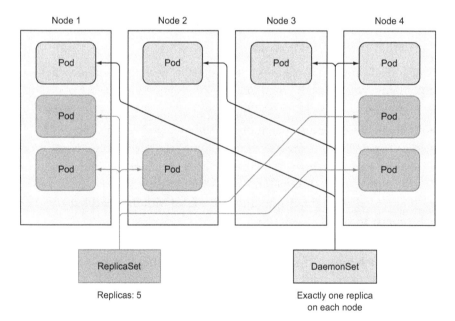

Figure 4.8   DaemonSets run only a single pod replica on each node, whereas ReplicaSets scatter them around the whole cluster randomly.

Outside of Kubernetes, such processes would usually be started through system init scripts or the systemd daemon during node boot up. On Kubernetes nodes, you can still use systemd to run your system processes, but then you can't take advantage of all the features Kubernetes provides.

4.4.1 Using a DaemonSet to run a pod on every node

To run a pod on all cluster nodes, you create a DaemonSet object, which is much like a ReplicationController or a ReplicaSet, except that pods created by a Daemon-Set already have a target node specified and skip the Kubernetes Scheduler. They aren't scattered around the cluster randomly.

A DaemonSet makes sure it creates as many pods as there are nodes and deploys each one on its own node, as shown in figure 4.8.

Whereas a ReplicaSet (or ReplicationController) makes sure that a desired number of pod replicas exist in the cluster, a DaemonSet doesn't have any notion of a desired replica count. It doesn't need it because its job is to ensure that a pod matching its pod selector is running on each node.

If a node goes down, the DaemonSet doesn't cause the pod to be created elsewhere. But when a new node is added to the cluster, the DaemonSet immediately deploys a new pod instance to it. It also does the same if someone inadvertently deletes one of the pods, leaving the node without the DaemonSet's pod. Like a Replica-Set, a DaemonSet creates the pod from the pod template configured in it.

4.4.2 Using a DaemonSet to run pods only on certain nodes

A DaemonSet deploys pods to all nodes in the cluster, unless you specify that the pods should only run on a subset of all the nodes. This is done by specifying the node-Selector property in the pod template, which is part of the DaemonSet definition (similar to the pod template in a ReplicaSet or ReplicationController).

You've already used node selectors to deploy a pod onto specific nodes in chapter 3. A node selector in a DaemonSet is similar—it defines the nodes the DaemonSet must deploy its pods to.

> **NOTE** Later in the book, you'll learn that nodes can be made unschedulable, preventing pods from being deployed to them. A DaemonSet will deploy pods even to such nodes, because the unschedulable attribute is only used by the Scheduler, whereas pods managed by a DaemonSet bypass the Scheduler completely. This is usually desirable, because DaemonSets are meant to run system services, which usually need to run even on unschedulable nodes.

EXPLAINING DAEMONSETS WITH AN EXAMPLE

Let's imagine having a daemon called ssd-monitor that needs to run on all nodes that contain a solid-state drive (SSD). You'll create a DaemonSet that runs this dae-mon on all nodes that are marked as having an SSD. The cluster administrators have added the disk=ssd label to all such nodes, so you'll create the DaemonSet with a node selector that only selects nodes with that label, as shown in figure 4.9.

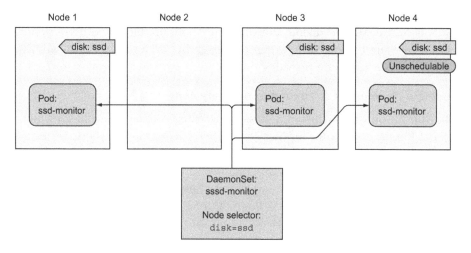

Figure 4.9   Using a DaemonSet with a node selector to deploy system pods only on certain nodes

CREATING A DAEMONSET YAML DEFINITION

You'll create a DaemonSet that runs a mock `ssd-monitor` process, which prints "SSD OK" to the standard output every five seconds. I've already prepared the mock container image and pushed it to Docker Hub, so you can use it instead of building your own. Create the YAML for the DaemonSet, as shown in the following listing.

Listing 4.10   A YAML for a DaemonSet: ssd-monitor-daemonset.yaml

```
apiVersion: apps/v1beta2          ⎫  DaemonSets are in the
kind: DaemonSet                   ⎬  apps API group,
metadata:                         ⎭  version v1beta2.
  name: ssd-monitor
spec:
  selector:
    matchLabels:
      app: ssd-monitor
  template:
    metadata:
      labels:
        app: ssd-monitor
    spec:                         ⎫  The pod template includes a
      nodeSelector:               ⎬  node selector, which selects
        disk: ssd                 ⎭  nodes with the disk=ssd label.
      containers:
      - name: main
        image: luksa/ssd-monitor
```

You're defining a DaemonSet that will run a pod with a single container based on the `luksa/ssd-monitor` container image. An instance of this pod will be created for each node that has the `disk=ssd` label.

CREATING THE DAEMONSET

You'll create the DaemonSet like you always create resources from a YAML file:

```
$ kubectl create -f ssd-monitor-daemonset.yaml
daemonset "ssd-monitor" created
```

Let's see the created DaemonSet:

```
$ kubectl get ds
NAME         DESIRED  CURRENT  READY  UP-TO-DATE  AVAILABLE  NODE-SELECTOR
ssd-monitor  0        0        0      0           0          disk=ssd
```

Those zeroes look strange. Didn't the DaemonSet deploy any pods? List the pods:

```
$ kubectl get po
No resources found.
```

Where are the pods? Do you know what's going on? Yes, you forgot to label your nodes with the disk=ssd label. No problem—you can do that now. The DaemonSet should detect that the nodes' labels have changed and deploy the pod to all nodes with a matching label. Let's see if that's true.

ADDING THE REQUIRED LABEL TO YOUR NODE(S)

Regardless if you're using Minikube, GKE, or another multi-node cluster, you'll need to list the nodes first, because you'll need to know the node's name when labeling it:

```
$ kubectl get node
NAME      STATUS  AGE  VERSION
minikube  Ready   4d   v1.6.0
```

Now, add the disk=ssd label to one of your nodes like this:

```
$ kubectl label node minikube disk=ssd
node "minikube" labeled
```

> **NOTE** Replace minikube with the name of one of your nodes if you're not using Minikube.

The DaemonSet should have created one pod now. Let's see:

```
$ kubectl get po
NAME                READY  STATUS   RESTARTS  AGE
ssd-monitor-hgxwq   1/1    Running  0         35s
```

Okay; so far so good. If you have multiple nodes and you add the same label to further nodes, you'll see the DaemonSet spin up pods for each of them.

REMOVING THE REQUIRED LABEL FROM THE NODE

Now, imagine you've made a mistake and have mislabeled one of the nodes. It has a spinning disk drive, not an SSD. What happens if you change the node's label?

```
$ kubectl label node minikube disk=hdd --overwrite
node "minikube" labeled
```

Let's see if the change has any effect on the pod that was running on that node:

```
$ kubectl get po
NAME                READY     STATUS        RESTARTS    AGE
ssd-monitor-hgxwq   1/1       Terminating   0           4m
```

The pod is being terminated. But you knew that was going to happen, right? This wraps up your exploration of DaemonSets, so you may want to delete your `ssd-monitor` DaemonSet. If you still have any other daemon pods running, you'll see that deleting the DaemonSet deletes those pods as well.

4.5   *Running pods that perform a single completable task*

Up to now, we've only talked about pods than need to run continuously. You'll have cases where you only want to run a task that terminates after completing its work. ReplicationControllers, ReplicaSets, and DaemonSets run continuous tasks that are never considered completed. Processes in such pods are restarted when they exit. But in a completable task, after its process terminates, it should not be restarted again.

4.5.1   *Introducing the Job resource*

Kubernetes includes support for this through the Job resource, which is similar to the other resources we've discussed in this chapter, but it allows you to run a pod whose container isn't restarted when the process running inside finishes successfully. Once it does, the pod is considered complete.

In the event of a node failure, the pods on that node that are managed by a Job will be rescheduled to other nodes the way ReplicaSet pods are. In the event of a failure of the process itself (when the process returns an error exit code), the Job can be configured to either restart the container or not.

Figure 4.10 shows how a pod created by a Job is rescheduled to a new node if the node it was initially scheduled to fails. The figure also shows both a managed pod, which isn't rescheduled, and a pod backed by a ReplicaSet, which is.

For example, Jobs are useful for ad hoc tasks, where it's crucial that the task finishes properly. You could run the task in an unmanaged pod and wait for it to finish, but in the event of a node failing or the pod being evicted from the node while it is performing its task, you'd need to manually recreate it. Doing this manually doesn't make sense—especially if the job takes hours to complete.

An example of such a job would be if you had data stored somewhere and you needed to transform and export it somewhere. You're going to emulate this by running a container image built on top of the `busybox` image, which invokes the `sleep` command for two minutes. I've already built the image and pushed it to Docker Hub, but you can peek into its Dockerfile in the book's code archive.

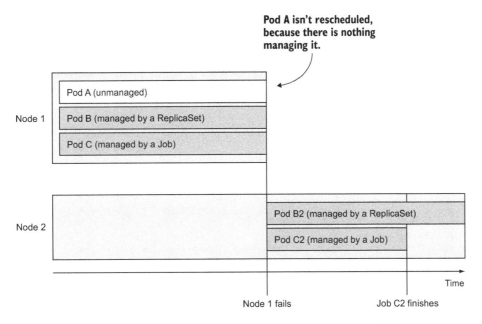

Figure 4.10   Pods managed by Jobs are rescheduled until they finish successfully.

4.5.2   Defining a Job resource

Create the Job manifest as in the following listing.

Listing 4.11   A YAML definition of a Job: exporter.yaml

```
apiVersion: batch/v1            Jobs are in the batch
kind: Job                       API group, version v1.
metadata:
  name: batch-job
spec:
  template:                     You're not specifying a pod
    metadata:                   selector (it will be created
      labels:                   based on the labels in the
        app. batch job          pod template).
    spec:
      restartPolicy: OnFailure      Jobs can't use the
      containers:                   default restart policy,
      - name: main                  which is Always.
        image: luksa/batch-job
```

Jobs are part of the `batch` API group and `v1` API version. The YAML defines a resource of type Job that will run the `luksa/batch-job` image, which invokes a process that runs for exactly 120 seconds and then exits.

In a pod's specification, you can specify what Kubernetes should do when the processes running in the container finish. This is done through the `restartPolicy` pod spec property, which defaults to `Always`. Job pods can't use the default policy, because they're not meant to run indefinitely. Therefore, you need to explicitly set the restart policy to either `OnFailure` or `Never`. This setting is what prevents the container from being restarted when it finishes (not the fact that the pod is being managed by a Job resource).

4.5.3   *Seeing a Job run a pod*

After you create this Job with the `kubectl create` command, you should see it start up a pod immediately:

```
$ kubectl get jobs
NAME         DESIRED    SUCCESSFUL    AGE
batch-job    1          0             2s

$ kubectl get po
NAME              READY      STATUS      RESTARTS    AGE
batch-job-28qf4   1/1        Running     0           4s
```

After the two minutes have passed, the pod will no longer show up in the pod list and the Job will be marked as completed. By default, completed pods aren't shown when you list pods, unless you use the `--show-all` (or `-a`) switch:

```
$ kubectl get po -a
NAME              READY      STATUS       RESTARTS    AGE
batch-job-28qf4   0/1        Completed    0           2m
```

The reason the pod isn't deleted when it completes is to allow you to examine its logs; for example:

```
$ kubectl logs batch-job-28qf4
Fri Apr 29 09:58:22 UTC 2016 Batch job starting
Fri Apr 29 10:00:22 UTC 2016 Finished succesfully
```

The pod will be deleted when you delete it or the Job that created it. Before you do that, let's look at the Job resource again:

```
$ kubectl get job
NAME         DESIRED    SUCCESSFUL    AGE
batch-job    1          1             9m
```

The Job is shown as having completed successfully. But why is that piece of information shown as a number instead of as `yes` or `true`? And what does the `DESIRED` column indicate?

4.5.4   *Running multiple pod instances in a Job*

Jobs may be configured to create more than one pod instance and run them in parallel or sequentially. This is done by setting the `completions` and the `parallelism` properties in the Job spec.

RUNNING JOB PODS SEQUENTIALLY

If you need a Job to run more than once, you set completions to how many times you
want the Job's pod to run. The following listing shows an example.

Listing 4.12 A Job requiring multiple completions: multi-completion-batch-job.yaml

```
apiVersion: batch/v1
kind: Job
metadata:
  name: multi-completion-batch-job          Setting completions to
spec:                                        5 makes this Job run
  completions: 5                       ◁──┘  five pods sequentially.
  template:
    <template is the same as in listing 4.11>
```

This Job will run five pods one after the other. It initially creates one pod, and when
the pod's container finishes, it creates the second pod, and so on, until five pods complete successfully. If one of the pods fails, the Job creates a new pod, so the Job may
create more than five pods overall.

RUNNING JOB PODS IN PARALLEL

Instead of running single Job pods one after the other, you can also make the Job run
multiple pods in parallel. You specify how many pods are allowed to run in parallel
with the parallelism Job spec property, as shown in the following listing.

Listing 4.13 Running Job pods in parallel: multi-completion-parallel-batch-job.yaml

```
apiVersion: batch/v1
kind: Job
metadata:                                    This job must ensure
  name: multi-completion-batch-job           five pods complete
spec:                                        successfully.
  completions: 5                       ◁──┘
  parallelism: 2                       ◁──┐  Up to two pods
  template:                                │  can run in parallel.
    <same as in listing 4.11>
```

By setting parallelism to 2, the Job creates two pods and runs them in parallel:

```
$ kubectl get po
NAME                                 READY   STATUS    RESTARTS   AGE
multi-completion-batch-job-lmmnk     1/1     Running   0          21s
multi-completion-batch-job-qx4nq     1/1     Running   0          21s
```

As soon as one of them finishes, the Job will run the next pod, until five pods finish
successfully.

SCALING A JOB

You can even change a Job's `parallelism` property while the Job is running. This is
similar to scaling a ReplicaSet or ReplicationController, and can be done with the
`kubectl scale` command:

```
$ kubectl scale job multi-completion-batch-job --replicas 3
job "multi-completion-batch-job" scaled
```

Because you've increased `parallelism` from 2 to 3, another pod is immediately spun
up, so three pods are now running.

4.5.5   Limiting the time allowed for a Job pod to complete

We need to discuss one final thing about Jobs. How long should the Job wait for a pod
to finish? What if the pod gets stuck and can't finish at all (or it can't finish fast
enough)?

A pod's time can be limited by setting the `activeDeadlineSeconds` property in the
pod spec. If the pod runs longer than that, the system will try to terminate it and will
mark the Job as failed.

> **NOTE** You can configure how many times a Job can be retried before it is
> marked as failed by specifying the `spec.backoffLimit` field in the Job mani-
> fest. If you don't explicitly specify it, it defaults to 6.

4.6   Scheduling Jobs to run periodically or once in the future

Job resources run their pods immediately when you create the Job resource. But many
batch jobs need to be run at a specific time in the future or repeatedly in the specified
interval. In Linux- and UNIX-like operating systems, these jobs are better known as
cron jobs. Kubernetes supports them, too.

A cron job in Kubernetes is configured by creating a CronJob resource. The
schedule for running the job is specified in the well-known cron format, so if you're
familiar with regular cron jobs, you'll understand Kubernetes' CronJobs in a matter
of seconds.

At the configured time, Kubernetes will create a Job resource according to the Job
template configured in the CronJob object. When the Job resource is created, one or
more pod replicas will be created and started according to the Job's pod template, as
you learned in the previous section. There's nothing more to it.

Let's look at how to create CronJobs.

4.6.1   Creating a CronJob

Imagine you need to run the batch job from your previous example every 15 minutes.
To do that, create a CronJob resource with the following specification.

Listing 4.14   YAML for a CronJob resource: cronjob.yaml

```
apiVersion: batch/v1beta1        ◁─┐  API group is batch,
kind: CronJob                      │  version is v1beta1
metadata:
  name: batch-job-every-fifteen-minutes
spec:                                      This job should run at the
  schedule: "0,15,30,45 * * * *"    ◁─┐    0, 15, 30 and 45 minutes of
  jobTemplate:                           every hour, every day.
    spec:
      template:
        metadata:
          labels:
            app: periodic-batch-job     The template for the
        spec:                           Job resources that
          restartPolicy: OnFailure      will be created by
          containers:                   this CronJob
          - name: main
            image: luksa/batch-job
```

As you can see, it's not too complicated. You've specified a schedule and a template from which the Job objects will be created.

CONFIGURING THE SCHEDULE

If you're unfamiliar with the cron schedule format, you'll find great tutorials and explanations online, but as a quick introduction, from left to right, the schedule contains the following five entries:

- Minute
- Hour
- Day of month
- Month
- Day of week.

In the example, you want to run the job every 15 minutes, so the schedule needs to be "0,15,30,45 * * * *", which means at the 0, 15, 30 and 45 minutes mark of every hour (first asterisk), of every day of the month (second asterisk), of every month (third asterisk) and on every day of the week (fourth asterisk).

If, instead, you wanted it to run every 30 minutes, but only on the first day of the month, you'd set the schedule to "0,30 * 1 * *", and if you want it to run at 3AM every Sunday, you'd set it to "0 3 * * 0" (the last zero stands for Sunday).

CONFIGURING THE JOB TEMPLATE

A CronJob creates Job resources from the jobTemplate property configured in the CronJob spec, so refer to section 4.5 for more information on how to configure it.

4.6.2   *Understanding how scheduled jobs are run*

Job resources will be created from the CronJob resource at approximately the scheduled time. The Job then creates the pods.

It may happen that the Job or pod is created and run relatively late. You may have a hard requirement for the job to not be started too far over the scheduled time. In that case, you can specify a deadline by specifying the `startingDeadlineSeconds` field in the CronJob specification as shown in the following listing.

```
apiVersion: batch/v1beta1
kind: CronJob
spec:
  schedule: "0,15,30,45 * * * *"
  startingDeadlineSeconds: 15
  ...
```

At the latest, the pod must start running at 15 seconds past the scheduled time.

In the example in listing 4.15, one of the times the job is supposed to run is 10:30:00. If it doesn't start by 10:30:15 for whatever reason, the job will not run and will be shown as Failed.

In normal circumstances, a CronJob always creates only a single Job for each execution configured in the schedule, but it may happen that two Jobs are created at the same time, or none at all. To combat the first problem, your jobs should be idempotent (running them multiple times instead of once shouldn't lead to unwanted results). For the second problem, make sure that the next job run performs any work that should have been done by the previous (missed) run.

4.7   Summary

You've now learned how to keep pods running and have them rescheduled in the event of node failures. You should now know that

- You can specify a liveness probe to have Kubernetes restart your container as soon as it's no longer healthy (where the app defines what's considered healthy).
- Pods shouldn't be created directly, because they will not be re-created if they're deleted by mistake, if the node they're running on fails, or if they're evicted from the node.
- ReplicationControllers always keep the desired number of pod replicas running.
- Scaling pods horizontally is as easy as changing the desired replica count on a ReplicationController.
- Pods aren't owned by the ReplicationControllers and can be moved between them if necessary.
- A ReplicationController creates new pods from a pod template. Changing the template has no effect on existing pods.

- ReplicationControllers should be replaced with ReplicaSets and Deployments, which provide the same functionality, but with additional powerful features.
- ReplicationControllers and ReplicaSets schedule pods to random cluster nodes, whereas DaemonSets make sure every node runs a single instance of a pod defined in the DaemonSet.
- Pods that perform a batch task should be created through a Kubernetes Job resource, not directly or through a ReplicationController or similar object.
- Jobs that need to run sometime in the future can be created through CronJob resources.

Services: enabling clients to discover and talk to pods

This chapter covers

- Creating Service resources to expose a group of pods at a single address
- Discovering services in the cluster
- Exposing services to external clients
- Connecting to external services from inside the cluster
- Controlling whether a pod is ready to be part of the service or not
- Troubleshooting services

You've learned about pods and how to deploy them through ReplicaSets and similar resources to ensure they keep running. Although certain pods can do their work independently of an external stimulus, many applications these days are meant to respond to external requests. For example, in the case of microservices, pods will usually respond to HTTP requests coming either from other pods inside the cluster or from clients outside the cluster.

Pods need a way of finding other pods if they want to consume the services they provide. Unlike in the non-Kubernetes world, where a sysadmin would configure each client app by specifying the exact IP address or hostname of the server providing the service in the client's configuration files, doing the same in Kubernetes wouldn't work, because

- *Pods are ephemeral*—They may come and go at any time, whether it's because a pod is removed from a node to make room for other pods, because someone scaled down the number of pods, or because a cluster node has failed.
- *Kubernetes assigns an IP address to a pod after the pod has been scheduled to a node and before it's started*—Clients thus can't know the IP address of the server pod up front.
- *Horizontal scaling means multiple pods may provide the same service*—Each of those pods has its own IP address. Clients shouldn't care how many pods are backing the service and what their IPs are. They shouldn't have to keep a list of all the individual IPs of pods. Instead, all those pods should be accessible through a single IP address.

To solve these problems, Kubernetes also provides another resource type—Services—that we'll discuss in this chapter.

5.1 *Introducing services*

A Kubernetes Service is a resource you create to make a single, constant point of entry to a group of pods providing the same service. Each service has an IP address and port that never change while the service exists. Clients can open connections to that IP and port, and those connections are then routed to one of the pods backing that service. This way, clients of a service don't need to know the location of individual pods providing the service, allowing those pods to be moved around the cluster at any time.

EXPLAINING SERVICES WITH AN EXAMPLE

Let's revisit the example where you have a frontend web server and a backend database server. There may be multiple pods that all act as the frontend, but there may only be a single backend database pod. You need to solve two problems to make the system function:

- External clients need to connect to the frontend pods without caring if there's only a single web server or hundreds.
- The frontend pods need to connect to the backend database. Because the database runs inside a pod, it may be moved around the cluster over time, causing its IP address to change. You don't want to reconfigure the frontend pods every time the backend database is moved.

By creating a service for the frontend pods and configuring it to be accessible from outside the cluster, you expose a single, constant IP address through which external clients can connect to the pods. Similarly, by also creating a service for the backend pod, you create a stable address for the backend pod. The service address doesn't change even if the pod's IP address changes. Additionally, by creating the service, you also enable the frontend pods to easily find the backend service by its name through either environment variables or DNS. All the components of your system (the two services, the two sets of pods backing those services, and the interdependencies between them) are shown in figure 5.1.

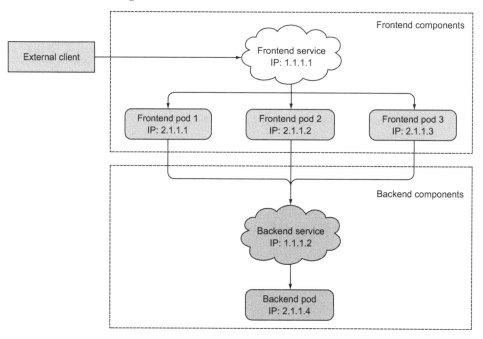

Figure 5.1   Both internal and external clients usually connect to pods through services.

You now understand the basic idea behind services. Now, let's dig deeper by first seeing how they can be created.

5.1.1   Creating services

As you've seen, a service can be backed by more than one pod. Connections to the service are load-balanced across all the backing pods. But how exactly do you define which pods are part of the service and which aren't?

You probably remember label selectors and how they're used in Replication-Controllers and other pod controllers to specify which pods belong to the same set. The same mechanism is used by services in the same way, as you can see in figure 5.2.

In the previous chapter, you created a ReplicationController which then ran three instances of the pod containing the Node.js app. Create the ReplicationController again and verify three pod instances are up and running. After that, you'll create a Service for those three pods.

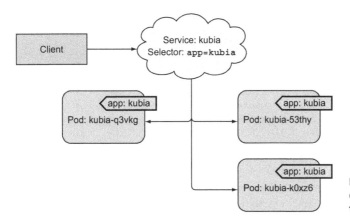

Figure 5.2 Label selectors determine which pods belong to the Service.

CREATING A SERVICE THROUGH KUBECTL EXPOSE

The easiest way to create a service is through `kubectl expose`, which you've already used in chapter 2 to expose the ReplicationController you created earlier. The expose command created a Service resource with the same pod selector as the one used by the ReplicationController, thereby exposing all its pods through a single IP address and port.

Now, instead of using the `expose` command, you'll create a service manually by posting a YAML to the Kubernetes API server.

CREATING A SERVICE THROUGH A YAML DESCRIPTOR

Create a file called kubia-svc.yaml with the following listing's contents.

Listing 5.1 A definition of a service: kubia-svc.yaml

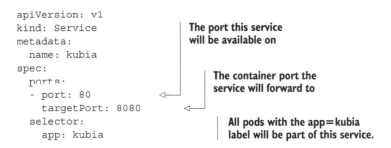

You're defining a service called `kubia`, which will accept connections on port 80 and route each connection to port 8080 of one of the pods matching the `app=kubia` label selector.

Go ahead and create the service by posting the file using `kubectl create`.

EXAMINING YOUR NEW SERVICE

After posting the YAML, you can list all Service resources in your namespace and see that an internal cluster IP has been assigned to your service:

```
$ kubectl get svc
NAME            CLUSTER-IP        EXTERNAL-IP    PORT(S)    AGE
kubernetes      10.111.240.1      <none>         443/TCP    30d
kubia           10.111.249.153    <none>         80/TCP     6m
```

Here's your service.

The list shows that the IP address assigned to the service is 10.111.249.153. Because this is the cluster IP, it's only accessible from inside the cluster. The primary purpose of services is exposing groups of pods to other pods in the cluster, but you'll usually also want to expose services externally. You'll see how to do that later. For now, let's use your service from inside the cluster and see what it does.

TESTING YOUR SERVICE FROM WITHIN THE CLUSTER

You can send requests to your service from within the cluster in a few ways:

- The obvious way is to create a pod that will send the request to the service's cluster IP and log the response. You can then examine the pod's log to see what the service's response was.
- You can ssh into one of the Kubernetes nodes and use the curl command.
- You can execute the curl command inside one of your existing pods through the kubectl exec command.

Let's go for the last option, so you also learn how to run commands in existing pods.

REMOTELY EXECUTING COMMANDS IN RUNNING CONTAINERS

The kubectl exec command allows you to remotely run arbitrary commands inside an existing container of a pod. This comes in handy when you want to examine the contents, state, and/or environment of a container. List the pods with the kubectl get pods command and choose one as your target for the exec command (in the following example, I've chosen the kubia-7nog1 pod as the target). You'll also need to obtain the cluster IP of your service (using kubectl get svc, for example). When running the following commands yourself, be sure to replace the pod name and the service IP with your own:

```
$ kubectl exec kubia-7nog1 -- curl -s http://10.111.249.153
You've hit kubia-gzwli
```

If you've used ssh to execute commands on a remote system before, you'll recognize that kubectl exec isn't much different.

Why the double dash?

The double dash (--) in the command signals the end of command options for `kubectl`. Everything after the double dash is the command that should be executed inside the pod. Using the double dash isn't necessary if the command has no arguments that start with a dash. But in your case, if you don't use the double dash there, the -s option would be interpreted as an option for `kubectl exec` and would result in the following strange and highly misleading error:

```
$ kubectl exec kubia-7nog1 curl -s http://10.111.249.153
The connection to the server 10.111.249.153 was refused - did you
    specify the right host or port?
```

This has nothing to do with your service refusing the connection. It's because `kubectl` is not able to connect to an API server at 10.111.249.153 (the -s option is used to tell `kubectl` to connect to a different API server than the default).

Let's go over what transpired when you ran the command. Figure 5.3 shows the sequence of events. You instructed Kubernetes to execute the `curl` command inside the container of one of your pods. Curl sent an HTTP request to the service IP, which is backed by three pods. The Kubernetes service proxy intercepted the connection, selected a random pod among the three pods, and forwarded the request to it. Node.js running inside that pod then handled the request and returned an HTTP response containing the pod's name. Curl then printed the response to the standard output, which was intercepted and printed to its standard output on your local machine by `kubectl`.

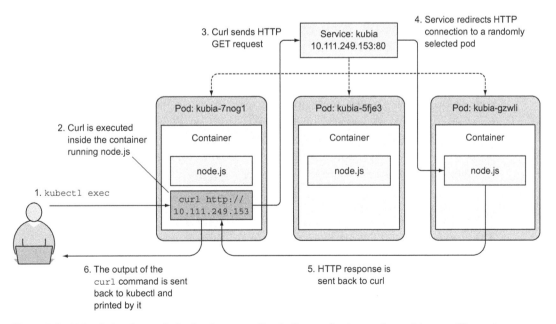

Figure 5.3   Using kubectl exec to test out a connection to the service by running curl in one of the pods

In the previous example, you executed the `curl` command as a separate process, but inside the pod's main container. This isn't much different from the actual main process in the container talking to the service.

CONFIGURING SESSION AFFINITY ON THE SERVICE

If you execute the same command a few more times, you should hit a different pod with every invocation, because the service proxy normally forwards each connection to a randomly selected backing pod, even if the connections are coming from the same client.

If, on the other hand, you want all requests made by a certain client to be redirected to the same pod every time, you can set the service's `sessionAffinity` property to `ClientIP` (instead of `None`, which is the default), as shown in the following listing.

Listing 5.2   A example of a service with `ClientIP` session affinity configured

```
apiVersion: v1
kind: Service
spec:
  sessionAffinity: ClientIP
  ...
```

This makes the service proxy redirect all requests originating from the same client IP to the same pod. As an exercise, you can create an additional service with session affinity set to `ClientIP` and try sending requests to it.

Kubernetes supports only two types of service session affinity: `None` and `ClientIP`. You may be surprised it doesn't have a cookie-based session affinity option, but you need to understand that Kubernetes services don't operate at the HTTP level. Services deal with TCP and UDP packets and don't care about the payload they carry. Because cookies are a construct of the HTTP protocol, services don't know about them, which explains why session affinity cannot be based on cookies.

EXPOSING MULTIPLE PORTS IN THE SAME SERVICE

Your service exposes only a single port, but services can also support multiple ports. For example, if your pods listened on two ports—let's say 8080 for HTTP and 8443 for HTTPS—you could use a single service to forward both port 80 and 443 to the pod's ports 8080 and 8443. You don't need to create two different services in such cases. Using a single, multi-port service exposes all the service's ports through a single cluster IP.

> **NOTE** When creating a service with multiple ports, you must specify a name for each port.

The spec for a multi-port service is shown in the following listing.

Listing 5.3   Specifying multiple ports in a service definition

```
apiVersion: v1
kind: Service
metadata:
  name: kubia
```

```
spec:
  ports:
  - name: http
    port: 80
    targetPort: 8080
  - name: https
    port: 443
    targetPort: 8443
  selector:
    app: kubia
```

Port 80 is mapped to the pods' port 8080.

Port 443 is mapped to pods' port 8443.

The label selector always applies to the whole service.

NOTE The label selector applies to the service as a whole—it can't be configured for each port individually. If you want different ports to map to different subsets of pods, you need to create two services.

Because your kubia pods don't listen on multiple ports, creating a multi-port service and a multi-port pod is left as an exercise to you.

USING NAMED PORTS

In all these examples, you've referred to the target port by its number, but you can also give a name to each pod's port and refer to it by name in the service spec. This makes the service spec slightly clearer, especially if the port numbers aren't well-known.

For example, suppose your pod defines names for its ports as shown in the following listing.

Listing 5.4   Specifying port names in a pod definition

```
kind: Pod
spec:
  containers:
  - name: kubia
    ports:
    - name: http
      containerPort: 8080
    - name: https
      containerPort: 8443
```

Container's port 8080 is called http

Port 8443 is called https.

You can then refer to those ports by name in the service spec, as shown in the following listing.

Listing 5.5   Referring to named ports in a service

```
apiVersion: v1
kind: Service
spec:
  ports:
  - name: http
    port: 80
    targetPort: http
  - name: https
    port: 443
    targetPort: https
```

Port 80 is mapped to the container's port called http.

Port 443 is mapped to the container's port, whose name is https.

But why should you even bother with naming ports? The biggest benefit of doing so is that it enables you to change port numbers later without having to change the service spec. Your pod currently uses port 8080 for http, but what if you later decide you'd like to move that to port 80?

If you're using named ports, all you need to do is change the port number in the pod spec (while keeping the port's name unchanged). As you spin up pods with the new ports, client connections will be forwarded to the appropriate port numbers, depending on the pod receiving the connection (port 8080 on old pods and port 80 on the new ones).

5.1.2 Discovering services

By creating a service, you now have a single and stable IP address and port that you can hit to access your pods. This address will remain unchanged throughout the whole lifetime of the service. Pods behind this service may come and go, their IPs may change, their number can go up or down, but they'll always be accessible through the service's single and constant IP address.

But how do the client pods know the IP and port of a service? Do you need to create the service first, then manually look up its IP address and pass the IP to the configuration options of the client pod? Not really. Kubernetes also provides ways for client pods to discover a service's IP and port.

DISCOVERING SERVICES THROUGH ENVIRONMENT VARIABLES

When a pod is started, Kubernetes initializes a set of environment variables pointing to each service that exists at that moment. If you create the service before creating the client pods, processes in those pods can get the IP address and port of the service by inspecting their environment variables.

Let's see what those environment variables look like by examining the environment of one of your running pods. You've already learned that you can use the `kubectl exec` command to run a command in the pod, but because you created the service only after your pods had been created, the environment variables for the service couldn't have been set yet. You'll need to address that first.

Before you can see environment variables for your service, you first need to delete all the pods and let the ReplicationController create new ones. You may remember you can delete all pods without specifying their names like this:

```
$ kubectl delete po --all
pod "kubia-7nog1" deleted
pod "kubia-bf50t" deleted
pod "kubia-gzwli" deleted
```

Now you can list the new pods (I'm sure you know how to do that) and pick one as your target for the `kubectl exec` command. Once you've selected your target pod, you can list environment variables by running the `env` command inside the container, as shown in the following listing.

Listing 5.6 Service-related environment variables in a container

```
$ kubectl exec kubia-3inly env
PATH=/usr/local/sbin:/usr/local/bin:/usr/sbin:/usr/bin:/sbin:/bin
HOSTNAME=kubia-3inly
KUBERNETES_SERVICE_HOST=10.111.240.1
KUBERNETES_SERVICE_PORT=443
...
KUBIA_SERVICE_HOST=10.111.249.153
KUBIA_SERVICE_PORT=80
...
```

Here's the cluster
IP of the service.

And here's the port the
service is available on.

Two services are defined in your cluster: the kubernetes and the kubia service (you saw this earlier with the kubectl get svc command); consequently, two sets of service-related environment variables are in the list. Among the variables that pertain to the kubia service you created at the beginning of the chapter, you'll see the KUBIA_SERVICE _HOST and the KUBIA_SERVICE_PORT environment variables, which hold the IP address and port of the kubia service, respectively.

Turning back to the frontend-backend example we started this chapter with, when you have a frontend pod that requires the use of a backend database server pod, you can expose the backend pod through a service called backend-database and then have the frontend pod look up its IP address and port through the environment variables BACKEND_DATABASE_SERVICE_HOST and BACKEND_DATABASE_SERVICE_PORT.

> **NOTE** Dashes in the service name are converted to underscores and all letters are uppercased when the service name is used as the prefix in the environment variable's name.

Environment variables are one way of looking up the IP and port of a service, but isn't this usually the domain of DNS? Why doesn't Kubernetes include a DNS server and allow you to look up service IPs through DNS instead? As it turns out, it does!

DISCOVERING SERVICES THROUGH DNS

Remember in chapter 3 when you listed pods in the kube-system namespace? One of the pods was called kube-dns. The kube-system namespace also includes a corresponding service with the same name.

As the name suggests, the pod runs a DNS server, which all other pods running in the cluster are automatically configured to use (Kubernetes does that by modifying each container's /etc/resolv.conf file). Any DNS query performed by a process running in a pod will be handled by Kubernetes' own DNS server, which knows all the services running in your system.

> **NOTE** Whether a pod uses the internal DNS server or not is configurable through the dnsPolicy property in each pod's spec.

Each service gets a DNS entry in the internal DNS server, and client pods that know the name of the service can access it through its fully qualified domain name (FQDN) instead of resorting to environment variables.

CONNECTING TO THE SERVICE THROUGH ITS FQDN

To revisit the frontend-backend example, a frontend pod can connect to the backend-database service by opening a connection to the following FQDN:

```
backend-database.default.svc.cluster.local
```

backend-database corresponds to the service name, default stands for the namespace the service is defined in, and svc.cluster.local is a configurable cluster domain suffix used in all cluster local service names.

> **NOTE** The client must still know the service's port number. If the service is using a standard port (for example, 80 for HTTP or 5432 for Postgres), that shouldn't be a problem. If not, the client can get the port number from the environment variable.

Connecting to a service can be even simpler than that. You can omit the svc.cluster .local suffix and even the namespace, when the frontend pod is in the same namespace as the database pod. You can thus refer to the service simply as backend-database. That's incredibly simple, right?

Let's try this. You'll try to access the kubia service through its FQDN instead of its IP. Again, you'll need to do that inside an existing pod. You already know how to use kubectl exec to run a single command in a pod's container, but this time, instead of running the curl command directly, you'll run the bash shell instead, so you can then run multiple commands in the container. This is similar to what you did in chapter 2 when you entered the container you ran with Docker by using the docker exec -it bash command.

RUNNING A SHELL IN A POD'S CONTAINER

You can use the kubectl exec command to run bash (or any other shell) inside a pod's container. This way you're free to explore the container as long as you want, without having to perform a kubectl exec for every command you want to run.

> **NOTE** The shell's binary executable must be available in the container image for this to work.

To use the shell properly, you need to pass the -it option to kubectl exec:

```
$ kubectl exec -it kubia-3inly bash
root@kubia-3inly:/#
```

You're now inside the container. You can use the curl command to access the kubia service in any of the following ways:

```
root@kubia-3inly:/# curl http://kubia.default.svc.cluster.local
You've hit kubia-5asi2

root@kubia-3inly:/# curl http://kubia.default
You've hit kubia-3inly
```

```
root@kubia-3inly:/# curl http://kubia
You've hit kubia-8awf3
```

You can hit your service by using the service's name as the hostname in the requested URL. You can omit the namespace and the `svc.cluster.local` suffix because of how the DNS resolver inside each pod's container is configured. Look at the /etc/resolv.conf file in the container and you'll understand:

```
root@kubia-3inly:/# cat /etc/resolv.conf
search default.svc.cluster.local svc.cluster.local cluster.local ...
```

UNDERSTANDING WHY YOU CAN'T PING A SERVICE IP

One last thing before we move on. You know how to create services now, so you'll soon create your own. But what if, for whatever reason, you can't access your service?

You'll probably try to figure out what's wrong by entering an existing pod and trying to access the service like you did in the last example. Then, if you still can't access the service with a simple `curl` command, maybe you'll try to ping the service IP to see if it's up. Let's try that now:

```
root@kubia-3inly:/# ping kubia
PING kubia.default.svc.cluster.local (10.111.249.153): 56 data bytes
^C--- kubia.default.svc.cluster.local ping statistics ---
54 packets transmitted, 0 packets received, 100% packet loss
```

Hmm. `curl`-ing the service works, but pinging it doesn't. That's because the service's cluster IP is a virtual IP, and only has meaning when combined with the service port. We'll explain what that means and how services work in chapter 11. I wanted to mention that here because it's the first thing users do when they try to debug a broken service and it catches most of them off guard.

5.2 Connecting to services living outside the cluster

Up to now, we've talked about services backed by one or more pods running inside the cluster. But cases exist when you'd like to expose external services through the Kubernetes services feature. Instead of having the service redirect connections to pods in the cluster, you want it to redirect to external IP(s) and port(s).

This allows you to take advantage of both service load balancing and service discovery. Client pods running in the cluster can connect to the external service like they connect to internal services.

5.2.1 Introducing service endpoints

Before going into how to do this, let me first shed more light on services. Services don't link to pods directly. Instead, a resource sits in between—the Endpoints resource. You may have already noticed endpoints if you used the `kubectl describe` command on your service, as shown in the following listing.

Listing 5.7   Full details of a service displayed with kubectl describe

```
$ kubectl describe svc kubia
Name:              kubia
Namespace:         default
Labels:            <none>
Selector:          app=kubia
Type:              ClusterIP
IP:                10.111.249.153
Port:              <unset> 80/TCP
Endpoints:         10.108.1.4:8080,10.108.2.5:8080,10.108.2.6:8080
Session Affinity:  None
No events.
```

The service's pod selector is used to create the list of endpoints.

The list of pod IPs and ports that represent the endpoints of this service

An Endpoints resource (yes, plural) is a list of IP addresses and ports exposing a service. The Endpoints resource is like any other Kubernetes resource, so you can display its basic info with kubectl get:

```
$ kubectl get endpoints kubia
NAME    ENDPOINTS                                            AGE
kubia   10.108.1.4:8080,10.108.2.5:8080,10.108.2.6:8080     1h
```

Although the pod selector is defined in the service spec, it's not used directly when redirecting incoming connections. Instead, the selector is used to build a list of IPs and ports, which is then stored in the Endpoints resource. When a client connects to a service, the service proxy selects one of those IP and port pairs and redirects the incoming connection to the server listening at that location.

5.2.2   *Manually configuring service endpoints*

You may have probably realized this already, but having the service's endpoints decoupled from the service allows them to be configured and updated manually.

If you create a service without a pod selector, Kubernetes won't even create the Endpoints resource (after all, without a selector, it can't know which pods to include in the service). It's up to you to create the Endpoints resource to specify the list of endpoints for the service.

To create a service with manually managed endpoints, you need to create both a Service and an Endpoints resource.

CREATING A SERVICE WITHOUT A SELECTOR
You'll first create the YAML for the service itself, as shown in the following listing.

Listing 5.8   A service without a pod selector: external-service.yaml

```
apiVersion: v1
kind: Service
metadata:
  name: external-service
spec:
  ports:
  - port: 80
```

The name of the service must match the name of the Endpoints object (see next listing).

This service has no selector defined.

You're defining a service called `external-service` that will accept incoming connections on port 80. You didn't define a pod selector for the service.

CREATING AN ENDPOINTS RESOURCE FOR A SERVICE WITHOUT A SELECTOR

Endpoints are a separate resource and not an attribute of a service. Because you created the service without a selector, the corresponding Endpoints resource hasn't been created automatically, so it's up to you to create it. The following listing shows its YAML manifest.

Listing 5.9   A manually created Endpoints resource: external-service-endpoints.yaml

```
apiVersion: v1
kind: Endpoints                          The name of the Endpoints object
metadata:                                must match the name of the
  name: external-service                 service (see previous listing).
subsets:
  - addresses:
    - ip: 11.11.11.11                     The IPs of the endpoints that the
    - ip: 22.22.22.22                     service will forward connections to
    ports:
    - port: 80                            The target port of the endpoints
```

The Endpoints object needs to have the same name as the service and contain the list of target IP addresses and ports for the service. After both the Service and the Endpoints resource are posted to the server, the service is ready to be used like any regular service with a pod selector. Containers created after the service is created will include the environment variables for the service, and all connections to its IP:port pair will be load balanced between the service's endpoints.

Figure 5.4 shows three pods connecting to the service with external endpoints.

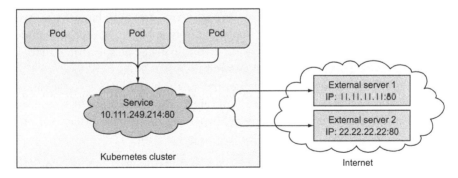

Figure 5.4   Pods consuming a service with two external endpoints.

If you later decide to migrate the external service to pods running inside Kubernetes, you can add a selector to the service, thereby making its Endpoints managed automatically. The same is also true in reverse—by removing the selector from a Service,

Kubernetes stops updating its Endpoints. This means a service IP address can remain constant while the actual implementation of the service is changed.

5.2.3 Creating an alias for an external service

Instead of exposing an external service by manually configuring the service's Endpoints, a simpler method allows you to refer to an external service by its fully qualified domain name (FQDN).

CREATING AN EXTERNALNAME SERVICE

To create a service that serves as an alias for an external service, you create a Service resource with the `type` field set to `ExternalName`. For example, let's imagine there's a public API available at api.somecompany.com. You can define a service that points to it as shown in the following listing.

> **Listing 5.10   An `ExternalName`-type service: external-service-externalname.yaml**

```
apiVersion: v1
kind: Service
metadata:
  name: external-service
spec:
  type: ExternalName                              Service type is set
  externalName: someapi.somecompany.com           to ExternalName
  ports:                                          The fully qualified domain
  - port: 80                                      name of the actual service
```

After the service is created, pods can connect to the external service through the `external-service.default.svc.cluster.local` domain name (or even `external-service`) instead of using the service's actual FQDN. This hides the actual service name and its location from pods consuming the service, allowing you to modify the service definition and point it to a different service any time later, by only changing the `externalName` attribute or by changing the type back to `ClusterIP` and creating an Endpoints object for the service—either manually or by specifying a label selector on the service and having it created automatically.

`ExternalName` services are implemented solely at the DNS level—a simple `CNAME` DNS record is created for the service. Therefore, clients connecting to the service will connect to the external service directly, bypassing the service proxy completely. For this reason, these types of services don't even get a cluster IP.

> **NOTE**   A `CNAME` record points to a fully qualified domain name instead of a numeric IP address.

5.3 Exposing services to external clients

Up to now, we've only talked about how services can be consumed by pods from inside the cluster. But you'll also want to expose certain services, such as frontend webservers, to the outside, so external clients can access them, as depicted in figure 5.5.

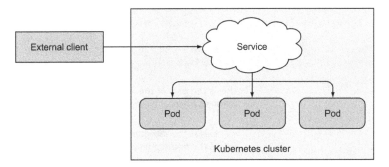

Figure 5.5 Exposing a service to external clients

You have a few ways to make a service accessible externally:

- *Setting the service type to* NodePort—For a NodePort service, each cluster node opens a port on the node itself (hence the name) and redirects traffic received on that port to the underlying service. The service isn't accessible only at the internal cluster IP and port, but also through a dedicated port on all nodes.
- *Setting the service type to* LoadBalancer, *an extension of the* NodePort *type*—This makes the service accessible through a dedicated load balancer, provisioned from the cloud infrastructure Kubernetes is running on. The load balancer redirects traffic to the node port across all the nodes. Clients connect to the service through the load balancer's IP.
- *Creating an Ingress resource, a radically different mechanism for exposing multiple services through a single IP address*—It operates at the HTTP level (network layer 7) and can thus offer more features than layer 4 services can. We'll explain Ingress resources in section 5.4.

5.3.1 Using a NodePort service

The first method of exposing a set of pods to external clients is by creating a service and setting its type to NodePort. By creating a NodePort service, you make Kubernetes reserve a port on all its nodes (the same port number is used across all of them) and forward incoming connections to the pods that are part of the service.

This is similar to a regular service (their actual type is ClusterIP), but a NodePort service can be accessed not only through the service's internal cluster IP, but also through any node's IP and the reserved node port.

This will make more sense when you try interacting with a NodePort service.

CREATING A NODEPORT SERVICE

You'll now create a NodePort service to see how you can use it. The following listing shows the YAML for the service.

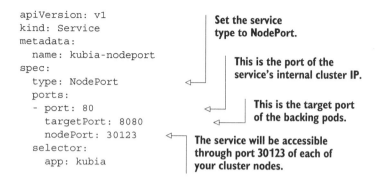

Listing 5.11   A `NodePort` service definition: kubia-svc-nodeport.yaml

```
apiVersion: v1
kind: Service
metadata:
  name: kubia-nodeport
spec:
  type: NodePort
  ports:
  - port: 80
    targetPort: 8080
    nodePort: 30123
  selector:
    app: kubia
```

Set the service type to NodePort.

This is the port of the service's internal cluster IP.

This is the target port of the backing pods.

The service will be accessible through port 30123 of each of your cluster nodes.

You set the type to `NodePort` and specify the node port this service should be bound to across all cluster nodes. Specifying the port isn't mandatory; Kubernetes will choose a random port if you omit it.

> **NOTE**   When you create the service in GKE, `kubectl` prints out a warning about having to configure firewall rules. We'll see how to do that soon.

EXAMINING YOUR NODEPORT SERVICE

Let's see the basic information of your service to learn more about it:

```
$ kubectl get svc kubia-nodeport
NAME             CLUSTER-IP       EXTERNAL-IP    PORT(S)       AGE
kubia-nodeport   10.111.254.223   <nodes>        80:30123/TCP  2m
```

Look at the `EXTERNAL-IP` column. It shows `<nodes>`, indicating the service is accessible through the IP address of any cluster node. The `PORT(S)` column shows both the internal port of the cluster IP (`80`) and the node port (`30123`). The service is accessible at the following addresses:

- `10.111.254.223:80`
- `<1st node's IP>:30123`
- `<2nd node's IP>:30123`, and so on.

Figure 5.6 shows your service exposed on port 30123 of both of your cluster nodes (this applies if you're running this on GKE; Minikube only has a single node, but the principle is the same). An incoming connection to one of those ports will be redirected to a randomly selected pod, which may or may not be the one running on the node the connection is being made to.

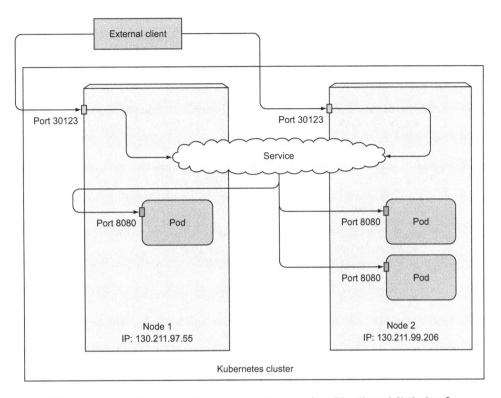

Figure 5.6   An external client connecting to a `NodePort` service either through Node 1 or 2

A connection received on port 30123 of the first node might be forwarded either to the pod running on the first node or to one of the pods running on the second node.

CHANGING FIREWALL RULES TO LET EXTERNAL CLIENTS ACCESS OUR NODEPORT SERVICE

As I've mentioned previously, before you can access your service through the node port, you need to configure the Google Cloud Platform's firewalls to allow external connections to your nodes on that port. You'll do this now:

```
$ gcloud compute firewall-rules create kubia-svc-rule --allow=tcp:30123
Created [https://www.googleapis.com/compute/v1/projects/kubia-
    1295/global/firewalls/kubia-svc-rule].
NAME            NETWORK   SRC_RANGES   RULES       SRC_TAGS   TARGET_TAGS
kubia-svc-rule  default   0.0.0.0/0    tcp:30123
```

You can access your service through port 30123 of one of the node's IPs. But you need to figure out the IP of a node first. Refer to the sidebar on how to do that.

Using JSONPath to get the IPs of all your nodes

You can find the IP in the JSON or YAML descriptors of the nodes. But instead of sifting through the relatively large JSON, you can tell `kubectl` to print out only the node IP instead of the whole service definition:

```
$ kubectl get nodes -o jsonpath='{.items[*].status.
    addresses[?(@.type=="ExternalIP")].address}'
130.211.97.55 130.211.99.206
```

You're telling `kubectl` to only output the information you want by specifying a JSONPath. You're probably familiar with XPath and how it's used with XML. JSONPath is basically XPath for JSON. The JSONPath in the previous example instructs `kubectl` to do the following:

- Go through all the elements in the `items` attribute.
- For each element, enter the `status` attribute.
- Filter elements of the `addresses` attribute, taking only those that have the `type` attribute set to `ExternalIP`.
- Finally, print the `address` attribute of the filtered elements.

To learn more about how to use JSONPath with `kubectl`, refer to the documentation at http://kubernetes.io/docs/user-guide/jsonpath.

Once you know the IPs of your nodes, you can try accessing your service through them:

```
$ curl http://130.211.97.55:30123
You've hit kubia-ym8or
$ curl http://130.211.99.206:30123
You've hit kubia-xueq1
```

> **TIP**   When using Minikube, you can easily access your `NodePort` services through your browser by running `minikube service <service-name> [-n <namespace>]`.

As you can see, your pods are now accessible to the whole internet through port 30123 on any of your nodes. It doesn't matter what node a client sends the request to. But if you only point your clients to the first node, when that node fails, your clients can't access the service anymore. That's why it makes sense to put a load balancer in front of the nodes to make sure you're spreading requests across all healthy nodes and never sending them to a node that's offline at that moment.

If your Kubernetes cluster supports it (which is mostly true when Kubernetes is deployed on cloud infrastructure), the load balancer can be provisioned automatically by creating a `LoadBalancer` instead of a `NodePort` service. We'll look at this next.

5.3.2   *Exposing a service through an external load balancer*

Kubernetes clusters running on cloud providers usually support the automatic provision of a load balancer from the cloud infrastructure. All you need to do is set the service's type to `LoadBalancer` instead of `NodePort`. The load balancer will have its own unique, publicly accessible IP address and will redirect all connections to your service. You can thus access your service through the load balancer's IP address.

If Kubernetes is running in an environment that doesn't support `LoadBalancer` services, the load balancer will not be provisioned, but the service will still behave like a `NodePort` service. That's because a `LoadBalancer` service is an extension of a `Node-Port` service. You'll run this example on Google Kubernetes Engine, which supports `LoadBalancer` services. Minikube doesn't, at least not as of this writing.

CREATING A LOADBALANCER SERVICE

To create a service with a load balancer in front, create the service from the following YAML manifest, as shown in the following listing.

> **Listing 5.12   A `LoadBalancer`-type service: kubia-svc-loadbalancer.yaml**

```
apiVersion: v1
kind: Service
metadata:
  name: kubia-loadbalancer
spec:
  type: LoadBalancer          ◁── This type of service obtains
  ports:                          a load balancer from the
  - port: 80                      infrastructure hosting the
    targetPort: 8080              Kubernetes cluster.
  selector:
    app: kubia
```

The service type is set to `LoadBalancer` instead of `NodePort`. You're not specifying a specific node port, although you could (you're letting Kubernetes choose one instead).

CONNECTING TO THE SERVICE THROUGH THE LOAD BALANCER

After you create the service, it takes time for the cloud infrastructure to create the load balancer and write its IP address into the Service object. Once it does that, the IP address will be listed as the external IP address of your service:

```
$ kubectl get svc kubia-loadbalancer
NAME                 CLUSTER-IP       EXTERNAL-IP      PORT(S)       AGE
kubia-loadbalancer   10.111.241.153   130.211.53.173   80:32143/TCP  1m
```

In this case, the load balancer is available at IP 130.211.53.173, so you can now access the service at that IP address:

```
$ curl http://130.211.53.173
You've hit kubia-xueq1
```

Success! As you may have noticed, this time you didn't need to mess with firewalls the way you had to before with the `NodePort` service.

Session affinity and web browsers

Because your service is now exposed externally, you may try accessing it with your web browser. You'll see something that may strike you as odd—the browser will hit the exact same pod every time. Did the service's session affinity change in the meantime? With `kubectl describe`, you can double-check that the service's session affinity is still set to `None`, so why don't different browser requests hit different pods, as is the case when using `curl`?

Let me explain what's happening. The browser is using keep-alive connections and sends all its requests through a single connection, whereas `curl` opens a new connection every time. Services work at the connection level, so when a connection to a service is first opened, a random pod is selected and then all network packets belonging to that connection are all sent to that single pod. Even if session affinity is set to `None`, users will always hit the same pod (until the connection is closed).

See figure 5.7 to see how HTTP requests are delivered to the pod. External clients (`curl` in your case) connect to port 80 of the load balancer and get routed to the

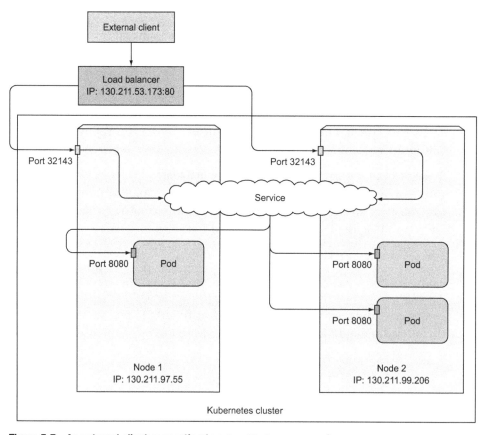

Figure 5.7   An external client connecting to a `LoadBalancer` service

implicitly assigned node port on one of the nodes. From there, the connection is forwarded to one of the pod instances.

As already mentioned, a `LoadBalancer`-type service is a `NodePort` service with an additional infrastructure-provided load balancer. If you use `kubectl describe` to display additional info about the service, you'll see that a node port has been selected for the service. If you were to open the firewall for this port, the way you did in the previous section about `NodePort` services, you could access the service through the node IPs as well.

> **TIP** If you're using Minikube, even though the load balancer will never be provisioned, you can still access the service through the node port (at the Minikube VM's IP address).

5.3.3 *Understanding the peculiarities of external connections*

You must be aware of several things related to externally originating connections to services.

UNDERSTANDING AND PREVENTING UNNECESSARY NETWORK HOPS

When an external client connects to a service through the node port (this also includes cases when it goes through the load balancer first), the randomly chosen pod may or may not be running on the same node that received the connection. An additional network hop is required to reach the pod, but this may not always be desirable.

You can prevent this additional hop by configuring the service to redirect external traffic only to pods running on the node that received the connection. This is done by setting the `externalTrafficPolicy` field in the service's spec section:

```
spec:
  externalTrafficPolicy: Local
  ...
```

If a service definition includes this setting and an external connection is opened through the service's node port, the service proxy will choose a locally running pod. If no local pods exist, the connection will hang (it won't be forwarded to a random global pod, the way connections are when not using the annotation). You therefore need to ensure the load balancer forwards connections only to nodes that have at least one such pod.

Using this annotation also has other drawbacks. Normally, connections are spread evenly across all the pods, but when using this annotation, that's no longer the case.

Imagine having two nodes and three pods. Let's say node A runs one pod and node B runs the other two. If the load balancer spreads connections evenly across the two nodes, the pod on node A will receive 50% of all connections, but the two pods on node B will only receive 25% each, as shown in figure 5.8.

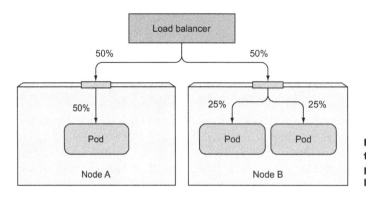

Figure 5.8 **A Service using the** `Local` **external traffic policy may lead to uneven load distribution across pods.**

BEING AWARE OF THE NON-PRESERVATION OF THE CLIENT'S IP

Usually, when clients inside the cluster connect to a service, the pods backing the service can obtain the client's IP address. But when the connection is received through a node port, the packets' source IP is changed, because Source Network Address Translation (SNAT) is performed on the packets.

The backing pod can't see the actual client's IP, which may be a problem for some applications that need to know the client's IP. In the case of a web server, for example, this means the access log won't show the browser's IP.

The `Local` external traffic policy described in the previous section affects the preservation of the client's IP, because there's no additional hop between the node receiving the connection and the node hosting the target pod (SNAT isn't performed).

5.4 *Exposing services externally through an Ingress resource*

You've now seen two ways of exposing a service to clients outside the cluster, but another method exists—creating an Ingress resource.

> **DEFINITION** *Ingress* (noun)—The act of going in or entering; the right to enter; a means or place of entering; entryway.

Let me first explain why you need another way to access Kubernetes services from the outside.

UNDERSTANDING WHY INGRESSES ARE NEEDED

One important reason is that each `LoadBalancer` service requires its own load balancer with its own public IP address, whereas an Ingress only requires one, even when providing access to dozens of services. When a client sends an HTTP request to the Ingress, the host and path in the request determine which service the request is forwarded to, as shown in figure 5.9.

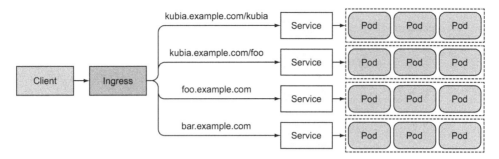

Figure 5.9   Multiple services can be exposed through a single Ingress.

Ingresses operate at the application layer of the network stack (HTTP) and can provide features such as cookie-based session affinity and the like, which services can't.

UNDERSTANDING THAT AN INGRESS CONTROLLER IS REQUIRED

Before we go into the features an Ingress object provides, let me emphasize that to make Ingress resources work, an Ingress controller needs to be running in the cluster. Different Kubernetes environments use different implementations of the controller, but several don't provide a default controller at all.

For example, Google Kubernetes Engine uses Google Cloud Platform's own HTTP load-balancing features to provide the Ingress functionality. Initially, Minikube didn't provide a controller out of the box, but it now includes an add-on that can be enabled to let you try out the Ingress functionality. Follow the instructions in the following sidebar to ensure it's enabled.

Enabling the Ingress add-on in Minikube

If you're using Minikube to run the examples in this book, you'll need to ensure the Ingress add-on is enabled. You can check whether it is by listing all the add-ons:

```
$ minikube addons list
- default-storageclass: enabled
- kube-dns: enabled
- heapster: disabled
- ingress: disabled          <--- The Ingress add-on
- registry-creds: disabled        isn't enabled.
- addon-manager: enabled
- dashboard: enabled
```

You'll learn about what these add-ons are throughout the book, but it should be pretty clear what the `dashboard` and the `kube-dns` add-ons do. Enable the Ingress add-on so you can see Ingresses in action:

```
$ minikube addons enable ingress
ingress was successfully enabled
```

(continued)

This should have spun up an Ingress controller as another pod. Most likely, the controller pod will be in the `kube-system` namespace, but not necessarily, so list all the running pods across all namespaces by using the `--all-namespaces` option:

```
$ kubectl get po --all-namespaces
NAMESPACE     NAME                               READY  STATUS    RESTARTS AGE
default       kubia-rsv5m                        1/1    Running   0        13h
default       kubia-fe4ad                        1/1    Running   0        13h
default       kubia-ke823                        1/1    Running   0        13h
kube-system   default-http-backend-5wb0h         1/1    Running   0        18m
kube-system   kube-addon-manager-minikube        1/1    Running   3        6d
kube-system   kube-dns-v20-101vq                 3/3    Running   9        6d
kube-system   kubernetes-dashboard-jxd91         1/1    Running   3        6d
kube-system   nginx-ingress-controller-gdts0     1/1    Running   0        18m
```

At the bottom of the output, you see the Ingress controller pod. The name suggests that Nginx (an open-source HTTP server and reverse proxy) is used to provide the Ingress functionality.

TIP   The `--all-namespaces` option mentioned in the sidebar is handy when you don't know what namespace your pod (or other type of resource) is in, or if you want to list resources across all namespaces.

5.4.1   *Creating an Ingress resource*

You've confirmed there's an Ingress controller running in your cluster, so you can now create an Ingress resource. The following listing shows what the YAML manifest for the Ingress looks like.

> **Listing 5.13   An Ingress resource definition: kubia-ingress.yaml**

```
apiVersion: extensions/v1beta1
kind: Ingress
metadata:
  name: kubia
spec:
  rules:
  - host: kubia.example.com        ◁──  This Ingress maps the
    http:                               kubia.example.com domain
      paths:                            name to your service.
      - path: /
        backend:                        All requests will be sent to
          serviceName: kubia-nodeport   port 80 of the kubia-
          servicePort: 80               nodeport service.
```

This defines an Ingress with a single rule, which makes sure all HTTP requests received by the Ingress controller, in which the host `kubia.example.com` is requested, will be sent to the `kubia-nodeport` service on port `80`.

NOTE Ingress controllers on cloud providers (in GKE, for example) require the Ingress to point to a `NodePort` service. But that's not a requirement of Kubernetes itself.

5.4.2 Accessing the service through the Ingress

To access your service through http://kubia.example.com, you'll need to make sure the domain name resolves to the IP of the Ingress controller.

OBTAINING THE IP ADDRESS OF THE INGRESS

To look up the IP, you need to list Ingresses:

```
$ kubectl get ingresses
NAME     HOSTS               ADDRESS          PORTS   AGE
kubia    kubia.example.com   192.168.99.100   80      29m
```

NOTE When running on cloud providers, the address may take time to appear, because the Ingress controller provisions a load balancer behind the scenes.

The IP is shown in the `ADDRESS` column.

ENSURING THE HOST CONFIGURED IN THE INGRESS POINTS TO THE INGRESS' IP ADDRESS

Once you know the IP, you can then either configure your DNS servers to resolve kubia.example.com to that IP or you can add the following line to /etc/hosts (or C:\windows\system32\drivers\etc\hosts on Windows):

```
192.168.99.100    kubia.example.com
```

ACCESSING PODS THROUGH THE INGRESS

Everything is now set up, so you can access the service at http://kubia.example.com (using a browser or `curl`):

```
$ curl http://kubia.example.com
You've hit kubia-ke823
```

You've successfully accessed the service through an Ingress. Let's take a better look at how that unfolded.

UNDERSTANDING HOW INGRESSES WORK

Figure 5.10 shows how the client connected to one of the pods through the Ingress controller. The client first performed a DNS lookup of kubia.example.com, and the DNS server (or the local operating system) returned the IP of the Ingress controller. The client then sent an HTTP request to the Ingress controller and specified kubia.example.com in the Host header. From that header, the controller determined which service the client is trying to access, looked up the pod IPs through the Endpoints object associated with the service, and forwarded the client's request to one of the pods.

As you can see, the Ingress controller didn't forward the request to the service. It only used it to select a pod. Most, if not all, controllers work like this.

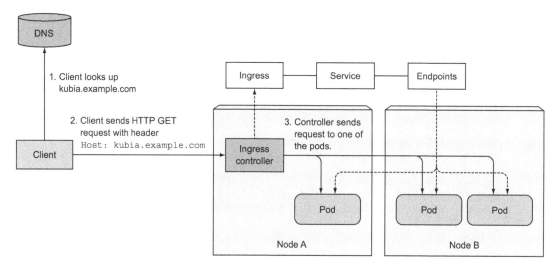

Figure 5.10 Accessing pods through an Ingress

5.4.3 *Exposing multiple services through the same Ingress*

If you look at the Ingress spec closely, you'll see that both `rules` and `paths` are arrays, so they can contain multiple items. An Ingress can map multiple hosts and paths to multiple services, as you'll see next. Let's focus on `paths` first.

MAPPING DIFFERENT SERVICES TO DIFFERENT PATHS OF THE SAME HOST

You can map multiple `paths` on the same host to different services, as shown in the following listing.

Listing 5.14   Ingress exposing multiple services on same host, but different `paths`

```
...
  - host: kubia.example.com
    http:
      paths:
      - path: /kubia
        backend:                          Requests to kubia.example.com/kubia
          serviceName: kubia              will be routed to the kubia service.
          servicePort: 80
      - path: /bar
        backend:                          Requests to kubia.example.com/bar
          serviceName: bar                will be routed to the bar service.
          servicePort: 80
```

In this case, requests will be sent to two different services, depending on the path in the requested URL. Clients can therefore reach two different services through a single IP address (that of the Ingress controller).

Mapping different services to different hosts

Similarly, you can use an Ingress to map to different services based on the host in the HTTP request instead of (only) the path, as shown in the next listing.

Listing 5.15   Ingress exposing multiple services on different hosts

```
spec:
  rules:
  - host: foo.example.com        ◁───┐
    http:                             │  Requests for
      paths:                          │  foo.example.com will be
      - path: /                       │  routed to service foo.
        backend:
          serviceName: foo     ◁───┘
          servicePort: 80
  - host: bar.example.com        ◁───┐
    http:                             │  Requests for
      paths:                          │  bar.example.com will be
      - path: /                       │  routed to service bar.
        backend:
          serviceName: bar     ◁───┘
          servicePort: 80
```

Requests received by the controller will be forwarded to either service `foo` or `bar`, depending on the `Host` header in the request (the way virtual hosts are handled in web servers). DNS needs to point both the foo.example.com and the bar.example.com domain names to the Ingress controller's IP address.

5.4.4 Configuring Ingress to handle TLS traffic

You've seen how an Ingress forwards HTTP traffic. But what about HTTPS? Let's take a quick look at how to configure Ingress to support TLS.

Creating a TLS certificate for the Ingress

When a client opens a TLS connection to an Ingress controller, the controller terminates the TLS connection. The communication between the client and the controller is encrypted, whereas the communication between the controller and the backend pod isn't. The application running in the pod doesn't need to support TLS. For example, if the pod runs a web server, it can accept only HTTP traffic and let the Ingress controller take care of everything related to TLS. To enable the controller to do that, you need to attach a certificate and a private key to the Ingress. The two need to be stored in a Kubernetes resource called a Secret, which is then referenced in the Ingress manifest. We'll explain Secrets in detail in chapter 7. For now, you'll create the Secret without paying too much attention to it.

First, you need to create the private key and certificate:

```
$ openssl genrsa -out tls.key 2048
$ openssl req -new -x509 -key tls.key -out tls.cert -days 360 -subj
➥ /CN=kubia.example.com
```

Then you create the Secret from the two files like this:

```
$ kubectl create secret tls tls-secret --cert=tls.cert --key=tls.key
secret "tls-secret" created
```

Signing certificates through the CertificateSigningRequest resource

Instead of signing the certificate ourselves, you can get the certificate signed by creating a CertificateSigningRequest (CSR) resource. Users or their applications can create a regular certificate request, put it into a CSR, and then either a human operator or an automated process can approve the request like this:

```
$ kubectl certificate approve <name of the CSR>
```

The signed certificate can then be retrieved from the CSR's status.certificate field.

Note that a certificate signer component must be running in the cluster; otherwise creating CertificateSigningRequest and approving or denying them won't have any effect.

The private key and the certificate are now stored in the Secret called tls-secret. Now, you can update your Ingress object so it will also accept HTTPS requests for kubia.example.com. The Ingress manifest should now look like the following listing.

Listing 5.16   Ingress handling TLS traffic: kubia-ingress-tls.yaml

```
apiVersion: extensions/v1beta1
kind: Ingress
metadata:
  name: kubia
spec:
  tls:                                    ◁─┐   The whole TLS configuration
  - hosts:                                      is under this attribute.
    - kubia.example.com                         TLS connections will be accepted for
    secretName: tls-secret          ◁─┐         the kubia.example.com hostname.
  rules:
  - host: kubia.example.com                     The private key and the certificate
    http:                                       should be obtained from the tls-
      paths:                                    secret you created previously.
      - path: /
        backend:
          serviceName: kubia-nodeport
          servicePort: 80
```

TIP   Instead of deleting the Ingress and re-creating it from the new file, you can invoke kubectl apply -f kubia-ingress-tls.yaml, which updates the Ingress resource with what's specified in the file.

You can now use HTTPS to access your service through the Ingress:

```
$ curl -k -v https://kubia.example.com/kubia
* About to connect() to kubia.example.com port 443 (#0)
...
* Server certificate:
*    subject: CN=kubia.example.com
...
> GET /kubia HTTP/1.1
> ...
You've hit kubia-xueq1
```

The command's output shows the response from the app, as well as the server certificate you configured the Ingress with.

> **NOTE** Support for Ingress features varies between the different Ingress controller implementations, so check the implementation-specific documentation to see what's supported.

Ingresses are a relatively new Kubernetes feature, so you can expect to see many improvements and new features in the future. Although they currently support only L7 (HTTP/HTTPS) load balancing, support for L4 load balancing is also planned.

5.5 *Signaling when a pod is ready to accept connections*

There's one more thing we need to cover regarding both Services and Ingresses. You've already learned that pods are included as endpoints of a service if their labels match the service's pod selector. As soon as a new pod with proper labels is created, it becomes part of the service and requests start to be redirected to the pod. But what if the pod isn't ready to start serving requests immediately?

The pod may need time to load either configuration or data, or it may need to perform a warm-up procedure to prevent the first user request from taking too long and affecting the user experience. In such cases you don't want the pod to start receiving requests immediately, especially when the already-running instances can process requests properly and quickly. It makes sense to not forward requests to a pod that's in the process of starting up until it's fully ready.

5.5.1 *Introducing readiness probes*

In the previous chapter you learned about liveness probes and how they help keep your apps healthy by ensuring unhealthy containers are restarted automatically. Similar to liveness probes, Kubernetes allows you to also define a readiness probe for your pod.

The readiness probe is invoked periodically and determines whether the specific pod should receive client requests or not. When a container's readiness probe returns success, it's signaling that the container is ready to accept requests.

This notion of being ready is obviously something that's specific to each container. Kubernetes can merely check if the app running in the container responds to a simple

GET / request or it can hit a specific URL path, which causes the app to perform a whole list of checks to determine if it's ready. Such a detailed readiness probe, which takes the app's specifics into account, is the app developer's responsibility.

TYPES OF READINESS PROBES

Like liveness probes, three types of readiness probes exist:

- An *Exec* probe, where a process is executed. The container's status is determined by the process' exit status code.
- An *HTTP GET* probe, which sends an HTTP GET request to the container and the HTTP status code of the response determines whether the container is ready or not.
- A *TCP Socket* probe, which opens a TCP connection to a specified port of the container. If the connection is established, the container is considered ready.

UNDERSTANDING THE OPERATION OF READINESS PROBES

When a container is started, Kubernetes can be configured to wait for a configurable amount of time to pass before performing the first readiness check. After that, it invokes the probe periodically and acts based on the result of the readiness probe. If a pod reports that it's not ready, it's removed from the service. If the pod then becomes ready again, it's re-added.

Unlike liveness probes, if a container fails the readiness check, it won't be killed or restarted. This is an important distinction between liveness and readiness probes. Liveness probes keep pods healthy by killing off unhealthy containers and replacing them with new, healthy ones, whereas readiness probes make sure that only pods that are ready to serve requests receive them. This is mostly necessary during container start up, but it's also useful after the container has been running for a while.

As you can see in figure 5.11, if a pod's readiness probe fails, the pod is removed from the Endpoints object. Clients connecting to the service will not be redirected to the pod. The effect is the same as when the pod doesn't match the service's label selector at all.

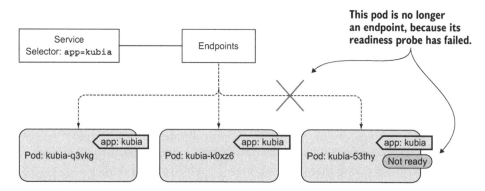

Figure 5.11   A pod whose readiness probe fails is removed as an endpoint of a service.

UNDERSTANDING WHY READINESS PROBES ARE IMPORTANT

Imagine that a group of pods (for example, pods running application servers) depends on a service provided by another pod (a backend database, for example). If at any point one of the frontend pods experiences connectivity problems and can't reach the database anymore, it may be wise for its readiness probe to signal to Kubernetes that the pod isn't ready to serve any requests at that time. If other pod instances aren't experiencing the same type of connectivity issues, they can serve requests normally. A readiness probe makes sure clients only talk to those healthy pods and never notice there's anything wrong with the system.

5.5.2 Adding a readiness probe to a pod

Next you'll add a readiness probe to your existing pods by modifying the Replication-Controller's pod template.

ADDING A READINESS PROBE TO THE POD TEMPLATE

You'll use the `kubectl edit` command to add the probe to the pod template in your existing ReplicationController:

```
$ kubectl edit rc kubia
```

When the ReplicationController's YAML opens in the text editor, find the container specification in the pod template and add the following readiness probe definition to the first container under `spec.template.spec.containers`. The YAML should look like the following listing.

Listing 5.17　RC creating a pod with a readiness probe: kubia-rc-readinessprobe.yaml

```
apiVersion: v1
kind: ReplicationController
...
spec:
  ...
  template:
    ...
    spec:
      containers:
      - name: kubia
        image: luksa/kubia
        readinessProbe:            A readinessProbe may
          exec:                    be defined for each
            command:               container in the pod.
            - ls
            - /var/ready
        ...
```

The readiness probe will periodically perform the command `ls /var/ready` inside the container. The `ls` command returns exit code zero if the file exists, or a non-zero exit code otherwise. If the file exists, the readiness probe will succeed; otherwise, it will fail.

The reason you're defining such a strange readiness probe is so you can toggle its result by creating or removing the file in question. The file doesn't exist yet, so all the pods should now report not being ready, right? Well, not exactly. As you may remember from the previous chapter, changing a ReplicationController's pod template has no effect on existing pods.

In other words, all your existing pods still have no readiness probe defined. You can see this by listing the pods with `kubectl get pods` and looking at the READY column. You need to delete the pods and have them re-created by the Replication-Controller. The new pods will fail the readiness check and won't be included as endpoints of the service until you create the /var/ready file in each of them.

OBSERVING AND MODIFYING THE PODS' READINESS STATUS

List the pods again and inspect whether they're ready or not:

```
$ kubectl get po
NAME            READY     STATUS      RESTARTS    AGE
kubia-2r1qb     0/1       Running     0           1m
kubia-3rax1     0/1       Running     0           1m
kubia-3yw4s     0/1       Running     0           1m
```

The READY column shows that none of the containers are ready. Now make the readiness probe of one of them start returning success by creating the /var/ready file, whose existence makes your mock readiness probe succeed:

```
$ kubectl exec kubia-2r1qb -- touch /var/ready
```

You've used the `kubectl exec` command to execute the `touch` command inside the container of the kubia-2r1qb pod. The `touch` command creates the file if it doesn't yet exist. The pod's readiness probe command should now exit with status code 0, which means the probe is successful, and the pod should now be shown as ready. Let's see if it is:

```
$ kubectl get po kubia-2r1qb
NAME            READY     STATUS      RESTARTS    AGE
kubia-2r1qb     0/1       Running     0           2m
```

The pod still isn't ready. Is there something wrong or is this the expected result? Take a more detailed look at the pod with `kubectl describe`. The output should contain the following line:

```
Readiness: exec [ls /var/ready] delay=0s timeout=1s period=10s #success=1
  ⇒  #failure=3
```

The readiness probe is checked periodically—every 10 seconds by default. The pod isn't ready because the readiness probe hasn't been invoked yet. But in 10 seconds at the latest, the pod should become ready and its IP should be listed as the only endpoint of the service (run `kubectl get endpoints kubia-loadbalancer` to confirm).

HITTING THE SERVICE WITH THE SINGLE READY POD

You can now hit the service URL a few times to see that each and every request is redirected to this one pod:

```
$ curl http://130.211.53.173
You've hit kubia-2r1qb
$ curl http://130.211.53.173
You've hit kubia-2r1qb
...
$ curl http://130.211.53.173
You've hit kubia-2r1qb
```

Even though there are three pods running, only a single pod is reporting as being ready and is therefore the only pod receiving requests. If you now delete the file, the pod will be removed from the service again.

5.5.3   *Understanding what real-world readiness probes should do*

This mock readiness probe is useful only for demonstrating what readiness probes do. In the real world, the readiness probe should return success or failure depending on whether the app can (and wants to) receive client requests or not.

Manually removing pods from services should be performed by either deleting the pod or changing the pod's labels instead of manually flipping a switch in the probe.

> **TIP** If you want to add or remove a pod from a service manually, add `enabled=true` as a label to your pod and to the label selector of your service. Remove the label when you want to remove the pod from the service.

ALWAYS DEFINE A READINESS PROBE

Before we conclude this section, there are two final notes about readiness probes that I need to emphasize. First, if you don't add a readiness probe to your pods, they'll become service endpoints almost immediately. If your application takes too long to start listening for incoming connections, client requests hitting the service will be forwarded to the pod while it's still starting up and not ready to accept incoming connections. Clients will therefore see "Connection refused" types of errors.

> **TIP** You should always define a readiness probe, even if it's as simple as sending an HTTP request to the base URL.

DON'T INCLUDE POD SHUTDOWN LOGIC INTO YOUR READINESS PROBES

The other thing I need to mention applies to the other end of the pod's life (pod shutdown) and is also related to clients experiencing connection errors.

When a pod is being shut down, the app running in it usually stops accepting connections as soon as it receives the termination signal. Because of this, you might think you need to make your readiness probe start failing as soon as the shutdown procedure is initiated, ensuring the pod is removed from all services it's part of. But that's not necessary, because Kubernetes removes the pod from all services as soon as you delete the pod.

5.6   *Using a headless service for discovering individual pods*

You've seen how services can be used to provide a stable IP address allowing clients to connect to pods (or other endpoints) backing each service. Each connection to the service is forwarded to one randomly selected backing pod. But what if the client needs to connect to all of those pods? What if the backing pods themselves need to each connect to all the other backing pods? Connecting through the service clearly isn't the way to do this. What is?

For a client to connect to all pods, it needs to figure out the the IP of each individual pod. One option is to have the client call the Kubernetes API server and get the list of pods and their IP addresses through an API call, but because you should always strive to keep your apps Kubernetes-agnostic, using the API server isn't ideal.

Luckily, Kubernetes allows clients to discover pod IPs through DNS lookups. Usually, when you perform a DNS lookup for a service, the DNS server returns a single IP—the service's cluster IP. But if you tell Kubernetes you don't need a cluster IP for your service (you do this by setting the `clusterIP` field to `None` in the service specification), the DNS server will return the pod IPs instead of the single service IP.

Instead of returning a single DNS A record, the DNS server will return multiple A records for the service, each pointing to the IP of an individual pod backing the service at that moment. Clients can therefore do a simple DNS A record lookup and get the IPs of all the pods that are part of the service. The client can then use that information to connect to one, many, or all of them.

5.6.1   *Creating a headless service*

Setting the `clusterIP` field in a service spec to `None` makes the service *headless*, as Kubernetes won't assign it a cluster IP through which clients could connect to the pods backing it.

You'll create a headless service called `kubia-headless` now. The following listing shows its definition.

> **Listing 5.18   A headless service: kubia-svc-headless.yaml**

```
apiVersion: v1
kind: Service
metadata:
  name: kubia-headless
spec:
  clusterIP: None          This makes the
  ports:                   service headless.
  - port: 80
    targetPort: 8080
  selector:
    app: kubia
```

After you create the service with `kubectl create`, you can inspect it with `kubectl get` and `kubectl describe`. You'll see it has no cluster IP and its endpoints include (part of) the pods matching its pod selector. I say "part of" because your pods contain a readiness probe, so only pods that are ready will be listed as endpoints of the service. Before continuing, please make sure at least two pods report being ready, by creating the /var/ready file, as in the previous example:

```
$ kubectl exec <pod name> -- touch /var/ready
```

5.6.2 *Discovering pods through DNS*

With your pods ready, you can now try performing a DNS lookup to see if you get the actual pod IPs or not. You'll need to perform the lookup from inside one of the pods. Unfortunately, your kubia container image doesn't include the nslookup (or the dig) binary, so you can't use it to perform the DNS lookup.

All you're trying to do is perform a DNS lookup from inside a pod running in the cluster. Why not run a new pod based on an image that contains the binaries you need? To perform DNS-related actions, you can use the tutum/dnsutils container image, which is available on Docker Hub and contains both the nslookup and the dig binaries. To run the pod, you can go through the whole process of creating a YAML manifest for it and passing it to kubectl create, but that's too much work, right? Luckily, there's a faster way.

RUNNING A POD WITHOUT WRITING A YAML MANIFEST

In chapter 1, you already created pods without writing a YAML manifest by using the kubectl run command. But this time you want to create only a pod—you don't need to create a ReplicationController to manage the pod. You can do that like this:

```
$ kubectl run dnsutils --image=tutum/dnsutils --generator=run-pod/v1
➥ --command -- sleep infinity
pod "dnsutils" created
```

The trick is in the --generator=run-pod/v1 option, which tells kubectl to create the pod directly, without any kind of ReplicationController or similar behind it.

UNDERSTANDING DNS A RECORDS RETURNED FOR A HEADLESS SERVICE

Let's use the newly created pod to perform a DNS lookup:

```
$ kubectl exec dnsutils nslookup kubia-headless
...
Name:    kubia-headless.default.svc.cluster.local
Address: 10.108.1.4
Name:    kubia-headless.default.svc.cluster.local
Address: 10.108.2.5
```

The DNS server returns two different IPs for the kubia-headless.default.svc .cluster.local FQDN. Those are the IPs of the two pods that are reporting being ready. You can confirm this by listing pods with kubectl get pods -o wide, which shows the pods' IPs.

This is different from what DNS returns for regular (non-headless) services, such as for your kubia service, where the returned IP is the service's cluster IP:

```
$ kubectl exec dnsutils nslookup kubia
...
Name:    kubia.default.svc.cluster.local
Address: 10.111.249.153
```

Although headless services may seem different from regular services, they aren't that different from the clients' perspective. Even with a headless service, clients can connect to its pods by connecting to the service's DNS name, as they can with regular services. But with headless services, because DNS returns the pods' IPs, clients connect directly to the pods, instead of through the service proxy.

NOTE   A headless services still provides load balancing across pods, but through the DNS round-robin mechanism instead of through the service proxy.

5.6.3   *Discovering all pods—even those that aren't ready*

You've seen that only pods that are ready become endpoints of services. But sometimes you want to use the service discovery mechanism to find all pods matching the service's label selector, even those that aren't ready.

Luckily, you don't have to resort to querying the Kubernetes API server. You can use the DNS lookup mechanism to find even those unready pods. To tell Kubernetes you want all pods added to a service, regardless of the pod's readiness status, you must add the following annotation to the service:

```
kind: Service
metadata:
  annotations:
    service.alpha.kubernetes.io/tolerate-unready-endpoints: "true"
```

WARNING   As the annotation name suggests, as I'm writing this, this is an alpha feature. The Kubernetes Service API already supports a new service spec field called publishNotReadyAddresses, which will replace the tolerate-unready-endpoints annotation. In Kubernetes version 1.9.0, the field is not honored yet (the annotation is what determines whether unready endpoints are included in the DNS or not). Check the documentation to see whether that's changed.

5.7   *Troubleshooting services*

Services are a crucial Kubernetes concept and the source of frustration for many developers. I've seen many developers lose heaps of time figuring out why they can't connect to their pods through the service IP or FQDN. For this reason, a short look at how to troubleshoot services is in order.

When you're unable to access your pods through the service, you should start by going through the following list:

- First, make sure you're connecting to the service's cluster IP from within the cluster, not from the outside.
- Don't bother pinging the service IP to figure out if the service is accessible (remember, the service's cluster IP is a virtual IP and pinging it will never work).
- If you've defined a readiness probe, make sure it's succeeding; otherwise the pod won't be part of the service.
- To confirm that a pod is part of the service, examine the corresponding Endpoints object with `kubectl get endpoints`.
- If you're trying to access the service through its FQDN or a part of it (for example, myservice.mynamespace.svc.cluster.local or myservice.mynamespace) and it doesn't work, see if you can access it using its cluster IP instead of the FQDN.
- Check whether you're connecting to the port exposed by the service and not the target port.
- Try connecting to the pod IP directly to confirm your pod is accepting connections on the correct port.
- If you can't even access your app through the pod's IP, make sure your app isn't only binding to localhost.

This should help you resolve most of your service-related problems. You'll learn much more about how services work in chapter 11. By understanding exactly how they're implemented, it should be much easier for you to troubleshoot them.

5.8 Summary

In this chapter, you've learned how to create Kubernetes Service resources to expose the services available in your application, regardless of how many pod instances are providing each service. You've learned how Kubernetes

- Exposes multiple pods that match a certain label selector under a single, stable IP address and port
- Makes services accessible from inside the cluster by default, but allows you to make the service accessible from outside the cluster by setting its type to either `NodePort` or `LoadBalancer`
- Enables pods to discover services together with their IP addresses and ports by looking up environment variables
- Allows discovery of and communication with services residing outside the cluster by creating a Service resource without specifying a selector, by creating an associated Endpoints resource instead
- Provides a DNS `CNAME` alias for external services with the `ExternalName` service type
- Exposes multiple HTTP services through a single Ingress (consuming a single IP)

- Uses a pod container's readiness probe to determine whether a pod should or shouldn't be included as a service endpoint
- Enables discovery of pod IPs through DNS when you create a headless service

Along with getting a better understanding of services, you've also learned how to

- Troubleshoot them
- Modify firewall rules in Google Kubernetes/Compute Engine
- Execute commands in pod containers through `kubectl exec`
- Run a `bash` shell in an existing pod's container
- Modify Kubernetes resources through the `kubectl apply` command
- Run an unmanaged ad hoc pod with `kubectl run --generator=run-pod/v1`

Volumes: attaching
disk storage to containers

6

This chapter covers

- Creating multi-container pods
- Creating a volume to share disk storage between containers
- Using a Git repository inside a pod
- Attaching persistent storage such as a GCE Persistent Disk to pods
- Using pre-provisioned persistent storage
- Dynamic provisioning of persistent storage

In the previous three chapters, we introduced pods and other Kubernetes resources that interact with them, namely ReplicationControllers, ReplicaSets, DaemonSets, Jobs, and Services. Now, we're going back inside the pod to learn how its containers can access external disk storage and/or share storage between them.

We've said that pods are similar to logical hosts where processes running inside them share resources such as CPU, RAM, network interfaces, and others. One would expect the processes to also share disks, but that's not the case. You'll remember that each container in a pod has its own isolated filesystem, because the filesystem comes from the container's image.

Every new container starts off with the exact set of files that was added to the image at build time. Combine this with the fact that containers in a pod get restarted (either because the process died or because the liveness probe signaled to Kubernetes that the container wasn't healthy anymore) and you'll realize that the new container will not see anything that was written to the filesystem by the previous container, even though the newly started container runs in the same pod.

In certain scenarios you want the new container to continue where the last one finished, such as when restarting a process on a physical machine. You may not need (or want) the whole filesystem to be persisted, but you do want to preserve the directories that hold actual data.

Kubernetes provides this by defining storage *volumes*. They aren't top-level resources like pods, but are instead defined as a part of a pod and share the same lifecycle as the pod. This means a volume is created when the pod is started and is destroyed when the pod is deleted. Because of this, a volume's contents will persist across container restarts. After a container is restarted, the new container can see all the files that were written to the volume by the previous container. Also, if a pod contains multiple containers, the volume can be used by all of them at once.

6.1 Introducing volumes

Kubernetes volumes are a component of a pod and are thus defined in the pod's specification—much like containers. They aren't a standalone Kubernetes object and cannot be created or deleted on their own. A volume is available to all containers in the pod, but it must be mounted in each container that needs to access it. In each container, you can mount the volume in any location of its filesystem.

6.1.1 Explaining volumes in an example

Imagine you have a pod with three containers (shown in figure 6.1). One container runs a web server that serves HTML pages from the /var/htdocs directory and stores the access log to /var/logs. The second container runs an agent that creates HTML files and stores them in /var/html. The third container processes the logs it finds in the /var/logs directory (rotates them, compresses them, analyzes them, or whatever).

Each container has a nicely defined single responsibility, but on its own each container wouldn't be of much use. Creating a pod with these three containers without them sharing disk storage doesn't make any sense, because the content generator would write the generated HTML files inside its own container and the web server couldn't access those files, as it runs in a separate isolated container. Instead, it would serve an empty directory or whatever you put in the /var/htdocs directory in its container image. Similarly, the log rotator would never have anything to do, because its /var/logs directory would always remain empty with nothing writing logs there. A pod with these three containers and no volumes basically does nothing.

But if you add two volumes to the pod and mount them at appropriate paths inside the three containers, as shown in figure 6.2, you've created a system that's much more

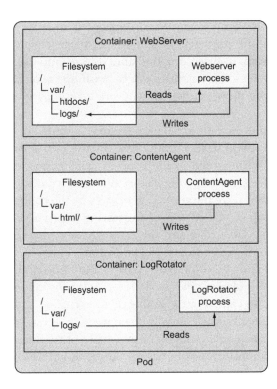

Figure 6.1 Three containers of the same pod without shared storage

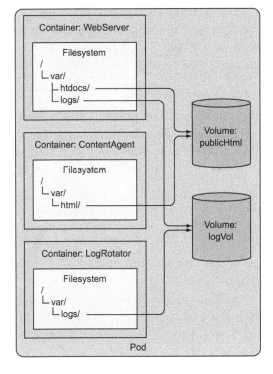

Figure 6.2 Three containers sharing two volumes mounted at various mount paths

than the sum of its parts. Linux allows you to mount a filesystem at arbitrary locations in the file tree. When you do that, the contents of the mounted filesystem are accessible in the directory it's mounted into. By mounting the same volume into two containers, they can operate on the same files. In your case, you're mounting two volumes in three containers. By doing this, your three containers can work together and do something useful. Let me explain how.

First, the pod has a volume called `publicHtml`. This volume is mounted in the Web-Server container at /var/htdocs, because that's the directory the web server serves files from. The same volume is also mounted in the `ContentAgent` container, but at /var/html, because that's where the agent writes the files to. By mounting this single volume like that, the web server will now serve the content generated by the content agent.

Similarly, the pod also has a volume called `logVol` for storing logs. This volume is mounted at /var/logs in both the `WebServer` and the `LogRotator` containers. Note that it isn't mounted in the `ContentAgent` container. The container cannot access its files, even though the container and the volume are part of the same pod. It's not enough to define a volume in the pod; you need to define a `VolumeMount` inside the container's spec also, if you want the container to be able to access it.

The two volumes in this example can both initially be empty, so you can use a type of volume called `emptyDir`. Kubernetes also supports other types of volumes that are either populated during initialization of the volume from an external source, or an existing directory is mounted inside the volume. This process of populating or mounting a volume is performed before the pod's containers are started.

A volume is bound to the lifecycle of a pod and will stay in existence only while the pod exists, but depending on the volume type, the volume's files may remain intact even after the pod and volume disappear, and can later be mounted into a new volume. Let's see what types of volumes exist.

6.1.2   *Introducing available volume types*

A wide variety of volume types is available. Several are generic, while others are specific to the actual storage technologies used underneath. Don't worry if you've never heard of those technologies—I hadn't heard of at least half of them. You'll probably only use volume types for the technologies you already know and use. Here's a list of several of the available volume types:

- `emptyDir`—A simple empty directory used for storing transient data.
- `hostPath`—Used for mounting directories from the worker node's filesystem into the pod.
- `gitRepo`—A volume initialized by checking out the contents of a Git repository.
- `nfs`—An NFS share mounted into the pod.
- `gcePersistentDisk` (Google Compute Engine Persistent Disk), `awsElastic-BlockStore` (Amazon Web Services Elastic Block Store Volume), `azureDisk` (Microsoft Azure Disk Volume)—Used for mounting cloud provider-specific storage.

- cinder, cephfs, iscsi, flocker, glusterfs, quobyte, rbd, flexVolume, vsphere-Volume, photonPersistentDisk, scaleIO—Used for mounting other types of network storage.
- configMap, secret, downwardAPI—Special types of volumes used to expose certain Kubernetes resources and cluster information to the pod.
- persistentVolumeClaim—A way to use a pre- or dynamically provisioned persistent storage. (We'll talk about them in the last section of this chapter.)

These volume types serve various purposes. You'll learn about some of them in the following sections. Special types of volumes (secret, downwardAPI, configMap) are covered in the next two chapters, because they aren't used for storing data, but for exposing Kubernetes metadata to apps running in the pod.

A single pod can use multiple volumes of different types at the same time, and, as we've mentioned before, each of the pod's containers can either have the volume mounted or not.

6.2 *Using volumes to share data between containers*

Although a volume can prove useful even when used by a single container, let's first focus on how it's used for sharing data between multiple containers in a pod.

6.2.1 *Using an emptyDir volume*

The simplest volume type is the emptyDir volume, so let's look at it in the first example of how to define a volume in a pod. As the name suggests, the volume starts out as an empty directory. The app running inside the pod can then write any files it needs to it. Because the volume's lifetime is tied to that of the pod, the volume's contents are lost when the pod is deleted.

An emptyDir volume is especially useful for sharing files between containers running in the same pod. But it can also be used by a single container for when a container needs to write data to disk temporarily, such as when performing a sort operation on a large dataset, which can't fit into the available memory. The data could also be written to the container's filesystem itself (remember the top read-write layer in a container?), but subtle differences exist between the two options. A container's filesystem may not even be writable (we'll talk about this toward the end of the book), so writing to a mounted volume might be the only option.

USING AN EMPTYDIR VOLUME IN A POD

Let's revisit the previous example where a web server, a content agent, and a log rotator share two volumes, but let's simplify a bit. You'll build a pod with only the web server container and the content agent and a single volume for the HTML.

You'll use Nginx as the web server and the UNIX fortune command to generate the HTML content. The fortune command prints out a random quote every time you run it. You'll create a script that invokes the fortune command every 10 seconds and stores its output in index.html. You'll find an existing Nginx image available on

Docker Hub, but you'll need to either create the `fortune` image yourself or use the one I've already built and pushed to Docker Hub under `luksa/fortune`. If you want a refresher on how to build Docker images, refer to the sidebar.

Building the fortune container image

Here's how to build the image. Create a new directory called fortune and then inside it, create a `fortuneloop.sh` shell script with the following contents:

```
#!/bin/bash
trap "exit" SIGINT
while :
do
  echo $(date) Writing fortune to /var/htdocs/index.html
  /usr/games/fortune > /var/htdocs/index.html
  sleep 10
done
```

Then, in the same directory, create a file called Dockerfile containing the following:

```
FROM ubuntu:latest
RUN apt-get update ; apt-get -y install fortune
ADD fortuneloop.sh /bin/fortuneloop.sh
ENTRYPOINT /bin/fortuneloop.sh
```

The image is based on the `ubuntu:latest` image, which doesn't include the `fortune` binary by default. That's why in the second line of the Dockerfile you install it with `apt-get`. After that, you add the `fortuneloop.sh` script to the image's `/bin` folder. In the last line of the Dockerfile, you specify that the `fortuneloop.sh` script should be executed when the image is run.

After preparing both files, build and upload the image to Docker Hub with the following two commands (replace `luksa` with your own Docker Hub user ID):

```
$ docker build -t luksa/fortune .
$ docker push luksa/fortune
```

CREATING THE POD

Now that you have the two images required to run your pod, it's time to create the pod manifest. Create a file called fortune-pod.yaml with the contents shown in the following listing.

Listing 6.1   A pod with two containers sharing the same volume: fortune-pod.yaml

```
apiVersion: v1
kind: Pod
metadata:
  name: fortune
spec:
  containers:
```

```
    - image: luksa/fortune
      name: html-generator
      volumeMounts:
      - name: html
        mountPath: /var/htdocs
    - image: nginx:alpine
      name: web-server
      volumeMounts:
      - name: html
        mountPath: /usr/share/nginx/html
        readOnly: true
      ports:
      - containerPort: 80
        protocol: TCP
    volumes:
    - name: html
      emptyDir: {}
```

> The first container is called html-generator and runs the luksa/fortune image.
>
> The volume called html is mounted at /var/htdocs in the container.
>
> The second container is called web-server and runs the nginx:alpine image.
>
> The same volume as above is mounted at /usr/share/nginx/html as read-only.
>
> A single emptyDir volume called html that's mounted in the two containers above

The pod contains two containers and a single volume that's mounted in both of them, yet at different paths. When the `html-generator` container starts, it starts writing the output of the `fortune` command to the /var/htdocs/index.html file every 10 seconds. Because the volume is mounted at /var/htdocs, the index.html file is written to the volume instead of the container's top layer. As soon as the `web-server` container starts, it starts serving whatever HTML files are in the /usr/share/nginx/html directory (this is the default directory Nginx serves files from). Because you mounted the volume in that exact location, Nginx will serve the index.html file written there by the container running the fortune loop. The end effect is that a client sending an HTTP request to the pod on port 80 will receive the current fortune message as the response.

SEEING THE POD IN ACTION

To see the fortune message, you need to enable access to the pod. You'll do that by forwarding a port from your local machine to the pod:

```
$ kubectl port-forward fortune 8080:80
Forwarding from 127.0.0.1:8080 -> 80
Forwarding from [::1]:8080 -> 80
```

> **NOTE** As an exercise, you can also expose the pod through a service instead of using port forwarding.

Now you can access the Nginx server through port 8080 of your local machine. Use `curl` to do that:

```
$ curl http://localhost:8080
Beware of a tall blond man with one black shoe.
```

If you wait a few seconds and send another request, you should receive a different message. By combining two containers, you created a simple app to see how a volume can glue together two containers and enhance what each of them does.

SPECIFYING THE MEDIUM TO USE FOR THE EMPTYDIR

The emptyDir you used as the volume was created on the actual disk of the worker node hosting your pod, so its performance depends on the type of the node's disks. But you can tell Kubernetes to create the emptyDir on a tmpfs filesystem (in memory instead of on disk). To do this, set the emptyDir's medium to Memory like this:

```
volumes:
  - name: html
    emptyDir:
      medium: Memory
```

This emptyDir's files should be stored in memory.

An emptyDir volume is the simplest type of volume, but other types build upon it. After the empty directory is created, they populate it with data. One such volume type is the gitRepo volume type, which we'll introduce next.

6.2.2   *Using a Git repository as the starting point for a volume*

A gitRepo volume is basically an emptyDir volume that gets populated by cloning a Git repository and checking out a specific revision when the pod is starting up (but before its containers are created). Figure 6.3 shows how this unfolds.

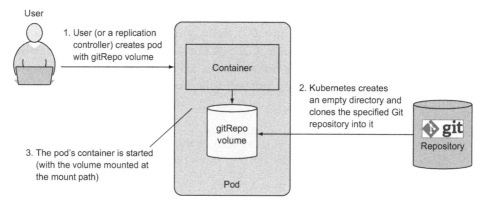

Figure 6.3   A gitRepo **volume is an** emptyDir **volume initially populated with the contents of a Git repository.**

> **NOTE**   After the gitRepo volume is created, it isn't kept in sync with the repo it's referencing. The files in the volume will not be updated when you push additional commits to the Git repository. However, if your pod is managed by a ReplicationController, deleting the pod will result in a new pod being created and this new pod's volume will then contain the latest commits.

For example, you can use a Git repository to store static HTML files of your website and create a pod containing a web server container and a gitRepo volume. Every time the pod is created, it pulls the latest version of your website and starts serving it. The only drawback to this is that you need to delete the pod every time you push changes to the `gitRepo` and want to start serving the new version of the website.

Let's do this right now. It's not that different from what you did before.

RUNNING A WEB SERVER POD SERVING FILES FROM A CLONED GIT REPOSITORY

Before you create your pod, you'll need an actual Git repository with HTML files in it. I've created a repo on GitHub at https://github.com/luksa/kubia-website-example.git. You'll need to fork it (create your own copy of the repo on GitHub) so you can push changes to it later.

Once you've created your fork, you can move on to creating the pod. This time, you'll only need a single Nginx container and a single `gitRepo` volume in the pod (be sure to point the `gitRepo` volume to your own fork of my repository), as shown in the following listing.

Listing 6.2   A pod using a `gitRepo` volume: gitrepo-volume-pod.yaml

```
apiVersion: v1
kind: Pod
metadata:
  name: gitrepo-volume-pod
spec:
  containers:
  - image: nginx:alpine
    name: web-server
    volumeMounts:
    - name: html
      mountPath: /usr/share/nginx/html
      readOnly: true
    ports:
    - containerPort: 80
      protocol: TCP
  volumes:
  - name: html
    gitRepo:                                              You're creating a
      repository: https://github.com/luksa/kubia-website-example.git    gitRepo volume.
      revision: master
      directory: .
```

> You're creating a gitRepo volume.
> The volume will clone this Git repository.
> You want the repo to be cloned into the root dir of the volume.
> The master branch will be checked out.

When you create the pod, the volume is first initialized as an empty directory and then the specified Git repository is cloned into it. If you hadn't set the directory to . (dot), the repository would have been cloned into the kubia-website-example subdirectory, which isn't what you want. You want the repo to be cloned into the root directory of your volume. Along with the repository, you also specified you want Kubernetes to check out whatever revision the master branch is pointing to at the time the volume is created.

With the pod running, you can try hitting it through port forwarding, a service, or by executing the `curl` command from within the pod (or any other pod inside the cluster).

CONFIRMING THE FILES AREN'T KEPT IN SYNC WITH THE GIT REPO

Now you'll make changes to the index.html file in your GitHub repository. If you don't use Git locally, you can edit the file on GitHub directly—click on the file in your GitHub repository to open it and then click on the pencil icon to start editing it. Change the text and then commit the changes by clicking the button at the bottom.

The master branch of the Git repository now includes the changes you made to the HTML file. These changes will not be visible on your Nginx web server yet, because the gitRepo volume isn't kept in sync with the Git repository. You can confirm this by hitting the pod again.

To see the new version of the website, you need to delete the pod and create it again. Instead of having to delete the pod every time you make changes, you could run an additional process, which keeps your volume in sync with the Git repository. I won't explain in detail how to do this. Instead, try doing this yourself as an exercise, but here are a few pointers.

INTRODUCING SIDECAR CONTAINERS

The Git sync process shouldn't run in the same container as the Nginx web server, but in a second container: a *sidecar container*. A sidecar container is a container that augments the operation of the main container of the pod. You add a sidecar to a pod so you can use an existing container image instead of cramming additional logic into the main app's code, which would make it overly complex and less reusable.

To find an existing container image, which keeps a local directory synchronized with a Git repository, go to Docker Hub and search for "git sync." You'll find many images that do that. Then use the image in a new container in the pod from the previous example, mount the pod's existing gitRepo volume in the new container, and configure the Git sync container to keep the files in sync with your Git repo. If you set everything up correctly, you should see that the files the web server is serving are kept in sync with your GitHub repo.

> **NOTE** An example in chapter 18 includes using a Git sync container like the one explained here, so you can wait until you reach chapter 18 and follow the step-by-step instructions then instead of doing this exercise on your own now.

USING A GITREPO VOLUME WITH PRIVATE GIT REPOSITORIES

There's one other reason for having to resort to Git sync sidecar containers. We haven't talked about whether you can use a gitRepo volume with a private Git repo. It turns out you can't. The current consensus among Kubernetes developers is to keep the gitRepo volume simple and not add any support for cloning private repositories through the SSH protocol, because that would require adding additional config options to the gitRepo volume.

If you want to clone a private Git repo into your container, you should use a git-sync sidecar or a similar method instead of a gitRepo volume.

WRAPPING UP THE GITREPO VOLUME

A `gitRepo` volume, like the `emptyDir` volume, is basically a dedicated directory created specifically for, and used exclusively by, the pod that contains the volume. When the pod is deleted, the volume and its contents are deleted. Other types of volumes, however, don't create a new directory, but instead mount an existing external directory into the pod's container's filesystem. The contents of that volume can survive multiple pod instantiations. We'll learn about those types of volumes next.

6.3 Accessing files on the worker node's filesystem

Most pods should be oblivious of their host node, so they shouldn't access any files on the node's filesystem. But certain system-level pods (remember, these will usually be managed by a DaemonSet) do need to either read the node's files or use the node's filesystem to access the node's devices through the filesystem. Kubernetes makes this possible through a `hostPath` volume.

6.3.1 Introducing the hostPath volume

A `hostPath` volume points to a specific file or directory on the node's filesystem (see figure 6.4). Pods running on the same node and using the same path in their `host-Path` volume see the same files.

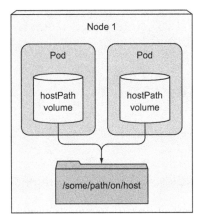
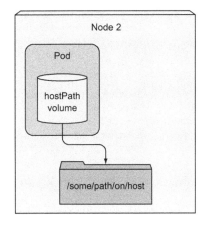

Figure 6.4   A `hostPath` volume mounts a file or directory on the worker node into the container's filesystem.

`hostPath` volumes are the first type of persistent storage we're introducing, because both the `gitRepo` and `emptyDir` volumes' contents get deleted when a pod is torn down, whereas a `hostPath` volume's contents don't. If a pod is deleted and the next pod uses a `hostPath` volume pointing to the same path on the host, the new pod will see whatever was left behind by the previous pod, but only if it's scheduled to the same node as the first pod.

If you're thinking of using a `hostPath` volume as the place to store a database's data directory, think again. Because the volume's contents are stored on a specific node's filesystem, when the database pod gets rescheduled to another node, it will no longer see the data. This explains why it's not a good idea to use a `hostPath` volume for regular pods, because it makes the pod sensitive to what node it's scheduled to.

6.3.2   *Examining system pods that use hostPath volumes*

Let's see how a `hostPath` volume can be used properly. Instead of creating a new pod, let's see if any existing system-wide pods are already using this type of volume. As you may remember from one of the previous chapters, several such pods are running in the `kube-system` namespace. Let's list them again:

```
$ kubectl get pod s --namespace kube-system
NAME                            READY   STATUS    RESTARTS   AGE
fluentd-kubia-4ebc2f1e-9a3e     1/1     Running   1          4d
fluentd-kubia-4ebc2f1e-e2vz     1/1     Running   1          31d
...
```

Pick the first one and see what kinds of volumes it uses (shown in the following listing).

Listing 6.3   A pod using `hostPath` volumes to access the node's logs

```
$ kubectl describe po fluentd-kubia-4ebc2f1e-9a3e --namespace kube-system
Name:           fluentd-cloud-logging-gke-kubia-default-pool-4ebc2f1e-9a3e
Namespace:      kube-system
...
Volumes:
  varlog:
    Type:       HostPath (bare host directory volume)
    Path:       /var/log
  varlibdockercontainers:
    Type:       HostPath (bare host directory volume)
    Path:       /var/lib/docker/containers
```

TIP   If you're using Minikube, try the `kube-addon-manager-minikube` pod.

Aha! The pod uses two `hostPath` volumes to gain access to the node's /var/log and the /var/lib/docker/containers directories. You'd think you were lucky to find a pod using a `hostPath` volume on the first try, but not really (at least not on GKE). Check the other pods, and you'll see most use this type of volume either to access the node's log files, kubeconfig (the Kubernetes config file), or the CA certificates.

If you inspect the other pods, you'll see none of them uses the `hostPath` volume for storing their own data. They all use it to get access to the node's data. But as we'll see later in the chapter, `hostPath` volumes are often used for trying out persistent storage in single-node clusters, such as the one created by Minikube. Read on to learn about the types of volumes you should use for storing persistent data properly even in a multi-node cluster.

TIP Remember to use `hostPath` volumes only if you need to read or write system files on the node. Never use them to persist data across pods.

6.4 *Using persistent storage*

When an application running in a pod needs to persist data to disk and have that same data available even when the pod is rescheduled to another node, you can't use any of the volume types we've mentioned so far. Because this data needs to be accessible from any cluster node, it must be stored on some type of network-attached storage (NAS).

To learn about volumes that allow persisting data, you'll create a pod that will run the MongoDB document-oriented NoSQL database. Running a database pod without a volume or with a non-persistent volume doesn't make sense, except for testing purposes, so you'll add an appropriate type of volume to the pod and mount it in the MongoDB container.

6.4.1 *Using a GCE Persistent Disk in a pod volume*

If you've been running these examples on Google Kubernetes Engine, which runs your cluster nodes on Google Compute Engine (GCE), you'll use a GCE Persistent Disk as your underlying storage mechanism.

In the early versions, Kubernetes didn't provision the underlying storage automatically—you had to do that manually. Automatic provisioning is now possible, and you'll learn about it later in the chapter, but first, you'll start by provisioning the storage manually. It will give you a chance to learn exactly what's going on underneath.

CREATING A GCE PERSISTENT DISK

You'll start by creating the GCE persistent disk first. You need to create it in the same zone as your Kubernetes cluster. If you don't remember what zone you created the cluster in, you can see it by listing your Kubernetes clusters with the `gcloud` command like this:

```
$ gcloud container clusters list
NAME    ZONE            MASTER_VERSION  MASTER_IP      ...
kubia   europe-west1-b  1.2.5           104.155.84.137
```

This shows you've created your cluster in zone `europe-west1-b`, so you need to create the GCE persistent disk in the same zone as well. You create the disk like this:

```
$ gcloud compute disks create --size=1GiB --zone=europe-west1-b mongodb
WARNING: You have selected a disk size of under [200GB]. This may result in
    poor I/O performance. For more information, see:
        https://developers.google.com/compute/docs/disks#pdperformance.
Created [https://www.googleapis.com/compute/v1/projects/rapid-pivot-
    136513/zones/europe-west1-b/disks/mongodb].
NAME     ZONE            SIZE_GB  TYPE         STATUS
mongodb  europe-west1-b  1        pd-standard  READY
```

This command creates a 1 GiB large GCE persistent disk called mongodb. You can ignore the warning about the disk size, because you don't care about the disk's performance for the tests you're about to run.

CREATING A POD USING A GCEPERSISTENTDISK VOLUME

Now that you have your physical storage properly set up, you can use it in a volume inside your MongoDB pod. You're going to prepare the YAML for the pod, which is shown in the following listing.

Listing 6.4 A pod using a `gcePersistentDisk` volume: mongodb-pod-gcepd.yaml

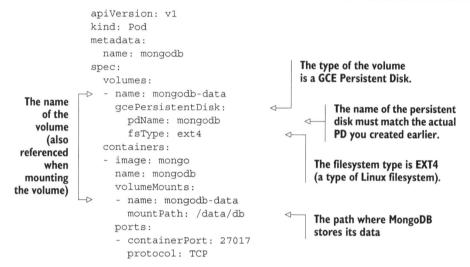

```
apiVersion: v1
kind: Pod
metadata:
  name: mongodb
spec:
  volumes:
  - name: mongodb-data
    gcePersistentDisk:
      pdName: mongodb
      fsType: ext4
  containers:
  - image: mongo
    name: mongodb
    volumeMounts:
    - name: mongodb-data
      mountPath: /data/db
    ports:
    - containerPort: 27017
      protocol: TCP
```

The name of the volume (also referenced when mounting the volume)

The type of the volume is a GCE Persistent Disk.

The name of the persistent disk must match the actual PD you created earlier.

The filesystem type is EXT4 (a type of Linux filesystem).

The path where MongoDB stores its data

NOTE If you're using Minikube, you can't use a GCE Persistent Disk, but you can deploy mongodb-pod-hostpath.yaml, which uses a hostPath volume instead of a GCE PD.

The pod contains a single container and a single volume backed by the GCE Persistent Disk you've created (as shown in figure 6.5). You're mounting the volume inside the container at /data/db, because that's where MongoDB stores its data.

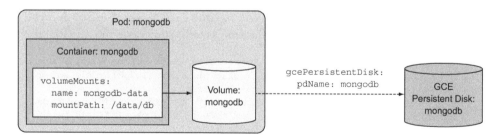

Figure 6.5 A pod with a single container running MongoDB, which mounts a volume referencing an external GCE Persistent Disk

WRITING DATA TO THE PERSISTENT STORAGE BY ADDING DOCUMENTS TO YOUR MONGODB DATABASE

Now that you've created the pod and the container has been started, you can run the MongoDB shell inside the container and use it to write some data to the data store.

You'll run the shell as shown in the following listing.

Listing 6.5 Entering the MongoDB shell inside the `mongodb` **pod**

```
$ kubectl exec -it mongodb mongo
MongoDB shell version: 3.2.8
connecting to: mongodb://127.0.0.1:27017
Welcome to the MongoDB shell.
For interactive help, type "help".
For more comprehensive documentation, see
    http://docs.mongodb.org/
Questions? Try the support group
    http://groups.google.com/group/mongodb-user
...
>
```

MongoDB allows storing JSON documents, so you'll store one to see if it's stored persistently and can be retrieved after the pod is re-created. Insert a new JSON document with the following commands:

```
> use mystore
switched to db mystore
> db.foo.insert({name:'foo'})
WriteResult({ "nInserted" : 1 })
```

You've inserted a simple JSON document with a single property (name: ′foo′). Now, use the find() command to see the document you inserted:

```
> db.foo.find()
{ "_id" : ObjectId("57a61eb9de0cfd512374cc75"), "name" : "foo" }
```

There it is. The document should be stored in your GCE persistent disk now.

RE-CREATING THE POD AND VERIFYING THAT IT CAN READ THE DATA PERSISTED BY THE PREVIOUS POD

You can now exit the `mongodb` shell (type `exit` and press Enter), and then delete the pod and recreate it:

```
$ kubectl delete pod mongodb
pod "mongodb" deleted
$ kubectl create -f mongodb-pod-gcepd.yaml
pod "mongodb" created
```

The new pod uses the exact same GCE persistent disk as the previous pod, so the MongoDB container running inside it should see the exact same data, even if the pod is scheduled to a different node.

> **TIP** You can see what node a pod is scheduled to by running `kubectl get po -o wide`.

Once the container is up, you can again run the MongoDB shell and check to see if the document you stored earlier can still be retrieved, as shown in the following listing.

Listing 6.6   Retrieving MongoDB's persisted data in a new pod

```
$ kubectl exec -it mongodb mongo
MongoDB shell version: 3.2.8
connecting to: mongodb://127.0.0.1:27017
Welcome to the MongoDB shell.
...
> use mystore
switched to db mystore
> db.foo.find()
{ "_id" : ObjectId("57a61eb9de0cfd512374cc75"), "name" : "foo" }
```

As expected, the data is still there, even though you deleted the pod and re-created it. This confirms you can use a GCE persistent disk to persist data across multiple pod instances.

You're done playing with the MongoDB pod, so go ahead and delete it again, but hold off on deleting the underlying GCE persistent disk. You'll use it again later in the chapter.

6.4.2   *Using other types of volumes with underlying persistent storage*

The reason you created the GCE Persistent Disk volume is because your Kubernetes cluster runs on Google Kubernetes Engine. When you run your cluster elsewhere, you should use other types of volumes, depending on the underlying infrastructure.

If your Kubernetes cluster is running on Amazon's AWS EC2, for example, you can use an `awsElasticBlockStore` volume to provide persistent storage for your pods. If your cluster runs on Microsoft Azure, you can use the `azureFile` or the `azureDisk` volume. We won't go into detail on how to do that here, but it's virtually the same as in the previous example. First, you need to create the actual underlying storage, and then set the appropriate properties in the volume definition.

USING AN AWS ELASTIC BLOCK STORE VOLUME

For example, to use an AWS elastic block store instead of the GCE Persistent Disk, you'd only need to change the volume definition as shown in the following listing (see those lines printed in bold).

Listing 6.7   A pod using an `awsElasticBlockStore` volume: mongodb-pod-aws.yaml

```
apiVersion: v1
kind: Pod
metadata:
  name: mongodb
spec:
  volumes:
  - name: mongodb-data                    Using awsElasticBlockStore
    awsElasticBlockStore:       ⟵         instead of gcePersistentDisk
```

```
        volumeId: my-volume
        fsType: ext4
      containers:
      - ...
```

The filesystem type is EXT4 as before.

Specify the ID of the EBS volume you created.

USING AN NFS VOLUME

If your cluster is running on your own set of servers, you have a vast array of other supported options for mounting external storage inside your volume. For example, to mount a simple NFS share, you only need to specify the NFS server and the path exported by the server, as shown in the following listing.

Listing 6.8 A pod using an `nfs` volume: mongodb-pod-nfs.yaml

```
volumes:
- name: mongodb-data
  nfs:
    server: 1.2.3.4
    path: /some/path
```

This volume is backed by an NFS share.

The IP of the NFS server

The path exported by the server

USING OTHER STORAGE TECHNOLOGIES

Other supported options include `iscsi` for mounting an ISCSI disk resource, `glusterfs` for a GlusterFS mount, `rbd` for a RADOS Block Device, `flexVolume`, `cinder`, `cephfs`, `flocker`, `fc` (Fibre Channel), and others. You don't need to know all of them if you're not using them. They're mentioned here to show you that Kubernetes supports a broad range of storage technologies and you can use whichever you prefer and are used to.

To see details on what properties you need to set for each of these volume types, you can either turn to the Kubernetes API definitions in the Kubernetes API reference or look up the information through `kubectl explain`, as shown in chapter 3. If you're already familiar with a particular storage technology, using the `explain` command should allow you to easily figure out how to mount a volume of the proper type and use it in your pods.

But does a developer need to know all this stuff? Should a developer, when creating a pod, have to deal with infrastructure-related storage details, or should that be left to the cluster administrator?

Having a pod's volumes refer to the actual underlying infrastructure isn't what Kubernetes is about, is it? For example, for a developer to have to specify the hostname of the NFS server feels wrong. And that's not even the worst thing about it.

Including this type of infrastructure-related information into a pod definition means the pod definition is pretty much tied to a specific Kubernetes cluster. You can't use the same pod definition in another one. That's why using volumes like this isn't the best way to attach persistent storage to your pods. You'll learn how to improve on this in the next section.

6.5   *Decoupling pods from the underlying storage technology*

All the persistent volume types we've explored so far have required the developer of the pod to have knowledge of the actual network storage infrastructure available in the cluster. For example, to create a NFS-backed volume, the developer has to know the actual server the NFS export is located on. This is against the basic idea of Kubernetes, which aims to hide the actual infrastructure from both the application and its developer, leaving them free from worrying about the specifics of the infrastructure and making apps portable across a wide array of cloud providers and on-premises datacenters.

Ideally, a developer deploying their apps on Kubernetes should never have to know what kind of storage technology is used underneath, the same way they don't have to know what type of physical servers are being used to run their pods. Infrastructure-related dealings should be the sole domain of the cluster administrator.

When a developer needs a certain amount of persistent storage for their application, they can request it from Kubernetes, the same way they can request CPU, memory, and other resources when creating a pod. The system administrator can configure the cluster so it can give the apps what they request.

6.5.1   *Introducing PersistentVolumes and PersistentVolumeClaims*

To enable apps to request storage in a Kubernetes cluster without having to deal with infrastructure specifics, two new resources were introduced. They are Persistent-Volumes and PersistentVolumeClaims. The names may be a bit misleading, because as you've seen in the previous few sections, even regular Kubernetes volumes can be used to store persistent data.

Using a PersistentVolume inside a pod is a little more complex than using a regular pod volume, so let's illustrate how pods, PersistentVolumeClaims, PersistentVolumes, and the actual underlying storage relate to each other in figure 6.6.

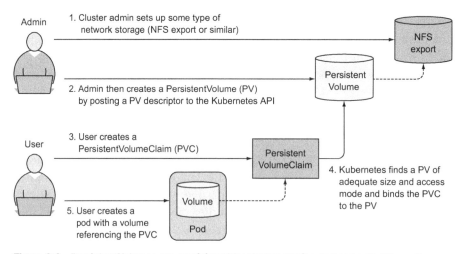

Figure 6.6   PersistentVolumes are provisioned by cluster admins and consumed by pods through PersistentVolumeClaims.

Instead of the developer adding a technology-specific volume to their pod, it's the cluster administrator who sets up the underlying storage and then registers it in Kubernetes by creating a PersistentVolume resource through the Kubernetes API server. When creating the PersistentVolume, the admin specifies its size and the access modes it supports.

When a cluster user needs to use persistent storage in one of their pods, they first create a PersistentVolumeClaim manifest, specifying the minimum size and the access mode they require. The user then submits the PersistentVolumeClaim manifest to the Kubernetes API server, and Kubernetes finds the appropriate PersistentVolume and binds the volume to the claim.

The PersistentVolumeClaim can then be used as one of the volumes inside a pod. Other users cannot use the same PersistentVolume until it has been released by deleting the bound PersistentVolumeClaim.

6.5.2   *Creating a PersistentVolume*

Let's revisit the MongoDB example, but unlike before, you won't reference the GCE Persistent Disk in the pod directly. Instead, you'll first assume the role of a cluster administrator and create a PersistentVolume backed by the GCE Persistent Disk. Then you'll assume the role of the application developer and first claim the PersistentVolume and then use it inside your pod.

In section 6.4.1 you set up the physical storage by provisioning the GCE Persistent Disk, so you don't need to do that again. All you need to do is create the PersistentVolume resource in Kubernetes by preparing the manifest shown in the following listing and posting it to the API server.

Listing 6.9   A `gcePersistentDisk` PersistentVolume: mongodb-pv-gcepd.yaml

```
apiVersion: v1
kind: PersistentVolume
metadata:
  name: mongodb-pv
spec:
  capacity:                                    Defining the
    storage: 1Gi                               PersistentVolume's size          It can either be mounted by a single
  accessModes:                                                                  client for reading and writing or by
  - ReadWriteOnce                                                               multiple clients for reading only.
  - ReadOnlyMany
  persistentVolumeReclaimPolicy: Retain                                         After the claim is released,
  gcePersistentDisk:                                                            the PersistentVolume
    pdName: mongodb                                                             should be retained (not
    fsType: ext4                               The PersistentVolume is          erased or deleted).
                                               backed by the GCE Persistent
                                               Disk you created earlier.
```

> **NOTE** If you're using Minikube, create the PV using the mongodb-pv-host-path.yaml file.

When creating a PersistentVolume, the administrator needs to tell Kubernetes what its capacity is and whether it can be read from and/or written to by a single node or by multiple nodes at the same time. They also need to tell Kubernetes what to do with the PersistentVolume when it's released (when the PersistentVolumeClaim it's bound to is deleted). And last, but certainly not least, they need to specify the type, location, and other properties of the actual storage this PersistentVolume is backed by. If you look closely, this last part is exactly the same as earlier, when you referenced the GCE Persistent Disk in the pod volume directly (shown again in the following listing).

Listing 6.10   Referencing a GCE PD in a pod's volume

```
spec:
  volumes:
  - name: mongodb-data
    gcePersistentDisk:
      pdName: mongodb
      fsType: ext4
  ...
```

After you create the PersistentVolume with the `kubectl create` command, it should be ready to be claimed. See if it is by listing all PersistentVolumes:

```
$ kubectl get pv
NAME          CAPACITY    RECLAIMPOLICY    ACCESSMODES    STATUS       CLAIM
mongodb-pv    1Gi         Retain           RWO,ROX        Available
```

> **NOTE** Several columns are omitted. Also, `pv` is used as a shorthand for `persistentvolume`.

As expected, the PersistentVolume is shown as Available, because you haven't yet created the PersistentVolumeClaim.

> **NOTE** PersistentVolumes don't belong to any namespace (see figure 6.7). They're cluster-level resources like nodes.

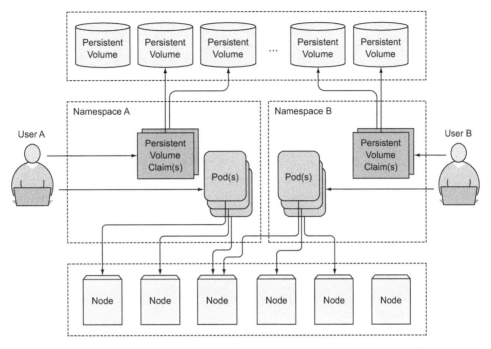

Figure 6.7 PersistentVolumes, like cluster Nodes, don't belong to any namespace, unlike pods and PersistentVolumeClaims.

6.5.3 *Claiming a PersistentVolume by creating a PersistentVolumeClaim*

Now let's lay down our admin hats and put our developer hats back on. Say you need to deploy a pod that requires persistent storage. You'll use the PersistentVolume you created earlier. But you can't use it directly in the pod. You need to claim it first.

Claiming a PersistentVolume is a completely separate process from creating a pod, because you want the same PersistentVolumeClaim to stay available even if the pod is rescheduled (remember, rescheduling means the previous pod is deleted and a new one is created).

CREATING A PERSISTENTVOLUMECLAIM

You'll create the claim now. You need to prepare a PersistentVolumeClaim manifest like the one shown in the following listing and post it to the Kubernetes API through `kubectl create`.

Listing 6.11   A `PersistentVolumeClaim`: mongodb-pvc.yaml

```
apiVersion: v1
kind: PersistentVolumeClaim
metadata:
  name: mongodb-pvc
```
> The name of your claim—you'll need this later when using the claim as the pod's volume.

```
spec:
  resources:
    requests:
      storage: 1Gi          Requesting 1 GiB of storage
  accessModes:
  - ReadWriteOnce             You want the storage to support a single
  storageClassName: ""   ◁    client (performing both reads and writes).
                              You'll learn about this in the section
                              about dynamic provisioning.
```

As soon as you create the claim, Kubernetes finds the appropriate PersistentVolume and binds it to the claim. The PersistentVolume's capacity must be large enough to accommodate what the claim requests. Additionally, the volume's access modes must include the access modes requested by the claim. In your case, the claim requests 1 GiB of storage and a `ReadWriteOnce` access mode. The PersistentVolume you created earlier matches those two requirements so it is bound to your claim. You can see this by inspecting the claim.

LISTING PERSISTENTVOLUMECLAIMS

List all PersistentVolumeClaims to see the state of your PVC:

```
$ kubectl get pvc
NAME          STATUS    VOLUME        CAPACITY    ACCESSMODES    AGE
mongodb-pvc   Bound     mongodb-pv    1Gi         RWO,ROX        3s
```

> **NOTE**   We're using `pvc` as a shorthand for `persistentvolumeclaim`.

The claim is shown as `Bound` to PersistentVolume `mongodb-pv`. Note the abbreviations used for the access modes:

- `RWO`—`ReadWriteOnce`—Only a single node can mount the volume for reading and writing.
- `ROX`—`ReadOnlyMany`—Multiple nodes can mount the volume for reading.
- `RWX`—`ReadWriteMany`—Multiple nodes can mount the volume for both reading and writing.

> **NOTE**   `RWO`, `ROX`, and `RWX` pertain to the number of worker nodes that can use the volume at the same time, not to the number of pods!

LISTING PERSISTENTVOLUMES

You can also see that the PersistentVolume is now `Bound` and no longer `Available` by inspecting it with `kubectl get`:

```
$ kubectl get pv
NAME         CAPACITY    ACCESSMODES    STATUS    CLAIM                  AGE
mongodb-pv   1Gi         RWO,ROX        Bound     default/mongodb-pvc    1m
```

The PersistentVolume shows it's bound to claim `default/mongodb-pvc`. The `default` part is the namespace the claim resides in (you created the claim in the default namespace). We've already said that PersistentVolume resources are cluster-scoped and thus cannot be created in a specific namespace, but PersistentVolumeClaims can only be created in a specific namespace. They can then only be used by pods in the same namespace.

6.5.4   *Using a PersistentVolumeClaim in a pod*

The PersistentVolume is now yours to use. Nobody else can claim the same volume until you release it. To use it inside a pod, you need to reference the Persistent-VolumeClaim by name inside the pod's volume (yes, the PersistentVolumeClaim, not the PersistentVolume directly!), as shown in the following listing.

Listing 6.12   A pod using a PersistentVolumeClaim volume: mongodb-pod-pvc.yaml

```
apiVersion: v1
kind: Pod
metadata:
  name: mongodb
spec:
  containers:
  - image: mongo
    name: mongodb
    volumeMounts:
    - name: mongodb-data
      mountPath: /data/db
    ports:
    - containerPort: 27017
      protocol: TCP
  volumes:
  - name: mongodb-data
    persistentVolumeClaim:            Referencing the PersistentVolumeClaim
      claimName: mongodb-pvc          by name in the pod volume
```

Go ahead and create the pod. Now, check to see if the pod is indeed using the same PersistentVolume and its underlying GCE PD. You should see the data you stored earlier by running the MongoDB shell again, as shown in the following listing.

Listing 6.13   Retrieving MongoDB's persisted data in the pod using the PVC and PV

```
$ kubectl exec -it mongodb mongo
MongoDB shell version: 3.2.8
connecting to: mongodb://127.0.0.1:27017
Welcome to the MongoDB shell.
...
> use mystore
switched to db mystore
> db.foo.find()
{ "_id" : ObjectId("57a61eb9de0cfd512374cc75"), "name" : "foo" }
```

And there it is. You're able to retrieve the document you stored into MongoDB previously.

6.5.5   *Understanding the benefits of using PersistentVolumes and claims*

Examine figure 6.8, which shows both ways a pod can use a GCE Persistent Disk—directly or through a PersistentVolume and claim.

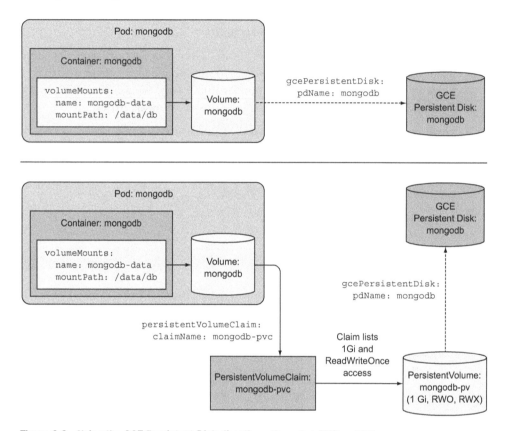

Figure 6.8   Using the GCE Persistent Disk directly or through a PVC and PV

Consider how using this indirect method of obtaining storage from the infrastructure is much simpler for the application developer (or cluster user). Yes, it does require the additional steps of creating the PersistentVolume and the PersistentVolumeClaim, but the developer doesn't have to know anything about the actual storage technology used underneath.

Additionally, the same pod and claim manifests can now be used on many different Kubernetes clusters, because they don't refer to anything infrastructure-specific. The claim states, "I need *x* amount of storage and I need to be able to read and write to it by a single client at once," and then the pod references the claim by name in one of its volumes.

6.5.6   *Recycling PersistentVolumes*

Before you wrap up this section on PersistentVolumes, let's do one last quick experiment. Delete the pod and the PersistentVolumeClaim:

```
$ kubectl delete pod mongodb
pod "mongodb" deleted
$ kubectl delete pvc mongodb-pvc
persistentvolumeclaim "mongodb-pvc" deleted
```

What if you create the PersistentVolumeClaim again? Will it be bound to the Persistent-Volume or not? After you create the claim, what does kubectl get pvc show?

```
$ kubectl get pvc
NAME          STATUS     VOLUME     CAPACITY   ACCESSMODES   AGE
mongodb-pvc   Pending                                        13s
```

The claim's status is shown as Pending. Interesting. When you created the claim earlier, it was immediately bound to the PersistentVolume, so why wasn't it bound now? Maybe listing the PersistentVolumes can shed more light on this:

```
$ kubectl get pv
NAME        CAPACITY   ACCESSMODES   STATUS     CLAIM                  REASON AGE
mongodb-pv  1Gi        RWO,ROX       Released   default/mongodb-pvc           5m
```

The STATUS column shows the PersistentVolume as Released, not Available like before. Because you've already used the volume, it may contain data and shouldn't be bound to a completely new claim without giving the cluster admin a chance to clean it up. Without this, a new pod using the same PersistentVolume could read the data stored there by the previous pod, even if the claim and pod were created in a different namespace (and thus likely belong to a different cluster tenant).

RECLAIMING PERSISTENTVOLUMES MANUALLY

You told Kubernetes you wanted your PersistentVolume to behave like this when you created it—by setting its persistentVolumeReclaimPolicy to Retain. You wanted Kubernetes to retain the volume and its contents after it's released from its claim. As far as I'm aware, the only way to manually recycle the PersistentVolume to make it available again is to delete and recreate the PersistentVolume resource. As you do that, it's your decision what to do with the files on the underlying storage: you can either delete them or leave them alone so they can be reused by the next pod.

RECLAIMING PERSISTENTVOLUMES AUTOMATICALLY

Two other possible reclaim policies exist: Recycle and Delete. The first one deletes the volume's contents and makes the volume available to be claimed again. This way, the PersistentVolume can be reused multiple times by different PersistentVolume-Claims and different pods, as you can see in figure 6.9.

The Delete policy, on the other hand, deletes the underlying storage. Note that the Recycle option is currently not available for GCE Persistent Disks. This type of

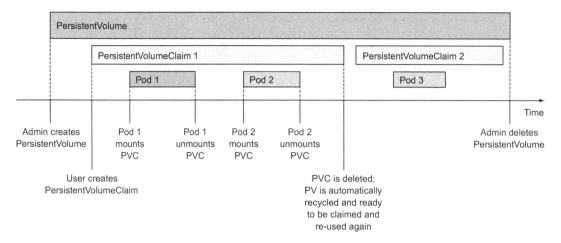

Figure 6.9   The lifespan of a PersistentVolume, PersistentVolumeClaims, and pods using them

PersistentVolume only supports the `Retain` or `Delete` policies. Other Persistent-Volume types may or may not support each of these options, so before creating your own PersistentVolume, be sure to check what reclaim policies are supported for the specific underlying storage you'll use in the volume.

TIP   You can change the PersistentVolume reclaim policy on an existing PersistentVolume. For example, if it's initially set to `Delete`, you can easily change it to `Retain` to prevent losing valuable data.

6.6   *Dynamic provisioning of PersistentVolumes*

You've seen how using PersistentVolumes and PersistentVolumeClaims makes it easy to obtain persistent storage without the developer having to deal with the actual storage technology used underneath. But this still requires a cluster administrator to provision the actual storage up front. Luckily, Kubernetes can also perform this job automatically through dynamic provisioning of PersistentVolumes.

The cluster admin, instead of creating PersistentVolumes, can deploy a Persistent-Volume provisioner and define one or more StorageClass objects to let users choose what type of PersistentVolume they want. The users can refer to the `StorageClass` in their PersistentVolumeClaims and the provisioner will take that into account when provisioning the persistent storage.

NOTE   Similar to PersistentVolumes, StorageClass resources aren't namespaced.

Kubernetes includes provisioners for the most popular cloud providers, so the administrator doesn't always need to deploy a provisioner. But if Kubernetes is deployed on-premises, a custom provisioner needs to be deployed.

Instead of the administrator pre-provisioning a bunch of PersistentVolumes, they need to define one or two (or more) StorageClasses and let the system create a new PersistentVolume each time one is requested through a PersistentVolumeClaim. The great thing about this is that it's impossible to run out of PersistentVolumes (obviously, you can run out of storage space).

6.6.1 Defining the available storage types through StorageClass resources

Before a user can create a PersistentVolumeClaim, which will result in a new Persistent-Volume being provisioned, an admin needs to create one or more StorageClass resources. Let's look at an example of one in the following listing.

> **Listing 6.14   A StorageClass definition: storageclass-fast-gcepd.yaml**

```
apiVersion: storage.k8s.io/v1
kind: StorageClass
metadata:
  name: fast
provisioner: kubernetes.io/gce-pd        ◁──────  The volume plugin to
parameters:                                        use for provisioning
  type: pd-ssd            The parameters passed     the PersistentVolume
  zone: europe-west1-b    to the provisioner
```

NOTE If using Minikube, deploy the file storageclass-fast-hostpath.yaml.

The StorageClass resource specifies which provisioner should be used for provisioning the PersistentVolume when a PersistentVolumeClaim requests this StorageClass. The parameters defined in the StorageClass definition are passed to the provisioner and are specific to each provisioner plugin.

The StorageClass uses the Google Compute Engine (GCE) Persistent Disk (PD) provisioner, which means it can be used when Kubernetes is running in GCE. For other cloud providers, other provisioners need to be used.

6.6.2 Requesting the storage class in a PersistentVolumeClaim

After the StorageClass resource is created, users can refer to the storage class by name in their PersistentVolumeClaims.

CREATING A PVC DEFINITION REQUESTING A SPECIFIC STORAGE CLASS

You can modify your `mongodb-pvc` to use dynamic provisioning. The following listing shows the updated YAML definition of the PVC.

> **Listing 6.15   A PVC with dynamic provisioning: mongodb-pvc-dp.yaml**

```
apiVersion: v1
kind: PersistentVolumeClaim
metadata:
  name: mongodb-pvc
```

```
spec:
  storageClassName: fast          ◁─┐  This PVC requests the
  resources:                          custom storage class.
    requests:
      storage: 100Mi
  accessModes:
    - ReadWriteOnce
```

Apart from specifying the size and access modes, your PersistentVolumeClaim now also specifies the class of storage you want to use. When you create the claim, the PersistentVolume is created by the provisioner referenced in the `fast` StorageClass resource. The provisioner is used even if an existing manually provisioned Persistent-Volume matches the PersistentVolumeClaim.

> **NOTE** If you reference a non-existing storage class in a PVC, the provisioning of the PV will fail (you'll see a `ProvisioningFailed` event when you use `kubectl describe` on the PVC).

EXAMINING THE CREATED PVC AND THE DYNAMICALLY PROVISIONED PV

Next you'll create the PVC and then use `kubectl get` to see it:

```
$ kubectl get pvc mongodb-pvc
NAME          STATUS   VOLUME        CAPACITY   ACCESSMODES   STORAGECLASS
mongodb-pvc   Bound    pvc-1e6bc048  1Gi        RWO           fast
```

The `VOLUME` column shows the PersistentVolume that's bound to this claim (the actual name is longer than what's shown above). You can try listing PersistentVolumes now to see that a new PV has indeed been created automatically:

```
$ kubectl get pv
NAME           CAPACITY   ACCESSMODES   RECLAIMPOLICY   STATUS      STORAGECLASS
mongodb-pv     1Gi        RWO,ROX       Retain          Released
pvc-1e6bc048   1Gi        RWO           Delete          Bound       fast
```

> **NOTE** Only pertinent columns are shown.

You can see the dynamically provisioned PersistentVolume. Its capacity and access modes are what you requested in the PVC. Its reclaim policy is `Delete`, which means the PersistentVolume will be deleted when the PVC is deleted. Beside the PV, the provisioner also provisioned the actual storage. Your `fast` StorageClass is configured to use the `kubernetes.io/gce-pd` provisioner, which provisions GCE Persistent Disks. You can see the disk with the following command:

```
$ gcloud compute disks list
NAME                           ZONE            SIZE_GB   TYPE          STATUS
gke-kubia-dyn-pvc-1e6bc048     europe-west1-d  1         pd-ssd        READY
gke-kubia-default-pool-71df    europe-west1-d  100       pd-standard   READY
gke-kubia-default-pool-79cd    europe-west1-d  100       pd-standard   READY
gke-kubia-default-pool-b1c4    europe-west1-d  100       pd-standard   READY
mongodb                        europe-west1-d  1         pd-standard   READY
```

As you can see, the first persistent disk's name suggests it was provisioned dynamically and its type shows it's an SSD, as specified in the storage class you created earlier.

UNDERSTANDING HOW TO USE STORAGE CLASSES

The cluster admin can create multiple storage classes with different performance or other characteristics. The developer then decides which one is most appropriate for each claim they create.

The nice thing about StorageClasses is the fact that claims refer to them by name. The PVC definitions are therefore portable across different clusters, as long as the StorageClass names are the same across all of them. To see this portability yourself, you can try running the same example on Minikube, if you've been using GKE up to this point. As a cluster admin, you'll have to create a different storage class (but with the same name). The storage class defined in the storageclass-fast-hostpath.yaml file is tailor-made for use in Minikube. Then, once you deploy the storage class, you as a cluster user can deploy the exact same PVC manifest and the exact same pod manifest as before. This shows how the pods and PVCs are portable across different clusters.

6.6.3 *Dynamic provisioning without specifying a storage class*

As we've progressed through this chapter, attaching persistent storage to pods has become ever simpler. The sections in this chapter reflect how provisioning of storage has evolved from early Kubernetes versions to now. In this final section, we'll look at the latest and simplest way of attaching a PersistentVolume to a pod.

LISTING STORAGE CLASSES

When you created your custom storage class called `fast`, you didn't check if any existing storage classes were already defined in your cluster. Why don't you do that now? Here are the storage classes available in GKE:

```
$ kubectl get sc
NAME                TYPE
fast                kubernetes.io/gce-pd
standard (default)  kubernetes.io/gce-pd
```

> **NOTE** We're using sc as shorthand for storageclass.

Beside the `fast` storage class, which you created yourself, a `standard` storage class exists and is marked as default. You'll learn what that means in a moment. Let's list the storage classes available in Minikube, so we can compare:

```
$ kubectl get sc
NAME                TYPE
fast                k8s.io/minikube-hostpath
standard (default)  k8s.io/minikube-hostpath
```

Again, the `fast` storage class was created by you and a default `standard` storage class exists here as well. Comparing the TYPE columns in the two listings, you see GKE is using the `kubernetes.io/gce-pd` provisioner, whereas Minikube is using `k8s.io/minikube-hostpath`.

EXAMINING THE DEFAULT STORAGE CLASS

You're going to use `kubectl get` to see more info about the standard storage class in a GKE cluster, as shown in the following listing.

Listing 6.16 The definition of the standard storage class on GKE

```
$ kubectl get sc standard -o yaml
apiVersion: storage.k8s.io/v1
kind: StorageClass
metadata:
  annotations:
    storageclass.beta.kubernetes.io/is-default-class: "true"    ← This annotation marks the storage class as default.
  creationTimestamp: 2017-05-16T15:24:11Z
  labels:
    addonmanager.kubernetes.io/mode: EnsureExists
    kubernetes.io/cluster-service: "true"
  name: standard
  resourceVersion: "180"
  selfLink: /apis/storage.k8s.io/v1/storageclassesstandard
  uid: b6498511-3a4b-11e7-ba2c-42010a840014
parameters:
  type: pd-standard    ← The type parameter is used by the provisioner to know what type of GCE PD to create.
provisioner: kubernetes.io/gce-pd    ← The GCE Persistent Disk provisioner is used to provision PVs of this class.
```

If you look closely toward the top of the listing, the storage class definition includes an annotation, which makes this the default storage class. The default storage class is what's used to dynamically provision a PersistentVolume if the PersistentVolumeClaim doesn't explicitly say which storage class to use.

CREATING A PERSISTENTVOLUMECLAIM WITHOUT SPECIFYING A STORAGE CLASS

You can create a PVC without specifying the `storageClassName` attribute and (on Google Kubernetes Engine) a GCE Persistent Disk of type `pd-standard` will be provisioned for you. Try this by creating a claim from the YAML in the following listing.

Listing 6.17 PVC with no storage class defined: mongodb-pvc-dp-nostorageclass.yaml

```
apiVersion: v1
kind: PersistentVolumeClaim
metadata:
  name: mongodb-pvc2
spec:
  resources:
    requests:
      storage: 100Mi    ← You're not specifying the storageClassName attribute (unlike earlier examples).
  accessModes:
    - ReadWriteOnce
```

This PVC definition includes only the storage size request and the desired access modes, but no storage class. When you create the PVC, whatever storage class is marked as default will be used. You can confirm that's the case:

```
$ kubectl get pvc mongodb-pvc2
NAME          STATUS   VOLUME         CAPACITY   ACCESSMODES   STORAGECLASS
mongodb-pvc2  Bound    pvc-95a5ec12   1Gi        RWO           standard

$ kubectl get pv pvc-95a5ec12
NAME          CAPACITY   ACCESSMODES   RECLAIMPOLICY   STATUS   STORAGECLASS
pvc-95a5ec12  1Gi        RWO           Delete          Bound    standard

$ gcloud compute disks list
NAME                          ZONE            SIZE_GB   TYPE          STATUS
gke-kubia-dyn-pvc-95a5ec12    europe-west1-d  1         pd-standard   READY
...
```

FORCING A PERSISTENTVOLUMECLAIM TO BE BOUND TO ONE OF THE PRE-PROVISIONED PERSISTENTVOLUMES

This finally brings us to why you set storageClassName to an empty string in listing 6.11 (when you wanted the PVC to bind to the PV you'd provisioned manually). Let me repeat the relevant lines of that PVC definition here:

```
kind: PersistentVolumeClaim
spec:
  storageClassName: ""
```

Specifying an empty string as the storage class name ensures the PVC binds to a pre-provisioned PV instead of dynamically provisioning a new one.

If you hadn't set the storageClassName attribute to an empty string, the dynamic volume provisioner would have provisioned a new PersistentVolume, despite there being an appropriate pre-provisioned PersistentVolume. At that point, I wanted to demonstrate how a claim gets bound to a manually pre-provisioned PersistentVolume. I didn't want the dynamic provisioner to interfere.

> **TIP** Explicitly set storageClassName to "" if you want the PVC to use a pre-provisioned PersistentVolume.

UNDERSTANDING THE COMPLETE PICTURE OF DYNAMIC PERSISTENTVOLUME PROVISIONING

This brings us to the end of this chapter. To summarize, the best way to attach persistent storage to a pod is to only create the PVC (with an explicitly specified storageClassName if necessary) and the pod (which refers to the PVC by name). Everything else is taken care of by the dynamic PersistentVolume provisioner.

To get a complete picture of the steps involved in getting a dynamically provisioned PersistentVolume, examine figure 6.10.

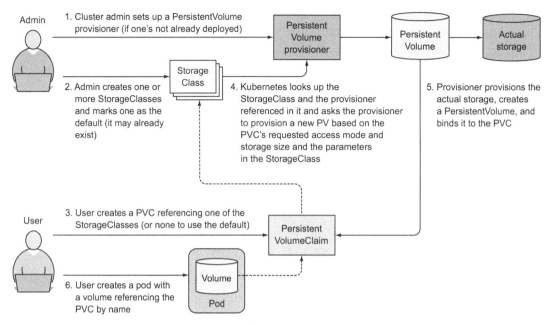

Figure 6.10   The complete picture of dynamic provisioning of PersistentVolumes

6.7   *Summary*

This chapter has shown you how volumes are used to provide either temporary or persistent storage to a pod's containers. You've learned how to

- Create a multi-container pod and have the pod's containers operate on the same files by adding a volume to the pod and mounting it in each container
- Use the `emptyDir` volume to store temporary, non-persistent data
- Use the `gitRepo` volume to easily populate a directory with the contents of a Git repository at pod startup
- Use the `hostPath` volume to access files from the host node
- Mount external storage in a volume to persist pod data across pod restarts
- Decouple the pod from the storage infrastructure by using PersistentVolumes and PersistentVolumeClaims
- Have PersistentVolumes of the desired (or the default) storage class dynamically provisioned for each PersistentVolumeClaim
- Prevent the dynamic provisioner from interfering when you want the PersistentVolumeClaim to be bound to a pre-provisioned PersistentVolume

In the next chapter, you'll see what mechanisms Kubernetes provides to deliver configuration data, secret information, and metadata about the pod and container to the processes running inside a pod. This is done with the special types of volumes we've mentioned in this chapter, but not yet explored.

ConfigMaps and Secrets: configuring applications

This chapter covers

- Changing the main process of a container
- Passing command-line options to the app
- Setting environment variables exposed to the app
- Configuring apps through ConfigMaps
- Passing sensitive information through Secrets

Up to now you haven't had to pass any kind of configuration data to the apps you've run in the exercises in this book. Because almost all apps require configuration (settings that differ between deployed instances, credentials for accessing external systems, and so on), which shouldn't be baked into the built app itself, let's see how to pass configuration options to your app when running it in Kubernetes.

7.1 Configuring containerized applications

Before we go over how to pass configuration data to apps running in Kubernetes, let's look at how containerized applications are usually configured.

If you skip the fact that you can bake the configuration into the application itself, when starting development of a new app, you usually start off by having the

191

app configured through command-line arguments. Then, as the list of configuration options grows, you can move the configuration into a config file.

Another way of passing configuration options to an application that's widely popular in containerized applications is through environment variables. Instead of having the app read a config file or command-line arguments, the app looks up the value of a certain environment variable. The official MySQL container image, for example, uses an environment variable called MYSQL_ROOT_PASSWORD for setting the password for the root super-user account.

But why are environment variables so popular in containers? Using configuration files inside Docker containers is a bit tricky, because you'd have to bake the config file into the container image itself or mount a volume containing the file into the container. Obviously, baking files into the image is similar to hardcoding configuration into the source code of the application, because it requires you to rebuild the image every time you want to change the config. Plus, everyone with access to the image can see the config, including any information that should be kept secret, such as credentials or encryption keys. Using a volume is better, but still requires you to make sure the file is written to the volume before the container is started.

If you've read the previous chapter, you might think of using a gitRepo volume as a configuration source. That's not a bad idea, because it allows you to keep the config nicely versioned and enables you to easily rollback a config change if necessary. But a simpler way allows you to put the configuration data into a top-level Kubernetes resource and store it and all the other resource definitions in the same Git repository or in any other file-based storage. The Kubernetes resource for storing configuration data is called a ConfigMap. We'll learn how to use it in this chapter.

Regardless if you're using a ConfigMap to store configuration data or not, you can configure your apps by

- Passing command-line arguments to containers
- Setting custom environment variables for each container
- Mounting configuration files into containers through a special type of volume

We'll go over all these options in the next few sections, but before we start, let's look at config options from a security perspective. Though most configuration options don't contain any sensitive information, several can. These include credentials, private encryption keys, and similar data that needs to be kept secure. This type of information needs to be handled with special care, which is why Kubernetes offers another type of first-class object called a Secret. We'll learn about it in the last part of this chapter.

7.2   *Passing command-line arguments to containers*

In all the examples so far, you've created containers that ran the default command defined in the container image, but Kubernetes allows overriding the command as part of the pod's container definition when you want to run a different executable instead of the one specified in the image, or want to run it with a different set of command-line arguments. We'll look at how to do that now.

7.2.1 *Defining the command and arguments in Docker*

The first thing I need to explain is that the whole command that gets executed in the container is composed of two parts: the *command* and the *arguments*.

UNDERSTANDING ENTRYPOINT AND CMD

In a Dockerfile, two instructions define the two parts:

- ENTRYPOINT defines the executable invoked when the container is started.
- CMD specifies the arguments that get passed to the ENTRYPOINT.

Although you can use the CMD instruction to specify the command you want to execute when the image is run, the correct way is to do it through the ENTRYPOINT instruction and to only specify the CMD if you want to define the default arguments. The image can then be run without specifying any arguments

```
$ docker run <image>
```

or with additional arguments, which override whatever's set under CMD in the Dockerfile:

```
$ docker run <image> <arguments>
```

UNDERSTANDING THE DIFFERENCE BETWEEN THE SHELL AND EXEC FORMS

But there's more. Both instructions support two different forms:

- shell form—For example, ENTRYPOINT node app.js.
- exec form—For example, ENTRYPOINT ["node", "app.js"].

The difference is whether the specified command is invoked inside a shell or not.

In the kubia image you created in chapter 2, you used the exec form of the ENTRY-POINT instruction:

```
ENTRYPOINT ["node", "app.js"]
```

This runs the node process directly (not inside a shell), as you can see by listing the processes running inside the container:

```
$ docker exec 4675d ps x
  PID TTY      STAT   TIME COMMAND
    1 ?        Ssl    0:00 node app.js
   12 ?        Rs     0:00 ps x
```

If you'd used the shell form (ENTRYPOINT node app.js), these would have been the container's processes:

```
$ docker exec -it e4bad ps x
  PID TTY      STAT   TIME COMMAND
    1 ?        Ss     0:00 /bin/sh -c node app.js
```

```
  7 ?       Sl      0:00 node app.js
 13 ?       Rs+     0:00 ps x
```

As you can see, in that case, the main process (PID 1) would be the `shell` process instead of the node process. The node process (PID 7) would be started from that shell. The `shell` process is unnecessary, which is why you should always use the `exec` form of the ENTRYPOINT instruction.

MAKING THE INTERVAL CONFIGURABLE IN YOUR FORTUNE IMAGE

Let's modify your fortune script and image so the delay interval in the loop is configurable. You'll add an `INTERVAL` variable and initialize it with the value of the first command-line argument, as shown in the following listing.

> **Listing 7.1   Fortune script with interval configurable through argument: fortune-args/
> fortuneloop.sh**

```
#!/bin/bash
trap "exit" SIGINT
INTERVAL=$1
echo Configured to generate new fortune every $INTERVAL seconds
mkdir -p /var/htdocs
while :
do
  echo $(date) Writing fortune to /var/htdocs/index.html
  /usr/games/fortune > /var/htdocs/index.html
  sleep $INTERVAL
done
```

You've added or modified the lines in bold font. Now, you'll modify the Dockerfile so it uses the `exec` version of the ENTRYPOINT instruction and sets the default interval to 10 seconds using the CMD instruction, as shown in the following listing.

> **Listing 7.2   Dockerfile for the updated `fortune` image: fortune-args/Dockerfile**

```
FROM ubuntu:latest
RUN apt-get update ; apt-get -y install fortune     The exec form of the
ADD fortuneloop.sh /bin/fortuneloop.sh              ENTRYPOINT instruction
ENTRYPOINT ["/bin/fortuneloop.sh"]                  The default argument
CMD ["10"]                                          for the executable
```

You can now build and push the image to Docker Hub. This time, you'll tag the image as args instead of `latest`:

```
$ docker build -t docker.io/luksa/fortune:args .
$ docker push docker.io/luksa/fortune:args
```

You can test the image by running it locally with Docker:

```
$ docker run -it docker.io/luksa/fortune:args
Configured to generate new fortune every 10 seconds
Fri May 19 10:39:44 UTC 2017 Writing fortune to /var/htdocs/index.html
```

NOTE　You can stop the script with Control+C.

And you can override the default sleep interval by passing it as an argument:

```
$ docker run -it docker.io/luksa/fortune:args 15
Configured to generate new fortune every 15 seconds
```

Now that you're sure your image honors the argument passed to it, let's see how to use it in a pod.

7.2.2 Overriding the command and arguments in Kubernetes

In Kubernetes, when specifying a container, you can choose to override both ENTRY-POINT and CMD. To do that, you set the properties `command` and `args` in the container specification, as shown in the following listing.

Listing 7.3　A pod definition specifying a custom command and arguments

```
kind: Pod
spec:
  containers:
  - image: some/image
    command: ["/bin/command"]
    args: ["arg1", "arg2", "arg3"]
```

In most cases, you'll only set custom arguments and rarely override the command (except in general-purpose images such as `busybox`, which doesn't define an ENTRY-POINT at all).

NOTE　The `command` and `args` fields can't be updated after the pod is created.

The two Dockerfile instructions and the equivalent pod spec fields are shown in table 7.1.

Table 7.1　Specifying the executable and its arguments in Docker vs Kubernetes

Docker	Kubernetes	Description
ENTRYPOINT	command	The executable that's executed inside the container
CMD	args	The arguments passed to the executable

RUNNING THE FORTUNE POD WITH A CUSTOM INTERVAL

To run the fortune pod with a custom delay interval, you'll copy your fortune-pod.yaml into fortune-pod-args.yaml and modify it as shown in the following listing.

Listing 7.4　Passing an argument in the pod definition: fortune-pod-args.yaml

```
apiVersion: v1
kind: Pod
metadata:
  name: fortune2s          ⟵┐ You changed the
                             └ pod's name.
```

```
spec:
  containers:
  - image: luksa/fortune:args      ◁──┐  Using fortune:args
    args: ["2"]                     ◁──┘  instead of fortune:latest
    name: html-generator                 This argument makes the
    volumeMounts:                         script generate a new fortune
    - name: html                          every two seconds.
      mountPath: /var/htdocs
...
```

You added the `args` array to the container definition. Try creating this pod now. The values of the array will be passed to the container as command-line arguments when it is run.

The array notation used in this listing is great if you have one argument or a few. If you have several, you can also use the following notation:

```
args:
- foo
- bar
- "15"
```

> **TIP** You don't need to enclose string values in quotations marks (but you must enclose numbers).

Specifying arguments is one way of passing config options to your containers through command-line arguments. Next, you'll see how to do it through environment variables.

7.3 *Setting environment variables for a container*

As I've already mentioned, containerized applications often use environment variables as a source of configuration options. Kubernetes allows you to specify a custom list of environment variables for each container of a pod, as shown in figure 7.1. Although it would be useful to also define environment variables at the pod level and have them be inherited by its containers, no such option currently exists.

> **NOTE** Like the container's command and arguments, the list of environment variables also cannot be updated after the pod is created.

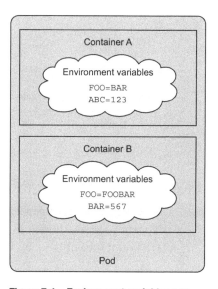

Figure 7.1 **Environment variables can be set per container.**

MAKING THE INTERVAL IN YOUR FORTUNE IMAGE CONFIGURABLE THROUGH AN ENVIRONMENT VARIABLE

Let's see how to modify your fortuneloop.sh script once again to allow it to be configured from an environment variable, as shown in the following listing.

> **Listing 7.5 Fortune script with interval configurable through env var: fortune-env/
> fortuneloop.sh**

```
#!/bin/bash
trap "exit" SIGINT
echo Configured to generate new fortune every $INTERVAL seconds
mkdir -p /var/htdocs
while :
do
  echo $(date) Writing fortune to /var/htdocs/index.html
  /usr/games/fortune > /var/htdocs/index.html
  sleep $INTERVAL
done
```

All you had to do was remove the row where the INTERVAL variable is initialized. Because your "app" is a simple bash script, you didn't need to do anything else. If the app was written in Java you'd use System.getenv("INTERVAL"), whereas in Node.JS you'd use process.env.INTERVAL, and in Python you'd use os.environ['INTERVAL'].

7.3.1 Specifying environment variables in a container definition

After building the new image (I've tagged it as luksa/fortune:env this time) and pushing it to Docker Hub, you can run it by creating a new pod, in which you pass the environment variable to the script by including it in your container definition, as shown in the following listing.

> **Listing 7.6 Defining an environment variable in a pod: fortune-pod-env.yaml**

```
kind: Pod
spec:
 containers:
 - image: luksa/fortune:env
   env:
   - name: INTERVAL          Adding a single variable to
     value: "30"             the environment variable list
   name: html-generator
...
```

As mentioned previously, you set the environment variable inside the container definition, not at the pod level.

> **NOTE** Don't forget that in each container, Kubernetes also automatically exposes environment variables for each service in the same namespace. These environment variables are basically auto-injected configuration.

7.3.2 Referring to other environment variables in a variable's value

In the previous example, you set a fixed value for the environment variable, but you can also reference previously defined environment variables or any other existing variables by using the $(VAR) syntax. If you define two environment variables, the second one can include the value of the first one as shown in the following listing.

> **Listing 7.7 Referring to an environment variable inside another one**

```
env:
- name: FIRST_VAR
  value: "foo"
- name: SECOND_VAR
  value: "$(FIRST_VAR)bar"
```

In this case, the SECOND_VAR's value will be "foobar". Similarly, both the command and args attributes you learned about in section 7.2 can also refer to environment variables like this. You'll use this method in section 7.4.5.

7.3.3 Understanding the drawback of hardcoding environment variables

Having values effectively hardcoded in the pod definition means you need to have separate pod definitions for your production and your development pods. To reuse the same pod definition in multiple environments, it makes sense to decouple the configuration from the pod descriptor. Luckily, you can do that using a ConfigMap resource and using it as a source for environment variable values using the valueFrom instead of the value field. You'll learn about this next.

7.4 Decoupling configuration with a ConfigMap

The whole point of an app's configuration is to keep the config options that vary between environments, or change frequently, separate from the application's source code. If you think of a pod descriptor as source code for your app (and in microservices architectures that's what it really is, because it defines how to compose the individual components into a functioning system), it's clear you should move the configuration out of the pod description.

7.4.1 Introducing ConfigMaps

Kubernetes allows separating configuration options into a separate object called a ConfigMap, which is a map containing key/value pairs with the values ranging from short literals to full config files.

An application doesn't need to read the ConfigMap directly or even know that it exists. The contents of the map are instead passed to containers as either environment variables or as files in a volume (see figure 7.2). And because environment variables can be referenced in command-line arguments using the $(ENV_VAR) syntax, you can also pass ConfigMap entries to processes as command-line arguments.

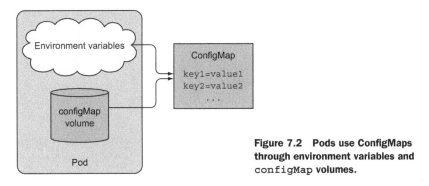

Figure 7.2 Pods use ConfigMaps through environment variables and configMap **volumes.**

Sure, the application can also read the contents of a ConfigMap directly through the Kubernetes REST API endpoint if needed, but unless you have a real need for this, you should keep your app Kubernetes-agnostic as much as possible.

Regardless of how an app consumes a ConfigMap, having the config in a separate standalone object like this allows you to keep multiple manifests for ConfigMaps with the same name, each for a different environment (development, testing, QA, production, and so on). Because pods reference the ConfigMap by name, you can use a different config in each environment while using the same pod specification across all of them (see figure 7.3).

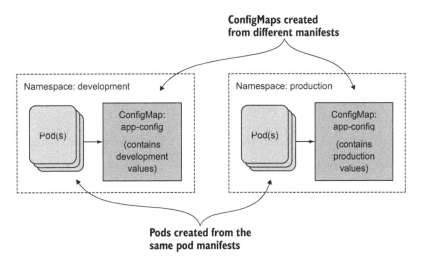

Figure 7.3   Two different ConfigMaps with the same name used in different environments

7.4.2 Creating a ConfigMap

Let's see how to use a ConfigMap in one of your pods. To start with the simplest example, you'll first create a map with a single key and use it to fill the INTERVAL environment variable from your previous example. You'll create the ConfigMap with the special kubectl create configmap command instead of posting a YAML with the generic kubectl create -f command.

USING THE KUBECTL CREATE CONFIGMAP COMMAND

You can define the map's entries by passing literals to the kubectl command or you can create the ConfigMap from files stored on your disk. Use a simple literal first:

```
$ kubectl create configmap fortune-config --from-literal=sleep-interval=25
configmap "fortune-config" created
```

> **NOTE** ConfigMap keys must be a valid DNS subdomain (they may only contain alphanumeric characters, dashes, underscores, and dots). They may optionally include a leading dot.

This creates a ConfigMap called fortune-config with the single-entry sleep-interval=25 (figure 7.4).

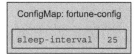

Figure 7.4 The fortune-config **ConfigMap containing a single entry**

ConfigMaps usually contain more than one entry. To create a ConfigMap with multiple literal entries, you add multiple --from-literal arguments:

```
$ kubectl create configmap myconfigmap
    --from-literal=foo=bar --from-literal=bar=baz --from-literal=one=two
```

Let's inspect the YAML descriptor of the ConfigMap you created by using the kubectl get command, as shown in the following listing.

Listing 7.8 A ConfigMap definition

```
$ kubectl get configmap fortune-config -o yaml         The single entry
apiVersion: v1                                         in this map
data:
  sleep-interval: "25"                                 This descriptor
kind: ConfigMap                                        describes a ConfigMap.
metadata:
  creationTimestamp: 2016-08-11T20:31:08Z              The name of this map
  name: fortune-config                                 (you're referencing it
  namespace: default                                   by this name)
  resourceVersion: "910025"
  selfLink: /api/v1/namespaces/default/configmaps/fortune-config
  uid: 88c4167e-6002-11e6-a50d-42010af00237
```

Nothing extraordinary. You could easily have written this YAML yourself (you wouldn't need to specify anything but the name in the `metadata` section, of course) and posted it to the Kubernetes API with the well-known

```
$ kubectl create -f fortune-config.yaml
```

CREATING A CONFIGMAP ENTRY FROM THE CONTENTS OF A FILE

ConfigMaps can also store coarse-grained config data, such as complete config files. To do this, the `kubectl create configmap` command also supports reading files from disk and storing them as individual entries in the ConfigMap:

```
$ kubectl create configmap my-config --from-file=config-file.conf
```

When you run the previous command, kubectl looks for the file `config-file.conf` in the directory you run `kubectl` in. It will then store the contents of the file under the key `config-file.conf` in the ConfigMap (the filename is used as the map key), but you can also specify a key manually like this:

```
$ kubectl create configmap my-config --from-file=customkey=config-file.conf
```

This command will store the file's contents under the key `customkey`. As with literals, you can add multiple files by using the `--from-file` argument multiple times.

CREATING A CONFIGMAP FROM FILES IN A DIRECTORY

Instead of importing each file individually, you can even import all files from a file directory:

```
$ kubectl create configmap my-config --from-file=/path/to/dir
```

In this case, kubectl will create an individual map entry for each file in the specified directory, but only for files whose name is a valid ConfigMap key.

COMBINING DIFFERENT OPTIONS

When creating ConfigMaps, you can use a combination of all the options mentioned here (note that these files aren't included in the book's code archive—you can create them yourself if you'd like to try out the command):

```
$ kubectl create configmap my-config
    --from-file=foo.json              A single file
    --from-file=bar=foobar.conf       A file stored under
    --from-file=config-opts/          a custom key
    --from-literal=some=thing         A whole directory
                                      A literal value
```

Here, you've created the ConfigMap from multiple sources: a whole directory, a file, another file (but stored under a custom key instead of using the filename as the key), and a literal value. Figure 7.5 shows all these sources and the resulting ConfigMap.

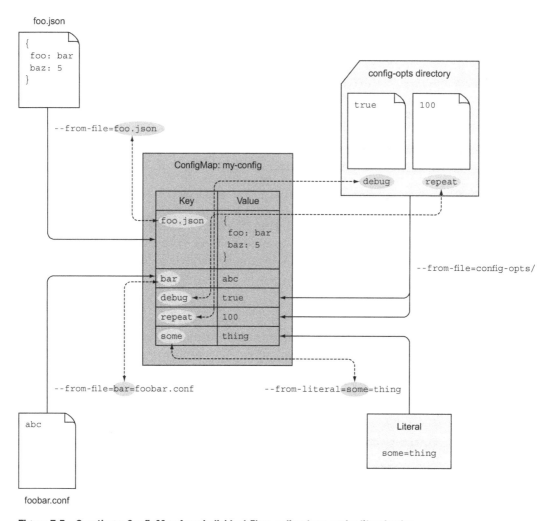

Figure 7.5   Creating a ConfigMap from individual files, a directory, and a literal value

7.4.3   *Passing a ConfigMap entry to a container as an environment variable*

How do you now get the values from this map into a pod's container? You have three options. Let's start with the simplest—setting an environment variable. You'll use the `valueFrom` field I mentioned in section 7.3.3. The pod descriptor should look like the following listing.

Listing 7.9   Pod with `env var` from a config map: fortune-pod-env-configmap.yaml

```
apiVersion: v1
kind: Pod
```

```
metadata:
  name: fortune-env-from-configmap
spec:
  containers:
  - image: luksa/fortune:env
    env:
    - name: INTERVAL
      valueFrom:
        configMapKeyRef:
          name: fortune-config
          key: sleep-interval
  ...
```

You're setting the environment variable called **INTERVAL**.

Instead of setting a fixed value, you're initializing it from a ConfigMap key.

The name of the ConfigMap you're referencing

You're setting the variable to whatever is stored under this key in the ConfigMap.

You defined an environment variable called INTERVAL and set its value to whatever is stored in the fortune-config ConfigMap under the key sleep-interval. When the process running in the html-generator container reads the INTERVAL environment variable, it will see the value 25 (shown in figure 7.6).

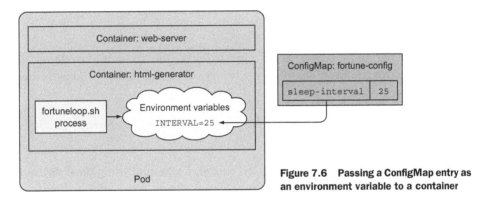

Figure 7.6   Passing a ConfigMap entry as an environment variable to a container

REFERENCING NON-EXISTING CONFIGMAPS IN A POD

You might wonder what happens if the referenced ConfigMap doesn't exist when you create the pod. Kubernetes schedules the pod normally and tries to run its containers. The container referencing the non-existing ConfigMap will fail to start, but the other container will start normally. If you then create the missing ConfigMap, the failed container is started without requiring you to recreate the pod.

> **NOTE**   You can also mark a reference to a ConfigMap as optional (by setting configMapKeyRef.optional: true). In that case, the container starts even if the ConfigMap doesn't exist.

This example shows you how to decouple the configuration from the pod specification. This allows you to keep all the configuration options closely together (even for multiple pods) instead of having them splattered around the pod definition (or duplicated across multiple pod manifests).

7.4.4   *Passing all entries of a ConfigMap as environment variables at once*

When your ConfigMap contains more than just a few entries, it becomes tedious and error-prone to create environment variables from each entry individually. Luckily, Kubernetes version 1.6 provides a way to expose all entries of a ConfigMap as environment variables.

Imagine having a ConfigMap with three keys called FOO, BAR, and FOO-BAR. You can expose them all as environment variables by using the envFrom attribute, instead of env the way you did in previous examples. The following listing shows an example.

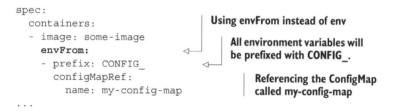

Listing 7.10   Pod with env vars from all entries of a ConfigMap

As you can see, you can also specify a prefix for the environment variables (CONFIG_ in this case). This results in the following two environment variables being present inside the container: CONFIG_FOO and CONFIG_BAR.

> **NOTE**   The prefix is optional, so if you omit it the environment variables will have the same name as the keys.

Did you notice I said two variables, but earlier, I said the ConfigMap has three entries (FOO, BAR, and FOO-BAR)? Why is there no environment variable for the FOO-BAR ConfigMap entry?

The reason is that CONFIG_FOO-BAR isn't a valid environment variable name because it contains a dash. Kubernetes doesn't convert the keys in any way (it doesn't convert dashes to underscores, for example). If a ConfigMap key isn't in the proper format, it skips the entry (but it does record an event informing you it skipped it).

7.4.5   *Passing a ConfigMap entry as a command-line argument*

Now, let's also look at how to pass values from a ConfigMap as arguments to the main process running in the container. You can't reference ConfigMap entries directly in the pod.spec.containers.args field, but you can first initialize an environment variable from the ConfigMap entry and then refer to the variable inside the arguments as shown in figure 7.7.

Listing 7.11 shows an example of how to do this in the YAML.

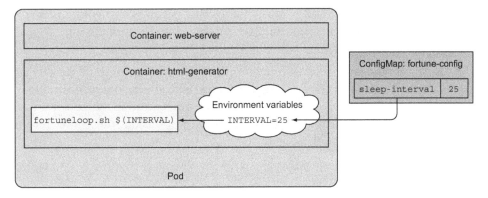

Figure 7.7 Passing a ConfigMap entry as a command-line argument

Listing 7.11 Using ConfigMap entries as arguments: fortune-pod-args-configmap.yaml

```
apiVersion: v1
kind: Pod
metadata:
  name: fortune-args-from-configmap        Using the image that takes the
spec:                                       interval from the first argument,
  containers:                               not from an environment variable
  - image: luksa/fortune:args        ◁────┘
    env:
    - name: INTERVAL
      valueFrom:                            Defining the
        configMapKeyRef:                    environment variable
          name: fortune-config              exactly as before
          key: sleep-interval
    args: ["$(INTERVAL)"]          ◁────┐
  ...                                    Referencing the environment
                                         variable in the argument
```

You defined the environment variable exactly as you did before, but then you used the $(ENV_VARIABLE_NAME) syntax to have Kubernetes inject the value of the variable into the argument.

7.4.6 *Using a configMap volume to expose ConfigMap entries as files*

Passing configuration options as environment variables or command-line arguments is usually used for short variable values. A ConfigMap, as you've seen, can also contain whole config files. When you want to expose those to the container, you can use one of the special volume types I mentioned in the previous chapter, namely a configMap volume.

A configMap volume will expose each entry of the ConfigMap as a file. The process running in the container can obtain the entry's value by reading the contents of the file.

Although this method is mostly meant for passing large config files to the container, nothing prevents you from passing short single values this way.

CREATING THE CONFIGMAP

Instead of modifying your fortuneloop.sh script once again, you'll now try a different example. You'll use a config file to configure the Nginx web server running inside the fortune pod's web-server container. Let's say you want your Nginx server to compress responses it sends to the client. To enable compression, the config file for Nginx needs to look like the following listing.

Listing 7.12   An Nginx config with enabled gzip compression: my-nginx-config.conf

```
server {
  listen          80;
  server_name     www.kubia-example.com;

  gzip on;                                         This enables gzip compression
  gzip_types text/plain application/xml;            for plain text and XML files.

  location / {
    root   /usr/share/nginx/html;
    index  index.html index.htm;
  }
}
```

Now delete your existing `fortune-config` ConfigMap with `kubectl delete config-map fortune-config`, so that you can replace it with a new one, which will include the Nginx config file. You'll create the ConfigMap from files stored on your local disk.

Create a new directory called configmap-files and store the Nginx config from the previous listing into configmap-files/my-nginx-config.conf. To make the ConfigMap also contain the `sleep-interval` entry, add a plain text file called sleep-interval to the same directory and store the number 25 in it (see figure 7.8).

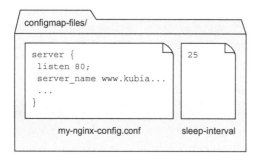

Figure 7.8   The contents of the configmap-files directory and its files

Now create a ConfigMap from all the files in the directory like this:

```
$ kubectl create configmap fortune-config --from-file=configmap-files
configmap "fortune-config" created
```

The following listing shows what the YAML of this ConfigMap looks like.

Listing 7.13 YAML definition of a config map created from a file

```
$ kubectl get configmap fortune-config -o yaml
apiVersion: v1
data:
  my-nginx-config.conf: |
    server {
      listen              80;
      server_name         www.kubia-example.com;

      gzip on;
      gzip_types text/plain application/xml;

      location / {
       root    /usr/share/nginx/html;
       index   index.html index.htm;
      }
    }
  sleep-interval: |
    25
kind: ConfigMap
...
```

The entry holding the
Nginx config file's
contents

The sleep-interval entry

NOTE   The pipeline character after the colon in the first line of both entries signals that a literal multi-line value follows.

The ConfigMap contains two entries, with keys corresponding to the actual names of the files they were created from. You'll now use the ConfigMap in both of your pod's containers.

USING THE CONFIGMAP'S ENTRIES IN A VOLUME

Creating a volume populated with the contents of a ConfigMap is as easy as creating a volume that references the ConfigMap by name and mounting the volume in a container. You already learned how to create volumes and mount them, so the only thing left to learn is how to initialize the volume with files created from a Config-Map's entries.

Nginx reads its config file from /etc/nginx/nginx.conf. The Nginx image already contains this file with default configuration options, which you don't want to override, so you don't want to replace this file as a whole. Luckily, the default config file automatically includes all .conf files in the /etc/nginx/conf.d/ subdirectory as well, so you should add your config file in there. Figure 7.9 shows what you want to achieve.

The pod descriptor is shown in listing 7.14 (the irrelevant parts are omitted, but you'll find the complete file in the code archive).

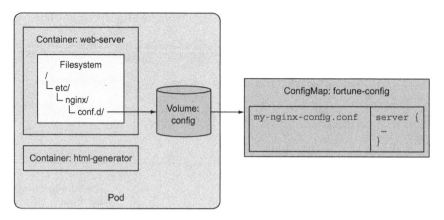

Figure 7.9   Passing ConfigMap entries to a pod as files in a volume

Listing 7.14   A pod with ConfigMap entries mounted as files: fortune-pod-configmap-volume.yaml

```
apiVersion: v1
kind: Pod
metadata:
  name: fortune-configmap-volume
spec:
  containers:
  - image: nginx:alpine
    name: web-server
    volumeMounts:
    ...
    - name: config
      mountPath: /etc/nginx/conf.d          ◁── You're mounting the
      readOnly: true                             configMap volume at
    ...                                          this location.
  volumes:
  ...
  - name: config
    configMap:                                   The volume refers to your
      name: fortune-config                       fortune-config ConfigMap.
  ...
```

This pod definition includes a volume, which references your `fortune-config` ConfigMap. You mount the volume into the /etc/nginx/conf.d directory to make Nginx use it.

VERIFYING NGINX IS USING THE MOUNTED CONFIG FILE

The web server should now be configured to compress the responses it sends. You can verify this by enabling port-forwarding from localhost:8080 to the pod's port 80 and checking the server's response with `curl`, as shown in the following listing.

Listing 7.15   Seeing if nginx responses have compression enabled

```
$ kubectl port-forward fortune-configmap-volume 8080:80 &
Forwarding from 127.0.0.1:8080 -> 80
Forwarding from [::1]:8080 -> 80
$ curl -H "Accept-Encoding: gzip" -I localhost:8080
HTTP/1.1 200 OK
Server: nginx/1.11.1
Date: Thu, 18 Aug 2016 11:52:57 GMT
Content-Type: text/html
Last-Modified: Thu, 18 Aug 2016 11:52:55 GMT
Connection: keep-alive
ETag: W/"57b5a197-37"
Content-Encoding: gzip
```
This shows the response is compressed.

EXAMINING THE MOUNTED CONFIGMAP VOLUME'S CONTENTS

The response shows you achieved what you wanted, but let's look at what's in the /etc/nginx/conf.d directory now:

```
$ kubectl exec fortune-configmap-volume -c web-server ls /etc/nginx/conf.d
my-nginx-config.conf
sleep-interval
```

Both entries from the ConfigMap have been added as files to the directory. The sleep-interval entry is also included, although it has no business being there, because it's only meant to be used by the fortuneloop container. You could create two different ConfigMaps and use one to configure the fortuneloop container and the other one to configure the web-server container. But somehow it feels wrong to use multiple ConfigMaps to configure containers of the same pod. After all, having containers in the same pod implies that the containers are closely related and should probably also be configured as a unit.

EXPOSING CERTAIN CONFIGMAP ENTRIES IN THE VOLUME

Luckily, you can populate a configMap volume with only part of the ConfigMap's entries—in your case, only the my-nginx-config.conf entry. This won't affect the fortuneloop container, because you're passing the sleep-interval entry to it through an environment variable and not through the volume.

To define which entries should be exposed as files in a configMap volume, use the volume's items attribute as shown in the following listing.

Listing 7.16   A pod with a specific ConfigMap entry mounted into a file directory: fortune-pod-configmap-volume-with-items.yaml

```
volumes:
- name: config
  configMap:
    name: fortune-config
    items:
    - key: my-nginx-config.conf
      path: gzip.conf
```
Selecting which entries to include in the volume by listing them

You want the entry under this key included.

The entry's value should be stored in this file.

When specifying individual entries, you need to set the filename for each individual entry, along with the entry's key. If you run the pod from the previous listing, the /etc/nginx/conf.d directory is kept nice and clean, because it only contains the gzip.conf file and nothing else.

UNDERSTANDING THAT MOUNTING A DIRECTORY HIDES EXISTING FILES IN THAT DIRECTORY

There's one important thing to discuss at this point. In both this and in your previous example, you mounted the volume as a directory, which means you've hidden any files that are stored in the /etc/nginx/conf.d directory in the container image itself.

This is generally what happens in Linux when you mount a filesystem into a nonempty directory. The directory then only contains the files from the mounted filesystem, whereas the original files in that directory are inaccessible for as long as the filesystem is mounted.

In your case, this has no terrible side effects, but imagine mounting a volume to the /etc directory, which usually contains many important files. This would most likely break the whole container, because all of the original files that should be in the /etc directory would no longer be there. If you need to add a file to a directory like /etc, you can't use this method at all.

MOUNTING INDIVIDUAL CONFIGMAP ENTRIES AS FILES WITHOUT HIDING OTHER FILES IN THE DIRECTORY

Naturally, you're now wondering how to add individual files from a ConfigMap into an existing directory without hiding existing files stored in it. An additional subPath property on the volumeMount allows you to mount either a single file or a single directory from the volume instead of mounting the whole volume. Perhaps this is easier to explain visually (see figure 7.10).

Say you have a configMap volume containing a myconfig.conf file, which you want to add to the /etc directory as someconfig.conf. You can use the subPath property to mount it there without affecting any other files in that directory. The relevant part of the pod definition is shown in the following listing.

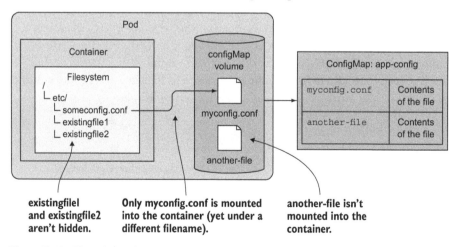

Figure 7.10   Mounting a single file from a volume

Listing 7.17　A pod with a specific config map entry mounted into a specific file

```
spec:
  containers:
  - image: some/image
    volumeMounts:
    - name: myvolume
      mountPath: /etc/someconfig.conf    <---
      subPath: myconfig.conf             <---
```

You're mounting into a file, not a directory.

Instead of mounting the whole volume, you're only mounting the myconfig.conf entry.

The subPath property can be used when mounting any kind of volume. Instead of mounting the whole volume, you can mount part of it. But this method of mounting individual files has a relatively big deficiency related to updating files. You'll learn more about this in the following section, but first, let's finish talking about the initial state of a configMap volume by saying a few words about file permissions.

SETTING THE FILE PERMISSIONS FOR FILES IN A CONFIGMAP VOLUME

By default, the permissions on all files in a configMap volume are set to 644 (-rw-r-r--). You can change this by setting the defaultMode property in the volume spec, as shown in the following listing.

Listing 7.18　Setting file permissions: fortune-pod-configmap-volume-defaultMode.yaml

```
volumes:
- name: config
  configMap:
    name: fortune-config
    defaultMode: "6600"    <---
```

This sets the permissions for all files to -rw-rw------.

Although ConfigMaps should be used for non-sensitive configuration data, you may want to make the file readable and writable only to the user and group the file is owned by, as the example in the previous listing shows.

7.4.7　Updating an app's config without having to restart the app

We've said that one of the drawbacks of using environment variables or command-line arguments as a configuration source is the inability to update them while the process is running. Using a ConfigMap and exposing it through a volume brings the ability to update the configuration without having to recreate the pod or even restart the container.

　When you update a ConfigMap, the files in all the volumes referencing it are updated. It's then up to the process to detect that they've been changed and reload them. But Kubernetes will most likely eventually also support sending a signal to the container after updating the files.

> **WARNING**　Be aware that as I'm writing this, it takes a surprisingly long time for the files to be updated after you update the ConfigMap (it can take up to one whole minute).

EDITING A CONFIGMAP

Let's see how you can change a ConfigMap and have the process running in the pod reload the files exposed in the `configMap` volume. You'll modify the Nginx config file from your previous example and make Nginx use the new config without restarting the pod. Try switching gzip compression off by editing the `fortune-config` Config-Map with `kubectl edit`:

```
$ kubectl edit configmap fortune-config
```

Once your editor opens, change the `gzip on` line to `gzip off`, save the file, and then close the editor. The ConfigMap is then updated, and soon afterward, the actual file in the volume is updated as well. You can confirm this by printing the contents of the file with `kubectl exec`:

```
$ kubectl exec fortune-configmap-volume -c web-server
⮡   cat /etc/nginx/conf.d/my-nginx-config.conf
```

If you don't see the update yet, wait a while and try again. It takes a while for the files to get updated. Eventually, you'll see the change in the config file, but you'll find this has no effect on Nginx, because it doesn't watch the files and reload them automatically.

SIGNALING NGINX TO RELOAD THE CONFIG

Nginx will continue to compress its responses until you tell it to reload its config files, which you can do with the following command:

```
$ kubectl exec fortune-configmap-volume -c web-server -- nginx -s reload
```

Now, if you try hitting the server again with `curl`, you should see the response is no longer compressed (it no longer contains the `Content-Encoding: gzip` header). You've effectively changed the app's config without having to restart the container or recreate the pod.

UNDERSTANDING HOW THE FILES ARE UPDATED ATOMICALLY

You may wonder what happens if an app can detect config file changes on its own and reloads them before Kubernetes has finished updating all the files in the `configMap` volume. Luckily, this can't happen, because all the files are updated atomically, which means all updates occur at once. Kubernetes achieves this by using symbolic links. If you list all the files in the mounted `configMap` volume, you'll see something like the following listing.

Listing 7.19   Files in a mounted `configMap` volume

```
$ kubectl exec -it fortune-configmap-volume -c web-server -- ls -lA
⮡   /etc/nginx/conf.d
total 4
drwxr-xr-x  ... 12:15 ..4984_09_04_12_15_06.865837643
```

```
lrwxrwxrwx  ... 12:15 ..data -> ..4984_09_04_12_15_06.865837643
lrwxrwxrwx  ... 12:15 my-nginx-config.conf -> ..data/my-nginx-config.conf
lrwxrwxrwx  ... 12:15 sleep-interval -> ..data/sleep-interval
```

As you can see, the files in the mounted `configMap` volume are symbolic links pointing to files in the `..data` dir. The `..data` dir is also a symbolic link pointing to a directory called `..4984_09_04_something`. When the ConfigMap is updated, Kubernetes creates a new directory like this, writes all the files to it, and then re-links the `..data` symbolic link to the new directory, effectively changing all files at once.

UNDERSTANDING THAT FILES MOUNTED INTO EXISTING DIRECTORIES DON'T GET UPDATED

One big caveat relates to updating ConfigMap-backed volumes. If you've mounted a single file in the container instead of the whole volume, the file will not be updated! At least, this is true at the time of writing this chapter.

For now, if you need to add an individual file and have it updated when you update its source ConfigMap, one workaround is to mount the whole volume into a different directory and then create a symbolic link pointing to the file in question. The symlink can either be created in the container image itself, or you could create the symlink when the container starts.

UNDERSTANDING THE CONSEQUENCES OF UPDATING A CONFIGMAP

One of the most important features of containers is their immutability, which allows us to be certain that no differences exist between multiple running containers created from the same image, so is it wrong to bypass this immutability by modifying a Config-Map used by running containers?

The main problem occurs when the app doesn't support reloading its configuration. This results in different running instances being configured differently—those pods that are created after the ConfigMap is changed will use the new config, whereas the old pods will still use the old one. And this isn't limited to new pods. If a pod's container is restarted (for whatever reason), the new process will also see the new config. Therefore, if the app doesn't reload its config automatically, modifying an existing ConfigMap (while pods are using it) may not be a good idea.

If the app does support reloading, modifying the ConfigMap usually isn't such a big deal, but you do need to be aware that because files in the ConfigMap volumes aren't updated synchronously across all running instances, the files in individual pods may be out of sync for up to a whole minute.

7.5 *Using Secrets to pass sensitive data to containers*

All the information you've passed to your containers so far is regular, non-sensitive configuration data that doesn't need to be kept secure. But as we mentioned at the start of the chapter, the config usually also includes sensitive information, such as credentials and private encryption keys, which need to be kept secure.

7.5.1 *Introducing Secrets*

To store and distribute such information, Kubernetes provides a separate object called a Secret. Secrets are much like ConfigMaps—they're also maps that hold key-value pairs. They can be used the same way as a ConfigMap. You can

- Pass Secret entries to the container as environment variables
- Expose Secret entries as files in a volume

Kubernetes helps keep your Secrets safe by making sure each Secret is only distributed to the nodes that run the pods that need access to the Secret. Also, on the nodes themselves, Secrets are always stored in memory and never written to physical storage, which would require wiping the disks after deleting the Secrets from them.

On the master node itself (more specifically in etcd), Secrets used to be stored in unencrypted form, which meant the master node needs to be secured to keep the sensitive data stored in Secrets secure. This didn't only include keeping the etcd storage secure, but also preventing unauthorized users from using the API server, because anyone who can create pods can mount the Secret into the pod and gain access to the sensitive data through it. From Kubernetes version 1.7, etcd stores Secrets in encrypted form, making the system much more secure. Because of this, it's imperative you properly choose when to use a Secret or a ConfigMap. Choosing between them is simple:

- Use a ConfigMap to store non-sensitive, plain configuration data.
- Use a Secret to store any data that is sensitive in nature and needs to be kept under key. If a config file includes both sensitive and not-sensitive data, you should store the file in a Secret.

You already used Secrets in chapter 5, when you created a Secret to hold the TLS certificate needed for the Ingress resource. Now you'll explore Secrets in more detail.

7.5.2 *Introducing the default token Secret*

You'll start learning about Secrets by examining a Secret that's mounted into every container you run. You may have noticed it when using kubectl describe on a pod. The command's output has always contained something like this:

```
Volumes:
  default-token-cfee9:
    Type:       Secret (a volume populated by a Secret)
    SecretName: default-token-cfee9
```

Every pod has a secret volume attached to it automatically. The volume in the previous kubectl describe output refers to a Secret called default-token-cfee9. Because Secrets are resources, you can list them with kubectl get secrets and find the default-token Secret in that list. Let's see:

```
$ kubectl get secrets
NAME                  TYPE                                  DATA   AGE
default-token-cfee9   kubernetes.io/service-account-token   3      39d
```

You can also use `kubectl describe` to learn a bit more about it, as shown in the following listing.

Listing 7.20 Describing a Secret

```
$ kubectl describe secrets
Name:          default-token-cfee9
Namespace:     default
Labels:        <none>
Annotations:   kubernetes.io/service-account.name=default
               kubernetes.io/service-account.uid=cc04bb39-b53f-42010af00237
Type:          kubernetes.io/service-account-token

Data
====
ca.crt:        1139 bytes
namespace:     7 bytes
token:         eyJhbGciOiJSUzI1NiIsInR5cCI6IkpXVCJ9...
```

> **This secret contains three entries.**

You can see that the Secret contains three entries—`ca.crt`, `namespace`, and `token`—which represent everything you need to securely talk to the Kubernetes API server from within your pods, should you need to do that. Although ideally you want your application to be completely Kubernetes-agnostic, when there's no alternative other than to talk to Kubernetes directly, you'll use the files provided through this `secret` volume.

The `kubectl describe pod` command shows where the secret volume is mounted:

```
Mounts:
  /var/run/secrets/kubernetes.io/serviceaccount from default-token-cfee9
```

> **NOTE** By default, the `default-token` Secret is mounted into every container, but you can disable that in each pod by setting the `automountService-AccountToken` field in the pod spec to `false` or by setting it to `false` on the service account the pod is using. (You'll learn about service accounts later in the book.)

To help you visualize where and how the default token Secret is mounted, see figure 7.11.

We've said Secrets are like ConfigMaps, so because this Secret contains three entries, you can expect to see three files in the directory the `secret` volume is mounted into. You can check this easily with `kubectl exec`:

```
$ kubectl exec mypod ls /var/run/secrets/kubernetes.io/serviceaccount/
ca.crt
namespace
token
```

You'll see how your app can use these files to access the API server in the next chapter.

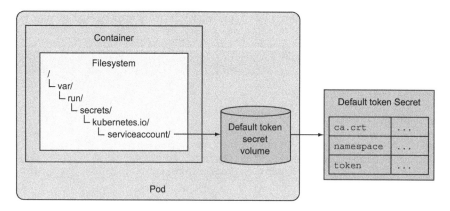

Figure 7.11 The `default-token` **Secret is created automatically and a corresponding volume is mounted in each pod automatically.**

7.5.3   Creating a Secret

Now, you'll create your own little Secret. You'll improve your fortune-serving Nginx container by configuring it to also serve HTTPS traffic. For this, you need to create a certificate and a private key. The private key needs to be kept secure, so you'll put it and the certificate into a Secret.

First, generate the certificate and private key files (do this on your local machine). You can also use the files in the book's code archive (the cert and key files are in the `fortune-https` directory):

```
$ openssl genrsa -out https.key 2048
$ openssl req -new -x509 -key https.key -out https.cert -days 3650 -subj
    /CN=www.kubia-example.com
```

Now, to help better demonstrate a few things about Secrets, create an additional dummy file called foo and make it contain the string `bar`. You'll understand why you need to do this in a moment or two:

```
$ echo bar > foo
```

Now you can use `kubectl create secret` to create a Secret from the three files:

```
$ kubectl create secret generic fortune-https --from-file=https.key
    --from-file=https.cert --from-file=foo
secret "fortune-https" created
```

This isn't very different from creating ConfigMaps. In this case, you're creating a `generic` Secret called `fortune-https` and including two entries in it (https.key with the contents of the https.key file and likewise for the https.cert key/file). As you learned earlier, you could also include the whole directory with `--from-file=fortune-https` instead of specifying each file individually.

NOTE You're creating a generic Secret, but you could also have created a `tls` Secret with the `kubectl create secret tls` command, as you did in chapter 5. This would create the Secret with different entry names, though.

7.5.4 *Comparing ConfigMaps and Secrets*

Secrets and ConfigMaps have a pretty big difference. This is what drove Kubernetes developers to create ConfigMaps after Kubernetes had already supported Secrets for a while. The following listing shows the YAML of the Secret you created.

Listing 7.21   A Secret's YAML definition

```
$ kubectl get secret fortune-https -o yaml
apiVersion: v1
data:
  foo: YmFyCg==
  https.cert: LS0tLS1CRUdJTiBDRVJUSUZJQ0FURS0tLS0tCk1JSURRekNDNNDQ...
  https.key: LS0tLS1CRUdJTiBSU0EgUFJJVkFURSBLRVktLS0tLQpNSUlFcE...
kind: Secret
...
```

Now compare this to the YAML of the ConfigMap you created earlier, which is shown in the following listing.

Listing 7.22   A ConfigMap's YAML definition

```
$ kubectl get configmap fortune-config -o yaml
apiVersion: v1
data:
  my-nginx-config.conf: |
    server {
      ...
    }
  sleep-interval: |
    25
kind: ConfigMap
...
```

Notice the difference? The contents of a Secret's entries are shown as Base64-encoded strings, whereas those of a ConfigMap are shown in clear text. This initially made working with Secrets in YAML and JSON manifests a bit more painful, because you had to encode and decode them when setting and reading their entries.

USING SECRETS FOR BINARY DATA

The reason for using Base64 encoding is simple. A Secret's entries can contain binary values, not only plain-text. Base64 encoding allows you to include the binary data in YAML or JSON, which are both plain-text formats.

TIP You can use Secrets even for non-sensitive binary data, but be aware that the maximum size of a Secret is limited to 1MB.

INTRODUCING THE STRINGDATA FIELD

Because not all sensitive data is in binary form, Kubernetes also allows setting a Secret's values through the `stringData` field. The following listing shows how it's used.

Listing 7.23   Adding plain text entries to a `Secret` using the `stringData` field

```
kind: Secret                    The stringData can be used
apiVersion: v1                  for non-binary Secret data.
stringData:           ◁──┘
  foo: plain text          ◁──┘  See, "plain text" is not Base64-encoded.
data:
  https.cert: LS0tLS1CRUdJTiBDRVJUSUZJQ0FURS0tLS0tCk1JSURCekNDQQ...
  https.key: LS0tLS1CRUdJTiBSU0EgUFJJVkFURSBLRVktLS0tLQpNSUlFcE...
```

The `stringData` field is write-only (note: write-only, not read-only). It can only be used to set values. When you retrieve the Secret's YAML with `kubectl get -o yaml`, the `stringData` field will not be shown. Instead, all entries you specified in the `string-Data` field (such as the `foo` entry in the previous example) will be shown under `data` and will be Base64-encoded like all the other entries.

READING A SECRET'S ENTRY IN A POD

When you expose the Secret to a container through a `secret` volume, the value of the Secret entry is decoded and written to the file in its actual form (regardless if it's plain text or binary). The same is also true when exposing the Secret entry through an environment variable. In both cases, the app doesn't need to decode it, but can read the file's contents or look up the environment variable value and use it directly.

7.5.5   *Using the Secret in a pod*

With your fortune-https Secret containing both the cert and key files, all you need to do now is configure Nginx to use them.

MODIFYING THE FORTUNE-CONFIG CONFIGMAP TO ENABLE HTTPS

For this, you need to modify the config file again by editing the ConfigMap:

```
$ kubectl edit configmap fortune-config
```

After the text editor opens, modify the part that defines the contents of the `my-nginx-config.conf` entry so it looks like the following listing.

Listing 7.24   Modifying the `fortune-config` ConfigMap's data

```
...
data:
  my-nginx-config.conf: |
    server {
      listen              80;
      listen              443 ssl;
      server_name         www.kubia-example.com;
```

```
    ssl_certificate       certs/https.cert;
    ssl_certificate_key certs/https.key;
    ssl_protocols         TLSv1 TLSv1.1 TLSv1.2;
    ssl_ciphers           HIGH:!aNULL:!MD5;

    location / {
      root    /usr/share/nginx/html;
      index   index.html index.htm;
    }
  }
sleep-interval: |
...
```

The paths are relative to /etc/nginx.

This configures the server to read the certificate and key files from /etc/nginx/certs, so you'll need to mount the secret volume there.

MOUNTING THE FORTUNE-HTTPS SECRET IN A POD

Next, you'll create a new fortune-https pod and mount the secret volume holding the certificate and key into the proper location in the web-server container, as shown in the following listing.

Listing 7.25 YAML definition of the `fortune-https` pod: fortune-pod-https.yaml

```
apiVersion: v1
kind: Pod
metadata:
  name: fortune-https
spec:
  containers:
  - image: luksa/fortune:env
    name: html-generator
    env:
    - name: INTERVAL
      valueFrom:
        configMapKeyRef:
          name: fortune-config
          key: sleep-interval
    volumeMounts:
    - name: html
      mountPath: /var/htdocs
  - image: nginx:alpine
    name: web-server
    volumeMounts:
    - name: html
      mountPath: /usr/share/nginx/html
      readOnly: true
    - name: config
      mountPath: /etc/nginx/conf.d
      readOnly: true
    - name: certs
      mountPath: /etc/nginx/certs/
      readOnly: true
    ports:
    - containerPort: 80
```

You configured Nginx to read the cert and key file from /etc/nginx/certs, so you need to mount the Secret volume there.

```
      - containerPort: 443
volumes:
- name: html
  emptyDir: {}
- name: config
  configMap:
    name: fortune-config
    items:
    - key: my-nginx-config.conf
      path: https.conf
- name: certs
  secret:
    secretName: fortune-https
```

> **You define the secret volume here, referring to the fortune-https Secret.**

Much is going on in this pod descriptor, so let me help you visualize it. Figure 7.12 shows the components defined in the YAML. The `default-token` Secret, volume, and volume mount, which aren't part of the YAML, but are added to your pod automatically, aren't shown in the figure.

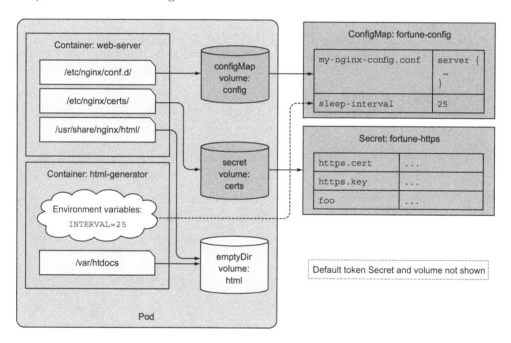

Figure 7.12   Combining a ConfigMap and a Secret to run your fortune-https pod

NOTE   Like `configMap` volumes, `secret` volumes also support specifying file permissions for the files exposed in the volume through the `defaultMode` property.

TESTING WHETHER NGINX IS USING THE CERT AND KEY FROM THE SECRET

Once the pod is running, you can see if it's serving HTTPS traffic by opening a port-forward tunnel to the pod's port 443 and using it to send a request to the server with `curl`:

```
$ kubectl port-forward fortune-https 8443:443 &
Forwarding from 127.0.0.1:8443 -> 443
Forwarding from [::1]:8443 -> 443
$ curl https://localhost:8443 -k
```

If you configured the server properly, you should get a response. You can check the server's certificate to see if it matches the one you generated earlier. This can also be done with `curl` by turning on verbose logging using the `-v` option, as shown in the following listing.

Listing 7.26   Displaying the server certificate sent by Nginx

```
$ curl https://localhost:8443 -k -v
* About to connect() to localhost port 8443 (#0)
*   Trying ::1...
* Connected to localhost (::1) port 8443 (#0)
* Initializing NSS with certpath: sql:/etc/pki/nssdb
* skipping SSL peer certificate verification
* SSL connection using TLS_ECDHE_RSA_WITH_AES_256_GCM_SHA384
* Server certificate:
*    subject: CN=www.kubia-example.com          The certificate
*    start date: aug 16 18:43:13 2016 GMT        matches the one you
*    expire date: aug 14 18:43:13 2026 GMT       created and stored
*    common name: www.kubia-example.com          in the Secret.
*    issuer: CN=www.kubia-example.com
```

UNDERSTANDING SECRET VOLUMES ARE STORED IN MEMORY

You successfully delivered your certificate and private key to your container by mounting a `secret` volume in its directory tree at /etc/nginx/certs. The `secret` volume uses an in-memory filesystem (tmpfs) for the Secret files. You can see this if you list mounts in the container:

```
$ kubectl exec fortune-https -c web-server -- mount | grep certs
tmpfs on /etc/nginx/certs type tmpfs (ro,relatime)
```

Because tmpfs is used, the sensitive data stored in the Secret is never written to disk, where it could be compromised.

EXPOSING A SECRET'S ENTRIES THROUGH ENVIRONMENT VARIABLES

Instead of using a volume, you could also have exposed individual entries from the `secret` as environment variables, the way you did with the `sleep-interval` entry from the ConfigMap. For example, if you wanted to expose the `foo` key from your Secret as environment variable `FOO_SECRET`, you'd add the snippet from the following listing to the container definition.

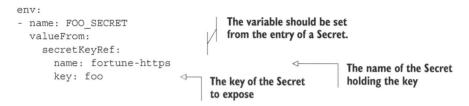

Listing 7.27   Exposing a Secret's entry as an environment variable

```
env:
- name: FOO_SECRET
  valueFrom:                          The variable should be set
    secretKeyRef:                     from the entry of a Secret.
      name: fortune-https                             The name of the Secret
      key: foo                 The key of the Secret  holding the key
                               to expose
```

This is almost exactly like when you set the INTERVAL environment variable, except that this time you're referring to a Secret by using `secretKeyRef` instead of `config-MapKeyRef`, which is used to refer to a ConfigMap.

Even though Kubernetes enables you to expose Secrets through environment variables, it may not be the best idea to use this feature. Applications usually dump environment variables in error reports or even write them to the application log at startup, which may unintentionally expose them. Additionally, child processes inherit all the environment variables of the parent process, so if your app runs a third-party binary, you have no way of knowing what happens with your secret data.

> **TIP**   Think twice before using environment variables to pass your Secrets to your container, because they may get exposed inadvertently. To be safe, always use `secret` volumes for exposing Secrets.

7.5.6   *Understanding image pull Secrets*

You've learned how to pass Secrets to your applications and use the data they contain. But sometimes Kubernetes itself requires you to pass credentials to it—for example, when you'd like to use images from a private container image registry. This is also done through Secrets.

Up to now all your container images have been stored on public image registries, which don't require any special credentials to pull images from them. But most organizations don't want their images to be available to everyone and thus use a private image registry. When deploying a pod, whose container images reside in a private registry, Kubernetes needs to know the credentials required to pull the image. Let's see how to do that.

USING A PRIVATE IMAGE REPOSITORY ON DOCKER HUB

Docker Hub, in addition to public image repositories, also allows you to create private repositories. You can mark a repository as private by logging in at http://hub.docker .com with your web browser, finding the repository and checking a checkbox.

To run a pod, which uses an image from the private repository, you need to do two things:

- Create a Secret holding the credentials for the Docker registry.
- Reference that Secret in the `imagePullSecrets` field of the pod manifest.

CREATING A SECRET FOR AUTHENTICATING WITH A DOCKER REGISTRY

Creating a Secret holding the credentials for authenticating with a Docker registry isn't that different from creating the generic Secret you created in section 7.5.3. You use the same `kubectl create secret` command, but with a different type and options:

```
$ kubectl create secret docker-registry mydockerhubsecret \
  --docker-username=myusername --docker-password=mypassword \
  --docker-email=my.email@provider.com
```

Rather than create a `generic` secret, you're creating a `docker-registry` Secret called `mydockerhubsecret`. You're specifying your Docker Hub username, password, and email. If you inspect the contents of the newly created Secret with `kubectl describe`, you'll see that it includes a single entry called `.dockercfg`. This is equivalent to the .dockercfg file in your home directory, which is created by Docker when you run the `docker login` command.

USING THE DOCKER-REGISTRY SECRET IN A POD DEFINITION

To have Kubernetes use the Secret when pulling images from your private Docker Hub repository, all you need to do is specify the Secret's name in the pod spec, as shown in the following listing.

Listing 7.28   A pod definition using an image pull Secret: pod-with-private-image.yaml

```
apiVersion: v1
kind: Pod
metadata:
  name: private-pod
spec:
  imagePullSecrets:            This enables pulling images
  - name: mydockerhubsecret    from a private image registry.
  containers:
  - image: username/private:tag
    name: main
```

In the pod definition in the previous listing, you're specifying the `mydockerhubsecret` Secret as one of the `imagePullSecrets`. I suggest you try this out yourself, because it's likely you'll deal with private container images soon.

NOT HAVING TO SPECIFY IMAGE PULL SECRETS ON EVERY POD

Given that people usually run many different pods in their systems, it makes you wonder if you need to add the same image pull Secrets to every pod. Luckily, that's not the case. In chapter 12 you'll learn how image pull Secrets can be added to all your pods automatically if you add the Secrets to a ServiceAccount.

7.6   Summary

This wraps up this chapter on how to pass configuration data to containers. You've learned how to

- Override the default command defined in a container image in the pod definition
- Pass command-line arguments to the main container process
- Set environment variables for a container
- Decouple configuration from a pod specification and put it into a ConfigMap
- Store sensitive data in a Secret and deliver it securely to containers
- Create a `docker-registry` Secret and use it to pull images from a private image registry

In the next chapter, you'll learn how to pass pod and container metadata to applications running inside them. You'll also see how the default token Secret, which we learned about in this chapter, is used to talk to the API server from within a pod.

Accessing pod metadata and other resources from applications

This chapter covers

- Using the Downward API to pass information into containers
- Exploring the Kubernetes REST API
- Leaving authentication and server verification to `kubectl proxy`
- Accessing the API server from within a container
- Understanding the ambassador container pattern
- Using Kubernetes client libraries

Applications often need information about the environment they're running in, including details about themselves and that of other components in the cluster. You've already seen how Kubernetes enables service discovery through environment variables or DNS, but what about other information? In this chapter, you'll see how certain pod and container metadata can be passed to the container and how easy it is for an app running inside a container to talk to the Kubernetes API server to get information about the resources deployed in the cluster and even how to create or modify those resources.

8.1   Passing metadata through the Downward API

In the previous chapter you saw how you can pass configuration data to your applications through environment variables or through configMap and secret volumes. This works well for data that you set yourself and that is known before the pod is scheduled to a node and run there. But what about data that isn't known up until that point—such as the pod's IP, the host node's name, or even the pod's own name (when the name is generated; for example, when the pod is created by a ReplicaSet or similar controller)? And what about data that's already specified elsewhere, such as a pod's labels and annotations? You don't want to repeat the same information in multiple places.

Both these problems are solved by the Kubernetes Downward API. It allows you to pass metadata about the pod and its environment through environment variables or files (in a downwardAPI volume). Don't be confused by the name. The Downward API isn't like a REST endpoint that your app needs to hit so it can get the data. It's a way of having environment variables or files populated with values from the pod's specification or status, as shown in figure 8.1.

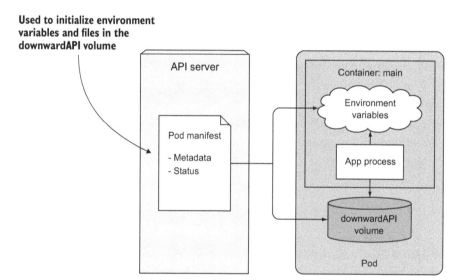

Figure 8.1   The Downward API exposes pod metadata through environment variables or files.

8.1.1   Understanding the available metadata

The Downward API enables you to expose the pod's own metadata to the processes running inside that pod. Currently, it allows you to pass the following information to your containers:

- The pod's name
- The pod's IP address

- The namespace the pod belongs to
- The name of the node the pod is running on
- The name of the service account the pod is running under
- The CPU and memory requests for each container
- The CPU and memory limits for each container
- The pod's labels
- The pod's annotations

Most of the items in the list shouldn't require further explanation, except perhaps the service account and CPU/memory requests and limits, which we haven't introduced yet. We'll cover service accounts in detail in chapter 12. For now, all you need to know is that a service account is the account that the pod authenticates as when talking to the API server. CPU and memory requests and limits are explained in chapter 14. They're the amount of CPU and memory guaranteed to a container and the maximum amount it can get.

Most items in the list can be passed to containers either through environment variables or through a downwardAPI volume, but labels and annotations can only be exposed through the volume. Part of the data can be acquired by other means (for example, from the operating system directly), but the Downward API provides a simpler alternative.

Let's look at an example to pass metadata to your containerized process.

8.1.2   *Exposing metadata through environment variables*

First, let's look at how you can pass the pod's and container's metadata to the container through environment variables. You'll create a simple single-container pod from the following listing's manifest.

> **Listing 8.1   Downward API used in environment variables: downward-api-env.yaml**

```yaml
apiVersion: v1
kind: Pod
metadata:
  name: downward
spec:
  containers:
  - name: main
    image: busybox
    command: ["sleep", "9999999"]
    resources:
      requests:
        cpu: 15m
        memory: 100Ki
      limits:
        cpu: 100m
        memory: 4Mi
    env:
    - name: POD_NAME
```

```
      valueFrom:
        fieldRef:
          fieldPath: metadata.name
  - name: POD_NAMESPACE
    valueFrom:
      fieldRef:
        fieldPath: metadata.namespace
  - name: POD_IP
    valueFrom:
      fieldRef:
        fieldPath: status.podIP
  - name: NODE_NAME
    valueFrom:
      fieldRef:
        fieldPath: spec.nodeName
  - name: SERVICE_ACCOUNT
    valueFrom:
      fieldRef:
        fieldPath: spec.serviceAccountName
  - name: CONTAINER_CPU_REQUEST_MILLICORES
    valueFrom:
      resourceFieldRef:
        resource: requests.cpu
        divisor: 1m
  - name: CONTAINER_MEMORY_LIMIT_KIBIBYTES
    valueFrom:
      resourceFieldRef:
        resource: limits.memory
        divisor: 1Ki
```

> **Instead of specifying an absolute value, you're referencing the metadata.name field from the pod manifest.**

> **A container's CPU and memory requests and limits are referenced by using resourceFieldRef instead of fieldRef.**

> **For resource fields, you define a divisor to get the value in the unit you need.**

When your process runs, it can look up all the environment variables you defined in the pod spec. Figure 8.2 shows the environment variables and the sources of their values. The pod's name, IP, and namespace will be exposed through the POD_NAME, POD_IP, and POD_NAMESPACE environment variables, respectively. The name of the node the container is running on will be exposed through the NODE_NAME variable. The name of the service account is made available through the SERVICE_ACCOUNT environment variable. You're also creating two environment variables that will hold the amount of CPU requested for this container and the maximum amount of memory the container is allowed to consume.

For environment variables exposing resource limits or requests, you specify a divisor. The actual value of the limit or the request will be divided by the divisor and the result exposed through the environment variable. In the previous example, you're setting the divisor for CPU requests to 1m (one milli-core, or one one-thousandth of a CPU core). Because you've set the CPU request to 15m, the environment variable CONTAINER_CPU_REQUEST_MILLICORES will be set to 15. Likewise, you set the memory limit to 4Mi (4 mebibytes) and the divisor to 1Ki (1 Kibibyte), so the CONTAINER_MEMORY _LIMIT_KIBIBYTES environment variable will be set to 4096.

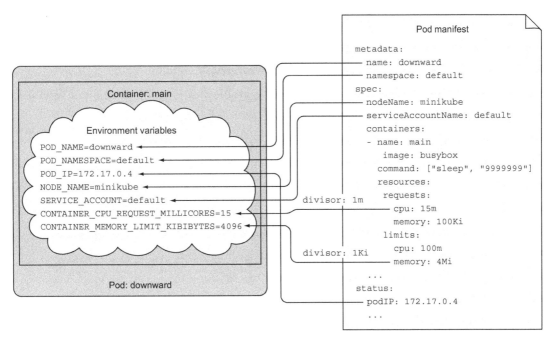

Figure 8.2 Pod metadata and attributes can be exposed to the pod through environment variables.

The divisor for CPU limits and requests can be either 1, which means one whole core, or 1m, which is one millicore. The divisor for memory limits/requests can be 1 (byte), 1k (kilobyte) or 1Ki (kibibyte), 1M (megabyte) or 1Mi (mebibyte), and so on.

After creating the pod, you can use kubectl exec to see all these environment variables in your container, as shown in the following listing.

Listing 8.2 Environment variables in the downward pod

```
$ kubectl exec downward env
PATH=/usr/local/sbin:/usr/local/bin:/usr/sbin:/usr/bin:/sbin:/bin
HOSTNAME=downward
CONTAINER_MEMORY_LIMIT_KIBIBYTES=4096
POD_NAME=downward
POD_NAMESPACE=default
POD_IP=10.0.0.10
NODE_NAME=gke-kubia-default-pool-32a2cac8-sgl7
SERVICE_ACCOUNT=default
CONTAINER_CPU_REQUEST_MILLICORES=15
KUBERNETES_SERVICE_HOST=10.3.240.1
KUBERNETES_SERVICE_PORT=443
...
```

All processes running inside the container can read those variables and use them however they need.

8.1.3 *Passing metadata through files in a downwardAPI volume*

If you prefer to expose the metadata through files instead of environment variables, you can define a downwardAPI volume and mount it into your container. You must use a downwardAPI volume for exposing the pod's labels or its annotations, because neither can be exposed through environment variables. We'll discuss why later.

As with environment variables, you need to specify each metadata field explicitly if you want to have it exposed to the process. Let's see how to modify the previous example to use a volume instead of environment variables, as shown in the following listing.

Listing 8.3 Pod with a `downwardAPI` volume: downward-api-volume.yaml

```
apiVersion: v1
kind: Pod
metadata:
  name: downward
  labels:
    foo: bar
  annotations:
    key1: value1
    key2: |
      multi
      line
      value
spec:
  containers:
  - name: main
    image: busybox
    command: ["sleep", "9999999"]
    resources:
      requests:
        cpu: 15m
        memory: 100Ki
      limits:
        cpu: 100m
        memory: 4Mi
    volumeMounts:
    - name: downward
      mountPath: /etc/downward
  volumes:
  - name: downward
    downwardAPI:
      items:
      - path: "podName"
        fieldRef:
          fieldPath: metadata.name
      - path: "podNamespace"
        fieldRef:
          fieldPath: metadata.namespace
```

These labels and annotations will be exposed through the downwardAPI volume.

You're mounting the downward volume under /etc/downward.

You're defining a downwardAPI volume with the name downward.

The pod's name (from the metadata.name field in the manifest) will be written to the podName file.

```
          - path: "labels"
            fieldRef:
               fieldPath: metadata.labels
          - path: "annotations"
            fieldRef:
               fieldPath: metadata.annotations
          - path: "containerCpuRequestMilliCores"
            resourceFieldRef:
               containerName: main
               resource: requests.cpu
               divisor: 1m
          - path: "containerMemoryLimitBytes"
            resourceFieldRef:
               containerName: main
               resource: limits.memory
               divisor: 1
```

**The pod's labels will be written
to the /etc/downward/labels file.**

**The pod's annotations will be
written to the /etc/downward/
annotations file.**

Instead of passing the metadata through environment variables, you're defining a volume called `downward` and mounting it in your container under /etc/downward. The files this volume will contain are configured under the `downwardAPI.items` attribute in the volume specification.

Each item specifies the `path` (the filename) where the metadata should be written to and references either a pod-level field or a container resource field whose value you want stored in the file (see figure 8.3).

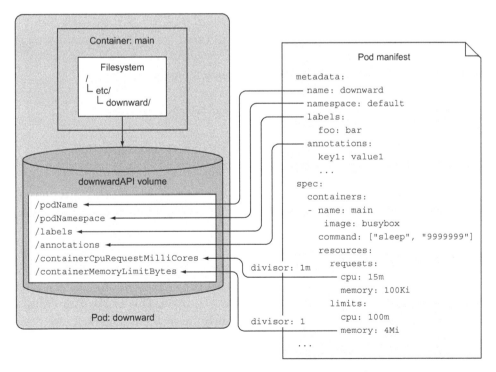

Figure 8.3   Using a `downwardAPI` volume to pass metadata to the container

Delete the previous pod and create a new one from the manifest in the previous listing. Then look at the contents of the mounted downwardAPI volume directory. You
mounted the volume under /etc/downward/, so list the files in there, as shown in the
following listing.

Listing 8.4   Files in the downwardAPI volume

```
$ kubectl exec downward ls -1L /etc/downward
-rw-r--r--   1 root    root    134 May 25 10:23 annotations
-rw-r--r--   1 root    root      2 May 25 10:23 containerCpuRequestMilliCores
-rw-r--r--   1 root    root      7 May 25 10:23 containerMemoryLimitBytes
-rw-r--r--   1 root    root      9 May 25 10:23 labels
-rw-r--r--   1 root    root      8 May 25 10:23 podName
-rw-r--r--   1 root    root      7 May 25 10:23 podNamespace
```

> **NOTE**   As with the configMap and secret volumes, you can change the file
> permissions through the downwardAPI volume's defaultMode property in the
> pod spec.

Each file corresponds to an item in the volume's definition. The contents of files,
which correspond to the same metadata fields as in the previous example, are the
same as the values of environment variables you used before, so we won't show them
here. But because you couldn't expose labels and annotations through environment
variables before, examine the following listing for the contents of the two files you
exposed them in.

Listing 8.5   Displaying labels and annotations in the downwardAPI volume

```
$ kubectl exec downward cat /etc/downward/labels
foo="bar"

$ kubectl exec downward cat /etc/downward/annotations
key1="value1"
key2="multi\nline\nvalue\n"
kubernetes.io/config.seen="2016-11-28T14:27:45.664924282Z"
kubernetes.io/config.source="api"
```

As you can see, each label/annotation is written in the key=value format on a separate line. Multi-line values are written to a single line with newline characters denoted
with \n.

UPDATING LABELS AND ANNOTATIONS

You may remember that labels and annotations can be modified while a pod is running. As you might expect, when they change, Kubernetes updates the files holding
them, allowing the pod to always see up-to-date data. This also explains why labels and
annotations can't be exposed through environment variables. Because environment
variable values can't be updated afterward, if the labels or annotations of a pod were
exposed through environment variables, there's no way to expose the new values after
they're modified.

REFERRING TO CONTAINER-LEVEL METADATA IN THE VOLUME SPECIFICATION

Before we wrap up this section, we need to point out one thing. When exposing container-level metadata, such as a container's resource limit or requests (done using `resourceFieldRef`), you need to specify the name of the container whose resource field you're referencing, as shown in the following listing.

Listing 8.6 Referring to container-level metadata in a `downwardAPI` volume

```
spec:
  volumes:
  - name: downward
    downwardAPI:
      items:
      - path: "containerCpuRequestMilliCores"
        resourceFieldRef:                          Container name
          containerName: main          ◁─┘        must be specified
          resource: requests.cpu
          divisor: 1m
```

The reason for this becomes obvious if you consider that volumes are defined at the pod level, not at the container level. When referring to a container's resource field inside a volume specification, you need to explicitly specify the name of the container you're referring to. This is true even for single-container pods.

Using volumes to expose a container's resource requests and/or limits is slightly more complicated than using environment variables, but the benefit is that it allows you to pass one container's resource fields to a different container if needed (but both containers need to be in the same pod). With environment variables, a container can only be passed its own resource limits and requests.

UNDERSTANDING WHEN TO USE THE DOWNWARD API

As you've seen, using the Downward API isn't complicated. It allows you to keep the application Kubernetes-agnostic. This is especially useful when you're dealing with an existing application that expects certain data in environment variables. The Downward API allows you to expose the data to the application without having to rewrite the application or wrap it in a shell script, which collects the data and then exposes it through environment variables.

But the metadata available through the Downward API is fairly limited. If you need more, you'll need to obtain it from the Kubernetes API server directly. You'll learn how to do that next.

8.2   *Talking to the Kubernetes API server*

We've seen how the Downward API provides a simple way to pass certain pod and container metadata to the process running inside them. It only exposes the pod's own metadata and a subset of all of the pod's data. But sometimes your app will need to know more about other pods and even other resources defined in your cluster. The Downward API doesn't help in those cases.

As you've seen throughout the book, information about services and pods can be obtained by looking at the service-related environment variables or through DNS. But when the app needs data about other resources or when it requires access to the most up-to-date information as possible, it needs to talk to the API server directly (as shown in figure 8.4).

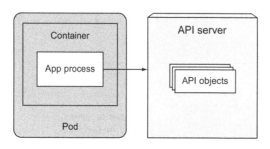

Figure 8.4   Talking to the API server from inside a pod to get information about other API objects

Before you see how apps within pods can talk to the Kubernetes API server, let's first explore the server's REST endpoints from your local machine, so you can see what talking to the API server looks like.

8.2.1   Exploring the Kubernetes REST API

You've learned about different Kubernetes resource types. But if you're planning on developing apps that talk to the Kubernetes API, you'll want to know the API first.

To do that, you can try hitting the API server directly. You can get its URL by running kubectl cluster-info:

```
$ kubectl cluster-info
Kubernetes master is running at https://192.168.99.100:8443
```

Because the server uses HTTPS and requires authentication, it's not simple to talk to it directly. You can try accessing it with curl and using curl's --insecure (or -k) option to skip the server certificate check, but that doesn't get you far:

```
$ curl https://192.168.99.100:8443 -k
Unauthorized
```

Luckily, rather than dealing with authentication yourself, you can talk to the server through a proxy by running the kubectl proxy command.

ACCESSING THE API SERVER THROUGH KUBECTL PROXY

The kubectl proxy command runs a proxy server that accepts HTTP connections on your local machine and proxies them to the API server while taking care of authentication, so you don't need to pass the authentication token in every request. It also makes sure you're talking to the actual API server and not a man in the middle (by verifying the server's certificate on each request).

Running the proxy is trivial. All you need to do is run the following command:

```
$ kubectl proxy
Starting to serve on 127.0.0.1:8001
```

You don't need to pass in any other arguments, because `kubectl` already knows everything it needs (the API server URL, authorization token, and so on). As soon as it starts up, the proxy starts accepting connections on local port 8001. Let's see if it works:

```
$ curl localhost:8001
{
  "paths": [
    "/api",
    "/api/v1",
    ...
```

Voila! You sent the request to the proxy, it sent a request to the API server, and then the proxy returned whatever the server returned. Now, let's start exploring.

EXPLORING THE KUBERNETES API THROUGH THE KUBECTL PROXY

You can continue to use `curl`, or you can open your web browser and point it to http://localhost:8001. Let's examine what the API server returns when you hit its base URL more closely. The server responds with a list of paths, as shown in the following listing.

> **Listing 8.7 Listing the API server's REST endpoints: http://localhost:8001**

```
$ curl http://localhost:8001
{
  "paths": [
    "/api",                          Most resource types
    "/api/v1",                       can be found here.
    "/apis",
    "/apis/apps",
    "/apis/apps/v1beta1",
    ...
    "/apis/batch",                   The batch API
    "/apis/batch/v1",                group and its
    "/apis/batch/v2alpha1",          two versions
    ...
```

These paths correspond to the API groups and versions you specify in your resource definitions when creating resources such as Pods, Services, and so on.

You may recognize the `batch/v1` in the `/apis/batch/v1` path as the API group and version of the Job resources you learned about in chapter 4. Likewise, the `/api/v1` corresponds to the `apiVersion: v1` you refer to in the common resources you created (Pods, Services, ReplicationControllers, and so on). The most common resource types, which were introduced in the earliest versions of Kubernetes, don't belong to any specific group, because Kubernetes initially didn't even use the concept of API groups; they were introduced later.

> **NOTE**   These initial resource types without an API group are now considered to belong to the core API group.

EXPLORING THE BATCH API GROUP'S REST ENDPOINT

Let's explore the Job resource API. You'll start by looking at what's behind the /apis/batch path (you'll omit the version for now), as shown in the following listing.

> **Listing 8.8   Listing endpoints under /apis/batch: http://localhost:8001/apis/batch**

```
$ curl http://localhost:8001/apis/batch
{
  "kind": "APIGroup",
  "apiVersion": "v1",
  "name": "batch",
  "versions": [
    {
      "groupVersion": "batch/v1",
      "version": "v1"
    },
    {
      "groupVersion": "batch/v2alpha1",
      "version": "v2alpha1"
    }
  ],
  "preferredVersion": {
    "groupVersion": "batch/v1",
    "version": "v1"
  },
  "serverAddressByClientCIDRs": null
}
```

The batch API group contains two versions.

Clients should use the v1 version instead of v2alpha1.

The response shows a description of the batch API group, including the available versions and the preferred version clients should use. Let's continue and see what's behind the /apis/batch/v1 path. It's shown in the following listing.

> **Listing 8.9   Resource types in batch/v1: http://localhost:8001/apis/batch/v1**

```
$ curl http://localhost:8001/apis/batch/v1
{
  "kind": "APIResourceList",
  "apiVersion": "v1",
  "groupVersion": "batch/v1",
  "resources": [
    {
      "name": "jobs",
      "namespaced": true,
      "kind": "Job",
```

This is a list of API resources in the batch/v1 API group.

Here's an array holding all the resource types in this group.

This describes the Job resource, which is namespaced.

```
    "verbs": [
      "create",
      "delete",
      "deletecollection",
      "get",
      "list",
      "patch",
      "update",
      "watch"
    ]
  },
  {
    "name": "jobs/status",
    "namespaced": true,
    "kind": "Job",
    "verbs": [
      "get",
      "patch",
      "update"
    ]
  }
  ]
}
```

Here are the verbs that can be used with this resource (you can create Jobs; delete individual ones or a collection of them; and retrieve, watch, and update them).

Resources also have a special REST endpoint for modifying their status.

The status can be retrieved, patched, or updated.

As you can see, the API server returns a list of resource types and REST endpoints in the batch/v1 API group. One of those is the Job resource. In addition to the name of the resource and the associated kind, the API server also includes information on whether the resource is namespaced or not, its short name (if it has one; Jobs don't), and a list of verbs you can use with the resource.

The returned list describes the REST resources exposed in the API server. The "name": "jobs" line tells you that the API contains the /apis/batch/v1/jobs endpoint. The "verbs" array says you can retrieve, update, and delete Job resources through that endpoint. For certain resources, additional API endpoints are also exposed (such as the jobs/status path, which allows modifying only the status of a Job).

LISTING ALL JOB INSTANCES IN THE CLUSTER

To get a list of Jobs in your cluster, perform a GET request on path /apis/batch/v1/jobs, as shown in the following listing.

Listing 8.10   List of Jobs: http://localhost:8001/apis/batch/v1/jobs

```
$ curl http://localhost:8001/apis/batch/v1/jobs
{
  "kind": "JobList",
  "apiVersion": "batch/v1",
  "metadata": {
    "selfLink": "/apis/batch/v1/jobs",
    "resourceVersion": "225162"
  },
```

```
"items": [
  {
    "metadata": {
      "name": "my-job",
      "namespace": "default",
      ...
```

You probably have no Job resources deployed in your cluster, so the items array will be empty. You can try deploying the Job in Chapter08/my-job.yaml and hitting the REST endpoint again to get the same output as in listing 8.10.

RETRIEVING A SPECIFIC JOB INSTANCE BY NAME

The previous endpoint returned a list of all Jobs across all namespaces. To get back only one specific Job, you need to specify its name and namespace in the URL. To retrieve the Job shown in the previous listing (name: `my-job`; namespace: `default`), you need to request the following path: `/apis/batch/v1/namespaces/default/jobs/my-job`, as shown in the following listing.

Listing 8.11 Retrieving a resource in a specific namespace by name

```
$ curl http://localhost:8001/apis/batch/v1/namespaces/default/jobs/my-job
{
  "kind": "Job",
  "apiVersion": "batch/v1",
  "metadata": {
    "name": "my-job",
    "namespace": "default",
    ...
```

As you can see, you get back the complete JSON definition of the `my-job` Job resource, exactly like you do if you run:

```
$ kubectl get job my-job -o json
```

You've seen that you can browse the Kubernetes REST API server without using any special tools, but to fully explore the REST API and interact with it, a better option is described at the end of this chapter. For now, exploring it with `curl` like this is enough to make you understand how an application running in a pod talks to Kubernetes.

8.2.2 *Talking to the API server from within a pod*

You've learned how to talk to the API server from your local machine, using the `kubectl` proxy. Now, let's see how to talk to it from within a pod, where you (usually) don't have `kubectl`. Therefore, to talk to the API server from inside a pod, you need to take care of three things:

- Find the location of the API server.
- Make sure you're talking to the API server and not something impersonating it.
- Authenticate with the server; otherwise it won't let you see or do anything.

You'll see how this is done in the next three sections.

RUNNING A POD TO TRY OUT COMMUNICATION WITH THE API SERVER

The first thing you need is a pod from which to talk to the API server. You'll run a pod that does nothing (it runs the `sleep` command in its only container), and then run a shell in the container with `kubectl exec`. Then you'll try to access the API server from within that shell using `curl`.

Therefore, you need to use a container image that contains the `curl` binary. If you search for such an image on, say, Docker Hub, you'll find the `tutum/curl` image, so use it (you can also use any other existing image containing the `curl` binary or you can build your own). The pod definition is shown in the following listing.

> **Listing 8.12   A pod for trying out communication with the API server: curl.yaml**

```
apiVersion: v1
kind: Pod
metadata:
  name: curl
spec:
  containers:
  - name: main
    image: tutum/curl          ◁────┐   Using the tutum/curl image,
    command: ["sleep", "9999999"]    │   because you need curl
                                     │   available in the container
                            ◁────────┘
                                         You're running the sleep
                                         command with a long delay to
                                         keep your container running.
```

After creating the pod, run `kubectl exec` to run a bash shell inside its container:

```
$ kubectl exec -it curl bash
root@curl:/#
```

You're now ready to talk to the API server.

FINDING THE API SERVER'S ADDRESS

First, you need to find the IP and port of the Kubernetes API server. This is easy, because a Service called `kubernetes` is automatically exposed in the default namespace and configured to point to the API server. You may remember seeing it every time you listed services with `kubectl get svc`:

```
$ kubectl get svc
NAME         CLUSTER-IP   EXTERNAL-IP   PORT(S)   AGE
kubernetes   10.0.0.1     <none>        443/TCP   46d
```

And you'll remember from chapter 5 that environment variables are configured for each service. You can get both the IP address and the port of the API server by looking up the `KUBERNETES_SERVICE_HOST` and `KUBERNETES_SERVICE_PORT` variables (inside the container):

```
root@curl:/# env | grep KUBERNETES_SERVICE
KUBERNETES_SERVICE_PORT=443
KUBERNETES_SERVICE_HOST=10.0.0.1
KUBERNETES_SERVICE_PORT_HTTPS=443
```

You may also remember that each service also gets a DNS entry, so you don't even need to look up the environment variables, but instead simply point `curl` to https://kubernetes. To be fair, if you don't know which port the service is available at, you also either need to look up the environment variables or perform a DNS SRV record lookup to get the service's actual port number.

The environment variables shown previously say that the API server is listening on port 443, which is the default port for HTTPS, so try hitting the server through HTTPS:

```
root@curl:/# curl https://kubernetes
curl: (60) SSL certificate problem: unable to get local issuer certificate
...
If you'd like to turn off curl's verification of the certificate, use
  the -k (or --insecure) option.
```

Although the simplest way to get around this is to use the proposed `-k` option (and this is what you'd normally use when playing with the API server manually), let's look at the longer (and correct) route. Instead of blindly trusting that the server you're connecting to is the authentic API server, you'll verify its identity by having `curl` check its certificate.

> **TIP** Never skip checking the server's certificate in an actual application. Doing so could make your app expose its authentication token to an attacker using a man-in-the-middle attack.

VERIFYING THE SERVER'S IDENTITY

In the previous chapter, while discussing Secrets, we looked at an automatically created Secret called `default-token-xyz`, which is mounted into each container at /var/run/secrets/kubernetes.io/serviceaccount/. Let's see the contents of that Secret again, by listing files in that directory:

```
root@curl:/#ls/var/run/secrets/kubernetes.io/serviceaccount/
ca.crt    namespace    token
```

The Secret has three entries (and therefore three files in the Secret volume). Right now, we'll focus on the ca.crt file, which holds the certificate of the certificate authority (CA) used to sign the Kubernetes API server's certificate. To verify you're talking to the API server, you need to check if the server's certificate is signed by the CA. `curl` allows you to specify the CA certificate with the `--cacert` option, so try hitting the API server again:

```
root@curl:/# curl --cacert /var/run/secrets/kubernetes.io/serviceaccount
          /ca.crt https://kubernetes
Unauthorized
```

> **NOTE** You may see a longer error description than "Unauthorized."

Okay, you've made progress. `curl` verified the server's identity because its certificate was signed by the CA you trust. As the `Unauthorized` response suggests, you still need to take care of authentication. You'll do that in a moment, but first let's see how to make life easier by setting the `CURL_CA_BUNDLE` environment variable, so you don't need to specify `--cacert` every time you run `curl`:

```
root@curl:/# export CURL_CA_BUNDLE=/var/run/secrets/kubernetes.io/
          ➥ serviceaccount/ca.crt
```

You can now hit the API server without using `--cacert`:

```
root@curl:/# curl https://kubernetes
Unauthorized
```

This is much nicer now. Your client (`curl`) trusts the API server now, but the API server itself says you're not authorized to access it, because it doesn't know who you are.

AUTHENTICATING WITH THE API SERVER

You need to authenticate with the server, so it allows you to read and even update and/or delete the API objects deployed in the cluster. To authenticate, you need an authentication token. Luckily, the token is provided through the default-token Secret mentioned previously, and is stored in the `token` file in the `secret` volume. As the Secret's name suggests, that's the primary purpose of the Secret.

You're going to use the token to access the API server. First, load the token into an environment variable:

```
root@curl:/# TOKEN=$(cat /var/run/secrets/kubernetes.io/
          ➥ serviceaccount/token)
```

The token is now stored in the `TOKEN` environment variable. You can use it when sending requests to the API server, as shown in the following listing.

Listing 8.13 Getting a proper response from the API server

```
root@curl:/# curl -H "Authorization: Bearer $TOKEN" https://kubernetes
{
  "paths": [
    "/api",
    "/api/v1",
    "/apis",
    "/apis/apps",
    "/apis/apps/v1beta1",
    "/apis/authorization.k8s.io",
    ...
    "/ui/",
    "/version"
  ]
}
```

Disabling role-based access control (RBAC)

If you're using a Kubernetes cluster with RBAC enabled, the service account may not be authorized to access (parts of) the API server. You'll learn about service accounts and RBAC in chapter 12. For now, the simplest way to allow you to query the API server is to work around RBAC by running the following command:

```
$ kubectl create clusterrolebinding permissive-binding \
  --clusterrole=cluster-admin \
  --group=system:serviceaccounts
```

This gives all service accounts (we could also say all pods) cluster-admin privileges, allowing them to do whatever they want. Obviously, doing this is dangerous and should never be done on production clusters. For test purposes, it's fine.

As you can see, you passed the token inside the `Authorization` HTTP header in the request. The API server recognized the token as authentic and returned a proper response. You can now explore all the resources in your cluster, the way you did a few sections ago.

For example, you could list all the pods in the same namespace. But first you need to know what namespace the `curl` pod is running in.

GETTING THE NAMESPACE THE POD IS RUNNING IN

In the first part of this chapter, you saw how to pass the namespace to the pod through the Downward API. But if you're paying attention, you probably noticed your `secret` volume also contains a file called namespace. It contains the namespace the pod is running in, so you can read the file instead of having to explicitly pass the namespace to your pod through an environment variable. Load the contents of the file into the NS environment variable and then list all the pods, as shown in the following listing.

Listing 8.14   Listing pods in the pod's own namespace

```
root@curl:/# NS=$(cat /var/run/secrets/kubernetes.io/
         ➥ serviceaccount/namespace)
root@curl:/# curl -H "Authorization: Bearer $TOKEN"
         ➥ https://kubernetes/api/v1/namespaces/$NS/pods
{
  "kind": "PodList",
  "apiVersion": "v1",
  ...
```

And there you go. By using the three files in the mounted `secret` volume directory, you listed all the pods running in the same namespace as your pod. In the same manner, you could also retrieve other API objects and even update them by sending PUT or PATCH instead of simple GET requests.

RECAPPING HOW PODS TALK TO KUBERNETES

Let's recap how an app running inside a pod can access the Kubernetes API properly:

- The app should verify whether the API server's certificate is signed by the certificate authority, whose certificate is in the ca.crt file.
- The app should authenticate itself by sending the `Authorization` header with the bearer token from the `token` file.
- The `namespace` file should be used to pass the namespace to the API server when performing CRUD operations on API objects inside the pod's namespace.

DEFINITION CRUD stands for Create, Read, Update, and Delete. The corresponding HTTP methods are POST, GET, PATCH/PUT, and DELETE, respectively.

All three aspects of pod to API server communication are displayed in figure 8.5.

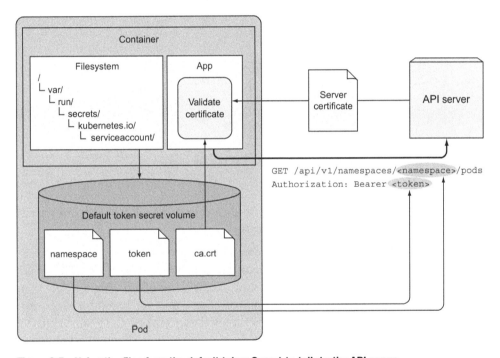

Figure 8.5   Using the files from the default-token Secret to talk to the API server

8.2.3   Simplifying API server communication with ambassador containers

Dealing with HTTPS, certificates, and authentication tokens sometimes seems too complicated to developers. I've seen developers disable validation of server certificates on way too many occasions (and I'll admit to doing it myself a few times). Luckily, you can make the communication much simpler while keeping it secure.

Remember the `kubectl proxy` command we mentioned in section 8.2.1? You ran the command on your local machine to make it easier to access the API server. Instead of sending requests to the API server directly, you sent them to the proxy and let it take care of authentication, encryption, and server verification. The same method can be used inside your pods, as well.

INTRODUCING THE AMBASSADOR CONTAINER PATTERN

Imagine having an application that (among other things) needs to query the API server. Instead of it talking to the API server directly, as you did in the previous section, you can run `kubectl proxy` in an ambassador container alongside the main container and communicate with the API server through it.

Instead of talking to the API server directly, the app in the main container can connect to the ambassador through HTTP (instead of HTTPS) and let the ambassador proxy handle the HTTPS connection to the API server, taking care of security transparently (see figure 8.6). It does this by using the files from the default token's `secret` volume.

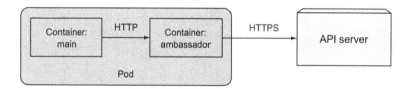

Figure 8.6   Using an ambassador to connect to the API server

Because all containers in a pod share the same loopback network interface, your app can access the proxy through a port on localhost.

RUNNING THE CURL POD WITH AN ADDITIONAL AMBASSADOR CONTAINER

To see the ambassador container pattern in action, you'll create a new pod like the curl pod you created earlier, but this time, instead of running a single container in the pod, you'll run an additional ambassador container based on a general-purpose `kubectl-proxy` container image I've created and pushed to Docker Hub. You'll find the Dockerfile for the image in the code archive (in /Chapter08/kubectl-proxy/) if you want to build it yourself.

The pod's manifest is shown in the following listing.

> **Listing 8.15   A pod with an ambassador container: curl-with-ambassador.yaml**

```
apiVersion: v1
kind: Pod
metadata:
  name: curl-with-ambassador
spec:
  containers:
  - name: main
```

```
    image: tutum/curl
    command: ["sleep", "9999999"]
  - name: ambassador
    image: luksa/kubectl-proxy:1.6.2
```
**The ambassador container,
running the kubectl-proxy image**

The pod spec is almost the same as before, but with a different pod name and an additional container. Run the pod and then enter the main container with

```
$ kubectl exec -it curl-with-ambassador -c main bash
root@curl-with-ambassador:/#
```

Your pod now has two containers, and you want to run bash in the main container, hence the -c main option. You don't need to specify the container explicitly if you want to run the command in the pod's first container. But if you want to run a command inside any other container, you do need to specify the container's name using the -c option.

TALKING TO THE API SERVER THROUGH THE AMBASSADOR

Next you'll try connecting to the API server through the ambassador container. By default, kubectl proxy binds to port 8001, and because both containers in the pod share the same network interfaces, including loopback, you can point curl to local-host:8001, as shown in the following listing.

Listing 8.16   Accessing the API server through the ambassador container

```
root@curl-with-ambassador:/# curl localhost:8001
{
  "paths": [
    "/api",
    ...
  ]
}
```

Success! The output printed by curl is the same response you saw earlier, but this time you didn't need to deal with authentication tokens and server certificates.

To get a clear picture of what exactly happened, refer to figure 8.7. curl sent the plain HTTP request (without any authentication headers) to the proxy running inside the ambassador container, and then the proxy sent an HTTPS request to the API server, handling the client authentication by sending the token and checking the server's identity by validating its certificate.

This is a great example of how an ambassador container can be used to hide the complexities of connecting to an external service and simplify the app running in the main container. The ambassador container is reusable across many different apps, regardless of what language the main app is written in. The downside is that an additional process is running and consuming additional resources.

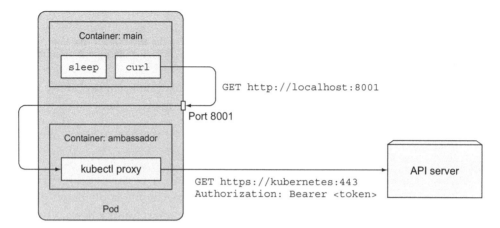

Figure 8.7   **Offloading encryption, authentication, and server verification to `kubectl proxy` in an ambassador container**

8.2.4   *Using client libraries to talk to the API server*

If your app only needs to perform a few simple operations on the API server, you can often use a regular HTTP client library and perform simple HTTP requests, especially if you take advantage of the `kubectl-proxy` ambassador container the way you did in the previous example. But if you plan on doing more than simple API requests, it's better to use one of the existing Kubernetes API client libraries.

USING EXISTING CLIENT LIBRARIES

Currently, two Kubernetes API client libraries exist that are supported by the API Machinery special interest group (SIG):

- *Golang client*—https://github.com/kubernetes/client-go
- *Python*—https://github.com/kubernetes-incubator/client-python

NOTE   The Kubernetes community has a number of Special Interest Groups (SIGs) and Working Groups that focus on specific parts of the Kubernetes ecosystem. You'll find a list of them at https://github.com/kubernetes/community/blob/master/sig-list.md.

In addition to the two officially supported libraries, here's a list of user-contributed client libraries for many other languages:

- *Java client by Fabric8*—https://github.com/fabric8io/kubernetes-client
- *Java client by Amdatu*—https://bitbucket.org/amdatulabs/amdatu-kubernetes
- *Node.js client by tenxcloud*—https://github.com/tenxcloud/node-kubernetes-client
- *Node.js client by GoDaddy*—https://github.com/godaddy/kubernetes-client
- *PHP*—https://github.com/devstub/kubernetes-api-php-client
- *Another PHP client*—https://github.com/maclof/kubernetes-client

- *Ruby*—https://github.com/Ch00k/kubr
- *Another Ruby client*—https://github.com/abonas/kubeclient
- *Clojure*—https://github.com/yanatan16/clj-kubernetes-api
- *Scala*—https://github.com/doriordan/skuber
- *Perl*—https://metacpan.org/pod/Net::Kubernetes

These libraries usually support HTTPS and take care of authentication, so you won't need to use the ambassador container.

AN EXAMPLE OF INTERACTING WITH KUBERNETES WITH THE FABRIC8 JAVA CLIENT

To give you a sense of how client libraries enable you to talk to the API server, the following listing shows an example of how to list services in a Java app using the Fabric8 Kubernetes client.

Listing 8.17   Listing, creating, updating, and deleting pods with the Fabric8 Java client

```java
import java.util.Arrays;
import io.fabric8.kubernetes.api.model.Pod;
import io.fabric8.kubernetes.api.model.PodList;
import io.fabric8.kubernetes.client.DefaultKubernetesClient;
import io.fabric8.kubernetes.client.KubernetesClient;

public class Test {
  public static void main(String[] args) throws Exception {
    KubernetesClient client = new DefaultKubernetesClient();

    // list pods in the default namespace
    PodList pods = client.pods().inNamespace("default").list();
    pods.getItems().stream()
      .forEach(s -> System.out.println("Found pod: " +
              s.getMetadata().getName()));

    // create a pod
    System.out.println("Creating a pod");
    Pod pod = client.pods().inNamespace("default")
      .createNew()
      .withNewMetadata()
        .withName("programmatically-created-pod")
      .endMetadata()
      .withNewSpec()
        .addNewContainer()
          .withName("main")
          .withImage("busybox")
          .withCommand(Arrays.asList("sleep", "99999"))
        .endContainer()
      .endSpec()
      .done();
    System.out.println("Created pod: " + pod);

    // edit the pod (add a label to it)
    client.pods().inNamespace("default")
      .withName("programmatically-created-pod")
      .edit()
      .editMetadata()
```

```
        .addToLabels("foo", "bar")
      .endMetadata()
      .done();
    System.out.println("Added label foo=bar to pod");

    System.out.println("Waiting 1 minute before deleting pod...");
    Thread.sleep(60000);

    // delete the pod
    client.pods().inNamespace("default")
      .withName("programmatically-created-pod")
      .delete();
    System.out.println("Deleted the pod");
  }
}
```

The code should be self-explanatory, especially because the Fabric8 client exposes a nice, fluent Domain-Specific-Language (DSL) API, which is easy to read and understand.

BUILDING YOUR OWN LIBRARY WITH SWAGGER AND OPENAPI

If no client is available for your programming language of choice, you can use the Swagger API framework to generate the client library and documentation. The Kubernetes API server exposes Swagger API definitions at /swaggerapi and OpenAPI spec at /swagger.json.

To find out more about the Swagger framework, visit the website at http://swagger.io.

EXPLORING THE API WITH SWAGGER UI

Earlier in the chapter I said I'd point you to a better way of exploring the REST API instead of hitting the REST endpoints with `curl`. Swagger, which I mentioned in the previous section, is not just a tool for specifying an API, but also provides a web UI for exploring REST APIs if they expose the Swagger API definitions. The better way of exploring REST APIs is through this UI.

Kubernetes not only exposes the Swagger API, but it also has Swagger UI integrated into the API server, though it's not enabled by default. You can enable it by running the API server with the `--enable-swagger-ui=true` option.

> **TIP** If you're using Minikube, you can enable Swagger UI when starting the cluster: `minikube start --extra-config=apiserver.Features.Enable-SwaggerUI=true`

After you enable the UI, you can open it in your browser by pointing it to:

```
http(s)://<api server>:<port>/swagger-ui
```

I urge you to give Swagger UI a try. It not only allows you to browse the Kubernetes API, but also interact with it (you can POST JSON resource manifests, PATCH resources, or DELETE them, for example).

8.3   Summary

After reading this chapter, you now know how your app, running inside a pod, can get data about itself, other pods, and other components deployed in the cluster. You've learned

- How a pod's name, namespace, and other metadata can be exposed to the process either through environment variables or files in a `downwardAPI` volume
- How CPU and memory requests and limits are passed to your app in any unit the app requires
- How a pod can use `downwardAPI` volumes to get up-to-date metadata, which may change during the lifetime of the pod (such as labels and annotations)
- How you can browse the Kubernetes REST API through `kubectl proxy`
- How pods can find the API server's location through environment variables or DNS, similar to any other Service defined in Kubernetes
- How an application running in a pod can verify that it's talking to the API server and how it can authenticate itself
- How using an ambassador container can make talking to the API server from within an app much simpler
- How client libraries can get you interacting with Kubernetes in minutes

In this chapter, you learned how to talk to the API server, so the next step is learning more about how it works. You'll do that in chapter 11, but before we dive into such details, you still need to learn about two other Kubernetes resources—Deployments and StatefulSets. They're explained in the next two chapters.

Deployments: updating applications declaratively

This chapter covers

- Replacing pods with newer versions
- Updating managed pods
- Updating pods declaratively using Deployment resources
- Performing rolling updates
- Automatically blocking rollouts of bad versions
- Controlling the rate of the rollout
- Reverting pods to a previous version

You now know how to package your app components into containers, group them into pods, provide them with temporary or permanent storage, pass both secret and non-secret config data to them, and allow pods to find and talk to each other. You know how to run a full-fledged system composed of independently running smaller components—microservices, if you will. Is there anything else?

Eventually, you're going to want to update your app. This chapter covers how to update apps running in a Kubernetes cluster and how Kubernetes helps you move toward a true zero-downtime update process. Although this can be achieved using only ReplicationControllers or ReplicaSets, Kubernetes also provides a Deployment resource that sits on top of ReplicaSets and enables declarative application updates. If you're not completely sure what that means, keep reading—it's not as complicated as it sounds.

9.1 Updating applications running in pods

Let's start off with a simple example. Imagine having a set of pod instances providing a service to other pods and/or external clients. After reading this book up to this point, you likely recognize that these pods are backed by a ReplicationController or a ReplicaSet. A Service also exists through which clients (apps running in other pods or external clients) access the pods. This is how a basic application looks in Kubernetes (shown in figure 9.1).

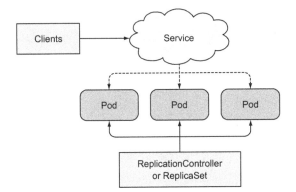

Figure 9.1   The basic outline of an application running in Kubernetes

Initially, the pods run the first version of your application—let's suppose its image is tagged as v1. You then develop a newer version of the app and push it to an image repository as a new image, tagged as v2. You'd next like to replace all the pods with this new version. Because you can't change an existing pod's image after the pod is created, you need to remove the old pods and replace them with new ones running the new image.

You have two ways of updating all those pods. You can do one of the following:

- Delete all existing pods first and then start the new ones.
- Start new ones and, once they're up, delete the old ones. You can do this either by adding all the new pods and then deleting all the old ones at once, or sequentially, by adding new pods and removing old ones gradually.

Both these strategies have their benefits and drawbacks. The first option would lead to a short period of time when your application is unavailable. The second option requires your app to handle running two versions of the app at the same time. If your app stores data in a data store, the new version shouldn't modify the data schema or the data in such a way that breaks the previous version.

How do you perform these two update methods in Kubernetes? First, let's look at how to do this manually; then, once you know what's involved in the process, you'll learn how to have Kubernetes perform the update automatically.

9.1.1 Deleting old pods and replacing them with new ones

You already know how to get a ReplicationController to replace all its pod instances with pods running a new version. You probably remember the pod template of a ReplicationController can be updated at any time. When the ReplicationController creates new instances, it uses the updated pod template to create them.

If you have a ReplicationController managing a set of v1 pods, you can easily replace them by modifying the pod template so it refers to version v2 of the image and then deleting the old pod instances. The ReplicationController will notice that no pods match its label selector and it will spin up new instances. The whole process is shown in figure 9.2.

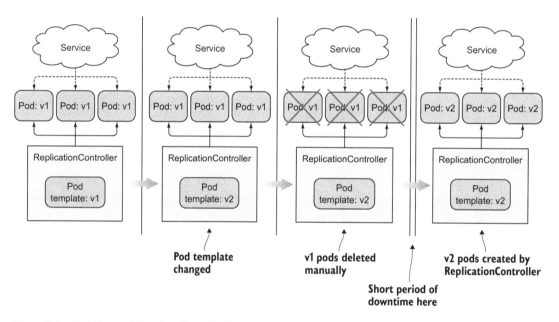

Figure 9.2   Updating pods by changing a ReplicationController's pod template and deleting old Pods

This is the simplest way to update a set of pods, if you can accept the short downtime between the time the old pods are deleted and new ones are started.

9.1.2 Spinning up new pods and then deleting the old ones

If you don't want to see any downtime and your app supports running multiple versions at once, you can turn the process around and first spin up all the new pods and only then delete the old ones. This will require more hardware resources, because you'll have double the number of pods running at the same time for a short while.

This is a slightly more complex method compared to the previous one, but you should be able to do it by combining what you've learned about ReplicationControllers and Services so far.

SWITCHING FROM THE OLD TO THE NEW VERSION AT ONCE

Pods are usually fronted by a Service. It's possible to have the Service front only the initial version of the pods while you bring up the pods running the new version. Then, once all the new pods are up, you can change the Service's label selector and have the Service switch over to the new pods, as shown in figure 9.3. This is called a *blue-green deployment*. After switching over, and once you're sure the new version functions correctly, you're free to delete the old pods by deleting the old ReplicationController.

NOTE You can change a Service's pod selector with the kubectl set selector command.

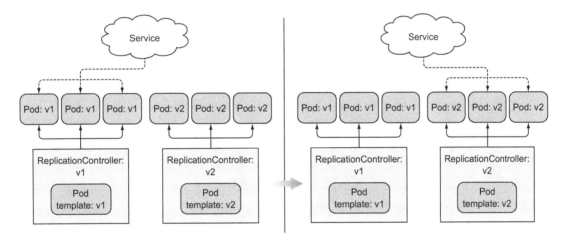

Figure 9.3 Switching a Service from the old pods to the new ones

PERFORMING A ROLLING UPDATE

Instead of bringing up all the new pods and deleting the old pods at once, you can also perform a rolling update, which replaces pods step by step. You do this by slowly scaling down the previous ReplicationController and scaling up the new one. In this case, you'll want the Service's pod selector to include both the old and the new pods, so it directs requests toward both sets of pods. See figure 9.4.

Doing a rolling update manually is laborious and error-prone. Depending on the number of replicas, you'd need to run a dozen or more commands in the proper order to perform the update process. Luckily, Kubernetes allows you to perform the rolling update with a single command. You'll learn how in the next section.

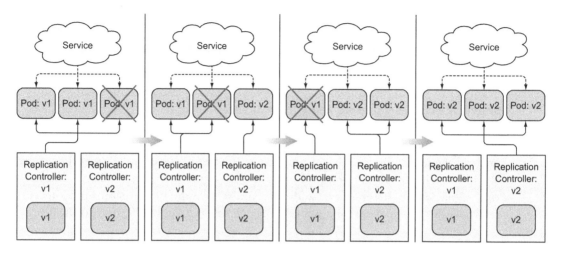

Figure 9.4   **A rolling update of pods using two ReplicationControllers**

9.2   *Performing an automatic rolling update with a ReplicationController*

Instead of performing rolling updates using ReplicationControllers manually, you can have kubectl perform them. Using kubectl to perform the update makes the process much easier, but, as you'll see later, this is now an outdated way of updating apps. Nevertheless, we'll walk through this option first, because it was historically the first way of doing an automatic rolling update, and also allows us to discuss the process without introducing too many additional concepts.

9.2.1   *Running the initial version of the app*

Obviously, before you can update an app, you need to have an app deployed. You're going to use a slightly modified version of the kubia NodeJS app you created in chapter 2 as your initial version. In case you don't remember what it does, it's a simple web-app that returns the pod's hostname in the HTTP response.

CREATING THE V1 APP

You'll change the app so it also returns its version number in the response, which will allow you to distinguish between the different versions you're about to build. I've already built and pushed the app image to Docker Hub under luksa/kubia:v1. The following listing shows the app's code.

> Listing 9.1   **The v1 version of our app: v1/app.js**

```
const http = require('http');
const os = require('os');

console.log("Kubia server starting...");
```

```
var handler = function(request, response) {
  console.log("Received request from " + request.connection.remoteAddress);
  response.writeHead(200);
  response.end("This is v1 running in pod " + os.hostname() + "\n");
};

var www = http.createServer(handler);
www.listen(8080);
```

RUNNING THE APP AND EXPOSING IT THROUGH A SERVICE USING A SINGLE YAML FILE

To run your app, you'll create a ReplicationController and a `LoadBalancer` Service to enable you to access the app externally. This time, rather than create these two resources separately, you'll create a single YAML for both of them and post it to the Kubernetes API with a single `kubectl create` command. A YAML manifest can contain multiple objects delimited with a line containing three dashes, as shown in the following listing.

> **Listing 9.2 A YAML containing an RC and a Service: kubia-rc-and-service-v1.yaml**

```
apiVersion: v1
kind: ReplicationController
metadata:
  name: kubia-v1
spec:
  replicas: 3
  template:
    metadata:
      name: kubia
      labels:
        app: kubia
    spec:
      containers:
      - image: luksa/kubia:v1     ◁── You're creating a
        name: nodejs                  ReplicationController for
---                              ◁     pods running this image.
apiVersion: v1                       YAML files can contain
kind: Service                        multiple resource
metadata:                            definitions separated by
  name: kubia                        a line with three dashes.
spec:
  type: LoadBalancer                 The Service fronts all
  selector:                          pods created by the
    app: kubia                       ReplicationController.
  ports:
  - port: 80
    targetPort: 8080
```

The YAML defines a ReplicationController called `kubia-v1` and a Service called `kubia`. Go ahead and post the YAML to Kubernetes. After a while, your three `v1` pods and the load balancer should all be running, so you can look up the Service's external IP and start hitting the service with `curl`, as shown in the following listing.

Listing 9.3   Getting the Service's external IP and hitting the service in a loop with `curl`

```
$ kubectl get svc kubia
NAME       CLUSTER-IP      EXTERNAL-IP      PORT(S)        AGE
kubia      10.3.246.195    130.211.109.222  80:32143/TCP   5m
$ while true; do curl http://130.211.109.222; done
This is v1 running in pod kubia-v1-qr192
This is v1 running in pod kubia-v1-kbtsk
This is v1 running in pod kubia-v1-qr192
This is v1 running in pod kubia-v1-2321o
...
```

NOTE   If you're using Minikube or any other Kubernetes cluster where load balancer services aren't supported, you can use the Service's node port to access the app. This was explained in chapter 5.

9.2.2   *Performing a rolling update with kubectl*

Next you'll create version 2 of the app. To keep things simple, all you'll do is change the response to say, "This is v2":

```
response.end("This is v2 running in pod " + os.hostname() + "\n");
```

This new version is available in the image `luksa/kubia:v2` on Docker Hub, so you don't need to build it yourself.

Pushing updates to the same image tag

Modifying an app and pushing the changes to the same image tag isn't a good idea, but we all tend to do that during development. If you're modifying the `latest` tag, that's not a problem, but when you're tagging an image with a different tag (for example, tag `v1` instead of `latest`), once the image is pulled by a worker node, the image will be stored on the node and not pulled again when a new pod using the same image is run (at least that's the default policy for pulling images).

That means any changes you make to the image won't be picked up if you push them to the same tag. If a new pod is scheduled to the same node, the Kubelet will run the old version of the image. On the other hand, nodes that haven't run the old version will pull and run the new image, so you might end up with two different versions of the pod running. To make sure this doesn't happen, you need to set the container's `imagePullPolicy` property to `Always`.

You need to be aware that the default `imagePullPolicy` depends on the image tag. If a container refers to the `latest` tag (either explicitly or by not specifying the tag at all), `imagePullPolicy` defaults to `Always`, but if the container refers to any other tag, the policy defaults to `IfNotPresent`.

When using a tag other than `latest`, you need to set the `imagePullPolicy` properly if you make changes to an image without changing the tag. Or better yet, make sure you always push changes to an image under a new tag.

Keep the `curl` loop running and open another terminal, where you'll get the rolling update started. To perform the update, you'll run the `kubectl rolling-update` command. All you need to do is tell it which ReplicationController you're replacing, give a name for the new ReplicationController, and specify the new image you'd like to replace the original one with. The following listing shows the full command for performing the rolling update.

Listing 9.4   Initiating a rolling-update of a ReplicationController using `kubectl`

```
$ kubectl rolling-update kubia-v1 kubia-v2 --image=luksa/kubia:v2
Created kubia-v2
Scaling up kubia-v2 from 0 to 3, scaling down kubia-v1 from 3 to 0 (keep 3
    pods available, don't exceed 4 pods)
...
```

Because you're replacing ReplicationController `kubia-v1` with one running version 2 of your kubia app, you'd like the new ReplicationController to be called `kubia-v2` and use the `luksa/kubia:v2` container image.

When you run the command, a new ReplicationController called `kubia-v2` is created immediately. The state of the system at this point is shown in figure 9.5.

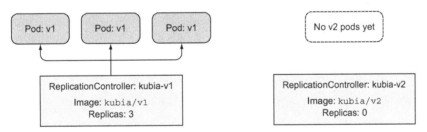

Figure 9.5   The state of the system immediately after starting the rolling update

The new ReplicationController's pod template references the `luksa/kubia:v2` image and its initial desired replica count is set to 0, as you can see in the following listing.

Listing 9.5   Describing the new ReplicationController created by the rolling update

```
$ kubectl describe rc kubia-v2                                    The new
Name:        kubia-v2                                             ReplicationController
Namespace:   default                                             refers to the v2 image.
Image(s):    luksa/kubia:v2              ◄─┘
Selector:    app=kubia,deployment=757d16a0f02f6a5c387f2b5edb62b155
Labels:      app=kubia
Replicas:    0 current / 0 desired       ◄──┐  Initially, the desired
...                                           │  number of replicas is zero.
```

UNDERSTANDING THE STEPS PERFORMED BY KUBECTL BEFORE THE ROLLING UPDATE COMMENCES

`kubectl` created this ReplicationController by copying the `kubia-v1` controller and changing the image in its pod template. If you look closely at the controller's label selector, you'll notice it has been modified, too. It includes not only a simple `app=kubia` label, but also an additional `deployment` label which the pods must have in order to be managed by this ReplicationController.

You probably know this already, but this is necessary to avoid having both the new and the old ReplicationControllers operating on the same set of pods. But even if pods created by the new controller have the additional `deployment` label in addition to the `app=kubia` label, doesn't this mean they'll be selected by the first ReplicationController's selector, because it's set to `app=kubia`?

Yes, that's exactly what would happen, but there's a catch. The rolling-update process has modified the selector of the first ReplicationController, as well:

```
$ kubectl describe rc kubia-v1
Name:       kubia-v1
Namespace:  default
Image(s):   luksa/kubia:v1
Selector:   app=kubia,deployment=3ddd307978b502a5b975ed4045ae4964-orig
```

Okay, but doesn't this mean the first controller now sees zero pods matching its selector, because the three pods previously created by it contain only the `app=kubia` label? No, because `kubectl` had also modified the labels of the live pods just before modifying the ReplicationController's selector:

```
$ kubectl get po --show-labels
NAME             READY   STATUS    RESTARTS   AGE   LABELS
kubia-v1-m33mv   1/1     Running   0          2m    app=kubia,deployment=3ddd...
kubia-v1-nmzw9   1/1     Running   0          2m    app=kubia,deployment=3ddd...
kubia-v1-cdtey   1/1     Running   0          2m    app=kubia,deployment=3ddd...
```

If this is getting too complicated, examine figure 9.6, which shows the pods, their labels, and the two ReplicationControllers, along with their pod selectors.

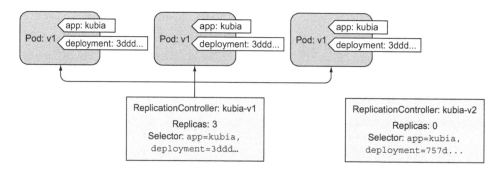

Figure 9.6   Detailed state of the old and new ReplicationControllers and pods at the start of a rolling update

kubectl had to do all this before even starting to scale anything up or down. Now imagine doing the rolling update manually. It's easy to see yourself making a mistake here and possibly having the ReplicationController kill off all your pods—pods that are actively serving your production clients!

REPLACING OLD PODS WITH NEW ONES BY SCALING THE TWO REPLICATIONCONTROLLERS

After setting up all this, kubectl starts replacing pods by first scaling up the new controller to 1. The controller thus creates the first v2 pod. kubectl then scales down the old ReplicationController by 1. This is shown in the next two lines printed by kubectl:

```
Scaling kubia-v2 up to 1
Scaling kubia-v1 down to 2
```

Because the Service is targeting all pods with the app=kubia label, you should start seeing your curl requests redirected to the new v2 pod every few loop iterations:

```
This is v2 running in pod kubia-v2-nmzw9
This is v1 running in pod kubia-v1-kbtsk
This is v1 running in pod kubia-v1-2321o
This is v2 running in pod kubia-v2-nmzw9
. . .
```

Requests hitting the pod running the new version

Figure 9.7 shows the current state of the system.

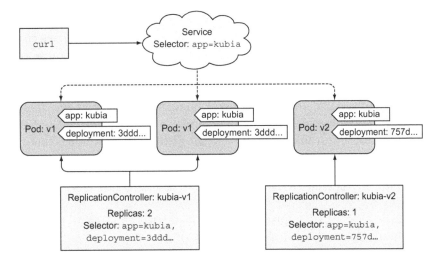

Figure 9.7   The Service is redirecting requests to both the old and new pods during the rolling update.

As kubectl continues with the rolling update, you start seeing a progressively bigger percentage of requests hitting v2 pods, as the update process deletes more of the v1 pods and replaces them with those running your new image. Eventually, the original

ReplicationController is scaled to zero, causing the last v1 pod to be deleted, which means the Service will now be backed by v2 pods only. At that point, kubectl will delete the original ReplicationController and the update process will be finished, as shown in the following listing.

Listing 9.6   **The final steps performed by** `kubectl rolling-update`

```
...
Scaling kubia-v2 up to 2
Scaling kubia-v1 down to 1
Scaling kubia-v2 up to 3
Scaling kubia-v1 down to 0
Update succeeded. Deleting kubia-v1
replicationcontroller "kubia-v1" rolling updated to "kubia-v2"
```

You're now left with only the kubia-v2 ReplicationController and three v2 pods. All throughout this update process, you've hit your service and gotten a response every time. You have, in fact, performed a rolling update with zero downtime.

9.2.3   *Understanding why kubectl rolling-update is now obsolete*

At the beginning of this section, I mentioned an even better way of doing updates than through kubectl rolling-update. What's so wrong with this process that a better one had to be introduced?

Well, for starters, I, for one, don't like Kubernetes modifying objects I've created. Okay, it's perfectly fine for the scheduler to assign a node to my pods after I create them, but Kubernetes modifying the labels of my pods and the label selectors of my ReplicationControllers is something that I don't expect and could cause me to go around the office yelling at my colleagues, "Who's been messing with my controllers!?!?"

But even more importantly, if you've paid close attention to the words I've used, you probably noticed that all this time I said explicitly that the kubectl client was the one performing all these steps of the rolling update.

You can see this by turning on verbose logging with the --v option when triggering the rolling update:

```
$ kubectl rolling-update kubia-v1 kubia-v2 --image=luksa/kubia:v2 --v 6
```

> **TIP**   Using the --v 6 option increases the logging level enough to let you see the requests kubectl is sending to the API server.

Using this option, kubectl will print out each HTTP request it sends to the Kubernetes API server. You'll see PUT requests to

```
/api/v1/namespaces/default/replicationcontrollers/kubia-v1
```

which is the RESTful URL representing your kubia-v1 ReplicationController resource. These requests are the ones scaling down your ReplicationController, which shows that the kubectl client is the one doing the scaling, instead of it being performed by the Kubernetes master.

> **TIP** Use the verbose logging option when running other kubectl commands, to learn more about the communication between kubectl and the API server.

But why is it such a bad thing that the update process is being performed by the client instead of on the server? Well, in your case, the update went smoothly, but what if you lost network connectivity while kubectl was performing the update? The update process would be interrupted mid-way. Pods and ReplicationControllers would end up in an intermediate state.

Another reason why performing an update like this isn't as good as it could be is because it's imperative. Throughout this book, I've stressed how Kubernetes is about you telling it the desired state of the system and having Kubernetes achieve that state on its own, by figuring out the best way to do it. This is how pods are deployed and how pods are scaled up and down. You never tell Kubernetes to add an additional pod or remove an excess one—you change the number of desired replicas and that's it.

Similarly, you will also want to change the desired image tag in your pod definitions and have Kubernetes replace the pods with new ones running the new image. This is exactly what drove the introduction of a new resource called a Deployment, which is now the preferred way of deploying applications in Kubernetes.

9.3 *Using Deployments for updating apps declaratively*

A Deployment is a higher-level resource meant for deploying applications and updating them declaratively, instead of doing it through a ReplicationController or a ReplicaSet, which are both considered lower-level concepts.

When you create a Deployment, a ReplicaSet resource is created underneath (eventually more of them). As you may remember from chapter 4, ReplicaSets are a new generation of ReplicationControllers, and should be used instead of them. Replica-Sets replicate and manage pods, as well. When using a Deployment, the actual pods are created and managed by the Deployment's ReplicaSets, not by the Deployment directly (the relationship is shown in figure 9.8).

Figure 9.8   A Deployment is backed by a ReplicaSet, which supervises the deployment's pods.

You might wonder why you'd want to complicate things by introducing another object on top of a ReplicationController or ReplicaSet, when they're what suffices to keep a set of pod instances running. As the rolling update example in section 9.2 demonstrates, when updating the app, you need to introduce an additional ReplicationController and coordinate the two controllers to dance around each other without stepping on each other's toes. You need something coordinating this dance. A Deployment resource takes care of that (it's not the Deployment resource itself, but the controller process running in the Kubernetes control plane that does that; but we'll get to that in chapter 11).

Using a Deployment instead of the lower-level constructs makes updating an app much easier, because you're defining the desired state through the single Deployment resource and letting Kubernetes take care of the rest, as you'll see in the next few pages.

9.3.1   *Creating a Deployment*

Creating a Deployment isn't that different from creating a ReplicationController. A Deployment is also composed of a label selector, a desired replica count, and a pod template. In addition to that, it also contains a field, which specifies a deployment strategy that defines how an update should be performed when the Deployment resource is modified.

CREATING A DEPLOYMENT MANIFEST

Let's see how to use the `kubia-v1` ReplicationController example from earlier in this chapter and modify it so it describes a Deployment instead of a ReplicationController. As you'll see, this requires only three trivial changes. The following listing shows the modified YAML.

Listing 9.7   A Deployment definition: kubia-deployment-v1.yaml

```
apiVersion: apps/v1beta1        ◁──   Deployments are in the apps
kind: Deployment        ◁──             API group, version v1beta1.
metadata:
  name: kubia        ◁──   You've changed the kind
spec:                       from ReplicationController
  replicas: 3               to Deployment.
  template:
    metadata:              There's no need to include
      name: kubia          the version in the name of
      labels:              the Deployment.
        app: kubia
    spec:
      containers:
      - image: luksa/kubia:v1
        name: nodejs
```

NOTE   You'll find an older version of the Deployment resource in `extensions/v1beta1`, and a newer one in `apps/v1beta2` with different required fields and different defaults. Be aware that `kubectl explain` shows the older version.

Because the ReplicationController from before was managing a specific version of the pods, you called it `kubia-v1`. A Deployment, on the other hand, is above that version stuff. At a given point in time, the Deployment can have multiple pod versions running under its wing, so its name shouldn't reference the app version.

CREATING THE DEPLOYMENT RESOURCE

Before you create this Deployment, make sure you delete any ReplicationControllers and pods that are still running, but keep the kubia Service for now. You can use the --all switch to delete all those ReplicationControllers like this:

```
$ kubectl delete rc --all
```

You're now ready to create the Deployment:

```
$ kubectl create -f kubia-deployment-v1.yaml --record
deployment "kubia" created
```

> **TIP** Be sure to include the --record command-line option when creating it. This records the command in the revision history, which will be useful later.

DISPLAYING THE STATUS OF THE DEPLOYMENT ROLLOUT

You can use the usual kubectl get deployment and the kubectl describe deployment commands to see details of the Deployment, but let me point you to an additional command, which is made specifically for checking a Deployment's status:

```
$ kubectl rollout status deployment kubia
deployment kubia successfully rolled out
```

According to this, the Deployment has been successfully rolled out, so you should see the three pod replicas up and running. Let's see:

```
$ kubectl get po
NAME                        READY   STATUS    RESTARTS   AGE
kubia-1506449474-otnnh      1/1     Running   0          14s
kubia-1506449474-vmn7s      1/1     Running   0          14s
kubia-1506449474-xis6m      1/1     Running   0          14s
```

UNDERSTANDING HOW DEPLOYMENTS CREATE REPLICASETS, WHICH THEN CREATE THE PODS

Take note of the names of these pods. Earlier, when you used a ReplicationController to create pods, their names were composed of the name of the controller plus a randomly generated string (for example, kubia-v1-m33mv). The three pods created by the Deployment include an additional numeric value in the middle of their names. What is that exactly?

The number corresponds to the hashed value of the pod template in the Deployment and the ReplicaSet managing these pods. As we said earlier, a Deployment doesn't manage pods directly. Instead, it creates ReplicaSets and leaves the managing to them, so let's look at the ReplicaSet created by your Deployment:

```
$ kubectl get replicasets
NAME              DESIRED   CURRENT   AGE
kubia-1506449474  3         3         10s
```

The ReplicaSet's name also contains the hash value of its pod template. As you'll see later, a Deployment creates multiple ReplicaSets—one for each version of the pod template. Using the hash value of the pod template like this allows the Deployment to always use the same (possibly existing) ReplicaSet for a given version of the pod template.

ACCESSING THE PODS THROUGH THE SERVICE

With the three replicas created by this ReplicaSet now running, you can use the Service you created a while ago to access them, because you made the new pods' labels match the Service's label selector.

Up until this point, you probably haven't seen a good-enough reason why you should use Deployments over ReplicationControllers. Luckily, creating a Deployment also hasn't been any harder than creating a ReplicationController. Now, you'll start doing things with this Deployment, which will make it clear why Deployments are superior. This will become clear in the next few moments, when you see how updating the app through a Deployment resource compares to updating it through a ReplicationController.

9.3.2 *Updating a Deployment*

Previously, when you ran your app using a ReplicationController, you had to explicitly tell Kubernetes to perform the update by running `kubectl rolling-update`. You even had to specify the name for the new ReplicationController that should replace the old one. Kubernetes replaced all the original pods with new ones and deleted the original ReplicationController at the end of the process. During the process, you basically had to stay around, keeping your terminal open and waiting for `kubectl` to finish the rolling update.

Now compare this to how you're about to update a Deployment. The only thing you need to do is modify the pod template defined in the Deployment resource and Kubernetes will take all the steps necessary to get the actual system state to what's defined in the resource. Similar to scaling a ReplicationController or ReplicaSet up or down, all you need to do is reference a new image tag in the Deployment's pod template and leave it to Kubernetes to transform your system so it matches the new desired state.

UNDERSTANDING THE AVAILABLE DEPLOYMENT STRATEGIES

How this new state should be achieved is governed by the deployment strategy configured on the Deployment itself. The default strategy is to perform a rolling update (the strategy is called `RollingUpdate`). The alternative is the `Recreate` strategy, which deletes all the old pods at once and then creates new ones, similar to modifying a ReplicationController's pod template and then deleting all the pods (we talked about this in section 9.1.1).

The `Recreate` strategy causes all old pods to be deleted before the new ones are created. Use this strategy when your application doesn't support running multiple versions in parallel and requires the old version to be stopped completely before the new one is started. This strategy does involve a short period of time when your app becomes completely unavailable.

The `RollingUpdate` strategy, on the other hand, removes old pods one by one, while adding new ones at the same time, keeping the application available throughout the whole process, and ensuring there's no drop in its capacity to handle requests. This is the default strategy. The upper and lower limits for the number of pods above or below the desired replica count are configurable. You should use this strategy only when your app can handle running both the old and new version at the same time.

SLOWING DOWN THE ROLLING UPDATE FOR DEMO PURPOSES

In the next exercise, you'll use the `RollingUpdate` strategy, but you need to slow down the update process a little, so you can see that the update is indeed performed in a rolling fashion. You can do that by setting the `minReadySeconds` attribute on the Deployment. We'll explain what this attribute does by the end of this chapter. For now, set it to 10 seconds with the `kubectl patch` command.

```
$ kubectl patch deployment kubia -p '{"spec": {"minReadySeconds": 10}}'
"kubia" patched
```

> **TIP** The `kubectl patch` command is useful for modifying a single property or a limited number of properties of a resource without having to edit its definition in a text editor.

You used the patch command to change the spec of the Deployment. This doesn't cause any kind of update to the pods, because you didn't change the pod template. Changing other Deployment properties, like the desired replica count or the deployment strategy, also doesn't trigger a rollout, because it doesn't affect the existing individual pods in any way.

TRIGGERING THE ROLLING UPDATE

If you'd like to track the update process as it progresses, first run the `curl` loop again in another terminal to see what's happening with the requests (don't forget to replace the IP with the actual external IP of your service):

```
$ while true; do curl http://130.211.109.222; done
```

To trigger the actual rollout, you'll change the image used in the single pod container to `luksa/kubia:v2`. Instead of editing the whole YAML of the Deployment object or using the `patch` command to change the image, you'll use the `kubectl set image` command, which allows changing the image of any resource that contains a container (ReplicationControllers, ReplicaSets, Deployments, and so on). You'll use it to modify your Deployment like this:

```
$ kubectl set image deployment kubia nodejs=luksa/kubia:v2
deployment "kubia" image updated
```

When you execute this command, you're updating the kubia Deployment's pod template so the image used in its `nodejs` container is changed to `luksa/kubia:v2` (from `:v1`). This is shown in figure 9.9.

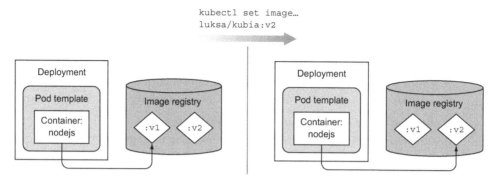

Figure 9.9   Updating a Deployment's pod template to point to a new image

Ways of modifying Deployments and other resources

Over the course of this book, you've learned several ways how to modify an existing object. Let's list all of them together to refresh your memory.

Table 9.1   Modifying an existing resource in Kubernetes

Method	What it does
kubectl edit	Opens the object's manifest in your default editor. After making changes, saving the file, and exiting the editor, the object is updated. Example: kubectl edit deployment kubia
kubectl patch	Modifies individual properties of an object. Example: kubectl patch deployment kubia -p '{"spec": {"template": {"spec": {"containers": [{"name": "nodejs", "image": "luksa/kubia:v2"}]}}}}'
kubectl apply	Modifies the object by applying property values from a full YAML or JSON file. If the object specified in the YAML/JSON doesn't exist yet, it's created. The file needs to contain the full definition of the resource (it can't include only the fields you want to update, as is the case with kubectl patch). Example: kubectl apply -f kubia-deployment-v2.yaml
kubectl replace	Replaces the object with a new one from a YAML/JSON file. In contrast to the apply command, this command requires the object to exist; otherwise it prints an error. Example: kubectl replace -f kubia-deployment-v2.yaml
kubectl set image	Changes the container image defined in a Pod, ReplicationController's template, Deployment, DaemonSet, Job, or ReplicaSet. Example: kubectl set image deployment kubia nodejs=luksa/kubia:v2

All these methods are equivalent as far as Deployments go. What they do is change the Deployment's specification. This change then triggers the rollout process.

If you've run the `curl` loop, you'll see requests initially hitting only the v1 pods; then more and more of them hit the v2 pods until, finally, all of them hit only the remaining v2 pods, after all v1 pods are deleted. This works much like the rolling update performed by `kubectl`.

UNDERSTANDING THE AWESOMENESS OF DEPLOYMENTS

Let's think about what has happened. By changing the pod template in your Deployment resource, you've updated your app to a newer version—by changing a single field!

The controllers running as part of the Kubernetes control plane then performed the update. The process wasn't performed by the `kubectl` client, like it was when you used `kubectl rolling-update`. I don't know about you, but I think that's simpler than having to run a special command telling Kubernetes what to do and then waiting around for the process to be completed.

> **NOTE** Be aware that if the pod template in the Deployment references a ConfigMap (or a Secret), modifying the ConfigMap will not trigger an update. One way to trigger an update when you need to modify an app's config is to create a new ConfigMap and modify the pod template so it references the new ConfigMap.

The events that occurred below the Deployment's surface during the update are similar to what happened during the `kubectl rolling-update`. An additional ReplicaSet was created and it was then scaled up slowly, while the previous ReplicaSet was scaled down to zero (the initial and final states are shown in figure 9.10).

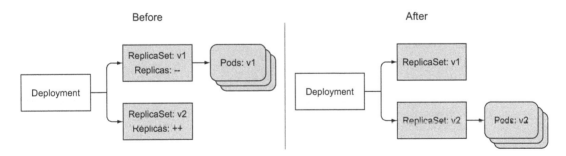

Figure 9.10 A Deployment at the start and end of a rolling update

You can still see the old ReplicaSet next to the new one if you list them:

```
$ kubectl get rs
NAME                DESIRED   CURRENT   AGE
kubia-1506449474    0         0         24m
kubia-1581357123    3         3         23m
```

Similar to ReplicationControllers, all your new pods are now managed by the new ReplicaSet. Unlike before, the old ReplicaSet is still there, whereas the old Replication-Controller was deleted at the end of the rolling-update process. You'll soon see what the purpose of this inactive ReplicaSet is.

But you shouldn't care about ReplicaSets here, because you didn't create them directly. You created and operated only on the Deployment resource; the underlying ReplicaSets are an implementation detail. You'll agree that managing a single Deployment object is much easier compared to dealing with and keeping track of multiple ReplicationControllers.

Although this difference may not be so apparent when everything goes well with a rollout, it becomes much more obvious when you hit a problem during the rollout process. Let's simulate one problem right now.

9.3.3   *Rolling back a deployment*

You're currently running version v2 of your image, so you'll need to prepare version 3 first.

CREATING VERSION 3 OF YOUR APP

In version 3, you'll introduce a bug that makes your app handle only the first four requests properly. All requests from the fifth request onward will return an internal server error (HTTP status code 500). You'll simulate this by adding an `if` statement at the beginning of the handler function. The following listing shows the new code, with all required changes shown in bold.

> **Listing 9.8   Version 3 of our app (a broken version): v3/app.js**

```
const http = require('http');
const os = require('os');

var requestCount = 0;

console.log("Kubia server starting...");

var handler = function(request, response) {
  console.log("Received request from " + request.connection.remoteAddress);
  if (++requestCount >= 5) {
    response.writeHead(500);
    response.end("Some internal error has occurred! This is pod " +
     os.hostname() + "\n");
    return;
  }
  response.writeHead(200);
  response.end("This is v3 running in pod " + os.hostname() + "\n");
};

var www = http.createServer(handler);
www.listen(8080);
```

As you can see, on the fifth and all subsequent requests, the code returns a 500 error with the message "Some internal error has occurred..."

DEPLOYING VERSION 3

I've made the v3 version of the image available as `luksa/kubia:v3`. You'll deploy this new version by changing the image in the Deployment specification again:

```
$ kubectl set image deployment kubia nodejs=luksa/kubia:v3
deployment "kubia" image updated
```

You can follow the progress of the rollout with `kubectl rollout status`:

```
$ kubectl rollout status deployment kubia
Waiting for rollout to finish: 1 out of 3 new replicas have been updated...
Waiting for rollout to finish: 2 out of 3 new replicas have been updated...
Waiting for rollout to finish: 1 old replicas are pending termination...
deployment "kubia" successfully rolled out
```

The new version is now live. As the following listing shows, after a few requests, your web clients start receiving errors.

Listing 9.9   Hitting your broken version 3

```
$ while true; do curl http://130.211.109.222; done
This is v3 running in pod kubia-1914148340-1almx
This is v3 running in pod kubia-1914148340-bz35w
This is v3 running in pod kubia-1914148340-w0voh
...
This is v3 running in pod kubia-1914148340-w0voh
Some internal error has occurred! This is pod kubia-1914148340-bz35w
This is v3 running in pod kubia-1914148340-w0voh
Some internal error has occurred! This is pod kubia-1914148340-1almx
This is v3 running in pod kubia-1914148340-w0voh
Some internal error has occurred! This is pod kubia-1914148340-1almx
Some internal error has occurred! This is pod kubia-1914148340-bz35w
Some internal error has occurred! This is pod kubia-1914148340-w0voh
```

UNDOING A ROLLOUT

You can't have your users experiencing internal server errors, so you need to do something about it fast. In section 9.3.6 you'll see how to block bad rollouts automatically, but for now, let's see what you can do about your bad rollout manually. Luckily, Deployments make it easy to roll back to the previously deployed version by telling Kubernetes to undo the last rollout of a Deployment:

```
$ kubectl rollout undo deployment kubia
deployment "kubia" rolled back
```

This rolls the Deployment back to the previous revision.

> **TIP**   The `undo` command can also be used while the rollout process is still in progress to essentially abort the rollout. Pods already created during the rollout process are removed and replaced with the old ones again.

DISPLAYING A DEPLOYMENT'S ROLLOUT HISTORY

Rolling back a rollout is possible because Deployments keep a revision history. As you'll see later, the history is stored in the underlying ReplicaSets. When a rollout completes, the old ReplicaSet isn't deleted, and this enables rolling back to any revision, not only the previous one. The revision history can be displayed with the `kubectl rollout history` command:

```
$ kubectl rollout history deployment kubia
deployments "kubia":
REVISION    CHANGE-CAUSE
2           kubectl set image deployment kubia nodejs=luksa/kubia:v2
3           kubectl set image deployment kubia nodejs=luksa/kubia:v3
```

Remember the `--record` command-line option you used when creating the Deployment? Without it, the `CHANGE-CAUSE` column in the revision history would be empty, making it much harder to figure out what's behind each revision.

ROLLING BACK TO A SPECIFIC DEPLOYMENT REVISION

You can roll back to a specific revision by specifying the revision in the `undo` command. For example, if you want to roll back to the first version, you'd execute the following command:

```
$ kubectl rollout undo deployment kubia --to-revision=1
```

Remember the inactive ReplicaSet left over when you modified the Deployment the first time? The ReplicaSet represents the first revision of your Deployment. All ReplicaSets created by a Deployment represent the complete revision history, as shown in figure 9.11. Each ReplicaSet stores the complete information of the Deployment at that specific revision, so you shouldn't delete it manually. If you do, you'll lose that specific revision from the Deployment's history, preventing you from rolling back to it.

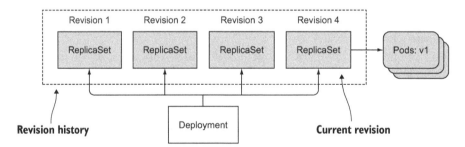

Figure 9.11   A Deployment's ReplicaSets also act as its revision history.

But having old ReplicaSets cluttering your ReplicaSet list is not ideal, so the length of the revision history is limited by the `revisionHistoryLimit` property on the Deployment resource. It defaults to two, so normally only the current and the previous revision are shown in the history (and only the current and the previous ReplicaSet are preserved). Older ReplicaSets are deleted automatically.

NOTE The extensions/v1beta1 version of Deployments doesn't have a default revisionHistoryLimit, whereas the default in version apps/v1beta2 is 10.

9.3.4 Controlling the rate of the rollout

When you performed the rollout to v3 and tracked its progress with the kubectl rollout status command, you saw that first a new pod was created, and when it became available, one of the old pods was deleted and another new pod was created. This continued until there were no old pods left. The way new pods are created and old ones are deleted is configurable through two additional properties of the rolling update strategy.

INTRODUCING THE MAXSURGE AND MAXUNAVAILABLE PROPERTIES OF THE ROLLING UPDATE STRATEGY
Two properties affect how many pods are replaced at once during a Deployment's rolling update. They are maxSurge and maxUnavailable and can be set as part of the rollingUpdate sub-property of the Deployment's strategy attribute, as shown in the following listing.

Listing 9.10 Specifying parameters for the rollingUpdate strategy

```
spec:
  strategy:
    rollingUpdate:
      maxSurge: 1
      maxUnavailable: 0
    type: RollingUpdate
```

What these properties do is explained in table 9.2.

Table 9.2 Properties for configuring the rate of the rolling update

Property	What it does
maxSurge	Determines how many pod instances you allow to exist above the desired replica count configured on the Deployment. It defaults to 25%, so there can be at most 25% more pod instances than the desired count. If the desired replica count is set to four, there will never be more than five pod instances running at the same time during an update. When converting a percentage to an absolute number, the number is rounded up. Instead of a percentage, the value can also be an absolute value (for example, one or two additional pods can be allowed).
maxUnavailable	Determines how many pod instances can be unavailable relative to the desired replica count during the update. It also defaults to 25%, so the number of available pod instances must never fall below 75% of the desired replica count. Here, when converting a percentage to an absolute number, the number is rounded down. If the desired replica count is set to four and the percentage is 25%, only one pod can be unavailable. There will always be at least three pod instances available to serve requests during the whole rollout. As with maxSurge, you can also specify an absolute value instead of a percentage.

Because the desired replica count in your case was three, and both these properties default to 25%, maxSurge allowed the number of all pods to reach four, and

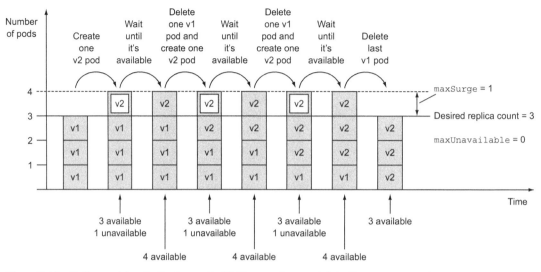

Figure 9.12 **Rolling update of a Deployment with three replicas and default `maxSurge` and `maxUnavailable`**

`maxUnavailable` disallowed having any unavailable pods (in other words, three pods had to be available at all times). This is shown in figure 9.12.

UNDERSTANDING THE MAXUNAVAILABLE PROPERTY

The `extensions/v1beta1` version of Deployments uses different defaults—it sets both `maxSurge` and `maxUnavailable` to 1 instead of 25%. In the case of three replicas, max-Surge is the same as before, but `maxUnavailable` is different (1 instead of 0). This makes the rollout process unwind a bit differently, as shown in figure 9.13.

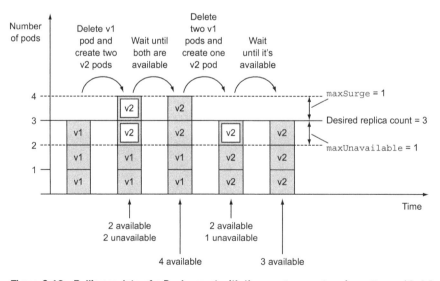

Figure 9.13 **Rolling update of a Deployment with the `maxSurge=1` and `maxUnavailable=1`**

In this case, one replica can be unavailable, so if the desired replica count is three, only two of them need to be available. That's why the rollout process immediately deletes one pod and creates two new ones. This ensures two pods are available and that the maximum number of pods isn't exceeded (the maximum is four in this case—three plus one from maxSurge). As soon as the two new pods are available, the two remaining old pods are deleted.

This is a bit hard to grasp, especially since the maxUnavailable property leads you to believe that that's the maximum number of unavailable pods that are allowed. If you look at the previous figure closely, you'll see two unavailable pods in the second column even though maxUnavailable is set to 1.

It's important to keep in mind that maxUnavailable is relative to the desired replica count. If the replica count is set to three and maxUnavailable is set to one, that means that the update process must always keep at least two (3 minus 1) pods available, while the number of pods that aren't available can exceed one.

9.3.5 *Pausing the rollout process*

After the bad experience with version 3 of your app, imagine you've now fixed the bug and pushed version 4 of your image. You're a little apprehensive about rolling it out across all your pods the way you did before. What you want is to run a single v4 pod next to your existing v2 pods and see how it behaves with only a fraction of all your users. Then, once you're sure everything's okay, you can replace all the old pods with new ones.

You could achieve this by running an additional pod either directly or through an additional Deployment, ReplicationController, or ReplicaSet, but you do have another option available on the Deployment itself. A Deployment can also be paused during the rollout process. This allows you to verify that everything is fine with the new version before proceeding with the rest of the rollout.

PAUSING THE ROLLOUT

I've prepared the v4 image, so go ahead and trigger the rollout by changing the image to luksa/kubia:v4, but then immediately (within a few seconds) pause the rollout:

```
$ kubectl set image deployment kubia nodejs=luksa/kubia:v4
deployment "kubia" image updated

$ kubectl rollout pause deployment kubia
deployment "kubia" paused
```

A single new pod should have been created, but all original pods should also still be running. Once the new pod is up, a part of all requests to the service will be redirected to the new pod. This way, you've effectively run a canary release. A canary release is a technique for minimizing the risk of rolling out a bad version of an application and it affecting all your users. Instead of rolling out the new version to everyone, you replace only one or a small number of old pods with new ones. This way only a small number of users will initially hit the new version. You can then verify whether the new version is working fine or not and then either continue the rollout across all remaining pods or roll back to the previous version.

RESUMING THE ROLLOUT

In your case, by pausing the rollout process, only a small portion of client requests will hit your v4 pod, while most will still hit the v3 pods. Once you're confident the new version works as it should, you can resume the deployment to replace all the old pods with new ones:

```
$ kubectl rollout resume deployment kubia
deployment "kubia" resumed
```

Obviously, having to pause the deployment at an exact point in the rollout process isn't what you want to do. In the future, a new upgrade strategy may do that automatically, but currently, the proper way of performing a canary release is by using two different Deployments and scaling them appropriately.

USING THE PAUSE FEATURE TO PREVENT ROLLOUTS

Pausing a Deployment can also be used to prevent updates to the Deployment from kicking off the rollout process, allowing you to make multiple changes to the Deployment and starting the rollout only when you're done making all the necessary changes. Once you're ready for changes to take effect, you resume the Deployment and the rollout process will start.

> **NOTE** If a Deployment is paused, the undo command won't undo it until you resume the Deployment.

9.3.6   *Blocking rollouts of bad versions*

Before you conclude this chapter, we need to discuss one more property of the Deployment resource. Remember the minReadySeconds property you set on the Deployment at the beginning of section 9.3.2? You used it to slow down the rollout, so you could see it was indeed performing a rolling update and not replacing all the pods at once. The main function of minReadySeconds is to prevent deploying malfunctioning versions, not slowing down a deployment for fun.

UNDERSTANDING THE APPLICABILITY OF MINREADYSECONDS

The minReadySeconds property specifies how long a newly created pod should be ready before the pod is treated as available. Until the pod is available, the rollout process will not continue (remember the maxUnavailable property?). A pod is ready when readiness probes of all its containers return a success. If a new pod isn't functioning properly and its readiness probe starts failing before minReadySeconds have passed, the rollout of the new version will effectively be blocked.

You used this property to slow down your rollout process by having Kubernetes wait 10 seconds after a pod was ready before continuing with the rollout. Usually, you'd set minReadySeconds to something much higher to make sure pods keep reporting they're ready after they've already started receiving actual traffic.

Although you should obviously test your pods both in a test and in a staging environment before deploying them into production, using `minReadySeconds` is like an airbag that saves your app from making a big mess after you've already let a buggy version slip into production.

With a properly configured readiness probe and a proper `minReadySeconds` setting, Kubernetes would have prevented us from deploying the buggy v3 version earlier. Let me show you how.

DEFINING A READINESS PROBE TO PREVENT OUR V3 VERSION FROM BEING ROLLED OUT FULLY

You're going to deploy version v3 again, but this time, you'll have the proper readiness probe defined on the pod. Your Deployment is currently at version v4, so before you start, roll back to version v2 again so you can pretend this is the first time you're upgrading to v3. If you wish, you can go straight from v4 to v3, but the text that follows assumes you returned to v2 first.

Unlike before, where you only updated the image in the pod template, you're now also going to introduce a readiness probe for the container at the same time. Up until now, because there was no explicit readiness probe defined, the container and the pod were always considered ready, even if the app wasn't truly ready or was returning errors. There was no way for Kubernetes to know that the app was malfunctioning and shouldn't be exposed to clients.

To change the image and introduce the readiness probe at once, you'll use the `kubectl apply` command. You'll use the following YAML to update the deployment (you'll store it as `kubia-deployment-v3-with-readinesscheck.yaml`), as shown in the following listing.

Listing 9.11   Deployment with a readiness probe: kubia-deployment-v3-with-readinesscheck.yaml

```
apiVersion: apps/v1beta1
kind: Deployment
metadata:
  name: kubia
spec:
  replicas: 3
  minReadySeconds: 10          ◁   You're keeping minReadySeconds set to 10.
  strategy:
    rollingUpdate:
      maxSurge: 1
      maxUnavailable: 0        ◁   You're keeping maxUnavailable set to 0 to make the deployment replace pods one by one
    type: RollingUpdate
  template:
    metadata:
      name: kubia
      labels:
        app: kubia
    spec:
      containers:
      - image: luksa/kubia:v3
```

```
name: nodejs
readinessProbe:
  periodSeconds: 1    ◁─┐
  httpGet:
    path: /
    port: 8080
```

You're defining a readiness probe that will be executed every second.

The readiness probe will perform an HTTP GET request against our container.

UPDATING A DEPLOYMENT WITH KUBECTL APPLY

To update the Deployment this time, you'll use `kubectl apply` like this:

```
$ kubectl apply -f kubia-deployment-v3-with-readinesscheck.yaml
deployment "kubia" configured
```

The `apply` command updates the Deployment with everything that's defined in the YAML file. It not only updates the image but also adds the readiness probe definition and anything else you've added or modified in the YAML. If the new YAML also contains the `replicas` field, which doesn't match the number of replicas on the existing Deployment, the apply operation will also scale the Deployment, which isn't usually what you want.

> **TIP**   To keep the desired replica count unchanged when updating a Deployment with `kubectl apply`, don't include the `replicas` field in the YAML.

Running the `apply` command will kick off the update process, which you can again follow with the `rollout status` command:

```
$ kubectl rollout status deployment kubia
Waiting for rollout to finish: 1 out of 3 new replicas have been updated...
```

Because the status says one new pod has been created, your service should be hitting it occasionally, right? Let's see:

```
$ while true; do curl http://130.211.109.222; done
This is v2 running in pod kubia-1765119474-jvslk
This is v2 running in pod kubia-1765119474-jvslk
This is v2 running in pod kubia-1765119474-xk5g3
This is v2 running in pod kubia-1765119474-pmb26
This is v2 running in pod kubia-1765119474-pmb26
This is v2 running in pod kubia-1765119474-xk5g3
...
```

Nope, you never hit the v3 pod. Why not? Is it even there? List the pods:

```
$ kubectl get po
NAME                       READY    STATUS     RESTARTS    AGE
kubia-1163142519-7ws0i     0/1      Running    0           30s
kubia-1765119474-jvslk     1/1      Running    0           9m
kubia-1765119474-pmb26     1/1      Running    0           9m
kubia-1765119474-xk5g3     1/1      Running    0           8m
```

Aha! There's your problem (or as you'll learn soon, your blessing)! The pod is shown as not ready, but I guess you've been expecting that, right? What has happened?

UNDERSTANDING HOW A READINESS PROBE PREVENTS BAD VERSIONS FROM BEING ROLLED OUT

As soon as your new pod starts, the readiness probe starts being hit every second (you set the probe's interval to one second in the pod spec). On the fifth request the readiness probe began failing, because your app starts returning HTTP status code 500 from the fifth request onward.

As a result, the pod is removed as an endpoint from the service (see figure 9.14). By the time you start hitting the service in the `curl` loop, the pod has already been marked as not ready. This explains why you never hit the new pod with `curl`. And that's exactly what you want, because you don't want clients to hit a pod that's not functioning properly.

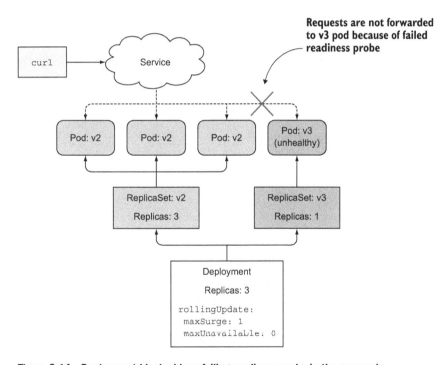

Figure 9.14 Deployment blocked by a failing readiness probe in the new pod

But what about the rollout process? The `rollout status` command shows only one new replica has started. Thankfully, the rollout process will not continue, because the new pod will never become available. To be considered available, it needs to be ready for at least 10 seconds. Until it's available, the rollout process will not create any new pods, and it also won't remove any original pods because you've set the `maxUnavailable` property to 0.

The fact that the deployment is stuck is a good thing, because if it had continued replacing the old pods with the new ones, you'd end up with a completely non-working service, like you did when you first rolled out version 3, when you weren't using the readiness probe. But now, with the readiness probe in place, there was virtually no negative impact on your users. A few users may have experienced the internal server error, but that's not as big of a problem as if the rollout had replaced all pods with the faulty version 3.

> **TIP**   If you only define the readiness probe without setting `minReadySeconds` properly, new pods are considered available immediately when the first invocation of the readiness probe succeeds. If the readiness probe starts failing shortly after, the bad version is rolled out across all pods. Therefore, you should set `minReadySeconds` appropriately.

CONFIGURING A DEADLINE FOR THE ROLLOUT

By default, after the rollout can't make any progress in 10 minutes, it's considered as failed. If you use the `kubectl describe` deployment command, you'll see it display a `ProgressDeadlineExceeded` condition, as shown in the following listing.

> **Listing 9.12   Seeing the conditions of a Deployment with `kubectl describe`**

```
$ kubectl describe deploy kubia
Name:                    kubia
...
Conditions:
  Type           Status   Reason
  ----           ------   ------
  Available      True     MinimumReplicasAvailable
  Progressing    False    ProgressDeadlineExceeded      ⊲─┐  The Deployment
                                                           took too long to
                                                           make progress.
```

The time after which the Deployment is considered failed is configurable through the `progressDeadlineSeconds` property in the Deployment spec.

> **NOTE**   The `extensions/v1beta1` version of Deployments doesn't set a deadline.

ABORTING A BAD ROLLOUT

Because the rollout will never continue, the only thing to do now is abort the rollout by undoing it:

```
$ kubectl rollout undo deployment kubia
deployment "kubia" rolled back
```

> **NOTE**   In future versions, the rollout will be aborted automatically when the time specified in `progressDeadlineSeconds` is exceeded.

9.4 *Summary*

This chapter has shown you how to make your life easier by using a declarative approach to deploying and updating applications in Kubernetes. Now that you've read this chapter, you should know how to

- Perform a rolling update of pods managed by a ReplicationController
- Create Deployments instead of lower-level ReplicationControllers or ReplicaSets
- Update your pods by editing the pod template in the Deployment specification
- Roll back a Deployment either to the previous revision or to any earlier revision still listed in the revision history
- Abort a Deployment mid-way
- Pause a Deployment to inspect how a single instance of the new version behaves in production before allowing additional pod instances to replace the old ones
- Control the rate of the rolling update through `maxSurge` and `maxUnavailable` properties
- Use `minReadySeconds` and readiness probes to have the rollout of a faulty version blocked automatically

In addition to these Deployment-specific tasks, you also learned how to

- Use three dashes as a separator to define multiple resources in a single YAML file
- Turn on `kubectl`'s verbose logging to see exactly what it's doing behind the curtains

You now know how to deploy and manage sets of pods created from the same pod template and thus share the same persistent storage. You even know how to update them declaratively. But what about running sets of pods, where each instance needs to use its own persistent storage? We haven't looked at that yet. That's the subject of our next chapter.

StatefulSets: deploying replicated stateful applications

This chapter covers

- Deploying stateful clustered applications
- Providing separate storage for each instance of a replicated pod
- Guaranteeing a stable name and hostname for pod replicas
- Starting and stopping pod replicas in a predictable order
- Discovering peers through DNS SRV records

You now know how to run both single-instance and replicated stateless pods, and even stateful pods utilizing persistent storage. You can run several replicated web-server pod instances and you can run a single database pod instance that uses persistent storage, provided either through plain pod volumes or through PersistentVolumes bound by a PersistentVolumeClaim. But can you employ a ReplicaSet to replicate the database pod?

10.1   *Replicating stateful pods*

ReplicaSets create multiple pod replicas from a single pod template. These replicas don't differ from each other, apart from their name and IP address. If the pod template includes a volume, which refers to a specific PersistentVolumeClaim, all replicas of the ReplicaSet will use the exact same PersistentVolumeClaim and therefore the same PersistentVolume bound by the claim (shown in figure 10.1).

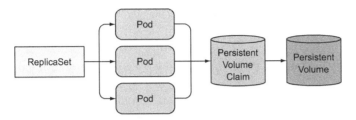

Figure 10.1   All pods from the same ReplicaSet always use the same PersistentVolumeClaim and PersistentVolume.

Because the reference to the claim is in the pod template, which is used to stamp out multiple pod replicas, you can't make each replica use its own separate PersistentVolumeClaim. You can't use a ReplicaSet to run a distributed data store, where each instance needs its own separate storage—at least not by using a single ReplicaSet. To be honest, none of the API objects you've seen so far make running such a data store possible. You need something else.

10.1.1 *Running multiple replicas with separate storage for each*

How does one run multiple replicas of a pod and have each pod use its own storage volume? ReplicaSets create exact copies (replicas) of a pod; therefore you can't use them for these types of pods. What can you use?

CREATING PODS MANUALLY

You could create pods manually and have each of them use its own PersistentVolumeClaim, but because no ReplicaSet looks after them, you'd need to manage them manually and recreate them when they disappear (as in the event of a node failure). Therefore, this isn't a viable option.

USING ONE REPLICASET PER POD INSTANCE

Instead of creating pods directly, you could create multiple ReplicaSets—one for each pod with each ReplicaSet's desired replica count set to one, and each ReplicaSet's pod template referencing a dedicated PersistentVolumeClaim (as shown in figure 10.2).

Although this takes care of the automatic rescheduling in case of node failures or accidental pod deletions, it's much more cumbersome compared to having a single ReplicaSet. For example, think about how you'd scale the pods in that case. You

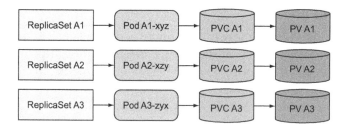

Figure 10.2   Using one ReplicaSet for each pod instance

couldn't change the desired replica count—you'd have to create additional Replica-Sets instead.

Using multiple ReplicaSets is therefore not the best solution. But could you maybe use a single ReplicaSet and have each pod instance keep its own persistent state, even though they're all using the same storage volume?

USING MULTIPLE DIRECTORIES IN THE SAME VOLUME

A trick you can use is to have all pods use the same PersistentVolume, but then have a separate file directory inside that volume for each pod (this is shown in figure 10.3).

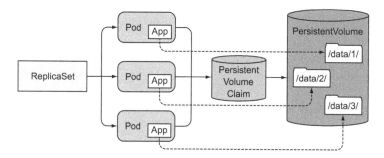

Figure 10.3   Working around the shared storage problem by having the app in each pod use a different file directory

Because you can't configure pod replicas differently from a single pod template, you can't tell each instance what directory it should use, but you can make each instance automatically select (and possibly also create) a data directory that isn't being used by any other instance at that time. This solution does require coordination between the instances, and isn't easy to do correctly. It also makes the shared storage volume the bottleneck.

10.1.2 *Providing a stable identity for each pod*

In addition to storage, certain clustered applications also require that each instance has a long-lived stable identity. Pods can be killed from time to time and replaced with new ones. When a ReplicaSet replaces a pod, the new pod is a completely new pod with a new hostname and IP, although the data in its storage volume may be that of the killed pod. For certain apps, starting up with the old instance's data but with a completely new network identity may cause problems.

Why do certain apps mandate a stable network identity? This requirement is fairly common in distributed stateful applications. Certain apps require the administrator to list all the other cluster members and their IP addresses (or hostnames) in each member's configuration file. But in Kubernetes, every time a pod is rescheduled, the new pod gets both a new hostname and a new IP address, so the whole application cluster would have to be reconfigured every time one of its members is rescheduled.

USING A DEDICATED SERVICE FOR EACH POD INSTANCE

A trick you can use to work around this problem is to provide a stable network address for cluster members by creating a dedicated Kubernetes Service for each individual member. Because service IPs are stable, you can then point to each member through its service IP (rather than the pod IP) in the configuration.

This is similar to creating a ReplicaSet for each member to provide them with individual storage, as described previously. Combining these two techniques results in the setup shown in figure 10.4 (an additional service covering all the cluster members is also shown, because you usually need one for clients of the cluster).

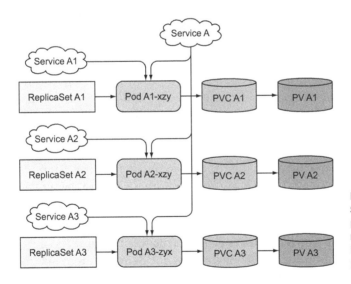

Figure 10.4 Using one Service and ReplicaSet per pod to provide a stable network address and an individual volume for each pod, respectively

The solution is not only ugly, but it still doesn't solve everything. The individual pods can't know which Service they are exposed through (and thus can't know their stable IP), so they can't self-register in other pods using that IP.

Luckily, Kubernetes saves us from resorting to such complex solutions. The proper clean and simple way of running these special types of applications in Kubernetes is through a StatefulSet.

10.2 Understanding StatefulSets

Instead of using a ReplicaSet to run these types of pods, you create a StatefulSet resource, which is specifically tailored to applications where instances of the application must be treated as non-fungible individuals, with each one having a stable name and state.

10.2.1 Comparing StatefulSets with ReplicaSets

To understand the purpose of StatefulSets, it's best to compare them to ReplicaSets or ReplicationControllers. But first let me explain them with a little analogy that's widely used in the field.

UNDERSTANDING STATEFUL PODS WITH THE PETS VS. CATTLE ANALOGY

You may have already heard of the pets vs. cattle analogy. If not, let me explain it. We can treat our apps either as pets or as cattle.

> **NOTE** StatefulSets were initially called PetSets. That name comes from the pets vs. cattle analogy explained here.

We tend to treat our app instances as pets, where we give each instance a name and take care of each instance individually. But it's usually better to treat instances as cattle and not pay special attention to each individual instance. This makes it easy to replace unhealthy instances without giving it a second thought, similar to the way a farmer replaces unhealthy cattle.

Instances of a stateless app, for example, behave much like heads of cattle. It doesn't matter if an instance dies—you can create a new instance and people won't notice the difference.

On the other hand, with stateful apps, an app instance is more like a pet. When a pet dies, you can't go buy a new one and expect people not to notice. To replace a lost pet, you need to find a new one that looks and behaves exactly like the old one. In the case of apps, this means the new instance needs to have the same state and identity as the old one.

COMPARING STATEFULSETS WITH REPLICASETS OR REPLICATIONCONTROLLERS

Pod replicas managed by a ReplicaSet or ReplicationController are much like cattle. Because they're mostly stateless, they can be replaced with a completely new pod replica at any time. Stateful pods require a different approach. When a stateful pod instance dies (or the node it's running on fails), the pod instance needs to be resurrected on another node, but the new instance needs to get the same name, network identity, and state as the one it's replacing. This is what happens when the pods are managed through a StatefulSet.

A StatefulSet makes sure pods are rescheduled in such a way that they retain their identity and state. It also allows you to easily scale the number of pets up and down. A StatefulSet, like a ReplicaSet, has a desired replica count field that determines how many pets you want running at that time. Similar to ReplicaSets, pods are created from a pod template specified as part of the StatefulSet (remember the cookie-cutter analogy?). But unlike pods created by ReplicaSets, pods created by the StatefulSet aren't exact replicas of each other. Each can have its own set of volumes—in other words, storage (and thus persistent state)—which differentiates it from its peers. Pet pods also have a predictable (and stable) identity instead of each new pod instance getting a completely random one.

10.2.2 Providing a stable network identity

Each pod created by a StatefulSet is assigned an ordinal index (zero-based), which is then used to derive the pod's name and hostname, and to attach stable storage to the pod. The names of the pods are thus predictable, because each pod's name is derived from the StatefulSet's name and the ordinal index of the instance. Rather than the pods having random names, they're nicely organized, as shown in the next figure.

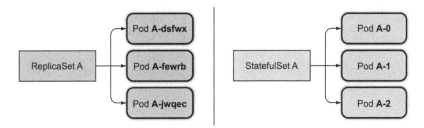

Figure 10.5 Pods created by a StatefulSet have predictable names (and hostnames), unlike those created by a ReplicaSet

INTRODUCING THE GOVERNING SERVICE

But it's not all about the pods having a predictable name and hostname. Unlike regular pods, stateful pods sometimes need to be addressable by their hostname, whereas stateless pods usually don't. After all, each stateless pod is like any other. When you need one, you pick any one of them. But with stateful pods, you usually want to operate on a specific pod from the group, because they differ from each other (they hold different state, for example).

For this reason, a StatefulSet requires you to create a corresponding governing headless Service that's used to provide the actual network identity to each pod. Through this Service, each pod gets its own DNS entry, so its peers and possibly other clients in the cluster can address the pod by its hostname. For example, if the governing Service belongs to the `default` namespace and is called `foo`, and one of the pods is called A-0, you can reach the pod through its fully qualified domain name, which is a-0.foo.default.svc.cluster.local. You can't do that with pods managed by a ReplicaSet.

Additionally, you can also use DNS to look up all the StatefulSet's pods' names by looking up SRV records for the foo.default.svc.cluster.local domain. We'll explain SRV records in section 10.4 and learn how they're used to discover members of a StatefulSet.

REPLACING LOST PETS

When a pod instance managed by a StatefulSet disappears (because the node the pod was running on has failed, it was evicted from the node, or someone deleted the pod object manually), the StatefulSet makes sure it's replaced with a new instance—similar to how ReplicaSets do it. But in contrast to ReplicaSets, the replacement pod gets the same name and hostname as the pod that has disappeared (this distinction between ReplicaSets and StatefulSets is illustrated in figure 10.6).

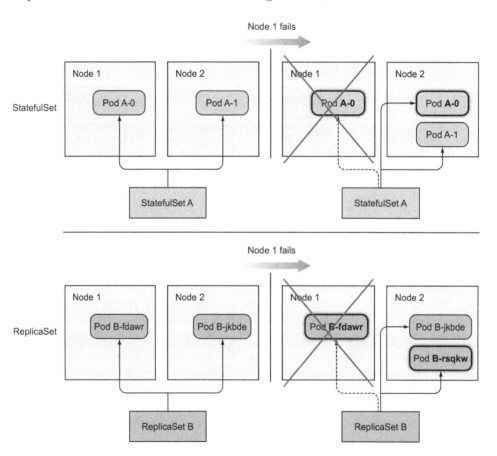

Figure 10.6   A StatefulSet replaces a lost pod with a new one with the same identity, whereas a ReplicaSet replaces it with a completely new unrelated pod.

The new pod isn't necessarily scheduled to the same node, but as you learned early on, what node a pod runs on shouldn't matter. This holds true even for stateful pods. Even if the pod is scheduled to a different node, it will still be available and reachable under the same hostname as before.

SCALING A STATEFULSET

Scaling the StatefulSet creates a new pod instance with the next unused ordinal index. If you scale up from two to three instances, the new instance will get index 2 (the existing instances obviously have indexes 0 and 1).

The nice thing about scaling down a StatefulSet is the fact that you always know what pod will be removed. Again, this is also in contrast to scaling down a ReplicaSet, where you have no idea what instance will be deleted, and you can't even specify which one you want removed first (but this feature may be introduced in the future). Scaling down a StatefulSet always removes the instances with the highest ordinal index first (shown in figure 10.7). This makes the effects of a scale-down predictable.

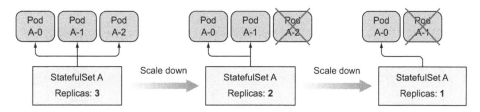

Figure 10.7 Scaling down a StatefulSet always removes the pod with the highest ordinal index first.

Because certain stateful applications don't handle rapid scale-downs nicely, Stateful-Sets scale down only one pod instance at a time. A distributed data store, for example, may lose data if multiple nodes go down at the same time. For example, if a replicated data store is configured to store two copies of each data entry, in cases where two nodes go down at the same time, a data entry would be lost if it was stored on exactly those two nodes. If the scale-down was sequential, the distributed data store has time to create an additional replica of the data entry somewhere else to replace the (single) lost copy.

For this exact reason, StatefulSets also never permit scale-down operations if any of the instances are unhealthy. If an instance is unhealthy, and you scale down by one at the same time, you've effectively lost two cluster members at once.

10.2.3 Providing stable dedicated storage to each stateful instance

You've seen how StatefulSets ensure stateful pods have a stable identity, but what about storage? Each stateful pod instance needs to use its own storage, plus if a stateful pod is rescheduled (replaced with a new instance but with the same identity as before), the new instance must have the same storage attached to it. How do Stateful-Sets achieve this?

Obviously, storage for stateful pods needs to be persistent and decoupled from the pods. In chapter 6 you learned about PersistentVolumes and PersistentVolume-Claims, which allow persistent storage to be attached to a pod by referencing the PersistentVolumeClaim in the pod by name. Because PersistentVolumeClaims map to PersistentVolumes one-to-one, each pod of a StatefulSet needs to reference a different PersistentVolumeClaim to have its own separate PersistentVolume. Because all pod instances are stamped from the same pod template, how can they each refer to a different PersistentVolumeClaim? And who creates these claims? Surely you're not expected to create as many PersistentVolumeClaims as the number of pods you plan to have in the StatefulSet upfront? Of course not.

TEAMING UP POD TEMPLATES WITH VOLUME CLAIM TEMPLATES

The StatefulSet has to create the PersistentVolumeClaims as well, the same way it's creating the pods. For this reason, a StatefulSet can also have one or more volume claim templates, which enable it to stamp out PersistentVolumeClaims along with each pod instance (see figure 10.8).

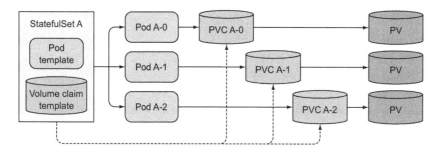

Figure 10.8   A StatefulSet creates both pods and PersistentVolumeClaims.

The PersistentVolumes for the claims can either be provisioned up-front by an administrator or just in time through dynamic provisioning of PersistentVolumes, as explained at the end of chapter 6.

UNDERSTANDING THE CREATION AND DELETION OF PERSISTENTVOLUMECLAIMS

Scaling up a StatefulSet by one creates two or more API objects (the pod and one or more PersistentVolumeClaims referenced by the pod). Scaling down, however, deletes only the pod, leaving the claims alone. The reason for this is obvious, if you consider what happens when a claim is deleted. After a claim is deleted, the PersistentVolume it was bound to gets recycled or deleted and its contents are lost.

Because stateful pods are meant to run stateful applications, which implies that the data they store in the volume is important, deleting the claim on scale-down of a Stateful-Set could be catastrophic—especially since triggering a scale-down is as simple as decreasing the `replicas` field of the StatefulSet. For this reason, you're required to delete PersistentVolumeClaims manually to release the underlying PersistentVolume.

REATTACHING THE PERSISTENTVOLUMECLAIM TO THE NEW INSTANCE OF THE SAME POD

The fact that the PersistentVolumeClaim remains after a scale-down means a subsequent scale-up can reattach the same claim along with the bound PersistentVolume and its contents to the new pod instance (shown in figure 10.9). If you accidentally scale down a StatefulSet, you can undo the mistake by scaling up again and the new pod will get the same persisted state again (as well as the same name).

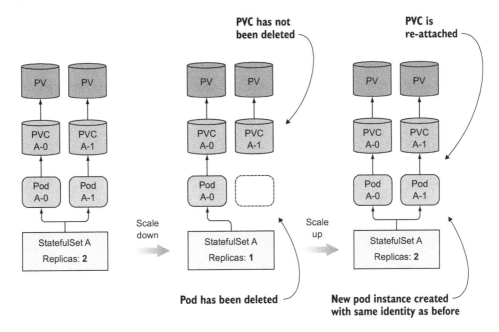

Figure 10.9 StatefulSets don't delete PersistentVolumeClaims when scaling down; then they reattach them when scaling back up.

10.2.4 *Understanding StatefulSet guarantees*

As you've seen so far, StatefulSets behave differently from ReplicaSets or Replication-Controllers. But this doesn't end with the pods having a stable identity and storage. StatefulSets also have different guarantees regarding their pods.

UNDERSTANDING THE IMPLICATIONS OF STABLE IDENTITY AND STORAGE

While regular, stateless pods are fungible, stateful pods aren't. We've already seen how a stateful pod is always replaced with an identical pod (one having the same name and hostname, using the same persistent storage, and so on). This happens when Kubernetes sees that the old pod is no longer there (for example, when you delete the pod manually).

But what if Kubernetes can't be sure about the state of the pod? If it creates a replacement pod with the same identity, two instances of the app with the same identity might be running in the system. The two would also be bound to the same storage, so two processes with the same identity would be writing over the same files. With pods managed by a ReplicaSet, this isn't a problem, because the apps are obviously made to work on the same files. Also, ReplicaSets create pods with a randomly generated identity, so there's no way for two processes to run with the same identity.

INTRODUCING STATEFULSET'S AT-MOST-ONE SEMANTICS

Kubernetes must thus take great care to ensure two stateful pod instances are never running with the same identity and are bound to the same PersistentVolumeClaim. A StatefulSet must guarantee *at-most-one* semantics for stateful pod instances.

This means a StatefulSet must be absolutely certain that a pod is no longer running before it can create a replacement pod. This has a big effect on how node failures are handled. We'll demonstrate this later in the chapter. Before we can do that, however, you need to create a StatefulSet and see how it behaves. You'll also learn a few more things about them along the way.

10.3   Using a StatefulSet

To properly show StatefulSets in action, you'll build your own little clustered data store. Nothing fancy—more like a data store from the Stone Age.

10.3.1   Creating the app and container image

You'll use the kubia app you've used throughout the book as your starting point. You'll expand it so it allows you to store and retrieve a single data entry on each pod instance.

The important parts of the source code of your data store are shown in the following listing.

Listing 10.1   A simple stateful app: kubia-pet-image/app.js

```
...
const dataFile = "/var/data/kubia.txt";
...
var handler = function(request, response) {
  if (request.method == 'POST') {
    var file = fs.createWriteStream(dataFile);
    file.on('open', function (fd) {
      request.pipe(file);
      console.log("New data has been received and stored.");
      response.writeHead(200);
      response.end("Data stored on pod " + os.hostname() + "\n");
    });
  } else {
    var data = fileExists(dataFile)
      ? fs.readFileSync(dataFile, 'utf8')
      : "No data posted yet";
    response.writeHead(200);
    response.write("You've hit " + os.hostname() + "\n");
    response.end("Data stored on this pod: " + data + "\n");
  }
};
```

On POST requests, store the request's body into a data file.

On GET (and all other types of) requests, return your hostname and the contents of the data file.

```
var www = http.createServer(handler);
www.listen(8080);
```

Whenever the app receives a POST request, it writes the data it receives in the body of the request to the file /var/data/kubia.txt. Upon a GET request, it returns the hostname and the stored data (contents of the file). Simple enough, right? This is the first version of your app. It's not clustered yet, but it's enough to get you started. You'll expand the app later in the chapter.

The Dockerfile for building the container image is shown in the following listing and hasn't changed from before.

Listing 10.2   Dockerfile for the stateful app: kubia-pet-image/Dockerfile

```
FROM node:7
ADD app.js /app.js
ENTRYPOINT ["node", "app.js"]
```

Go ahead and build the image now, or use the one I pushed to docker.io/luksa/kubia-pet.

10.3.2   Deploying the app through a StatefulSet

To deploy your app, you'll need to create two (or three) different types of objects:

- PersistentVolumes for storing your data files (you'll need to create these only if the cluster doesn't support dynamic provisioning of PersistentVolumes).
- A governing Service required by the StatefulSet.
- The StatefulSet itself.

For each pod instance, the StatefulSet will create a PersistentVolumeClaim that will bind to a PersistentVolume. If your cluster supports dynamic provisioning, you don't need to create any PersistentVolumes manually (you can skip the next section). If it doesn't, you'll need to create them as explained in the next section.

CREATING THE PERSISTENT VOLUMES

You'll need three PersistentVolumes, because you'll be scaling the StatefulSet up to three replicas. You must create more if you plan on scaling the StatefulSet up more than that.

If you're using Minikube, deploy the PersistentVolumes defined in the Chapter10/persistent-volumes-hostpath.yaml file in the book's code archive.

If you're using Google Kubernetes Engine, you'll first need to create the actual GCE Persistent Disks like this:

```
$ gcloud compute disks create --size=1GiB --zone=europe-west1-b pv-a
$ gcloud compute disks create --size=1GiB --zone=europe-west1-b pv-b
$ gcloud compute disks create --size=1GiB --zone=europe-west1-b pv-c
```

> **NOTE**   Make sure to create the disks in the same zone that your nodes are running in.

Then create the PersistentVolumes from the persistent-volumes-gcepd.yaml file, which is shown in the following listing.

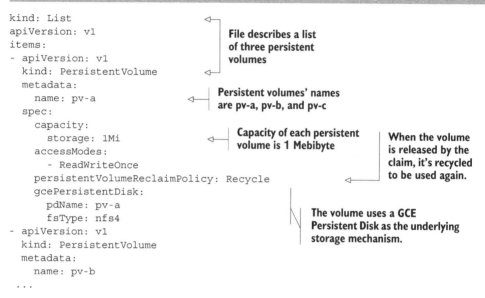

Listing 10.3   Three PersistentVolumes: persistent-volumes-gcepd.yaml

```
kind: List
apiVersion: v1
items:
- apiVersion: v1
  kind: PersistentVolume
  metadata:
    name: pv-a
  spec:
    capacity:
      storage: 1Mi
    accessModes:
      - ReadWriteOnce
    persistentVolumeReclaimPolicy: Recycle
    gcePersistentDisk:
      pdName: pv-a
      fsType: nfs4
- apiVersion: v1
  kind: PersistentVolume
  metadata:
    name: pv-b
...
```

File describes a list of three persistent volumes

Persistent volumes' names are pv-a, pv-b, and pv-c

Capacity of each persistent volume is 1 Mebibyte

When the volume is released by the claim, it's recycled to be used again.

The volume uses a GCE Persistent Disk as the underlying storage mechanism.

NOTE   In the previous chapter you specified multiple resources in the same YAML by delimiting them with a three-dash line. Here you're using a different approach by defining a List object and listing the resources as items of the object. Both methods are equivalent.

This manifest creates PersistentVolumes called `pv-a`, `pv-b`, and `pv-c`. They use GCE Persistent Disks as the underlying storage mechanism, so they're not appropriate for clusters that aren't running on Google Kubernetes Engine or Google Compute Engine. If you're running the cluster elsewhere, you must modify the PersistentVolume definition and use an appropriate volume type, such as NFS (Network File System), or similar.

CREATING THE GOVERNING SERVICE

As explained earlier, before deploying a StatefulSet, you first need to create a headless Service, which will be used to provide the network identity for your stateful pods. The following listing shows the Service manifest.

Listing 10.4   Headless service to be used in the StatefulSet: kubia-service-headless.yaml

```
apiVersion: v1
kind: Service
metadata:
  name: kubia
spec:
  clusterIP: None
```

Name of the Service

The StatefulSet's governing Service must be headless.

```
selector:
  app: kubia
ports:
- name: http
  port: 80
```

All pods with the app=kubia label belong to this service.

You're setting the `clusterIP` field to `None`, which makes this a headless Service. It will enable peer discovery between your pods (you'll need this later). Once you create the Service, you can move on to creating the actual StatefulSet.

CREATING THE STATEFULSET MANIFEST
Now you can finally create the StatefulSet. The following listing shows the manifest.

Listing 10.5   StatefulSet manifest: kubia-statefulset.yaml

```
apiVersion: apps/v1beta1
kind: StatefulSet
metadata:
  name: kubia
spec:
  serviceName: kubia
  replicas: 2
  template:
    metadata:
      labels:
        app: kubia
    spec:
      containers:
      - name: kubia
        image: luksa/kubia-pet
        ports:
        - name: http
          containerPort: 8080
        volumeMounts:
        - name: data
          mountPath: /var/data
  volumeClaimTemplates:
  - metadata:
      name: data
    spec:
      resources:
        requests:
          storage: 1Mi
      accessModes:
      - ReadWriteOnce
```

Pods created by the StatefulSet will have the app=kubia label.

The container inside the pod will mount the pvc volume at this path.

The PersistentVolumeClaims will be created from this template.

The StatefulSet manifest isn't that different from ReplicaSet or Deployment manifests you've created so far. What's new is the `volumeClaimTemplates` list. In it, you're defining one volume claim template called `data`, which will be used to create a PersistentVolumeClaim for each pod. As you may remember from chapter 6, a pod references a claim by including a `persistentVolumeClaim` volume in the manifest. In the previous pod template, you'll find no such volume. The StatefulSet adds it to the pod specification automatically and configures the volume to be bound to the claim the StatefulSet created for the specific pod.

CREATING THE STATEFULSET

You'll create the StatefulSet now:

```
$ kubectl create -f kubia-statefulset.yaml
statefulset "kubia" created
```

Now, list your pods:

```
$ kubectl get po
NAME        READY    STATUS             RESTARTS    AGE
kubia-0     0/1      ContainerCreating  0           1s
```

Notice anything strange? Remember how a ReplicationController or a ReplicaSet creates all the pod instances at the same time? Your StatefulSet is configured to create two replicas, but it created a single pod.

Don't worry, nothing is wrong. The second pod will be created only after the first one is up and ready. StatefulSets behave this way because certain clustered stateful apps are sensitive to race conditions if two or more cluster members come up at the same time, so it's safer to bring each member up fully before continuing to bring up the rest.

List the pods again to see how the pod creation is progressing:

```
$ kubectl get po
NAME        READY    STATUS             RESTARTS    AGE
kubia-0     1/1      Running            0           8s
kubia-1     0/1      ContainerCreating  0           2s
```

See, the first pod is now running, and the second one has been created and is being started.

EXAMINING THE GENERATED STATEFUL POD

Let's take a closer look at the first pod's spec in the following listing to see how the StatefulSet has constructed the pod from the pod template and the PersistentVolumeClaim template.

> **Listing 10.6   A stateful pod created by the StatefulSet**

```
$ kubectl get po kubia-0 -o yaml
apiVersion: v1
kind: Pod
metadata:
  ...
spec:
  containers:
  - image: luksa/kubia-pet
    ...
```

```
        volumeMounts:                              The volume mount, as
        - mountPath: /var/data                     specified in the manifest
          name: data
        - mountPath: /var/run/secrets/kubernetes.io/serviceaccount
          name: default-token-r2m41
          readOnly: true
      ...
      volumes:
      - name: data                                 The volume created
        persistentVolumeClaim:                     by the StatefulSet
          claimName: data-kubia-0
      - name: default-token-r2m41                   The claim referenced
        secret:                                     by this volume
          secretName: default-token-r2m41
```

The PersistentVolumeClaim template was used to create the PersistentVolumeClaim and the volume inside the pod, which refers to the created PersistentVolumeClaim.

EXAMINING THE GENERATED PERSISTENTVOLUMECLAIMS

Now list the generated PersistentVolumeClaims to confirm they were created:

```
$ kubectl get pvc
NAME            STATUS    VOLUME    CAPACITY    ACCESSMODES    AGE
data-kubia-0    Bound     pv-c      0                          37s
data-kubia-1    Bound     pv-a      0                          37s
```

The names of the generated PersistentVolumeClaims are composed of the name defined in the `volumeClaimTemplate` and the name of each pod. You can examine the claims' YAML to see that they match the template.

10.3.3 *Playing with your pods*

With the nodes of your data store cluster now running, you can start exploring it. You can't communicate with your pods through the Service you created because it's headless. You'll need to connect to individual pods directly (or create a regular Service, but that wouldn't allow you to talk to a specific pod).

You've already seen ways to connect to a pod directly: by piggybacking on another pod and running `curl` inside it, by using port-forwarding, and so on. This time, you'll try another option. You'll use the API server as a proxy to the pods.

COMMUNICATING WITH PODS THROUGH THE API SERVER

One useful feature of the API server is the ability to proxy connections directly to individual pods. If you want to perform requests against your `kubia-0` pod, you hit the following URL:

```
<apiServerHost>:<port>/api/v1/namespaces/default/pods/kubia-0/proxy/<path>
```

Because the API server is secured, sending requests to pods through the API server is cumbersome (among other things, you need to pass the authorization token in each request). Luckily, in chapter 8 you learned how to use `kubectl proxy` to talk to the

API server without having to deal with authentication and SSL certificates. Run the proxy again:

```
$ kubectl proxy
Starting to serve on 127.0.0.1:8001
```

Now, because you'll be talking to the API server through the kubectl proxy, you'll use localhost:8001 rather than the actual API server host and port. You'll send a request to the kubia-0 pod like this:

```
$ curl localhost:8001/api/v1/namespaces/default/pods/kubia-0/proxy/
You've hit kubia-0
Data stored on this pod: No data posted yet
```

The response shows that the request was indeed received and handled by the app running in your pod kubia-0.

> **NOTE**   If you receive an empty response, make sure you haven't left out that
> last slash character at the end of the URL (or make sure curl follows redirects
> by using its -L option).

Because you're communicating with the pod through the API server, which you're connecting to through the kubectl proxy, the request went through two different proxies (the first was the kubectl proxy and the other was the API server, which proxied the request to the pod). For a clearer picture, examine figure 10.10.

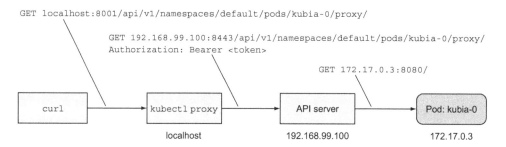

Figure 10.10   Connecting to a pod through both the kubectl proxy and API server proxy

The request you sent to the pod was a GET request, but you can also send POST requests through the API server. This is done by sending a POST request to the same proxy URL as the one you sent the GET request to.

When your app receives a POST request, it stores whatever's in the request body into a local file. Send a POST request to the kubia-0 pod:

```
$ curl -X POST -d "Hey there! This greeting was submitted to kubia-0."
➥ localhost:8001/api/v1/namespaces/default/pods/kubia-0/proxy/
Data stored on pod kubia-0
```

The data you sent should now be stored in that pod. Let's see if it returns the stored data when you perform a GET request again:

```
$ curl localhost:8001/api/v1/namespaces/default/pods/kubia-0/proxy/
You've hit kubia-0
Data stored on this pod: Hey there! This greeting was submitted to kubia-0.
```

Okay, so far so good. Now let's see what the other cluster node (the kubia-1 pod) says:

```
$ curl localhost:8001/api/v1/namespaces/default/pods/kubia-1/proxy/
You've hit kubia-1
Data stored on this pod: No data posted yet
```

As expected, each node has its own state. But is that state persisted? Let's find out.

DELETING A STATEFUL POD TO SEE IF THE RESCHEDULED POD IS REATTACHED TO THE SAME STORAGE

You're going to delete the kubia-0 pod and wait for it to be rescheduled. Then you'll see if it's still serving the same data as before:

```
$ kubectl delete po kubia-0
pod "kubia-0" deleted
```

If you list the pods, you'll see that the pod is terminating:

```
$ kubectl get po
NAME      READY    STATUS         RESTARTS    AGE
kubia-0   1/1      Terminating    0           3m
kubia-1   1/1      Running        0           3m
```

As soon as it terminates successfully, a new pod with the same name is created by the StatefulSet:

```
$ kubectl get po
NAME      READY    STATUS              RESTARTS    AGE
kubia-0   0/1      ContainerCreating   0           6s
kubia-1   1/1      Running             0           4m
$ kubectl get po
NAME      READY    STATUS    RESTARTS    AGE
kubia-0   1/1      Running   0           9s
kubia-1   1/1      Running   0           4m
```

Let me remind you again that this new pod may be scheduled to any node in the cluster, not necessarily the same node that the old pod was scheduled to. The old pod's whole identity (the name, hostname, and the storage) is effectively moved to the new node (as shown in figure 10.11). If you're using Minikube, you can't see this because it only runs a single node, but in a multi-node cluster, you may see the pod scheduled to a different node than before.

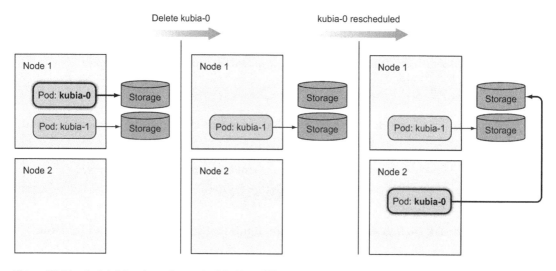

Figure 10.11   A stateful pod may be rescheduled to a different node, but it retains the name, hostname, and storage.

With the new pod now running, let's check to see if it has the exact same identity as in its previous incarnation. The pod's name is the same, but what about the hostname and persistent data? You can ask the pod itself to confirm:

```
$ curl localhost:8001/api/v1/namespaces/default/pods/kubia-0/proxy/
You've hit kubia-0
Data stored on this pod: Hey there! This greeting was submitted to kubia-0.
```

The pod's response shows that both the hostname and the data are the same as before, confirming that a StatefulSet always replaces a deleted pod with what's effectively the exact same pod.

SCALING A STATEFULSET

Scaling down a StatefulSet and scaling it back up after an extended time period should be no different than deleting a pod and having the StatefulSet recreate it immediately. Remember that scaling down a StatefulSet only deletes the pods, but leaves the PersistentVolumeClaims untouched. I'll let you try scaling down the StatefulSet yourself and confirm this behavior.

The key thing to remember is that scaling down (and up) is performed gradually—similar to how individual pods are created when the StatefulSet is created initially. When scaling down by more than one instance, the pod with the highest ordinal number is deleted first. Only after the pod terminates completely is the pod with the second highest ordinal number deleted.

EXPOSING STATEFUL PODS THROUGH A REGULAR, NON-HEADLESS SERVICE

Before you move on to the last part of this chapter, you're going to add a proper, non-headless Service in front of your pods, because clients usually connect to the pods through a Service rather than connecting directly.

You know how to create the Service by now, but in case you don't, the following listing shows the manifest.

```
apiVersion: v1
kind: Service
metadata:
  name: kubia-public
spec:
  selector:
    app: kubia
  ports:
  - port: 80
    targetPort: 8080
```

Because this isn't an externally exposed Service (it's a regular `ClusterIP` Service, not
a `NodePort` or a `LoadBalancer`-type Service), you can only access it from inside the
cluster. You'll need a pod to access it from, right? Not necessarily.

CONNECTING TO CLUSTER-INTERNAL SERVICES THROUGH THE API SERVER

Instead of using a piggyback pod to access the service from inside the cluster, you can
use the same proxy feature provided by the API server to access the service the way
you've accessed individual pods.

The URI path for proxy-ing requests to Services is formed like this:

```
/api/v1/namespaces/<namespace>/services/<service name>/proxy/<path>
```

Therefore, you can run `curl` on your local machine and access the service through the
kubectl proxy like this (you ran kubectl proxy earlier and it should still be running):

```
$ curl localhost:8001/api/v1/namespaces/default/services/kubia-
➥ public/proxy/
You've hit kubia-1
Data stored on this pod: No data posted yet
```

Likewise, clients (inside the cluster) can use the kubia-public service for storing to
and reading data from your clustered data store. Of course, each request lands on a
random cluster node, so you'll get the data from a random node each time. You'll
improve this next.

10.4 Discovering peers in a StatefulSet

We still need to cover one more important thing. An important requirement of clustered apps is peer discovery—the ability to find other members of the cluster. Each
member of a StatefulSet needs to easily find all the other members. Sure, it could do
that by talking to the API server, but one of Kubernetes' aims is to expose features that
help keep applications completely Kubernetes-agnostic. Having apps talk to the Kubernetes API is therefore undesirable.

How can a pod discover its peers without talking to the API? Is there an existing, well-known technology you can use that makes this possible? How about the Domain Name System (DNS)? Depending on how much you know about DNS, you probably understand what an A, CNAME, or MX record is used for. Other lesser-known types of DNS records also exist. One of them is the SRV record.

INTRODUCING SRV RECORDS

SRV records are used to point to hostnames and ports of servers providing a specific service. Kubernetes creates SRV records to point to the hostnames of the pods backing a headless service.

You're going to list the SRV records for your stateful pods by running the dig DNS lookup tool inside a new temporary pod. This is the command you'll use:

```
$ kubectl run -it srvlookup --image=tutum/dnsutils --rm
  --restart=Never -- dig SRV kubia.default.svc.cluster.local
```

The command runs a one-off pod (`--restart=Never`) called srvlookup, which is attached to the console (`-it`) and is deleted as soon as it terminates (`--rm`). The pod runs a single container from the tutum/dnsutils image and runs the following command:

```
dig SRV kubia.default.svc.cluster.local
```

The following listing shows what the command prints out.

Listing 10.8   Listing DNS SRV records of your headless Service

```
...
;; ANSWER SECTION:
k.d.s.c.l. 30 IN   SRV      10 33 0 kubia-0.kubia.default.svc.cluster.local.
k.d.s.c.l. 30 IN   SRV      10 33 0 kubia-1.kubia.default.svc.cluster.local.

;; ADDITIONAL SECTION:
kubia-0.kubia.default.svc.cluster.local. 30 IN A 172.17.0.4
kubia-1.kubia.default.svc.cluster.local. 30 IN A 172.17.0.6
...
```

> **NOTE**   I've had to shorten the actual name to get records to fit into a single line, so kubia.d.s.c.l is actually kubia.default.svc.cluster.local.

The ANSWER SECTION shows two SRV records pointing to the two pods backing your headless service. Each pod also gets its own A record, as shown in ADDITIONAL SECTION.

For a pod to get a list of all the other pods of a StatefulSet, all you need to do is perform an SRV DNS lookup. In Node.js, for example, the lookup is performed like this:

```
dns.resolveSrv("kubia.default.svc.cluster.local", callBackFunction);
```

You'll use this command in your app to enable each pod to discover its peers.

NOTE The order of the returned SRV records is random, because they all have the same priority. Don't expect to always see kubia-0 listed before kubia-1.

10.4.1 *Implementing peer discovery through DNS*

Your Stone Age data store isn't clustered yet. Each data store node runs completely independently of all the others—no communication exists between them. You'll get them talking to each other next.

Data posted by clients connecting to your data store cluster through the kubia-public Service lands on a random cluster node. The cluster can store multiple data entries, but clients currently have no good way to see all those entries. Because services forward requests to pods randomly, a client would need to perform many requests until it hit all the pods if it wanted to get the data from all the pods.

You can improve this by having the node respond with data from all the cluster nodes. To do this, the node needs to find all its peers. You're going to use what you learned about StatefulSets and SRV records to do this.

You'll modify your app's source code as shown in the following listing (the full source is available in the book's code archive; the listing shows only the important parts).

Listing 10.9 **Discovering peers in a sample app: kubia-pet-peers-image/app.js**

```
...
const dns = require('dns');

const dataFile = "/var/data/kubia.txt";
const serviceName = "kubia.default.svc.cluster.local";
const port = 8080;
...

var handler = function(request, response) {
  if (request.method == 'POST') {
    ...
  } else {
    response.writeHead(200);
    if (request.url == '/data') {
      var data = fileExists(dataFile)
        ? fs.readFileSync(dataFile, 'utf8')
        : "No data posted yet";
      response.end(data);
    } else {
      response.write("You've hit " + os.hostname() + "\n");
      response.write("Data stored in the cluster:\n");
      dns.resolveSrv(serviceName, function (err, addresses) {    <─┐  The app
        if (err) {                                                │  performs a DNS
          response.end("Could not look up DNS SRV records: " + err);  lookup to obtain
          return;                                                 │  SRV records.
        }
        var numResponses = 0;
        if (addresses.length == 0) {
          response.end("No peers discovered.");
        } else {
```

```
addresses.forEach(function (item) {                          ◁──
  var requestOptions = {                                              Each pod
    host: item.name,                                                  pointed to by
    port: port,                                                       an SRV record is
    path: '/data'                                                     then contacted
  };                                                                  to get its data.
  httpGet(requestOptions, function (returnedData) {        ◁──
    numResponses++;
    response.write("- " + item.name + ": " + returnedData);
    response.write("\n");
    if (numResponses == addresses.length) {
      response.end();
    }
  });
});
    }
  });
    }
  }
};
...
```

Figure 10.12 shows what happens when a GET request is received by your app. The server that receives the request first performs a lookup of SRV records for the headless `kubia` service and then sends a GET request to each of the pods backing the service (even to itself, which obviously isn't necessary, but I wanted to keep the code as simple as possible). It then returns a list of all the nodes along with the data stored on each of them.

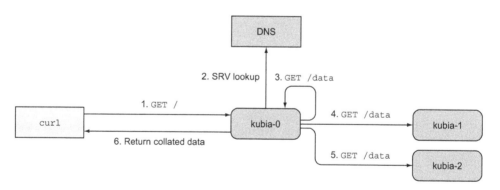

Figure 10.12   The operation of your simplistic distributed data store

The container image containing this new version of the app is available at docker.io/luksa/kubia-pet-peers.

10.4.2 Updating a StatefulSet

Your StatefulSet is already running, so let's see how to update its pod template so the pods use the new image. You'll also set the replica count to 3 at the same time. To update the StatefulSet, use the `kubectl edit` command (the `patch` command would be another option):

```
$ kubectl edit statefulset kubia
```

This opens the StatefulSet definition in your default editor. In the definition, change `spec.replicas` to 3 and modify the `spec.template.spec.containers.image` attribute so it points to the new image (`luksa/kubia-pet-peers` instead of `luksa/kubia-pet`). Save the file and exit the editor to update the StatefulSet. Two replicas were running previously, so you should now see an additional replica called `kubia-2` starting. List the pods to confirm:

```
$ kubectl get po
NAME       READY    STATUS              RESTARTS    AGE
kubia-0    1/1      Running             0           25m
kubia-1    1/1      Running             0           26m
kubia-2    0/1      ContainerCreating   0           4s
```

The new pod instance is running the new image. But what about the existing two replicas? Judging from their age, they don't seem to have been updated. This is expected, because initially, StatefulSets were more like ReplicaSets and not like Deployments, so they don't perform a rollout when the template is modified. You need to delete the replicas manually and the StatefulSet will bring them up again based on the new template:

```
$ kubectl delete po kubia-0 kubia-1
pod "kubia-0" deleted
pod "kubia-1" deleted
```

> **NOTE** Starting from Kubernetes version 1.7, StatefulSets support rolling updates the same way Deployments and DaemonSets do. See the StatefulSet's `spec.updateStrategy` field documentation using `kubectl explain` for more information.

10.4.3 *Trying out your clustered data store*

Once the two pods are up, you can see if your shiny new Stone Age data store works as expected. Post a few requests to the cluster, as shown in the following listing.

> **Listing 10.10 Writing to the clustered data store through the service**

```
$ curl -X POST -d "The sun is shining" \
  localhost:8001/api/v1/namespaces/default/services/kubia-public/proxy/
Data stored on pod kubia-1

$ curl -X POST -d "The weather is sweet" \
  localhost:8001/api/v1/namespaces/default/services/kubia-public/proxy/
Data stored on pod kubia-0
```

Now, read the stored data, as shown in the following listing.

```
Listing 10.11   Reading from the data store
```

```
$ curl localhost:8001/api/v1/namespaces/default/services
↪ /kubia-public/proxy/
You've hit kubia-2
Data stored on each cluster node:
- kubia-0.kubia.default.svc.cluster.local: The weather is sweet
- kubia-1.kubia.default.svc.cluster.local: The sun is shining
- kubia-2.kubia.default.svc.cluster.local: No data posted yet
```

Nice! When a client request reaches one of your cluster nodes, it discovers all its peers, gathers data from them, and sends all the data back to the client. Even if you scale the StatefulSet up or down, the pod servicing the client's request can always find all the peers running at that time.

The app itself isn't that useful, but I hope you found it a fun way to show how instances of a replicated stateful app can discover their peers and handle horizontal scaling with ease.

10.5   Understanding how StatefulSets deal with node failures

In section 10.2.4 we stated that Kubernetes must be absolutely sure that a stateful pod is no longer running before creating its replacement. When a node fails abruptly, Kubernetes can't know the state of the node or its pods. It can't know whether the pods are no longer running, or if they still are and are possibly even still reachable, and it's only the Kubelet that has stopped reporting the node's state to the master.

Because a StatefulSet guarantees that there will never be two pods running with the same identity and storage, when a node appears to have failed, the StatefulSet cannot and should not create a replacement pod until it knows for certain that the pod is no longer running.

It can only know that when the cluster administrator tells it so. To do that, the admin needs to either delete the pod or delete the whole node (doing so then deletes all the pods scheduled to the node).

As your final exercise in this chapter, you'll look at what happens to StatefulSets and their pods when one of the cluster nodes gets disconnected from the network.

10.5.1   Simulating a node's disconnection from the network

As in chapter 4, you'll simulate the node disconnecting from the network by shutting down the node's eth0 network interface. Because this example requires multiple nodes, you can't run it on Minikube. You'll use Google Kubernetes Engine instead.

SHUTTING DOWN THE NODE'S NETWORK ADAPTER

To shut down a node's eth0 interface, you need to ssh into one of the nodes like this:

```
$ gcloud compute ssh gke-kubia-default-pool-32a2cac8-m0g1
```

Then, inside the node, run the following command:

```
$ sudo ifconfig eth0 down
```

Your ssh session will stop working, so you'll need to open another terminal to continue.

CHECKING THE NODE'S STATUS AS SEEN BY THE KUBERNETES MASTER

With the node's network interface down, the Kubelet running on the node can no longer contact the Kubernetes API server and let it know that the node and all its pods are still running.

After a while, the control plane will mark the node as NotReady. You can see this when listing nodes, as the following listing shows.

> **Listing 10.12 Observing a failed node's status change to** NotReady

```
$ kubectl get node
NAME                                   STATUS     AGE    VERSION
gke-kubia-default-pool-32a2cac8-596v   Ready      16m    v1.6.2
gke-kubia-default-pool-32a2cac8-m0g1   NotReady   16m    v1.6.2
gke-kubia-default-pool-32a2cac8-sgl7   Ready      16m    v1.6.2
```

Because the control plane is no longer getting status updates from the node, the status of all pods on that node is Unknown. This is shown in the pod list in the following listing.

> **Listing 10.13 Observing the pod's status change after its node becomes** NotReady

```
$ kubectl get po
NAME      READY    STATUS     RESTARTS    AGE
kubia-0   1/1      Unknown    0           15m
kubia-1   1/1      Running    0           14m
kubia-2   1/1      Running    0           13m
```

As you can see, the kubia-0 pod's status is no longer known because the pod was (and still is) running on the node whose network interface you shut down.

UNDERSTANDING WHAT HAPPENS TO PODS WHOSE STATUS IS UNKNOWN

If the node were to come back online and report its and its pod statuses again, the pod would again be marked as Running. But if the pod's status remains unknown for more than a few minutes (this time is configurable), the pod is automatically evicted from the node. This is done by the master (the Kubernetes control plane). It evicts the pod by deleting the pod resource.

When the Kubelet sees that the pod has been marked for deletion, it starts terminating the pod. In your case, the Kubelet can no longer reach the master (because you disconnected the node from the network), which means the pod will keep running.

Let's examine the current situation. Use kubectl describe to display details about the kubia-0 pod, as shown in the following listing.

Listing 10.14   Displaying details of the pod with the unknown status

```
$ kubectl describe po kubia-0
Name:        kubia-0
Namespace:   default
Node:        gke-kubia-default-pool-32a2cac8-m0g1/10.132.0.2
...
Status:      Terminating (expires Tue, 23 May 2017 15:06:09 +0200)
Reason:      NodeLost
Message:     Node gke-kubia-default-pool-32a2cac8-m0g1 which was
             running pod kubia-0 is unresponsive
```

The pod is shown as Terminating, with NodeLost listed as the reason for the termination. The message says the node is considered lost because it's unresponsive.

> **NOTE** What's shown here is the control plane's view of the world. In reality, the pod's container is still running perfectly fine. It isn't terminating at all.

10.5.2 *Deleting the pod manually*

You know the node isn't coming back, but you need all three pods running to handle clients properly. You need to get the kubia-0 pod rescheduled to a healthy node. As mentioned earlier, you need to delete the node or the pod manually.

DELETING THE POD IN THE USUAL WAY

Delete the pod the way you've always deleted pods:

```
$ kubectl delete po kubia-0
pod "kubia-0" deleted
```

All done, right? By deleting the pod, the StatefulSet should immediately create a replacement pod, which will get scheduled to one of the remaining nodes. List the pods again to confirm:

```
$ kubectl get po
NAME       READY   STATUS    RESTARTS   AGE
kubia-0    1/1     Unknown   0          15m
kubia-1    1/1     Running   0          14m
kubia-2    1/1     Running   0          13m
```

That's strange. You deleted the pod a moment ago and kubectl said it had deleted it. Why is the same pod still there?

> **NOTE** The kubia-0 pod in the listing isn't a new pod with the same name—this is clear by looking at the AGE column. If it were new, its age would be merely a few seconds.

UNDERSTANDING WHY THE POD ISN'T DELETED

The pod was marked for deletion even before you deleted it. That's because the control plane itself already deleted it (in order to evict it from the node).

If you look at listing 10.14 again, you'll see that the pod's status is `Terminating`. The pod was already marked for deletion earlier and will be removed as soon as the Kubelet on its node notifies the API server that the pod's containers have terminated. Because the node's network is down, this will never happen.

FORCIBLY DELETING THE POD

The only thing you can do is tell the API server to delete the pod without waiting for the Kubelet to confirm that the pod is no longer running. You do that like this:

```
$ kubectl delete po kubia-0 --force --grace-period 0
warning: Immediate deletion does not wait for confirmation that the running
    resource has been terminated. The resource may continue to run on the
    cluster indefinitely.
pod "kubia-0" deleted
```

You need to use both the `--force` and `--grace-period 0` options. The warning displayed by `kubectl` notifies you of what you did. If you list the pods again, you'll finally see a new `kubia-0` pod created:

```
$ kubectl get po
NAME         READY    STATUS             RESTARTS    AGE
kubia-0      0/1      ContainerCreating  0           8s
kubia-1      1/1      Running            0           20m
kubia-2      1/1      Running            0           19m
```

> **WARNING** Don't delete stateful pods forcibly unless you know the node is no longer running or is unreachable (and will remain so forever).

Before continuing, you may want to bring the node you disconnected back online. You can do that by restarting the node through the GCE web console or in a terminal by issuing the following command:

```
$ gcloud compute instances reset <node name>
```

10.6 *Summary*

This concludes the chapter on using StatefulSets to deploy stateful apps. This chapter has shown you how to

- Give replicated pods individual storage
- Provide a stable identity to a pod
- Create a StatefulSet and a corresponding headless governing Service
- Scale and update a StatefulSet
- Discover other members of the StatefulSet through DNS

- Connect to other members through their host names
- Forcibly delete stateful pods

Now that you know the major building blocks you can use to have Kubernetes run and manage your apps, we can look more closely at how it does that. In the next chapter, you'll learn about the individual components that control the Kubernetes cluster and keep your apps running.

Understanding
Kubernetes internals

11

This chapter covers

- What components make up a Kubernetes cluster
- What each component does and how it does it
- How creating a Deployment object results in a running pod
- What a running pod is
- How the network between pods works
- How Kubernetes Services work
- How high-availability is achieved

By reading this book up to this point, you've become familiar with what Kubernetes has to offer and what it does. But so far, I've intentionally not spent much time explaining exactly how it does all this because, in my opinion, it makes no sense to go into details of how a system works until you have a good understanding of what the system does. That's why we haven't talked about exactly how a pod is scheduled or how the various controllers running inside the Controller Manager make deployed resources come to life. Because you now know most resources that can be deployed in Kubernetes, it's time to dive into how they're implemented.

11.1   *Understanding the architecture*

Before you look at how Kubernetes does what it does, let's take a closer look at the components that make up a Kubernetes cluster. In chapter 1, you saw that a Kubernetes cluster is split into two parts:

- The Kubernetes Control Plane
- The (worker) nodes

Let's look more closely at what these two parts do and what's running inside them.

COMPONENTS OF THE CONTROL PLANE

The Control Plane is what controls and makes the whole cluster function. To refresh your memory, the components that make up the Control Plane are

- The etcd distributed persistent storage
- The API server
- The Scheduler
- The Controller Manager

These components store and manage the state of the cluster, but they aren't what runs the application containers.

COMPONENTS RUNNING ON THE WORKER NODES

The task of running your containers is up to the components running on each worker node:

- The Kubelet
- The Kubernetes Service Proxy (kube-proxy)
- The Container Runtime (Docker, rkt, or others)

ADD-ON COMPONENTS

Beside the Control Plane components and the components running on the nodes, a few add-on components are required for the cluster to provide everything discussed so far. This includes

- The Kubernetes DNS server
- The Dashboard
- An Ingress controller
- Heapster, which we'll talk about in chapter 14
- The Container Network Interface network plugin (we'll explain it later in this chapter)

11.1.1   *The distributed nature of Kubernetes components*

The previously mentioned components all run as individual processes. The components and their inter-dependencies are shown in figure 11.1.

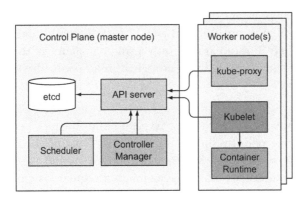

Figure 11.1 Kubernetes components of the Control Plane and the worker nodes

To get all the features Kubernetes provides, all these components need to be running. But several can also perform useful work individually without the other components. You'll see how as we examine each of them.

Checking the status of the Control Plane components

The API server exposes an API resource called ComponentStatus, which shows the health status of each Control Plane component. You can list the components and their statuses with kubectl:

```
$ kubectl get componentstatuses
NAME                   STATUS     MESSAGE              ERROR
scheduler              Healthy    ok
controller-manager     Healthy    ok
etcd-0                 Healthy    {"health": "true"}
```

HOW THESE COMPONENTS COMMUNICATE

Kubernetes system components communicate only with the API server. They don't talk to each other directly. The API server is the only component that communicates with etcd. None of the other components communicate with etcd directly, but instead modify the cluster state by talking to the API server.

Connections between the API server and the other components are almost always initiated by the components, as shown in figure 11.1. But the API server does connect to the Kubelet when you use kubectl to fetch logs, use kubectl attach to connect to a running container, or use the kubectl port-forward command.

> **NOTE** The kubectl attach command is similar to kubectl exec, but it attaches to the main process running in the container instead of running an additional one.

RUNNING MULTIPLE INSTANCES OF INDIVIDUAL COMPONENTS

Although the components on the worker nodes all need to run on the same node, the components of the Control Plane can easily be split across multiple servers. There can be more than one instance of each Control Plane component running to ensure high availability. While multiple instances of etcd and API server can be active at the same time and do perform their jobs in parallel, only a single instance of the Scheduler and the Controller Manager may be active at a given time—with the others in standby mode.

HOW COMPONENTS ARE RUN

The Control Plane components, as well as kube-proxy, can either be deployed on the system directly or they can run as pods (as shown in listing 11.1). You may be surprised to hear this, but it will all make sense later when we talk about the Kubelet.

The Kubelet is the only component that always runs as a regular system component, and it's the Kubelet that then runs all the other components as pods. To run the Control Plane components as pods, the Kubelet is also deployed on the master. The next listing shows pods in the `kube-system` namespace in a cluster created with `kubeadm`, which is explained in appendix B.

Listing 11.1   Kubernetes components running as pods

```
$ kubectl get po -o custom-columns=POD:metadata.name,NODE:spec.nodeName
➥ --sort-by spec.nodeName -n kube-system
POD                                NODE
kube-controller-manager-master     master
kube-dns-2334855451-37d9k          master
etcd-master                        master
kube-apiserver-master              master
kube-scheduler-master              master
kube-flannel-ds-tgj9k              node1
kube-proxy-ny3xm                   node1
kube-flannel-ds-0eek8              node2
kube-proxy-sp362                   node2
kube-flannel-ds-r5yf4              node3
kube-proxy-og9ac                   node3
```

etcd, API server, Scheduler, Controller Manager, and the DNS server are running on the master.

The three nodes each run a Kube Proxy pod and a Flannel networking pod.

As you can see in the listing, all the Control Plane components are running as pods on the master node. There are three worker nodes, and each one runs the kube-proxy and a Flannel pod, which provides the overlay network for the pods (we'll talk about Flannel later).

> **TIP**   As shown in the listing, you can tell `kubectl` to display custom columns with the `-o custom-columns` option and sort the resource list with `--sort-by`.

Now, let's look at each of the components up close, starting with the lowest level component of the Control Plane—the persistent storage.

11.1.2   *How Kubernetes uses etcd*

All the objects you've created throughout this book—Pods, ReplicationControllers, Services, Secrets, and so on—need to be stored somewhere in a persistent manner so their manifests survive API server restarts and failures. For this, Kubernetes uses etcd, which is a fast, distributed, and consistent key-value store. Because it's distributed, you can run more than one etcd instance to provide both high availability and better performance.

The only component that talks to etcd directly is the Kubernetes API server. All other components read and write data to etcd indirectly through the API server. This brings a few benefits, among them a more robust optimistic locking system as well as validation; and, by abstracting away the actual storage mechanism from all the other components, it's much simpler to replace it in the future. It's worth emphasizing that etcd is the *only* place Kubernetes stores cluster state and metadata.

About optimistic concurrency control

Optimistic concurrency control (sometimes referred to as optimistic locking) is a method where instead of locking a piece of data and preventing it from being read or updated while the lock is in place, the piece of data includes a version number. Every time the data is updated, the version number increases. When updating the data, the version number is checked to see if it has increased between the time the client read the data and the time it submits the update. If this happens, the update is rejected and the client must re-read the new data and try to update it again.

The result is that when two clients try to update the same data entry, only the first one succeeds.

All Kubernetes resources include a `metadata.resourceVersion` field, which clients need to pass back to the API server when updating an object. If the version doesn't match the one stored in etcd, the API server rejects the update.

HOW RESOURCES ARE STORED IN ETCD

As I'm writing this, Kubernetes can use either etcd version 2 or version 3, but version 3 is now recommended because of improved performance. etcd v2 stores keys in a hierarchical key space, which makes key-value pairs similar to files in a file system. Each key in etcd is either a directory, which contains other keys, or is a regular key with a corresponding value. etcd v3 doesn't support directories, but because the key format remains the same (keys can include slashes), you can still think of them as being grouped into directories. Kubernetes stores all its data in etcd under /registry. The following listing shows a list of keys stored under /registry.

> Listing 11.2   Top-level entries stored in etcd by Kubernetes

```
$ etcdctl ls /registry
/registry/configmaps
/registry/daemonsets
/registry/deployments
/registry/events
/registry/namespaces
/registry/pods
...
```

You'll recognize that these keys correspond to the resource types you learned about in the previous chapters.

> **NOTE** If you're using v3 of the etcd API, you can't use the `ls` command to see the contents of a directory. Instead, you can list all keys that start with a given prefix with `etcdctl get /registry --prefix=true`.

The following listing shows the contents of the /registry/pods directory.

Listing 11.3   Keys in the `/registry/pods` directory

```
$ etcdctl ls /registry/pods
/registry/pods/default
/registry/pods/kube-system
```

As you can infer from the names, these two entries correspond to the `default` and the `kube-system` namespaces, which means pods are stored per namespace. The following listing shows the entries in the /registry/pods/default directory.

Listing 11.4   etcd entries for pods in the `default` namespace

```
$ etcdctl ls /registry/pods/default
/registry/pods/default/kubia-159041347-xk0vc
/registry/pods/default/kubia-159041347-wt6ga
/registry/pods/default/kubia-159041347-hp2o5
```

Each entry corresponds to an individual pod. These aren't directories, but key-value entries. The following listing shows what's stored in one of them.

Listing 11.5   An etcd entry representing a pod

```
$ etcdctl get /registry/pods/default/kubia-159041347-wt6ga
{"kind":"Pod","apiVersion":"v1","metadata":{"name":"kubia-159041347-wt6ga",
"generateName":"kubia-159041347-","namespace":"default","selfLink":...
```

You'll recognize that this is nothing other than a pod definition in JSON format. The API server stores the complete JSON representation of a resource in etcd. Because of etcd's hierarchical key space, you can think of all the stored resources as JSON files in a filesystem. Simple, right?

> **WARNING** Prior to Kubernetes version 1.7, the JSON manifest of a `Secret` resource was also stored like this (it wasn't encrypted). If someone got direct access to etcd, they knew all your Secrets. From version 1.7, Secrets are encrypted and thus stored much more securely.

ENSURING THE CONSISTENCY AND VALIDITY OF STORED OBJECTS

Remember Google's Borg and Omega systems mentioned in chapter 1, which are what Kubernetes is based on? Like Kubernetes, Omega also uses a centralized store to hold the state of the cluster, but in contrast, multiple Control Plane components access the store directly. All these components need to make sure they all adhere to the same optimistic locking mechanism to handle conflicts properly. A single component not adhering fully to the mechanism may lead to inconsistent data.

Kubernetes improves this by requiring all other Control Plane components to go through the API server. This way updates to the cluster state are always consistent, because the optimistic locking mechanism is implemented in a single place, so less chance exists, if any, of error. The API server also makes sure that the data written to the store is always valid and that changes to the data are only performed by authorized clients.

ENSURING CONSISTENCY WHEN ETCD IS CLUSTERED

For ensuring high availability, you'll usually run more than a single instance of etcd. Multiple etcd instances will need to remain consistent. Such a distributed system needs to reach a consensus on what the actual state is. etcd uses the RAFT consensus algorithm to achieve this, which ensures that at any given moment, each node's state is either what the majority of the nodes agrees is the current state or is one of the previously agreed upon states.

Clients connecting to different nodes of an etcd cluster will either see the actual current state or one of the states from the past (in Kubernetes, the only etcd client is the API server, but there may be multiple instances).

The consensus algorithm requires a majority (or quorum) for the cluster to progress to the next state. As a result, if the cluster splits into two disconnected groups of nodes, the state in the two groups can never diverge, because to transition from the previous state to the new one, there needs to be more than half of the nodes taking part in the state change. If one group contains the majority of all nodes, the other one obviously doesn't. The first group can modify the cluster state, whereas the other one can't. When the two groups reconnect, the second group can catch up with the state in the first group (see figure 11.2).

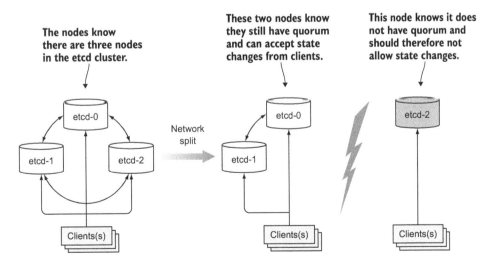

Figure 11.2 In a split-brain scenario, only the side which still has the majority (quorum) accepts state changes.

WHY THE NUMBER OF ETCD INSTANCES SHOULD BE AN ODD NUMBER

etcd is usually deployed with an odd number of instances. I'm sure you'd like to know why. Let's compare having two vs. having one instance. Having two instances requires both instances to be present to have a majority. If either of them fails, the etcd cluster can't transition to a new state because no majority exists. Having two instances is worse than having only a single instance. By having two, the chance of the whole cluster failing has increased by 100%, compared to that of a single-node cluster failing.

The same applies when comparing three vs. four etcd instances. With three instances, one instance can fail and a majority (of two) still exists. With four instances, you need three nodes for a majority (two aren't enough). In both three- and four-instance clusters, only a single instance may fail. But when running four instances, if one fails, a higher possibility exists of an additional instance of the three remaining instances failing (compared to a three-node cluster with one failed node and two remaining nodes).

Usually, for large clusters, an etcd cluster of five or seven nodes is sufficient. It can handle a two- or a three-node failure, respectively, which suffices in almost all situations.

11.1.3   *What the API server does*

The Kubernetes API server is the central component used by all other components and by clients, such as `kubectl`. It provides a CRUD (Create, Read, Update, Delete) interface for querying and modifying the cluster state over a RESTful API. It stores that state in etcd.

In addition to providing a consistent way of storing objects in etcd, it also performs validation of those objects, so clients can't store improperly configured objects (which they could if they were writing to the store directly). Along with validation, it also handles optimistic locking, so changes to an object are never overridden by other clients in the event of concurrent updates.

One of the API server's clients is the command-line tool `kubectl` you've been using from the beginning of the book. When creating a resource from a JSON file, for example, `kubectl` posts the file's contents to the API server through an HTTP POST request. Figure 11.3 shows what happens inside the API server when it receives the request. This is explained in more detail in the next few paragraphs.

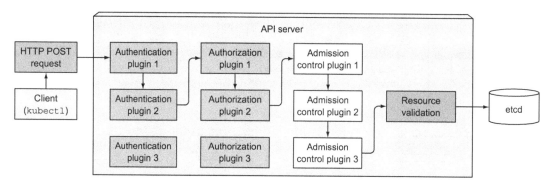

Figure 11.3   The operation of the API server

AUTHENTICATING THE CLIENT WITH AUTHENTICATION PLUGINS

First, the API server needs to authenticate the client sending the request. This is performed by one or more authentication plugins configured in the API server. The API server calls these plugins in turn, until one of them determines who is sending the request. It does this by inspecting the HTTP request.

Depending on the authentication method, the user can be extracted from the client's certificate or an HTTP header, such as `Authorization`, which you used in chapter 8. The plugin extracts the client's username, user ID, and groups the user belongs to. This data is then used in the next stage, which is authorization.

AUTHORIZING THE CLIENT WITH AUTHORIZATION PLUGINS

Besides authentication plugins, the API server is also configured to use one or more authorization plugins. Their job is to determine whether the authenticated user can perform the requested action on the requested resource. For example, when creating pods, the API server consults all authorization plugins in turn, to determine whether the user can create pods in the requested namespace. As soon as a plugin says the user can perform the action, the API server progresses to the next stage.

VALIDATING AND/OR MODIFYING THE RESOURCE IN THE REQUEST WITH ADMISSION CONTROL PLUGINS

If the request is trying to create, modify, or delete a resource, the request is sent through Admission Control. Again, the server is configured with multiple Admission Control plugins. These plugins can modify the resource for different reasons. They may initialize fields missing from the resource specification to the configured default values or even override them. They may even modify other related resources, which aren't in the request, and can also reject a request for whatever reason. The resource passes through all Admission Control plugins.

> **NOTE** When the request is only trying to read data, the request doesn't go through the Admission Control.

Examples of Admission Control plugins include

- `AlwaysPullImages`—Overrides the pod's `imagePullPolicy` to `Always`, forcing the image to be pulled every time the pod is deployed.
- `ServiceAccount`—Applies the default service account to pods that don't specify it explicitly.
- `NamespaceLifecycle`—Prevents creation of pods in namespaces that are in the process of being deleted, as well as in non-existing namespaces.
- `ResourceQuota`—Ensures pods in a certain namespace only use as much CPU and memory as has been allotted to the namespace. We'll learn more about this in chapter 14.

You'll find a list of additional Admission Control plugins in the Kubernetes documentation at https://kubernetes.io/docs/admin/admission-controllers/.

VALIDATING THE RESOURCE AND STORING IT PERSISTENTLY

After letting the request pass through all the Admission Control plugins, the API server then validates the object, stores it in etcd, and returns a response to the client.

11.1.4 Understanding how the API server notifies clients of resource changes

The API server doesn't do anything else except what we've discussed. For example, it doesn't create pods when you create a ReplicaSet resource and it doesn't manage the endpoints of a service. That's what controllers in the Controller Manager do.

But the API server doesn't even tell these controllers what to do. All it does is enable those controllers and other components to observe changes to deployed resources. A Control Plane component can request to be notified when a resource is created, modified, or deleted. This enables the component to perform whatever task it needs in response to a change of the cluster metadata.

Clients watch for changes by opening an HTTP connection to the API server. Through this connection, the client will then receive a stream of modifications to the watched objects. Every time an object is updated, the server sends the new version of the object to all connected clients watching the object. Figure 11.4 shows how clients can watch for changes to pods and how a change to one of the pods is stored into etcd and then relayed to all clients watching pods at that moment.

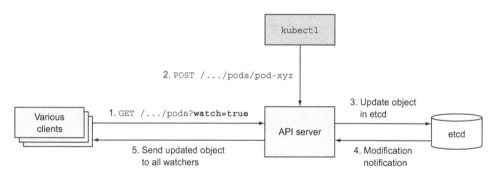

Figure 11.4   When an object is updated, the API server sends the updated object to all interested watchers.

One of the API server's clients is the kubectl tool, which also supports watching resources. For example, when deploying a pod, you don't need to constantly poll the list of pods by repeatedly executing kubectl get pods. Instead, you can use the --watch flag and be notified of each creation, modification, or deletion of a pod, as shown in the following listing.

> **Listing 11.6   Watching a pod being created and then deleted**

```
$ kubectl get pods --watch
NAME                    READY       STATUS              RESTARTS    AGE
```

```
kubia-159041347-14j3i    0/1    Pending              0    0s
kubia-159041347-14j3i    0/1    Pending              0    0s
kubia-159041347-14j3i    0/1    ContainerCreating    0    1s
kubia-159041347-14j3i    0/1    Running              0    3s
kubia-159041347-14j3i    1/1    Running              0    5s
kubia-159041347-14j3i    1/1    Terminating          0    9s
kubia-159041347-14j3i    0/1    Terminating          0    17s
kubia-159041347-14j3i    0/1    Terminating          0    17s
kubia-159041347-14j3i    0/1    Terminating          0    17s
```

You can even have kubectl print out the whole YAML on each watch event like this:

```
$ kubectl get pods -o yaml --watch
```

The watch mechanism is also used by the Scheduler, which is the next Control Plane component you're going to learn more about.

11.1.5 *Understanding the Scheduler*

You've already learned that you don't usually specify which cluster node a pod should run on. This is left to the Scheduler. From afar, the operation of the Scheduler looks simple. All it does is wait for newly created pods through the API server's watch mechanism and assign a node to each new pod that doesn't already have the node set.

The Scheduler doesn't instruct the selected node (or the Kubelet running on that node) to run the pod. All the Scheduler does is update the pod definition through the API server. The API server then notifies the Kubelet (again, through the watch mechanism described previously) that the pod has been scheduled. As soon as the Kubelet on the target node sees the pod has been scheduled to its node, it creates and runs the pod's containers.

Although a coarse-grained view of the scheduling process seems trivial, the actual task of selecting the best node for the pod isn't that simple. Sure, the simplest Scheduler could pick a random node and not care about the pods already running on that node. On the other side of the spectrum, the Scheduler could use advanced techniques such as machine learning to anticipate what kind of pods are about to be scheduled in the next minutes or hours and schedule pods to maximize future hardware utilization without requiring any rescheduling of existing pods. Kubernetes' default Scheduler falls somewhere in between.

UNDERSTANDING THE DEFAULT SCHEDULING ALGORITHM

The selection of a node can be broken down into two parts, as shown in figure 11.5:

- Filtering the list of all nodes to obtain a list of acceptable nodes the pod can be scheduled to.
- Prioritizing the acceptable nodes and choosing the best one. If multiple nodes have the highest score, round-robin is used to ensure pods are deployed across all of them evenly.

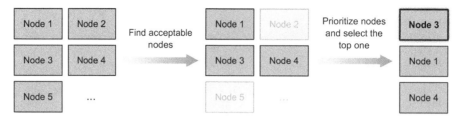

Figure 11.5   The Scheduler finds acceptable nodes for a pod and then selects the best node for the pod.

FINDING ACCEPTABLE NODES

To determine which nodes are acceptable for the pod, the Scheduler passes each node through a list of configured predicate functions. These check various things such as

- Can the node fulfill the pod's requests for hardware resources? You'll learn how to specify them in chapter 14.
- Is the node running out of resources (is it reporting a memory or a disk pressure condition)?
- If the pod requests to be scheduled to a specific node (by name), is this the node?
- Does the node have a label that matches the node selector in the pod specification (if one is defined)?
- If the pod requests to be bound to a specific host port (discussed in chapter 13), is that port already taken on this node or not?
- If the pod requests a certain type of volume, can this volume be mounted for this pod on this node, or is another pod on the node already using the same volume?
- Does the pod tolerate the taints of the node? Taints and tolerations are explained in chapter 16.
- Does the pod specify node and/or pod affinity or anti-affinity rules? If yes, would scheduling the pod to this node break those rules? This is also explained in chapter 16.

All these checks must pass for the node to be eligible to host the pod. After performing these checks on every node, the Scheduler ends up with a subset of the nodes. Any of these nodes could run the pod, because they have enough available resources for the pod and conform to all requirements you've specified in the pod definition.

SELECTING THE BEST NODE FOR THE POD

Even though all these nodes are acceptable and can run the pod, several may be a better choice than others. Suppose you have a two-node cluster. Both nodes are eligible, but one is already running 10 pods, while the other, for whatever reason, isn't running any pods right now. It's obvious the Scheduler should favor the second node in this case.

Or is it? If these two nodes are provided by the cloud infrastructure, it may be better to schedule the pod to the first node and relinquish the second node back to the cloud provider to save money.

ADVANCED SCHEDULING OF PODS

Consider another example. Imagine having multiple replicas of a pod. Ideally, you'd want them spread across as many nodes as possible instead of having them all scheduled to a single one. Failure of that node would cause the service backed by those pods to become unavailable. But if the pods were spread across different nodes, a single node failure would barely leave a dent in the service's capacity.

Pods belonging to the same Service or ReplicaSet are spread across multiple nodes by default. It's not guaranteed that this is always the case. But you can force pods to be spread around the cluster or kept close together by defining pod affinity and anti-affinity rules, which are explained in chapter 16.

Even these two simple cases show how complex scheduling can be, because it depends on a multitude of factors. Because of this, the Scheduler can either be configured to suit your specific needs or infrastructure specifics, or it can even be replaced with a custom implementation altogether. You could also run a Kubernetes cluster without a Scheduler, but then you'd have to perform the scheduling manually.

USING MULTIPLE SCHEDULERS

Instead of running a single Scheduler in the cluster, you can run multiple Schedulers. Then, for each pod, you specify the Scheduler that should schedule this particular pod by setting the `schedulerName` property in the pod spec.

Pods without this property set are scheduled using the default Scheduler, and so are pods with `schedulerName` set to `default-scheduler`. All other pods are ignored by the default Scheduler, so they need to be scheduled either manually or by another Scheduler watching for such pods.

You can implement your own Schedulers and deploy them in the cluster, or you can deploy an additional instance of Kubernetes' Scheduler with different configuration options.

11.1.6 Introducing the controllers running in the Controller Manager

As previously mentioned, the API server doesn't do anything except store resources in etcd and notify clients about the change. The Scheduler only assigns a node to the pod, so you need other active components to make sure the actual state of the system converges toward the desired state, as specified in the resources deployed through the API server. This work is done by controllers running inside the Controller Manager.

The single Controller Manager process currently combines a multitude of controllers performing various reconciliation tasks. Eventually those controllers will be split up into separate processes, enabling you to replace each one with a custom implementation if necessary. The list of these controllers includes the

- Replication Manager (a controller for ReplicationController resources)
- ReplicaSet, DaemonSet, and Job controllers

- Deployment controller
- StatefulSet controller
- Node controller
- Service controller
- Endpoints controller
- Namespace controller
- PersistentVolume controller
- Others

What each of these controllers does should be evident from its name. From the list, you can tell there's a controller for almost every resource you can create. Resources are descriptions of what should be running in the cluster, whereas the controllers are the active Kubernetes components that perform actual work as a result of the deployed resources.

UNDERSTANDING WHAT CONTROLLERS DO AND HOW THEY DO IT

Controllers do many different things, but they all watch the API server for changes to resources (Deployments, Services, and so on) and perform operations for each change, whether it's a creation of a new object or an update or deletion of an existing object. Most of the time, these operations include creating other resources or updating the watched resources themselves (to update the object's `status`, for example).

In general, controllers run a reconciliation loop, which reconciles the actual state with the desired state (specified in the resource's `spec` section) and writes the new actual state to the resource's `status` section. Controllers use the watch mechanism to be notified of changes, but because using watches doesn't guarantee the controller won't miss an event, they also perform a re-list operation periodically to make sure they haven't missed anything.

Controllers never talk to each other directly. They don't even know any other controllers exist. Each controller connects to the API server and, through the watch mechanism described in section 11.1.3, asks to be notified when a change occurs in the list of resources of any type the controller is responsible for.

We'll briefly look at what each of the controllers does, but if you'd like an in-depth view of what they do, I suggest you look at their source code directly. The sidebar explains how to get started.

A few pointers on exploring the controllers' source code

If you're interested in seeing exactly how these controllers operate, I strongly encourage you to browse through their source code. To make it easier, here are a few tips:

The source code for the controllers is available at https://github.com/kubernetes/kubernetes/blob/master/pkg/controller.

Each controller usually has a constructor in which it creates an `Informer`, which is basically a listener that gets called every time an API object gets updated. Usually, an Informer listens for changes to a specific type of resource. Looking at the constructor will show you which resources the controller is watching.

Next, go look for the `worker()` method. In it, you'll find the method that gets invoked each time the controller needs to do something. The actual function is often stored in a field called `syncHandler` or something similar. This field is also initialized in the constructor, so that's where you'll find the name of the function that gets called. That function is the place where all the magic happens.

THE REPLICATION MANAGER

The controller that makes ReplicationController resources come to life is called the Replication Manager. We talked about how ReplicationControllers work in chapter 4. It's not the ReplicationControllers that do the actual work, but the Replication Manager. Let's quickly review what the controller does, because this will help you understand the rest of the controllers.

In chapter 4, we said that the operation of a ReplicationController could be thought of as an infinite loop, where in each iteration, the controller finds the number of pods matching its pod selector and compares the number to the desired replica count.

Now that you know how the API server can notify clients through the watch mechanism, it's clear that the controller doesn't poll the pods in every iteration, but is instead notified by the watch mechanism of each change that may affect the desired replica count or the number of matched pods (see figure 11.6). Any such changes trigger the controller to recheck the desired vs. actual replica count and act accordingly.

You already know that when too few pod instances are running, the ReplicationController runs additional instances. But it doesn't actually run them itself. It creates

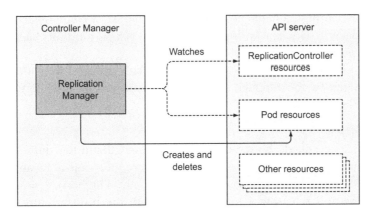

Figure 11.6   The Replication Manager watches for changes to API objects.

new Pod manifests, posts them to the API server, and lets the Scheduler and the Kubelet do their job of scheduling and running the pod.

The Replication Manager performs its work by manipulating Pod API objects through the API server. This is how all controllers operate.

THE REPLICASET, THE DAEMONSET, AND THE JOB CONTROLLERS

The ReplicaSet controller does almost the same thing as the Replication Manager described previously, so we don't have much to add here. The DaemonSet and Job controllers are similar. They create Pod resources from the pod template defined in their respective resources. Like the Replication Manager, these controllers don't run the pods, but post Pod definitions to the API server, letting the Kubelet create their containers and run them.

THE DEPLOYMENT CONTROLLER

The Deployment controller takes care of keeping the actual state of a deployment in sync with the desired state specified in the corresponding Deployment API object.

The Deployment controller performs a rollout of a new version each time a Deployment object is modified (if the modification should affect the deployed pods). It does this by creating a ReplicaSet and then appropriately scaling both the old and the new ReplicaSet based on the strategy specified in the Deployment, until all the old pods have been replaced with new ones. It doesn't create any pods directly.

THE STATEFULSET CONTROLLER

The StatefulSet controller, similarly to the ReplicaSet controller and other related controllers, creates, manages, and deletes Pods according to the spec of a StatefulSet resource. But while those other controllers only manage Pods, the StatefulSet controller also instantiates and manages PersistentVolumeClaims for each Pod instance.

THE NODE CONTROLLER

The Node controller manages the Node resources, which describe the cluster's worker nodes. Among other things, a Node controller keeps the list of Node objects in sync with the actual list of machines running in the cluster. It also monitors each node's health and evicts pods from unreachable nodes.

The Node controller isn't the only component making changes to Node objects. They're also changed by the Kubelet, and can obviously also be modified by users through REST API calls.

THE SERVICE CONTROLLER

In chapter 5, when we talked about Services, you learned that a few different types exist. One of them was the LoadBalancer service, which requests a load balancer from the infrastructure to make the service available externally. The Service controller is the one requesting and releasing a load balancer from the infrastructure, when a LoadBalancer-type Service is created or deleted.

THE ENDPOINTS CONTROLLER

You'll remember that Services aren't linked directly to pods, but instead contain a list of endpoints (IPs and ports), which is created and updated either manually or automatically according to the pod selector defined on the Service. The Endpoints controller is the active component that keeps the endpoint list constantly updated with the IPs and ports of pods matching the label selector.

As figure 11.7 shows, the controller watches both Services and Pods. When Services are added or updated or Pods are added, updated, or deleted, it selects Pods matching the Service's pod selector and adds their IPs and ports to the Endpoints resource. Remember, the Endpoints object is a standalone object, so the controller creates it if necessary. Likewise, it also deletes the Endpoints object when the Service is deleted.

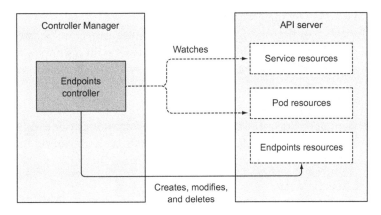

Figure 11.7   The Endpoints controller watches Service and Pod resources, and manages Endpoints.

THE NAMESPACE CONTROLLER

Remember namespaces (we talked about them in chapter 3)? Most resources belong to a specific namespace. When a Namespace resource is deleted, all the resources in that namespace must also be deleted. This is what the Namespace controller does. When it's notified of the deletion of a Namespace object, it deletes all the resources belonging to the namespace through the API server.

THE PERSISTENTVOLUME CONTROLLER

In chapter 6 you learned about PersistentVolumes and PersistentVolumeClaims. Once a user creates a PersistentVolumeClaim, Kubernetes must find an appropriate PersistentVolume and bind it to the claim. This is performed by the PersistentVolume controller.

When a PersistentVolumeClaim pops up, the controller finds the best match for the claim by selecting the smallest PersistentVolume with the access mode matching the one requested in the claim and the declared capacity above the capacity requested in the claim. It does this by keeping an ordered list of PersistentVolumes for each access mode by ascending capacity and returning the first volume from the list.

Then, when the user deletes the PersistentVolumeClaim, the volume is unbound and reclaimed according to the volume's reclaim policy (left as is, deleted, or emptied).

CONTROLLER WRAP-UP

You should now have a good feel for what each controller does and how controllers work in general. Again, all these controllers operate on the API objects through the API server. They don't communicate with the Kubelets directly or issue any kind of instructions to them. In fact, they don't even know Kubelets exist. After a controller updates a resource in the API server, the Kubelets and Kubernetes Service Proxies, also oblivious of the controllers' existence, perform their work, such as spinning up a pod's containers and attaching network storage to them, or in the case of services, setting up the actual load balancing across pods.

The Control Plane handles one part of the operation of the whole system, so to fully understand how things unfold in a Kubernetes cluster, you also need to understand what the Kubelet and the Kubernetes Service Proxy do. We'll learn that next.

11.1.7 *What the Kubelet does*

In contrast to all the controllers, which are part of the Kubernetes Control Plane and run on the master node(s), the Kubelet and the Service Proxy both run on the worker nodes, where the actual pods containers run. What does the Kubelet do exactly?

UNDERSTANDING THE KUBELET'S JOB

In a nutshell, the Kubelet is the component responsible for everything running on a worker node. Its initial job is to register the node it's running on by creating a Node resource in the API server. Then it needs to continuously monitor the API server for Pods that have been scheduled to the node, and start the pod's containers. It does this by telling the configured container runtime (which is Docker, CoreOS' rkt, or something else) to run a container from a specific container image. The Kubelet then constantly monitors running containers and reports their status, events, and resource consumption to the API server.

The Kubelet is also the component that runs the container liveness probes, restarting containers when the probes fail. Lastly, it terminates containers when their Pod is deleted from the API server and notifies the server that the pod has terminated.

RUNNING STATIC PODS WITHOUT THE API SERVER

Although the Kubelet talks to the Kubernetes API server and gets the pod manifests from there, it can also run pods based on pod manifest files in a specific local directory as shown in figure 11.8. This feature is used to run the containerized versions of the Control Plane components as pods, as you saw in the beginning of the chapter.

Instead of running Kubernetes system components natively, you can put their pod manifests into the Kubelet's manifest directory and have the Kubelet run and manage

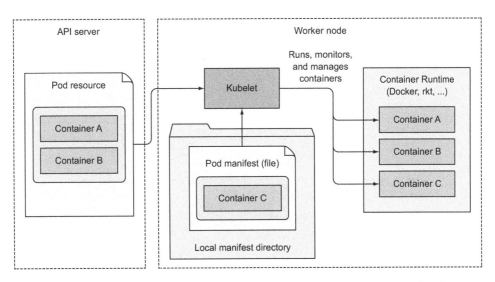

Figure 11.8 The Kubelet runs pods based on pod specs from the API server and a local file directory.

them. You can also use the same method to run your custom system containers, but doing it through a DaemonSet is the recommended method.

11.1.8 *The role of the Kubernetes Service Proxy*

Beside the Kubelet, every worker node also runs the kube-proxy, whose purpose is to make sure clients can connect to the services you define through the Kubernetes API. The kube-proxy makes sure connections to the service IP and port end up at one of the pods backing that service (or other, non-pod service endpoints). When a service is backed by more than one pod, the proxy performs load balancing across those pods.

WHY IT'S CALLED A PROXY

The initial implementation of the kube-proxy was the userspace proxy. It used an actual server process to accept connections and proxy them to the pods. To intercept connections destined to the service IPs, the proxy configured iptables rules (iptables is the tool for managing the Linux kernel's packet filtering features) to redirect the connections to the proxy server. A rough diagram of the userspace proxy mode is shown in figure 11.9.

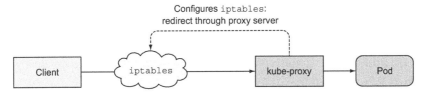

Figure 11.9 The userspace proxy mode

The kube-proxy got its name because it was an actual proxy, but the current, much better performing implementation only uses `iptables` rules to redirect packets to a randomly selected backend pod without passing them through an actual proxy server. This mode is called the `iptables` proxy mode and is shown in figure 11.10.

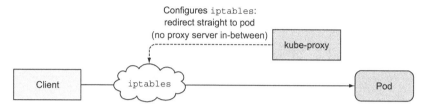

Figure 11.10   **The `iptables` proxy mode**

The major difference between these two modes is whether packets pass through the kube-proxy and must be handled in user space, or whether they're handled only by the Kernel (in kernel space). This has a major impact on performance.

Another smaller difference is that the `userspace` proxy mode balanced connections across pods in a true round-robin fashion, while the `iptables` proxy mode doesn't—it selects pods randomly. When only a few clients use a service, they may not be spread evenly across pods. For example, if a service has two backing pods but only five or so clients, don't be surprised if you see four clients connect to pod A and only one client connect to pod B. With a higher number of clients or pods, this problem isn't so apparent.

You'll learn exactly how `iptables` proxy mode works in section 11.5.

11.1.9 *Introducing Kubernetes add-ons*

We've now discussed the core components that make a Kubernetes cluster work. But in the beginning of the chapter, we also listed a few add-ons, which although not always required, enable features such as DNS lookup of Kubernetes services, exposing multiple HTTP services through a single external IP address, the Kubernetes web dashboard, and so on.

HOW ADD-ONS ARE DEPLOYED

These components are available as add-ons and are deployed as pods by submitting YAML manifests to the API server, the way you've been doing throughout the book. Some of these components are deployed through a Deployment resource or a ReplicationController resource, and some through a DaemonSet.

For example, as I'm writing this, in Minikube, the Ingress controller and the dashboard add-ons are deployed as ReplicationControllers, as shown in the following listing.

Listing 11.7   Add-ons deployed with ReplicationControllers in Minikube

```
$ kubectl get rc -n kube-system
NAME                      DESIRED   CURRENT   READY   AGE
default-http-backend      1         1         1       6d
kubernetes-dashboard      1         1         1       6d
nginx-ingress-controller  1         1         1       6d
```

The DNS add-on is deployed as a Deployment, as shown in the following listing.

Listing 11.8   The kube-dns Deployment

```
$ kubectl get deploy -n kube-system
NAME       DESIRED   CURRENT   UP-TO-DATE   AVAILABLE   AGE
kube-dns   1         1         1            1           6d
```

Let's see how DNS and the Ingress controllers work.

HOW THE DNS SERVER WORKS

All the pods in the cluster are configured to use the cluster's internal DNS server by default. This allows pods to easily look up services by name or even the pod's IP addresses in the case of headless services.

The DNS server pod is exposed through the kube-dns service, allowing the pod to be moved around the cluster, like any other pod. The service's IP address is specified as the nameserver in the /etc/resolv.conf file inside every container deployed in the cluster. The kube-dns pod uses the API server's watch mechanism to observe changes to Services and Endpoints and updates its DNS records with every change, allowing its clients to always get (fairly) up-to-date DNS information. I say fairly because during the time between the update of the Service or Endpoints resource and the time the DNS pod receives the watch notification, the DNS records may be invalid.

HOW (MOST) INGRESS CONTROLLERS WORK

Unlike the DNS add-on, you'll find a few different implementations of Ingress controllers, but most of them work in the same way. An Ingress controller runs a reverse proxy server (like Nginx, for example), and keeps it configured according to the Ingress, Service, and Endpoints resources defined in the cluster. The controller thus needs to observe those resources (again, through the watch mechanism) and change the proxy server's config every time one of them changes.

Although the Ingress resource's definition points to a Service, Ingress controllers forward traffic to the service's pod directly instead of going through the service IP. This affects the preservation of client IPs when external clients connect through the Ingress controller, which makes them preferred over Services in certain use cases.

USING OTHER ADD-ONS

You've seen how both the DNS server and the Ingress controller add-ons are similar to the controllers running in the Controller Manager, except that they also accept client connections instead of only observing and modifying resources through the API server.

Other add-ons are similar. They all need to observe the cluster state and perform the necessary actions when that changes. We'll introduce a few other add-ons in this and the remaining chapters.

11.1.10 Bringing it all together

You've now learned that the whole Kubernetes system is composed of relatively small, loosely coupled components with good separation of concerns. The API server, the Scheduler, the individual controllers running inside the Controller Manager, the Kubelet, and the kube-proxy all work together to keep the actual state of the system synchronized with what you specify as the desired state.

For example, submitting a pod manifest to the API server triggers a coordinated dance of various Kubernetes components, which eventually results in the pod's containers running. You'll learn how this dance unfolds in the next section.

11.2   How controllers cooperate

You now know about all the components that a Kubernetes cluster is comprised of. Now, to solidify your understanding of how Kubernetes works, let's go over what happens when a Pod resource is created. Because you normally don't create Pods directly, you're going to create a Deployment resource instead and see everything that must happen for the pod's containers to be started.

11.2.1 Understanding which components are involved

Even before you start the whole process, the controllers, the Scheduler, and the Kubelet are watching the API server for changes to their respective resource types. This is shown in figure 11.11. The components depicted in the figure will each play a part in the process you're about to trigger. The diagram doesn't include etcd, because it's hidden behind the API server, and you can think of the API server as the place where objects are stored.

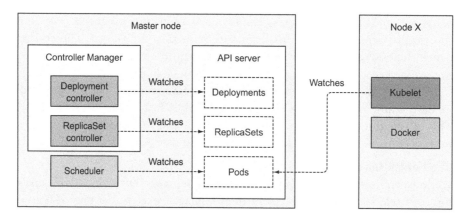

Figure 11.11   Kubernetes components watching API objects through the API server

11.2.2 *The chain of events*

Imagine you prepared the YAML file containing the Deployment manifest and you're about to submit it to Kubernetes through `kubectl`. `kubectl` sends the manifest to the Kubernetes API server in an HTTP POST request. The API server validates the Deployment specification, stores it in etcd, and returns a response to `kubectl`. Now a chain of events starts to unfold, as shown in figure 11.12.

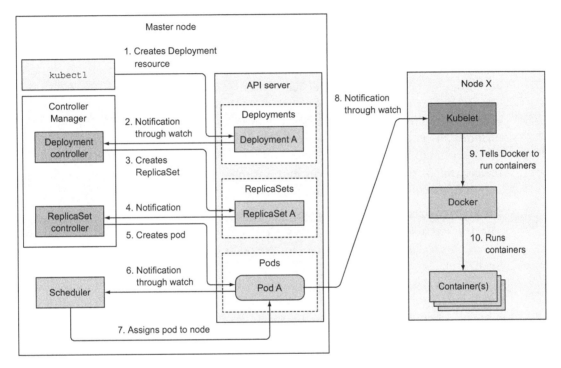

Figure 11.12 The chain of events that unfolds when a Deployment resource is posted to the API server

THE DEPLOYMENT CONTROLLER CREATES THE REPLICASET

All API server clients watching the list of Deployments through the API server's watch mechanism are notified of the newly created Deployment resource immediately after it's created. One of those clients is the Deployment controller, which, as we discussed earlier, is the active component responsible for handling Deployments.

As you may remember from chapter 9, a Deployment is backed by one or more ReplicaSets, which then create the actual pods. As a new Deployment object is detected by the Deployment controller, it creates a ReplicaSet for the current specification of the Deployment. This involves creating a new ReplicaSet resource through the Kubernetes API. The Deployment controller doesn't deal with individual pods at all.

THE REPLICASET CONTROLLER CREATES THE POD RESOURCES

The newly created ReplicaSet is then picked up by the ReplicaSet controller, which watches for creations, modifications, and deletions of ReplicaSet resources in the API server. The controller takes into consideration the replica count and pod selector defined in the ReplicaSet and verifies whether enough existing Pods match the selector.

The controller then creates the Pod resources based on the pod template in the ReplicaSet (the pod template was copied over from the Deployment when the Deployment controller created the ReplicaSet).

THE SCHEDULER ASSIGNS A NODE TO THE NEWLY CREATED PODS

These newly created Pods are now stored in etcd, but they each still lack one important thing—they don't have an associated node yet. Their `nodeName` attribute isn't set. The Scheduler watches for Pods like this, and when it encounters one, chooses the best node for the Pod and assigns the Pod to the node. The Pod's definition now includes the name of the node it should be running on.

Everything so far has been happening in the Kubernetes Control Plane. None of the controllers that have taken part in this whole process have done anything tangible except update the resources through the API server.

THE KUBELET RUNS THE POD'S CONTAINERS

The worker nodes haven't done anything up to this point. The pod's containers haven't been started yet. The images for the pod's containers haven't even been downloaded yet.

But with the Pod now scheduled to a specific node, the Kubelet on that node can finally get to work. The Kubelet, watching for changes to Pods on the API server, sees a new Pod scheduled to its node, so it inspects the Pod definition and instructs Docker, or whatever container runtime it's using, to start the pod's containers. The container runtime then runs the containers.

11.2.3   Observing cluster events

Both the Control Plane components and the Kubelet emit events to the API server as they perform these actions. They do this by creating Event resources, which are like any other Kubernetes resource. You've already seen events pertaining to specific resources every time you used `kubectl describe` to inspect those resources, but you can also retrieve events directly with `kubectl get events`.

Maybe it's me, but using `kubectl get` to inspect events is painful, because they're not shown in proper temporal order. Instead, if an event occurs multiple times, the event is displayed only once, showing when it was first seen, when it was last seen, and the number of times it occurred. Luckily, watching events with the `--watch` option is much easier on the eyes and useful for seeing what's happening in the cluster.

The following listing shows the events emitted in the process described previously (some columns have been removed and the output is edited heavily to make it legible in the limited space on the page).

Listing 11.9   Watching events emitted by the controllers

```
$ kubectl get events --watch
    NAME                KIND         REASON             SOURCE
... kubia               Deployment   ScalingReplicaSet  deployment-controller
                        ➥ Scaled up replica set kubia-193 to 3
... kubia-193           ReplicaSet   SuccessfulCreate   replicaset-controller
                        ➥ Created pod: kubia-193-w7ll2
... kubia-193-tpg6j     Pod          Scheduled          default-scheduler
                        ➥ Successfully assigned kubia-193-tpg6j to node1
... kubia-193           ReplicaSet   SuccessfulCreate   replicaset-controller
                        ➥ Created pod: kubia-193-39590
... kubia-193           ReplicaSet   SuccessfulCreate   replicaset-controller
                        ➥ Created pod: kubia-193-tpg6j
... kubia-193-39590     Pod          Scheduled          default-scheduler
                        ➥ Successfully assigned kubia-193-39590 to node2
... kubia-193-w7ll2     Pod          Scheduled          default-scheduler
                        ➥ Successfully assigned kubia-193-w7ll2 to node2
... kubia-193-tpg6j     Pod          Pulled             kubelet, node1
                        ➥ Container image already present on machine
... kubia-193-tpg6j     Pod          Created            kubelet, node1
                        ➥ Created container with id 13da752
... kubia-193-39590     Pod          Pulled             kubelet, node2
                        ➥ Container image already present on machine
... kubia-193-tpg6j     Pod          Started            kubelet, node1
                        ➥ Started container with id 13da752
... kubia-193-w7ll2     Pod          Pulled             kubelet, node2
                        ➥ Container image already present on machine
... kubia-193-39590     Pod          Created            kubelet, node2
                        ➥ Created container with id 8850184
...
```

As you can see, the SOURCE column shows the controller performing the action, and the NAME and KIND columns show the resource the controller is acting on. The REASON column and the MESSAGE column (shown in every second line) give more details about what the controller has done.

11.3 *Understanding what a running pod is*

With the pod now running, let's look more closely at what a running pod even is. If a pod contains a single container, do you think that the Kubelet just runs this single container, or is there more to it?

You've run several pods throughout this book. If you're the investigative type, you may have already snuck a peek at what exactly Docker ran when you created a pod. If not, let me explain what you'd see.

Imagine you run a single container pod. Let's say you create an Nginx pod:

```
$ kubectl run nginx --image=nginx
deployment "nginx" created
```

You can now ssh into the worker node running the pod and inspect the list of running Docker containers. I'm using Minikube to test this out, so to ssh into the single node, I use `minikube ssh`. If you're using GKE, you can `ssh` into a node with `gcloud compute ssh <node name>`.

Once you're inside the node, you can list all the running containers with `docker ps`, as shown in the following listing.

Listing 11.10   Listing running Docker containers

```
docker@minikubeVM:~$ docker ps
CONTAINER ID    IMAGE                 COMMAND                 CREATED
c917a6f3c3f7    nginx                 "nginx -g 'daemon off"  4 seconds ago
98b8bf797174    gcr.io/.../pause:3.0  "/pause"                7 seconds ago
...
```

> **NOTE** I've removed irrelevant information from the previous listing—this includes both columns and rows. I've also removed all the other running containers. If you're trying this out yourself, pay attention to the two containers that were created a few seconds ago.

As expected, you see the Nginx container, but also an additional container. Judging from the COMMAND column, this additional container isn't doing anything (the container's command is `"pause"`). If you look closely, you'll see that this container was created a few seconds before the Nginx container. What's its role?

This pause container is the container that holds all the containers of a pod together. Remember how all containers of a pod share the same network and other Linux namespaces? The pause container is an infrastructure container whose sole purpose is to hold all these namespaces. All other user-defined containers of the pod then use the namespaces of the pod infrastructure container (see figure 11.13).

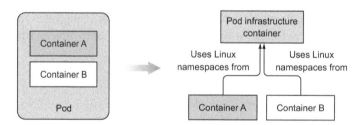

Figure 11.13   A two-container pod results in three running containers sharing the same Linux namespaces.

Actual application containers may die and get restarted. When such a container starts up again, it needs to become part of the same Linux namespaces as before. The infrastructure container makes this possible since its lifecycle is tied to that of the pod—the container runs from the time the pod is scheduled until the pod is deleted. If the infrastructure pod is killed in the meantime, the Kubelet recreates it and all the pod's containers.

11.4 *Inter-pod networking*

By now, you know that each pod gets its own unique IP address and can communicate with all other pods through a flat, NAT-less network. How exactly does Kubernetes achieve this? In short, it doesn't. The network is set up by the system administrator or by a Container Network Interface (CNI) plugin, not by Kubernetes itself.

11.4.1 *What the network must be like*

Kubernetes doesn't require you to use a specific networking technology, but it does mandate that the pods (or to be more precise, their containers) can communicate with each other, regardless if they're running on the same worker node or not. The network the pods use to communicate must be such that the IP address a pod sees as its own is the exact same address that all other pods see as the IP address of the pod in question.

Look at figure 11.14. When pod A connects to (sends a network packet to) pod B, the source IP pod B sees must be the same IP that pod A sees as its own. There should be no network address translation (NAT) performed in between—the packet sent by pod A must reach pod B with both the source and destination address unchanged.

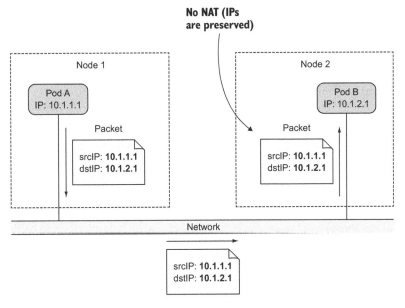

Figure 11.14 Kubernetes mandates pods are connected through a NAT-less network.

This is important, because it makes networking for applications running inside pods simple and exactly as if they were running on machines connected to the same network switch. The absence of NAT between pods enables applications running inside them to self-register in other pods.

For example, say you have a client pod X and pod Y, which provides a kind of notification service to all pods that register with it. Pod X connects to pod Y and tells it, "Hey, I'm pod X, available at IP 1.2.3.4; please send updates to me at this IP address." The pod providing the service can connect to the first pod by using the received IP address.

The requirement for NAT-less communication between pods also extends to pod-to-node and node-to-pod communication. But when a pod communicates with services out on the internet, the source IP of the packets the pod sends does need to be changed, because the pod's IP is private. The source IP of outbound packets is changed to the host worker node's IP address.

Building a proper Kubernetes cluster involves setting up the networking according to these requirements. There are various methods and technologies available to do this, each with its own benefits or drawbacks in a given scenario. Because of this, we're not going to go into specific technologies. Instead, let's explain how inter-pod networking works in general.

11.4.2 *Diving deeper into how networking works*

In section 11.3, we saw that a pod's IP address and network namespace are set up and held by the infrastructure container (the pause container). The pod's containers then use its network namespace. A pod's network interface is thus whatever is set up in the infrastructure container. Let's see how the interface is created and how it's connected to the interfaces in all the other pods. Look at figure 11.15. We'll discuss it next.

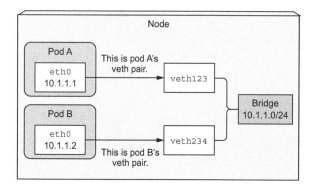

Figure 11.15 **Pods on a node are connected to the same bridge through virtual Ethernet interface pairs.**

ENABLING COMMUNICATION BETWEEN PODS ON THE SAME NODE

Before the infrastructure container is started, a virtual Ethernet interface pair (a veth pair) is created for the container. One interface of the pair remains in the host's namespace (you'll see it listed as vethXXX when you run ifconfig on the node), whereas the other is moved into the container's network namespace and renamed eth0. The two virtual interfaces are like two ends of a pipe (or like two network devices connected by an Ethernet cable)—what goes in on one side comes out on the other, and vice-versa.

The interface in the host's network namespace is attached to a network bridge that the container runtime is configured to use. The eth0 interface in the container is assigned an IP address from the bridge's address range. Anything that an application running inside the container sends to the eth0 network interface (the one in the container's namespace), comes out at the other veth interface in the host's namespace and is sent to the bridge. This means it can be received by any network interface that's connected to the bridge.

If pod A sends a network packet to pod B, the packet first goes through pod A's veth pair to the bridge and then through pod B's veth pair. All containers on a node are connected to the same bridge, which means they can all communicate with each other. But to enable communication between containers running on different nodes, the bridges on those nodes need to be connected somehow.

ENABLING COMMUNICATION BETWEEN PODS ON DIFFERENT NODES
You have many ways to connect bridges on different nodes. This can be done with overlay or underlay networks or by regular layer 3 routing, which we'll look at next.

You know pod IP addresses must be unique across the whole cluster, so the bridges across the nodes must use non-overlapping address ranges to prevent pods on different nodes from getting the same IP. In the example shown in figure 11.16, the bridge on node A is using the 10.1.1.0/24 IP range and the bridge on node B is using 10.1.2.0/24, which ensures no IP address conflicts exist.

Figure 11.16 shows that to enable communication between pods across two nodes with plain layer 3 networking, the node's physical network interface needs to be connected to the bridge as well. Routing tables on node A need to be configured so all packets destined for 10.1.2.0/24 are routed to node B, whereas node B's routing tables need to be configured so packets sent to 10.1.1.0/24 are routed to node A.

With this type of setup, when a packet is sent by a container on one of the nodes to a container on the other node, the packet first goes through the veth pair, then

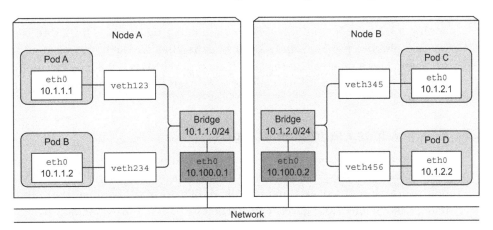

Figure 11.16   For pods on different nodes to communicate, the bridges need to be connected somehow.

through the bridge to the node's physical adapter, then over the wire to the other node's physical adapter, through the other node's bridge, and finally through the veth pair of the destination container.

This works only when nodes are connected to the same network switch, without any routers in between; otherwise those routers would drop the packets because they refer to pod IPs, which are private. Sure, the routers in between could be configured to route packets between the nodes, but this becomes increasingly difficult and error-prone as the number of routers between the nodes increases. Because of this, it's easier to use a Software Defined Network (SDN), which makes the nodes appear as though they're connected to the same network switch, regardless of the actual underlying network topology, no matter how complex it is. Packets sent from the pod are encapsulated and sent over the network to the node running the other pod, where they are de-encapsulated and delivered to the pod in their original form.

11.4.3 *Introducing the Container Network Interface*

To make it easier to connect containers into a network, a project called Container Network Interface (CNI) was started. The CNI allows Kubernetes to be configured to use any CNI plugin that's out there. These plugins include

- Calico
- Flannel
- Romana
- Weave Net
- And others

We're not going to go into the details of these plugins; if you want to learn more about them, refer to https://kubernetes.io/docs/concepts/cluster-administration/addons/.

Installing a network plugin isn't difficult. You only need to deploy a YAML containing a DaemonSet and a few other supporting resources. This YAML is provided on each plugin's project page. As you can imagine, the DaemonSet is used to deploy a network agent on all cluster nodes. It then ties into the CNI interface on the node, but be aware that the Kubelet needs to be started with `--network-plugin=cni` to use CNI.

11.5 *How services are implemented*

In chapter 5 you learned about Services, which allow exposing a set of pods at a long-lived, stable IP address and port. In order to focus on what Services are meant for and how they can be used, we intentionally didn't go into how they work. But to truly understand Services and have a better feel for where to look when things don't behave the way you expect, you need to understand how they are implemented.

11.5.1 Introducing the kube-proxy

Everything related to Services is handled by the kube-proxy process running on each node. Initially, the kube-proxy was an actual proxy waiting for connections and for each incoming connection, opening a new connection to one of the pods. This was called the userspace proxy mode. Later, a better-performing iptables proxy mode replaced it. This is now the default, but you can still configure Kubernetes to use the old mode if you want.

Before we continue, let's quickly review a few things about Services, which are relevant for understanding the next few paragraphs.

We've learned that each Service gets its own stable IP address and port. Clients (usually pods) use the service by connecting to this IP address and port. The IP address is virtual—it's not assigned to any network interfaces and is never listed as either the source or the destination IP address in a network packet when the packet leaves the node. A key detail of Services is that they consist of an IP and port pair (or multiple IP and port pairs in the case of multi-port Services), so the service IP by itself doesn't represent anything. That's why you can't ping them.

11.5.2 How kube-proxy uses iptables

When a service is created in the API server, the virtual IP address is assigned to it immediately. Soon afterward, the API server notifies all kube-proxy agents running on the worker nodes that a new Service has been created. Then, each kube-proxy makes that service addressable on the node it's running on. It does this by setting up a few iptables rules, which make sure each packet destined for the service IP/port pair is intercepted and its destination address modified, so the packet is redirected to one of the pods backing the service.

Besides watching the API server for changes to Services, kube-proxy also watches for changes to Endpoints objects. We talked about them in chapter 5, but let me refresh your memory, as it's easy to forget they even exist, because you rarely create them manually. An Endpoints object holds the IP/port pairs of all the pods that back the service (an IP/port pair can also point to something other than a pod). That's why the kube-proxy must also watch all Endpoints objects. After all, an Endpoints object changes every time a new backing pod is created or deleted, and when the pod's readiness status changes or the pod's labels change and it falls in or out of scope of the service.

Now let's see how kube-proxy enables clients to connect to those pods through the Service. This is shown in figure 11.17.

The figure shows what the kube-proxy does and how a packet sent by a client pod reaches one of the pods backing the Service. Let's examine what happens to the packet when it's sent by the client pod (pod A in the figure).

The packet's destination is initially set to the IP and port of the Service (in the example, the Service is at 172.30.0.1:80). Before being sent to the network, the

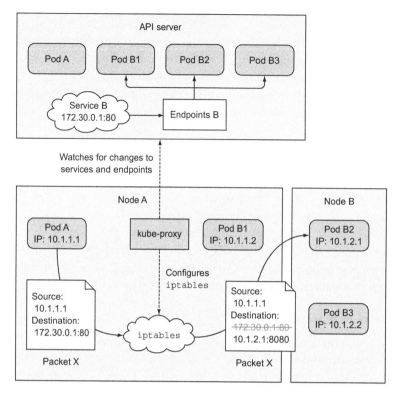

Figure 11.17 **Network packets sent to a Service's virtual IP/port pair are modified and redirected to a randomly selected backend pod.**

packet is first handled by node A's kernel according to the `iptables` rules set up on the node.

The kernel checks if the packet matches any of those `iptables` rules. One of them says that if any packet has the destination IP equal to 172.30.0.1 and destination port equal to 80, the packet's destination IP and port should be replaced with the IP and port of a randomly selected pod.

The packet in the example matches that rule and so its destination IP/port is changed. In the example, pod B2 was randomly selected, so the packet's destination IP is changed to 10.1.2.1 (pod B2's IP) and the port to 8080 (the target port specified in the Service spec). From here on, it's exactly as if the client pod had sent the packet to pod B directly instead of through the service.

It's slightly more complicated than that, but that's the most important part you need to understand.

11.6 *Running highly available clusters*

One of the reasons for running apps inside Kubernetes is to keep them running without interruption with no or limited manual intervention in case of infrastructure failures. For running services without interruption it's not only the apps that need to be up all the time, but also the Kubernetes Control Plane components. We'll look at what's involved in achieving high availability next.

11.6.1 *Making your apps highly available*

When running apps in Kubernetes, the various controllers make sure your app keeps running smoothly and at the specified scale even when nodes fail. To ensure your app is highly available, you only need to run them through a Deployment resource and configure an appropriate number of replicas; everything else is taken care of by Kubernetes.

RUNNING MULTIPLE INSTANCES TO REDUCE THE LIKELIHOOD OF DOWNTIME

This requires your apps to be horizontally scalable, but even if that's not the case in your app, you should still use a Deployment with its replica count set to one. If the replica becomes unavailable, it will be replaced with a new one quickly, although that doesn't happen instantaneously. It takes time for all the involved controllers to notice that a node has failed, create the new pod replica, and start the pod's containers. There will inevitably be a short period of downtime in between.

USING LEADER-ELECTION FOR NON-HORIZONTALLY SCALABLE APPS

To avoid the downtime, you need to run additional inactive replicas along with the active one and use a fast-acting lease or leader-election mechanism to make sure only one is active. In case you're unfamiliar with leader election, it's a way for multiple app instances running in a distributed environment to come to an agreement on which is the leader. That leader is either the only one performing tasks, while all others are waiting for the leader to fail and then becoming leaders themselves, or they can all be active, with the leader being the only instance performing writes, while all the others are providing read-only access to their data, for example. This ensures two instances are never doing the same job, if that would lead to unpredictable system behavior due to race conditions.

The mechanism doesn't need to be incorporated into the app itself. You can use a sidecar container that performs all the leader-election operations and signals the main container when it should become active. You'll find an example of leader election in Kubernetes at https://github.com/kubernetes/contrib/tree/master/election.

Ensuring your apps are highly available is relatively simple, because Kubernetes takes care of almost everything. But what if Kubernetes itself fails? What if the servers running the Kubernetes Control Plane components go down? How are those components made highly available?

11.6.2 *Making Kubernetes Control Plane components highly available*

In the beginning of this chapter, you learned about the few components that make up a Kubernetes Control Plane. To make Kubernetes highly available, you need to run multiple master nodes, which run multiple instances of the following components:

- etcd, which is the distributed data store where all the API objects are kept
- API server
- Controller Manager, which is the process in which all the controllers run
- Scheduler

Without going into the actual details of how to install and run these components, let's see what's involved in making each of these components highly available. Figure 11.18 shows an overview of a highly available cluster.

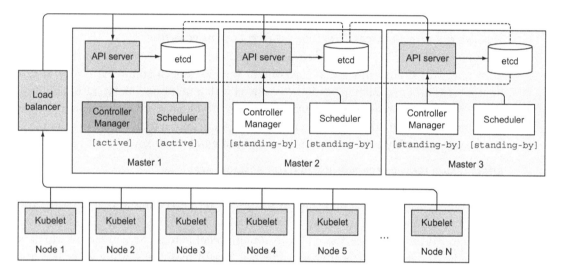

Figure 11.18   A highly-available cluster with three master nodes

RUNNING AN ETCD CLUSTER

Because etcd was designed as a distributed system, one of its key features is the ability to run multiple etcd instances, so making it highly available is no big deal. All you need to do is run it on an appropriate number of machines (three, five, or seven, as explained earlier in the chapter) and make them aware of each other. You do this by including the list of all the other instances in every instance's configuration. For example, when starting an instance, you specify the IPs and ports where the other etcd instances can be reached.

etcd will replicate data across all its instances, so a failure of one of the nodes when running a three-machine cluster will still allow the cluster to accept both read and write operations. To increase the fault tolerance to more than a single node, you need to run five or seven etcd nodes, which would allow the cluster to handle two or three node failures, respectively. Having more than seven etcd instances is almost never necessary and begins impacting performance.

RUNNING MULTIPLE INSTANCES OF THE API SERVER

Making the API server highly available is even simpler. Because the API server is (almost completely) stateless (all the data is stored in etcd, but the API server does cache it), you can run as many API servers as you need, and they don't need to be aware of each other at all. Usually, one API server is collocated with every etcd instance. By doing this, the etcd instances don't need any kind of load balancer in front of them, because every API server instance only talks to the local etcd instance.

The API servers, on the other hand, do need to be fronted by a load balancer, so clients (`kubectl`, but also the Controller Manager, Scheduler, and all the Kubelets) always connect only to the healthy API server instances.

ENSURING HIGH AVAILABILITY OF THE CONTROLLERS AND THE SCHEDULER

Compared to the API server, where multiple replicas can run simultaneously, running multiple instances of the Controller Manager or the Scheduler isn't as simple. Because controllers and the Scheduler all actively watch the cluster state and act when it changes, possibly modifying the cluster state further (for example, when the desired replica count on a ReplicaSet is increased by one, the ReplicaSet controller creates an additional pod), running multiple instances of each of those components would result in all of them performing the same action. They'd be racing each other, which could cause undesired effects (creating two new pods instead of one, as mentioned in the previous example).

For this reason, when running multiple instances of these components, only one instance may be active at any given time. Luckily, this is all taken care of by the components themselves (this is controlled with the `--leader-elect` option, which defaults to true). Each individual component will only be active when it's the elected leader. Only the leader performs actual work, whereas all other instances are standing by and waiting for the current leader to fail. When it does, the remaining instances elect a new leader, which then takes over the work. This mechanism ensures that two components are never operating at the same time and doing the same work (see figure 11.19).

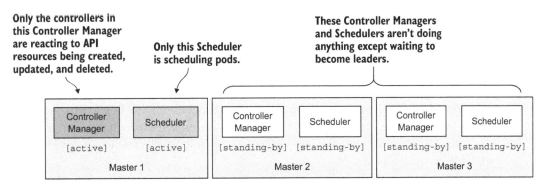

Figure 11.19   Only a single Controller Manager and a single Scheduler are active; others are standing by.

The Controller Manager and Scheduler can run collocated with the API server and etcd, or they can run on separate machines. When collocated, they can talk to the local API server directly; otherwise they connect to the API servers through the load balancer.

UNDERSTANDING THE LEADER ELECTION MECHANISM USED IN CONTROL PLANE COMPONENTS

What I find most interesting here is that these components don't need to talk to each other directly to elect a leader. The leader election mechanism works purely by creating a resource in the API server. And it's not even a special kind of resource—the Endpoints resource is used to achieve this (abused is probably a more appropriate term).

There's nothing special about using an Endpoints object to do this. It's used because it has no side effects as long as no Service with the same name exists. Any other resource could be used (in fact, the leader election mechanism will soon use ConfigMaps instead of Endpoints).

I'm sure you're interested in how a resource can be used for this purpose. Let's take the Scheduler, for example. All instances of the Scheduler try to create (and later update) an Endpoints resource called `kube-scheduler`. You'll find it in the `kube-system` namespace, as the following listing shows.

> **Listing 11.11   The `kube-scheduler` Endpoints resource used for leader-election**

```
$ kubectl get endpoints kube-scheduler -n kube-system -o yaml
apiVersion: v1
kind: Endpoints
metadata:
  annotations:
    control-plane.alpha.kubernetes.io/leader: '{"holderIdentity":
      "minikube","leaseDurationSeconds":15,"acquireTime":
      "2017-05-27T18:54:53Z","renewTime":"2017-05-28T13:07:49Z",
      "leaderTransitions":0}'
  creationTimestamp: 2017-05-27T18:54:53Z
  name: kube-scheduler
  namespace: kube-system
  resourceVersion: "654059"
  selfLink: /api/v1/namespaces/kube-system/endpoints/kube-scheduler
  uid: f847bd14-430d-11e7-9720-080027f8fa4e
subsets: []
```

The `control-plane.alpha.kubernetes.io/leader` annotation is the important part. As you can see, it contains a field called `holderIdentity`, which holds the name of the current leader. The first instance that succeeds in putting its name there becomes the leader. Instances race each other to do that, but there's always only one winner.

Remember the optimistic concurrency we explained earlier? That's what ensures that if multiple instances try to write their name into the resource only one of them succeeds. Based on whether the write succeeded or not, each instance knows whether it is or it isn't the leader.

Once becoming the leader, it must periodically update the resource (every two seconds by default), so all other instances know that it's still alive. When the leader fails, other instances see that the resource hasn't been updated for a while, and try to become the leader by writing their own name to the resource. Simple, right?

11.7 *Summary*

Hopefully, this has been an interesting chapter that has improved your knowledge of the inner workings of Kubernetes. This chapter has shown you

- What components make up a Kubernetes cluster and what each component is responsible for
- How the API server, Scheduler, various controllers running in the Controller Manager, and the Kubelet work together to bring a pod to life
- How the infrastructure container binds together all the containers of a pod
- How pods communicate with other pods running on the same node through the network bridge, and how those bridges on different nodes are connected, so pods running on different nodes can talk to each other
- How the kube-proxy performs load balancing across pods in the same service by configuring `iptables` rules on the node
- How multiple instances of each component of the Control Plane can be run to make the cluster highly available

Next, we'll look at how to secure the API server and, by extension, the cluster as a whole.

Securing the
Kubernetes API server

This chapter covers

- Understanding authentication
- What ServiceAccounts are and why they're used
- Understanding the role-based access control (RBAC) plugin
- Using Roles and RoleBindings
- Using ClusterRoles and ClusterRoleBindings
- Understanding the default roles and bindings

In chapter 8 you learned how applications running in pods can talk to the API server to retrieve or change the state of resources deployed in the cluster. To authenticate with the API server, you used the ServiceAccount token mounted into the pod. In this chapter, you'll learn what ServiceAccounts are and how to configure their permissions, as well as permissions for other subjects using the cluster.

12.1 Understanding authentication

In the previous chapter, we said the API server can be configured with one or more authentication plugins (and the same is true for authorization plugins). When a request is received by the API server, it goes through the list of authentication plugins, so they can each examine the request and try to determine who's sending the request. The first plugin that can extract that information from the request returns the username, user ID, and the groups the client belongs to back to the API server core. The API server stops invoking the remaining authentication plugins and continues onto the authorization phase.

Several authentication plugins are available. They obtain the identity of the client using the following methods:

- From the client certificate
- From an authentication token passed in an HTTP header
- Basic HTTP authentication
- Others

The authentication plugins are enabled through command-line options when starting the API server.

12.1.1 *Users and groups*

An authentication plugin returns the username and group(s) of the authenticated user. Kubernetes doesn't store that information anywhere; it uses it to verify whether the user is authorized to perform an action or not.

UNDERSTANDING USERS

Kubernetes distinguishes between two kinds of clients connecting to the API server:

- Actual humans (users)
- Pods (more specifically, applications running inside them)

Both these types of clients are authenticated using the aforementioned authentication plugins. Users are meant to be managed by an external system, such as a Single Sign On (SSO) system, but the pods use a mechanism called *service accounts*, which are created and stored in the cluster as ServiceAccount resources. In contrast, no resource represents user accounts, which means you can't create, update, or delete users through the API server.

We won't go into any details of how to manage users, but we will explore Service-Accounts in detail, because they're essential for running pods. For more information on how to configure the cluster for authentication of human users, cluster administrators should refer to the Kubernetes Cluster Administrator guide at http://kubernetes.io/docs/admin.

UNDERSTANDING GROUPS

Both human users and ServiceAccounts can belong to one or more groups. We've said that the authentication plugin returns groups along with the username and user ID. Groups are used to grant permissions to several users at once, instead of having to grant them to individual users.

Groups returned by the plugin are nothing but strings, representing arbitrary group names, but built-in groups have special meaning:

- The `system:unauthenticated` group is used for requests where none of the authentication plugins could authenticate the client.
- The `system:authenticated` group is automatically assigned to a user who was authenticated successfully.
- The `system:serviceaccounts` group encompasses all ServiceAccounts in the system.
- The `system:serviceaccounts:<namespace>` includes all ServiceAccounts in a specific namespace.

12.1.2   *Introducing ServiceAccounts*

Let's explore ServiceAccounts up close. You've already learned that the API server requires clients to authenticate themselves before they're allowed to perform operations on the server. And you've already seen how pods can authenticate by sending the contents of the file `/var/run/secrets/kubernetes.io/serviceaccount/token`, which is mounted into each container's filesystem through a `secret` volume.

But what exactly does that file represent? Every pod is associated with a ServiceAccount, which represents the identity of the app running in the pod. The token file holds the ServiceAccount's authentication token. When an app uses this token to connect to the API server, the authentication plugin authenticates the ServiceAccount and passes the ServiceAccount's username back to the API server core. ServiceAccount usernames are formatted like this:

```
system:serviceaccount:<namespace>:<service account name>
```

The API server passes this username to the configured authorization plugins, which determine whether the action the app is trying to perform is allowed to be performed by the ServiceAccount.

ServiceAccounts are nothing more than a way for an application running inside a pod to authenticate itself with the API server. As already mentioned, applications do that by passing the ServiceAccount's token in the request.

UNDERSTANDING THE SERVICEACCOUNT RESOURCE

ServiceAccounts are resources just like Pods, Secrets, ConfigMaps, and so on, and are scoped to individual namespaces. A default ServiceAccount is automatically created for each namespace (that's the one your pods have used all along).

You can list ServiceAccounts like you do other resources:

```
$ kubectl get sa
NAME      SECRETS   AGE
default   1         1d
```

NOTE   The shorthand for `serviceaccount` is `sa`.

As you can see, the current namespace only contains the `default` ServiceAccount. Additional ServiceAccounts can be added when required. Each pod is associated with exactly one ServiceAccount, but multiple pods can use the same ServiceAccount. As you can see in figure 12.1, a pod can only use a ServiceAccount from the same namespace.

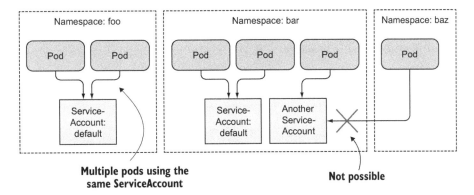

Figure 12.1   Each pod is associated with a single ServiceAccount in the pod's namespace.

UNDERSTANDING HOW SERVICEACCOUNTS TIE INTO AUTHORIZATION

You can assign a ServiceAccount to a pod by specifying the account's name in the pod manifest. If you don't assign it explicitly, the pod will use the default ServiceAccount in the namespace.

By assigning different ServiceAccounts to pods, you can control which resources each pod has access to. When a request bearing the authentication token is received by the API server, the server uses the token to authenticate the client sending the request and then determines whether or not the related ServiceAccount is allowed to perform the requested operation. The API server obtains this information from the system-wide authorization plugin configured by the cluster administrator. One of the available authorization plugins is the role-based access control (RBAC) plugin, which is discussed later in this chapter. From Kubernetes version 1.6 on, the RBAC plugin is the plugin most clusters should use.

12.1.3   Creating ServiceAccounts

We've said every namespace contains its own default ServiceAccount, but additional ones can be created if necessary. But why should you bother with creating Service-Accounts instead of using the default one for all your pods?

The obvious reason is cluster security. Pods that don't need to read any cluster metadata should run under a constrained account that doesn't allow them to retrieve or modify any resources deployed in the cluster. Pods that need to retrieve resource metadata should run under a ServiceAccount that only allows reading those objects' metadata, whereas pods that need to modify those objects should run under their own ServiceAccount allowing modifications of API objects.

Let's see how you can create additional ServiceAccounts, how they relate to Secrets, and how you can assign them to your pods.

CREATING A SERVICEACCOUNT

Creating a ServiceAccount is incredibly easy, thanks to the dedicated `kubectl create serviceaccount` command. Let's create a new ServiceAccount called `foo`:

```
$ kubectl create serviceaccount foo
serviceaccount "foo" created
```

Now, you can inspect the ServiceAccount with the `describe` command, as shown in the following listing.

Listing 12.1 Inspecting a ServiceAccount with `kubectl describe`

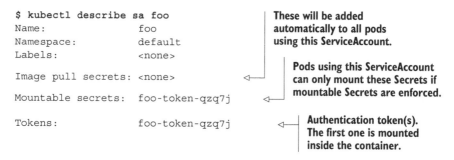

```
$ kubectl describe sa foo
Name:                  foo
Namespace:             default
Labels:                <none>

Image pull secrets:    <none>

Mountable secrets:     foo-token-qzq7j

Tokens:                foo-token-qzq7j
```

These will be added
automatically to all pods
using this ServiceAccount.

Pods using this ServiceAccount
can only mount these Secrets if
mountable Secrets are enforced.

Authentication token(s).
The first one is mounted
inside the container.

You can see that a custom token Secret has been created and associated with the ServiceAccount. If you look at the Secret's data with `kubectl describe secret foo-token-qzq7j`, you'll see it contains the same items (the CA certificate, namespace, and token) as the default ServiceAccount's token does (the token itself will obviously be different), as shown in the following listing.

Listing 12.2 Inspecting the custom ServiceAccount's Secret

```
$ kubectl describe secret foo-token-qzq7j
...
ca.crt:        1066 bytes
namespace:     7 bytes
token:         eyJhbGciOiJSUzI1NiIsInR5cCI6IkpXVCJ9...
```

NOTE You've probably heard of JSON Web Tokens (JWT). The authentication tokens used in ServiceAccounts are JWT tokens.

UNDERSTANDING A SERVICEACCOUNT'S MOUNTABLE SECRETS

The token is shown in the `Mountable secrets` list when you inspect a ServiceAccount with `kubectl describe`. Let me explain what that list represents. In chapter 7 you learned how to create Secrets and mount them inside a pod. By default, a pod can mount any Secret it wants. But the pod's ServiceAccount can be configured to only allow the pod to mount Secrets that are listed as mountable Secrets on the Service-Account. To enable this feature, the ServiceAccount must contain the following annotation: `kubernetes.io/enforce-mountable-secrets="true"`.

If the ServiceAccount is annotated with this annotation, any pods using it can mount only the ServiceAccount's mountable Secrets—they can't use any other Secret.

UNDERSTANDING A SERVICEACCOUNT'S IMAGE PULL SECRETS

A ServiceAccount can also contain a list of image pull Secrets, which we examined in chapter 7. In case you don't remember, they are Secrets that hold the credentials for pulling container images from a private image repository.

The following listing shows an example of a ServiceAccount definition, which includes the image pull Secret you created in chapter 7.

Listing 12.3   ServiceAccount with an image pull Secret: sa-image-pull-secrets.yaml

```
apiVersion: v1
kind: ServiceAccount
metadata:
  name: my-service-account
imagePullSecrets:
- name: my-dockerhub-secret
```

A ServiceAccount's image pull Secrets behave slightly differently than its mountable Secrets. Unlike mountable Secrets, they don't determine which image pull Secrets a pod can use, but which ones are added automatically to all pods using the Service-Account. Adding image pull Secrets to a ServiceAccount saves you from having to add them to each pod individually.

12.1.4 Assigning a ServiceAccount to a pod

After you create additional ServiceAccounts, you need to assign them to pods. This is done by setting the name of the ServiceAccount in the `spec.serviceAccountName` field in the pod definition.

> **NOTE** A pod's ServiceAccount must be set when creating the pod. It can't be changed later.

CREATING A POD WHICH USES A CUSTOM SERVICEACCOUNT

In chapter 8 you deployed a pod that ran a container based on the `tutum/curl` image and an ambassador container alongside it. You used it to explore the API server's REST interface. The ambassador container ran the `kubectl proxy` process, which used the pod's ServiceAccount's token to authenticate with the API server.

You can now modify the pod so it uses the `foo` ServiceAccount you created minutes ago. The next listing shows the pod definition.

Listing 12.4 Pod using a non-default ServiceAccount: curl-custom-sa.yaml

```
apiVersion: v1
kind: Pod
metadata:
  name: curl-custom-sa
spec:
  serviceAccountName: foo          ◁——  This pod uses the
  containers:                            foo ServiceAccount
  - name: main                           instead of the default.
    image: tutum/curl
    command: ["sleep", "9999999"]
  - name: ambassador
    image: luksa/kubectl-proxy:1.6.2
```

To confirm that the custom ServiceAccount's token is mounted into the two containers, you can print the contents of the token as shown in the following listing.

Listing 12.5 Inspecting the token mounted into the pod's container(s)

```
$ kubectl exec -it curl-custom-sa -c main
➥ cat /var/run/secrets/kubernetes.io/serviceaccount/token
eyJhbGciOiJSUzI1NiIsInR5cCI6IkpXVCJ9...
```

You can see the token is the one from the `foo` ServiceAccount by comparing the token string in listing 12.5 with the one in listing 12.2.

USING THE CUSTOM SERVICEACCOUNT'S TOKEN TO TALK TO THE API SERVER

Let's see if you can talk to the API server using this token. As mentioned previously, the ambassador container uses the token when talking to the server, so you can test the token by going through the ambassador, which listens on `localhost:8001`, as shown in the following listing.

Listing 12.6 Talking to the API server with a custom ServiceAccount

```
$ kubectl exec -it curl-custom-sa -c main curl localhost:8001/api/v1/pods
{
  "kind": "PodList",
  "apiVersion": "v1",
  "metadata": {
    "selfLink": "/api/v1/pods",
    "resourceVersion": "433895"
  },
  "items": [
  ...
```

Okay, you got back a proper response from the server, which means the custom ServiceAccount is allowed to list pods. This may be because your cluster doesn't use the RBAC authorization plugin, or you gave all ServiceAccounts full permissions, as instructed in chapter 8.

When your cluster isn't using proper authorization, creating and using additional ServiceAccounts doesn't make much sense, since even the default ServiceAccount is allowed to do anything. The only reason to use ServiceAccounts in that case is to enforce mountable Secrets or to provide image pull Secrets through the Service-Account, as explained earlier.

But creating additional ServiceAccounts is practically a must when you use the RBAC authorization plugin, which we'll explore next.

12.2 *Securing the cluster with role-based access control*

Starting with Kubernetes version 1.6.0, cluster security was ramped up considerably. In earlier versions, if you managed to acquire the authentication token from one of the pods, you could use it to do anything you want in the cluster. If you google around, you'll find demos showing how a *path traversal* (or *directory traversal*) attack (where clients can retrieve files located outside of the web server's web root directory) can be used to get the token and use it to run your malicious pods in an insecure Kubernetes cluster.

But in version 1.8.0, the RBAC authorization plugin graduated to GA (General Availability) and is now enabled by default on many clusters (for example, when deploying a cluster with kubadm, as described in appendix B). RBAC prevents unauthorized users from viewing or modifying the cluster state. The default Service-Account isn't allowed to view cluster state, let alone modify it in any way, unless you grant it additional privileges. To write apps that communicate with the Kubernetes API server (as described in chapter 8), you need to understand how to manage authorization through RBAC-specific resources.

> **NOTE** In addition to RBAC, Kubernetes also includes other authorization plugins, such as the Attribute-based access control (ABAC) plugin, a Web-Hook plugin and custom plugin implementations. RBAC is the standard, though.

12.2.1 *Introducing the RBAC authorization plugin*

The Kubernetes API server can be configured to use an authorization plugin to check whether an action is allowed to be performed by the user requesting the action. Because the API server exposes a REST interface, users perform actions by sending HTTP requests to the server. Users authenticate themselves by including credentials in the request (an authentication token, username and password, or a client certificate).

UNDERSTANDING ACTIONS

But what actions are there? As you know, REST clients send GET, POST, PUT, DELETE, and other types of HTTP requests to specific URL paths, which represent specific REST resources. In Kubernetes, those resources are Pods, Services, Secrets, and so on. Here are a few examples of actions in Kubernetes:

- Get Pods
- Create Services

- Update Secrets
- And so on

The verbs in those examples (get, create, update) map to HTTP methods (GET, POST, PUT) performed by the client (the complete mapping is shown in table 12.1). The nouns (Pods, Service, Secrets) obviously map to Kubernetes resources.

An authorization plugin such as RBAC, which runs inside the API server, determines whether a client is allowed to perform the requested verb on the requested resource or not.

Table 12.1   Mapping HTTP methods to authorization verbs

HTTP method	Verb for single resource	Verb for collection
GET, HEAD	get (and watch for watching)	list (and watch)
POST	create	n/a
PUT	update	n/a
PATCH	patch	n/a
DELETE	delete	deletecollection

NOTE   The additional verb use is used for PodSecurityPolicy resources, which are explained in the next chapter.

Besides applying security permissions to whole resource types, RBAC rules can also apply to specific instances of a resource (for example, a Service called `myservice`). And later you'll see that permissions can also apply to non-resource URL paths, because not every path the API server exposes maps to a resource (such as the `/api` path itself or the server health information at `/healthz`).

UNDERSTANDING THE RBAC PLUGIN

The RBAC authorization plugin, as the name suggests, uses user roles as the key factor in determining whether the user may perform the action or not. A subject (which may be a human, a ServiceAccount, or a group of users or ServiceAccounts) is associated with one or more roles and each role is allowed to perform certain verbs on certain resources.

If a user has multiple roles, they may do anything that any of their roles allows them to do. If none of the user's roles contains a permission to, for example, update Secrets, the API server will prevent the user from performing PUT or PATCH requests on Secrets.

Managing authorization through the RBAC plugin is simple. It's all done by creating four RBAC-specific Kubernetes resources, which we'll look at next.

12.2.2 Introducing RBAC resources

The RBAC authorization rules are configured through four resources, which can be grouped into two groups:

- Roles and ClusterRoles, which specify which verbs can be performed on which resources.
- RoleBindings and ClusterRoleBindings, which bind the above roles to specific users, groups, or ServiceAccounts.

Roles define *what* can be done, while bindings define *who* can do it (this is shown in figure 12.2).

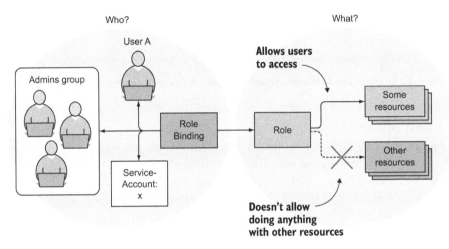

Figure 12.2   Roles grant permissions, whereas RoleBindings bind Roles to subjects.

The distinction between a Role and a ClusterRole, or between a RoleBinding and a ClusterRoleBinding, is that the Role and RoleBinding are namespaced resources, whereas the ClusterRole and ClusterRoleBinding are cluster-level resources (not namespaced). This is depicted in figure 12.3.

As you can see from the figure, multiple RoleBindings can exist in a single namespace (this is also true for Roles). Likewise, multiple ClusterRoleBindings and ClusterRoles can be created. Another thing shown in the figure is that although RoleBindings are namespaced, they can also reference ClusterRoles, which aren't.

The best way to learn about these four resources and what their effects are is by trying them out in a hands-on exercise. You'll do that now.

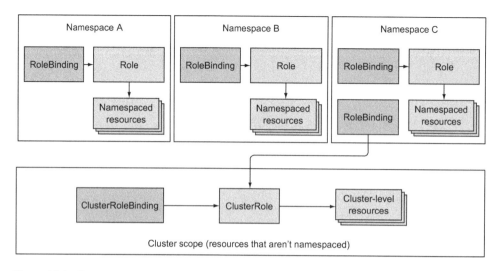

Figure 12.3   Roles and RoleBindings are namespaced; ClusterRoles and ClusterRoleBindings aren't.

SETTING UP YOUR EXERCISE

Before you can explore how RBAC resources affect what you can do through the API server, you need to make sure RBAC is enabled in your cluster. First, ensure you're using at least version 1.6 of Kubernetes and that the RBAC plugin is the only configured authorization plugin. There can be multiple plugins enabled in parallel and if one of them allows an action to be performed, the action is allowed.

> **NOTE** If you're using GKE 1.6 or 1.7, you need to explicitly disable legacy authorization by creating the cluster with the `--no-enable-legacy-authorization` option. If you're using Minikube, you also may need to enable RBAC by starting Minikube with `--extra-config=apiserver.Authorization.Mode=RBAC`

If you followed the instructions on how to disable RBAC in chapter 8, now's the time to re-enable it by running the following command:

```
$ kubectl delete clusterrolebinding permissive-binding
```

To try out RBAC, you'll run a pod through which you'll try to talk to the API server, the way you did in chapter 8. But this time you'll run two pods in different namespaces to see how per-namespace security behaves.

In the examples in chapter 8, you ran two containers to demonstrate how an application in one container uses the other container to talk to the API server. This time, you'll run a single container (based on the `kubectl-proxy` image) and use `kubectl exec` to run `curl` inside that container directly. The proxy will take care of authentication and HTTPS, so you can focus on the authorization aspect of API server security.

CREATING THE NAMESPACES AND RUNNING THE PODS

You're going to create one pod in namespace `foo` and the other one in namespace `bar`, as shown in the following listing.

> **Listing 12.7 Running test pods in different namespaces**

```
$ kubectl create ns foo
namespace "foo" created
$ kubectl run test --image=luksa/kubectl-proxy -n foo
deployment "test" created
$ kubectl create ns bar
namespace "bar" created
$ kubectl run test --image=luksa/kubectl-proxy -n bar
deployment "test" created
```

Now open two terminals and use `kubectl exec` to run a shell inside each of the two pods (one in each terminal). For example, to run the shell in the pod in namespace `foo`, first get the name of the pod:

```
$ kubectl get po -n foo
NAME                      READY    STATUS     RESTARTS    AGE
test-145485760-ttq36     1/1      Running    0           1m
```

Then use the name in the `kubectl exec` command:

```
$ kubectl exec -it test-145485760-ttq36 -n foo sh
/ #
```

Do the same in the other terminal, but for the pod in the `bar` namespace.

LISTING SERVICES FROM YOUR PODS

To verify that RBAC is enabled and preventing the pod from reading cluster state, use `curl` to list Services in the `foo` namespace:

```
/ # curl localhost:8001/api/v1/namespaces/foo/services
User "system:serviceaccount:foo:default" cannot list services in the
     namespace "foo".
```

You're connecting to `localhost:8001`, which is where the `kubectl proxy` process is listening (as explained in chapter 8). The process received your request and sent it to the API server while authenticating as the default ServiceAccount in the `foo` namespace (as evident from the API server's response).

The API server responded that the ServiceAccount isn't allowed to list Services in the `foo` namespace, even though the pod is running in that same namespace. You're seeing RBAC in action. The default permissions for a ServiceAccount don't allow it to list or modify any resources. Now, let's learn how to allow the ServiceAccount to do that. First, you'll need to create a Role resource.

12.2.3   *Using Roles and RoleBindings*

A Role resource defines what actions can be taken on which resources (or, as explained earlier, which types of HTTP requests can be performed on which RESTful resources). The following listing defines a Role, which allows users to `get` and `list` Services in the `foo` namespace.

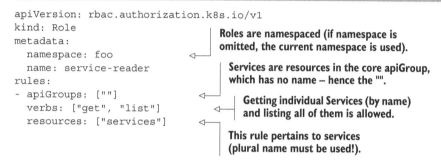

Listing 12.8   A definition of a `Role`: service-reader.yaml

```
apiVersion: rbac.authorization.k8s.io/v1
kind: Role
metadata:
  namespace: foo          ◁     Roles are namespaced (if namespace is
                                omitted, the current namespace is used).
  name: service-reader
rules:                          Services are resources in the core apiGroup,
- apiGroups: [""]         ◁     which has no name – hence the "".
  verbs: ["get", "list"]  ◁     Getting individual Services (by name)
  resources: ["services"] ◁     and listing all of them is allowed.
                                This rule pertains to services
                                (plural name must be used!).
```

WARNING   The plural form must be used when specifying resources.

This Role resource will be created in the `foo` namespace. In chapter 8, you learned that each resource type belongs to an API group, which you specify in the `apiVersion` field (along with the version) in the resource's manifest. In a Role definition, you need to specify the `apiGroup` for the resources listed in each rule included in the definition. If you're allowing access to resources belonging to different API groups, you use multiple rules.

NOTE   In the example, you're allowing access to all Service resources, but you could also limit access only to specific Service instances by specifying their names through an additional `resourceNames` field.

Figure 12.4 shows the Role, its verbs and resources, and the namespace it will be created in.

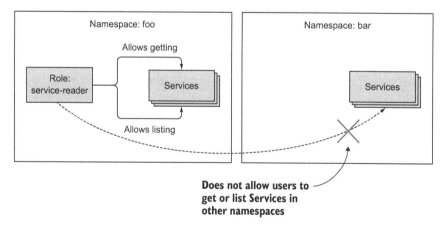

Figure 12.4   The service-reader Role allows getting and listing Services in the `foo` namespace.

CREATING A ROLE

Create the previous Role in the foo namespace now:

```
$ kubectl create -f service-reader.yaml -n foo
role "service-reader" created
```

> **NOTE** The -n option is shorthand for --namespace.

Note that if you're using GKE, the previous command may fail because you don't have cluster-admin rights. To grant the rights, run the following command:

```
$ kubectl create clusterrolebinding cluster-admin-binding
➥ --clusterrole=cluster-admin --user=your.email@address.com
```

Instead of creating the service-reader Role from a YAML file, you could also create it with the special kubectl create role command. Let's use this method to create the Role in the bar namespace:

```
$ kubectl create role service-reader --verb=get --verb=list
➥ --resource=services -n bar
role "service-reader" created
```

These two Roles will allow you to list Services in the foo and bar namespaces from within your two pods (running in the foo and bar namespace, respectively). But creating the two Roles isn't enough (you can check by executing the curl command again). You need to bind each of the Roles to the ServiceAccounts in their respective namespaces.

BINDING A ROLE TO A SERVICEACCOUNT

A Role defines what actions can be performed, but it doesn't specify who can perform them. To do that, you must bind the Role to a subject, which can be a user, a Service-Account, or a group (of users or ServiceAccounts).

Binding Roles to subjects is achieved by creating a RoleBinding resource. To bind the Role to the default ServiceAccount, run the following command:

```
$ kubectl create rolebinding test --role=service-reader
➥ --serviceaccount=foo:default -n foo
rolebinding "test" created
```

The command should be self-explanatory. You're creating a RoleBinding, which binds the service-reader Role to the default ServiceAccount in namespace foo. You're creating the RoleBinding in namespace foo. The RoleBinding and the referenced Service-Account and Role are shown in figure 12.5.

> **NOTE** To bind a Role to a user instead of a ServiceAccount, use the --user argument to specify the username. To bind it to a group, use --group.

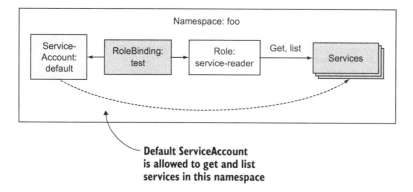

Figure 12.5   The `test` RoleBinding binds the `default` ServiceAccount with the `service-reader` Role.

The following listing shows the YAML of the RoleBinding you created.

Listing 12.9   A RoleBinding referencing a Role

```
$ kubectl get rolebinding test -n foo -o yaml
apiVersion: rbac.authorization.k8s.io/v1
kind: RoleBinding
metadata:
  name: test
  namespace: foo
  ...
roleRef:
  apiGroup: rbac.authorization.k8s.io
  kind: Role                             This RoleBinding references
  name: service-reader                   the service-reader Role.
subjects:
- kind: ServiceAccount                   And binds it to the
  name: default                          default ServiceAccount
  namespace: foo                         in the foo namespace.
```

As you can see, a RoleBinding always references a single Role (as evident from the `roleRef` property), but can bind the Role to multiple `subjects` (for example, one or more ServiceAccounts and any number of users or groups). Because this RoleBinding binds the Role to the ServiceAccount the pod in namespace `foo` is running under, you can now list Services from within that pod.

Listing 12.10   Getting Services from the API server

```
/ # curl localhost:8001/api/v1/namespaces/foo/services
{
  "kind": "ServiceList",
  "apiVersion": "v1",
  "metadata": {
    "selfLink": "/api/v1/namespaces/foo/services",
```

```
      "resourceVersion": "24906"
  },
  "items": []          ◁─────── The list of items is empty,
}                                because no Services exist.
```

INCLUDING SERVICEACCOUNTS FROM OTHER NAMESPACES IN A ROLEBINDING

The pod in namespace `bar` can't list the Services in its own namespace, and obviously also not those in the `foo` namespace. But you can edit your RoleBinding in the `foo` namespace and add the other pod's ServiceAccount, even though it's in a different namespace. Run the following command:

```
$ kubectl edit rolebinding test -n foo
```

Then add the following lines to the list of `subjects`, as shown in the following listing.

Listing 12.11 Referencing a ServiceAccount from another namespace

```
subjects:
- kind: ServiceAccount
  name: default            You're referencing the default
  namespace: bar           ServiceAccount in the bar namespace.
```

Now you can also list Services in the `foo` namespace from inside the pod running in the `bar` namespace. Run the same command as in listing 12.10, but do it in the other terminal, where you're running the shell in the other pod.

Before moving on to ClusterRoles and ClusterRoleBindings, let's summarize what RBAC resources you currently have. You have a RoleBinding in namespace `foo`, which references the `service-reader` Role (also in the `foo` namespace) and binds the `default` ServiceAccounts in both the `foo` and the `bar` namespaces, as depicted in figure 12.6.

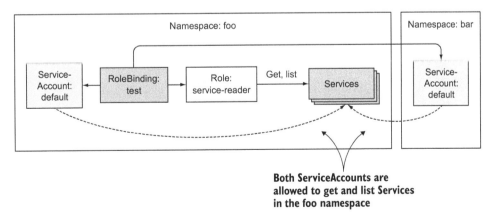

Figure 12.6 A RoleBinding binding ServiceAccounts from different namespaces to the same Role.

12.2.4 *Using ClusterRoles and ClusterRoleBindings*

Roles and RoleBindings are namespaced resources, meaning they reside in and apply to resources in a single namespace, but, as we saw, RoleBindings can refer to Service-Accounts from other namespaces, too.

In addition to these namespaced resources, two cluster-level RBAC resources also exist: ClusterRole and ClusterRoleBinding. They're not namespaced. Let's see why you need them.

A regular Role only allows access to resources in the same namespace the Role is in. If you want to allow someone access to resources across different namespaces, you have to create a Role and RoleBinding in every one of those namespaces. If you want to extend this to all namespaces (this is something a cluster administrator would probably need), you need to create the same Role and RoleBinding in each namespace. When creating an additional namespace, you have to remember to create the two resources there as well.

As you've learned throughout the book, certain resources aren't namespaced at all (this includes Nodes, PersistentVolumes, Namespaces, and so on). We've also mentioned the API server exposes some URL paths that don't represent resources (/healthz for example). Regular Roles can't grant access to those resources or non-resource URLs, but ClusterRoles can.

A ClusterRole is a cluster-level resource for allowing access to non-namespaced resources or non-resource URLs or used as a common role to be bound inside individual namespaces, saving you from having to redefine the same role in each of them.

ALLOWING ACCESS TO CLUSTER-LEVEL RESOURCES

As mentioned, a ClusterRole can be used to allow access to cluster-level resources. Let's look at how to allow your pod to list PersistentVolumes in your cluster. First, you'll create a ClusterRole called `pv-reader`:

```
$ kubectl create clusterrole pv-reader --verb=get,list
    --resource=persistentvolumes
clusterrole "pv-reader" created
```

The ClusterRole's YAML is shown in the following listing.

Listing 12.12   A ClusterRole definition

```
$ kubectl get clusterrole pv-reader -o yaml
apiVersion: rbac.authorization.k8s.io/v1
kind: ClusterRole
metadata:
  name: pv-reader
  resourceVersion: "39932"
  selfLink: ...
  uid: e9ac1099-30e2-11e7-955c-080027e6b159
```

> **ClusterRoles aren't namespaced, hence no namespace field.**

```
rules:
- apiGroups:
  - ""
  resources:
  - persistentvolumes
  verbs:
  - get
  - list
```

> **In this case, the
> rules are exactly
> like those in a
> regular Role.**

Before you bind this ClusterRole to your pod's ServiceAccount, verify whether the pod can list PersistentVolumes. Run the following command in the first terminal, where you're running the shell inside the pod in the `foo` namespace:

```
/ # curl localhost:8001/api/v1/persistentvolumes
User "system:serviceaccount:foo:default" cannot list persistentvolumes at the
    cluster scope.
```

> **NOTE** The URL contains no namespace, because PersistentVolumes aren't namespaced.

As expected, the default ServiceAccount can't list PersistentVolumes. You need to bind the ClusterRole to your ServiceAccount to allow it to do that. ClusterRoles can be bound to subjects with regular RoleBindings, so you'll create a RoleBinding now:

```
$ kubectl create rolebinding pv-test --clusterrole=pv-reader
➥ --serviceaccount=foo:default -n foo
rolebinding "pv-test" created
```

Can you list PersistentVolumes now?

```
/ # curl localhost:8001/api/v1/persistentvolumes
User "system:serviceaccount:foo:default" cannot list persistentvolumes at the
    cluster scope.
```

Hmm, that's strange. Let's examine the RoleBinding's YAML in the following listing. Can you tell what (if anything) is wrong with it?

Listing 12.13 A RoleBinding referencing a ClusterRole

```
$ kubectl get rolebindings pv-test -o yaml
apiVersion: rbac.authorization.k8s.io/v1
kind: RoleBinding
metadata:
  name: pv-test
  namespace: foo
  ...
roleRef:
  apiGroup: rbac.authorization.k8s.io
  kind: ClusterRole
  name: pv-reader
```

> **The binding references the
> pv-reader ClusterRole.**

```
subjects:
- kind: ServiceAccount          The bound subject is the
  name: default                 default ServiceAccount in
  namespace: foo                the foo namespace.
```

The YAML looks perfectly fine. You're referencing the correct ClusterRole and the correct ServiceAccount, as shown in figure 12.7, so what's wrong?

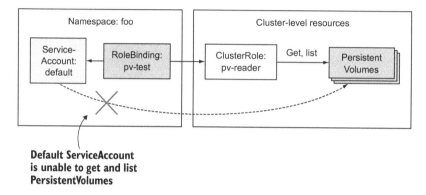

Default ServiceAccount is unable to get and list PersistentVolumes

Figure 12.7   A RoleBinding referencing a ClusterRole doesn't grant access to cluster-level resources.

Although you can create a RoleBinding and have it reference a ClusterRole when you want to enable access to namespaced resources, you can't use the same approach for cluster-level (non-namespaced) resources. To grant access to cluster-level resources, you must always use a ClusterRoleBinding.

Luckily, creating a ClusterRoleBinding isn't that different from creating a Role-Binding, but you'll clean up and delete the RoleBinding first:

```
$ kubectl delete rolebinding pv-test
rolebinding "pv-test" deleted
```

Now create the ClusterRoleBinding:

```
$ kubectl create clusterrolebinding pv-test --clusterrole=pv-reader
➥ --serviceaccount=foo:default
clusterrolebinding "pv-test" created
```

As you can see, you replaced `rolebinding` with `clusterrolebinding` in the command and didn't (need to) specify the namespace. Figure 12.8 shows what you have now.

Let's see if you can list PersistentVolumes now:

```
/ # curl localhost:8001/api/v1/persistentvolumes
{
  "kind": "PersistentVolumeList",
  "apiVersion": "v1",
...
```

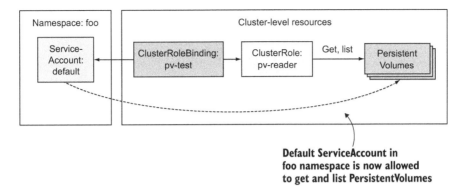

Figure 12.8　A ClusterRoleBinding and ClusterRole must be used to grant access to cluster-level resources.

You can! It turns out you must use a ClusterRole and a ClusterRoleBinding when granting access to cluster-level resources.

> **TIP**　Remember that a RoleBinding can't grant access to cluster-level resources, even if it references a ClusterRoleBinding.

ALLOWING ACCESS TO NON-RESOURCE URLS

We've mentioned that the API server also exposes non-resource URLs. Access to these URLs must also be granted explicitly; otherwise the API server will reject the client's request. Usually, this is done for you automatically through the `system:discovery` ClusterRole and the identically named ClusterRoleBinding, which appear among other predefined ClusterRoles and ClusterRoleBindings (we'll explore them in section 12.2.5).

Let's inspect the `system:discovery` ClusterRole shown in the following listing.

Listing 12.14　The default `system:discovery` ClusterRole

```
$ kubectl get clusterrole system:discovery -o yaml
apiVersion: rbac.authorization.k8s.io/v1
kind: ClusterRole
metadata:
  name: system:discovery
  ...
rules:
- nonResourceURLs:
  - /api
  - /api/*
  - /apis
  - /apis/*
  - /healthz
  - /swaggerapi
  - /swaggerapi/*
  - /version
```

Instead of referring to resources, this rule refers to non-resource URLs.

```
verbs:                    Only the HTTP GET method
- get                     is allowed for these URLs.
```

You can see this ClusterRole refers to URLs instead of resources (field `nonResource-URLs` is used instead of the `resources` field). The `verbs` field only allows the `GET` HTTP method to be used on these URLs.

> **NOTE** For non-resource URLs, plain HTTP verbs such as `post`, `put`, and `patch` are used instead of `create` or `update`. The verbs need to be specified in lowercase.

As with cluster-level resources, ClusterRoles for non-resource URLs must be bound with a ClusterRoleBinding. Binding them with a RoleBinding won't have any effect. The `system:discovery` ClusterRole has a corresponding system:discovery ClusterRoleBinding, so let's see what's in it by examining the following listing.

Listing 12.15   The default `system:discovery` ClusterRoleBinding

```
$ kubectl get clusterrolebinding system:discovery -o yaml
apiVersion: rbac.authorization.k8s.io/v1
kind: ClusterRoleBinding
metadata:
  name: system:discovery
  ...
roleRef:
  apiGroup: rbac.authorization.k8s.io
  kind: ClusterRole                        This ClusterRoleBinding references
  name: system:discovery                   the system:discovery ClusterRole.
subjects:
- apiGroup: rbac.authorization.k8s.io
  kind: Group                              It binds the ClusterRole
  name: system:authenticated              to all authenticated and
- apiGroup: rbac.authorization.k8s.io     unauthenticated users
  kind: Group                              (that is, everyone).
  name: system:unauthenticated
```

The YAML shows the ClusterRoleBinding refers to the `system:discovery` ClusterRole, as expected. It's bound to two groups, `system:authenticated` and `system:unauthenticated`, which makes it bound to all users. This means absolutely everyone can access the URLs listed in the ClusterRole.

> **NOTE** Groups are in the domain of the authentication plugin. When a request is received by the API server, it calls the authentication plugin to obtain the list of groups the user belongs to. This information is then used in authorization.

You can confirm this by accessing the /api URL path from inside the pod (through the `kubectl` proxy, which means you'll be authenticated as the pod's ServiceAccount) and from your local machine, without specifying any authentication tokens (making you an unauthenticated user):

```
$ curl https://$(minikube ip):8443/api -k
{
  "kind": "APIVersions",
  "versions": [
  ...
```

You've now used ClusterRoles and ClusterRoleBindings to grant access to cluster-level resources and non-resource URLs. Now let's look at how ClusterRoles can be used with namespaced RoleBindings to grant access to namespaced resources in the Role-Binding's namespace.

USING CLUSTERROLES TO GRANT ACCESS TO RESOURCES IN SPECIFIC NAMESPACES

ClusterRoles don't always need to be bound with cluster-level ClusterRoleBindings. They can also be bound with regular, namespaced RoleBindings. You've already started looking at predefined ClusterRoles, so let's look at another one called view, which is shown in the following listing.

Listing 12.16 The default view ClusterRole

```
$ kubectl get clusterrole view -o yaml
apiVersion: rbac.authorization.k8s.io/v1
kind: ClusterRole
metadata:
  name: view
  ...
rules:
- apiGroups:
  - ""
  resources:
  - configmaps
  - endpoints
  - persistentvolumeclaims          This rule applies to
  - pods                             these resources (note:
  - replicationcontrollers           they're all namespaced
  - replicationcontrollers/scale      resources).
  - serviceaccounts
  - services
  verbs:                     As the ClusterRole's name
  - get                      suggests, it only allows
  - list                     reading, not writing the
  - watch                    resources listed.
...
```

This ClusterRole has many rules. Only the first one is shown in the listing. The rule allows getting, listing, and watching resources like ConfigMaps, Endpoints, Persistent-VolumeClaims, and so on. These are namespaced resources, even though you're looking at a ClusterRole (not a regular, namespaced Role). What exactly does this ClusterRole do?

It depends whether it's bound with a ClusterRoleBinding or a RoleBinding (it can be bound with either). If you create a ClusterRoleBinding and reference the Cluster-Role in it, the subjects listed in the binding can view the specified resources across all namespaces. If, on the other hand, you create a RoleBinding, the subjects listed in the binding can only view resources in the namespace of the RoleBinding. You'll try both options now.

You'll see how the two options affect your test pod's ability to list pods. First, let's see what happens before any bindings are in place:

```
/ # curl localhost:8001/api/v1/pods
User "system:serviceaccount:foo:default" cannot list pods at the cluster
    scope./ #
/ # curl localhost:8001/api/v1/namespaces/foo/pods
User "system:serviceaccount:foo:default" cannot list pods in the namespace
    "foo".
```

With the first command, you're trying to list pods across all namespaces. With the second, you're trying to list pods in the foo namespace. The server doesn't allow you to do either.

Now, let's see what happens when you create a ClusterRoleBinding and bind it to the pod's ServiceAccount:

```
$ kubectl create clusterrolebinding view-test --clusterrole=view
➥  --serviceaccount=foo:default
clusterrolebinding "view-test" created
```

Can the pod now list pods in the foo namespace?

```
/ # curl localhost:8001/api/v1/namespaces/foo/pods
{
  "kind": "PodList",
  "apiVersion": "v1",
  ...
```

It can! Because you created a ClusterRoleBinding, it applies across all namespaces. The pod in namespace foo can list pods in the bar namespace as well:

```
/ # curl localhost:8001/api/v1/namespaces/bar/pods
{
  "kind": "PodList",
  "apiVersion": "v1",
  ...
```

Okay, the pod is allowed to list pods in a different namespace. It can also retrieve pods across all namespaces by hitting the /api/v1/pods URL path:

```
/ # curl localhost:8001/api/v1/pods
{
  "kind": "PodList",
  "apiVersion": "v1",
  ...
```

As expected, the pod can get a list of all the pods in the cluster. To summarize, combining a ClusterRoleBinding with a ClusterRole referring to namespaced resources allows the pod to access namespaced resources in any namespace, as shown in figure 12.9.

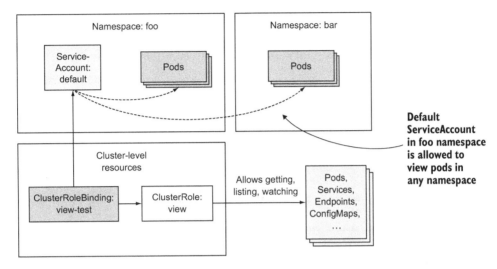

Figure 12.9   A ClusterRoleBinding and ClusterRole grants permission to resources across all namespaces.

Now, let's see what happens if you replace the ClusterRoleBinding with a RoleBinding. First, delete the ClusterRoleBinding:

```
$ kubectl delete clusterrolebinding view-test
clusterrolebinding "view-test" deleted
```

Next create a RoleBinding instead. Because a RoleBinding is namespaced, you need to specify the namespace you want to create it in. Create it in the foo namespace:

```
$ kubectl create rolebinding view-test --clusterrole=view
➥ --serviceaccount=foo:default -n foo
rolebinding "view-test" created
```

You now have a RoleBinding in the foo namespace, binding the default Service-Account in that same namespace with the view ClusterRole. What can your pod access now?

```
/ # curl localhost:8001/api/v1/namespaces/foo/pods
{
  "kind": "PodList",
  "apiVersion": "v1",
  ...
```

```
/ # curl localhost:8001/api/v1/namespaces/bar/pods
User "system:serviceaccount:foo:default" cannot list pods in the namespace
    "bar".
```

```
/ # curl localhost:8001/api/v1/pods
User "system:serviceaccount:foo:default" cannot list pods at the cluster
    scope.
```

As you can see, your pod can list pods in the foo namespace, but not in any other specific namespace or across all namespaces. This is visualized in figure 12.10.

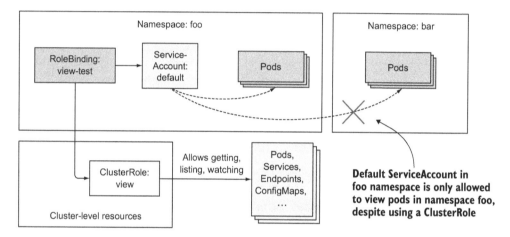

Figure 12.10   A RoleBinding referring to a ClusterRole only grants access to resources inside the RoleBinding's namespace.

SUMMARIZING ROLE, CLUSTERROLE, ROLEBINDING, AND CLUSTERROLEBINDING COMBINATIONS
We've covered many different combinations and it may be hard for you to remember when to use each one. Let's see if we can make sense of all these combinations by categorizing them per specific use case. Refer to table 12.2.

Table 12.2   When to use specific combinations of role and binding types

For accessing	Role type to use	Binding type to use
Cluster-level resources (Nodes, PersistentVolumes, ...)	ClusterRole	ClusterRoleBinding
Non-resource URLs (/api, /healthz, ...)	ClusterRole	ClusterRoleBinding
Namespaced resources in any namespace (and across all namespaces)	ClusterRole	ClusterRoleBinding
Namespaced resources in a specific namespace (reusing the same ClusterRole in multiple namespaces)	ClusterRole	RoleBinding
Namespaced resources in a specific namespace (Role must be defined in each namespace)	Role	RoleBinding

Hopefully, the relationships between the four RBAC resources are much clearer now. Don't worry if you still feel like you don't yet grasp everything. Things may clear up as we explore the pre-configured ClusterRoles and ClusterRoleBindings in the next section.

12.2.5 *Understanding default ClusterRoles and ClusterRoleBindings*

Kubernetes comes with a default set of ClusterRoles and ClusterRoleBindings, which are updated every time the API server starts. This ensures all the default roles and bindings are recreated if you mistakenly delete them or if a newer version of Kubernetes uses a different configuration of cluster roles and bindings.

You can see the default cluster roles and bindings in the following listing.

Listing 12.17 Listing all ClusterRoleBindings and ClusterRoles

```
$ kubectl get clusterrolebindings
NAME                                         AGE
cluster-admin                                1d
system:basic-user                            1d
system:controller:attachdetach-controller    1d
...
system:controller:ttl-controller             1d
system:discovery                             1d
system:kube-controller-manager               1d
system:kube-dns                              1d
system:kube-scheduler                        1d
system:node                                  1d
system:node-proxier                          1d

$ kubectl get clusterroles
NAME                                         AGE
admin                                        1d
cluster-admin                                1d
edit                                         1d
system:auth-delegator                        1d
system:basic-user                            1d
system:controller:attachdetach-controller    1d
...
system:controller:ttl-controller             1d
system:discovery                             1d
system:heapster                              1d
system:kube-aggregator                       1d
system:kube-controller-manager               1d
system:kube-dns                              1d
system:kube-scheduler                        1d
system:node                                  1d
system:node-bootstrapper                     1d
system:node-problem-detector                 1d
system:node-proxier                          1d
system:persistent-volume-provisioner         1d
view                                         1d
```

The most important roles are the `view`, `edit`, `admin`, and `cluster-admin` ClusterRoles. They're meant to be bound to ServiceAccounts used by user-defined pods.

ALLOWING READ-ONLY ACCESS TO RESOURCES WITH THE VIEW CLUSTERROLE

You already used the default `view` ClusterRole in the previous example. It allows reading most resources in a namespace, except for Roles, RoleBindings, and Secrets. You're probably wondering, why not Secrets? Because one of those Secrets might include an authentication token with greater privileges than those defined in the `view` ClusterRole and could allow the user to masquerade as a different user to gain additional privileges (privilege escalation).

ALLOWING MODIFYING RESOURCES WITH THE EDIT CLUSTERROLE

Next is the `edit` ClusterRole, which allows you to modify resources in a namespace, but also allows both reading and modifying Secrets. It doesn't, however, allow viewing or modifying Roles or RoleBindings—again, this is to prevent privilege escalation.

GRANTING FULL CONTROL OF A NAMESPACE WITH THE ADMIN CLUSTERROLE

Complete control of the resources in a namespace is granted in the `admin` ClusterRole. Subjects with this ClusterRole can read and modify any resource in the namespace, except ResourceQuotas (we'll learn what those are in chapter 14) and the Namespace resource itself. The main difference between the `edit` and the `admin` ClusterRoles is in the ability to view and modify Roles and RoleBindings in the namespace.

> **NOTE**   To prevent privilege escalation, the API server only allows users to create and update Roles if they already have all the permissions listed in that Role (and for the same scope).

ALLOWING COMPLETE CONTROL WITH THE CLUSTER-ADMIN CLUSTERROLE

Complete control of the Kubernetes cluster can be given by assigning the `cluster-admin` ClusterRole to a subject. As you've seen before, the `admin` ClusterRole doesn't allow users to modify the namespace's ResourceQuota objects or the Namespace resource itself. If you want to allow a user to do that, you need to create a RoleBinding that references the `cluster-admin` ClusterRole. This gives the user included in the RoleBinding complete control over all aspects of the namespace in which the RoleBinding is created.

If you've paid attention, you probably already know how to give users complete control of all the namespaces in the cluster. Yes, by referencing the `cluster-admin` ClusterRole in a ClusterRoleBinding instead of a RoleBinding.

UNDERSTANDING THE OTHER DEFAULT CLUSTERROLES

The list of default ClusterRoles includes a large number of other ClusterRoles, which start with the `system:` prefix. These are meant to be used by the various Kubernetes components. Among them, you'll find roles such as `system:kube-scheduler`, which is obviously used by the Scheduler, `system:node`, which is used by the Kubelets, and so on.

Although the Controller Manager runs as a single pod, each controller running inside it can use a separate ClusterRole and ClusterRoleBinding (they're prefixed with `system: controller:`).

Each of these system ClusterRoles has a matching ClusterRoleBinding, which binds it to the user the system component authenticates as. The `system:kube-scheduler` ClusterRoleBinding, for example, assigns the identically named ClusterRole to the `system:kube-scheduler` user, which is the username the scheduler Authenticates as.

12.2.6 *Granting authorization permissions wisely*

By default, the default ServiceAccount in a namespace has no permissions other than those of an unauthenticated user (as you may remember from one of the previous examples, the `system:discovery` ClusterRole and associated binding allow anyone to make GET requests on a few non-resource URLs). Therefore, pods, by default, can't even view cluster state. It's up to you to grant them appropriate permissions to do that.

Obviously, giving all your ServiceAccounts the `cluster-admin` ClusterRole is a bad idea. As is always the case with security, it's best to give everyone only the permissions they need to do their job and not a single permission more (*principle of least privilege*).

CREATING SPECIFIC SERVICEACCOUNTS FOR EACH POD

It's a good idea to create a specific ServiceAccount for each pod (or a set of pod replicas) and then associate it with a tailor-made Role (or a ClusterRole) through a RoleBinding (not a ClusterRoleBinding, because that would give the pod access to resources in other namespaces, which is probably not what you want).

If one of your pods (the application running within it) only needs to read pods, while the other also needs to modify them, then create two different ServiceAccounts and make those pods use them by specifying the `serviceAccountName` property in the pod spec, as you learned in the first part of this chapter. Don't add all the necessary permissions required by both pods to the default ServiceAccount in the namespace.

EXPECTING YOUR APPS TO BE COMPROMISED

Your aim is to reduce the possibility of an intruder getting hold of your cluster. Today's complex apps contain many vulnerabilities. You should expect unwanted persons to eventually get their hands on the ServiceAccount's authentication token, so you should always constrain the ServiceAccount to prevent them from doing any real damage.

12.3 *Summary*

This chapter has given you a foundation on how to secure the Kubernetes API server. You learned the following:

- Clients of the API server include both human users and applications running in pods.
- Applications in pods are associated with a ServiceAccount.
- Both users and ServiceAccounts are associated with groups.

- By default, pods run under the default ServiceAccount, which is created for each namespace automatically.
- Additional ServiceAccounts can be created manually and associated with a pod.
- ServiceAccounts can be configured to allow mounting only a constrained list of Secrets in a given pod.
- A ServiceAccount can also be used to attach image pull Secrets to pods, so you don't need to specify the Secrets in every pod.
- Roles and ClusterRoles define what actions can be performed on which resources.
- RoleBindings and ClusterRoleBindings bind Roles and ClusterRoles to users, groups, and ServiceAccounts.
- Each cluster comes with default ClusterRoles and ClusterRoleBindings.

In the next chapter, you'll learn how to protect the cluster nodes from pods and how to isolate pods from each other by securing the network.

Securing cluster nodes
and the network

This chapter covers

- Using the node's default Linux namespaces in pods
- Running containers as different users
- Running privileged containers
- Adding or dropping a container's kernel capabilities
- Defining security policies to limit what pods can do
- Securing the pod network

In the previous chapter, we talked about securing the API server. If an attacker gets access to the API server, they can run whatever they like by packaging their code into a container image and running it in a pod. But can they do any real damage? Aren't containers isolated from other containers and from the node they're running on?

Not necessarily. In this chapter, you'll learn how to allow pods to access the resources of the node they're running on. You'll also learn how to configure the cluster so users aren't able to do whatever they want with their pods. Then, in the last part of the chapter, you'll also learn how to secure the network the pods use to communicate.

13.1 *Using the host node's namespaces in a pod*

Containers in a pod usually run under separate Linux namespaces, which isolate their processes from processes running in other containers or in the node's default namespaces.

For example, we learned that each pod gets its own IP and port space, because it uses its own network namespace. Likewise, each pod has its own process tree, because it has its own PID namespace, and it also uses its own IPC namespace, allowing only processes in the same pod to communicate with each other through the Inter-Process Communication mechanism (IPC).

13.1.1 *Using the node's network namespace in a pod*

Certain pods (usually system pods) need to operate in the host's default namespaces, allowing them to see and manipulate node-level resources and devices. For example, a pod may need to use the node's network adapters instead of its own virtual network adapters. This can be achieved by setting the `hostNetwork` property in the pod spec to `true`.

In that case, the pod gets to use the node's network interfaces instead of having its own set, as shown in figure 13.1. This means the pod doesn't get its own IP address and if it runs a process that binds to a port, the process will be bound to the node's port.

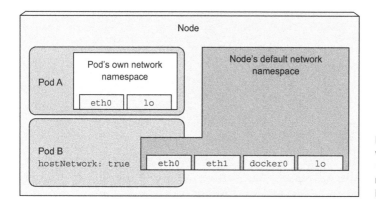

Figure 13.1 A pod with `hostNetwork: true` uses the node's network interfaces instead of its own.

You can try running such a pod. The next listing shows an example pod manifest.

Listing 13.1 A pod using the node's network namespace: pod-with-host-network.yaml

```
apiVersion: v1
kind: Pod
metadata:
  name: pod-with-host-network
```

```
spec:
  hostNetwork: true                    ◁──┐   Using the host node's
  containers:                                 network namespace
  - name: main
    image: alpine
    command: ["/bin/sleep", "999999"]
```

After you run the pod, you can use the following command to see that it's indeed using the host's network namespace (it sees all the host's network adapters, for example).

Listing 13.2 Network interfaces in a pod using the host's network namespace

```
$ kubectl exec pod-with-host-network ifconfig
docker0    Link encap:Ethernet  HWaddr 02:42:14:08:23:47
           inet addr:172.17.0.1  Bcast:0.0.0.0  Mask:255.255.0.0
           ...

eth0       Link encap:Ethernet  HWaddr 08:00:27:F8:FA:4E
           inet addr:10.0.2.15  Bcast:10.0.2.255  Mask:255.255.255.0
           ...

lo         Link encap:Local Loopback
           inet addr:127.0.0.1  Mask:255.0.0.0
           ...

veth1178d4f Link encap:Ethernet  HWaddr 1E:03:8D:D6:E1:2C
           inet6 addr: fe80::1c03:8dff:fed6:e12c/64 Scope:Link
           UP BROADCAST RUNNING MULTICAST  MTU:1500  Metric:1
...
```

When the Kubernetes Control Plane components are deployed as pods (such as when you deploy your cluster with kubeadm, as explained in appendix B), you'll find that those pods use the hostNetwork option, effectively making them behave as if they weren't running inside a pod.

13.1.2 Binding to a host port without using the host's network namespace

A related feature allows pods to bind to a port in the node's default namespace, but still have their own network namespace. This is done by using the hostPort property in one of the container's ports defined in the spec.containers.ports field.

Don't confuse pods using hostPort with pods exposed through a NodePort service. They're two different things, as explained in figure 13.2.

The first thing you'll notice in the figure is that when a pod is using a hostPort, a connection to the node's port is forwarded directly to the pod running on that node, whereas with a NodePort service, a connection to the node's port is forwarded to a randomly selected pod (possibly on another node). The other difference is that with pods using a hostPort, the node's port is only bound on nodes that run such pods, whereas NodePort services bind the port on all nodes, even on those that don't run such a pod (as on node 3 in the figure).

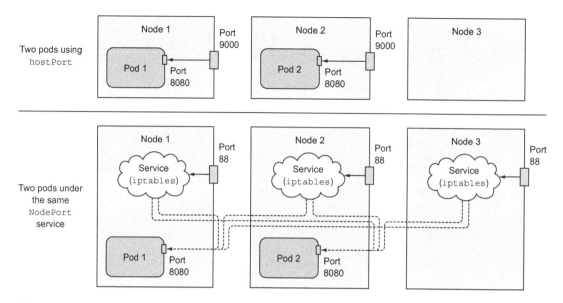

Figure 13.2 Difference between pods using a `hostPort` **and pods behind a** `NodePort` **service.**

It's important to understand that if a pod is using a specific host port, only one instance of the pod can be scheduled to each node, because two processes can't bind to the same host port. The Scheduler takes this into account when scheduling pods, so it doesn't schedule multiple pods to the same node, as shown in figure 13.3. If you have three nodes and want to deploy four pod replicas, only three will be scheduled (one pod will remain Pending).

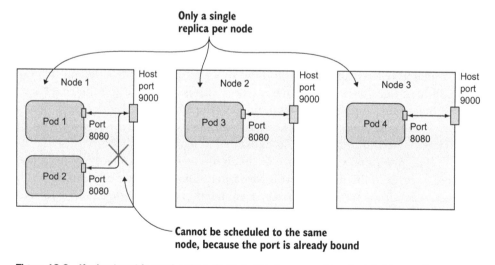

Figure 13.3 If a host port is used, only a single pod instance can be scheduled to a node.

Let's see how to define the hostPort in a pod's YAML definition. The following listing shows the YAML to run your kubia pod and bind it to the node's port 9000.

```
apiVersion: v1
kind: Pod
metadata:
  name: kubia-hostport
spec:
  containers:
  - image: luksa/kubia
    name: kubia
    ports:
    - containerPort: 8080
      hostPort: 9000
      protocol: TCP
```

The container can be reached on port 8080 of the pod's IP.

It can also be reached on port 9000 of the node it's deployed on.

After you create this pod, you can access it through port 9000 of the node it's scheduled to. If you have multiple nodes, you'll see you can't access the pod through that port on the other nodes.

NOTE If you're trying this on GKE, you need to configure the firewall properly using gcloud compute firewall-rules, the way you did in chapter 5.

The hostPort feature is primarily used for exposing system services, which are deployed to every node using DaemonSets. Initially, people also used it to ensure two replicas of the same pod were never scheduled to the same node, but now you have a better way of achieving this—it's explained in chapter 16.

13.1.3 Using the node's PID and IPC namespaces

Similar to the hostNetwork option are the hostPID and hostIPC pod spec properties. When you set them to true, the pod's containers will use the node's PID and IPC namespaces, allowing processes running in the containers to see all the other processes on the node or communicate with them through IPC, respectively. See the following listing for an example.

```
apiVersion: v1
kind: Pod
metadata:
  name: pod-with-host-pid-and-ipc
spec:
  hostPID: true
  hostIPC: true
  containers:
  - name: main
    image: alpine
    command: ["/bin/sleep", "999999"]
```

You want the pod to use the host's PID namespace.

You also want the pod to use the host's IPC namespace.

You'll remember that pods usually see only their own processes, but if you run this pod and then list the processes from within its container, you'll see all the processes running on the host node, not only the ones running in the container, as shown in the following listing.

Listing 13.5   Processes visible in a pod with `hostPID: true`

```
$ kubectl exec pod-with-host-pid-and-ipc ps aux
PID    USER     TIME    COMMAND
    1 root      0:01  /usr/lib/systemd/systemd --switched-root --system ...
    2 root      0:00  [kthreadd]
    3 root      0:00  [ksoftirqd/0]
    5 root      0:00  [kworker/0:0H]
    6 root      0:00  [kworker/u2:0]
    7 root      0:00  [migration/0]
    8 root      0:00  [rcu_bh]
    9 root      0:00  [rcu_sched]
   10 root      0:00  [watchdog/0]
...
```

By setting the `hostIPC` property to `true`, processes in the pod's containers can also communicate with all the other processes running on the node, through Inter-Process Communication.

13.2 *Configuring the container's security context*

Besides allowing the pod to use the host's Linux namespaces, other security-related features can also be configured on the pod and its container through the `security-Context` properties, which can be specified under the pod spec directly and inside the spec of individual containers.

UNDERSTANDING WHAT'S CONFIGURABLE IN THE SECURITY CONTEXT

Configuring the security context allows you to do various things:

- Specify the user (the user's ID) under which the process in the container will run.
- Prevent the container from running as root (the default user a container runs as is usually defined in the container image itself, so you may want to prevent containers from running as root).
- Run the container in privileged mode, giving it full access to the node's kernel.
- Configure fine-grained privileges, by adding or dropping capabilities—in contrast to giving the container all possible permissions by running it in privileged mode.
- Set SELinux (Security Enhanced Linux) options to strongly lock down a container.
- Prevent the process from writing to the container's filesystem.

We'll explore these options next.

RUNNING A POD WITHOUT SPECIFYING A SECURITY CONTEXT

First, run a pod with the default security context options (by not specifying them at all), so you can see how it behaves compared to pods with a custom security context:

```
$ kubectl run pod-with-defaults --image alpine --restart Never
➥  -- /bin/sleep 999999
pod "pod-with-defaults" created
```

Let's see what user and group ID the container is running as, and which groups it belongs to. You can see this by running the id command inside the container:

```
$ kubectl exec pod-with-defaults id
uid=0(root) gid=0(root) groups=0(root), 1(bin), 2(daemon), 3(sys), 4(adm),
    6(disk), 10(wheel), 11(floppy), 20(dialout), 26(tape), 27(video)
```

The container is running as user ID (uid) 0, which is root, and group ID (gid) 0 (also root). It's also a member of multiple other groups.

> **NOTE** What user the container runs as is specified in the container image. In a Dockerfile, this is done using the USER directive. If omitted, the container runs as root.

Now, you'll run a pod where the container runs as a different user.

13.2.1 *Running a container as a specific user*

To run a pod under a different user ID than the one that's baked into the container image, you'll need to set the pod's securityContext.runAsUser property. You'll make the container run as user guest, whose user ID in the alpine container image is 405, as shown in the following listing.

> **Listing 13.6 Running containers as a specific user: pod-as-user-guest.yaml**

```
apiVersion: v1
kind: Pod
metadata:
  name: pod-as-user-guest
spec:
  containers:
  - name: main
    image: alpine
    command: ["/bin/sleep", "999999"]
    securityContext:
      runAsUser: 405
```
> You need to specify a user ID, not a username (id 405 corresponds to the guest user).

Now, to see the effect of the runAsUser property, run the id command in this new pod, the way you did before:

```
$ kubectl exec pod-as-user-guest id
uid=405(guest) gid=100(users)
```

As requested, the container is running as the guest user.

13.2.2 Preventing a container from running as root

What if you don't care what user the container runs as, but you still want to prevent it from running as root?

Imagine having a pod deployed with a container image that was built with a USER daemon directive in the Dockerfile, which makes the container run under the daemon user. What if an attacker gets access to your image registry and pushes a different image under the same tag? The attacker's image is configured to run as the root user. When Kubernetes schedules a new instance of your pod, the Kubelet will download the attacker's image and run whatever code they put into it.

Although containers are mostly isolated from the host system, running their processes as root is still considered a bad practice. For example, when a host directory is mounted into the container, if the process running in the container is running as root, it has full access to the mounted directory, whereas if it's running as non-root, it won't.

To prevent the attack scenario described previously, you can specify that the pod's container needs to run as a non-root user, as shown in the following listing.

Listing 13.7 Preventing containers from running as root: pod-run-as-non-root.yaml

```
apiVersion: v1
kind: Pod
metadata:
  name: pod-run-as-non-root
spec:
  containers:
  - name: main
    image: alpine
    command: ["/bin/sleep", "999999"]
    securityContext:
      runAsNonRoot: true
```

This container will only be allowed to run as a non-root user.

If you deploy this pod, it gets scheduled, but is not allowed to run:

```
$ kubectl get po pod-run-as-non-root
NAME                  READY  STATUS
pod-run-as-non-root   0/1    container has runAsNonRoot and image will run
                                 ⇒  as root
```

Now, if anyone tampers with your container images, they won't get far.

13.2.3 Running pods in privileged mode

Sometimes pods need to do everything that the node they're running on can do, such as use protected system devices or other kernel features, which aren't accessible to regular containers.

An example of such a pod is the kube-proxy pod, which needs to modify the node's `iptables` rules to make services work, as was explained in chapter 11. If you follow the instructions in appendix B and deploy a cluster with `kubeadm`, you'll see every cluster node runs a kube-proxy pod and you can examine its YAML specification to see all the special features it's using.

To get full access to the node's kernel, the pod's container runs in privileged mode. This is achieved by setting the `privileged` property in the container's `security-Context` property to `true`. You'll create a privileged pod from the YAML in the following listing.

Listing 13.8 A pod with a privileged container: pod-privileged.yaml

```
apiVersion: v1
kind: Pod
metadata:
  name: pod-privileged
spec:
  containers:
  - name: main
    image: alpine
    command: ["/bin/sleep", "999999"]
    securityContext:              This container will
      privileged: true      ◁─── run in privileged
                                  mode
```

Go ahead and deploy this pod, so you can compare it with the non-privileged pod you ran earlier.

If you're familiar with Linux, you may know it has a special file directory called /dev, which contains device files for all the devices on the system. These aren't regular files on disk, but are special files used to communicate with devices. Let's see what devices are visible in the non-privileged container you deployed earlier (the `pod-with-defaults` pod), by listing files in its /dev directory, as shown in the following listing.

Listing 13.9 List of available devices in a non-privileged pod

```
$ kubectl exec -it pod-with-defaults ls /dev
core            null            stderr          urandom
fd              ptmx            stdin           zero
full            pts             stdout
fuse            random          termination-log
mqueue          shm             tty
```

The listing shows all the devices. The list is fairly short. Now, compare this with the following listing, which shows the device files your privileged pod can see.

Listing 13.10 List of available devices in a privileged pod

```
$ kubectl exec -it pod-privileged ls /dev
autofs          snd             tty46
bsg             sr0             tty47
```

```
btrfs-control          stderr                 tty48
core                   stdin                  tty49
cpu                    stdout                 tty5
cpu_dma_latency        termination-log        tty50
fd                     tty                    tty51
full                   tty0                   tty52
fuse                   tty1                   tty53
hpet                   tty10                  tty54
hwrng                  tty11                  tty55
...                    ...                    ...
```

I haven't included the whole list, because it's too long for the book, but it's evident that the device list is much longer than before. In fact, the privileged container sees all the host node's devices. This means it can use any device freely.

For example, I had to use privileged mode like this when I wanted a pod running on a Raspberry Pi to control LEDs connected it.

13.2.4 *Adding individual kernel capabilities to a container*

In the previous section, you saw one way of giving a container unlimited power. In the old days, traditional UNIX implementations only distinguished between privileged and unprivileged processes, but for many years, Linux has supported a much more fine-grained permission system through kernel *capabilities.*

Instead of making a container privileged and giving it unlimited permissions, a much safer method (from a security perspective) is to give it access only to the kernel features it really requires. Kubernetes allows you to add capabilities to each container or drop part of them, which allows you to fine-tune the container's permissions and limit the impact of a potential intrusion by an attacker.

For example, a container usually isn't allowed to change the system time (the hardware clock's time). You can confirm this by trying to set the time in your pod-with-defaults pod:

```
$ kubectl exec -it pod-with-defaults -- date +%T -s "12:00:00"
date: can't set date: Operation not permitted
```

If you want to allow the container to change the system time, you can add a capability called CAP_SYS_TIME to the container's capabilities list, as shown in the following listing.

> **Listing 13.11   Adding the CAP_SYS_TIME capability: pod-add-settime-capability.yaml**

```
apiVersion: v1
kind: Pod
metadata:
  name: pod-add-settime-capability
spec:
  containers:
  - name: main
    image: alpine
```

```
command: ["/bin/sleep", "999999"]
securityContext:
  capabilities:
    add:
    - SYS_TIME
```

Capabilities are added or dropped under the securityContext property.

You're adding the SYS_TIME capability.

NOTE Linux kernel capabilities are usually prefixed with `CAP_`. But when specifying them in a pod spec, you must leave out the prefix.

If you run the same command in this new pod's container, the system time is changed successfully:

```
$ kubectl exec -it pod-add-settime-capability -- date +%T -s "12:00:00"
12:00:00

$ kubectl exec -it pod-add-settime-capability -- date
Sun May  7 12:00:03 UTC 2017
```

WARNING If you try this yourself, be aware that it may cause your worker node to become unusable. In Minikube, although the system time was automatically reset back by the Network Time Protocol (NTP) daemon, I had to reboot the VM to schedule new pods.

You can confirm the node's time has been changed by checking the time on the node running the pod. In my case, I'm using Minikube, so I have only one node and I can get its time like this:

```
$ minikube ssh date
Sun May  7 12:00:07 UTC 2017
```

Adding capabilities like this is a much better way than giving a container full privileges with `privileged: true`. Admittedly, it does require you to know and understand what each capability does.

TIP You'll find the list of Linux kernel capabilities in the Linux man pages.

13.2.5 *Dropping capabilities from a container*

You've seen how to add capabilities, but you can also drop capabilities that may otherwise be available to the container. For example, the default capabilities given to a container include the `CAP_CHOWN` capability, which allows processes to change the ownership of files in the filesystem.

You can see that's the case by changing the ownership of the /tmp directory in your pod-with-defaults pod to the guest user, for example:

```
$ kubectl exec pod-with-defaults chown guest /tmp
$ kubectl exec pod-with-defaults -- ls -la / | grep tmp
drwxrwxrwt    2 guest    root         6 May 25 15:18 tmp
```

To prevent the container from doing that, you need to drop the capability by listing it under the container's `securityContext.capabilities.drop` property, as shown in the following listing.

Listing 13.12   Dropping a capability from a container: pod-drop-chown-capability.yaml

```
apiVersion: v1
kind: Pod
metadata:
  name: pod-drop-chown-capability
spec:
  containers:
  - name: main
    image: alpine
    command: ["/bin/sleep", "999999"]
    securityContext:
      capabilities:
        drop:
        - CHOWN
```

> **You're not allowing this container to change file ownership.**

By dropping the `CHOWN` capability, you're not allowed to change the owner of the /tmp directory in this pod:

```
$ kubectl exec pod-drop-chown-capability chown guest /tmp
chown: /tmp: Operation not permitted
```

You're almost done exploring the container's security context options. Let's look at one more.

13.2.6   *Preventing processes from writing to the container's filesystem*

You may want to prevent the processes running in the container from writing to the container's filesystem, and only allow them to write to mounted volumes. You'd want to do that mostly for security reasons.

Let's imagine you're running a PHP application with a hidden vulnerability, allowing an attacker to write to the filesystem. The PHP files are added to the container image at build time and are served from the container's filesystem. Because of the vulnerability, the attacker can modify those files and inject them with malicious code.

These types of attacks can be thwarted by preventing the container from writing to its filesystem, where the app's executable code is normally stored. This is done by setting the container's `securityContext.readOnlyRootFilesystem` property to `true`, as shown in the following listing.

Listing 13.13   A container with a read-only filesystem: pod-with-readonly-filesystem.yaml

```
apiVersion: v1
kind: Pod
metadata:
  name: pod-with-readonly-filesystem
```

```
spec:
  containers:
  - name: main
    image: alpine
    command: ["/bin/sleep", "999999"]
    securityContext:
      readOnlyRootFilesystem: true
    volumeMounts:
    - name: my-volume
      mountPath: /volume
      readOnly: false
  volumes:
  - name: my-volume
    emptyDir:
```

> This container's filesystem
> can't be written to...
>
> ...but writing to /volume is
> allowed, becase a volume
> is mounted there.

When you deploy this pod, the container is running as root, which has write permissions to the / directory, but trying to write a file there fails:

```
$ kubectl exec -it pod-with-readonly-filesystem touch /new-file
touch: /new-file: Read-only file system
```

On the other hand, writing to the mounted volume is allowed:

```
$ kubectl exec -it pod-with-readonly-filesystem touch /volume/newfile
$ kubectl exec -it pod-with-readonly-filesystem -- ls -la /volume/newfile
-rw-r--r--   1 root     root        0 May  7 19:11 /mountedVolume/newfile
```

As shown in the example, when you make the container's filesystem read-only, you'll probably want to mount a volume in every directory the application writes to (for example, logs, on-disk caches, and so on).

> **TIP** To increase security, when running pods in production, set their container's readOnlyRootFilesystem property to true.

SETTING SECURITY CONTEXT OPTIONS AT THE POD LEVEL

In all these examples, you've set the security context of an individual container. Several of these options can also be set at the pod level (through the pod.spec.security-Context property). They serve as a default for all the pod's containers but can be overridden at the container level. The pod-level security context also allows you to set additional properties, which we'll explain next.

13.2.7 *Sharing volumes when containers run as different users*

In chapter 6, we explained how volumes are used to share data between the pod's containers. You had no trouble writing files in one container and reading them in the other.

But this was only because both containers were running as root, giving them full access to all the files in the volume. Now imagine using the runAsUser option we explained earlier. You may need to run the two containers as two different users (perhaps you're using two third-party container images, where each one runs its process under its own specific user). If those two containers use a volume to share files, they may not necessarily be able to read or write files of one another.

That's why Kubernetes allows you to specify supplemental groups for all the pods running in the container, allowing them to share files, regardless of the user IDs they're running as. This is done using the following two properties:

- `fsGroup`
- `supplementalGroups`

What they do is best explained in an example, so let's see how to use them in a pod and then see what their effect is. The next listing describes a pod with two containers sharing the same volume.

Listing 13.14   `fsGroup` & `supplementalGroups`: pod-with-shared-volume-fsgroup.yaml

```
apiVersion: v1
kind: Pod
metadata:
  name: pod-with-shared-volume-fsgroup
spec:
  securityContext:              The fsGroup and supplementalGroups
    fsGroup: 555                are defined in the security context at
    supplementalGroups: [666, 777]   the pod level.
  containers:
  - name: first
    image: alpine
    command: ["/bin/sleep", "999999"]
    securityContext:            The first container
      runAsUser: 1111           runs as user ID 1111.
    volumeMounts:
    - name: shared-volume
      mountPath: /volume
      readOnly: false
  - name: second
    image: alpine
    command: ["/bin/sleep", "999999"]   Both containers
    securityContext:            use the same
      runAsUser: 2222           volume
    volumeMounts:
    - name: shared-volume
      mountPath: /volume
      readOnly: false
  volumes:
  - name: shared-volume
    emptyDir:
```

The second container runs as user ID 2222.

After you create this pod, run a shell in its first container and see what user and group IDs the container is running as:

```
$ kubectl exec -it pod-with-shared-volume-fsgroup -c first sh
/ $ id
uid=1111 gid=0(root) groups=555,666,777
```

The id command shows the container is running with user ID 1111, as specified in the pod definition. The effective group ID is 0 (root), but group IDs 555, 666, and 777 are also associated with the user.

   In the pod definition, you set fsGroup to 555. Because of this, the mounted volume will be owned by group ID 555, as shown here:

```
/ $ ls -l / | grep volume
drwxrwsrwx    2 root       555             6 May 29 12:23 volume
```

If you create a file in the mounted volume's directory, the file is owned by user ID 1111 (that's the user ID the container is running as) and by group ID 555:

```
/ $ echo foo > /volume/foo
/ $ ls -l /volume
total 4
-rw-r--r--    1 1111       555             4 May 29 12:25 foo
```

This is different from how ownership is otherwise set up for newly created files. Usually, the user's effective group ID, which is 0 in your case, is used when a user creates files. You can see this by creating a file in the container's filesystem instead of in the volume:

```
/ $ echo foo > /tmp/foo
/ $ ls -l /tmp
total 4
-rw-r--r--    1 1111       root            4 May 29 12:41 foo
```

As you can see, the fsGroup security context property is used when the process creates files in a volume (but this depends on the volume plugin used), whereas the supplementalGroups property defines a list of additional group IDs the user is associated with.

   This concludes this section about the configuration of the container's security context. Next, we'll see how a cluster administrator can restrict users from doing so.

13.3 *Restricting the use of security-related features in pods*

The examples in the previous sections have shown how a person deploying pods can do whatever they want on any cluster node, by deploying a privileged pod to the node, for example. Obviously, a mechanism must prevent users from doing part or all of what's been explained. The cluster admin can restrict the use of the previously described security-related features by creating one or more PodSecurityPolicy resources.

13.3.1 *Introducing the PodSecurityPolicy resource*

PodSecurityPolicy is a cluster-level (non-namespaced) resource, which defines what security-related features users can or can't use in their pods. The job of upholding the policies configured in PodSecurityPolicy resources is performed by the

PodSecurityPolicy admission control plugin running in the API server (we explained admission control plugins in chapter 11).

NOTE The PodSecurityPolicy admission control plugin may not be enabled in your cluster. Before running the following examples, ensure it's enabled. If you're using Minikube, refer to the next sidebar.

When someone posts a pod resource to the API server, the PodSecurityPolicy admission control plugin validates the pod definition against the configured PodSecurityPolicies. If the pod conforms to the cluster's policies, it's accepted and stored into etcd; otherwise it's rejected immediately. The plugin may also modify the pod resource according to defaults configured in the policy.

> **Enabling RBAC and PodSecurityPolicy admission control in Minikube**
>
> I'm using Minikube version v0.19.0 to run these examples. That version doesn't enable either the PodSecurityPolicy admission control plugin or RBAC authorization, which is required in part of the exercises. One exercise also requires authenticating as a different user, so you'll also need to enable the basic authentication plugin where users are defined in a file.
>
> To run Minikube with all these plugins enabled, you may need to use this (or a similar) command, depending on the version you're using:
>
> ```
> $ minikube start --extra-config apiserver.Authentication.PasswordFile.
>   BasicAuthFile=/etc/kubernetes/passwd --extra-config=apiserver.
>   Authorization.Mode=RBAC --extra-config=apiserver.GenericServerRun
>   Options.AdmissionControl=NamespaceLifecycle,LimitRanger,Service
>   Account,PersistentVolumeLabel,DefaultStorageClass,ResourceQuota,
>   DefaultTolerationSeconds,PodSecurityPolicy
> ```
>
> The API server won't start up until you create the password file you specified in the command line options. This is how to create the file:
>
> ```
> $ cat <<EOF | minikube ssh sudo tee /etc/kubernetes/passwd
> password,alice,1000,basic-user
> password,bob,2000,privileged-user
> EOF
> ```
>
> You'll find a shell script that runs both commands in the book's code archive in Chapter13/minikube-with-rbac-and-psp-enabled.sh.

UNDERSTANDING WHAT A PODSECURITYPOLICY CAN DO
A PodSecurityPolicy resource defines things like the following:

- Whether a pod can use the host's IPC, PID, or Network namespaces
- Which host ports a pod can bind to
- What user IDs a container can run as
- Whether a pod with privileged containers can be created

- Which kernel capabilities are allowed, which are added by default and which are always dropped
- What SELinux labels a container can use
- Whether a container can use a writable root filesystem or not
- Which filesystem groups the container can run as
- Which volume types a pod can use

If you've read this chapter up to this point, everything but the last item in the previous list should be familiar. The last item should also be fairly clear.

EXAMINING A SAMPLE PODSECURITYPOLICY

The following listing shows a sample PodSecurityPolicy, which prevents pods from using the host's IPC, PID, and Network namespaces, and prevents running privileged containers and the use of most host ports (except ports from 10000-11000 and 13000-14000). The policy doesn't set any constraints on what users, groups, or SELinux groups the container can run as.

Listing 13.15   An example PodSecurityPolicy: pod-security-policy.yaml

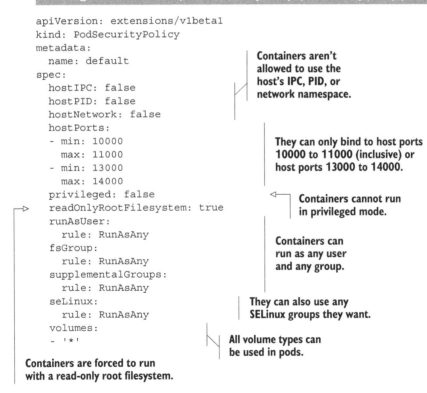

```
apiVersion: extensions/v1beta1
kind: PodSecurityPolicy
metadata:
  name: default
spec:
  hostIPC: false
  hostPID: false
  hostNetwork: false
  hostPorts:
  - min: 10000
    max: 11000
  - min: 13000
    max: 14000
  privileged: false
  readOnlyRootFilesystem: true
  runAsUser:
    rule: RunAsAny
  fsGroup:
    rule: RunAsAny
  supplementalGroups:
    rule: RunAsAny
  seLinux:
    rule: RunAsAny
  volumes:
  - '*'
```

Containers aren't allowed to use the host's IPC, PID, or network namespace.

They can only bind to host ports 10000 to 11000 (inclusive) or host ports 13000 to 14000.

Containers cannot run in privileged mode.

Containers can run as any user and any group.

They can also use any SELinux groups they want.

All volume types can be used in pods.

Containers are forced to run with a read-only root filesystem.

Most of the options specified in the example should be self-explanatory, especially if you've read the previous sections. After this PodSecurityPolicy resource is posted to the cluster, the API server will no longer allow you to deploy the privileged pod used earlier. For example

```
$ kubectl create -f pod-privileged.yaml
Error from server (Forbidden): error when creating "pod-privileged.yaml":
pods "pod-privileged" is forbidden: unable to validate against any pod
security policy: [spec.containers[0].securityContext.privileged: Invalid
value: true: Privileged containers are not allowed]
```

Likewise, you can no longer deploy pods that want to use the host's PID, IPC, or Network namespace. Also, because you set `readOnlyRootFilesystem` to `true` in the policy, the container filesystems in all pods will be read-only (containers can only write to volumes).

13.3.2 Understanding runAsUser, fsGroup, and supplementalGroups policies

The policy in the previous example doesn't impose any limits on which users and groups containers can run as, because you've used the `RunAsAny` rule for the `runAsUser`, `fsGroup`, and `supplementalGroups` fields. If you want to constrain the list of allowed user or group IDs, you change the rule to `MustRunAs` and specify the range of allowed IDs.

USING THE MUSTRUNAS RULE

Let's look at an example. To only allow containers to run as user ID `2` and constrain the default filesystem group and supplemental group IDs to be anything from `2-10` or `20-30` (all inclusive), you'd include the following snippet in the PodSecurityPolicy resource.

> **Listing 13.16   Specifying IDs containers must run as: psp-must-run-as.yaml**

```
runAsUser:
  rule: MustRunAs
  ranges:
  - min: 2              Add a single range with min equal
    max: 2              to max to set one specific ID.
fsGroup:
  rule: MustRunAs
  ranges:
  - min: 2
    max: 10
  - min: 20
    max: 30             Multiple ranges are
supplementalGroups:     supported—here,
  rule: MustRunAs       group IDs can be 2–10
  ranges:               or 20–30 (inclusive).
  - min: 2
    max: 10
  - min: 20
    max: 30
```

If the pod spec tries to set either of those fields to a value outside of these ranges, the pod will not be accepted by the API server. To try this, delete the previous PodSecurity-Policy and create the new one from the psp-must-run-as.yaml file.

> **NOTE**   Changing the policy has no effect on existing pods, because PodSecurity-Policies are enforced only when creating or updating pods.

DEPLOYING A POD WITH RUNASUSER OUTSIDE OF THE POLICY'S RANGE

If you try deploying the pod-as-user-guest.yaml file from earlier, which says the container should run as user ID 405, the API server rejects the pod:

```
$ kubectl create -f pod-as-user-guest.yaml
Error from server (Forbidden): error when creating "pod-as-user-guest.yaml"
: pods "pod-as-user-guest" is forbidden: unable to validate against any pod
security policy: [securityContext.runAsUser: Invalid value: 405: UID on
container main does not match required range.  Found 405, allowed: [{2 2}]]
```

Okay, that was obvious. But what happens if you deploy a pod without setting the runAs-User property, but the user ID is baked into the container image (using the USER directive in the Dockerfile)?

DEPLOYING A POD WITH A CONTAINER IMAGE WITH AN OUT-OF-RANGE USER ID

I've created an alternative image for the Node.js app you've used throughout the book. The image is configured so that the container will run as user ID 5. The Docker-file for the image is shown in the following listing.

> **Listing 13.17   Dockerfile with a USER directive: kubia-run-as-user-5/Dockerfile**

```
FROM node:7                    Containers run from
ADD app.js /app.js             this image will run
USER 5                    ◁─── as user ID 5.
ENTRYPOINT ["node", "app.js"]
```

I pushed the image to Docker Hub as `luksa/kubia-run-as-user-5`. If I deploy a pod with that image, the API server doesn't reject it:

```
$ kubectl run run-as-5 --image luksa/kubia-run-as-user-5 --restart Never
pod "run-as-5" created
```

Unlike before, the API server accepted the pod and the Kubelet has run its container. Let's see what user ID the container is running as:

```
$ kubectl exec run-as-5 -- id
uid=2(bin) gid=2(bin) groups=2(bin)
```

As you can see, the container is running as user ID 2, which is the ID you specified in the PodSecurityPolicy. The PodSecurityPolicy can be used to override the user ID hardcoded into a container image.

USING THE MUSTRUNASNONROOT RULE IN THE RUNASUSER FIELD

For the `runAsUser` field an additional rule can be used: `MustRunAsNonRoot`. As the name suggests, it prevents users from deploying containers that run as root. Either the container spec must specify a `runAsUser` field, which can't be zero (zero is the root user's ID), or the container image itself must run as a non-zero user ID. We explained why this is a good thing earlier.

13.3.3 Configuring allowed, default, and disallowed capabilities

As you learned, containers can run in privileged mode or not, and you can define a more fine-grained permission configuration by adding or dropping Linux kernel capabilities in each container. Three fields influence which capabilities containers can or cannot use:

- `allowedCapabilities`
- `defaultAddCapabilities`
- `requiredDropCapabilities`

We'll look at an example first, and then discuss what each of the three fields does. The following listing shows a snippet of a PodSecurityPolicy resource defining three fields related to capabilities.

Listing 13.18   Specifying capabilities in a PodSecurityPolicy: psp-capabilities.yaml

```
apiVersion: extensions/v1beta1
kind: PodSecurityPolicy
spec:
  allowedCapabilities:          Allow containers to
  - SYS_TIME                    add the SYS_TIME
  defaultAddCapabilities:       capability.
  - CHOWN                       Automatically add the CHOWN
  requiredDropCapabilities:     capability to every container.
  - SYS_ADMIN
  - SYS_MODULE                  Require containers to
  ...                           drop the SYS_ADMIN and
                                SYS_MODULE capabilities.
```

NOTE   The `SYS_ADMIN` capability allows a range of administrative operations, and the `SYS_MODULE` capability allows loading and unloading of Linux kernel modules.

SPECIFYING WHICH CAPABILITIES CAN BE ADDED TO A CONTAINER

The `allowedCapabilities` field is used to specify which capabilities pod authors can add in the `securityContext.capabilities` field in the container spec. In one of the previous examples, you added the `SYS_TIME` capability to your container. If the Pod-SecurityPolicy admission control plugin had been enabled, you wouldn't have been able to add that capability, unless it was specified in the PodSecurityPolicy as shown in listing 13.18.

ADDING CAPABILITIES TO ALL CONTAINERS

All capabilities listed under the `defaultAddCapabilities` field will be added to every deployed pod's containers. If a user doesn't want certain containers to have those capabilities, they need to explicitly drop them in the specs of those containers.

The example in listing 13.18 enables the automatic addition of the `CAP_CHOWN` capability to every container, thus allowing processes running in the container to change the ownership of files in the container (with the `chown` command, for example).

DROPPING CAPABILITIES FROM A CONTAINER

The final field in this example is `requiredDropCapabilities`. I must admit, this was a somewhat strange name for me at first, but it's not that complicated. The capabilities listed in this field are dropped automatically from every container (the PodSecurity-Policy Admission Control plugin will add them to every container's security-Context.capabilities.drop field).

If a user tries to create a pod where they explicitly add one of the capabilities listed in the policy's `requiredDropCapabilities` field, the pod is rejected:

```
$ kubectl create -f pod-add-sysadmin-capability.yaml
Error from server (Forbidden): error when creating "pod-add-sysadmin-
capability.yaml": pods "pod-add-sysadmin-capability" is forbidden: unable
to validate against any pod security policy: [capabilities.add: Invalid
value: "SYS_ADMIN": capability may not be added]
```

13.3.4 Constraining the types of volumes pods can use

The last thing a PodSecurityPolicy resource can do is define which volume types users can add to their pods. At the minimum, a PodSecurityPolicy should allow using at least the `emptyDir`, `configMap`, `secret`, `downwardAPI`, and the `persistentVolume-Claim` volumes. The pertinent part of such a PodSecurityPolicy resource is shown in the following listing.

> **Listing 13.19   A PSP snippet allowing the use of only certain volume types: psp-volumes.yaml**

```
kind: PodSecurityPolicy
spec:
  volumes:
  - emptyDir
  - configMap
  - secret
  - downwardAPI
  - persistentVolumeClaim
```

If multiple PodSecurityPolicy resources are in place, pods can use any volume type defined in any of the policies (the union of all `volumes` lists is used).

13.3.5   Assigning different PodSecurityPolicies to different users and groups

We mentioned that a PodSecurityPolicy is a cluster-level resource, which means it can't be stored in and applied to a specific namespace. Does that mean it always applies across all namespaces? No, because that would make them relatively unusable. After all, system pods must often be allowed to do things that regular pods shouldn't.

Assigning different policies to different users is done through the RBAC mechanism described in the previous chapter. The idea is to create as many policies as you need and make them available to individual users or groups by creating ClusterRole resources and pointing them to the individual policies by name. By binding those ClusterRoles to specific users or groups with ClusterRoleBindings, when the PodSecurityPolicy Admission Control plugin needs to decide whether to admit a pod definition or not, it will only consider the policies accessible to the user creating the pod.

You'll see how to do this in the next exercise. You'll start by creating an additional PodSecurityPolicy.

CREATING A PODSECURITYPOLICY ALLOWING PRIVILEGED CONTAINERS TO BE DEPLOYED

You'll create a special PodSecurityPolicy that will allow privileged users to create pods with privileged containers. The following listing shows the policy's definition.

Listing 13.20   A PodSecurityPolicy for privileged users: psp-privileged.yaml

```
apiVersion: extensions/v1beta1
kind: PodSecurityPolicy
metadata:
  name: privileged          The name of this
spec:                        policy is "privileged."
  privileged: true           It allows running
  runAsUser:                 privileged containers.
    rule: RunAsAny
  fsGroup:
    rule: RunAsAny
  supplementalGroups:
    rule: RunAsAny
  seLinux:
    rule: RunAsAny
  volumes:
  - '*'
```

After you post this policy to the API server, you have two policies in the cluster:

```
$ kubectl get psp
NAME          PRIV    CAPS    SELINUX     RUNASUSER    FSGROUP      ...
default       false   []      RunAsAny    RunAsAny     RunAsAny     ...
privileged    true    []      RunAsAny    RunAsAny     RunAsAny     ...
```

NOTE   The shorthand for PodSecurityPolicy is psp.

As you can see in the PRIV column, the default policy doesn't allow running privileged containers, whereas the privileged policy does. Because you're currently logged in as a cluster-admin, you can see all the policies. When creating pods, if any policy allows you to deploy a pod with certain features, the API server will accept your pod.

Now imagine two additional users are using your cluster: Alice and Bob. You want Alice to only deploy restricted (non-privileged) pods, but you want to allow Bob to also deploy privileged pods. You do this by making sure Alice can only use the default PodSecurityPolicy, while allowing Bob to use both.

USING RBAC TO ASSIGN DIFFERENT PODSECURITYPOLICIES TO DIFFERENT USERS

In the previous chapter, you used RBAC to grant users access to only certain resource types, but I mentioned that access can be granted to specific resource instances by referencing them by name. That's what you'll use to make users use different PodSecurityPolicy resources.

First, you'll create two ClusterRoles, each allowing the use of one of the policies. You'll call the first one psp-default and in it allow the use of the default PodSecurityPolicy resource. You can use kubectl create clusterrole to do that:

```
$ kubectl create clusterrole psp-default --verb=use
➥    --resource=podsecuritypolicies --resource-name=default
clusterrole "psp-default" created
```

> **NOTE** You're using the special verb use instead of get, list, watch, or similar.

As you can see, you're referring to a specific instance of a PodSecurityPolicy resource by using the --resource-name option. Now, create another ClusterRole called psp-privileged, pointing to the privileged policy:

```
$ kubectl create clusterrole psp-privileged --verb=use
➥    --resource=podsecuritypolicies --resource-name=privileged
clusterrole "psp-privileged" created
```

Now, you need to bind these two policies to users. As you may remember from the previous chapter, if you're binding a ClusterRole that grants access to cluster-level resources (which is what PodSecurityPolicy resources are), you need to use a ClusterRoleBinding instead of a (namespaced) RoleBinding.

You're going to bind the psp-default ClusterRole to all authenticated users, not only to Alice. This is necessary because otherwise no one could create any pods, because the Admission Control plugin would complain that no policy is in place. Authenticated users all belong to the system:authenticated group, so you'll bind the ClusterRole to the group:

```
$ kubectl create clusterrolebinding psp-all-users
➥    --clusterrole=psp-default --group=system:authenticated
clusterrolebinding "psp-all-users" created
```

You'll bind the `psp-privileged` ClusterRole only to Bob:

```
$ kubectl create clusterrolebinding psp-bob
➥  --clusterrole=psp-privileged --user=bob
clusterrolebinding "psp-bob" created
```

As an authenticated user, Alice should now have access to the `default` PodSecurity-Policy, whereas Bob should have access to both the `default` and the `privileged` Pod-SecurityPolicies. Alice shouldn't be able to create privileged pods, whereas Bob should. Let's see if that's true.

CREATING ADDITIONAL USERS FOR KUBECTL

But how do you authenticate as Alice or Bob instead of whatever you're authenticated as currently? The book's appendix A explains how `kubectl` can be used with multiple clusters, but also with multiple contexts. A context includes the user credentials used for talking to a cluster. Turn to appendix A to find out more. Here we'll show the bare commands enabling you to use `kubectl` as Alice or Bob.

First, you'll create two new users in `kubectl`'s config with the following two commands:

```
$ kubectl config set-credentials alice --username=alice --password=password
User "alice" set.
$ kubectl config set-credentials bob --username=bob --password=password
User "bob" set.
```

It should be obvious what the commands do. Because you're setting username and password credentials, `kubectl` will use basic HTTP authentication for these two users (other authentication methods include tokens, client certificates, and so on).

CREATING PODS AS A DIFFERENT USER

You can now try creating a privileged pod while authenticating as Alice. You can tell `kubectl` which user credentials to use by using the `--user` option:

```
$ kubectl --user alice create -f pod-privileged.yaml
Error from server (Forbidden): error when creating "pod-privileged.yaml":
    pods "pod-privileged" is forbidden: unable to validate against any pod
    security policy: [spec.containers[0].securityContext.privileged: Invalid
    value: true: Privileged containers are not allowed]
```

As expected, the API server doesn't allow Alice to create privileged pods. Now, let's see if it allows Bob to do that:

```
$ kubectl --user bob create -f pod-privileged.yaml
pod "pod-privileged" created
```

And there you go. You've successfully used RBAC to make the Admission Control plugin use different PodSecurityPolicy resources for different users.

13.4 Isolating the pod network

Up to now in this chapter, we've explored many security-related configuration options that apply to individual pods and their containers. In the remainder of this chapter, we'll look at how the network between pods can be secured by limiting which pods can talk to which pods.

Whether this is configurable or not depends on which container networking plugin is used in the cluster. If the networking plugin supports it, you can configure network isolation by creating NetworkPolicy resources.

A NetworkPolicy applies to pods that match its label selector and specifies either which sources can access the matched pods or which destinations can be accessed from the matched pods. This is configured through ingress and egress rules, respectively. Both types of rules can match only the pods that match a pod selector, all pods in a namespace whose labels match a namespace selector, or a network IP block specified using Classless Inter-Domain Routing (CIDR) notation (for example, 192.168.1.0/24).

We'll look at both ingress and egress rules and all three matching options.

> **NOTE** Ingress rules in a NetworkPolicy have nothing to do with the Ingress resource discussed in chapter 5.

13.4.1 Enabling network isolation in a namespace

By default, pods in a given namespace can be accessed by anyone. First, you'll need to change that. You'll create a `default-deny` NetworkPolicy, which will prevent all clients from connecting to any pod in your namespace. The NetworkPolicy definition is shown in the following listing.

Listing 13.21 A `default-deny` NetworkPolicy: network-policy-default-deny.yaml

```
apiVersion: networking.k8s.io/v1
kind: NetworkPolicy
metadata:
  name: default-deny            Empty pod selector
spec:                           matches all pods in the
  podSelector:            ◁──┘  same namespace
```

When you create this NetworkPolicy in a certain namespace, no one can connect to any pod in that namespace.

NOTE   The CNI plugin or other type of networking solution used in the cluster must support NetworkPolicy, or else there will be no effect on inter-pod connectivity.

13.4.2   *Allowing only some pods in the namespace to connect to a server pod*

To let clients connect to the pods in the namespace, you must now explicitly say who can connect to the pods. By who I mean which pods. Let's explore how to do this through an example.

Imagine having a PostgreSQL database pod running in namespace `foo` and a web-server pod that uses the database. Other pods are also in the namespace, and you don't want to allow them to connect to the database. To secure the network, you need to create the NetworkPolicy resource shown in the following listing in the same name-space as the database pod.

Listing 13.22   A NetworkPolicy for the Postgres pod: network-policy-postgres.yaml

```
apiVersion: networking.k8s.io/v1
kind: NetworkPolicy
metadata:
  name: postgres-netpolicy
spec:
  podSelector:                    This policy secures
    matchLabels:                  access to pods with
      app: database               app=database label.
  ingress:
  - from:                         It allows incoming connections
    - podSelector:                only from pods with the
        matchLabels:              app=webserver label.
          app: webserver
    ports:
    - port: 5432                  Connections to this
                                  port are allowed.
```

The example NetworkPolicy allows pods with the `app=webserver` label to connect to pods with the `app=database` label, and only on port 5432. Other pods can't connect to the database pods, and no one (not even the webserver pods) can connect to anything other than port 5432 of the database pods. This is shown in figure 13.4.

Client pods usually connect to server pods through a Service instead of directly to the pod, but that doesn't change anything. The NetworkPolicy is enforced when connecting through a Service, as well.

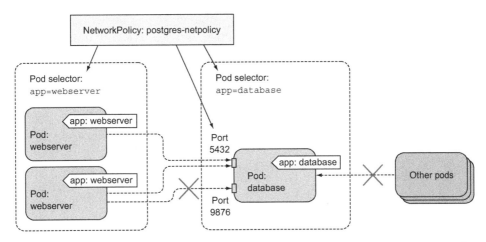

Figure 13.4   A NetworkPolicy allowing only some pods to access other pods and only on a specific port

13.4.3   *Isolating the network between Kubernetes namespaces*

Now let's look at another example, where multiple tenants are using the same Kubernetes cluster. Each tenant can use multiple namespaces, and each namespace has a label specifying the tenant it belongs to. For example, one of those tenants is Manning. All their namespaces have been labeled with `tenant: manning`. In one of their namespaces, they run a Shopping Cart microservice that needs to be available to all pods running in any of their namespaces. Obviously, they don't want any other tenants to access their microservice.

To secure their microservice, they create the NetworkPolicy resource shown in the following listing.

Listing 13.23   NetworkPolicy for the shopping cart pod(s): network-policy-cart.yaml

```
apiVersion: networking.k8s.io/v1
kind: NetworkPolicy
metadata:
  name: shoppingcart-netpolicy
spec:
  podSelector:                          This policy applies to
    matchLabels:                        pods labeled as app=
      app: shopping-cart                shopping-cart.
  ingress:
  - from:
    - namespaceSelector:                Only pods running in namespaces
        matchLabels:                    labeled as tenant=manning are
          tenant: manning               allowed to access the microservice.
    ports:
    - port: 80
```

This NetworkPolicy ensures only pods running in namespaces labeled as `tenant: manning` can access their Shopping Cart microservice, as shown in figure 13.5.

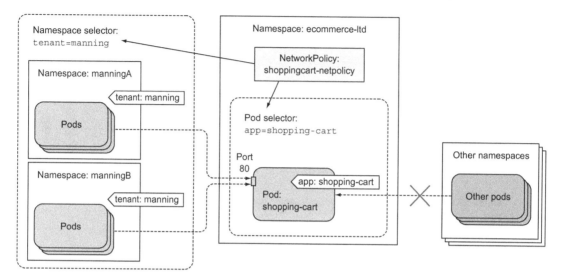

Figure 13.5 A NetworkPolicy only allowing pods in namespaces matching a `namespaceSelector` to access a specific pod.

If the shopping cart provider also wants to give access to other tenants (perhaps to one of their partner companies), they can either create an additional NetworkPolicy resource or add an additional ingress rule to their existing NetworkPolicy.

> **NOTE** In a multi-tenant Kubernetes cluster, tenants usually can't add labels (or annotations) to their namespaces themselves. If they could, they'd be able to circumvent the `namespaceSelector`-based ingress rules.

13.4.4 *Isolating using CIDR notation*

Instead of specifying a pod- or namespace selector to define who can access the pods targeted in the NetworkPolicy, you can also specify an IP block in CIDR notation. For example, to allow the `shopping-cart` pods from the previous section to only be accessible from IPs in the 192.168.1.1 to .255 range, you'd specify the ingress rule in the next listing.

Listing 13.24   Specifying an IP block in an ingress rule: network-policy-cidr.yaml

```
ingress:
- from:
  - ipBlock:                          This ingress rule only allows traffic from
      cidr: 192.168.1.0/24            clients in the 192.168.1.0/24 IP block.
```

13.4.5 *Limiting the outbound traffic of a set of pods*

In all previous examples, you've been limiting the inbound traffic to the pods that match the NetworkPolicy's pod selector using ingress rules, but you can also limit their outbound traffic through egress rules. An example is shown in the next listing.

Listing 13.25   Using egress rules in a NetworkPolicy: network-policy-egress.yaml

```
spec:
  podSelector:
    matchLabels:
      app: webserver
  egress:
  - to:
    - podSelector:
        matchLabels:
          app: database
```

This policy applies to pods with the app=webserver label.

It limits the pods' outbound traffic.

Webserver pods may only connect to pods with the app=database label.

The NetworkPolicy in the previous listing allows pods that have the app=webserver label to only access pods that have the app=database label and nothing else (neither other pods, nor any other IP, regardless of whether it's internal or external to the cluster).

13.5 *Summary*

In this chapter, you learned about securing cluster nodes from pods and pods from other pods. You learned that

- Pods can use the node's Linux namespaces instead of using their own.
- Containers can be configured to run as a different user and/or group than the one defined in the container image.
- Containers can also run in privileged mode, allowing them to access the node's devices that are otherwise not exposed to pods.
- Containers can be run as read-only, preventing processes from writing to the container's filesystem (and only allowing them to write to mounted volumes).
- Cluster-level PodSecurityPolicy resources can be created to prevent users from creating pods that could compromise a node.
- PodSecurityPolicy resources can be associated with specific users using RBAC's ClusterRoles and ClusterRoleBindings.
- NetworkPolicy resources are used to limit a pod's inbound and/or outbound traffic.

In the next chapter, you'll learn how computational resources available to pods can be constrained and how a pod's quality of service is configured.

Managing pods' computational resources

This chapter covers

- Requesting CPU, memory, and other computational resources for containers
- Setting a hard limit for CPU and memory
- Understanding Quality of Service guarantees for pods
- Setting default, min, and max resources for pods in a namespace
- Limiting the total amount of resources available in a namespace

Up to now you've created pods without caring about how much CPU and memory they're allowed to consume. But as you'll see in this chapter, setting both how much a pod is expected to consume and the maximum amount it's allowed to consume is a vital part of any pod definition. Setting these two sets of parameters makes sure that a pod takes only its fair share of the resources provided by the Kubernetes cluster and also affects how pods are scheduled across the cluster.

14.1 Requesting resources for a pod's containers

When creating a pod, you can specify the amount of CPU and memory that a container needs (these are called *requests*) and a hard limit on what it may consume (known as *limits*). They're specified for each container individually, not for the pod as a whole. The pod's resource requests and limits are the sum of the requests and limits of all its containers.

14.1.1 Creating pods with resource requests

Let's look at an example pod manifest, which has the CPU and memory requests specified for its single container, as shown in the following listing.

> **Listing 14.1   A pod with resource requests: requests-pod.yaml**

```
apiVersion: v1
kind: Pod
metadata:
  name: requests-pod
spec:
  containers:
  - image: busybox
    command: ["dd", "if=/dev/zero", "of=/dev/null"]
    name: main
    resources:
      requests:
        cpu: 200m
        memory: 10Mi
```

You're specifying resource requests for the main container.

The container requests 200 millicores (that is, 1/5 of a single CPU core's time).

The container also requests 10 mebibytes of memory.

In the pod manifest, your single container requires one-fifth of a CPU core (200 millicores) to run properly. Five such pods/containers can run sufficiently fast on a single CPU core.

When you don't specify a request for CPU, you're saying you don't care how much CPU time the process running in your container is allotted. In the worst case, it may not get any CPU time at all (this happens when a heavy demand by other processes exists on the CPU). Although this may be fine for low-priority batch jobs, which aren't time-critical, it obviously isn't appropriate for containers handling user requests.

In the pod spec, you're also requesting 10 mebibytes of memory for the container. By doing that, you're saying that you expect the processes running inside the container to use at most 10 mebibytes of RAM. They might use less, but you're not expecting them to use more than that in normal circumstances. Later in this chapter you'll see what happens if they do.

Now you'll run the pod. When the pod starts, you can take a quick look at the process' CPU consumption by running the `top` command inside the container, as shown in the following listing.

Listing 14.2   Examining CPU and memory usage from within a container

```
$ kubectl exec -it requests-pod top
Mem: 1288116K used, 760368K free, 9196K shrd, 25748K buff, 814840K cached
CPU:  9.1% usr 42.1% sys  0.0% nic 48.4% idle  0.0% io  0.0% irq  0.2% sirq
Load average: 0.79 0.52 0.29 2/481 10
  PID  PPID USER     STAT    VSZ %VSZ CPU %CPU COMMAND
    1     0 root     R      1192  0.0   1 50.2 dd if /dev/zero of /dev/null
    7     0 root     R      1200  0.0   0  0.0 top
```

The dd command you're running in the container consumes as much CPU as it can, but it only runs a single thread so it can only use a single core. The Minikube VM, which is where this example is running, has two CPU cores allotted to it. That's why the process is shown consuming 50% of the whole CPU.

Fifty percent of two cores is obviously one whole core, which means the container is using more than the 200 millicores you requested in the pod specification. This is expected, because requests don't limit the amount of CPU a container can use. You'd need to specify a CPU limit to do that. You'll try that later, but first, let's see how specifying resource requests in a pod affects the scheduling of the pod.

14.1.2 *Understanding how resource requests affect scheduling*

By specifying resource requests, you're specifying the minimum amount of resources your pod needs. This information is what the Scheduler uses when scheduling the pod to a node. Each node has a certain amount of CPU and memory it can allocate to pods. When scheduling a pod, the Scheduler will only consider nodes with enough unallocated resources to meet the pod's resource requirements. If the amount of unallocated CPU or memory is less than what the pod requests, Kubernetes will not schedule the pod to that node, because the node can't provide the minimum amount required by the pod.

UNDERSTANDING HOW THE SCHEDULER DETERMINES IF A POD CAN FIT ON A NODE

What's important and somewhat surprising here is that the Scheduler doesn't look at how much of each individual resource is being used at the exact time of scheduling but at the sum of resources requested by the existing pods deployed on the node. Even though existing pods may be using less than what they've requested, scheduling another pod based on actual resource consumption would break the guarantee given to the already deployed pods.

This is visualized in figure 14.1. Three pods are deployed on the node. Together, they've requested 80% of the node's CPU and 60% of the node's memory. Pod D, shown at the bottom right of the figure, cannot be scheduled onto the node because it requests 25% of the CPU, which is more than the 20% of unallocated CPU. The fact that the three pods are currently using only 70% of the CPU makes no difference.

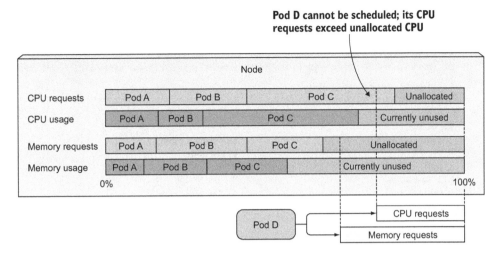

Pod D cannot be scheduled; its CPU requests exceed unallocated CPU

Figure 14.1 The Scheduler only cares about requests, not actual usage.

UNDERSTANDING HOW THE SCHEDULER USES PODS' REQUESTS WHEN SELECTING THE BEST NODE FOR A POD

You may remember from chapter 11 that the Scheduler first filters the list of nodes to exclude those that the pod can't fit on and then prioritizes the remaining nodes per the configured prioritization functions. Among others, two prioritization functions rank nodes based on the amount of resources requested: LeastRequestedPriority and MostRequestedPriority. The first one prefers nodes with fewer requested resources (with a greater amount of unallocated resources), whereas the second one is the exact opposite—it prefers nodes that have the most requested resources (a smaller amount of unallocated CPU and memory). But, as we've discussed, they both consider the amount of requested resources, not the amount of resources actually consumed.

The Scheduler is configured to use only one of those functions. You may wonder why anyone would want to use the MostRequestedPriority function. After all, if you have a set of nodes, you usually want to spread CPU load evenly across them. However, that's not the case when running on cloud infrastructure, where you can add and remove nodes whenever necessary. By configuring the Scheduler to use the Most-RequestedPriority function, you guarantee that Kubernetes will use the smallest possible number of nodes while still providing each pod with the amount of CPU/memory it requests. By keeping pods tightly packed, certain nodes are left vacant and can be removed. Because you're paying for individual nodes, this saves you money.

INSPECTING A NODE'S CAPACITY

Let's see the Scheduler in action. You'll deploy another pod with four times the amount of requested resources as before. But before you do that, let's see your node's capacity. Because the Scheduler needs to know how much CPU and memory each node has, the Kubelet reports this data to the API server, making it available through the Node resource. You can see it by using the kubectl describe command as in the following listing.

Listing 14.3   A node's capacity and allocatable resources

```
$ kubectl describe nodes
Name:        minikube
...
Capacity:
  cpu:            2
  memory:         2048484Ki
  pods:           110
Allocatable:
  cpu:            2
  memory:         1946084Ki
  pods:           110
...
```

The overall capacity of the node

The resources allocatable to pods

The output shows two sets of amounts related to the available resources on the node: the node's *capacity* and *allocatable* resources. The capacity represents the total resources of a node, which may not all be available to pods. Certain resources may be reserved for Kubernetes and/or system components. The Scheduler bases its decisions only on the allocatable resource amounts.

In the previous example, the node called minikube runs in a VM with two cores and has no CPU reserved, making the whole CPU allocatable to pods. Therefore, the Scheduler should have no problem scheduling another pod requesting 800 millicores.

Run the pod now. You can use the YAML file in the code archive, or run the pod with the kubectl run command like this:

```
$ kubectl run requests-pod-2 --image=busybox --restart Never
    --requests='cpu=800m,memory=20Mi' -- dd if=/dev/zero of=/dev/null
pod "requests-pod-2" created
```

Let's see if it was scheduled:

```
$ kubectl get po requests-pod-2
NAME             READY     STATUS     RESTARTS    AGE
requests-pod-2   1/1       Running    0           3m
```

Okay, the pod has been scheduled and is running.

CREATING A POD THAT DOESN'T FIT ON ANY NODE

You now have two pods deployed, which together have requested a total of 1,000 millicores or exactly 1 core. You should therefore have another 1,000 millicores available for additional pods, right? You can deploy another pod with a resource request of 1,000 millicores. Use a similar command as before:

```
$ kubectl run requests-pod-3 --image=busybox --restart Never
    --requests='cpu=1,memory=20Mi' -- dd if=/dev/zero of=/dev/null
pod "requests-pod-2" created
```

NOTE This time you're specifying the CPU request in whole cores (cpu=1) instead of millicores (cpu=1000m).

So far, so good. The pod has been accepted by the API server (you'll remember from the previous chapter that the API server can reject pods if they're invalid in any way). Now, check if the pod is running:

```
$ kubectl get po requests-pod-3
NAME             READY    STATUS     RESTARTS   AGE
requests-pod-3   0/1      Pending    0          4m
```

Even if you wait a while, the pod is still stuck at Pending. You can see more information on why that's the case by using the kubectl describe command, as shown in the following listing.

Listing 14.4 Examining why a pod is stuck at Pending with kubectl describe pod

```
$ kubectl describe po requests-pod-3
Name:        requests-pod-3
Namespace:   default
Node:        /
...
Conditions:
  Type              Status
  PodScheduled      False
...
Events:
... Warning  FailedScheduling    No nodes are available
                                 that match all of the
                                 following predicates::
                                 Insufficient cpu (1).
```

> No node is associated with the pod.

> The pod hasn't been scheduled.

> Scheduling has failed because of insufficient CPU.

The output shows that the pod hasn't been scheduled because it can't fit on any node due to insufficient CPU on your single node. But why is that? The sum of the CPU requests of all three pods equals 2,000 millicores or exactly two cores, which is exactly what your node can provide. What's wrong?

DETERMINING WHY A POD ISN'T BEING SCHEDULED

You can figure out why the pod isn't being scheduled by inspecting the node resource. Use the kubectl describe node command again and examine the output more closely in the following listing.

Listing 14.5 Inspecting allocated resources on a node with kubectl describe node

```
$ kubectl describe node
Name:               minikube
...
Non-terminated Pods:     (7 in total)
  Namespace    Name           CPU Requ.    CPU Lim.   Mem Req.     Mem Lim.
  ---------    ----           ---------    --------   ---------    --------
  default      requests-pod   200m (10%)   0 (0%)     10Mi (0%)    0 (0%)
```

```
default      requests-pod-2  800m (40%)   0 (0%)    20Mi (1%)    0 (0%)
kube-system  dflt-http-b...  10m (0%)    10m (0%)   20Mi (1%)   20Mi (1%)
kube-system  kube-addon-...  5m (0%)      0 (0%)    50Mi (2%)    0 (0%)
kube-system  kube-dns-26...  260m (13%)   0 (0%)   110Mi (5%)  170Mi (8%)
kube-system  kubernetes-...  0 (0%)       0 (0%)    0 (0%)       0 (0%)
kube-system  nginx-ingre...  0 (0%)       0 (0%)    0 (0%)       0 (0%)
Allocated resources:
 (Total limits may be over 100 percent, i.e., overcommitted.)
 CPU Requests   CPU Limits     Memory Requests  Memory Limits
 ------------   ----------     ---------------  -------------
 1275m (63%)    10m (0%)       210Mi (11%)      190Mi (9%)
```

If you look at the bottom left of the listing, you'll see a total of 1,275 millicores have been requested by the running pods, which is 275 millicores more than what you requested for the first two pods you deployed. Something is eating up additional CPU resources.

You can find the culprit in the list of pods in the previous listing. Three pods in the `kube-system` namespace have explicitly requested CPU resources. Those pods plus your two pods leave only 725 millicores available for additional pods. Because your third pod requested 1,000 millicores, the Scheduler won't schedule it to this node, as that would make the node overcommitted.

FREEING RESOURCES TO GET THE POD SCHEDULED

The pod will only be scheduled when an adequate amount of CPU is freed (when one of the first two pods is deleted, for example). If you delete your second pod, the Scheduler will be notified of the deletion (through the watch mechanism described in chapter 11) and will schedule your third pod as soon as the second pod terminates. This is shown in the following listing.

Listing 14.6   Pod is scheduled after deleting another pod

```
$ kubectl delete po requests-pod-2
pod "requests-pod-2" deleted

$ kubectl get po
NAME             READY      STATUS         RESTARTS     AGE
requests-pod     1/1        Running        0            2h
requests-pod-2   1/1        Terminating    0            1h
requests-pod-3   0/1        Pending        0            1h

$ kubectl get po
NAME             READY      STATUS    RESTARTS    AGE
requests-pod     1/1        Running   0           2h
requests-pod-3   1/1        Running   0           1h
```

In all these examples, you've specified a request for memory, but it hasn't played any role in the scheduling because your node has more than enough allocatable memory to accommodate all your pods' requests. Both CPU and memory requests are treated the same way by the Scheduler, but in contrast to memory requests, a pod's CPU requests also play a role elsewhere—while the pod is running. You'll learn about this next.

14.1.3 *Understanding how CPU requests affect CPU time sharing*

You now have two pods running in your cluster (you can disregard the system pods right now, because they're mostly idle). One has requested 200 millicores and the other one five times as much. At the beginning of the chapter, we said Kubernetes distinguishes between resource requests and limits. You haven't defined any limits yet, so the two pods are in no way limited when it comes to how much CPU they can each consume. If the process inside each pod consumes as much CPU time as it can, how much CPU time does each pod get?

The CPU requests don't only affect scheduling—they also determine how the remaining (unused) CPU time is distributed between pods. Because your first pod requested 200 millicores of CPU and the other one 1,000 millicores, any unused CPU will be split among the two pods in a 1 to 5 ratio, as shown in figure 14.2. If both pods consume as much CPU as they can, the first pod will get one sixth or 16.7% of the CPU time and the other one the remaining five sixths or 83.3%.

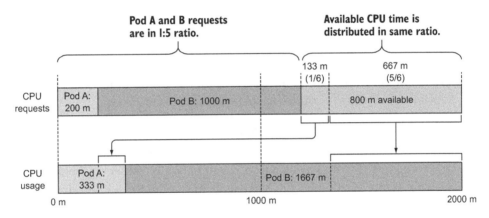

Figure 14.2 Unused CPU time is distributed to containers based on their CPU requests.

But if one container wants to use up as much CPU as it can, while the other one is sitting idle at a given moment, the first container will be allowed to use the whole CPU time (minus the small amount of time used by the second container, if any). After all, it makes sense to use all the available CPU if no one else is using it, right? As soon as the second container needs CPU time, it will get it and the first container will be throttled back.

14.1.4 *Defining and requesting custom resources*

Kubernetes also allows you to add your own custom resources to a node and request them in the pod's resource requests. Initially these were known as Opaque Integer Resources, but were replaced with Extended Resources in Kubernetes version 1.8.

First, you obviously need to make Kubernetes aware of your custom resource by adding it to the Node object's `capacity` field. This can be done by performing a `PATCH` HTTP request. The resource name can be anything, such as `example.org/my-resource`, as long as it doesn't start with the `kubernetes.io` domain. The quantity must be an integer (for example, you can't set it to 100 millis, because 0.1 isn't an integer; but you can set it to 1000m or 2000m or, simply, 1 or 2). The value will be copied from the `capacity` to the `allocatable` field automatically.

Then, when creating pods, you specify the same resource name and the requested quantity under the `resources.requests` field in the container spec or with `--requests` when using `kubectl run` like you did in previous examples. The Scheduler will make sure the pod is only deployed to a node that has the requested amount of the custom resource available. Every deployed pod obviously reduces the number of allocatable units of the resource.

An example of a custom resource could be the number of GPU units available on the node. Pods requiring the use of a GPU specify that in their requests. The Scheduler then makes sure the pod is only scheduled to nodes with at least one GPU still unallocated.

14.2 Limiting resources available to a container

Setting resource requests for containers in a pod ensures each container gets the minimum amount of resources it needs. Now let's see the other side of the coin—the maximum amount the container will be allowed to consume.

14.2.1 Setting a hard limit for the amount of resources a container can use

We've seen how containers are allowed to use up all the CPU if all the other processes are sitting idle. But you may want to prevent certain containers from using up more than a specific amount of CPU. And you'll always want to limit the amount of memory a container can consume.

CPU is a compressible resource, which means the amount used by a container can be throttled without affecting the process running in the container in an adverse way. Memory is obviously different—it's incompressible. Once a process is given a chunk of memory, that memory can't be taken away from it until it's released by the process itself. That's why you need to limit the maximum amount of memory a container can be given.

Without limiting memory, a container (or a pod) running on a worker node may eat up all the available memory and affect all other pods on the node and any new pods scheduled to the node (remember that new pods are scheduled to the node based on the memory requests and not actual memory usage). A single malfunctioning or malicious pod can practically make the whole node unusable.

CREATING A POD WITH RESOURCE LIMITS

To prevent this from happening, Kubernetes allows you to specify resource limits for every container (along with, and virtually in the same way as, resource requests). The following listing shows an example pod manifest with resource limits.

Listing 14.7   A pod with a hard limit on CPU and memory: limited-pod.yaml

```
apiVersion: v1
kind: Pod
metadata:
  name: limited-pod
spec:
  containers:
  - image: busybox
    command: ["dd", "if=/dev/zero", "of=/dev/null"]
    name: main
    resources:
      limits:
        cpu: 1
        memory: 20Mi
```

> Specifying resource
> limits for the container

> This container will be
> allowed to use at
> most 1 CPU core.

> The container will be
> allowed to use up to 20
> mebibytes of memory.

This pod's container has resource limits configured for both CPU and memory. The process or processes running inside the container will not be allowed to consume more than 1 CPU core and 20 mebibytes of memory.

> **NOTE**   Because you haven't specified any resource requests, they'll be set to the same values as the resource limits.

OVERCOMMITTING LIMITS

Unlike resource requests, resource limits aren't constrained by the node's allocatable resource amounts. The sum of all limits of all the pods on a node is allowed to exceed 100% of the node's capacity (figure 14.3). Restated, resource limits can be overcommitted. This has an important consequence—when 100% of the node's resources are used up, certain containers will need to be killed.

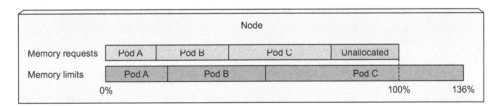

Figure 14.3   The sum of resource limits of all pods on a node can exceed 100% of the node's capacity.

You'll see how Kubernetes decides which containers to kill in section 14.3, but individual containers can be killed even if they try to use more than their resource limits specify. You'll learn more about this next.

14.2.2 *Exceeding the limits*

What happens when a process running in a container tries to use a greater amount of resources than it's allowed to?

You've already learned that CPU is a compressible resource, and it's only natural for a process to want to consume all of the CPU time when not waiting for an I/O operation. As you've learned, a process' CPU usage is throttled, so when a CPU limit is set for a container, the process isn't given more CPU time than the configured limit.

With memory, it's different. When a process tries to allocate memory over its limit, the process is killed (it's said the container is OOMKilled, where OOM stands for Out Of Memory). If the pod's restart policy is set to Always or OnFailure, the process is restarted immediately, so you may not even notice it getting killed. But if it keeps going over the memory limit and getting killed, Kubernetes will begin restarting it with increasing delays between restarts. You'll see a CrashLoopBackOff status in that case:

```
$ kubectl get po
NAME         READY    STATUS             RESTARTS    AGE
memoryhog    0/1      CrashLoopBackOff   3           1m
```

The CrashLoopBackOff status doesn't mean the Kubelet has given up. It means that after each crash, the Kubelet is increasing the time period before restarting the container. After the first crash, it restarts the container immediately and then, if it crashes again, waits for 10 seconds before restarting it again. On subsequent crashes, this delay is then increased exponentially to 20, 40, 80, and 160 seconds, and finally limited to 300 seconds. Once the interval hits the 300-second limit, the Kubelet keeps restarting the container indefinitely every five minutes until the pod either stops crashing or is deleted.

To examine why the container crashed, you can check the pod's log and/or use the kubectl describe pod command, as shown in the following listing.

> **Listing 14.8   Inspecting why a container terminated with kubectl describe pod**

```
$ kubectl describe pod
Name:          memoryhog
...
Containers:
  main:
    ...
    State:              Terminated
      Reason:           OOMKilled          │ The current container was
      Exit Code:        137                │ killed because it was out
      Started:          Tue, 27 Dec 2016 14:55:53 +0100   of memory (OOM).
      Finished:         Tue, 27 Dec 2016 14:55:58 +0100
    Last State:         Terminated
      Reason:           OOMKilled          │ The previous container
      Exit Code:        137                │ was also killed because
                                           │ it was  OOM
```

```
      Started:        Tue, 27 Dec 2016 14:55:37 +0100
      Finished:       Tue, 27 Dec 2016 14:55:50 +0100
   Ready:             False
...
```

The `OOMKilled` status tells you that the container was killed because it was out of memory. In the previous listing, the container went over its memory limit and was killed immediately.

It's important not to set memory limits too low if you don't want your container to be killed. But containers can get `OOMKilled` even if they aren't over their limit. You'll see why in section 14.3.2, but first, let's discuss something that catches most users off-guard the first time they start specifying limits for their containers.

14.2.3 Understanding how apps in containers see limits

If you haven't deployed the pod from listing 14.7, deploy it now:

```
$ kubectl create -f limited-pod.yaml
pod "limited-pod" created
```

Now, run the `top` command in the container, the way you did at the beginning of the chapter. The command's output is shown in the following listing.

Listing 14.9 Running the `top` command in a CPU- and memory-limited container

```
$ kubectl exec -it limited-pod top
Mem: 1450980K used, 597504K free, 22012K shrd, 65876K buff, 857552K cached
CPU: 10.0% usr 40.0% sys  0.0% nic 50.0% idle  0.0% io  0.0% irq  0.0% sirq
Load average: 0.17 1.19 2.47 4/503 10
  PID  PPID USER     STAT    VSZ %VSZ CPU %CPU COMMAND
    1     0 root     R      1192  0.0   1 49.9 dd if /dev/zero of /dev/null
    5     0 root     R      1196  0.0   0  0.0 top
```

First, let me remind you that the pod's CPU limit is set to 1 core and its memory limit is set to 20 MiB. Now, examine the output of the `top` command closely. Is there anything that strikes you as odd?

Look at the amount of used and free memory. Those numbers are nowhere near the 20 MiB you set as the limit for the container. Similarly, you set the CPU limit to one core and it seems like the main process is using only 50% of the available CPU time, even though the `dd` command, when used like you're using it, usually uses all the CPU it has available. What's going on?

UNDERSTANDING THAT CONTAINERS ALWAYS SEE THE NODE'S MEMORY, NOT THE CONTAINER'S

The `top` command shows the memory amounts of the whole node the container is running on. Even though you set a limit on how much memory is available to a container, the container will not be aware of this limit.

This has an unfortunate effect on any application that looks up the amount of memory available on the system and uses that information to decide how much memory it wants to reserve.

The problem is visible when running Java apps, especially if you don't specify the maximum heap size for the Java Virtual Machine with the -Xmx option. In that case, the JVM will set the maximum heap size based on the host's total memory instead of the memory available to the container. When you run your containerized Java apps in a Kubernetes cluster on your laptop, the problem doesn't manifest itself, because the difference between the memory limits you set for the pod and the total memory available on your laptop is not that great.

But when you deploy your pod onto a production system, where nodes have much more physical memory, the JVM may go over the container's memory limit you configured and will be OOMKilled.

And if you think setting the -Xmx option properly solves the issue, you're wrong, unfortunately. The -Xmx option only constrains the heap size, but does nothing about the JVM's off-heap memory. Luckily, new versions of Java alleviate that problem by taking the configured container limits into account.

UNDERSTANDING THAT CONTAINERS ALSO SEE ALL THE NODE'S CPU CORES

Exactly like with memory, containers will also see all the node's CPUs, regardless of the CPU limits configured for the container. Setting a CPU limit to one core doesn't magically only expose only one CPU core to the container. All the CPU limit does is constrain the amount of CPU time the container can use.

A container with a one-core CPU limit running on a 64-core CPU will get 1/64th of the overall CPU time. And even though its limit is set to one core, the container's processes will not run on only one core. At different points in time, its code may be executed on different cores.

Nothing is wrong with this, right? While that's generally the case, at least one scenario exists where this situation is catastrophic.

Certain applications look up the number of CPUs on the system to decide how many worker threads they should run. Again, such an app will run fine on a development laptop, but when deployed on a node with a much bigger number of cores, it's going to spin up too many threads, all competing for the (possibly) limited CPU time. Also, each thread requires additional memory, causing the apps memory usage to skyrocket.

You may want to use the Downward API to pass the CPU limit to the container and use it instead of relying on the number of CPUs your app can see on the system. You can also tap into the cgroups system directly to get the configured CPU limit by reading the following files:

- /sys/fs/cgroup/cpu/cpu.cfs_quota_us
- /sys/fs/cgroup/cpu/cpu.cfs_period_us

14.3 *Understanding pod QoS classes*

We've already mentioned that resource limits can be overcommitted and that a node can't necessarily provide all its pods the amount of resources specified in their resource limits.

Imagine having two pods, where pod A is using, let's say, 90% of the node's memory and then pod B suddenly requires more memory than what it had been using up to that point and the node can't provide the required amount of memory. Which container should be killed? Should it be pod B, because its request for memory can't be satisfied, or should pod A be killed to free up memory, so it can be provided to pod B?

Obviously, it depends. Kubernetes can't make a proper decision on its own. You need a way to specify which pods have priority in such cases. Kubernetes does this by categorizing pods into three Quality of Service (QoS) classes:

- BestEffort (the lowest priority)
- Burstable
- Guaranteed (the highest)

14.3.1 *Defining the QoS class for a pod*

You might expect these classes to be assignable to pods through a separate field in the manifest, but they aren't. The QoS class is derived from the combination of resource requests and limits for the pod's containers. Here's how.

ASSIGNING A POD TO THE BESTEFFORT CLASS

The lowest priority QoS class is the BestEffort class. It's assigned to pods that don't have any requests or limits set at all (in any of their containers). This is the QoS class that has been assigned to all the pods you created in previous chapters. Containers running in these pods have had no resource guarantees whatsoever. In the worst case, they may get almost no CPU time at all and will be the first ones killed when memory needs to be freed for other pods. But because a BestEffort pod has no memory limits set, its containers may use as much memory as they want, if enough memory is available.

ASSIGNING A POD TO THE GUARANTEED CLASS

On the other end of the spectrum is the Guaranteed QoS class. This class is given to pods whose containers' requests are equal to the limits for all resources. For a pod's class to be Guaranteed, three things need to be true:

- Requests and limits need to be set for both CPU and memory.
- They need to be set for each container.
- They need to be equal (the limit needs to match the request for each resource in each container).

Because a container's resource requests, if not set explicitly, default to the limits, specifying the limits for all resources (for each container in the pod) is enough for the pod to be Guaranteed. Containers in those pods get the requested amount of resources, but cannot consume additional ones (because their limits are no higher than their requests).

ASSIGNING THE BURSTABLE QoS CLASS TO A POD

In between BestEffort and Guaranteed is the Burstable QoS class. All other pods fall into this class. This includes single-container pods where the container's limits don't match its requests and all pods where at least one container has a resource request specified, but not the limit. It also includes pods where one container's requests match their limits, but another container has no requests or limits specified. Burstable pods get the amount of resources they request, but are allowed to use additional resources (up to the limit) if needed.

UNDERSTANDING HOW THE RELATIONSHIP BETWEEN REQUESTS AND LIMITS DEFINES THE QoS CLASS

All three QoS classes and their relationships with requests and limits are shown in figure 14.4.

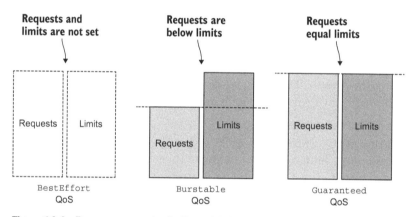

Figure 14.4   Resource requests, limits and QoS classes

Thinking about what QoS class a pod has can make your head spin, because it involves multiple containers, multiple resources, and all the possible relationships between requests and limits. It's easier if you start by thinking about QoS at the container level (although QoS classes are a property of pods, not containers) and then derive the pod's QoS class from the QoS classes of containers.

FIGURING OUT A CONTAINER'S QoS CLASS

Table 14.1 shows the QoS class based on how resource requests and limits are defined on a single container. For single-container pods, the QoS class applies to the pod as well.

Table 14.1 The QoS class of a single-container pod based on resource requests and limits

CPU requests vs. limits	Memory requests vs. limits	Container QoS class
None set	None set	`BestEffort`
None set	Requests < Limits	`Burstable`
None set	Requests = Limits	`Burstable`
Requests < Limits	None set	`Burstable`
Requests < Limits	Requests < Limits	`Burstable`
Requests < Limits	Requests = Limits	`Burstable`
Requests = Limits	Requests = Limits	`Guaranteed`

NOTE If only requests are set, but not limits, refer to the table rows where requests are less than the limits. If only limits are set, requests default to the limits, so refer to the rows where requests equal limits.

FIGURING OUT THE QoS CLASS OF A POD WITH MULTIPLE CONTAINERS

For multi-container pods, if all the containers have the same QoS class, that's also the pod's QoS class. If at least one container has a different class, the pod's QoS class is `Burstable`, regardless of what the container classes are. Table 14.2 shows how a two-container pod's QoS class relates to the classes of its two containers. You can easily extend this to pods with more than two containers.

Table 14.2 A Pod's QoS class derived from the classes of its containers

Container 1 QoS class	Container 2 QoS class	Pod's QoS class
`BestEffort`	`BestEffort`	`BestEffort`
`BestEffort`	`Burstable`	`Burstable`
`BestEffort`	`Guaranteed`	`Burstable`
`Burstable`	`Burstable`	`Burstable`
`Burstable`	`Guaranteed`	`Burstable`
`Guaranteed`	`Guaranteed`	`Guaranteed`

NOTE A pod's QoS class is shown when running `kubectl describe` pod and in the pod's YAML/JSON manifest in the `status.qosClass` field.

We've explained how QoS classes are determined, but we still need to look at how they determine which container gets killed in an overcommitted system.

14.3.2   *Understanding which process gets killed when memory is low*

When the system is overcommitted, the QoS classes determine which container gets killed first so the freed resources can be given to higher priority pods. First in line to get killed are pods in the `BestEffort` class, followed by `Burstable` pods, and finally `Guaranteed` pods, which only get killed if system processes need memory.

UNDERSTANDING HOW QoS CLASSES LINE UP

Let's look at the example shown in figure 14.5. Imagine having two single-container pods, where the first one has the `BestEffort` QoS class, and the second one's is `Burstable`. When the node's whole memory is already maxed out and one of the processes on the node tries to allocate more memory, the system will need to kill one of the processes (perhaps even the process trying to allocate additional memory) to honor the allocation request. In this case, the process running in the `BestEffort` pod will always be killed before the one in the `Burstable` pod.

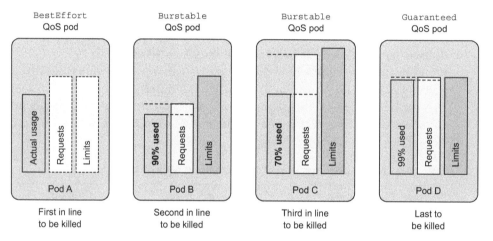

Figure 14.5   Which pods get killed first

Obviously, a `BestEffort` pod's process will also be killed before any `Guaranteed` pods' processes are killed. Likewise, a `Burstable` pod's process will also be killed before that of a `Guaranteed` pod. But what happens if there are only two `Burstable` pods? Clearly, the selection process needs to prefer one over the other.

UNDERSTANDING HOW CONTAINERS WITH THE SAME QoS CLASS ARE HANDLED

Each running process has an OutOfMemory (OOM) score. The system selects the process to kill by comparing OOM scores of all the running processes. When memory needs to be freed, the process with the highest score gets killed.

OOM scores are calculated from two things: the percentage of the available memory the process is consuming and a fixed OOM score adjustment, which is based on the pod's QoS class and the container's requested memory. When two single-container pods exist, both in the `Burstable` class, the system will kill the one using more of its requested memory than the other, percentage-wise. That's why in figure 14.5, pod B, using 90% of its requested memory, gets killed before pod C, which is only using 70%, even though it's using more megabytes of memory than pod B.

This shows you need to be mindful of not only the relationship between requests and limits, but also of requests and the expected actual memory consumption.

14.4 Setting default requests and limits for pods per namespace

We've looked at how resource requests and limits can be set for each individual container. If you don't set them, the container is at the mercy of all other containers that do specify resource requests and limits. It's a good idea to set requests and limits on every container.

14.4.1 Introducing the LimitRange resource

Instead of having to do this for every container, you can also do it by creating a Limit-Range resource. It allows you to specify (for each namespace) not only the minimum and maximum limit you can set on a container for each resource, but also the default resource requests for containers that don't specify requests explicitly, as depicted in figure 14.6.

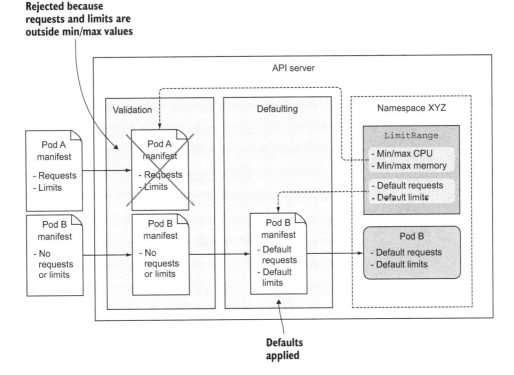

Figure 14.6 A LimitRange is used for validation and defaulting pods.

LimitRange resources are used by the LimitRanger Admission Control plugin (we explained what those plugins are in chapter 11). When a pod manifest is posted to the API server, the LimitRanger plugin validates the pod spec. If validation fails, the manifest is rejected immediately. Because of this, a great use-case for LimitRange objects is to prevent users from creating pods that are bigger than any node in the cluster. Without such a LimitRange, the API server will gladly accept the pod, but then never schedule it.

The limits specified in a LimitRange resource apply to each individual pod/container or other kind of object created in the same namespace as the LimitRange object. They don't limit the total amount of resources available across all the pods in the namespace. This is specified through ResourceQuota objects, which are explained in section 14.5.

14.4.2 Creating a LimitRange object

Let's look at a full example of a LimitRange and see what the individual properties do. The following listing shows the full definition of a LimitRange resource.

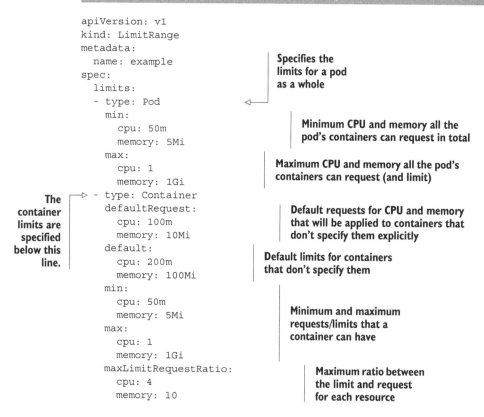

Listing 14.10   A LimitRange resource: limits.yaml

```
apiVersion: v1
kind: LimitRange
metadata:
  name: example
spec:
  limits:
  - type: Pod          ◁──  Specifies the
    min:                     limits for a pod
      cpu: 50m               as a whole
      memory: 5Mi                 Minimum CPU and memory all the
    max:                           pod's containers can request in total
      cpu: 1
      memory: 1Gi         Maximum CPU and memory all the pod's
                          containers can request (and limit)
  - type: Container
    defaultRequest:          Default requests for CPU and memory
      cpu: 100m              that will be applied to containers that
      memory: 10Mi          don't specify them explicitly
    default:            Default limits for containers
      cpu: 200m          that don't specify them
      memory: 100Mi
    min:
      cpu: 50m               Minimum and maximum
      memory: 5Mi            requests/limits that a
    max:                     container can have
      cpu: 1
      memory: 1Gi
    maxLimitRequestRatio:       Maximum ratio between
      cpu: 4                    the limit and request
      memory: 10                for each resource
```

The container limits are specified below this line.

```
      - type: PersistentVolumeClaim
        min:
          storage: 1Gi
        max:
          storage: 10Gi
```

**A LimitRange can also set
the minimum and maximum
amount of storage a PVC
can request.**

As you can see from the previous example, the minimum and maximum limits for a whole pod can be configured. They apply to the sum of all the pod's containers' requests and limits.

Lower down, at the container level, you can set not only the minimum and maximum, but also default resource requests (`defaultRequest`) and default limits (`default`) that will be applied to each container that doesn't specify them explicitly.

Beside the min, max, and default values, you can even set the maximum ratio of limits vs. requests. The previous listing sets the CPU `maxLimitRequestRatio` to 4, which means a container's CPU limits will not be allowed to be more than four times greater than its CPU requests. A container requesting 200 millicores will not be accepted if its CPU limit is set to 801 millicores or higher. For memory, the maximum ratio is set to 10.

In chapter 6 we looked at PersistentVolumeClaims (PVC), which allow you to claim a certain amount of persistent storage similarly to how a pod's containers claim CPU and memory. In the same way you're limiting the minimum and maximum amount of CPU a container can request, you should also limit the amount of storage a single PVC can request. A LimitRange object allows you to do that as well, as you can see at the bottom of the example.

The example shows a single LimitRange object containing limits for everything, but you could also split them into multiple objects if you prefer to have them organized per type (one for pod limits, another for container limits, and yet another for PVCs, for example). Limits from multiple LimitRange objects are all consolidated when validating a pod or PVC.

Because the validation (and defaults) configured in a LimitRange object is performed by the API server when it receives a new pod or PVC manifest, if you modify the limits afterwards, existing pods and PVCs will not be revalidated—the new limits will only apply to pods and PVCs created afterward.

14.4.3 *Enforcing the limits*

With your limits in place, you can now try creating a pod that requests more CPU than allowed by the LimitRange. You'll find the YAML for the pod in the code archive. The next listing only shows the part relevant to the discussion.

Listing 14.11   A pod with CPU requests greater than the limit: limits-pod-too-big.yaml

```
    resources:
      requests:
        cpu: 2
```

The pod's single container is requesting two CPUs, which is more than the maximum you set in the LimitRange earlier. Creating the pod yields the following result:

```
$ kubectl create -f limits-pod-too-big.yaml
Error from server (Forbidden): error when creating "limits-pod-too-big.yaml":
pods "too-big" is forbidden: [
  maximum cpu usage per Pod is 1, but request is 2.,
  maximum cpu usage per Container is 1, but request is 2.]
```

I've modified the output slightly to make it more legible. The nice thing about the error message from the server is that it lists all the reasons why the pod was rejected, not only the first one it encountered. As you can see, the pod was rejected for two reasons: you requested two CPUs for the container, but the maximum CPU limit for a container is one. Likewise, the pod as a whole requested two CPUs, but the maximum is one CPU (if this was a multi-container pod, even if each individual container requested less than the maximum amount of CPU, together they'd still need to request less than two CPUs to pass the maximum CPU for pods).

14.4.4 *Applying default resource requests and limits*

Now let's also see how default resource requests and limits are set on containers that don't specify them. Deploy the kubia-manual pod from chapter 3 again:

```
$ kubectl create -f ../Chapter03/kubia-manual.yaml
pod "kubia-manual" created
```

Before you set up your LimitRange object, all your pods were created without any resource requests or limits, but now the defaults are applied automatically when creating the pod. You can confirm this by describing the kubia-manual pod, as shown in the following listing.

Listing 14.12   Inspecting limits that were applied to a pod automatically
---

```
$ kubectl describe po kubia-manual
Name:          kubia-manual
...
Containers:
  kubia:
    Limits:
      cpu:        200m
      memory:     100Mi
    Requests:
      cpu:        100m
      memory:     10Mi
```

The container's requests and limits match the ones you specified in the LimitRange object. If you used a different LimitRange specification in another namespace, pods created in that namespace would obviously have different requests and limits. This allows admins to configure default, min, and max resources for pods per namespace.

If namespaces are used to separate different teams or to separate development, QA, staging, and production pods running in the same Kubernetes cluster, using a different LimitRange in each namespace ensures large pods can only be created in certain namespaces, whereas others are constrained to smaller pods.

But remember, the limits configured in a LimitRange only apply to each individual pod/container. It's still possible to create many pods and eat up all the resources available in the cluster. LimitRanges don't provide any protection from that. A ResourceQuota object, on the other hand, does. You'll learn about them next.

14.5 Limiting the total resources available in a namespace

As you've seen, LimitRanges only apply to individual pods, but cluster admins also need a way to limit the total amount of resources available in a namespace. This is achieved by creating a ResourceQuota object.

14.5.1 Introducing the ResourceQuota object

In chapter 10 we said that several Admission Control plugins running inside the API server verify whether the pod may be created or not. In the previous section, I said that the LimitRanger plugin enforces the policies configured in LimitRange resources. Similarly, the ResourceQuota Admission Control plugin checks whether the pod being created would cause the configured ResourceQuota to be exceeded. If that's the case, the pod's creation is rejected. Because resource quotas are enforced at pod creation time, a ResourceQuota object only affects pods created after the ResourceQuota object is created—creating it has no effect on existing pods.

A ResourceQuota limits the amount of computational resources the pods and the amount of storage PersistentVolumeClaims in a namespace can consume. It can also limit the number of pods, claims, and other API objects users are allowed to create inside the namespace. Because you've mostly dealt with CPU and memory so far, let's start by looking at how to specify quotas for them.

CREATING A RESOURCEQUOTA FOR CPU AND MEMORY

The overall CPU and memory all the pods in a namespace are allowed to consume is defined by creating a ResourceQuota object as shown in the following listing.

> **Listing 14.13   A ResourceQuota resource for CPU and memory: quota-cpu-memory.yaml**

```
apiVersion: v1
kind: ResourceQuota
metadata:
  name: cpu-and-mem
spec:
  hard:
    requests.cpu: 400m
    requests.memory: 200Mi
    limits.cpu: 600m
    limits.memory: 500Mi
```

Instead of defining a single total for each resource, you define separate totals for requests and limits for both CPU and memory. You'll notice the structure is a bit different, compared to that of a LimitRange. Here, both the requests and the limits for all resources are defined in a single place.

This ResourceQuota sets the maximum amount of CPU pods in the namespace can request to 400 millicores. The maximum total CPU limits in the namespace are set to 600 millicores. For memory, the maximum total requests are set to 200 MiB, whereas the limits are set to 500 MiB.

A ResourceQuota object applies to the namespace it's created in, like a LimitRange, but it applies to all the pods' resource requests and limits in total and not to each individual pod or container separately, as shown in figure 14.7.

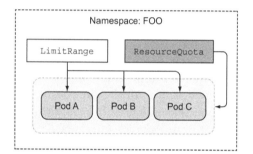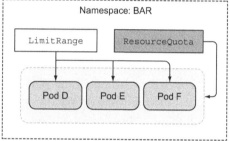

Figure 14.7 LimitRanges apply to individual pods; ResourceQuotas apply to all pods in the namespace.

INSPECTING THE QUOTA AND QUOTA USAGE

After you post the ResourceQuota object to the API server, you can use the `kubectl describe` command to see how much of the quota is already used up, as shown in the following listing.

Listing 14.14 Inspecting the ResourceQuota with `kubectl describe quota`

```
$ kubectl describe quota
Name:             cpu-and-mem
Namespace:        default
Resource          Used    Hard
--------          ----    ----
limits.cpu        200m    600m
limits.memory     100Mi   500Mi
requests.cpu      100m    400m
requests.memory   10Mi    200Mi
```

I only have the `kubia-manual` pod running, so the `Used` column matches its resource requests and limits. When I run additional pods, their requests and limits are added to the used amounts.

CREATING A LIMITRANGE ALONG WITH A RESOURCEQUOTA

One caveat when creating a ResourceQuota is that you will also want to create a Limit-Range object alongside it. In your case, you have a LimitRange configured from the previous section, but if you didn't have one, you couldn't run the kubia-manual pod, because it doesn't specify any resource requests or limits. Here's what would happen in that case:

```
$ kubectl create -f ../Chapter03/kubia-manual.yaml
Error from server (Forbidden): error when creating "../Chapter03/kubia-
    manual.yaml": pods "kubia-manual" is forbidden: failed quota: cpu-and-
    mem: must specify limits.cpu,limits.memory,requests.cpu,requests.memory
```

When a quota for a specific resource (CPU or memory) is configured (request or limit), pods need to have the request or limit (respectively) set for that same resource; otherwise the API server will not accept the pod. That's why having a LimitRange with defaults for those resources can make life a bit easier for people creating pods.

14.5.2 Specifying a quota for persistent storage

A ResourceQuota object can also limit the amount of persistent storage that can be claimed in the namespace, as shown in the following listing.

> **Listing 14.15   A ResourceQuota for storage: quota-storage.yaml**

```
apiVersion: v1
kind: ResourceQuota                                            The amount of
metadata:                                                      storage claimable
  name: storage                                                overall
spec:
  hard:                                                                   The amount
    requests.storage: 500Gi                          ◁─┘                  of claimable
    ssd.storageclass.storage.k8s.io/requests.storage: 300Gi    ◁─┤        storage in
    standard.storageclass.storage.k8s.io/requests.storage: 1Ti           StorageClass ssd
```

In this example, the amount of storage all PersistentVolumeClaims in a namespace can request is limited to 500 GiB (by the requests.storage entry in the Resource-Quota object). But as you'll remember from chapter 6, PersistentVolumeClaims can request a dynamically provisioned PersistentVolume of a specific StorageClass. That's why Kubernetes also makes it possible to define storage quotas for each StorageClass individually. The previous example limits the total amount of claimable SSD storage (designated by the ssd StorageClass) to 300 GiB. The less-performant HDD storage (StorageClass *standard*) is limited to 1 TiB.

14.5.3 Limiting the number of objects that can be created

A ResourceQuota can also be configured to limit the number of Pods, Replication-Controllers, Services, and other objects inside a single namespace. This allows the cluster admin to limit the number of objects users can create based on their payment plan, for example, and can also limit the number of public IPs or node ports Services can use.

The following listing shows what a ResourceQuota object that limits the number of objects may look like.

Listing 14.16   A ResourceQuota for max number of resources: quota-object-count.yaml

```
apiVersion: v1
kind: ResourceQuota
metadata:
  name: objects
spec:
  hard:
    pods: 10
    replicationcontrollers: 5
    secrets: 10
    configmaps: 10
    persistentvolumeclaims: 4
    services: 5
    services.loadbalancers: 1
    services.nodeports: 2
    ssd.storageclass.storage.k8s.io/persistentvolumeclaims: 2
```

Only 10 Pods, 5 ReplicationControllers, 10 Secrets, 10 ConfigMaps, and 4 PersistentVolumeClaims can be created in the namespace.

Five Services overall can be created, of which at most one can be a LoadBalancer Service and at most two can be NodePort Services.

Only two PVCs can claim storage with the ssd StorageClass.

The ResourceQuota in this listing allows users to create at most 10 Pods in the namespace, regardless if they're created manually or by a ReplicationController, ReplicaSet, DaemonSet, Job, and so on. It also limits the number of ReplicationControllers to five. A maximum of five Services can be created, of which only one can be a `LoadBalancer`-type Service, and only two can be `NodePort` Services. Similar to how the maximum amount of requested storage can be specified per StorageClass, the number of PersistentVolumeClaims can also be limited per StorageClass.

Object count quotas can currently be set for the following objects:

- Pods
- ReplicationControllers
- Secrets
- ConfigMaps
- PersistentVolumeClaims
- Services (in general), and for two specific types of Services, such as `LoadBalancer` Services (`services.loadbalancers`) and `NodePort` Services (`services.nodeports`)

Finally, you can even set an object count quota for ResourceQuota objects themselves. The number of other objects, such as ReplicaSets, Jobs, Deployments, Ingresses, and so on, cannot be limited yet (but this may have changed since the book was published, so please check the documentation for up-to-date information).

14.5.4 *Specifying quotas for specific pod states and/or QoS classes*

The quotas you've created so far have applied to all pods, regardless of their current state and QoS class. But quotas can also be limited to a set of *quota scopes*. Four scopes are currently available: `BestEffort`, `NotBestEffort`, `Terminating`, and `NotTerminating`.

The `BestEffort` and `NotBestEffort` scopes determine whether the quota applies to pods with the `BestEffort` QoS class or with one of the other two classes (that is, `Burstable` and `Guaranteed`).

The other two scopes (`Terminating` and `NotTerminating`) don't apply to pods that are (or aren't) in the process of shutting down, as the name might lead you to believe. We haven't talked about this, but you can specify how long each pod is allowed to run before it's terminated and marked as `Failed`. This is done by setting the `activeDeadlineSeconds` field in the pod spec. This property defines the number of seconds a pod is allowed to be active on the node relative to its start time before it's marked as `Failed` and then terminated. The `Terminating` quota scope applies to pods that have the `activeDeadlineSeconds` set, whereas the `NotTerminating` applies to those that don't.

When creating a ResourceQuota, you can specify the scopes that it applies to. A pod must match all the specified scopes for the quota to apply to it. Additionally, what a quota can limit depends on the quota's scope. `BestEffort` scope can only limit the number of pods, whereas the other three scopes can limit the number of pods, CPU/memory requests, and CPU/memory limits.

If, for example, you want the quota to apply only to `BestEffort`, `NotTerminating` pods, you can create the ResourceQuota object shown in the following listing.

Listing 14.17 ResourceQuota for `BestEffort/NotTerminating` pods: quota-scoped.yaml

```
apiVersion: v1
kind: ResourceQuota
metadata:
  name: besteffort-notterminating-pods
spec:
  scopes:
  - BestEffort
  - NotTerminating
  hard:
    pods: 4
```

This quota only applies to pods that have the BestEffort QoS and don't have an active deadline set.

Only four such pods can exist.

This quota ensures that at most four pods exist with the `BestEffort` QoS class, which don't have an active deadline. If the quota was targeting `NotBestEffort` pods instead, you could also specify `requests.cpu`, `requests.memory`, `limits.cpu`, and `limits.memory`.

> **NOTE** Before you move on to the next section of this chapter, please delete all the ResourceQuota and LimitRange resources you created. You won't

need them anymore and they may interfere with examples in the following chapters.

14.6   Monitoring pod resource usage

Properly setting resource requests and limits is crucial for getting the most out of your Kubernetes cluster. If requests are set too high, your cluster nodes will be underutilized and you'll be throwing money away. If you set them too low, your apps will be CPU-starved or even killed by the OOM Killer. How do you find the sweet spot for requests and limits?

You find it by monitoring the actual resource usage of your containers under the expected load levels. Once the application is exposed to the public, you should keep monitoring it and adjust the resource requests and limits if required.

14.6.1   Collecting and retrieving actual resource usages

How does one monitor apps running in Kubernetes? Luckily, the Kubelet itself already contains an agent called cAdvisor, which performs the basic collection of resource consumption data for both individual containers running on the node and the node as a whole. Gathering those statistics centrally for the whole cluster requires you to run an additional component called Heapster.

Heapster runs as a pod on one of the nodes and is exposed through a regular Kubernetes Service, making it accessible at a stable IP address. It collects the data from all cAdvisors in the cluster and exposes it in a single location. Figure 14.8 shows the flow of the metrics data from the pods, through cAdvisor and finally into Heapster.

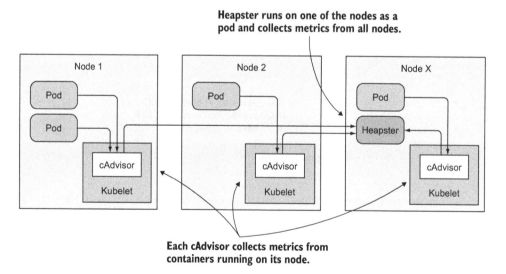

Figure 14.8   The flow of metrics data into Heapster

The arrows in the figure show how the metrics data flows. They don't show which component connects to which to get the data. The pods (or the containers running therein) don't know anything about cAdvisor, and cAdvisor doesn't know anything about Heapster. It's Heapster that connects to all the cAdvisors, and it's the cAdvisors that collect the container and node usage data without having to talk to the processes running inside the pods' containers.

ENABLING HEAPSTER

If you're running a cluster in Google Kubernetes Engine, Heapster is enabled by default. If you're using Minikube, it's available as an add-on and can be enabled with the following command:

```
$ minikube addons enable heapster
heapster was successfully enabled
```

To run Heapster manually in other types of Kubernetes clusters, you can refer to instructions located at https://github.com/kubernetes/heapster.

After enabling Heapster, you'll need to wait a few minutes for it to collect metrics before you can see resource usage statistics for your cluster, so be patient.

DISPLAYING CPU AND MEMORY USAGE FOR CLUSTER NODES

Running Heapster in your cluster makes it possible to obtain resource usages for nodes and individual pods through the `kubectl top` command. To see how much CPU and memory is being used on your nodes, you can run the command shown in the following listing.

> **Listing 14.18 Actual CPU and memory usage of nodes**

```
$ kubectl top node
NAME        CPU(cores)   CPU%    MEMORY(bytes)   MEMORY%
minikube    170m         8%      556Mi           27%
```

This shows the actual, current CPU and memory usage of all the pods running on the node, unlike the `kubectl describe node` command, which shows the amount of CPU and memory requests and limits instead of actual runtime usage data.

DISPLAYING CPU AND MEMORY USAGE FOR INDIVIDUAL PODS

To see how much each individual pod is using, you can use the `kubectl top pod` command, as shown in the following listing.

> **Listing 14.19 Actual CPU and memory usages of pods**

```
$ kubectl top pod --all-namespaces
NAMESPACE      NAME                     CPU(cores)   MEMORY(bytes)
kube-system    influxdb-grafana-2r2w9   1m           32Mi
kube-system    heapster-40j6d           0m           18Mi
```

```
default          kubia-3773182134-63bmb            0m       9Mi
kube-system      kube-dns-v20-z0hq6                1m       11Mi
kube-system      kubernetes-dashboard-r53mc        0m       14Mi
kube-system      kube-addon-manager-minikube       7m       33Mi
```

The outputs of both these commands are fairly simple, so you probably don't need me to explain them, but I do need to warn you about one thing. Sometimes the top pod command will refuse to show any metrics and instead print out an error like this:

```
$ kubectl top pod
W0312 22:12:58.021885   15126 top_pod.go:186] Metrics not available for pod
    default/kubia-3773182134-63bmb, age: 1h24m19.021873823s
error: Metrics not available for pod default/kubia-3773182134-63bmb, age:
    1h24m19.021873823s
```

If this happens, don't start looking for the cause of the error yet. Relax, wait a while, and rerun the command—it may take a few minutes, but the metrics should appear eventually. The kubectl top command gets the metrics from Heapster, which aggregates the data over a few minutes and doesn't expose it immediately.

> **TIP** To see resource usages across individual containers instead of pods, you can use the --containers option.

14.6.2 *Storing and analyzing historical resource consumption statistics*

The top command only shows current resource usages—it doesn't show you how much CPU or memory your pods consumed throughout the last hour, yesterday, or a week ago, for example. In fact, both cAdvisor and Heapster only hold resource usage data for a short window of time. If you want to analyze your pods' resource consumption over longer time periods, you'll need to run additional tools.

When using Google Kubernetes Engine, you can monitor your cluster with Google Cloud Monitoring, but when you're running your own local Kubernetes cluster (either through Minikube or other means), people usually use InfluxDB for storing statistics data and Grafana for visualizing and analyzing them.

INTRODUCING INFLUXDB AND GRAFANA

InfluxDB is an open source time-series database ideal for storing application metrics and other monitoring data. Grafana, also open source, is an analytics and visualization suite with a nice-looking web console that allows you to visualize the data stored in InfluxDB and discover how your application's resource usage behaves over time (an example showing three Grafana charts is shown in figure 14.9).

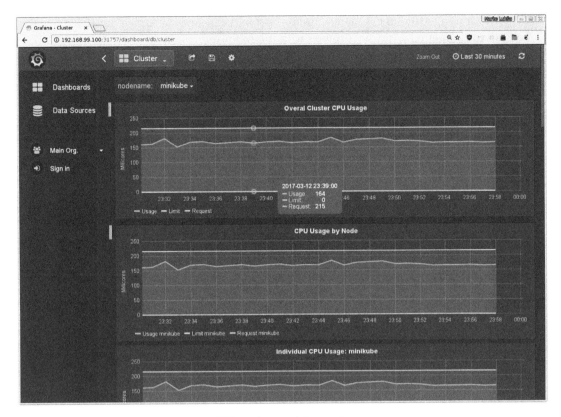

Figure 14.9   Grafana dashboard showing CPU usage across the cluster

RUNNING INFLUXDB AND GRAFANA IN YOUR CLUSTER

Both InfluxDB and Grafana can run as pods. Deploying them is straightforward. All the necessary manifests are available in the Heapster Git repository at http://github .com/kubernetes/heapster/tree/master/deploy/kube-config/influxdb.

When using Minikube, you don't even need to deploy them manually, because they're deployed along with Heapster when you enable the Heapster add-on.

ANALYZING RESOURCE USAGE WITH GRAFANA

To discover how much of each resource your pod requires over time, open the Grafana web console and explore the predefined dashboards. Generally, you can find out the URL of Grafana's web console with `kubectl cluster-info`:

```
$ kubectl cluster-info
...
monitoring-grafana is running at
    https://192.168.99.100:8443/api/v1/proxy/namespaces/kube-
    system/services/monitoring-grafana
```

When using Minikube, Grafana's web console is exposed through a `NodePort` Service, so you can open it in your browser with the following command:

```
$ minikube service monitoring-grafana -n kube-system
Opening kubernetes service kube-system/monitoring-grafana in default
    browser...
```

A new browser window or tab will open and show the Grafana Home screen. On the right-hand side, you'll see a list of dashboards containing two entries:

- Cluster
- Pods

To see the resource usage statistics of the nodes, open the Cluster dashboard. There you'll see several charts showing the overall cluster usage, usage by node, and the individual usage for CPU, memory, network, and filesystem. The charts will not only show the actual usage, but also the requests and limits for those resources (where they apply).

If you then switch over to the Pods dashboard, you can examine the resource usages for each individual pod, again with both requests and limits shown alongside the actual usage.

Initially, the charts show the statistics for the last 30 minutes, but you can zoom out and see the data for much longer time periods: days, months, or even years.

USING THE INFORMATION SHOWN IN THE CHARTS

By looking at the charts, you can quickly see if the resource requests or limits you've set for your pods need to be raised or whether they can be lowered to allow more pods to fit on your nodes. Let's look at an example. Figure 14.10 shows the CPU and memory charts for a pod.

At the far right of the top chart, you can see the pod is using more CPU than was requested in the pod's manifest. Although this isn't problematic when this is the only pod running on the node, you should keep in mind that a pod is only guaranteed as much of a resource as it requests through resource requests. Your pod may be running fine now, but when other pods are deployed to the same node and start using the CPU, your pod's CPU time may be throttled. Because of this, to ensure the pod can use as much CPU as it needs to at any time, you should raise the CPU resource request for the pod's container.

The bottom chart shows the pod's memory usage and request. Here the situation is the exact opposite. The amount of memory the pod is using is well below what was requested in the pod's spec. The requested memory is reserved for the pod and won't be available to other pods. The unused memory is therefore wasted. You should decrease the pod's memory request to make the memory available to other pods running on the node.

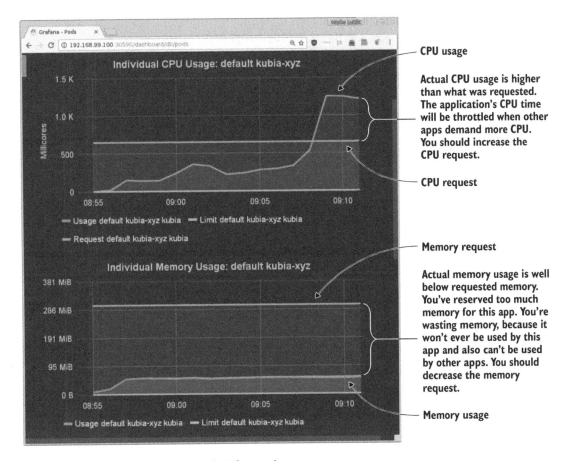

Figure 14.10 CPU and memory usage chart for a pod

14.7 Summary

This chapter has shown you that you need to consider your pod's resource usage and configure both the resource requests and the limits for your pod to keep everything running smoothly. The key takeaways from this chapter are

- Specifying resource requests helps Kubernetes schedule pods across the cluster.
- Specifying resource limits keeps pods from starving other pods of resources.
- Unused CPU time is allocated based on containers' CPU requests.
- Containers never get killed if they try to use too much CPU, but they are killed if they try to use too much memory.
- In an overcommitted system, containers also get killed to free memory for more important pods, based on the pods' QoS classes and actual memory usage.

- You can use LimitRange objects to define the minimum, maximum, and default resource requests and limits for individual pods.
- You can use ResourceQuota objects to limit the amount of resources available to all the pods in a namespace.
- To know how high to set a pod's resource requests and limits, you need to monitor how the pod uses resources over a long-enough time period.

In the next chapter, you'll see how these metrics can be used by Kubernetes to automatically scale your pods.

Automatic scaling
of pods and cluster nodes

This chapter covers

- Configuring automatic horizontal scaling of pods based on CPU utilization
- Configuring automatic horizontal scaling of pods based on custom metrics
- Understanding why vertical scaling of pods isn't possible yet
- Understanding automatic horizontal scaling of cluster nodes

Applications running in pods can be scaled out manually by increasing the `replicas` field in the ReplicationController, ReplicaSet, Deployment, or other scalable resource. Pods can also be scaled vertically by increasing their container's resource requests and limits (though this can currently only be done at pod creation time, not while the pod is running). Although manual scaling is okay for times when you can anticipate load spikes in advance or when the load changes gradually over longer periods of time, requiring manual intervention to handle sudden, unpredictable traffic increases isn't ideal.

Luckily, Kubernetes can monitor your pods and scale them up automatically as soon as it detects an increase in the CPU usage or some other metric. If running on a cloud infrastructure, it can even spin up additional nodes if the existing ones can't accept any more pods. This chapter will explain how to get Kubernetes to do both pod and node autoscaling.

The autoscaling feature in Kubernetes was completely rewritten between the 1.6 and the 1.7 version, so be aware you may find outdated information on this subject online.

15.1   *Horizontal pod autoscaling*

Horizontal pod autoscaling is the automatic scaling of the number of pod replicas managed by a controller. It's performed by the Horizontal controller, which is enabled and configured by creating a HorizontalPodAutoscaler (HPA) resource. The controller periodically checks pod metrics, calculates the number of replicas required to meet the target metric value configured in the HorizontalPodAutoscaler resource, and adjusts the `replicas` field on the target resource (Deployment, ReplicaSet, Replication-Controller, or StatefulSet).

15.1.1   *Understanding the autoscaling process*

The autoscaling process can be split into three steps:

- Obtain metrics of all the pods managed by the scaled resource object.
- Calculate the number of pods required to bring the metrics to (or close to) the specified target value.
- Update the `replicas` field of the scaled resource.

Let's examine all three steps next.

OBTAINING POD METRICS

The Autoscaler doesn't perform the gathering of the pod metrics itself. It gets the metrics from a different source. As we saw in the previous chapter, pod and node metrics are collected by an agent called *cAdvisor*, which runs in the Kubelet on each node, and then aggregated by the cluster-wide component called Heapster. The horizontal pod autoscaler controller gets the metrics of all the pods by querying Heapster through REST calls. The flow of metrics data is shown in figure 15.1 (although all the connections are initiated in the opposite direction).

Figure 15.1   Flow of metrics from the pod(s) to the HorizontalPodAutoscaler(s)

This implies that Heapster must be running in the cluster for autoscaling to work. If you're using Minikube and were following along in the previous chapter, Heapster should already be enabled in your cluster. If not, make sure to enable the Heapster add-on before trying out any autoscaling examples.

Although you don't need to query Heapster directly, if you're interested in doing so, you'll find both the Heapster Pod and the Service it's exposed through in the `kube-system` namespace.

A look at changes related to how the Autoscaler obtains metrics

Prior to Kubernetes version 1.6, the HorizontalPodAutoscaler obtained the metrics from Heapster directly. In version 1.8, the Autoscaler can get the metrics through an aggregated version of the resource metrics API by starting the Controller Manager with the `--horizontal-pod-autoscaler-use-rest-clients=true` flag. From version 1.9, this behavior will be enabled by default.

The core API server will not expose the metrics itself. From version 1.7, Kubernetes allows registering multiple API servers and making them appear as a single API server. This allows it to expose metrics through one of those underlying API servers. We'll explain API server aggregation in the last chapter.

Selecting what metrics collector to use in their clusters will be up to cluster administrators. A simple translation layer is usually required to expose the metrics in the appropriate API paths and in the appropriate format.

CALCULATING THE REQUIRED NUMBER OF PODS

Once the Autoscaler has metrics for all the pods belonging to the resource the Autoscaler is scaling (the Deployment, ReplicaSet, ReplicationController, or StatefulSet resource), it can use those metrics to figure out the required number of replicas. It needs to find the number that will bring the average value of the metric across all those replicas as close to the configured target value as possible. The input to this calculation is a set of pod metrics (possibly multiple metrics per pod) and the output is a single integer (the number of pod replicas).

When the Autoscaler is configured to consider only a single metric, calculating the required replica count is simple. All it takes is summing up the metrics values of all the pods, dividing that by the target value set on the HorizontalPodAutoscaler resource, and then rounding it up to the next-larger integer. The actual calculation is a bit more involved than this, because it also makes sure the Autoscaler doesn't thrash around when the metric value is unstable and changes rapidly.

When autoscaling is based on multiple pod metrics (for example, both CPU usage and Queries-Per-Second [QPS]), the calculation isn't that much more complicated. The Autoscaler calculates the replica count for each metric individually and then takes the highest value (for example, if four pods are required to achieve the target CPU usage, and three pods are required to achieve the target QPS, the Autoscaler will scale to four pods). Figure 15.2 shows this example.

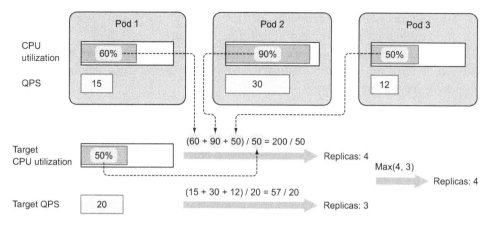

Figure 15.2   Calculating the number of replicas from two metrics

UPDATING THE DESIRED REPLICA COUNT ON THE SCALED RESOURCE

The final step of an autoscaling operation is updating the desired replica count field on the scaled resource object (a ReplicaSet, for example) and then letting the Replica-Set controller take care of spinning up additional pods or deleting excess ones.

The Autoscaler controller modifies the `replicas` field of the scaled resource through the Scale sub-resource. It enables the Autoscaler to do its work without knowing any details of the resource it's scaling, except for what's exposed through the Scale sub-resource (see figure 15.3).

Figure 15.3   The Horizontal Pod Autoscaler modifies only on the Scale sub-resource.

This allows the Autoscaler to operate on any scalable resource, as long as the API server exposes the Scale sub-resource for it. Currently, it's exposed for

- Deployments
- ReplicaSets
- ReplicationControllers
- StatefulSets

These are currently the only objects you can attach an Autoscaler to.

UNDERSTANDING THE WHOLE AUTOSCALING PROCESS

You now understand the three steps involved in autoscaling, so let's visualize all the components involved in the autoscaling process. They're shown in figure 15.4.

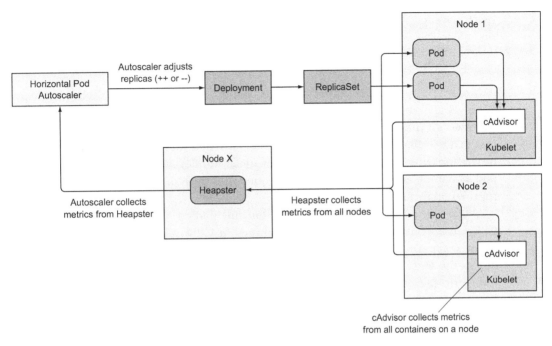

Figure 15.4   How the autoscaler obtains metrics and rescales the target deployment

The arrows leading from the pods to the cAdvisors, which continue on to Heapster and finally to the Horizontal Pod Autoscaler, indicate the direction of the flow of metrics data. It's important to be aware that each component gets the metrics from the other components periodically (that is, cAdvisor gets the metrics from the pods in a continuous loop; the same is also true for Heapster and for the HPA controller). The end effect is that it takes quite a while for the metrics data to be propagated and a rescaling action to be performed. It isn't immediate. Keep this in mind when you observe the Autoscaler in action next.

15.1.2   *Scaling based on CPU utilization*

Perhaps the most important metric you'll want to base autoscaling on is the amount of CPU consumed by the processes running inside your pods. Imagine having a few pods providing a service. When their CPU usage reaches 100% it's obvious they can't cope with the demand anymore and need to be scaled either up (vertical scaling—increasing the amount of CPU the pods can use) or out (horizontal scaling—increasing the number of pods). Because we're talking about the horizontal pod autoscaler here, we're only focusing on scaling out (increasing the number of pods). By doing that, the average CPU usage should come down.

Because CPU usage is usually unstable, it makes sense to scale out even before the CPU is completely swamped—perhaps when the average CPU load across the pods reaches or exceeds 80%. But 80% of *what*, exactly?

> **TIP**   Always set the target CPU usage well below 100% (and definitely never above 90%) to leave enough room for handling sudden load spikes.

As you may remember from the previous chapter, the process running inside a container is guaranteed the amount of CPU requested through the resource requests specified for the container. But at times when no other processes need CPU, the process may use all the available CPU on the node. When someone says a pod is consuming 80% of the CPU, it's not clear if they mean 80% of the node's CPU, 80% of the pod's guaranteed CPU (the resource request), or 80% of the hard limit configured for the pod through resource limits.

As far as the Autoscaler is concerned, only the pod's guaranteed CPU amount (the CPU requests) is important when determining the CPU utilization of a pod. The Autoscaler compares the pod's actual CPU consumption and its CPU requests, which means the pods you're autoscaling need to have CPU requests set (either directly or indirectly through a LimitRange object) for the Autoscaler to determine the CPU utilization percentage.

CREATING A HORIZONTALPODAUTOSCALER BASED ON CPU USAGE

Let's see how to create a HorizontalPodAutoscaler now and configure it to scale pods based on their CPU utilization. You'll create a Deployment similar to the one in chapter 9, but as we've discussed, you'll need to make sure the pods created by the Deployment all have the CPU resource requests specified in order to make autoscaling possible. You'll have to add a CPU resource request to the Deployment's pod template, as shown in the following listing.

Listing 15.1   Deployment with CPU requests set: deployment.yaml

```
apiVersion: extensions/v1beta1
kind: Deployment
metadata:
  name: kubia
spec:
  replicas: 3                        Manually setting the
  template:                          (initial) desired number
    metadata:                        of replicas to three
      name: kubia
      labels:
        app: kubia
    spec:
      containers:
      - image: luksa/kubia:v1        Running the
        name: nodejs                 kubia:v1 image
```

```
    resources:
      requests:
        cpu: 100m
```
Requesting 100 millicores of CPU per pod

This is a regular Deployment object—it doesn't use autoscaling yet. It will run three instances of the `kubia` NodeJS app, with each instance requesting 100 millicores of CPU.

After creating the Deployment, to enable horizontal autoscaling of its pods, you need to create a HorizontalPodAutoscaler (HPA) object and point it to the Deployment. You could prepare and post the YAML manifest for the HPA, but an easier way exists—using the `kubectl autoscale` command:

```
$ kubectl autoscale deployment kubia --cpu-percent=30 --min=1 --max=5
deployment "kubia" autoscaled
```

This creates the HPA object for you and sets the Deployment called `kubia` as the scaling target. You're setting the target CPU utilization of the pods to 30% and specifying the minimum and maximum number of replicas. The Autoscaler will constantly keep adjusting the number of replicas to keep their CPU utilization around 30%, but it will never scale down to less than one or scale up to more than five replicas.

TIP Always make sure to autoscale Deployments instead of the underlying ReplicaSets. This way, you ensure the desired replica count is preserved across application updates (remember that a Deployment creates a new ReplicaSet for each version). The same rule applies to manual scaling, as well.

Let's look at the definition of the HorizontalPodAutoscaler resource to gain a better understanding of it. It's shown in the following listing.

Listing 15.2   A HorizontalPodAutoscaler YAML definition

```
$ kubectl get hpa.v2beta1.autoscaling kubia -o yaml
apiVersion: autoscaling/v2beta1
kind: HorizontalPodAutoscaler
metadata:
  name: kubia
  ...
spec:
  maxReplicas: 5
  metrics:
  - resource:
      name: cpu
      targetAverageUtilization: 30
    type: Resource
  minReplicas: 1
  scaleTargetRef:
    apiVersion: extensions/v1beta1
    kind: Deployment
    name: kubia
```

HPA resources are in the autoscaling API group.

Each HPA has a name (it doesn't need to match the name of the Deployment as in this case).

The minimum and maximum number of replicas you specified

You'd like the Autoscaler to adjust the number of pods so they each utilize 30% of requested CPU.

The target resource which this Autoscaler will act upon

```
status:
  currentMetrics: []
  currentReplicas: 3
  desiredReplicas: 0
```
The current status
of the Autoscaler

NOTE Multiple versions of HPA resources exist: the new `autoscaling/v2beta1` and the old `autoscaling/v1`. You're requesting the new version here.

SEEING THE FIRST AUTOMATIC RESCALE EVENT

It takes a while for cAdvisor to get the CPU metrics and for Heapster to collect them before the Autoscaler can take action. During that time, if you display the HPA resource with `kubectl get`, the TARGETS column will show `<unknown>`:

```
$ kubectl get hpa
NAME       REFERENCE          TARGETS          MINPODS   MAXPODS   REPLICAS
kubia      Deployment/kubia   <unknown> / 30%  1         5         0
```

Because you're running three pods that are currently receiving no requests, which means their CPU usage should be close to zero, you should expect the Autoscaler to scale them down to a single pod, because even with a single pod, the CPU utilization will still be below the 30% target.

And sure enough, the autoscaler does exactly that. It soon scales the Deployment down to a single replica:

```
$ kubectl get deployment
NAME      DESIRED   CURRENT   UP-TO-DATE   AVAILABLE   AGE
kubia     1         1         1            1           23m
```

Remember, the autoscaler only adjusts the desired replica count on the Deployment. The Deployment controller then takes care of updating the desired replica count on the ReplicaSet object, which then causes the ReplicaSet controller to delete two excess pods, leaving one pod running.

You can use `kubectl describe` to see more information on the HorizontalPod-Autoscaler and the operation of the underlying controller, as the following listing shows.

Listing 15.3   Inspecting a HorizontalPodAutoscaler with `kubectl describe`

```
$ kubectl describe hpa
Name:                                      kubia
Namespace:                                 default
Labels:                                    <none>
Annotations:                               <none>
CreationTimestamp:                         Sat, 03 Jun 2017 12:59:57 +0200
Reference:                                 Deployment/kubia
Metrics:                                   ( current / target )
  resource cpu on pods
  (as a percentage of request):           0% (0) / 30%
Min replicas:                              1
Max replicas:                              5
```

```
Events:
From                            Reason            Message
----                            ------            ---
horizontal-pod-autoscaler       SuccessfulRescale New size: 1; reason: All
                                                  metrics below target
```

NOTE The output has been modified to make it more readable.

Turn your focus to the table of events at the bottom of the listing. You see the horizontal pod autoscaler has successfully rescaled to one replica, because all metrics were below target.

TRIGGERING A SCALE-UP

You've already witnessed your first automatic rescale event (a scale-down). Now, you'll start sending requests to your pod, thereby increasing its CPU usage, and you should see the autoscaler detect this and start up additional pods.

You'll need to expose the pods through a Service, so you can hit all of them through a single URL. You may remember that the easiest way to do that is with kubectl expose:

```
$ kubectl expose deployment kubia --port=80 --target-port=8080
service "kubia" exposed
```

Before you start hitting your pod(s) with requests, you may want to run the following command in a separate terminal to keep an eye on what's happening with the HorizontalPodAutoscaler and the Deployment, as shown in the following listing.

Listing 15.4 Watching multiple resources in parallel

```
$ watch -n 1 kubectl get hpa,deployment
Every 1.0s: kubectl get hpa,deployment

NAME        REFERENCE        TARGETS    MINPODS  MAXPODS  REPLICAS  AGE
hpa/kubia   Deployment/kubia 0% / 30%   1        5        1         45m

NAME          DESIRED   CURRENT   UP-TO-DATE   AVAILABLE   AGE
deploy/kubia  1         1         1            1           56m
```

TIP List multiple resource types with kubectl get by delimiting them with a comma.

If you're using OSX, you'll have to replace the watch command with a loop, manually run kubectl get periodically, or use kubectl's --watch option. But although a plain kubectl get can show multiple types of resources at once, that's not the case when using the aforementioned --watch option, so you'll need to use two terminals if you want to watch both the HPA and the Deployment objects.

Keep an eye on the state of those two objects while you run a load-generating pod. You'll run the following command in another terminal:

```
$ kubectl run -it --rm --restart=Never loadgenerator --image=busybox
➥ -- sh -c "while true; do wget -O - -q http://kubia.default; done"
```

This will run a pod which repeatedly hits the kubia Service. You've seen the `-it` option a few times when running the kubectl exec command. As you can see, it can also be used with kubectl run. It allows you to attach the console to the process, which will not only show you the process' output directly, but will also terminate the process as soon as you press CTRL+C. The `--rm` option causes the pod to be deleted afterward, and the `--restart=Never` option causes kubectl run to create an unmanaged pod directly instead of through a Deployment object, which you don't need. This combination of options is useful for running commands inside the cluster without having to piggyback on an existing pod. It not only behaves the same as if you were running the command locally, it even cleans up everything when the command terminates.

SEEING THE AUTOSCALER SCALE UP THE DEPLOYMENT

As the load-generator pod runs, you'll see it initially hitting the single pod. As before, it takes time for the metrics to be updated, but when they are, you'll see the autoscaler increase the number of replicas. In my case, the pod's CPU utilization initially jumped to 108%, which caused the autoscaler to increase the number of pods to four. The utilization on the individual pods then decreased to 74% and then stabilized at around 26%.

> **NOTE** If the CPU load in your case doesn't exceed 30%, try running additional load-generators.

Again, you can inspect autoscaler events with kubectl describe to see what the autoscaler has done (only the most important information is shown in the following listing).

Listing 15.5   Events of a HorizontalPodAutoscaler

```
From      Reason              Message
----      ------              -------
h-p-a     SuccessfulRescale   New size: 1; reason: All metrics below target
h-p-a     SuccessfulRescale   New size: 4; reason: cpu resource utilization
                              (percentage of request) above target
```

Does it strike you as odd that the initial average CPU utilization in my case, when I only had one pod, was 108%, which is more than 100%? Remember, a container's CPU utilization is the container's actual CPU usage divided by its requested CPU. The requested CPU defines the minimum, not maximum amount of CPU available to the container, so a container may consume more than the requested CPU, bringing the percentage over 100.

Before we go on, let's do a little math and see how the autoscaler concluded that four replicas are needed. Initially, there was one replica handling requests and its CPU usage spiked to 108%. Dividing 108 by 30 (the target CPU utilization percentage) gives 3.6, which the autoscaler then rounded up to 4. If you divide 108 by 4, you get 27%. If the autoscaler scales up to four pods, their average CPU utilization is expected to be somewhere in the neighborhood of 27%, which is close to the target value of 30% and almost exactly what the observed CPU utilization was.

UNDERSTANDING THE MAXIMUM RATE OF SCALING

In my case, the CPU usage shot up to 108%, but in general, the initial CPU usage could spike even higher. Even if the initial average CPU utilization was higher (say 150%), requiring five replicas to achieve the 30% target, the autoscaler would still only scale up to four pods in the first step, because it has a limit on how many replicas can be added in a single scale-up operation. The autoscaler will at most double the number of replicas in a single operation, if more than two current replicas exist. If only one or two exist, it will scale up to a maximum of four replicas in a single step.

Additionally, it has a limit on how soon a subsequent autoscale operation can occur after the previous one. Currently, a scale-up will occur only if no rescaling event occurred in the last three minutes. A scale-down event is performed even less frequently—every five minutes. Keep this in mind so you don't wonder why the autoscaler refuses to perform a rescale operation even if the metrics clearly show that it should.

MODIFYING THE TARGET METRIC VALUE ON AN EXISTING HPA OBJECT

To wrap up this section, let's do one last exercise. Maybe your initial CPU utilization target of 30% was a bit too low, so increase it to 60%. You do this by editing the HPA resource with the `kubectl edit` command. When the text editor opens, change the `targetAverageUtilization` field to 60, as shown in the following listing.

> **Listing 15.6　Increasing the target CPU utilization by editing the HPA resource**

```
...
spec:
  maxReplicas: 5
  metrics:
  - resource:
      name: cpu
      targetAverageUtilization: 60        Change this
    type: Resource                        from 30 to 60.
...
```

As with most other resources, after you modify the resource, your changes will be detected by the autoscaler controller and acted upon. You could also delete the resource and recreate it with different target values, because by deleting the HPA resource, you only disable autoscaling of the target resource (a Deployment in this case) and leave it at the scale it is at that time. The automatic scaling will resume after you create a new HPA resource for the Deployment.

15.1.3 *Scaling based on memory consumption*

You've seen how easily the horizontal Autoscaler can be configured to keep CPU uti-lization at the target level. But what about autoscaling based on the pods' memory usage?

Memory-based autoscaling is much more problematic than CPU-based autoscal-ing. The main reason is because after scaling up, the old pods would somehow need to be forced to release memory. This needs to be done by the app itself—it can't be done by the system. All the system could do is kill and restart the app, hoping it would use less memory than before. But if the app then uses the same amount as before, the Autoscaler would scale it up again. And again, and again, until it reaches the maxi-mum number of pods configured on the HPA resource. Obviously, this isn't what any-one wants. Memory-based autoscaling was introduced in Kubernetes version 1.8, and is configured exactly like CPU-based autoscaling. Exploring it is left up to the reader.

15.1.4 *Scaling based on other and custom metrics*

You've seen how easy it is to scale pods based on their CPU usage. Initially, this was the only autoscaling option that was usable in practice. To have the autoscaler use custom, app-defined metrics to drive its autoscaling decisions was fairly complicated. The ini-tial design of the autoscaler didn't make it easy to move beyond simple CPU-based scaling. This prompted the Kubernetes Autoscaling Special Interest Group (SIG) to redesign the autoscaler completely.

If you're interested in learning how complicated it was to use the initial autoscaler with custom metrics, I invite you to read my blog post entitled "Kubernetes autoscal-ing based on custom metrics without using a host port," which you'll find online at http://medium.com/@marko.luksa. You'll learn about all the other problems I encountered when trying to set up autoscaling based on custom metrics. Luckily, newer versions of Kubernetes don't have those problems. I'll cover the subject in a new blog post.

Instead of going through a complete example here, let's quickly go over how to configure the autoscaler to use different metrics sources. We'll start by examining how we defined what metric to use in our previous example. The following listing shows how your previous HPA object was configured to use the CPU usage metric.

Listing 15.7   HorizontalPodAutoscaler definition for CPU-based autoscaling

```
...
spec:
  maxReplicas: 5
  metrics:
  - type: Resource            ◁─┐      Defines the type
    resource:                   │      of metric
      name: cpu                 │      The resource, whose
      targetAverageUtilization: 30      utilization will be monitored
...                       ◁─────┘      The target utilization
                          ◁            of this resource
```

As you can see, the metrics field allows you to define more than one metric to use. In the listing, you're using a single metric. Each entry defines the type of metric—in this case, a Resource metric. You have three types of metrics you can use in an HPA object:

- Resource
- Pods
- Object

UNDERSTANDING THE RESOURCE METRIC TYPE

The Resource type makes the autoscaler base its autoscaling decisions on a resource metric, like the ones specified in a container's resource requests. We've already seen how to do that, so let's focus on the other two types.

UNDERSTANDING THE PODS METRIC TYPE

The Pods type is used to refer to any other (including custom) metric related to the pod directly. An example of such a metric could be the already mentioned Queries-Per-Second (QPS) or the number of messages in a message broker's queue (when the message broker is running as a pod). To configure the autoscaler to use the pod's QPS metric, the HPA object would need to include the entry shown in the following listing under its metrics field.

Listing 15.8   Referring to a custom pod metric in the HPA

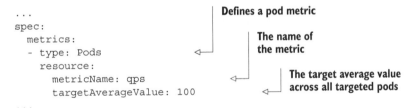

```
...
spec:
  metrics:
  - type: Pods            ◁─┘   The name of
    resource:                   the metric
      metricName: qps     ◁─┘   The target average value
      targetAverageValue: 100 ◁─ across all targeted pods
...
```

Defines a pod metric

The example in the listing configures the autoscaler to keep the average QPS of all the pods managed by the ReplicaSet (or other) controller targeted by this HPA resource at 100.

UNDERSTANDING THE OBJECT METRIC TYPE

The Object metric type is used when you want to make the autoscaler scale pods based on a metric that doesn't pertain directly to those pods. For example, you may want to scale pods according to a metric of another cluster object, such as an Ingress object. The metric could be QPS as in listing 15.8, the average request latency, or something else completely.

Unlike in the previous case, where the autoscaler needed to obtain the metric for all targeted pods and then use the average of those values, when you use an Object metric type, the autoscaler obtains a single metric from the single object. In the HPA definition, you need to specify the target object and the target value. The following listing shows an example.

Listing 15.9   Referring to a metric of a different object in the HPA

```
...
spec:
  metrics:
  - type: Object                      ⟵  Use metric of a
    resource:                            specific object
      metricName: latencyMillis       ⟵  The name of
      target:                              the metric
        apiVersion: extensions/v1beta1
        kind: Ingress                    The specific object whose metric
        name: frontend                   the autoscaler should obtain
      targetValue: 20
  scaleTargetRef:
    apiVersion: extensions/v1beta1
    kind: Deployment                     The scalable resource the
    name: kubia                          autoscaler will scale
...
```

The Autoscaler should scale so the value of the metric stays close to this.

In this example, the HPA is configured to use the `latencyMillis` metric of the `frontend` Ingress object. The target value for the metric is `20`. The horizontal pod autoscaler will monitor the Ingress' metric and if it rises too far above the target value, the autoscaler will scale the `kubia` Deployment resource.

15.1.5 *Determining which metrics are appropriate for autoscaling*

You need to understand that not all metrics are appropriate for use as the basis of autoscaling. As mentioned previously, the pods' containers' memory consumption isn't a good metric for autoscaling. The autoscaler won't function properly if increasing the number of replicas doesn't result in a linear decrease of the average value of the observed metric (or at least close to linear).

For example, if you have only a single pod instance and the value of the metric is X and the autoscaler scales up to two replicas, the metric needs to fall to somewhere close to X/2. An example of such a custom metric is Queries per Second (QPS), which in the case of web applications reports the number of requests the application is receiving per second. Increasing the number of replicas will always result in a pro-portionate decrease of QPS, because a greater number of pods will be handling the same total number of requests.

Before you decide to base the autoscaler on your app's own custom metric, be sure to think about how its value will behave when the number of pods increases or decreases.

15.1.6 *Scaling down to zero replicas*

The horizontal pod autoscaler currently doesn't allow setting the `minReplicas` field to 0, so the autoscaler will never scale down to zero, even if the pods aren't doing anything. Allowing the number of pods to be scaled down to zero can dramatically increase the utilization of your hardware. When you run services that get requests only once every few hours or even days, it doesn't make sense to have them running all the time, eating up resources that could be used by other pods. But you still want to have those services available immediately when a client request comes in.

This is known as idling and un-idling. It allows pods that provide a certain service to be scaled down to zero. When a new request comes in, the request is blocked until the pod is brought up and then the request is finally forwarded to the pod.

Kubernetes currently doesn't provide this feature yet, but it will eventually. Check the documentation to see if idling has been implemented yet.

15.2 *Vertical pod autoscaling*

Horizontal scaling is great, but not every application can be scaled horizontally. For such applications, the only option is to scale them vertically—give them more CPU and/or memory. Because a node usually has more resources than a single pod requests, it should almost always be possible to scale a pod vertically, right?

Because a pod's resource requests are configured through fields in the pod manifest, vertically scaling a pod would be performed by changing those fields. I say "would" because it's currently not possible to change either resource requests or limits of existing pods. Before I started writing the book (well over a year ago), I was sure that by the time I wrote this chapter, Kubernetes would already support proper vertical pod autoscaling, so I included it in my proposal for the table of contents. Sadly, what seems like a lifetime later, vertical pod autoscaling is still not available yet.

15.2.1 *Automatically configuring resource requests*

An experimental feature sets the CPU and memory requests on newly created pods, if their containers don't have them set explicitly. The feature is provided by an Admission Control plugin called InitialResources. When a new pod without resource requests is created, the plugin looks at historical resource usage data of the pod's containers (per the underlying container image and tag) and sets the requests accordingly.

You can deploy pods without specifying resource requests and rely on Kubernetes to eventually figure out what each container's resource needs are. Effectively, Kubernetes is vertically scaling the pod. For example, if a container keeps running out of memory, the next time a pod with that container image is created, its resource request for memory will be set higher automatically.

15.2.2 *Modifying resource requests while a pod is running*

Eventually, the same mechanism will be used to modify an existing pod's resource requests, which means it will vertically scale the pod while it's running. As I'm writing this, a new vertical pod autoscaling proposal is being finalized. Please refer to the

Kubernetes documentation to find out whether vertical pod autoscaling is already implemented or not.

15.3   *Horizontal scaling of cluster nodes*

The Horizontal Pod Autoscaler creates additional pod instances when the need for them arises. But what about when all your nodes are at capacity and can't run any more pods? Obviously, this problem isn't limited only to when new pod instances are created by the Autoscaler. Even when creating pods manually, you may encounter the problem where none of the nodes can accept the new pods, because the node's resources are used up by existing pods.

In that case, you'd need to delete several of those existing pods, scale them down vertically, or add additional nodes to your cluster. If your Kubernetes cluster is running on premises, you'd need to physically add a new machine and make it part of the Kubernetes cluster. But if your cluster is running on a cloud infrastructure, adding additional nodes is usually a matter of a few clicks or an API call to the cloud infrastructure. This can be done automatically, right?

Kubernetes includes the feature to automatically request additional nodes from the cloud provider as soon as it detects additional nodes are needed. This is performed by the Cluster Autoscaler.

15.3.1   *Introducing the Cluster Autoscaler*

The Cluster Autoscaler takes care of automatically provisioning additional nodes when it notices a pod that can't be scheduled to existing nodes because of a lack of resources on those nodes. It also de-provisions nodes when they're underutilized for longer periods of time.

REQUESTING ADDITIONAL NODES FROM THE CLOUD INFRASTRUCTURE

A new node will be provisioned if, after a new pod is created, the Scheduler can't schedule it to any of the existing nodes. The Cluster Autoscaler looks out for such pods and asks the cloud provider to start up an additional node. But before doing that, it checks whether the new node can even accommodate the pod. After all, if that's not the case, it makes no sense to start up such a node.

Cloud providers usually group nodes into groups (or pools) of same-sized nodes (or nodes having the same features). The Cluster Autoscaler thus can't simply say "Give me an additional node." It needs to also specify the node type.

The Cluster Autoscaler does this by examining the available node groups to see if at least one node type would be able to fit the unscheduled pod. If exactly one such node group exists, the Autoscaler can increase the size of the node group to have the cloud provider add another node to the group. If more than one option is available, the Autoscaler must pick the best one. The exact meaning of "best" will obviously need to be configurable. In the worst case, it selects a random one. A simple overview of how the cluster Autoscaler reacts to an unschedulable pod is shown in figure 15.5.

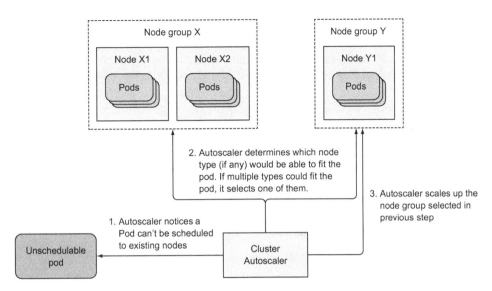

Figure 15.5 The Cluster Autoscaler scales up when it finds a pod that can't be scheduled to existing nodes.

When the new node starts up, the Kubelet on that node contacts the API server and registers the node by creating a Node resource. From then on, the node is part of the Kubernetes cluster and pods can be scheduled to it.

Simple, right? What about scaling down?

RELINQUISHING NODES

The Cluster Autoscaler also needs to scale down the number of nodes when they aren't being utilized enough. The Autoscaler does this by monitoring the requested CPU and memory on all the nodes. If the CPU and memory requests of all the pods running on a given node are below 50%, the node is considered unnecessary.

That's not the only determining factor in deciding whether to bring a node down. The Autoscaler also checks to see if any system pods are running (only) on that node (apart from those that are run on every node, because they're deployed by a Daemon-Set, for example). If a system pod is running on a node, the node won't be relinquished. The same is also true if an unmanaged pod or a pod with local storage is running on the node, because that would cause disruption to the service the pod is providing. In other words, a node will only be returned to the cloud provider if the Cluster Autoscaler knows the pods running on the node will be rescheduled to other nodes.

When a node is selected to be shut down, the node is first marked as unschedulable and then all the pods running on the node are evicted. Because all those pods belong to ReplicaSets or other controllers, their replacements are created and scheduled to the remaining nodes (that's why the node that's being shut down is first marked as unschedulable).

Manually cordoning and draining nodes

A node can also be marked as unschedulable and drained manually. Without going into specifics, this is done with the following `kubectl` commands:

- `kubectl cordon <node>` marks the node as unschedulable (but doesn't do anything with pods running on that node).
- `kubectl drain <node>` marks the node as unschedulable and then evicts all the pods from the node.

In both cases, no new pods are scheduled to the node until you uncordon it again with `kubectl uncordon <node>`.

15.3.2 *Enabling the Cluster Autoscaler*

Cluster autoscaling is currently available on

- Google Kubernetes Engine (GKE)
- Google Compute Engine (GCE)
- Amazon Web Services (AWS)
- Microsoft Azure

How you start the Autoscaler depends on where your Kubernetes cluster is running. For your `kubia` cluster running on GKE, you can enable the Cluster Autoscaler like this:

```
$ gcloud container clusters update kubia --enable-autoscaling \
  --min-nodes=3 --max-nodes=5
```

If your cluster is running on GCE, you need to set three environment variables before running `kube-up.sh`:

- `KUBE_ENABLE_CLUSTER_AUTOSCALER=true`
- `KUBE_AUTOSCALER_MIN_NODES=3`
- `KUBE_AUTOSCALER_MAX_NODES=5`

Refer to the Cluster Autoscaler GitHub repo at https://github.com/kubernetes/autoscaler/tree/master/cluster-autoscaler for information on how to enable it on other platforms.

> **NOTE** The Cluster Autoscaler publishes its status to the `cluster-autoscaler-status` ConfigMap in the `kube-system` namespace.

15.3.3 *Limiting service disruption during cluster scale-down*

When a node fails unexpectedly, nothing you can do will prevent its pods from becoming unavailable. But when a node is shut down voluntarily, either by the Cluster Autoscaler or by a human operator, you can make sure the operation doesn't disrupt the service provided by the pods running on that node through an additional feature.

Certain services require that a minimum number of pods always keeps running; this is especially true for quorum-based clustered applications. For this reason, Kubernetes provides a way of specifying the minimum number of pods that need to keep running while performing these types of operations. This is done by creating a PodDisruptionBudget resource.

Even though the name of the resource sounds complex, it's one of the simplest Kubernetes resources available. It contains only a pod label selector and a number specifying the minimum number of pods that must always be available or, starting from Kubernetes version 1.7, the maximum number of pods that can be unavailable. We'll look at what a PodDisruptionBudget (PDB) resource manifest looks like, but instead of creating it from a YAML file, you'll create it with `kubectl create poddisruptionbudget` and then obtain and examine the YAML later.

If you want to ensure three instances of your `kubia` pod are always running (they have the label `app=kubia`), create the PodDisruptionBudget resource like this:

```
$ kubectl create pdb kubia-pdb --selector=app=kubia --min-available=3
poddisruptionbudget "kubia-pdb" created
```

Simple, right? Now, retrieve the PDB's YAML. It's shown in the next listing.

Listing 15.10 A PodDisruptionBudget definition

```
$ kubectl get pdb kubia-pdb -o yaml
apiVersion: policy/v1beta1
kind: PodDisruptionBudget
metadata:
  name: kubia-pdb
spec:
  minAvailable: 3          <── How many pods should
  selector:                     always be available
    matchLabels:
      app: kubia                The label selector that
status:                         determines which pods
  ...                           this budget applies to
```

You can also use a percentage instead of an absolute number in the `minAvailable` field. For example, you could state that 60% of all pods with the `app=kubia` label need to be running at all times.

> **NOTE** Starting with Kubernetes 1.7, the PodDisruptionBudget resource also supports the `maxUnavailable` field, which you can use instead of `minAvailable` if you want to block evictions when more than that many pods are unavailable.

We don't have much more to say about this resource. As long as it exists, both the Cluster Autoscaler and the `kubectl drain` command will adhere to it and will never evict a pod with the `app=kubia` label if that would bring the number of such pods below three.

For example, if there were four pods altogether and `minAvailable` was set to three as in the example, the pod eviction process would evict pods one by one, waiting for the evicted pod to be replaced with a new one by the ReplicaSet controller, before evicting another pod.

15.4 Summary

This chapter has shown you how Kubernetes can scale not only your pods, but also your nodes. You've learned that

- Configuring the automatic horizontal scaling of pods is as easy as creating a HorizontalPodAutoscaler object and pointing it to a Deployment, ReplicaSet, or ReplicationController and specifying the target CPU utilization for the pods.
- Besides having the Horizontal Pod Autoscaler perform scaling operations based on the pods' CPU utilization, you can also configure it to scale based on your own application-provided custom metrics or metrics related to other objects deployed in the cluster.
- Vertical pod autoscaling isn't possible yet.
- Even cluster nodes can be scaled automatically if your Kubernetes cluster runs on a supported cloud provider.
- You can run one-off processes in a pod and have the pod stopped and deleted automatically as soon you press CTRL+C by using `kubectl run` with the `-it` and `--rm` options.

In the next chapter, you'll explore advanced scheduling features, such as how to keep certain pods away from certain nodes and how to schedule pods either close together or apart.

Advanced scheduling

This chapter covers

- Using node taints and pod tolerations to keep pods away from certain nodes
- Defining node affinity rules as an alternative to node selectors
- Co-locating pods using pod affinity
- Keeping pods away from each other using pod anti-affinity

Kubernetes allows you to affect where pods are scheduled. Initially, this was only done by specifying a node selector in the pod specification, but additional mechanisms were later added that expanded this functionality. They're covered in this chapter.

16.1 *Using taints and tolerations to repel pods from certain nodes*

The first two features related to advanced scheduling that we'll explore here are the node taints and pods' tolerations of those taints. They're used for restricting which pods can use a certain node. A pod can only be scheduled to a node if it tolerates the node's taints.

This is somewhat different from using node selectors and node affinity, which you'll learn about later in this chapter. Node selectors and node affinity rules make it possible to select which nodes a pod can or can't be scheduled to by specifically adding that information to the pod, whereas taints allow rejecting deployment of pods to certain nodes by only adding taints to the node without having to modify existing pods. Pods that you want deployed on a tainted node need to opt in to use the node, whereas with node selectors, pods explicitly specify which node(s) they want to be deployed to.

16.1.1 Introducing taints and tolerations

The best path to learn about node taints is to see an existing taint. Appendix B shows how to set up a multi-node cluster with the `kubeadm` tool. By default, the master node in such a cluster is tainted, so only Control Plane pods can be deployed on it.

DISPLAYING A NODE'S TAINTS

You can see the node's taints using `kubectl describe` node, as shown in the following listing.

Listing 16.1   Describing the master node in a cluster created with `kubeadm`

```
$ kubectl describe node master.k8s
Name:          master.k8s
Role:
Labels:        beta.kubernetes.io/arch=amd64
               beta.kubernetes.io/os=linux
               kubernetes.io/hostname=master.k8s
               node-role.kubernetes.io/master=
Annotations:   node.alpha.kubernetes.io/ttl=0
               volumes.kubernetes.io/controller-managed-attach-detach=true
Taints:        node-role.kubernetes.io/master:NoSchedule     ◁───┐  The master node
...                                                                 has one taint.
```

The master node has a single taint. Taints have a *key*, *value*, and an *effect*, and are represented as `<key>=<value>:<effect>`. The master node's taint shown in the previous listing has the key `node-role.kubernetes.io/master`, a `null` value (not shown in the taint), and the effect of `NoSchedule`.

This taint prevents pods from being scheduled to the master node, unless those pods tolerate this taint. The pods that tolerate it are usually system pods (see figure 16.1).

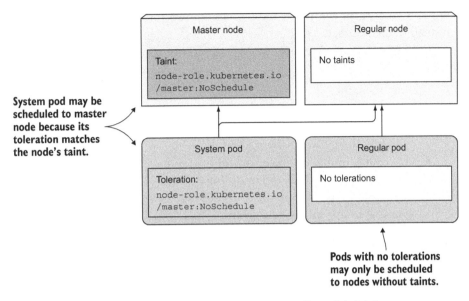

Figure 16.1 A pod is only scheduled to a node if it tolerates the node's taints.

DISPLAYING A POD'S TOLERATIONS

In a cluster installed with kubeadm, the kube-proxy cluster component runs as a pod on every node, including the master node, because master components that run as pods may also need to access Kubernetes Services. To make sure the kube-proxy pod also runs on the master node, it includes the appropriate toleration. In total, the pod has three tolerations, which are shown in the following listing.

Listing 16.2 A pod's tolerations

```
$ kubectl describe po kube-proxy-80wqm -n kube-system
...
Tolerations:    node-role.kubernetes.io/master=:NoSchedule
                node.alpha.kubernetes.io/notReady=:Exists:NoExecute
                node.alpha.kubernetes.io/unreachable=:Exists:NoExecute
...
```

As you can see, the first toleration matches the master node's taint, allowing this kube-proxy pod to be scheduled to the master node.

> **NOTE** Disregard the equal sign, which is shown in the pod's tolerations, but not in the node's taints. Kubectl apparently displays taints and tolerations differently when the taint's/toleration's value is null.

UNDERSTANDING TAINT EFFECTS

The two other tolerations on the kube-proxy pod define how long the pod is allowed to run on nodes that aren't ready or are unreachable (the time in seconds isn't shown, but can be seen in the pod's YAML). Those two tolerations refer to the `NoExecute` instead of the `NoSchedule` effect.

Each taint has an effect associated with it. Three possible effects exist:

- `NoSchedule`, which means pods won't be scheduled to the node if they don't tolerate the taint.
- `PreferNoSchedule` is a soft version of `NoSchedule`, meaning the scheduler will try to avoid scheduling the pod to the node, but will schedule it to the node if it can't schedule it somewhere else.
- `NoExecute`, unlike `NoSchedule` and `PreferNoSchedule` that only affect scheduling, also affects pods already running on the node. If you add a `NoExecute` taint to a node, pods that are already running on that node and don't tolerate the `NoExecute` taint will be evicted from the node.

16.1.2 *Adding custom taints to a node*

Imagine having a single Kubernetes cluster where you run both production and non-production workloads. It's of the utmost importance that non-production pods never run on the production nodes. This can be achieved by adding a taint to your production nodes. To add a taint, you use the `kubectl taint` command:

```
$ kubectl taint node node1.k8s node-type=production:NoSchedule
node "node1.k8s" tainted
```

This adds a taint with key `node-type`, value `production` and the `NoSchedule` effect. If you now deploy multiple replicas of a regular pod, you'll see none of them are scheduled to the node you tainted, as shown in the following listing.

> **Listing 16.3 Deploying pods without a toleration**

```
$ kubectl run test --image busybox --replicas 5 -- sleep 99999
deployment "test" created

$ kubectl get po -o wide
NAME                 READY  STATUS   RESTARTS  AGE  IP         NODE
test-196686-46ngl    1/1    Running  0         12s  10.47.0.1  node2.k8s
test-196686-73p89    1/1    Running  0         12s  10.47.0.7  node2.k8s
test-196686-77280    1/1    Running  0         12s  10.47.0.6  node2.k8s
test-196686-h9m8f    1/1    Running  0         12s  10.47.0.5  node2.k8s
test-196686-p85ll    1/1    Running  0         12s  10.47.0.4  node2.k8s
```

Now, no one can inadvertently deploy pods onto the production nodes.

16.1.3 *Adding tolerations to pods*

To deploy production pods to the production nodes, they need to tolerate the taint you added to the nodes. The manifests of your production pods need to include the YAML snippet shown in the following listing.

Listing 16.4 A production Deployment with a toleration: production-deployment.yaml

```
apiVersion: extensions/v1beta1
kind: Deployment
metadata:
  name: prod
spec:
  replicas: 5
  template:
    spec:
      ...
      tolerations:
      - key: node-type            This toleration allows the
        operator: Equal           pod to be scheduled to
        value: production         production nodes.
        effect: NoSchedule
```

If you deploy this Deployment, you'll see its pods get deployed to the production node, as shown in the next listing.

Listing 16.5 Pods with the toleration are deployed on production node1

```
$ kubectl get po -o wide
NAME                 READY   STATUS    RESTARTS   AGE   IP           NODE
prod-350605-1ph5h    0/1     Running   0          16s   10.44.0.3    node1.k8s
prod-350605-ctqcr    1/1     Running   0          16s   10.47.0.4    node2.k8s
prod-350605-f7pcc    0/1     Running   0          17s   10.44.0.6    node1.k8s
prod-350605-k7c8g    1/1     Running   0          17s   10.47.0.9    node2.k8s
prod-350605-rp1nv    0/1     Running   0          17s   10.44.0.4    node1.k8s
```

As you can see in the listing, production pods were also deployed to node2, which isn't a production node. To prevent that from happening, you'd also need to taint the non-production nodes with a taint such as `node-type=non-production:NoSchedule`. Then you'd also need to add the matching toleration to all your non-production pods.

16.1.4 Understanding what taints and tolerations can be used for

Nodes can have more than one taint and pods can have more than one toleration. As you've seen, taints can only have a key and an effect and don't require a value. Tolerations can tolerate a specific value by specifying the `Equal` operator (that's also the default operator if you don't specify one), or they can tolerate any value for a specific taint key if you use the `Exists` operator.

USING TAINTS AND TOLERATIONS DURING SCHEDULING

Taints can be used to prevent scheduling of new pods (`NoSchedule` effect) and to define unpreferred nodes (`PreferNoSchedule` effect) and even evict existing pods from a node (`NoExecute`).

You can set up taints and tolerations any way you see fit. For example, you could partition your cluster into multiple partitions, allowing your development teams to schedule pods only to their respective nodes. You can also use taints and tolerations when several of your nodes provide special hardware and only part of your pods need to use it.

CONFIGURING HOW LONG AFTER A NODE FAILURE A POD IS RESCHEDULED

You can also use a toleration to specify how long Kubernetes should wait before rescheduling a pod to another node if the node the pod is running on becomes unready or unreachable. If you look at the tolerations of one of your pods, you'll see two tolerations, which are shown in the following listing.

> #### Listing 16.6 Pod with default tolerations

```
$ kubectl get po prod-350605-1ph5h -o yaml
...
  tolerations:
  - effect: NoExecute
    key: node.alpha.kubernetes.io/notReady
    operator: Exists
    tolerationSeconds: 300
  - effect: NoExecute
    key: node.alpha.kubernetes.io/unreachable
    operator: Exists
    tolerationSeconds: 300
```

The pod tolerates the node being notReady for 300 seconds, before it needs to be rescheduled.

The same applies to the node being unreachable.

These two tolerations say that this pod tolerates a node being notReady or unreachable for 300 seconds. The Kubernetes Control Plane, when it detects that a node is no longer ready or no longer reachable, will wait for 300 seconds before it deletes the pod and reschedules it to another node.

These two tolerations are automatically added to pods that don't define them. If that five-minute delay is too long for your pods, you can make the delay shorter by adding those two tolerations to the pod's spec.

> **NOTE** This is currently an alpha feature, so it may change in future versions of Kubernetes. Taint-based evictions also aren't enabled by default. You enable them by running the Controller Manager with the `--feature-gates=Taint-BasedEvictions=true` option.

16.2 *Using node affinity to attract pods to certain nodes*

As you've learned, taints are used to keep pods away from certain nodes. Now you'll learn about a newer mechanism called *node affinity*, which allows you to tell Kubernetes to schedule pods only to specific subsets of nodes.

COMPARING NODE AFFINITY TO NODE SELECTORS

The initial node affinity mechanism in early versions of Kubernetes was the node-Selector field in the pod specification. The node had to include all the labels specified in that field to be eligible to become the target for the pod.

Node selectors get the job done and are simple, but they don't offer everything that you may need. Because of that, a more powerful mechanism was introduced.

Node selectors will eventually be deprecated, so it's important you understand the new node affinity rules.

Similar to node selectors, each pod can define its own node affinity rules. These allow you to specify either hard requirements or preferences. By specifying a preference, you tell Kubernetes which nodes you prefer for a specific pod, and Kubernetes will try to schedule the pod to one of those nodes. If that's not possible, it will choose one of the other nodes.

EXAMINING THE DEFAULT NODE LABELS

Node affinity selects nodes based on their labels, the same way node selectors do. Before you see how to use node affinity, let's examine the labels of one of the nodes in a Google Kubernetes Engine cluster (GKE) to see what the default node labels are. They're shown in the following listing.

> **Listing 16.7 Default labels of a node in GKE**

```
$ kubectl describe node gke-kubia-default-pool-db274c5a-mjnf
Name:      gke-kubia-default-pool-db274c5a-mjnf
Role:
Labels:    beta.kubernetes.io/arch=amd64
           beta.kubernetes.io/fluentd-ds-ready=true
           beta.kubernetes.io/instance-type=f1-micro
           beta.kubernetes.io/os=linux
           cloud.google.com/gke-nodepool=default-pool
           failure-domain.beta.kubernetes.io/region=europe-west1
           failure-domain.beta.kubernetes.io/zone=europe-west1-d
           kubernetes.io/hostname=gke-kubia-default-pool-db274c5a-mjnf
```

These three labels are the most important ones related to node affinity.

The node has many labels, but the last three are the most important when it comes to node affinity and pod affinity, which you'll learn about later. The meaning of those three labels is as follows:

- `failure-domain.beta.kubernetes.io/region` specifies the geographical region the node is located in.
- `failure-domain.beta.kubernetes.io/zone` specifies the availability zone the node is in.
- `kubernetes.io/hostname` is obviously the node's hostname.

These and other labels can be used in pod affinity rules. In chapter 3, you already learned how you can add a custom label to nodes and use it in a pod's node selector. You used the custom label to deploy pods only to nodes with that label by adding a node selector to the pods. Now, you'll see how to do the same using node affinity rules.

16.2.1 Specifying hard node affinity rules

In the example in chapter 3, you used the node selector to deploy a pod that requires a GPU only to nodes that have a GPU. The pod spec included the `nodeSelector` field shown in the following listing.

Listing 16.8 A pod using a node selector: kubia-gpu-nodeselector.yaml

```
apiVersion: v1
kind: Pod
metadata:
  name: kubia-gpu
spec:
  nodeSelector:
    gpu: "true"
  ...
```

This pod is only scheduled to nodes that have the gpu=true label.

The `nodeSelector` field specifies that the pod should only be deployed on nodes that include the gpu=true label. If you replace the node selector with a node affinity rule, the pod definition will look like the following listing.

Listing 16.9 A pod using a `nodeAffinity` rule: kubia-gpu-nodeaffinity.yaml

```
apiVersion: v1
kind: Pod
metadata:
  name: kubia-gpu
spec:
  affinity:
    nodeAffinity:
      requiredDuringSchedulingIgnoredDuringExecution:
        nodeSelectorTerms:
        - matchExpressions:
          - key: gpu
            operator: In
            values:
            - "true"
```

The first thing you'll notice is that this is much more complicated than a simple node selector. But that's because it's much more expressive. Let's examine the rule in detail.

MAKING SENSE OF THE LONG NODEAFFINITY ATTRIBUTE NAME

As you can see, the pod's spec section contains an `affinity` field that contains a `nodeAffinity` field, which contains a field with an extremely long name, so let's focus on that first.

Let's break it down into two parts and examine what they mean:

- `requiredDuringScheduling...` means the rules defined under this field specify the labels the node must have for the pod to be scheduled to the node.
- `...IgnoredDuringExecution` means the rules defined under the field don't affect pods already executing on the node.

At this point, let me make things easier for you by letting you know that affinity currently only affects pod scheduling and never causes a pod to be evicted from a node. That's why all the rules right now always end with `IgnoredDuringExecution`. Eventually, Kubernetes will also support `RequiredDuringExecution`, which means that if you remove a label from a node, pods that require the node to have that label will be evicted from such a node. As I've said, that's not yet supported in Kubernetes, so let's not concern ourselves with the second part of that long field any longer.

UNDERSTANDING NODESELECTORTERMS

By keeping what was explained in the previous section in mind, it's easy to understand that the nodeSelectorTerms field and the matchExpressions field define which expressions the node's labels must match for the pod to be scheduled to the node. The single expression in the example is simple to understand. The node must have a gpu label whose value is set to true.

This pod will therefore only be scheduled to nodes that have the gpu=true label, as shown in figure 16.2.

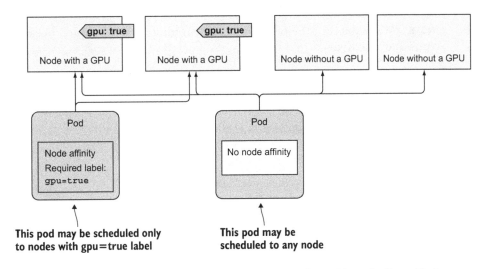

Figure 16.2 A pod's node affinity specifies which labels a node must have for the pod to be scheduled to it.

Now comes the more interesting part. Node also affinity allows you to prioritize nodes during scheduling. We'll look at that next.

16.2.2 *Prioritizing nodes when scheduling a pod*

The biggest benefit of the newly introduced node affinity feature is the ability to specify which nodes the Scheduler should prefer when scheduling a specific pod. This is done through the preferredDuringSchedulingIgnoredDuringExecution field.

Imagine having multiple datacenters across different countries. Each datacenter represents a separate availability zone. In each zone, you have certain machines meant only for your own use and others that your partner companies can use. You now want to deploy a few pods and you'd prefer them to be scheduled to zone1 and to the machines reserved for your company's deployments. If those machines don't have enough room for the pods or if other important reasons exist that prevent them from being scheduled there, you're okay with them being scheduled to the machines your partners use and to the other zones. Node affinity allows you to do that.

LABELING NODES

First, the nodes need to be labeled appropriately. Each node needs to have a label that designates the availability zone the node belongs to and a label marking it as either a dedicated or a shared node.

Appendix B explains how to set up a three-node cluster (one master and two worker nodes) in VMs running locally. In the following examples, I'll use the two worker nodes in that cluster, but you can also use Google Kubernetes Engine or any other multi-node cluster.

> **NOTE** Minikube isn't the best choice for running these examples, because it runs only one node.

First, label the nodes, as shown in the next listing.

Listing 16.10   Labeling nodes

```
$ kubectl label node node1.k8s availability-zone=zone1
node "node1.k8s" labeled
$ kubectl label node node1.k8s share-type=dedicated
node "node1.k8s" labeled
$ kubectl label node node2.k8s availability-zone=zone2
node "node2.k8s" labeled
$ kubectl label node node2.k8s share-type=shared
node "node2.k8s" labeled
$ kubectl get node -L availability-zone -L share-type
NAME         STATUS    AGE     VERSION    AVAILABILITY-ZONE    SHARE-TYPE
master.k8s   Ready     4d      v1.6.4     <none>               <none>
node1.k8s    Ready     4d      v1.6.4     zone1                dedicated
node2.k8s    Ready     4d      v1.6.4     zone2                shared
```

SPECIFYING PREFERENTIAL NODE AFFINITY RULES

With the node labels set up, you can now create a Deployment that prefers `dedicated` nodes in `zone1`. The following listing shows the Deployment manifest.

Listing 16.11   Deployment with preferred node affinity: preferred-deployment.yaml

```
apiVersion: extensions/v1beta1
kind: Deployment
metadata:
  name: pref
spec:
  template:
    ...
    spec:
      affinity:
        nodeAffinity:
```

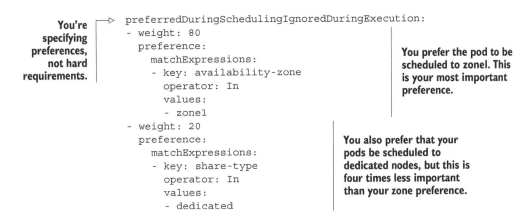

You're specifying preferences, not hard requirements.

```
preferredDuringSchedulingIgnoredDuringExecution:
- weight: 80
  preference:
    matchExpressions:
    - key: availability-zone
      operator: In
      values:
      - zone1
- weight: 20
  preference:
    matchExpressions:
    - key: share-type
      operator: In
      values:
      - dedicated
...
```

You prefer the pod to be scheduled to zone1. This is your most important preference.

You also prefer that your pods be scheduled to dedicated nodes, but this is four times less important than your zone preference.

Let's examine the listing closely. You're defining a node affinity preference, instead of a hard requirement. You want the pods scheduled to nodes that include the labels `availability-zone=zone1` and `share-type=dedicated`. You're saying that the first preference rule is important by setting its `weight` to `80`, whereas the second one is much less important (`weight` is set to `20`).

UNDERSTANDING HOW NODE PREFERENCES WORK

If your cluster had many nodes, when scheduling the pods of the Deployment in the previous listing, the nodes would be split into four groups, as shown in figure 16.3. Nodes whose `availability-zone` and `share-type` labels match the pod's node affinity are ranked the highest. Then, because of how the weights in the pod's node affinity rules are configured, next come the `shared` nodes in `zone1`, then come the `dedicated` nodes in the other zones, and at the lowest priority are all the other nodes.

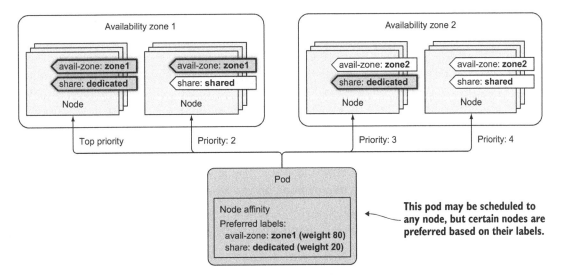

This pod may be scheduled to any node, but certain nodes are preferred based on their labels.

Figure 16.3   Prioritizing nodes based on a pod's node affinity preferences

DEPLOYING THE PODS IN THE TWO-NODE CLUSTER

If you create this Deployment in your two-node cluster, you should see most (if not all) of your pods deployed to `node1`. Examine the following listing to see if that's true.

Listing 16.12 Seeing where pods were scheduled

```
$ kubectl get po -o wide
NAME                   READY   STATUS    RESTARTS   AGE   IP           NODE
pref-607515-1rnwv      1/1     Running   0          4m    10.47.0.1    node2.k8s
pref-607515-27wp0      1/1     Running   0          4m    10.44.0.8    node1.k8s
pref-607515-5xd0z      1/1     Running   0          4m    10.44.0.5    node1.k8s
pref-607515-jx9wt      1/1     Running   0          4m    10.44.0.4    node1.k8s
pref-607515-mlgqm      1/1     Running   0          4m    10.44.0.6    node1.k8s
```

Out of the five pods that were created, four of them landed on `node1` and only one landed on `node2`. Why did one of them land on `node2` instead of `node1`? The reason is that besides the node affinity prioritization function, the Scheduler also uses other prioritization functions to decide where to schedule a pod. One of those is the `Selector-SpreadPriority` function, which makes sure pods belonging to the same ReplicaSet or Service are spread around different nodes so a node failure won't bring the whole service down. That's most likely what caused one of the pods to be scheduled to `node2`.

You can try scaling the Deployment up to 20 or more and you'll see the majority of pods will be scheduled to `node1`. In my test, only two out of the 20 were scheduled to `node2`. If you hadn't defined any node affinity preferences, the pods would have been spread around the two nodes evenly.

16.3 *Co-locating pods with pod affinity and anti-affinity*

You've seen how node affinity rules are used to influence which node a pod is scheduled to. But these rules only affect the affinity between a pod and a node, whereas sometimes you'd like to have the ability to specify the affinity between pods themselves.

For example, imagine having a frontend and a backend pod. Having those pods deployed near to each other reduces latency and improves the performance of the app. You could use node affinity rules to ensure both are deployed to the same node, rack, or datacenter, but then you'd have to specify exactly which node, rack, or datacenter to schedule them to, which is not the best solution. It's better to let Kubernetes deploy your pods anywhere it sees fit, while keeping the frontend and backend pods close together. This can be achieved using *pod affinity*. Let's learn more about it with an example.

16.3.1 *Using inter-pod affinity to deploy pods on the same node*

You'll deploy a backend pod and five frontend pod replicas with pod affinity configured so that they're all deployed on the same node as the backend pod.

First, deploy the backend pod:

```
$ kubectl run backend -l app=backend --image busybox -- sleep 999999
deployment "backend" created
```

This Deployment is not special in any way. The only thing you need to note is the app=backend label you added to the pod using the -1 option. This label is what you'll use in the frontend pod's podAffinity configuration.

SPECIFYING POD AFFINITY IN A POD DEFINITION

The frontend pod's definition is shown in the following listing.

Listing 16.13   Pod using `podAffinity`: frontend-podaffinity-host.yaml

```
apiVersion: extensions/v1beta1
kind: Deployment
metadata:
  name: frontend
spec:
  replicas: 5
  template:
    ...
    spec:
      affinity:
        podAffinity:
          requiredDuringSchedulingIgnoredDuringExecution:
          - topologyKey: kubernetes.io/hostname
            labelSelector:
              matchLabels:
                app: backend
    ...
```

Defining
podAffinity rules

Defining a hard
requirement, not
a preference

The pods of this Deployment
must be deployed on the
same node as the pods that
match the selector.

The listing shows that this Deployment will create pods that have a hard requirement to be deployed on the same node (specified by the topologyKey field) as pods that have the app=backend label (see figure 16.4).

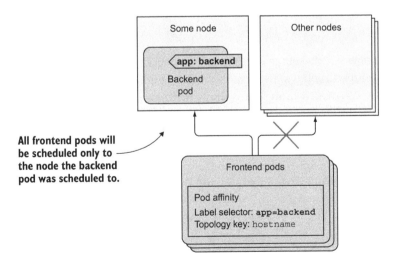

Figure 16.4   Pod affinity allows scheduling pods to the node where other pods with a specific label are.

NOTE   Instead of the simpler `matchLabels` field, you could also use the more expressive `matchExpressions` field.

DEPLOYING A POD WITH POD AFFINITY

Before you create this Deployment, let's see which node the backend pod was scheduled to earlier:

```
$ kubectl get po -o wide
NAME                   READY   STATUS    RESTARTS   AGE   IP           NODE
backend-257820-qhqj6   1/1     Running   0          8m    10.47.0.1    node2.k8s
```

When you create the frontend pods, they should be deployed to `node2` as well. You're going to create the Deployment and see where the pods are deployed. This is shown in the next listing.

Listing 16.14   **Deploying frontend pods and seeing which node they're scheduled to**

```
$ kubectl create -f frontend-podaffinity-host.yaml
deployment "frontend" created

$ kubectl get po -o wide
NAME                    READY   STATUS    RESTARTS   AGE   IP           NODE
backend-257820-qhqj6    1/1     Running   0          8m    10.47.0.1    node2.k8s
frontend-121895-2c1ts   1/1     Running   0          13s   10.47.0.6    node2.k8s
frontend-121895-776m7   1/1     Running   0          13s   10.47.0.4    node2.k8s
frontend-121895-7ffsm   1/1     Running   0          13s   10.47.0.8    node2.k8s
frontend-121895-fpgm6   1/1     Running   0          13s   10.47.0.7    node2.k8s
frontend-121895-vb9ll   1/1     Running   0          13s   10.47.0.5    node2.k8s
```

All the frontend pods were indeed scheduled to the same node as the backend pod. When scheduling the frontend pod, the Scheduler first found all the pods that match the `labelSelector` defined in the frontend pod's `podAffinity` configuration and then scheduled the frontend pod to the same node.

UNDERSTANDING HOW THE SCHEDULER USES POD AFFINITY RULES

What's interesting is that if you now delete the backend pod, the Scheduler will schedule the pod to `node2` even though it doesn't define any pod affinity rules itself (the rules are only on the frontend pods). This makes sense, because otherwise if the backend pod were to be deleted by accident and rescheduled to a different node, the frontend pods' affinity rules would be broken.

You can confirm the Scheduler takes other pods' pod affinity rules into account, if you increase the Scheduler's logging level and then check its log. The following listing shows the relevant log lines.

Listing 16.15   **Scheduler log showing why the backend pod is scheduled to** `node2`

```
... Attempting to schedule pod: default/backend-257820-qhqj6
... ...
... backend-qhqj6 -> node2.k8s: Taint Toleration Priority, Score: (10)
```

```
... backend-qhqj6 -> node1.k8s: Taint Toleration Priority, Score: (10)
... backend-qhqj6 -> node2.k8s: InterPodAffinityPriority, Score: (10)
... backend-qhqj6 -> node1.k8s: InterPodAffinityPriority, Score: (0)
... backend-qhqj6 -> node2.k8s: SelectorSpreadPriority, Score: (10)
... backend-qhqj6 -> node1.k8s: SelectorSpreadPriority, Score: (10)
... backend-qhqj6 -> node2.k8s: NodeAffinityPriority, Score: (0)
... backend-qhqj6 -> node1.k8s: NodeAffinityPriority, Score: (0)
... Host node2.k8s => Score 100030
... Host node1.k8s => Score 100022
... Attempting to bind backend-257820-qhqj6 to node2.k8s
```

If you focus on the two lines in bold, you'll see that during the scheduling of the back-end pod, node2 received a higher score than node1 because of inter-pod affinity.

16.3.2 *Deploying pods in the same rack, availability zone, or geographic region*

In the previous example, you used podAffinity to deploy frontend pods onto the same node as the backend pods. You probably don't want all your frontend pods to run on the same machine, but you'd still like to keep them close to the backend pod—for example, run them in the same availability zone.

CO-LOCATING PODS IN THE SAME AVAILABILITY ZONE

The cluster I'm using runs in three VMs on my local machine, so all the nodes are in the same availability zone, so to speak. But if the nodes were in different zones, all I'd need to do to run the frontend pods in the same zone as the backend pod would be to change the topologyKey property to failure-domain.beta.kubernetes.io/zone.

CO-LOCATING PODS IN THE SAME GEOGRAPHICAL REGION

To allow the pods to be deployed in the same region instead of the same zone (cloud providers usually have datacenters located in different geographical regions and split into multiple availability zones in each region), the topologyKey would be set to failure-domain.beta.kubernetes.io/region.

UNDERSTANDING HOW TOPOLOGYKEY WORKS

The way topologyKey works is simple. The three keys we've mentioned so far aren't special. If you want, you can easily use your own topologyKey, such as rack, to have the pods scheduled to the same server rack. The only prerequisite is to add a rack label to your nodes. This scenario is shown in figure 16.5.

For example, if you had 20 nodes, with 10 in each rack, you'd label the first ten as rack=rack1 and the others as rack=rack2. Then, when defining a pod's podAffinity, you'd set the toplogyKey to rack.

When the Scheduler is deciding where to deploy a pod, it checks the pod's pod-Affinity config, finds the pods that match the label selector, and looks up the nodes they're running on. Specifically, it looks up the nodes' label whose key matches the topologyKey field specified in podAffinity. Then it selects all the nodes whose label

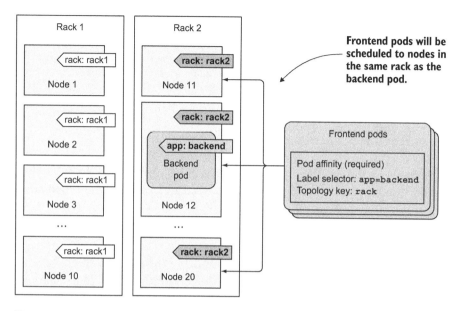

Figure 16.5 The `topologyKey` in `podAffinity` **determines the scope of where the pod should be scheduled to.**

matches the values of the pods it found earlier. In figure 16.5, the label selector matched the backend pod, which runs on Node 12. The value of the `rack` label on that node equals `rack2`, so when scheduling a frontend pod, the Scheduler will only select among the nodes that have the `rack=rack2` label.

> **NOTE** By default, the label selector only matches pods in the same namespace as the pod that's being scheduled. But you can also select pods from other namespaces by adding a `namespaces` field at the same level as `label-Selector`.

16.3.3 *Expressing pod affinity preferences instead of hard requirements*

Earlier, when we talked about node affinity, you saw that `nodeAffinity` can be used to express a hard requirement, which means a pod is only scheduled to nodes that match the node affinity rules. It can also be used to specify node preferences, to instruct the Scheduler to schedule the pod to certain nodes, while allowing it to schedule it anywhere else if those nodes can't fit the pod for any reason.

The same also applies to `podAffinity`. You can tell the Scheduler you'd prefer to have your frontend pods scheduled onto the same node as your backend pod, but if that's not possible, you're okay with them being scheduled elsewhere. An example of a Deployment using the `preferredDuringSchedulingIgnoredDuringExecution` pod affinity rule is shown in the next listing.

Listing 16.16   Pod affinity preference

```
apiVersion: extensions/v1beta1
kind: Deployment
metadata:
  name: frontend
spec:
  replicas: 5
  template:
    ...
    spec:
      affinity:
        podAffinity:
          preferredDuringSchedulingIgnoredDuringExecution:    ◁──
          - weight: 80
            podAffinityTerm:
              topologyKey: kubernetes.io/hostname
              labelSelector:
                matchLabels:
                  app: backend
      containers: ...
```

Preferred instead of Required

A weight and a podAffinity term is specified as in the previous example

As in `nodeAffinity` preference rules, you need to define a weight for each rule. You also need to specify the `topologyKey` and `labelSelector`, as in the hard-requirement `podAffinity` rules. Figure 16.6 shows this scenario.

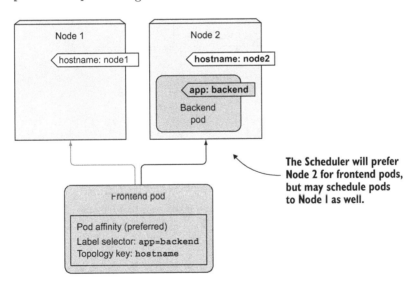

Figure 16.6   Pod affinity can be used to make the Scheduler prefer nodes where pods with a certain label are running.

Deploying this pod, as with your `nodeAffinity` example, deploys four pods on the same node as the backend pod, and one pod on the other node (see the following listing).

Listing 16.17   Pods deployed with `podAffinity` preferences

```
$ kubectl get po -o wide
NAME                      READY   STATUS    RESTARTS   AGE   IP           NODE
backend-257820-ssrgj      1/1     Running   0          1h    10.47.0.9    node2.k8s
frontend-941083-3mff9     1/1     Running   0          8m    10.44.0.4    node1.k8s
frontend-941083-7fp7d     1/1     Running   0          8m    10.47.0.6    node2.k8s
frontend-941083-cq23b     1/1     Running   0          8m    10.47.0.1    node2.k8s
frontend-941083-m70sw     1/1     Running   0          8m    10.47.0.5    node2.k8s
frontend-941083-wsjv8     1/1     Running   0          8m    10.47.0.4    node2.k8s
```

16.3.4 *Scheduling pods away from each other with pod anti-affinity*

You've seen how to tell the Scheduler to co-locate pods, but sometimes you may want the exact opposite. You may want to keep pods away from each other. This is called pod anti-affinity. It's specified the same way as pod affinity, except that you use the `podAntiAffinity` property instead of `podAffinity`, which results in the Scheduler never choosing nodes where pods matching the `podAntiAffinity`'s label selector are running, as shown in figure 16.7.

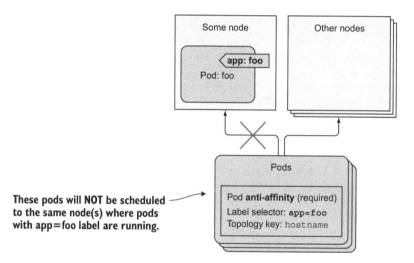

Figure 16.7   Using pod anti-affinity to keep pods away from nodes that run pods with a certain label.

An example of why you'd want to use pod anti-affinity is when two sets of pods interfere with each other's performance if they run on the same node. In that case, you want to tell the Scheduler to never schedule those pods on the same node. Another example would be to force the Scheduler to spread pods of the same group across different availability zones or regions, so that a failure of a whole zone (or region) never brings the service down completely.

USING ANTI-AFFINITY TO SPREAD APART PODS OF THE SAME DEPLOYMENT

Let's see how to force your frontend pods to be scheduled to different nodes. The following listing shows how the pods' anti-affinity is configured.

Listing 16.18   Pods with anti-affinity: frontend-podantiaffinity-host.yaml

```
apiVersion: extensions/v1beta1
kind: Deployment
metadata:
  name: frontend
spec:
  replicas: 5
  template:
    metadata:
      labels:
        app: frontend          The frontend pods have
                                the app=frontend label.
      spec:
        affinity:                                              Defining hard-
          podAntiAffinity:                                     requirements for
            requiredDuringSchedulingIgnoredDuringExecution:    pod anti-affinity
            - topologyKey: kubernetes.io/hostname     A frontend pod must not
              labelSelector:                          be scheduled to the same
                matchLabels:                          machine as a pod with
                  app: frontend                       app=frontend label.
        containers: ...
```

This time, you're defining `podAntiAffinity` instead of `podAffinity`, and you're making the `labelSelector` match the same pods that the Deployment creates. Let's see what happens when you create this Deployment. The pods created by it are shown in the following listing.

Listing 16.19   Pods created by the Deployment

```
$ kubectl get po -l app=frontend -o wide
NAME                    READY  STATUS   RESTARTS  AGE  IP          NODE
frontend-286632-0lffz   0/1    Pending  0         1m   <none>
frontend-286632-2rkcz   1/1    Running  0         1m   10.47.0.1   node2.k8s
frontend-286632-4nwhp   0/1    Pending  0         1m   <none>
frontend-286632-l4686   0/1    Pending  0         1m   <none>
frontend-286632-st222   1/1    Running  0         1m   10.44.0.4   node1.k8s
```

As you can see, only two pods were scheduled—one to node1, the other to node2. The three remaining pods are all `Pending`, because the Scheduler isn't allowed to schedule them to the same nodes.

USING PREFERENTIAL POD ANTI-AFFINITY

In this case, you probably should have specified a soft requirement instead (using the `preferredDuringSchedulingIgnoredDuringExecution` property). After all, it's not such a big problem if two frontend pods run on the same node. But in scenarios where that's a problem, using `requiredDuringScheduling` is appropriate.

As with pod affinity, the `topologyKey` property determines the scope of where the pod shouldn't be deployed to. You can use it to ensure pods aren't deployed to the same rack, availability zone, region, or any custom scope you create using custom node labels.

16.4 Summary

In this chapter, we looked at how to ensure pods aren't scheduled to certain nodes or are only scheduled to specific nodes, either because of the node's labels or because of the pods running on them.

You learned that

- If you add a taint to a node, pods won't be scheduled to that node unless they tolerate that taint.
- Three types of taints exist: `NoSchedule` completely prevents scheduling, `Prefer-NoSchedule` isn't as strict, and `NoExecute` even evicts existing pods from a node.
- The `NoExecute` taint is also used to specify how long the Control Plane should wait before rescheduling the pod when the node it runs on becomes unreachable or unready.
- Node affinity allows you to specify which nodes a pod should be scheduled to. It can be used to specify a hard requirement or to only express a node preference.
- Pod affinity is used to make the Scheduler deploy pods to the same node where another pod is running (based on the pod's labels).
- Pod affinity's `topologyKey` specifies how close the pod should be deployed to the other pod (onto the same node or onto a node in the same rack, availability zone, or availability region).
- Pod anti-affinity can be used to keep certain pods away from each other.
- Both pod affinity and anti-affinity, like node affinity, can either specify hard requirements or preferences.

In the next chapter, you'll learn about best practices for developing apps and how to make them run smoothly in a Kubernetes environment.

Best practices
for developing apps

This chapter covers

- Understanding which Kubernetes resources appear in a typical application
- Adding post-start and pre-stop pod lifecycle hooks
- Properly terminating an app without breaking client requests
- Making apps easy to manage in Kubernetes
- Using init containers in a pod
- Developing locally with Minikube

We've now covered most of what you need to know to run your apps in Kubernetes. We've explored what each individual resource does and how it's used. Now we'll see how to combine them in a typical application running on Kubernetes. We'll also look at how to make an application run smoothly. After all, that's the whole point of using Kubernetes, isn't it?

Hopefully, this chapter will help to clear up any misunderstandings and explain things that weren't explained clearly yet. Along the way, we'll also introduce a few additional concepts that haven't been mentioned up to this point.

17.1 *Bringing everything together*

Let's start by looking at what an actual application consists of. This will also give you a chance to see if you remember everything you've learned so far and look at the big picture. Figure 17.1 shows the Kubernetes components used in a typical application.

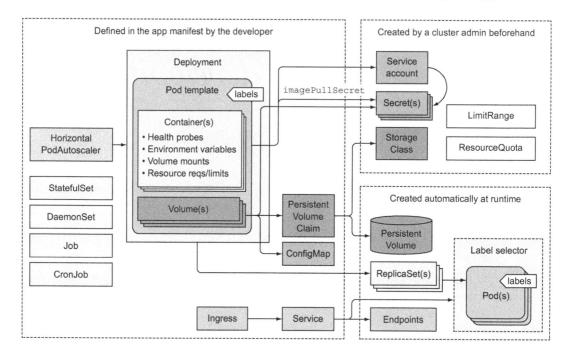

Figure 17.1   Resources in a typical application

A typical application manifest contains one or more Deployment and/or StatefulSet objects. Those include a pod template containing one or more containers, with a liveness probe for each of them and a readiness probe for the service(s) the container provides (if any). Pods that provide services to others are exposed through one or more Services. When they need to be reachable from outside the cluster, the Services are either configured to be `LoadBalancer` or `NodePort`-type Services, or exposed through an Ingress resource.

The pod templates (and the pods created from them) usually reference two types of Secrets—those for pulling container images from private image registries and those used directly by the process running inside the pods. The Secrets themselves are usually not part of the application manifest, because they aren't configured by the application developers but by the operations team. Secrets are usually assigned to ServiceAccounts, which are assigned to individual pods.

The application also contains one or more ConfigMaps, which are either used to initialize environment variables or mounted as a `configMap` volume in the pod. Certain pods use additional volumes, such as an `emptyDir` or a `gitRepo` volume, whereas pods requiring persistent storage use `persistentVolumeClaim` volumes. The Persistent-VolumeClaims are also part of the application manifest, whereas StorageClasses referenced by them are created by system administrators upfront.

In certain cases, an application also requires the use of Jobs or CronJobs. Daemon-Sets aren't normally part of application deployments, but are usually created by sysadmins to run system services on all or a subset of nodes. HorizontalPodAutoscalers are either included in the manifest by the developers or added to the system later by the ops team. The cluster administrator also creates LimitRange and ResourceQuota objects to keep compute resource usage of individual pods and all the pods (as a whole) under control.

After the application is deployed, additional objects are created automatically by the various Kubernetes controllers. These include service Endpoints objects created by the Endpoints controller, ReplicaSets created by the Deployment controller, and the actual pods created by the ReplicaSet (or Job, CronJob, StatefulSet, or DaemonSet) controllers.

Resources are often labeled with one or more labels to keep them organized. This doesn't apply only to pods but to all other resources as well. In addition to labels, most resources also contain annotations that describe each resource, list the contact information of the person or team responsible for it, or provide additional metadata for management and other tools.

At the center of all this is the Pod, which arguably is the most important Kubernetes resource. After all, each of your applications runs inside it. To make sure you know how to develop apps that make the most out of their environment, let's take one last close look at pods—this time from the application's perspective.

17.2 *Understanding the pod's lifecycle*

We've said that pods can be compared to VMs dedicated to running only a single application. Although an application running inside a pod is not unlike an application running in a VM, significant differences do exist. One example is that apps running in a pod can be killed any time, because Kubernetes needs to relocate the pod to another node for a reason or because of a scale-down request. We'll explore this aspect next.

17.2.1 *Applications must expect to be killed and relocated*

Outside Kubernetes, apps running in VMs are seldom moved from one machine to another. When an operator moves the app, they can also reconfigure the app and manually check that the app is running fine in the new location. With Kubernetes, apps are relocated much more frequently and automatically—no human operator reconfigures them and makes sure they still run properly after the move. This means application developers need to make sure their apps allow being moved relatively often.

EXPECTING THE LOCAL IP AND HOSTNAME TO CHANGE

When a pod is killed and run elsewhere (technically, it's a new pod instance replacing the old one; the pod isn't relocated), it not only has a new IP address but also a new name and hostname. Most stateless apps can usually handle this without any adverse effects, but stateful apps usually can't. We've learned that stateful apps can be run through a StatefulSet, which ensures that when the app starts up on a new node after being rescheduled, it will still see the same host name and persistent state as before. The pod's IP will change nevertheless. Apps need to be prepared for that to happen. The application developer therefore should never base membership in a clustered app on the member's IP address, and if basing it on the hostname, should always use a StatefulSet.

EXPECTING THE DATA WRITTEN TO DISK TO DISAPPEAR

Another thing to keep in mind is that if the app writes data to disk, that data may not be available after the app is started inside a new pod, unless you mount persistent storage at the location the app is writing to. It should be clear this happens when the pod is rescheduled, but files written to disk will disappear even in scenarios that don't involve any rescheduling. Even during the lifetime of a single pod, the files written to disk by the app running in the pod may disappear. Let me explain this with an example.

Imagine an app that has a long and computationally intensive initial startup procedure. To help the app come up faster on subsequent startups, the developers make the app cache the results of the initial startup on disk (an example of this would be the scanning of all Java classes for annotations at startup and then writing the results to an index file). Because apps in Kubernetes run in containers by default, these files are written to the container's filesystem. If the container is then restarted, they're all lost, because the new container starts off with a completely new writable layer (see figure 17.2).

Don't forget that individual containers may be restarted for several reasons, such as because the process crashes, because the liveness probe returned a failure, or because the node started running out of memory and the process was killed by the OOMKiller. When this happens, the pod is still the same, but the container itself is completely new. The Kubelet doesn't run the same container again; it always creates a new container.

USING VOLUMES TO PRESERVE DATA ACROSS CONTAINER RESTARTS

When its container is restarted, the app in the example will need to perform the intensive startup procedure again. This may or may not be desired. To make sure data like this isn't lost, you need to use at least a pod-scoped volume. Because volumes live and die together with the pod, the new container will be able to reuse the data written to the volume by the previous container (figure 17.3).

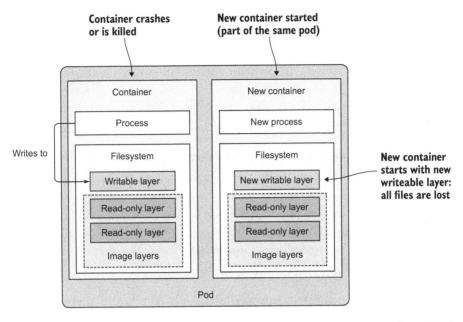

Figure 17.2 Files written to the container's filesystem are lost when the container is restarted.

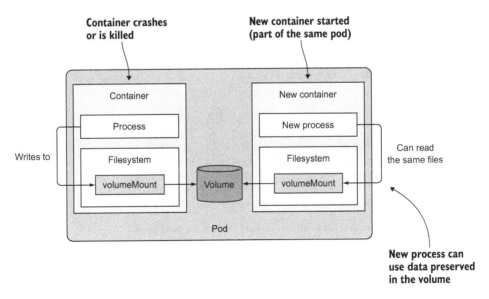

Figure 17.3 Using a volume to persist data across container restarts

Using a volume to preserve files across container restarts is a great idea sometimes, but not always. What if the data gets corrupted and causes the newly created process to crash again? This will result in a continuous crash loop (the pod will show the `CrashLoopBackOff` status). If you hadn't used a volume, the new container would start from scratch and most likely not crash. Using volumes to preserve files across container restarts like this is a double-edged sword. You need to think carefully about whether to use them or not.

17.2.2 *Rescheduling of dead or partially dead pods*

If a pod's container keeps crashing, the Kubelet will keep restarting it indefinitely. The time between restarts will be increased exponentially until it reaches five minutes. During those five minute intervals, the pod is essentially dead, because its container's process isn't running. To be fair, if it's a multi-container pod, certain containers may be running normally, so the pod is only partially dead. But if a pod contains only a single container, the pod is effectively dead and completely useless, because no process is running in it anymore.

You may find it surprising to learn that such pods aren't automatically removed and rescheduled, even if they're part of a ReplicaSet or similar controller. If you create a ReplicaSet with a desired replica count of three, and then one of the containers in one of those pods starts crashing, Kubernetes will not delete and replace the pod. The end result is a ReplicaSet with only two properly running replicas instead of the desired three (figure 17.4).

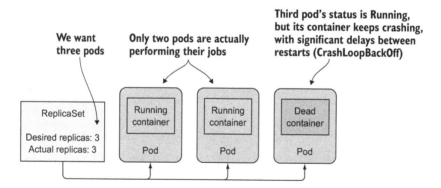

Figure 17.4 A ReplicaSet controller doesn't reschedule dead pods.

You'd probably expect the pod to be deleted and replaced with another pod instance that might run successfully on another node. After all, the container may be crashing because of a node-related problem that doesn't manifest itself on other nodes. Sadly, that isn't the case. The ReplicaSet controller doesn't care if the pods are dead—all it cares about is that the number of pods matches the desired replica count, which in this case, it does.

If you'd like to see for yourself, I've included a YAML manifest for a ReplicaSet whose pods will keep crashing (see file replicaset-crashingpods.yaml in the code archive). If you create the ReplicaSet and inspect the pods that are created, the following listing is what you'll see.

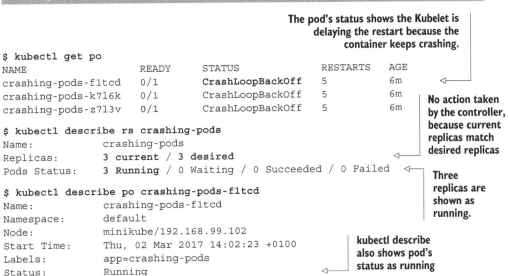

> **Listing 17.1   ReplicaSet and pods that keep crashing**

```
                                              The pod's status shows the Kubelet is
                                               delaying the restart because the
                                                  container keeps crashing.

$ kubectl get po
NAME                   READY    STATUS            RESTARTS    AGE
crashing-pods-f1tcd    0/1      CrashLoopBackOff  5           6m
crashing-pods-k716k    0/1      CrashLoopBackOff  5           6m      No action taken
crashing-pods-z7l3v    0/1      CrashLoopBackOff  5           6m      by the controller,
                                                                     because current
$ kubectl describe rs crashing-pods                                  replicas match
Name:           crashing-pods                                        desired replicas
Replicas:       3 current / 3 desired
Pods Status:    3 Running / 0 Waiting / 0 Succeeded / 0 Failed       Three
                                                                     replicas are
$ kubectl describe po crashing-pods-f1tcd                            shown as
Name:           crashing-pods-f1tcd                                  running.
Namespace:      default
Node:           minikube/192.168.99.102               kubectl describe
Start Time:     Thu, 02 Mar 2017 14:02:23 +0100       also shows pod's
Labels:         app=crashing-pods                     status as running
Status:         Running
```

In a way, it's understandable that Kubernetes behaves this way. The container will be restarted every five minutes in the hope that the underlying cause of the crash will be resolved. The rationale is that rescheduling the pod to another node most likely wouldn't fix the problem anyway, because the app is running inside a container and all the nodes should be mostly equivalent. That's not always the case, but it is most of the time.

17.2.3   *Starting pods in a specific order*

One other difference between apps running in pods and those managed manually is that the ops person deploying those apps knows about the dependencies between them. This allows them to start the apps in order.

UNDERSTANDING HOW PODS ARE STARTED

When you use Kubernetes to run your multi-pod applications, you don't have a built-in way to tell Kubernetes to run certain pods first and the rest only when the first pods are already up and ready to serve. Sure, you could post the manifest for the first app and then wait for the pod(s) to be ready before you post the second manifest, but your whole system is usually defined in a single YAML or JSON containing multiple Pods, Services, and other objects.

The Kubernetes API server does process the objects in the YAML/JSON in the order they're listed, but this only means they're written to etcd in that order. You have no guarantee that pods will also be started in that order.

But you *can* prevent a pod's main container from starting until a precondition is met. This is done by including an init containers in the pod.

INTRODUCING INIT CONTAINERS

In addition to regular containers, pods can also include init containers. As the name suggests, they can be used to initialize the pod—this often means writing data to the pod's volumes, which are then mounted into the pod's main container(s).

A pod may have any number of init containers. They're executed sequentially and only after the last one completes are the pod's main containers started. This means init containers can also be used to delay the start of the pod's main container(s)—for example, until a certain precondition is met. An init container could wait for a service required by the pod's main container to be up and ready. When it is, the init container terminates and allows the main container(s) to be started. This way, the main container wouldn't use the service before it's ready.

Let's look at an example of a pod using an init container to delay the start of the main container. Remember the `fortune` pod you created in chapter 7? It's a web server that returns a fortune quote as a response to client requests. Now, let's imagine you have a `fortune-client` pod that requires the `fortune` Service to be up and running before its main container starts. You can add an init container, which checks whether the Service is responding to requests. Until that's the case, the init container keeps retrying. Once it gets a response, the init container terminates and lets the main container start.

ADDING AN INIT CONTAINER TO A POD

Init containers can be defined in the pod spec like main containers but through the `spec.initContainers` field. You'll find the complete YAML for the fortune-client pod in the book's code archive. The following listing shows the part where the init container is defined.

Listing 17.2   An init container defined in a pod: fortune-client.yaml

```
spec:
  initContainers:
  - name: init                    ◁── You're defining
    image: busybox                    an init container,
    command:                          not a regular
    - sh                              container.
    - -c
    - 'while true; do echo "Waiting for fortune service to come up...";   The init container runs a
      wget http://fortune -q -T 1 -O /dev/null >/dev/null 2>/dev/null     loop that runs until the
      && break; sleep 1; done; echo "Service is up! Starting main         fortune Service is up.
      container."'
```

When you deploy this pod, only its init container is started. This is shown in the pod's status when you list pods with `kubectl get`:

```
$ kubectl get po
NAME              READY    STATUS      RESTARTS    AGE
fortune-client    0/1      Init:0/1    0           1m
```

The `STATUS` column shows that zero of one init containers have finished. You can see the log of the init container with `kubectl logs`:

```
$ kubectl logs fortune-client -c init
Waiting for fortune service to come up...
```

When running the `kubectl logs` command, you need to specify the name of the init container with the `-c` switch (in the example, the name of the pod's init container is init, as you can see in listing 17.2).

The main container won't run until you deploy the `fortune` Service and the `fortune-server` pod. You'll find them in the fortune-server.yaml file.

BEST PRACTICES FOR HANDLING INTER-POD DEPENDENCIES

You've seen how an init container can be used to delay starting the pod's main container(s) until a precondition is met (making sure the Service the pod depends on is ready, for example), but it's much better to write apps that don't require every service they rely on to be ready before the app starts up. After all, the service may also go offline later, while the app is already running.

The application needs to handle internally the possibility that its dependencies aren't ready. And don't forget readiness probes. If an app can't do its job because one of its dependencies is missing, it should signal that through its readiness probe, so Kubernetes knows it, too, isn't ready. You'll want to do this not only because it prevents the app from being added as a service endpoint, but also because the app's readiness is also used by the Deployment controller when performing a rolling update, thereby preventing a rollout of a bad version.

17.2.4 Adding lifecycle hooks

We've talked about how init containers can be used to hook into the startup of the pod, but pods also allow you to define two lifecycle hooks:

- *Post-start* hooks
- *Pre-stop* hooks

These lifecycle hooks are specified per container, unlike init containers, which apply to the whole pod. As their names suggest, they're executed when the container starts and before it stops.

Lifecycle hooks are similar to liveness and readiness probes in that they can either

- Execute a command inside the container
- Perform an HTTP GET request against a URL

Let's look at the two hooks individually to see what effect they have on the container lifecycle.

USING A POST-START CONTAINER LIFECYCLE HOOK

A post-start hook is executed immediately after the container's main process is started. You use it to perform additional operations when the application starts. Sure, if you're the author of the application running in the container, you can always perform those operations inside the application code itself. But when you're running an application developed by someone else, you mostly don't want to (or can't) modify its source code. Post-start hooks allow you to run additional commands without having to touch the app. These may signal to an external listener that the app is starting, or they may initialize the application so it can start doing its job.

The hook is run in parallel with the main process. The name might be somewhat misleading, because it doesn't wait for the main process to start up fully (if the process has an initialization procedure, the Kubelet obviously can't wait for the procedure to complete, because it has no way of knowing when that is).

But even though the hook runs asynchronously, it does affect the container in two ways. Until the hook completes, the container will stay in the `Waiting` state with the reason `ContainerCreating`. Because of this, the pod's status will be `Pending` instead of `Running`. If the hook fails to run or returns a non-zero exit code, the main container will be killed.

A pod manifest containing a post-start hook looks like the following listing.

Listing 17.3   A pod with a post-start lifecycle hook: post-start-hook.yaml

```
apiVersion: v1
kind: Pod
metadata:
  name: pod-with-poststart-hook
spec:
  containers:
  - image: luksa/kubia
    name: kubia
    lifecycle:              The hook is executed as
      postStart:            the container starts.
        exec:
          command:
          - sh
          - -c
          - "echo 'hook will fail with exit code 15'; sleep 5; exit 15"
```

It executes the postStart.sh script in the /bin directory inside the container.

In the example, the `echo`, `sleep`, and `exit` commands are executed along with the container's main process as soon as the container is created. Rather than run a command like this, you'd typically run a shell script or a binary executable file stored in the container image.

Sadly, if the process started by the hook logs to the standard output, you can't see the output anywhere. This makes debugging lifecycle hooks painful. If the hook fails, you'll only see a `FailedPostStartHook` warning among the pod's events (you can see them using `kubectl describe pod`). A while later, you'll see more information on why the hook failed, as shown in the following listing.

Listing 17.4   Pod's events showing the exit code of the failed command-based hook

```
FailedSync    Error syncing pod, skipping: failed to "StartContainer" for
              "kubia" with PostStart handler: command 'sh -c echo 'hook
              will fail with exit code 15'; sleep 5 ; exit 15' exited
              with 15: : "PostStart Hook Failed"
```

The number 15 in the last line is the exit code of the command. When using an HTTP GET hook handler, the reason may look like the following listing (you can try this by deploying the post-start-hook-httpget.yaml file from the book's code archive).

Listing 17.5   Pod's events showing the reason why an HTTP GET hook failed

```
FailedSync    Error syncing pod, skipping: failed to "StartContainer" for
              "kubia" with PostStart handler: Get
              http://10.32.0.2:9090/postStart: dial tcp 10.32.0.2:9090:
              getsockopt: connection refused: "PostStart Hook Failed"
```

> **NOTE** The post-start hook is intentionally misconfigured to use port 9090 instead of the correct port 8080, to show what happens when the hook fails.

The standard and error outputs of command-based post-start hooks aren't logged anywhere, so you may want to have the process the hook invokes log to a file in the container's filesystem, which will allow you to examine the contents of the file with something like this:

```
$ kubectl exec my-pod cat logfile.txt
```

If the container gets restarted for whatever reason (including because the hook failed), the file may be gone before you can examine it. You can work around that by mounting an `emptyDir` volume into the container and having the hook write to it.

USING A PRE-STOP CONTAINER LIFECYCLE HOOK

A pre-stop hook is executed immediately before a container is terminated. When a container needs to be terminated, the Kubelet will run the pre-stop hook, if configured, and only then send a `SIGTERM` to the process (and later kill the process if it doesn't terminate gracefully).

A pre-stop hook can be used to initiate a graceful shutdown of the container, if it doesn't shut down gracefully upon receipt of a `SIGTERM` signal. They can also be used to perform arbitrary operations before shutdown without having to implement those operations in the application itself (this is useful when you're running a third-party app, whose source code you don't have access to and/or can't modify).

Configuring a pre-stop hook in a pod manifest isn't very different from adding a post-start hook. The previous example showed a post-start hook that executes a command, so we'll look at a pre-stop hook that performs an HTTP GET request now. The following listing shows how to define a pre-stop HTTP GET hook in a pod.

Listing 17.6   A pre-stop hook YAML snippet: pre-stop-hook-httpget.yaml

```
lifecycle:
  preStop:                    This is a pre-stop hook that
    httpGet:                  performs an HTTP GET request.
      port: 8080
      path: shutdown          The request is sent to
                              http://POD_IP:8080/shutdown.
```

The pre-stop hook defined in this listing performs an HTTP GET request to http://POD_IP:8080/shutdown as soon as the Kubelet starts terminating the container. Apart from the `port` and `path` shown in the listing, you can also set the fields `scheme` (HTTP or HTTPS) and `host`, as well as `httpHeaders` that should be sent in the request. The `host` field defaults to the pod IP. Be sure not to set it to localhost, because localhost would refer to the node, not the pod.

In contrast to the post-start hook, the container will be terminated regardless of the result of the hook—an error HTTP response code or a non-zero exit code when using a command-based hook will not prevent the container from being terminated. If the pre-stop hook fails, you'll see a `FailedPreStopHook` warning event among the pod's events, but because the pod is deleted soon afterward (after all, the pod's deletion is what triggered the pre-stop hook in the first place), you may not even notice that the pre-stop hook failed to run properly.

> **TIP** If the successful completion of the pre-stop hook is critical to the proper operation of your system, verify whether it's being executed at all. I've witnessed situations where the pre-stop hook didn't run and the developer wasn't even aware of that.

USING A PRE-STOP HOOK BECAUSE YOUR APP DOESN'T RECEIVE THE SIGTERM SIGNAL

Many developers make the mistake of defining a pre-stop hook solely to send a SIGTERM signal to their apps in the pre-stop hook. They do this because they don't see their application receive the SIGTERM signal sent by the Kubelet. The reason why the signal isn't received by the application isn't because Kubernetes isn't sending it, but because the signal isn't being passed to the app process inside the container itself. If your container image is configured to run a shell, which in turn runs the app process, the signal may be eaten up by the shell itself, instead of being passed down to the child process.

In such cases, instead of adding a pre-stop hook to send the signal directly to your app, the proper fix is to make sure the shell passes the signal to the app. This can be achieved by handling the signal in the shell script running as the main container process and then passing it on to the app. Or you could not configure the container image to run a shell at all and instead run the application binary directly. You do this by using the exec form of ENTRYPOINT or CMD in the Dockerfile: ENTRYPOINT ["/mybinary"] instead of ENTRYPOINT /mybinary.

A container using the first form runs the `mybinary` executable as its main process, whereas the second form runs a shell as the main process with the `mybinary` process executed as a child of the shell process.

UNDERSTANDING THAT LIFECYCLE HOOKS TARGET CONTAINERS, NOT PODS

As a final thought on post-start and pre-stop hooks, let me emphasize that these lifecycle hooks relate to containers, not pods. You shouldn't use a pre-stop hook for running actions that need to be performed when the pod is terminating. The reason is that the pre-stop hook gets called when the container is being terminated (most likely because of a failed liveness probe). This may happen multiple times in the pod's lifetime, not only when the pod is in the process of being shut down.

17.2.5 *Understanding pod shutdown*

We've touched on the subject of pod termination, so let's explore this subject in more detail and go over exactly what happens during pod shutdown. This is important for understanding how to cleanly shut down an application running in a pod.

Let's start at the beginning. A pod's shut-down is triggered by the deletion of the Pod object through the API server. Upon receiving an HTTP DELETE request, the API server doesn't delete the object yet, but only sets a `deletionTimestamp` field in it. Pods that have the `deletionTimestamp` field set are terminating.

Once the Kubelet notices the pod needs to be terminated, it starts terminating each of the pod's containers. It gives each container time to shut down gracefully, but the time is limited. That time is called the termination grace period and is configurable per pod. The timer starts as soon as the termination process starts. Then the following sequence of events is performed:

1 Run the pre-stop hook, if one is configured, and wait for it to finish.
2 Send the `SIGTERM` signal to the main process of the container.
3 Wait until the container shuts down cleanly or until the termination grace period runs out.
4 Forcibly kill the process with `SIGKILL`, if it hasn't terminated gracefully yet.

The sequence of events is illustrated in figure 17.5.

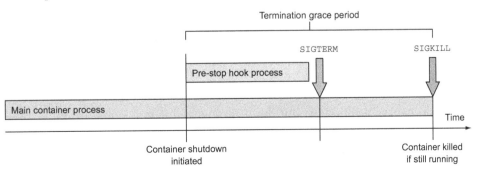

Figure 17.5 The container termination sequence

SPECIFYING THE TERMINATION GRACE PERIOD

The termination grace period can be configured in the pod spec by setting the `spec.terminationGracePeriodSeconds` field. It defaults to 30, which means the pod's containers will be given 30 seconds to terminate gracefully before they're killed forcibly.

> **TIP** You should set the grace period to long enough so your process can finish cleaning up in that time.

The grace period specified in the pod spec can also be overridden when deleting the pod like this:

```
$ kubectl delete po mypod --grace-period=5
```

This will make the Kubelet wait five seconds for the pod to shut down cleanly. When all the pod's containers stop, the Kubelet notifies the API server and the Pod resource is finally deleted. You can force the API server to delete the resource immediately, without waiting for confirmation, by setting the grace period to zero and adding the `--force` option like this:

```
$ kubectl delete po mypod --grace-period=0 --force
```

Be careful when using this option, especially with pods of a StatefulSet. The StatefulSet controller takes great care to never run two instances of the same pod at the same time (two pods with the same ordinal index and name and attached to the same PersistentVolume). By force-deleting a pod, you'll cause the controller to create a replacement pod without waiting for the containers of the deleted pod to shut down. In other words, two instances of the same pod might be running at the same time, which may cause your stateful cluster to malfunction. Only delete stateful pods forcibly when you're absolutely sure the pod isn't running anymore or can't talk to the other members of the cluster (you can be sure of this when you confirm that the node that hosted the pod has failed or has been disconnected from the network and can't reconnect).

Now that you understand how containers are shut down, let's look at it from the application's perspective and go over how applications should handle the shutdown procedure.

IMPLEMENTING THE PROPER SHUTDOWN HANDLER IN YOUR APPLICATION

Applications should react to a SIGTERM signal by starting their shut-down procedure and terminating when it finishes. Instead of handling the SIGTERM signal, the application can be notified to shut down through a pre-stop hook. In both cases, the app then only has a fixed amount of time to terminate cleanly.

But what if you can't predict how long the app will take to shut down cleanly? For example, imagine your app is a distributed data store. On scale-down, one of the pod instances will be deleted and therefore shut down. In the shut-down procedure, the pod needs to migrate all its data to the remaining pods to make sure it's not lost. Should the pod start migrating the data upon receiving a termination signal (through either the SIGTERM signal or through a pre-stop hook)?

Absolutely not! This is not recommended for at least the following two reasons:

- A container terminating doesn't necessarily mean the whole pod is being terminated.
- You have no guarantee the shut-down procedure will finish before the process is killed.

This second scenario doesn't happen only when the grace period runs out before the application has finished shutting down gracefully, but also when the node running the pod fails in the middle of the container shut-down sequence. Even if the node then starts up again, the Kubelet will not restart the shut-down procedure (it won't even start up the container again). There are absolutely no guarantees that the pod will be allowed to complete its whole shut-down procedure.

REPLACING CRITICAL SHUT-DOWN PROCEDURES WITH DEDICATED SHUT-DOWN PROCEDURE PODS

How do you ensure that a critical shut-down procedure that absolutely must run to completion does run to completion (for example, to ensure that a pod's data is migrated to other pods)?

One solution is for the app (upon receipt of a termination signal) to create a new Job resource that would run a new pod, whose sole job is to migrate the deleted pod's data to the remaining pods. But if you've been paying attention, you'll know that you have no guarantee the app will indeed manage to create the Job object every single time. What if the node fails exactly when the app tries to do that?

The proper way to handle this problem is by having a dedicated, constantly running pod that keeps checking for the existence of orphaned data. When this pod finds the orphaned data, it can migrate it to the remaining pods. Rather than a constantly running pod, you can also use a CronJob resource and run the pod periodically.

You may think StatefulSets could help here, but they don't. As you'll remember, scaling down a StatefulSet leaves PersistentVolumeClaims orphaned, leaving the data stored on the PersistentVolume stranded. Yes, upon a subsequent scale-up, the Persistent-Volume will be reattached to the new pod instance, but what if that scale-up never happens (or happens after a long time)? For this reason, you may want to run a data-migrating pod also when using StatefulSets (this scenario is shown in figure 17.6). To prevent the migration from occurring during an application upgrade, the data-migrating pod could be configured to wait a while to give the stateful pod time to come up again before performing the migration.

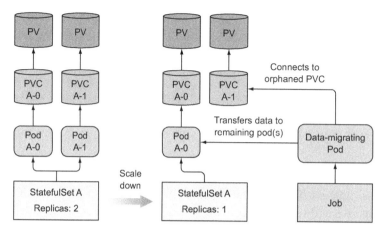

Figure 17.6   Using a dedicated pod to migrate data

17.3 *Ensuring all client requests are handled properly*

You now have a good sense of how to make pods shut down cleanly. Now, we'll look at the pod's lifecycle from the perspective of the pod's clients (clients consuming the service the pod is providing). This is important to understand if you don't want clients to run into problems when you scale pods up or down.

It goes without saying that you want all client requests to be handled properly. You obviously don't want to see broken connections when pods are starting up or shutting down. By itself, Kubernetes doesn't prevent this from happening. Your app needs to follow a few rules to prevent broken connections. First, let's focus on making sure all connections are handled properly when the pod starts up.

17.3.1 *Preventing broken client connections when a pod is starting up*

Ensuring each connection is handled properly at pod startup is simple if you understand how Services and service Endpoints work. When a pod is started, it's added as an endpoint to all the Services, whose label selector matches the pod's labels. As you may remember from chapter 5, the pod also needs to signal to Kubernetes that it's ready. Until it is, it won't become a service endpoint and therefore won't receive any requests from clients.

If you don't specify a readiness probe in your pod spec, the pod is always considered ready. It will start receiving requests almost immediately—as soon as the first kube-proxy updates the `iptables` rules on its node and the first client pod tries to connect to the service. If your app isn't ready to accept connections by then, clients will see "connection refused" types of errors.

All you need to do is make sure that your readiness probe returns success only when your app is ready to properly handle incoming requests. A good first step is to add an HTTP GET readiness probe and point it to the base URL of your app. In many cases that gets you far enough and saves you from having to implement a special readiness endpoint in your app.

17.3.2 Preventing broken connections during pod shut-down

Now let's see what happens at the other end of a pod's life—when the pod is deleted and its containers are terminated. We've already talked about how the pod's containers should start shutting down cleanly as soon they receive the SIGTERM signal (or when its pre-stop hook is executed). But does that ensure all client requests are handled properly?

How should the app behave when it receives a termination signal? Should it continue to accept requests? What about requests that have already been received but haven't completed yet? What about persistent HTTP connections, which may be in between requests, but are open (when no active request exists on the connection)? Before we can answer those questions, we need to take a detailed look at the chain of events that unfolds across the cluster when a Pod is deleted.

UNDERSTANDING THE SEQUENCE OF EVENTS OCCURRING AT POD DELETION

In chapter 11 we took an in-depth look at what components make up a Kubernetes cluster. You need to always keep in mind that those components run as separate processes on multiple machines. They aren't all part of a single big monolithic process. It takes time for all the components to be on the same page regarding the state of the cluster. Let's explore this fact by looking at what happens across the cluster when a Pod is deleted.

When a request for a pod deletion is received by the API server, it first modifies the state in etcd and then notifies its watchers of the deletion. Among those watchers are the Kubelet and the Endpoints controller. The two sequences of events, which happen in parallel (marked with either A or B), are shown in figure 17.7.

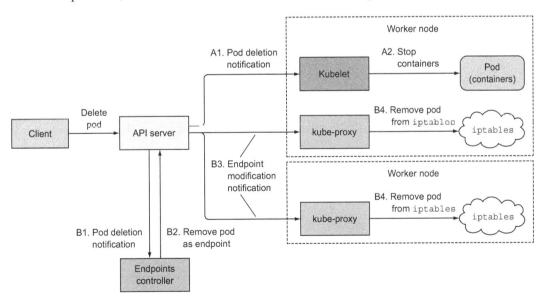

Figure 17.7　Sequence of events that occurs when a Pod is deleted

In the A sequence of events, you'll see that as soon as the Kubelet receives the notification that the pod should be terminated, it initiates the shutdown sequence as explained in section 17.2.5 (run the pre-stop hook, send SIGTERM, wait for a period of time, and then forcibly kill the container if it hasn't yet terminated on its own). If the app responds to the SIGTERM by immediately ceasing to receive client requests, any client trying to connect to it will receive a Connection Refused error. The time it takes for this to happen from the time the pod is deleted is relatively short because of the direct path from the API server to the Kubelet.

Now, let's look at what happens in the other sequence of events—the one leading up to the pod being removed from the iptables rules (sequence B in the figure). When the Endpoints controller (which runs in the Controller Manager in the Kubernetes Control Plane) receives the notification of the Pod being deleted, it removes the pod as an endpoint in all services that the pod is a part of. It does this by modifying the Endpoints API object by sending a REST request to the API server. The API server then notifies all clients watching the Endpoints object. Among those watchers are all the kube-proxies running on the worker nodes. Each of these proxies then updates the iptables rules on its node, which is what prevents new connections from being forwarded to the terminating pod. An important detail here is that removing the iptables rules has no effect on existing connections—clients who are already connected to the pod will still send additional requests to the pod through those existing connections.

Both of these sequences of events happen in parallel. Most likely, the time it takes to shut down the app's process in the pod is slightly shorter than the time required for the iptables rules to be updated. The chain of events that leads to iptables rules being updated is considerably longer (see figure 17.8), because the event must first reach the Endpoints controller, which then sends a new request to the API server, and

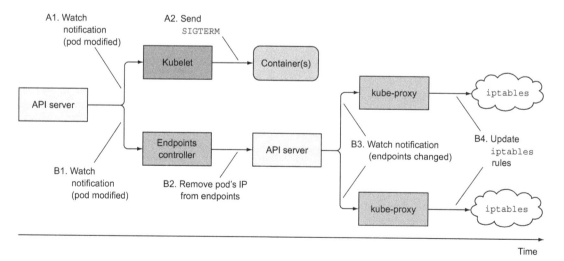

Figure 17.8 Timeline of events when pod is deleted

then the API server must notify the kube-proxy before the proxy finally modifies the `iptables` rules. A high probability exists that the `SIGTERM` signal will be sent well before the `iptables` rules are updated on all nodes.

The end result is that the pod may still receive client requests after it was sent the termination signal. If the app closes the server socket and stops accepting connections immediately, this will cause clients to receive "Connection Refused" types of errors (similar to what happens at pod startup if your app isn't capable of accepting connections immediately and you don't define a readiness probe for it).

SOLVING THE PROBLEM

Googling solutions to this problem makes it seem as though adding a readiness probe to your pod will solve the problem. Supposedly, all you need to do is make the readiness probe start failing as soon as the pod receives the `SIGTERM`. This is supposed to cause the pod to be removed as the endpoint of the service. But the removal would happen only after the readiness probe fails for a few consecutive times (this is configurable in the readiness probe spec). And, obviously, the removal then still needs to reach the kube-proxy before the pod is removed from `iptables` rules.

In reality, the readiness probe has absolutely no bearing on the whole process at all. The Endpoints controller removes the pod from the service Endpoints as soon as it receives notice of the pod being deleted (when the `deletionTimestamp` field in the pod's spec is no longer `null`). From that point on, the result of the readiness probe is irrelevant.

What's the proper solution to the problem? How can you make sure all requests are handled fully?

It's clear the pod needs to keep accepting connections even after it receives the termination signal up until all the kube-proxies have finished updating the `iptables` rules. Well, it's not only the kube-proxies. There may also be Ingress controllers or load balancers forwarding connections to the pod directly, without going through the Service (`iptables`). This also includes clients using client-side load-balancing. To ensure none of the clients experience broken connections, you'd have to wait until all of them somehow notify you they'll no longer forward connections to the pod.

That's impossible, because all those components are distributed across many different computers. Even if you knew the location of every one of them and could wait until all of them say it's okay to shut down the pod, what do you do if one of them doesn't respond? How long do you wait for the response? Remember, during that time, you're holding up the shut-down process.

The only reasonable thing you can do is wait for a long-enough time to ensure all the proxies have done their job. But how long is long enough? A few seconds should be enough in most situations, but there's no guarantee it will suffice every time. When the API server or the Endpoints controller is overloaded, it may take longer for the notification to reach the kube-proxy. It's important to understand that you can't solve the problem perfectly, but even adding a 5- or 10-second delay should improve the user experience considerably. You can use a longer delay, but don't go overboard, because the delay will prevent the container from shutting down promptly and will cause the pod to be shown in lists long after it has been deleted, which is always frustrating to the user deleting the pod.

WRAPPING UP THIS SECTION

To recap—properly shutting down an application includes these steps:

- Wait for a few seconds, then stop accepting new connections.
- Close all keep-alive connections not in the middle of a request.
- Wait for all active requests to finish.
- Then shut down completely.

To understand what's happening with the connections and requests during this process, examine figure 17.9 carefully.

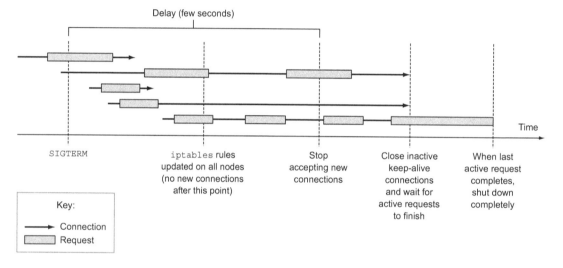

Figure 17.9   Properly handling existing and new connections after receiving a termination signal

Not as simple as exiting the process immediately upon receiving the termination signal, right? Is it worth going through all this? That's for you to decide. But the least you can do is add a pre-stop hook that waits a few seconds, like the one in the following listing, perhaps.

Listing 17.7   A pre-stop hook for preventing broken connections

```
lifecycle:
  preStop:
    exec:
      command:
      - sh
      - -c
      - "sleep 5"
```

This way, you don't need to modify the code of your app at all. If your app already ensures all in-flight requests are processed completely, this pre-stop delay may be all you need.

17.4 Making your apps easy to run and manage in Kubernetes

I hope you now have a better sense of how to make your apps handle clients nicely. Now we'll look at other aspects of how an app should be built to make it easier to manage in Kubernetes.

17.4.1 Making manageable container images

When you package your app into an image, you can choose to include the app's binary executable and any additional libraries it needs, or you can package up a whole OS filesystem along with the app. Way too many people do this, even though it's usually unnecessary.

Do you need every single file from an OS distribution in your image? Probably not. Most of the files will never be used and will make your image larger than it needs to be. Sure, the layering of images makes sure each individual layer is downloaded only once, but even having to wait longer than necessary the first time a pod is scheduled to a node is undesirable.

Deploying new pods and scaling them should be fast. This demands having small images without unnecessary cruft. If you're building apps using the Go language, your images don't need to include anything else apart from the app's single binary executable file. This makes Go-based container images extremely small and perfect for Kubernetes.

> **TIP** Use the FROM scratch directive in the Dockerfile for these images.

But in practice, you'll soon see these minimal images are extremely difficult to debug. The first time you need to run a tool such as ping, dig, curl, or something similar inside the container, you'll realize how important it is for container images to also include at least a limited set of these tools. I can't tell you what to include and what not to include in your images, because it depends on how you do things, so you'll need to find the sweet spot yourself.

17.4.2 Properly tagging your images and using imagePullPolicy wisely

You'll also soon learn that referring to the latest image tag in your pod manifests will cause problems, because you can't tell which version of the image each individual pod replica is running. Even if initially all your pod replicas run the same image version, if you push a new version of the image under the latest tag, and then pods are rescheduled (or you scale up your Deployment), the new pods will run the new version, whereas the old ones will still be running the old one. Also, using the latest tag makes it impossible to roll back to a previous version (unless you push the old version of the image again).

It's almost mandatory to use tags containing a proper version designator instead of `latest`, except maybe in development. Keep in mind that if you use mutable tags (you push changes to the same tag), you'll need to set the `imagePullPolicy` field in the pod spec to `Always`. But if you use that in production pods, be aware of the big caveat associated with it. If the image pull policy is set to `Always`, the container run-time will contact the image registry every time a new pod is deployed. This slows down pod startup a bit, because the node needs to check if the image has been modified. Worse yet, this policy prevents the pod from starting up when the registry cannot be contacted.

17.4.3   *Using multi-dimensional instead of single-dimensional labels*

Don't forget to label all your resources, not only Pods. Make sure you add multiple labels to each resource, so they can be selected across each individual dimension. You (or the ops team) will be grateful you did it when the number of resources increases.

Labels may include things like

- The name of the application (or perhaps microservice) the resource belongs to
- Application tier (front-end, back-end, and so on)
- Environment (development, QA, staging, production, and so on)
- Version
- Type of release (stable, canary, green or blue for green/blue deployments, and so on)
- Tenant (if you're running separate pods for each tenant instead of using namespaces)
- Shard for sharded systems

This will allow you to manage resources in groups instead of individually and make it easy to see where each resource belongs.

17.4.4   *Describing each resource through annotations*

To add additional information to your resources use annotations. At the least, resources should contain an annotation describing the resource and an annotation with contact information of the person responsible for it.

In a microservices architecture, pods could contain an annotation that lists the names of the other services the pod is using. This makes it possible to show dependencies between pods. Other annotations could include build and version information and metadata used by tooling or graphical user interfaces (icon names, and so on).

Both labels and annotations make managing running applications much easier, but nothing is worse than when an application starts crashing and you don't know why.

17.4.5   *Providing information on why the process terminated*

Nothing is more frustrating than having to figure out why a container terminated (or is even terminating continuously), especially if it happens at the worst possible moment. Be nice to the ops people and make their lives easier by including all the necessary debug information in your log files.

But to make triage even easier, you can use one other Kubernetes feature that makes it possible to show the reason why a container terminated in the pod's status. You do this by having the process write a termination message to a specific file in the container's filesystem. The contents of this file are read by the Kubelet when the container terminates and are shown in the output of kubectl describe pod. If an application uses this mechanism, an operator can quickly see why the app terminated without even having to look at the container logs.

The default file the process needs to write the message to is /dev/termination-log, but it can be changed by setting the terminationMessagePath field in the container definition in the pod spec.

You can see this in action by running a pod whose container dies immediately, as shown in the following listing.

Listing 17.8 Pod writing a termination message: termination-message.yaml

```
apiVersion: v1
kind: Pod
metadata:
  name: pod-with-termination-message
spec:
  containers:
  - image: busybox
    name: main
    terminationMessagePath: /var/termination-reason
    command:
    - sh
    - -c
    - 'echo "I''ve had enough" > /var/termination-reason ; exit 1'
```

> You're overriding the default path of the termination message file.

> The container will write the message to the file just before exiting.

When running this pod, you'll soon see the pod's status shown as CrashLoopBackOff. If you then use kubectl describe, you can see why the container died, without having to dig down into its logs, as shown in the following listing.

Listing 17.9 Seeing the container's termination message with kubectl describe

```
$ kubectl describe po
Name:          pod-with-termination-message
...
Containers:
...
    State:        Waiting
      Reason:     CrashLoopBackOff
    Last State:   Terminated
      Reason:     Error
      Message:    I've had enough
      Exit Code:     1
      Started:       Tue, 21 Feb 2017 21:38:31 +0100
      Finished:      Tue, 21 Feb 2017 21:38:31 +0100
```

> You can see the reason why the container died without having to inspect its logs.

```
Ready:                 False
Restart Count:         6
```

As you can see, the "I've had enough" message the process wrote to the file /var/ter-mination-reason is shown in the container's Last State section. Note that this mechanism isn't limited only to containers that crash. It can also be used in pods that run a completable task and terminate successfully (you'll find an example in the file termination-message-success.yaml).

This mechanism is great for terminated containers, but you'll probably agree that a similar mechanism would also be useful for showing app-specific status messages of running, not only terminated, containers. Kubernetes currently doesn't provide any such functionality and I'm not aware of any plans to introduce it.

> **NOTE** If the container doesn't write the message to any file, you can set the terminationMessagePolicy field to FallbackToLogsOnError. In that case, the last few lines of the container's log are used as its termination message (but only when the container terminates unsuccessfully).

17.4.6 *Handling application logs*

While we're on the subject of application logging, let's reiterate that apps should write to the standard output instead of files. This makes it easy to view logs with the kubectl logs command.

> **TIP** If a container crashes and is replaced with a new one, you'll see the new container's log. To see the previous container's logs, use the --previous option with kubectl logs.

If the application logs to a file instead of the standard output, you can display the log file using an alternative approach:

```
$ kubectl exec <pod> cat <logfile>
```

This executes the cat command inside the container and streams the logs back to kubectl, which prints them out in your terminal.

COPYING LOG AND OTHER FILES TO AND FROM A CONTAINER

You can also copy the log file to your local machine using the kubectl cp command, which we haven't looked at yet. It allows you to copy files from and into a container. For example, if a pod called foo-pod and its single container contains a file at /var/log/foo.log, you can transfer it to your local machine with the following command:

```
$ kubectl cp foo-pod:/var/log/foo.log foo.log
```

To copy a file from your local machine into the pod, specify the pod's name in the second argument:

```
$ kubectl cp localfile foo-pod:/etc/remotefile
```

This copies the file localfile to /etc/remotefile inside the pod's container. If the pod has more than one container, you specify the container using the `-c containerName` option.

USING CENTRALIZED LOGGING

In a production system, you'll want to use a centralized, cluster-wide logging solution, so all your logs are collected and (permanently) stored in a central location. This allows you to examine historical logs and analyze trends. Without such a system, a pod's logs are only available while the pod exists. As soon as it's deleted, its logs are deleted also.

Kubernetes by itself doesn't provide any kind of centralized logging. The components necessary for providing a centralized storage and analysis of all the container logs must be provided by additional components, which usually run as regular pods in the cluster.

Deploying centralized logging solutions is easy. All you need to do is deploy a few YAML/JSON manifests and you're good to go. On Google Kubernetes Engine, it's even easier. Check the Enable Stackdriver Logging checkbox when setting up the cluster. Setting up centralized logging on an on-premises Kubernetes cluster is beyond the scope of this book, but I'll give you a quick overview of how it's usually done.

You may have already heard of the ELK stack composed of ElasticSearch, Logstash, and Kibana. A slightly modified variation is the EFK stack, where Logstash is replaced with FluentD.

When using the EFK stack for centralized logging, each Kubernetes cluster node runs a FluentD agent (usually as a pod deployed through a DaemonSet), which is responsible for gathering the logs from the containers, tagging them with pod-specific information, and delivering them to ElasticSearch, which stores them persistently. ElasticSearch is also deployed as a pod somewhere in the cluster. The logs can then be viewed and analyzed in a web browser through Kibana, which is a web tool for visualizing ElasticSearch data. It also usually runs as a pod and is exposed through a Service. The three components of the EFK stack are shown in the following figure.

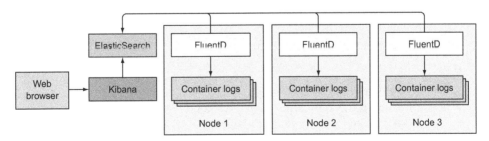

Figure 17.10 Centralized logging with FluentD, ElasticSearch, and Kibana

NOTE In the next chapter, you'll learn about Helm charts. You can use charts created by the Kubernetes community to deploy the EFK stack instead of creating your own YAML manifests.

HANDLING MULTI-LINE LOG STATEMENTS

The FluentD agent stores each line of the log file as an entry in the ElasticSearch data store. There's one problem with that. Log statements spanning multiple lines, such as exception stack traces in Java, appear as separate entries in the centralized logging system.

To solve this problem, you can have the apps output JSON instead of plain text. This way, a multiline log statement can be stored and shown in Kibana as a single entry. But that makes viewing logs with `kubectl logs` much less human-friendly.

The solution may be to keep outputting human-readable logs to standard output, while writing JSON logs to a file and having them processed by FluentD. This requires configuring the node-level FluentD agent appropriately or adding a logging sidecar container to every pod.

17.5   *Best practices for development and testing*

We've talked about what to be mindful of when developing apps, but we haven't talked about the development and testing workflows that will help you streamline those processes. I don't want to go into too much detail here, because everyone needs to find what works best for them, but here are a few starting points.

17.5.1   *Running apps outside of Kubernetes during development*

When you're developing an app that will run in a production Kubernetes cluster, does that mean you also need to run it in Kubernetes during development? Not really. Having to build the app after each minor change, then build the container image, push it to a registry, and then re-deploy the pods would make development slow and painful. Luckily, you don't need to go through all that trouble.

You can always develop and run apps on your local machine, the way you're used to. After all, an app running in Kubernetes is a regular (although isolated) process running on one of the cluster nodes. If the app depends on certain features the Kubernetes environment provides, you can easily replicate that environment on your development machine.

I'm not even talking about running the app in a container. Most of the time, you don't need that—you can usually run the app directly from your IDE.

CONNECTING TO BACKEND SERVICES

In production, if the app connects to a backend Service and uses the `BACKEND_SERVICE _HOST` and `BACKEND_SERVICE_PORT` environment variables to find the Service's coordinates, you can obviously set those environment variables on your local machine manually and point them to the backend Service, regardless of if it's running outside or inside a Kubernetes cluster. If it's running inside Kubernetes, you can always (at least temporarily) make the Service accessible externally by changing it to a `NodePort` or a `LoadBalancer`-type Service.

CONNECTING TO THE API SERVER

Similarly, if your app requires access to the Kubernetes API server when running inside a Kubernetes cluster, it can easily talk to the API server from outside the cluster during development. If it uses the ServiceAccount's token to authenticate itself, you can always copy the ServiceAccount's Secret's files to your local machine with `kubectl cp`. The API server doesn't care if the client accessing it is inside or outside the cluster.

If the app uses an ambassador container like the one described in chapter 8, you don't even need those Secret files. Run `kubectl proxy` on your local machine, run your app locally, and it should be ready to talk to your local `kubectl proxy` (as long as it and the ambassador container bind the proxy to the same port).

In this case, you'll need to make sure the user account your local `kubectl` is using has the same privileges as the ServiceAccount the app will run under.

RUNNING INSIDE A CONTAINER EVEN DURING DEVELOPMENT

When during development you absolutely have to run the app in a container for whatever reason, there is a way of avoiding having to build the container image every time. Instead of baking the binaries into the image, you can always mount your local filesystem into the container through Docker volumes, for example. This way, after you build a new version of the app's binaries, all you need to do is restart the container (or not even that, if hot-redeploy is supported). No need to rebuild the image.

17.5.2 *Using Minikube in development*

As you can see, nothing forces you to run your app inside Kubernetes during development. But you may do that anyway to see how the app behaves in a true Kubernetes environment.

You may have used Minikube to run examples in this book. Although a Minikube cluster runs only a single worker node, it's nevertheless a valuable method of trying out your app in Kubernetes (and, of course, developing all the resource manifests that make up your complete application). Minikube doesn't offer everything that a proper multi-node Kubernetes cluster usually provides, but in most cases, that doesn't matter.

MOUNTING LOCAL FILES INTO THE MINIKUBE VM AND THEN INTO YOUR CONTAINERS

When you're developing with Minikube and you'd like to try out every change to your app in your Kubernetes cluster, you can mount your local filesystem into the Minikube VM using the `minikube mount` command and then mount it into your containers through a `hostPath` volume. You'll find additional instructions on how to do that in the Minikube documentation at https://github.com/kubernetes/minikube/tree/master/docs.

USING THE DOCKER DAEMON INSIDE THE MINIKUBE VM TO BUILD YOUR IMAGES

If you're developing your app with Minikube and planning to build the container image after every change, you can use the Docker daemon inside the Minikube VM to do the building, instead of having to build the image through your local Docker daemon, push it to a registry, and then have it pulled by the daemon in the VM. To use

Minikube's Docker daemon, all you need to do is point your DOCKER_HOST environment variable to it. Luckily, this is much easier than it sounds. All you need to do is run the following command on your local machine:

```
$ eval $(minikube docker-env)
```

This will set all the required environment variables for you. You then build your images the same way as if the Docker daemon was running on your local machine. After you build the image, you don't need to push it anywhere, because it's already stored locally on the Minikube VM, which means new pods can use the image immediately. If your pods are already running, you either need to delete them or kill their containers so they're restarted.

BUILDING IMAGES LOCALLY AND COPYING THEM OVER TO THE MINIKUBE VM DIRECTLY

If you can't use the daemon inside the VM to build the images, you still have a way to avoid having to push the image to a registry and have the Kubelet running in the Minikube VM pull it. If you build the image on your local machine, you can copy it over to the Minikube VM with the following command:

```
$ docker save <image> | (eval $(minikube docker-env) && docker load)
```

As before, the image is immediately ready to be used in a pod. But make sure the imagePullPolicy in your pod spec isn't set to Always, because that would cause the image to be pulled from the external registry again and you'd lose the changes you've copied over.

COMBINING MINIKUBE WITH A PROPER KUBERNETES CLUSTER

You have virtually no limit when developing apps with Minikube. You can even combine a Minikube cluster with a proper Kubernetes cluster. I sometimes run my development workloads in my local Minikube cluster and have them talk to my other workloads that are deployed in a remote multi-node Kubernetes cluster thousands of miles away.

Once I'm finished with development, I can move my local workloads to the remote cluster with no modifications and with absolutely no problems thanks to how Kubernetes abstracts away the underlying infrastructure from the app.

17.5.3   *Versioning and auto-deploying resource manifests*

Because Kubernetes uses a declarative model, you never have to figure out the current state of your deployed resources and issue imperative commands to bring that state to what you desire. All you need to do is tell Kubernetes your desired state and it will take all the necessary actions to reconcile the cluster state with the desired state.

You can store your collection of resource manifests in a Version Control System, enabling you to perform code reviews, keep an audit trail, and roll back changes whenever necessary. After each commit, you can run the kubectl apply command to have your changes reflected in your deployed resources.

If you run an agent that periodically (or when it detects a new commit) checks out your manifests from the Version Control System (VCS), and then runs the `apply` command, you can manage your running apps simply by committing changes to the VCS without having to manually talk to the Kubernetes API server. Luckily, the people at Box (which coincidently was used to host this book's manuscript and other materials) developed and released a tool called `kube-applier`, which does exactly what I described. You'll find the tool's source code at https://github.com/box/kube-applier.

You can use multiple branches to deploy the manifests to a development, QA, staging, and production cluster (or in different namespaces in the same cluster).

17.5.4 Introducing Ksonnet as an alternative to writing YAML/JSON manifests

We've seen a number of YAML manifests throughout the book. I don't see writing YAML as too big of a problem, especially once you learn how to use `kubectl explain` to see the available options, but some people do.

Just as I was finalizing the manuscript for this book, a new tool called Ksonnet was announced. It's a library built on top of Jsonnet, which is a data templating language for building JSON data structures. Instead of writing the complete JSON by hand, it lets you define parameterized JSON fragments, give them a name, and then build a full JSON manifest by referencing those fragments by name, instead of repeating the same JSON code in multiple locations—much like you use functions or methods in a programming language.

Ksonnet defines the fragments you'd find in Kubernetes resource manifests, allowing you to quickly build a complete Kubernetes resource JSON manifest with much less code. The following listing shows an example.

> **Listing 17.10 The `kubia` Deployment written with Ksonnet: kubia.ksonnet**

```
local k = import "../ksonnet-lib/ksonnet.beta.1/k.libsonnet";

local container = k.core.v1.container;
local deployment = k.apps.v1beta1.deployment;

local kubiaContainer =
  container.default("kubia", "luksa/kubia:v1") +
  container.helpers.namedPort("http", 8080);

deployment.default("kubia", kubiaContainer) +
deployment.mixin.spec.replicas(3)
```

This defines a container called kubia, which uses the luksa/kubia:v1 image and includes a port called http.

This will be expanded into a full Deployment resource. The kubiaContainer defined here will be included in the Deployment's pod template.

The kubia.ksonnet file shown in the listing is converted to a full JSON Deployment manifest when you run the following command:

```
$ jsonnet kubia.ksonnet
```

The power of Ksonnet and Jsonnet becomes apparent when you realize you can define your own higher-level fragments and make all your manifests consistent and duplication-free. You'll find more information on using and installing Ksonnet and Jsonnet at https://github.com/ksonnet/ksonnet-lib.

17.5.5 *Employing Continuous Integration and Continuous Delivery (CI/CD)*

We've touched on automating the deployment of Kubernetes resources two sections back, but you may want to set up a complete CI/CD pipeline for building your application binaries, container images, and resource manifests and then deploying them in one or more Kubernetes clusters.

You'll find many online resources talking about this subject. Here, I'd like to point you specifically to the Fabric8 project (http://fabric8.io), which is an integrated development platform for Kubernetes. It includes Jenkins, the well-known, open-source automation system, and various other tools to deliver a full CI/CD pipeline for DevOps-style development, deployment, and management of microservices on Kubernetes.

If you'd like to build your own solution, I also suggest looking at one of the Google Cloud Platform's online labs that talks about this subject. It's available at https://github.com/GoogleCloudPlatform/continuous-deployment-on-kubernetes.

17.6 *Summary*

Hopefully, the information in this chapter has given you an even deeper insight into how Kubernetes works and will help you build apps that feel right at home when deployed to a Kubernetes cluster. The aim of this chapter was to

- Show you how all the resources covered in this book come together to represent a typical application running in Kubernetes.
- Make you think about the difference between apps that are rarely moved between machines and apps running as pods, which are relocated much more frequently.
- Help you understand that your multi-component apps (or microservices, if you will) shouldn't rely on a specific start-up order.
- Introduce init containers, which can be used to initialize a pod or delay the start of the pod's main containers until a precondition is met.
- Teach you about container lifecycle hooks and when to use them.
- Gain a deeper insight into the consequences of the distributed nature of Kubernetes components and its eventual consistency model.
- Learn how to make your apps shut down properly without breaking client connections.

- Give you a few small tips on how to make your apps easier to manage by keeping image sizes small, adding annotations and multi-dimensional labels to all your resources, and making it easier to see why an application terminated.
- Teach you how to develop Kubernetes apps and run them locally or in Minikube before deploying them on a proper multi-node cluster.

In the next and final chapter, we'll learn how you can extend Kubernetes with your own custom API objects and controllers and how others have done it to create complete Platform-as-a-Service solutions on top of Kubernetes.

Extending Kubernetes

This chapter covers

- Adding custom objects to Kubernetes
- Creating a controller for the custom object
- Adding custom API servers
- Self-provisioning of services with the Kubernetes Service Catalog
- Red Hat's OpenShift Container Platform
- Deis Workflow and Helm

You're almost done. To wrap up, we'll look at how you can define your own API objects and create controllers for those objects. We'll also look at how others have extended Kubernetes and built Platform-as-a-Service solutions on top of it.

18.1 Defining custom API objects

Throughout the book, you've learned about the API objects that Kubernetes provides and how they're used to build application systems. Currently, Kubernetes users mostly use only these objects even though they represent relatively low-level, generic concepts.

As the Kubernetes ecosystem evolves, you'll see more and more high-level objects, which will be much more specialized than the resources Kubernetes supports today. Instead of dealing with Deployments, Services, ConfigMaps, and the like, you'll create and manage objects that represent whole applications or software services. A custom controller will observe those high-level objects and create low-level objects based on them. For example, to run a messaging broker inside a Kubernetes cluster, all you'll need to do is create an instance of a Queue resource and all the necessary Secrets, Deployments, and Services will be created by a custom Queue controller. Kubernetes already provides ways of adding custom resources like this.

18.1.1 *Introducing CustomResourceDefinitions*

To define a new resource type, all you need to do is post a CustomResourceDefinition object (CRD) to the Kubernetes API server. The CustomResourceDefinition object is the description of the custom resource type. Once the CRD is posted, users can then create instances of the custom resource by posting JSON or YAML manifests to the API server, the same as with any other Kubernetes resource.

> **NOTE** Prior to Kubernetes 1.7, custom resources were defined through Third-PartyResource objects, which were similar to CustomResourceDefinitions, but were removed in version 1.8.

Creating a CRD so that users can create objects of the new type isn't a useful feature if those objects don't make something tangible happen in the cluster. Each CRD will usually also have an associated controller (an active component doing something based on the custom objects), the same way that all the core Kubernetes resources have an associated controller, as was explained in chapter 11. For this reason, to properly show what CustomResourceDefinitions allow you to do other than adding instances of a custom object, a controller must be deployed as well. You'll do that in the next example.

INTRODUCING THE EXAMPLE CUSTOMRESOURCEDEFINITION

Let's imagine you want to allow users of your Kubernetes cluster to run static websites as easily as possible, without having to deal with Pods, Services, and other Kubernetes resources. What you want to achieve is for users to create objects of type Website that contain nothing more than the website's name and the source from which the website's files (HTML, CSS, PNG, and others) should be obtained. You'll use a Git repository as the source of those files. When a user creates an instance of the Website resource, you want Kubernetes to spin up a new web server pod and expose it through a Service, as shown in figure 18.1.

To create the Website resource, you want users to post manifests along the lines of the one shown in the following listing.

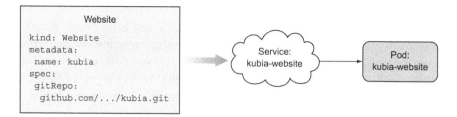

Figure 18.1   Each Website object should result in the creation of a Service and an HTTP server Pod.

Listing 18.1   An imaginary custom resource: imaginary-kubia-website.yaml

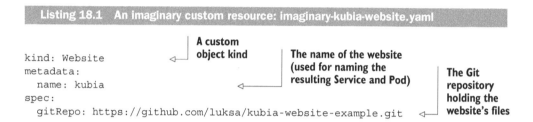

Like all other resources, your resource contains a `kind` and a `metadata.name` field, and like most resources, it also contains a `spec` section. It contains a single field called `gitRepo` (you can choose the name)—it specifies the Git repository containing the website's files. You'll also need to include an `apiVersion` field, but you don't know yet what its value must be for custom resources.

If you try posting this resource to Kubernetes, you'll receive an error because Kubernetes doesn't know what a Website object is yet:

```
$ kubectl create -f imaginary-kubia-website.yaml
error: unable to recognize "imaginary-kubia-website.yaml": no matches for
⇒ /, Kind=Website
```

Before you can create instances of your custom object, you need to make Kubernetes recognize them.

CREATING A CUSTOMRESOURCEDEFINITION OBJECT

To make Kubernetes accept your custom Website resource instances, you need to post the CustomResourceDefinition shown in the following listing to the API server.

Listing 18.2   A CustomResourceDefinition manifest: website-crd.yaml

```
                    apiVersion: apiextensions.k8s.io/v1beta1       CustomResourceDefinitions belong
The full            kind: CustomResourceDefinition                 to this API group and version.
name of             metadata:
your          ┌───▷   name: websites.extensions.example.com        You want Website resources
custom              spec:                                          to be namespaced.
object                scope: Namespaced        ◁
```

```
group: extensions.example.com          Define an API group and version
version: v1                             of the Website resource.
names:
  kind: Website                     You need to specify the various
  singular: website                 forms of the custom object's name.
  plural: websites
```

After you post the descriptor to Kubernetes, it will allow you to create any number of instances of the custom Website resource.

You can create the CRD from the website-crd.yaml file available in the code archive:

```
$ kubectl create -f website-crd-definition.yaml
customresourcedefinition "websites.extensions.example.com" created
```

I'm sure you're wondering about the long name of the CRD. Why not call it Website? The reason is to prevent name clashes. By adding a suffix to the name of the CRD (which will usually include the name of the organization that created the CRD), you keep CRD names unique. Luckily, the long name doesn't mean you'll need to create your Website resources with kind: websites.extensions.example.com, but as kind: Website, as specified in the names.kind property of the CRD. The extensions.example.com part is the API group of your resource.

You've seen how creating Deployment objects requires you to set apiVersion to apps/v1beta1 instead of v1. The part before the slash is the API group (Deployments belong to the apps API group), and the part after it is the version name (v1beta1 in the case of Deployments). When creating instances of the custom Website resource, the apiVersion property will need to be set to extensions.example.com/v1.

CREATING AN INSTANCE OF A CUSTOM RESOURCE

Considering what you learned, you'll now create a proper YAML for your Website resource instance. The YAML manifest is shown in the following listing.

> **Listing 18.3 A custom Website resource: kubia-website.yaml**

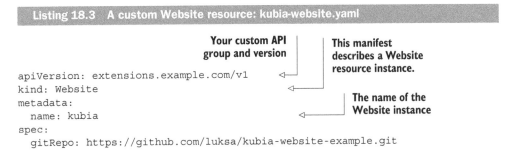

```
                              Your custom API        This manifest
                              group and version      describes a Website
                                                     resource instance.
apiVersion: extensions.example.com/v1   ◁─┘
kind: Website                                    ◁─
metadata:                                              The name of the
  name: kubia                              ◁──────┘    Website instance
spec:
  gitRepo: https://github.com/luksa/kubia-website-example.git
```

The kind of your resource is Website, and the apiVersion is composed of the API group and the version number you defined in the CustomResourceDefinition.

Create your Website object now:

```
$ kubectl create -f kubia-website.yaml
website "kubia" created
```

The response tells you that the API server has accepted and stored your custom Website object. Let's see if you can now retrieve it.

RETRIEVING INSTANCES OF A CUSTOM RESOURCE

List all the websites in your cluster:

```
$ kubectl get websites
NAME       KIND
kubia      Website.v1.extensions.example.com
```

As with existing Kubernetes resources, you can create and then list instances of custom resources. You can also use `kubectl describe` to see the details of your custom object, or retrieve the whole YAML with `kubectl get`, as in the following listing.

Listing 18.4   Full Website resource definition retrieved from the API server

```
$ kubectl get website kubia -o yaml
apiVersion: extensions.example.com/v1
kind: Website
metadata:
  creationTimestamp: 2017-02-26T15:53:21Z
  name: kubia
  namespace: default
  resourceVersion: "57047"
  selfLink: /apis/extensions.example.com/v1/.../default/websites/kubia
  uid: b2eb6d99-fc3b-11e6-bd71-0800270a1c50
spec:
  gitRepo: https://github.com/luksa/kubia-website-example.git
```

Note that the resource includes everything that was in the original YAML definition, and that Kubernetes has initialized additional metadata fields the way it does with all other resources.

DELETING AN INSTANCE OF A CUSTOM OBJECT

Obviously, in addition to creating and retrieving custom object instances, you can also delete them:

```
$ kubectl delete website kubia
website "kubia" deleted
```

> **NOTE** You're deleting an instance of a Website, not the Website CRD resource. You could also delete the CRD object itself, but let's hold off on that for a while, because you'll be creating additional Website instances in the next section.

Let's go over everything you've done. By creating a CustomResourceDefinition object, you can now store, retrieve, and delete custom objects through the Kubernetes API server. These objects don't do anything yet. You'll need to create a controller to make them do something.

In general, the point of creating custom objects like this isn't always to make something happen when the object is created. Certain custom objects are used to store data instead of using a more generic mechanism such as a ConfigMap. Applications running inside pods can query the API server for those objects and read whatever is stored in them.

But in this case, we said you wanted the existence of a Website object to result in the spinning up of a web server serving the contents of the Git repository referenced in the object. We'll look at how to do that next.

18.1.2 *Automating custom resources with custom controllers*

To make your Website objects run a web server pod exposed through a Service, you'll need to build and deploy a Website controller, which will watch the API server for the creation of Website objects and then create the Service and the web server Pod for each of them.

To make sure the Pod is managed and survives node failures, the controller will create a Deployment resource instead of an unmanaged Pod directly. The controller's operation is summarized in figure 18.2.

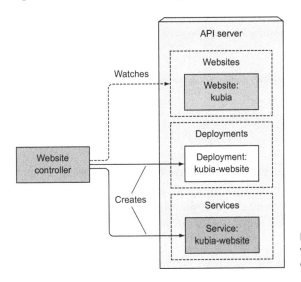

Figure 18.2   The Website controller watches for Website objects and creates a Deployment and a Service.

I've written a simple initial version of the controller, which works well enough to show CRDs and the controller in action, but it's far from being production-ready, because it's overly simplified. The container image is available at docker.io/luksa/website-controller:latest, and the source code is at https://github.com/luksa/k8s-website-controller. Instead of going through its source code, I'll explain what the controller does.

UNDERSTANDING WHAT THE WEBSITE CONTROLLER DOES

Immediately upon startup, the controller starts to watch Website objects by requesting the following URL:

```
http://localhost:8001/apis/extensions.example.com/v1/websites?watch=true
```

You may recognize the hostname and port—the controller isn't connecting to the API server directly, but is instead connecting to the kubectl proxy process, which runs in a sidecar container in the same pod and acts as the ambassador to the API server (we examined the ambassador pattern in chapter 8). The proxy forwards the request to the API server, taking care of both TLS encryption and authentication (see figure 18.3).

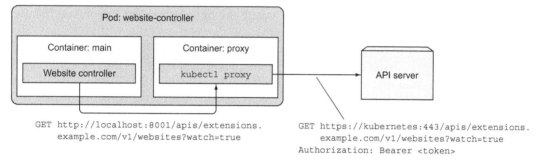

Figure 18.3   The Website controller talks to the API server through a proxy (in the ambassador container).

Through the connection opened by this HTTP GET request, the API server will send watch events for every change to any Website object.

The API server sends the ADDED watch event every time a new Website object is created. When the controller receives such an event, it extracts the Website's name and the URL of the Git repository from the Website object it received in the watch event and creates a Deployment and a Service object by posting their JSON manifests to the API server.

The Deployment resource contains a template for a pod with two containers (shown in figure 18.4): one running an nginx server and another one running a git-sync process, which keeps a local directory synced with the contents of a Git repo. The local directory is shared with the nginx container through an emptyDir volume (you did something similar to that in chapter 6, but instead of keeping the local directory synced with a Git repo, you used a gitRepo volume to download the Git repo's contents at pod startup; the volume's contents weren't kept in sync with the Git repo afterward). The Service is a NodePort Service, which exposes your web server pod through a random port on each node (the same port is used on all nodes). When a pod is created by the Deployment object, clients can access the website through the node port.

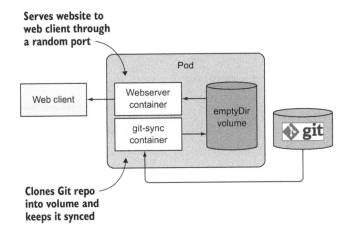

Serves website to web client through a random port

Clones Git repo into volume and keeps it synced

Figure 18.4   The pod serving the website specified in the Website object

The API server also sends a DELETED watch event when a Website resource instance is deleted. Upon receiving the event, the controller deletes the Deployment and the Service resources it created earlier. As soon as a user deletes the Website instance, the controller will shut down and remove the web server serving that website.

> **NOTE**   My oversimplified controller isn't implemented properly. The way it watches the API objects doesn't guarantee it won't miss individual watch events. The proper way to watch objects through the API server is to not only watch them, but also periodically re-list all objects in case any watch events were missed.

RUNNING THE CONTROLLER AS A POD

During development, I ran the controller on my local development laptop and used a locally running kubectl proxy process (not running as a pod) as the ambassador to the Kubernetes API server. This allowed me to develop quickly, because I didn't need to build a container image after every change to the source code and then run it inside Kubernetes.

When I'm ready to deploy the controller into production, the best way is to run the controller inside Kubernetes itself, the way you do with all the other core controllers. To run the controller in Kubernetes, you can deploy it through a Deployment resource. The following listing shows an example of such a Deployment.

Listing 18.5   A Website controller Deployment: website-controller.yaml

```
apiVersion: apps/v1beta1
kind: Deployment
metadata:
  name: website-controller
spec:
  replicas: 1                    ◁── You'll run a single
  template:                            replica of the
                                       controller.
```

```
metadata:
  name: website-controller
  labels:                                    It will run
    app: website-controller                  under a special
spec:                                        ServiceAccount.
  serviceAccountName: website-controller  ◁⌐
  containers:
  - name: main                               Two containers: the
    image: luksa/website-controller         main container and
  - name: proxy                              the proxy sidecar
    image: luksa/kubectl-proxy:1.6.2
```

As you can see, the Deployment deploys a single replica of a two-container pod. One container runs your controller, whereas the other one is the ambassador container used for simpler communication with the API server. The pod runs under its own special ServiceAccount, so you'll need to create it before you deploy the controller:

```
$ kubectl create serviceaccount website-controller
serviceaccount "website-controller" created
```

If Role Based Access Control (RBAC) is enabled in your cluster, Kubernetes will not allow the controller to watch Website resources or create Deployments or Services. To allow it to do that, you'll need to bind the `website-controller` ServiceAccount to the `cluster-admin` ClusterRole, by creating a ClusterRoleBinding like this:

```
$ kubectl create clusterrolebinding website-controller
➥  --clusterrole=cluster-admin
➥  --serviceaccount=default:website-controller
clusterrolebinding "website-controller" created
```

Once you have the ServiceAccount and ClusterRoleBinding in place, you can deploy the controller's Deployment.

SEEING THE CONTROLLER IN ACTION

With the controller now running, create the `kubia` Website resource again:

```
$ kubectl create -f kubia-website.yaml
website "kubia" created
```

Now, let's check the controller's logs (shown in the following listing) to see if it has received the watch event.

Listing 18.6 Displaying logs of the Website controller

```
$ kubectl logs website-controller-2429717411-q43zs -c main
2017/02/26 16:54:41 website-controller started.
2017/02/26 16:54:47 Received watch event: ADDED: kubia: https://github.c...
2017/02/26 16:54:47 Creating services with name kubia-website in namespa...
2017/02/26 16:54:47 Response status: 201 Created
2017/02/26 16:54:47 Creating deployments with name kubia-website in name...
2017/02/26 16:54:47 Response status: 201 Created
```

The logs show that the controller received the ADDED event and that it created a Service and a Deployment for the kubia-website Website. The API server responded with a 201 Created response, which means the two resources should now exist. Let's verify that the Deployment, Service and the resulting Pod were created. The following listing lists all Deployments, Services and Pods.

Listing 18.7 The Deployment, Service, and Pod created for the kubia-website

```
$ kubectl get deploy,svc,po
NAME                              DESIRED   CURRENT   UP-TO-DATE   AVAILABLE   AGE
deploy/kubia-website              1         1         1            1           4s
deploy/website-controller         1         1         1            1           5m

NAME                  CLUSTER-IP     EXTERNAL-IP   PORT(S)        AGE
svc/kubernetes        10.96.0.1      <none>        443/TCP        38d
svc/kubia-website     10.101.48.23   <nodes>       80:32589/TCP   4s

NAME                                     READY   STATUS    RESTARTS   AGE
po/kubia-website-1029415133-rs715        2/2     Running   0          4s
po/website-controller-1571685839-qzmg6   2/2     Running   1          5m
```

There they are. The kubia-website Service, through which you can access your website, is available on port 32589 on all cluster nodes. You can access it with your browser. Awesome, right?

Users of your Kubernetes cluster can now deploy static websites in seconds, without knowing anything about Pods, Services, or any other Kubernetes resources, except your custom Website resource.

Obviously, you still have room for improvement. The controller could, for example, watch for Service objects and as soon as the node port is assigned, write the URL the website is accessible at into the status section of the Website resource instance itself. Or it could also create an Ingress object for each website. I'll leave the implementation of these additional features to you as an exercise.

18.1.3 *Validating custom objects*

You may have noticed that you didn't specify any kind of validation schema in the Website CustomResourceDefinition. Users can include any field they want in the YAML of their Website object. The API server doesn't validate the contents of the YAML (except the usual fields like apiVersion, kind, and metadata), so users can create invalid Website objects (without a gitRepo field, for example).

Is it possible to add validation to the controller and prevent invalid objects from being accepted by the API server? It isn't, because the API server first stores the object, then returns a success response to the client (kubectl), and only then notifies all the watchers (the controller is one of them). All the controller can really do is validate the object when it receives it in a watch event, and if the object is invalid, write the error message to the Website object (by updating the object through a new request to the API server). The user wouldn't be notified of the error automatically. They'd have to notice the error message by querying the API server for the Website object. Unless the user does this, they have no way of knowing whether the object is valid or not.

This obviously isn't ideal. You'd want the API server to validate the object and reject invalid objects immediately. Validation of custom objects was introduced in Kubernetes version 1.8 as an alpha feature. To have the API server validate your custom objects, you need to enable the `CustomResourceValidation` feature gate in the API server and specify a JSON schema in the CRD.

18.1.4 *Providing a custom API server for your custom objects*

A better way of adding support for custom objects in Kubernetes is to implement your own API server and have the clients talk directly to it.

INTRODUCING API SERVER AGGREGATION

In Kubernetes version 1.7, you can integrate your custom API server with the main Kubernetes API server, through API server aggregation. Initially, the Kubernetes API server was a single monolithic component. From Kubernetes version 1.7, multiple aggregated API servers will be exposed at a single location. Clients can connect to the aggregated API and have their requests transparently forwarded to the appropriate API server. This way, the client wouldn't even be aware that multiple API servers handle different objects behind the scenes. Even the core Kubernetes API server may eventually end up being split into multiple smaller API servers and exposed as a single server through the aggregator, as shown in figure 18.5.

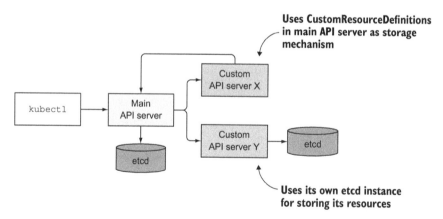

Figure 18.5   API server aggregation

In your case, you could create an API server responsible for handling your Website objects. It could validate those objects the way the core Kubernetes API server validates them. You'd no longer need to create a CRD to represent those objects, because you'd implement the Website object type into the custom API server directly.

Generally, each API server is responsible for storing their own resources. As shown in figure 18.5, it can either run its own instance of etcd (or a whole etcd cluster), or it can store its resources in the core API server's etcd store by creating CRD instances in the core API server. In that case, it needs to create a CRD object first, before creating instances of the CRD, the way you did in the example.

REGISTERING A CUSTOM API SERVER

To add a custom API server to your cluster, you'd deploy it as a pod and expose it through a Service. Then, to integrate it into the main API server, you'd deploy a YAML manifest describing an APIService resource like the one in the following listing.

Listing 18.8   An `APIService` YAML definition

```
apiVersion: apiregistration.k8s.io/v1beta1          This is an APIService
kind: APIService                                     resource.
metadata:
  name: v1alpha1.extensions.example.com             The API group this API
spec:                                                server is responsible for
  group: extensions.example.com
  version: v1alpha1                            The supported API version
  priority: 150
  service:                                 The Service the custom API
    name: website-api                      server is exposed through
    namespace: default
```

After creating the APIService resource from the previous listing, client requests sent to the main API server that contain any resource from the extensions.example.com API group and version v1alpha1 would be forwarded to the custom API server pod(s) exposed through the website-api Service.

CREATING CUSTOM CLIENTS

While you can create custom resources from YAML files using the regular kubectl client, to make deployment of custom objects even easier, in addition to providing a custom API server, you can also build a custom CLI tool. This will allow you to add dedicated commands for manipulating those objects, similar to how kubectl allows creating Secrets, Deployments, and other resources through resource-specific commands like kubectl create secret or kubectl create deployment.

As I've already mentioned, custom API servers, API server aggregation, and other features related to extending Kubernetes are currently being worked on intensively, so they may change after the book is published. To get up-to-date information on the subject, refer to the Kubernetes GitHub repos at http://github.com/kubernetes.

18.2   Extending Kubernetes with the Kubernetes Service Catalog

One of the first additional API servers that will be added to Kubernetes through API server aggregation is the Service Catalog API server. The Service Catalog is a hot topic in the Kubernetes community, so you may want to know about it.

Currently, for a pod to consume a service (here I use the term generally, not in relation to Service resources; for example, a database service includes everything required to allow users to use a database in their app), someone needs to deploy the pods providing the service, a Service resource, and possibly a Secret so the client pod can use it to authenticate with the service. That someone is usually the same user deploying the client pod or, if a team is dedicated to deploying these types of general services, the user needs to file a ticket and wait for the team to provision the service. This means the user needs to either create the manifests for all the components of the service, know where to find an existing set of manifests, know how to configure it properly, and deploy it manually, or wait for the other team to do it.

But Kubernetes is supposed to be an easy-to-use, self-service system. Ideally, users whose apps require a certain service (for example, a web application requiring a back-end database), should be able to say to Kubernetes. "Hey, I need a PostgreSQL database. Please provision one and tell me where and how I can connect to it." This will soon be possible through the Kubernetes Service Catalog.

18.2.1 *Introducing the Service Catalog*

As the name suggests, the Service Catalog is a catalog of services. Users can browse through the catalog and provision instances of the services listed in the catalog by themselves without having to deal with Pods, Services, ConfigMaps, and other resources required for the service to run. You'll recognize that this is similar to what you did with the Website custom resource.

Instead of adding custom resources to the API server for each type of service, the Service Catalog introduces the following four generic API resources:

- A ClusterServiceBroker, which describes an (external) system that can provision services
- A ClusterServiceClass, which describes a type of service that can be provisioned
- A ServiceInstance, which is one instance of a service that has been provisioned
- A ServiceBinding, which represents a binding between a set of clients (pods) and a ServiceInstance

The relationships between those four resources are shown in the figure 18.6 and explained in the following paragraphs.

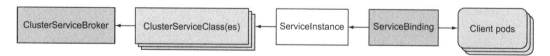

Figure 18.6   The relationships between Service Catalog API resources.

In a nutshell, a cluster admin creates a ClusterServiceBroker resource for each service broker whose services they'd like to make available in the cluster. Kubernetes then asks the broker for a list of services that it can provide and creates a ClusterServiceClass resource for each of them. When a user requires a service to be provisioned, they create an ServiceInstance resource and then a ServiceBinding to bind that ServiceInstance to their pods. Those pods are then injected with a Secret that holds all the necessary credentials and other data required to connect to the provisioned ServiceInstance.

The Service Catalog system architecture is shown in figure 18.7.

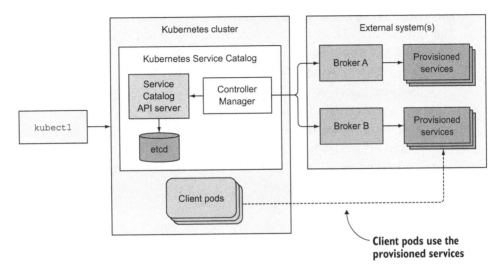

Figure 18.7 The architecture of the Service Catalog

The components shown in the figure are explained in the following sections.

18.2.2 *Introducing the Service Catalog API server and Controller Manager*

Similar to core Kubernetes, the Service Catalog is a distributed system composed of three components:

- Service Catalog API Server
- etcd as the storage
- Controller Manager, where all the controllers run

The four Service Catalog–related resources we introduced earlier are created by posting YAML/JSON manifests to the API server. It then stores them into its own etcd instance or uses CustomResourceDefinitions in the main API server as an alternative storage mechanism (in that case, no additional etcd instance is required).

The controllers running in the Controller Manager are the ones doing something with those resources. They obviously talk to the Service Catalog API server, the way other core Kubernetes controllers talk to the core API server. Those controllers don't provision the requested services themselves. They leave that up to external service brokers, which are registered by creating ServiceBroker resources in the Service Catalog API.

18.2.3   *Introducing Service Brokers and the OpenServiceBroker API*

A cluster administrator can register one or more external ServiceBrokers in the Service Catalog. Every broker must implement the OpenServiceBroker API.

INTRODUCING THE OPENSERVICEBROKER API

The Service Catalog talks to the broker through that API. The API is relatively simple. It's a REST API providing the following operations:

- Retrieving the list of services with `GET /v2/catalog`
- Provisioning a service instance (`PUT /v2/service_instances/:id`)
- Updating a service instance (`PATCH /v2/service_instances/:id`)
- Binding a service instance (`PUT /v2/service_instances/:id/service_bindings/:binding_id`)
- Unbinding an instance (`DELETE /v2/service_instances/:id/service_bindings/:binding_id`)
- Deprovisioning a service instance (`DELETE /v2/service_instances/:id`)

You'll find the OpenServiceBroker API spec at https://github.com/openservicebrokerapi/servicebroker.

REGISTERING BROKERS IN THE SERVICE CATALOG

The cluster administrator registers a broker by posting a ServiceBroker resource manifest to the Service Catalog API, like the one shown in the following listing.

> **Listing 18.9   A ClusterServiceBroker manifest: database-broker.yaml**

```
apiVersion: servicecatalog.k8s.io/v1alpha1          The resource kind and
kind: ClusterServiceBroker                          the API group and version
metadata:
  name: database-broker          ◁——————— The name of this broker
spec:
  url: http://database-osbapi.myorganization.org  ◁———┐

                                                    Where the Service Catalog
                                                    can contact the broker
                                            (its OpenServiceBroker [OSB] API URL)
```

The listing describes an imaginary broker that can provision databases of different types. After the administrator creates the ClusterServiceBroker resource, a controller in the Service Catalog Controller Manager connects to the URL specified in the resource to retrieve the list of services this broker can provision.

After the Service Catalog retrieves the list of services, it creates a ClusterServiceClass resource for each of them. Each ClusterServiceClass resource describes a single type of service that can be provisioned (an example of a ClusterServiceClass is "PostgreSQL database"). Each ClusterServiceClass has one or more service plans associated with it. These allow the user to choose the level of service they need (for example, a database ClusterServiceClass could provide a "Free" plan, where the size of the database is limited and the underlying storage is a spinning disk, and a "Premium" plan, with unlimited size and SSD storage).

LISTING THE AVAILABLE SERVICES IN A CLUSTER

Users of the Kubernetes cluster can retrieve a list of all services that can be provisioned in the cluster with `kubectl get serviceclasses`, as shown in the following listing.

Listing 18.10   List of ClusterServiceClasses in a cluster

```
$ kubectl get clusterserviceclasses
NAME                     KIND
postgres-database        ClusterServiceClass.v1alpha1.servicecatalog.k8s.io
mysql-database           ServiceClass.v1alpha1.servicecatalog.k8s.io
mongodb-database         ServiceClass.v1alpha1.servicecatalog.k8s.io
```

The listing shows ClusterServiceClasses for services that your imaginary database broker could provide. You can compare ClusterServiceClasses to StorageClasses, which we discussed in chapter 6. StorageClasses allow you to select the type of storage you'd like to use in your pods, while ClusterServiceClasses allow you to select the type of service.

You can see details of one of the ClusterServiceClasses by retrieving its YAML. An example is shown in the following listing.

Listing 18.11   A ClusterServiceClass definition

```
$ kubectl get serviceclass postgres-database -o yaml
apiVersion: servicecatalog.k8s.io/v1alpha1
bindable: true
brokerName: database-broker                ◁──── This ClusterServiceClass
description: A PostgreSQL database                is provided by the
kind: ClusterServiceClass                         database-broker.
metadata:
  name: postgres-database
  ...
planUpdatable: false
plans:
- description: A free (but slow) PostgreSQL instance
  name: free                                    A free plan for
  osbFree: true                                 this service
  ...
- description: A paid (very fast) PostgreSQL instance
  name: premium                                 A paid plan
  osbFree: false
  ...
```

The ClusterServiceClass in the listing contains two plans—a `free` plan, and a `premium` plan. You can see that this ClusterServiceClass is provided by the `database-broker` broker.

18.2.4 *Provisioning and using a service*

Let's imagine the pods you're deploying need to use a database. You've inspected the list of available ClusterServiceClasses and have chosen to use the `free` plan of the `postgres-database` ClusterServiceClass.

PROVISIONING A SERVICEINSTANCE

To have the database provisioned for you, all you need to do is create a Service-Instance resource, as shown in the following listing.

Listing 18.12   A ServiceInstance manifest: database-instance.yaml

```
apiVersion: servicecatalog.k8s.io/v1alpha1
kind: ServiceInstance
metadata:
  name: my-postgres-db                              ◁── You're giving this
spec:                                                    Instance a name.
  clusterServiceClassName: postgres-database        │ The ServiceClass
  clusterServicePlanName: free                       │ and Plan you want
  parameters:
    init-db-args: --data-checksums                  ◁── Additional parameters
                                                         passed to the broker
```

You created a ServiceInstance called `my-postgres-db` (that will be the name of the resource you're deploying) and specified the ClusterServiceClass and the chosen plan. You're also specifying a parameter, which is specific for each broker and Cluster-ServiceClass. Let's imagine you looked up the possible parameters in the broker's documentation.

As soon as you create this resource, the Service Catalog will contact the broker the ClusterServiceClass belongs to and ask it to provision the service. It will pass on the chosen ClusterServiceClass and plan names, as well as all the parameters you specified.

It's then completely up to the broker to know what to do with this information. In your case, your database broker will probably spin up a new instance of a PostgreSQL database somewhere—not necessarily in the same Kubernetes cluster or even in Kubernetes at all. It could run a Virtual Machine and run the database in there. The Service Catalog doesn't care, and neither does the user requesting the service.

You can check if the service has been provisioned successfully by inspecting the `status` section of the my-postgres-db ServiceInstance you created, as shown in the following listing.

Listing 18.13   Inspecting the status of a ServiceInstance

```
$ kubectl get instance my-postgres-db -o yaml
apiVersion: servicecatalog.k8s.io/v1alpha1
kind: ServiceInstance
...
status:
  asyncOpInProgress: false
  conditions:
```

```
- lastTransitionTime: 2017-05-17T13:57:22Z
  message: The instance was provisioned successfully
  reason: ProvisionedSuccessfully
  status: "True"
  type: Ready
```
The database was provisioned successfully.

It's ready to be used.

A database instance is now running somewhere, but how do you use it in your pods? To do that, you need to bind it.

BINDING A SERVICEINSTANCE

To use a provisioned ServiceInstance in your pods, you create a ServiceBinding resource, as shown in the following listing.

Listing 18.14 A ServiceBinding: my-postgres-db-binding.yaml

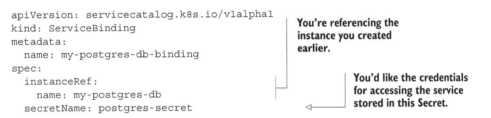

```
apiVersion: servicecatalog.k8s.io/v1alpha1
kind: ServiceBinding
metadata:
  name: my-postgres-db-binding
spec:
  instanceRef:
    name: my-postgres-db
  secretName: postgres-secret
```
You're referencing the instance you created earlier.

You'd like the credentials for accessing the service stored in this Secret.

The listing shows that you're defining a ServiceBinding resource called my-postgres-db-binding, in which you're referencing the my-postgres-db service instance you created earlier. You're also specifying a name of a Secret. You want the Service Catalog to put all the necessary credentials for accessing the service instance into a Secret called postgres-secret. But where are you binding the ServiceInstance to your pods? Nowhere, actually.

Currently, the Service Catalog doesn't yet make it possible to inject pods with the ServiceInstance's credentials. This will be possible when a new Kubernetes feature called PodPresets is available. Until then, you can choose a name for the Secret where you want the credentials to be stored in and mount that Secret into your pods manually.

When you submit the ServiceBinding resource from the previous listing to the Service Catalog API server, the controller will contact the Database broker once again and create a binding for the ServiceInstance you provisioned earlier. The broker responds with a list of credentials and other data necessary for connecting to the database. The Service Catalog creates a new Secret with the name you specified in the ServiceBinding resource and stores all that data in the Secret.

USING THE NEWLY CREATED SECRET IN CLIENT PODS

The Secret created by the Service Catalog system can be mounted into pods, so they can read its contents and use them to connect to the provisioned service instance (a PostgreSQL database in the example). The Secret could look like the one in the following listing.

Listing 18.15   A Secret holding the credentials for connecting to the service instance

```
$ kubectl get secret postgres-secret -o yaml
apiVersion: v1
data:
  host: <base64-encoded hostname of the database>
  username: <base64-encoded username>
  password: <base64-encoded password>
kind: Secret
metadata:
  name: postgres-secret
  namespace: default
  ...
type: Opaque
```

> **This is what the pod should use to connect to the database service.**

Because you can choose the name of the Secret yourself, you can deploy pods before provisioning or binding the service. As you learned in chapter 7, the pods won't be started until such a Secret exists.

If necessary, multiple bindings can be created for different pods. The service broker can choose to use the same set of credentials in every binding, but it's better to create a new set of credentials for every binding instance. This way, pods can be prevented from using the service by deleting the ServiceBinding resource.

18.2.5 *Unbinding and deprovisioning*

Once you no longer need a ServiceBinding, you can delete it the way you delete other resources:

```
$ kubectl delete servicebinding my-postgres-db-binding
servicebinding "my-postgres-db-binding" deleted
```

When you do this, the Service Catalog controller will delete the Secret and call the broker to perform an unbinding operation. The service instance (in your case a PostgreSQL database) is still running. You can therefore create a new ServiceBinding if you want.

But if you don't need the database instance anymore, you should delete the Service-Instance resource also:

```
$ kubectl delete serviceinstance my-postgres-db
serviceinstance "my-postgres-db " deleted
```

Deleting the ServiceInstance resource causes the Service Catalog to perform a deprovisioning operation on the service broker. Again, exactly what that means is up to the service broker, but in your case, the broker should shut down the PostgreSQL database instance that it created when we provisioned the service instance.

18.2.6 *Understanding what the Service Catalog brings*

As you've learned, the Service Catalog enables service providers make it possible to expose those services in any Kubernetes cluster by registering the broker in that cluster.

For example, I've been involved with the Service Catalog since early on and have implemented a broker, which makes it trivial to provision messaging systems and expose them to pods in a Kubernetes cluster. Another team has implemented a broker that makes it easy to provision Amazon Web Services.

In general, service brokers allow easy provisioning and exposing of services in Kubernetes and will make Kubernetes an even more awesome platform for deploying your applications.

18.3 Platforms built on top of Kubernetes

I'm sure you'll agree that Kubernetes is a great system by itself. Given that it's easily extensible across all its components, it's no wonder companies that had previously developed their own custom platforms are now re-implementing them on top of Kubernetes. Kubernetes is, in fact, becoming a widely accepted foundation for the new generation of Platform-as-a-Service offerings.

Among the best-known PaaS systems built on Kubernetes are Deis Workflow and Red Hat's OpenShift. We'll do a quick overview of both systems to give you a sense of what they offer on top of all the awesome stuff Kubernetes already offers.

18.3.1 Red Hat OpenShift Container Platform

Red Hat OpenShift is a Platform-as-a-Service and as such, it has a strong focus on developer experience. Among its goals are enabling rapid development of applications, as well as easy deployment, scaling, and long-term maintenance of those apps. OpenShift has been around much longer than Kubernetes. Versions 1 and 2 were built from the ground up and had nothing to do with Kubernetes, but when Kubernetes was announced, Red Hat decided to rebuild OpenShift version 3 from scratch—this time on top of Kubernetes. When a company such as Red Hat decides to throw away an old version of their software and build a new one on top of an existing technology like Kubernetes, it should be clear to everyone how great Kubernetes is.

Kubernetes automates rollouts and application scaling, whereas OpenShift also automates the actual building of application images and their automatic deployment without requiring you to integrate a Continuous Integration solution into your cluster.

OpenShift also provides user and group management, which allows you to run a properly secured multi-tenant Kubernetes cluster, where individual users are only allowed to access their own Kubernetes namespaces and the apps running in those namespaces are also fully network-isolated from each other by default.

INTRODUCING ADDITIONAL RESOURCES AVAILABLE IN OPENSHIFT

OpenShift provides some additional API objects in addition to all those available in Kubernetes. We'll explain them in the next few paragraphs to give you a good overview of what OpenShift does and what it provides.

The additional resources include

- Users & Groups
- Projects

- Templates
- BuildConfigs
- DeploymentConfigs
- ImageStreams
- Routes
- And others

UNDERSTANDING USERS, GROUPS, AND PROJECTS

We've said that OpenShift provides a proper multi-tenant environment to its users. Unlike Kubernetes, which doesn't have an API object for representing an individual user of the cluster (but does have ServiceAccounts that represent services running in it), OpenShift provides powerful user management features, which make it possible to specify what each user can do and what they cannot. These features pre-date the Role-Based Access Control, which is now the standard in vanilla Kubernetes.

Each user has access to certain Projects, which are nothing more than Kubernetes Namespaces with additional annotations. Users can only act on resources that reside in the projects the user has access to. Access to the project is granted by a cluster administrator.

INTRODUCING APPLICATION TEMPLATES

Kubernetes makes it possible to deploy a set of resources through a single JSON or YAML manifest. OpenShift takes this a step further by allowing that manifest to be parameterizable. A parameterizable list in OpenShift is called a *Template*; it's a list of objects whose definitions can include placeholders that get replaced with parameter values when you process and then instantiate a template (see figure 18.8).

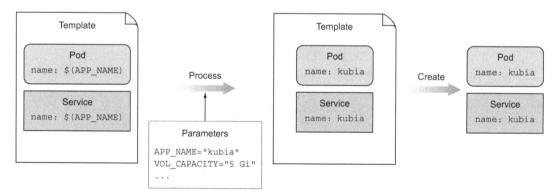

Figure 18.8   OpenShift templates

The template itself is a JSON or YAML file containing a list of parameters that are referenced in resources defined in that same JSON/YAML. The template can be stored in the API server like any other object. Before a template can be instantiated, it needs to be processed. To process a template, you supply the values for the template's parameters and then OpenShift replaces the references to the parameters with those values. The result is a processed template, which is exactly like a Kubernetes resource list that can then be created with a single POST request.

OpenShift provides a long list of pre-fabricated templates that allow users to quickly run complex applications by specifying a few arguments (or none at all, if the template provides good defaults for those arguments). For example, a template can enable the creation of all the Kubernetes resources necessary to run a Java EE application inside an Application Server, which connects to a back-end database, also deployed as part of that same template. All those components can be deployed with a single command.

BUILDING IMAGES FROM SOURCE USING BUILDCONFIGS

One of the best features of OpenShift is the ability to have OpenShift build and immediately deploy an application in the OpenShift cluster by pointing it to a Git repository holding the application's source code. You don't need to build the container image at all—OpenShift does that for you. This is done by creating a resource called Build-Config, which can be configured to trigger builds of container images immediately after a change is committed to the source Git repository.

Although OpenShift doesn't monitor the Git repository itself, a hook in the repository can notify OpenShift of the new commit. OpenShift will then pull the changes from the Git repository and start the build process. A build mechanism called *Source To Image* can detect what type of application is in the Git repository and run the proper build procedure for it. For example, if it detects a pom.xml file, which is used in Java Maven-formatted projects, it runs a Maven build. The resulting artifacts are packaged into an appropriate container image, and are then pushed to an internal container registry (provided by OpenShift). From there, they can be pulled and run in the cluster immediately.

By creating a BuildConfig object, developers can thus point to a Git repo and not worry about building container images. Developers have almost no need to know anything about containers. Once the ops team deploys an OpenShift cluster and gives developers access to it, those developers can develop their code, commit, and push it to a Git repo, the same way they used to before we started packaging apps into containers. Then OpenShift takes care of building, deploying, and managing apps from that code.

AUTOMATICALLY DEPLOYING NEWLY BUILT IMAGES WITH DEPLOYMENTCONFIGS

Once a new container image is built, it can also automatically be deployed in the cluster. This is enabled by creating a DeploymentConfig object and pointing it to an ImageStream. As the name suggests, an ImageStream is a stream of images. When an image is built, it's added to the ImageStream. This enables the DeploymentConfig to notice the newly built image and allows it to take action and initiate a rollout of the new image (see figure 18.9).

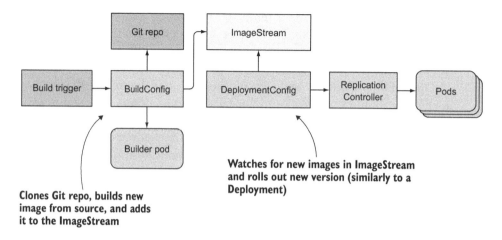

Figure 18.9   BuildConfigs and DeploymentConfigs in OpenShift

A DeploymentConfig is almost identical to the Deployment object in Kubernetes, but it pre-dates it. Like a Deployment object, it has a configurable strategy for transitioning between Deployments. It contains a pod template used to create the actual pods, but it also allows you to configure pre- and post-deployment hooks. In contrast to a Kubernetes Deployment, it creates ReplicationControllers instead of ReplicaSets and provides a few additional features.

EXPOSING SERVICES EXTERNALLY USING ROUTES

Early on, Kubernetes didn't provide Ingress objects. To expose Services to the outside world, you needed to use `NodePort` or `LoadBalancer`-type Services. But at that time, OpenShift already provided a better option through a Route resource. A Route is similar to an Ingress, but it provides additional configuration related to TLS termination and traffic splitting.

Similar to an Ingress controller, a Route needs a Router, which is a controller that provides the load balancer or proxy. In contrast to Kubernetes, the Router is available out of the box in OpenShift.

TRYING OUT OPENSHIFT

If you're interested in trying out OpenShift, you can start by using Minishift, which is the OpenShift equivalent of Minikube, or you can try OpenShift Online Starter at https://manage.openshift.com, which is a free multi-tenant, hosted solution provided to get you started with OpenShift.

18.3.2 *Deis Workflow and Helm*

A company called Deis, which has recently been acquired by Microsoft, also provides a PaaS called Workflow, which is also built on top of Kubernetes. Besides Workflow, they've also developed a tool called Helm, which is gaining traction in the Kubernetes community as a standard way of deploying existing apps in Kubernetes. We'll take a brief look at both.

INTRODUCING DEIS WORKFLOW

You can deploy Deis Workflow to any existing Kubernetes cluster (unlike OpenShift, which is a complete cluster with a modified API server and other Kubernetes components). When you run Workflow, it creates a set of Services and ReplicationControllers, which then provide developers with a simple, developer-friendly environment.

Deploying new versions of your app is triggered by pushing your changes with `git push deis master` and letting Workflow take care of the rest. Similar to OpenShift, Workflow also provides a source to image mechanism, application rollouts and rollbacks, edge routing, and also log aggregation, metrics, and alerting, which aren't available in core Kubernetes.

To run Workflow in your Kubernetes cluster, you first need to install the Deis Workflow and Helm CLI tools and then install Workflow into your cluster. We won't go into how to do that here, but if you'd like to learn more, visit the website at https://deis .com/workflow. What we'll explore here is the Helm tool, which can be used without Workflow and has gained popularity in the community.

DEPLOYING RESOURCES THROUGH HELM

Helm is a package manager for Kubernetes (similar to OS package managers like `yum` or `apt` in Linux or `homebrew` in MacOS).

Helm is comprised of two things:

- A `helm` CLI tool (the client).
- Tiller, a server component running as a Pod inside the Kubernetes cluster.

Those two components are used to deploy and manage application packages in a Kubernetes cluster. Helm application packages are called Charts. They're combined with a Config, which contains configuration information and is merged into a Chart to create a Release, which is a running instance of an application (a combined Chart and Config). You deploy and manage Releases using the `helm` CLI tool, which talks to the Tiller server, which is the component that creates all the necessary Kubernetes resources defined in the Chart, as shown in figure 18.10.

You can create charts yourself and keep them on your local disk, or you can use any existing chart, which is available in the growing list of helm charts maintained by the community at https://github.com/kubernetes/charts. The list includes charts for applications such as PostgreSQL, MySQL, MariaDB, Magento, Memcached, MongoDB, OpenVPN, PHPBB, RabbitMQ, Redis, WordPress, and others.

Similar to how you don't build and install apps developed by other people to your Linux system manually, you probably don't want to build and manage your own Kubernetes manifests for such applications, right? That's why you'll want to use Helm and the charts available in the GitHub repository I mentioned.

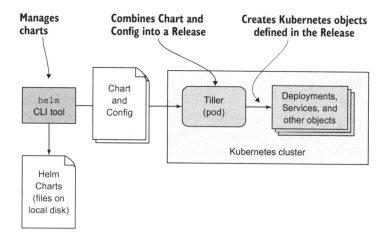

Figure 18.10   Overview of Helm

When you want to run a PostgreSQL or a MySQL database in your Kubernetes cluster, don't start writing manifests for them. Instead, check if someone else has already gone through the trouble and prepared a Helm chart for it.

Once someone prepares a Helm chart for a specific application and adds it to the Helm chart GitHub repo, installing the whole application takes a single one-line command. For example, to run MySQL in your Kubernetes cluster, all you need to do is clone the charts Git repo to your local machine and run the following command (provided you have Helm's CLI tool and Tiller running in your cluster):

```
$ helm install --name my-database stable/mysql
```

This will create all the necessary Deployments, Services, Secrets, and PersistentVolumeClaims needed to run MySQL in your cluster. You don't need to concern yourself with what components you need and how to configure them to run MySQL properly. I'm sure you'll agree this is awesome.

> **TIP** One of the most interesting charts available in the repo is an OpenVPN chart, which runs an OpenVPN server inside your Kubernetes cluster and allows you to enter the pod network through VPN and access Services as if your local machine was a pod in the cluster. This is useful when you're developing apps and running them locally.

These were several examples of how Kubernetes can be extended and how companies like Red Hat and Deis (now Microsoft) have extended it. Now go and start riding the Kubernetes wave yourself!

18.4 Summary

This final chapter has shown you how you can go beyond the existing functionalities Kubernetes provides and how companies like Dies and Red Hat have done it. You've learned how

- Custom resources can be registered in the API server by creating a Custom-ResourceDefinition object.
- Instances of custom objects can be stored, retrieved, updated, and deleted without having to change the API server code.
- A custom controller can be implemented to bring those objects to life.
- Kubernetes can be extended with custom API servers through API aggregation.
- Kubernetes Service Catalog makes it possible to self-provision external services and expose them to pods running in the Kubernetes cluster.
- Platforms-as-a-Service built on top of Kubernetes make it easy to build containerized applications inside the same Kubernetes cluster that then runs them.
- A package manager called Helm makes deploying existing apps without requiring you to build resource manifests for them.

Thank you for taking the time to read through this long book. I hope you've learned as much from reading it as I have from writing it.

appendix A
Using kubectl
with multiple clusters

A.1 Switching between Minikube and Google Kubernetes Engine

The examples in this book can either be run in a cluster created with Minikube, or one created with Google Kubernetes Engine (GKE). If you plan on using both, you need to know how to switch between them. A detailed explanation of how to use kubectl with multiple clusters is described in the next section. Here we look at how to switch between Minikube and GKE.

SWITCHING TO MINIKUBE

Luckily, every time you start up a Minikube cluster with minikube start, it also reconfigures kubectl to use it:

```
$ minikube start
Starting local Kubernetes cluster...
...
Setting up kubeconfig...
Kubectl is now configured to use the cluster.
```

Minikube sets up kubectl every time you start the cluster.

After switching from Minikube to GKE, you can switch back by stopping Minikube and starting it up again. kubectl will then be re-configured to use the Minikube cluster again.

SWITCHING TO GKE

To switch to using the GKE cluster, you can use the following command:

```
$ gcloud container clusters get-credentials my-gke-cluster
```

This will configure kubectl to use the GKE cluster called my-gke-cluster.

These two methods should be enough to get you started quickly, but to understand the complete picture of using `kubectl` with multiple clusters, study the next section.

A.2 Using kubectl with multiple clusters or namespaces

If you need to switch between different Kubernetes clusters, or if you want to work in a different namespace than the default and don't want to specify the `--namespace` option every time you run `kubectl`, here's how to do it.

A.2.1 Configuring the location of the kubeconfig file

The config used by `kubectl` is usually stored in the ~/.kube/config file. If it's stored somewhere else, the KUBECONFIG environment variable needs to point to its location.

> **NOTE** You can use multiple config files and have `kubectl` use them all at once by specifying all of them in the KUBECONFIG environment variable (separate them with a colon).

A.2.2 Understanding the contents of the kubeconfig file

An example config file is shown in the following listing.

Listing A.1   Example kubeconfig file

```
apiVersion: v1
clusters:
- cluster:
    certificate-authority: /home/luksa/.minikube/ca.crt       Contains
    server: https://192.168.99.100:8443                       information about a
  name: minikube                                              Kubernetes cluster
contexts:
- context:
    cluster: minikube                   Defines a
    user: minikube                      kubectl
    namespace: default                  context
  name: minikube
current-context: minikube               The current context
kind: Config                            kubectl uses
preferences: {}
users:
- name: minikube                                              Contains
  user:                                                       a user's
    client-certificate: /home/luksa/.minikube/apiserver.crt   credentials
    client-key: /home/luksa/.minikube/apiserver.key
```

The kubeconfig file consists of four sections:

- A list of clusters
- A list of users
- A list of contexts
- The name of the current context

Each cluster, user, and context has a name. The name is used to refer to the context, user, or cluster.

CLUSTERS

A cluster entry represents a Kubernetes cluster and contains the URL of the API server, the certificate authority (CA) file, and possibly a few other configuration options related to communication with the API server. The CA certificate can be stored in a separate file and referenced in the kubeconfig file, or it can be included in it directly in the `certificate-authority-data` field.

USERS

Each user defines the credentials to use when talking to an API server. This can be a username and password pair, an authentication token, or a client key and certificate. The certificate and key can be included in the kubeconfig file (through the `client-certificate-data` and `client-key-data` properties) or stored in separate files and referenced in the config file, as shown in listing A.1.

CONTEXTS

A context ties together a cluster, a user, and the default namespace `kubectl` should use when performing commands. Multiple contexts can point to the same user or cluster.

THE CURRENT CONTEXT

While there can be multiple contexts defined in the kubeconfig file, at any given time only one of them is the current context. Later we'll see how the current context can be changed.

A.2.3 Listing, adding, and modifying kube config entries

You can edit the file manually to add, modify, and remove clusters, users, or contexts, but you can also do it through one of the `kubectl config` commands.

ADDING OR MODIFYING A CLUSTER

To add another cluster, use the `kubectl config set-cluster` command:

```
$ kubectl config set-cluster my-other-cluster
➥ --server=https://k8s.example.com:6443
➥ --certificate-authority=path/to/the/cafile
```

This will add a cluster called `my-other-cluster` with the API server located at https://k8s.example.com:6443. To see additional options you can pass to the command, run `kubectl config set-cluster` to have it print out usage examples.

If a cluster by that name already exists, the `set-cluster` command will overwrite its configuration options.

ADDING OR MODIFYING USER CREDENTIALS

Adding and modifying users is similar to adding or modifying a cluster. To add a user that authenticates with the API server using a username and password, run the following command:

```
$ kubectl config set-credentials foo --username=foo --password=pass
```

To use token-based authentication, run the following instead:

```
$ kubectl config set-credentials foo --token=mysecrettokenXFDJIQ1234
```

Both these examples store user credentials under the name foo. If you use the same credentials for authenticating against different clusters, you can define a single user and use it with both clusters.

TYING CLUSTERS AND USER CREDENTIALS TOGETHER

A context defines which user to use with which cluster, but can also define the namespace that kubectl should use, when you don't specify the namespace explicitly with the --namespace or -n option.

The following command is used to create a new context that ties together the cluster and the user you created:

```
$ kubectl config set-context some-context --cluster=my-other-cluster
➥ --user=foo --namespace=bar
```

This creates a context called some-context that uses the my-other-cluster cluster and the foo user credentials. The default namespace in this context is set to bar.

You can also use the same command to change the namespace of your current context, for example. You can get the name of the current context like so:

```
$ kubectl config current-context
minikube
```

You then change the namespace like this:

```
$ kubectl config set-context minikube --namespace=another-namespace
```

Running this simple command once is much more user-friendly compared to having to include the --namespace option every time you run kubectl.

> **TIP** To easily switch between namespaces, define an alias like this: alias kcd='kubectl config set-context $(kubectl config current-context) --namespace '. You can then switch between namespaces with kcd some-namespace.

A.2.4 *Using kubectl with different clusters, users, and contexts*

When you run kubectl commands, the cluster, user, and namespace defined in the kubeconfig's current context are used, but you can override them using the following command-line options:

- --user to use a different user from the kubeconfig file.
- --username and --password to use a different username and/or password (they don't need to be specified in the config file). If using other types of authentication, you can use --client-key and --client-certificate or --token.
- --cluster to use a different cluster (must be defined in the config file).

- `--server` to specify the URL of a different server (which isn't in the config file).
- `--namespace` to use a different namespace.

A.2.5   *Switching between contexts*

Instead of modifying the current context as in one of the previous examples, you can also use the `set-context` command to create an additional context and then switch between contexts. This is handy when working with multiple clusters (use `set-cluster` to create cluster entries for them).

Once you have multiple contexts set up, switching between them is trivial:

```
$ kubectl config use-context my-other-context
```

This switches the current context to `my-other-context`.

A.2.6   *Listing contexts and clusters*

To list all the contexts defined in your kubeconfig file, run the following command:

```
$ kubectl config get-contexts
CURRENT   NAME          CLUSTER       AUTHINFO            NAMESPACE
*         minikube      minikube      minikube            default
          rpi-cluster   rpi-cluster   admin/rpi-cluster
          rpi-foo       rpi-cluster   admin/rpi-cluster   foo
```

As you can see, I'm using three different contexts. The `rpi-cluster` and the `rpi-foo` contexts use the same cluster and credentials, but default to different namespaces.

Listing clusters is similar:

```
$ kubectl config get-clusters
NAME
rpi-cluster
minikube
```

Credentials can't be listed for security reasons.

A.2.7   *Deleting contexts and clusters*

To clean up the list of contexts or clusters, you can either delete the entries from the kubeconfig file manually or use the following two commands:

```
$ kubectl config delete-context my-unused-context
```

and

```
$ kubectl config delete-cluster my-old-cluster
```

appendix B
Setting up a multi-node cluster with kubeadm

This appendix shows how to install a Kubernetes cluster with multiple nodes. You'll run the nodes inside virtual machines through VirtualBox, but you can also use a different virtualization tool or bare-metal machines. To set up both the master and the worker nodes, you'll use the `kubeadm` tool.

B.1 Setting up the OS and required packages

First, you need to download and install VirtualBox, if you don't have it installed already. You can download it from https://www.virtualbox.org/wiki/Downloads. Once you have it running, download the CentOS 7 minimal ISO image from www.centos.org/download. You can also use a different Linux distribution, but make sure it's supported by checking the http://kubernetes.io website.

B.1.1 Creating the virtual machine

Next, you'll create the VM for your Kubernetes master. Start by clicking the New icon in the upper-left corner. Then enter "k8s-master" as the name, and select Linux as the Type and Red Hat (64-bit) as the version, as shown in figure B.1.

After clicking the Next button, you can set the VM's memory size and set up the hard disk. If you have enough memory, select at least 2GB (keep in mind you'll run three such VMs). When creating the hard disk, leave the default options selected. Here's what they were in my case:

- Hard disk file type: VDI (VirtualBox Disk Image)
- Storage on physical hard disk: Dynamically allocated
- File location and size: k8s-master, size 8GB

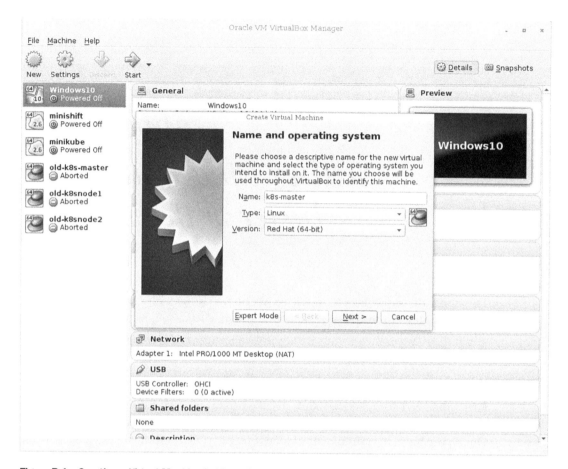

Figure B.1 Creating a Virtual Machine in VirtualBox

B.1.2 Configuring the network adapter for the VM

Once you're done creating the VM, you need to configure its network adapter, because the default won't allow you to run multiple nodes properly. You'll configure the adapter so it uses the Bridged Adapter mode. This will connect your VMs to the same network your host computer is in. Each VM will get its own IP address, the same way as if it were a physical machine connected to the same switch your host computer is connected to. Other options are much more complicated, because they usually require two network adapters to be set up.

To configure the network adapter, make sure the VM is selected in the main Virtual-Box window and then click the Settings icon (next to the New icon you clicked before).

A window like the one shown in figure B.2 will appear. On the left-hand side, select Network and then, in the main panel on the right, select Attached to: Bridged Adapter, as shown in the figure. In the Name drop-down menu, select your host machine's adapter, which you use to connect your machine to the network.

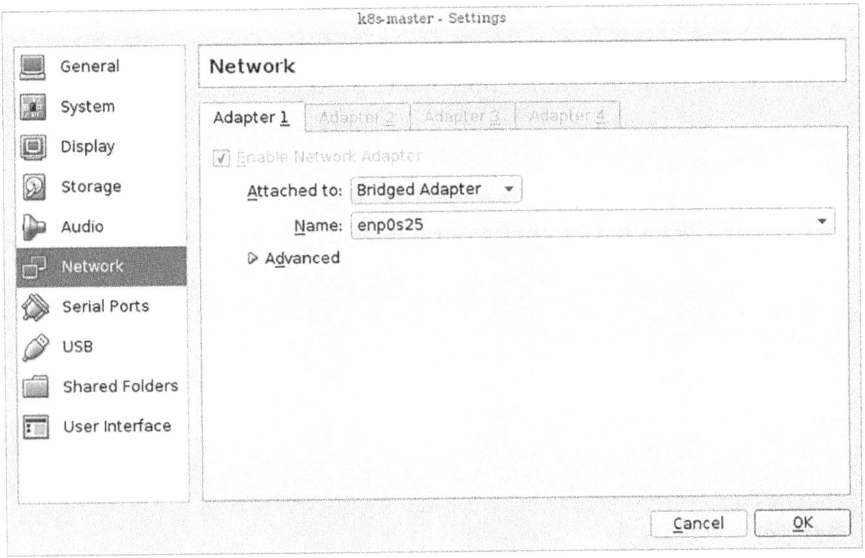

Figure B.2   Configuring the network adapter for the VM

B.1.3   *Installing the operating system*

You're now ready to run the VM and install the operating system. Ensure the VM is still selected in the list and click on the Start icon at the top of the VirtualBox main window.

SELECTING THE START-UP DISK

Before the VM starts up, VirtualBox will ask you what start-up disk to use. Click the icon next to the drop-down list (shown in figure B.3) and then find and select the CentOS ISO image you downloaded earlier. Then click Start to boot up the VM.

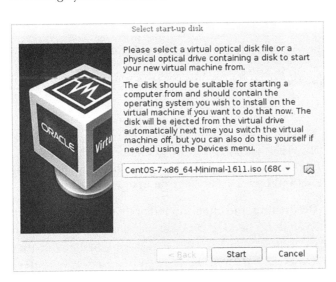

Figure B.3   Selecting the installation ISO image

INITIATING THE INSTALL
When the VM starts up, a textual menu screen will appear. Use the cursor up key to select the Install CentOS Linux 7 option and press the Enter button.

SETTING INSTALLATION OPTIONS
After a few moments, a graphical Welcome to CentOS Linux 7 screen will appear, allowing you to select the language you wish to use. I suggest you keep the language set to English. Click the Continue button to get to the main setup screen as shown in figure B.4.

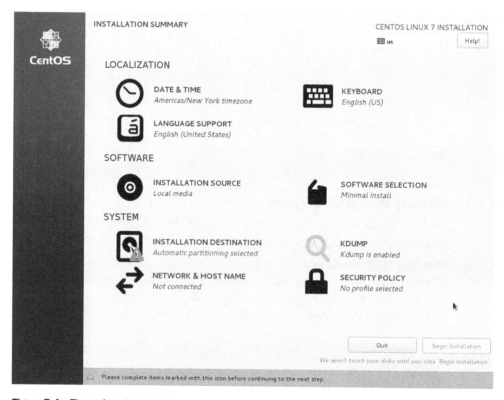

Figure B.4   The main setup screen

TIP When you click into the VM's window, your keyboard and mouse will be captured by the VM. To release them, press the key shown at the bottom-right corner of the VirtualBox window the VM is running in. This is usually the Right Control key on Windows and Linux or the left Command key on MacOS.

First, click Installation Destination and then immediately click the Done button on the screen that appears (you don't need to click anywhere else).

Then click on Network & Host Name. On the next screen, first enable the network adapter by clicking the ON/OFF switch in the top right corner. Then enter the host name into the field at the bottom left, as shown in figure B.5. You're currently setting up the master, so set the host name to master.k8s. Click the Apply button next to the text field to confirm the new host name.

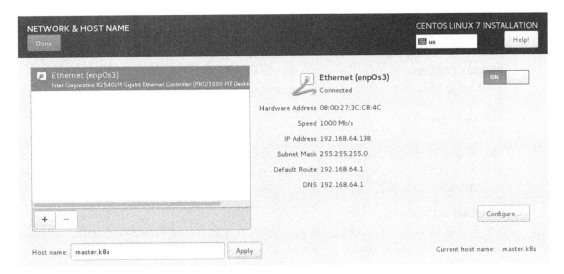

Figure B.5   Setting the hostname and configuring the network adapter

To return to the main setup screen, click the Done button in the top-left corner.

You also need to set the correct time zone. Click Date & Time and then, on the screen that opens, select the Region and City or click your location on the map. Return to the main screen by clicking the Done button in the top-left corner.

RUNNING THE INSTALL

To start the installation, click the Begin Installation button in the bottom-right corner. A screen like the one in figure B.6 will appear. While the OS is being installed, set the

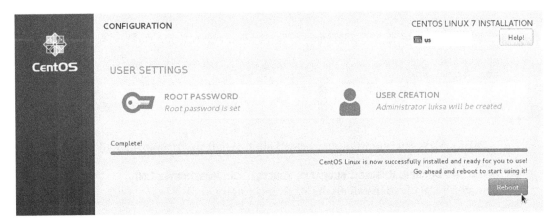

Figure B.6   Setting the root password while the OS is being installed and rebooting afterward

root password and create a user account, if you want. When the installation completes, click the Reboot button at the bottom right.

B.1.4 *Installing Docker and Kubernetes*

Log into the machine as root. First, you need to disable two security features: SELinux and the firewall.

DISABLING SELINUX

To disable SELinux, run the following command:

```
# setenforce 0
```

But this only disables it temporarily (until the next reboot). To disable it permanently, edit the /etc/selinux/config file and change the SELINUX=enforcing line to SELINUX=permissive.

DISABLING THE FIREWALL

You'll also disable the firewall, so you don't run into any firewall-related problems. Run the following command:

```
# systemctl disable firewalld && systemctl stop firewalld
Removed symlink /etc/systemd/system/dbus-org.fedoraproject.FirewallD1...
Removed symlink /etc/systemd/system/basic.target.wants/firewalld.service.
```

ADDING THE KUBERNETES YUM REPO

To make the Kubernetes RPM packages available to the yum package manager, you'll add a kubernetes.repo file to the /etc/yum.repos.d/ directory as shown in the following listing.

Listing B.1 Adding the Kubernetes RPM repo

```
# cat <<EOF > /etc/yum.repos.d/kubernetes.repo
[kubernetes]
name=Kubernetes
baseurl=http://yum.kubernetes.io/repos/kubernetes-el7-x86_64
enabled=1
gpgcheck=1
repo_gpgcheck=1
gpgkey=https://packages.cloud.google.com/yum/doc/yum-key.gpg
        https://packages.cloud.google.com/yum/doc/rpm-package-key.gpg
EOF
```

> **NOTE**   Make sure no whitespace exists after EOF if you're copying and pasting.

INSTALLING DOCKER, KUBELET, KUBEADM, KUBECTL, AND KUBERNETES-CNI

Now you're ready to install all the packages you need:

```
# yum install -y docker kubelet kubeadm kubectl kubernetes-cni
```

As you can see, you're installing quite a few packages. Here's what they are:

- `docker`—The container runtime
- `kubelet`—The Kubernetes node agent, which will run everything for you
- `kubeadm`—A tool for deploying multi-node Kubernetes clusters
- `kubectl`—The command line tool for interacting with Kubernetes
- `kubernetes-cni`—The Kubernetes Container Networking Interface

Once they're all installed, you need to manually enable the `docker` and the `kubelet` services:

```
# systemctl enable docker && systemctl start docker
# systemctl enable kubelet && systemctl start kubelet
```

ENABLING THE NET.BRIDGE.BRIDGE-NF-CALL-IPTABLES KERNEL OPTION

I've noticed that something disables the `bridge-nf-call-iptables` kernel parameter, which is required for Kubernetes services to operate properly. To rectify the problem, you need to run the following two commands:

```
# sysctl -w net.bridge.bridge-nf-call-iptables=1
# echo "net.bridge.bridge-nf-call-iptables=1" > /etc/sysctl.d/k8s.conf
```

DISABLING SWAP

The Kubelet won't run if swap is enabled, so you'll disable it with the following command:

```
# swapoff -a &&  sed -i '/ swap / s/^/#/' /etc/fstab
```

B.1.5 Cloning the VM

Everything you've done up to this point must be done on every machine you plan to use in your cluster. If you're doing this on bare metal, you need to repeat the process described in the previous section at least two more times—for each worker node. If you're building the cluster using virtual machines, now's the time to clone the VM, so you end up with three different VMs.

SHUTTING DOWN THE VM

To clone the machine in VirtualBox, first shut down the VM by running the shutdown command:

```
# shutdown now
```

CLONING THE VM

Now, right-click on the VM in the VirtualBox UI and select Clone. Enter the name for the new machine as shown in figure B.7 (for example, k8s-node1 for the first clone or k8s-node2 for the second one). Make sure you check the Reinitialize the MAC address of all network cards option, so each VM uses different MAC addresses (because they're going to be located in the same network).

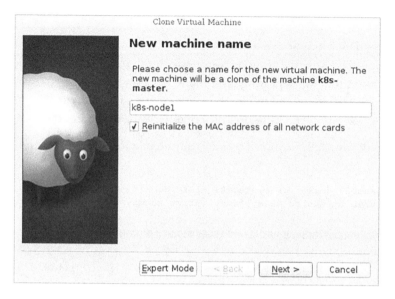

Figure B.7   Cloning the master VM

Click the Next button and then make sure the Full clone option is selected before clicking Next again. Then, on the next screen, click Clone (leave the Current machine state option selected).

Repeat the process for the VM for the second node and then start all three VMs by selecting all three and clicking the Start icon.

CHANGING THE HOSTNAME ON THE CLONED VMS

Because you created two clones from your master VM, all three VMs have the same hostname configured. Therefore, you need to change the hostnames of the two clones. To do that, log into each of the two nodes (as root) and run the following command:

```
# hostnamectl --static set-hostname node1.k8s
```

NOTE   Be sure to set the hostname to node2.k8s on the second node.

CONFIGURING NAME RESOLUTION FOR ALL THREE HOSTS

You need to ensure that all three nodes are resolvable either by adding records to a DNS server or by editing the /etc/hosts file on all of them. For example, you need to add the following three lines to the hosts file (replace the IPs with those of your VMs), as shown in the following listing.

Listing B.2   Entries to add to /etc/hosts on each cluster node

```
192.168.64.138 master.k8s
192.168.64.139 node1.k8s
192.168.64.140 node2.k8s
```

You can get each node's IP by logging into the node as root, running `ip addr` and finding the IP address associated with the enp0s3 network adapter, as shown in the following listing.

```
# ip addr
1: lo: <LOOPBACK,UP,LOWER_UP> mtu 65536 qdisc noqueue state UNKNOWN qlen 1
    link/loopback 00:00:00:00:00:00 brd 00:00:00:00:00:00
    inet 127.0.0.1/8 scope host lo
       valid_lft forever preferred_lft forever
    inet6 ::1/128 scope host
       valid_lft forever preferred_lft forever
2: enp0s3: <BROADCAST,MULTICAST,UP,LOWER_UP> mtu 1500 qdisc pfifo_fast state
    UP qlen 1000
    link/ether 08:00:27:db:c3:a4 brd ff:ff:ff:ff:ff:ff
    inet 192.168.64.138/24 brd 192.168.64.255 scope global dynamic enp0s3
       valid_lft 59414sec preferred_lft 59414sec
    inet6 fe80::77a9:5ad6:2597:2e1b/64 scope link
       valid_lft forever preferred_lft forever
```

The command's output in the previous listing shows that the machine's IP address is 192.168.64.138. You'll need to run this command on each of your nodes to get all their IPs.

B.2 *Configuring the master with kubeadm*

You're now ready to finally set up the Kubernetes Control Plane on your master node.

RUNNING KUBEADM INIT TO INITIALIZE THE MASTER

Thanks to the awesome `kubeadm` tool, all you need to do to initialize the master is run a single command, as shown in the following listing.

Listing B.4 Initializing the master node with kubeadm init

```
# kubeadm init
[kubeadm] WARNING: kubeadm is in beta, please do not use it for production
    clusters.
[init] Using Kubernetes version: v1.8.4
...
You should now deploy a pod network to the cluster.
Run "kubectl apply -f [podnetwork].yaml" with one of the options listed at:
  http://kubernetes.io/docs/admin/addons/

You can now join any number of machines by running the following on each node
    as root:

kubeadm join --token eb3877.3585d0423978c549 192.168.64.138:6443
    --discovery-token-ca-cert-hash
    sha256:037d2c5505294af196048a17f184a79411c7b1eac48aaa0ad137075be3d7a847
```

NOTE Write down the command shown in the last line of kubeadm init's output. You'll need it later.

Kubeadm has deployed all the necessary Control Plane components, including etcd, the API server, Scheduler, and Controller Manager. It has also deployed the kube-proxy, making Kubernetes services available from the master node.

B.2.1   Understanding how kubeadm runs the components

All these components are running as containers. You can use the `docker ps` command to confirm this. But kubeadm doesn't use Docker directly to run them. It deploys their YAML descriptors to the /etc/kubernetes/manifests directory. This directory is monitored by the Kubelet, which then runs these components through Docker. The components run as Pods. You can see them with the `kubectl get` command. But first, you need to configure `kubectl`.

RUNNING KUBECTL ON THE MASTER

You installed `kubectl` along with `docker`, `kubeadm`, and other packages in one of the initial steps. But you can't use `kubectl` to talk to your cluster without first configuring it through a kubeconfig file.

Luckily, the necessary configuration is stored in the /etc/kubernetes/admin.conf file. All you need to do is make `kubectl` use it by setting the KUBECONFIG environment variable, as explained in appendix A:

```
# export KUBECONFIG=/etc/kubernetes/admin.conf
```

LISTING THE PODS

To test `kubectl`, you can list the pods of the Control Plane (they're in the kube-system namespace), as shown in the following listing.

Listing B.5   System pods in the kube-system namespace

```
# kubectl get po -n kube-system
NAME                                      READY    STATUS     RESTARTS    AGE
etcd-master.k8s                           1/1      Running    0           21m
kube-apiserver-master.k8s                 1/1      Running    0           22m
kube-controller-manager-master.k8s        1/1      Running    0           21m
kube-dns-3913472980-cn6kz                 0/3      Pending    0           22m
kube-proxy-qb709                          1/1      Running    0           22m
kube-scheduler-master.k8s                 1/1      Running    0           21m
```

LISTING NODES

You're finished with setting up the master, but you still need to set up the nodes. Although you already installed the Kubelet on both of your two worker nodes (you either installed each node separately or cloned the initial VM after you installed all the required packages), they aren't part of your Kubernetes cluster yet. You can see that by listing nodes with `kubectl`:

```
# kubectl get node
NAME         STATUS      ROLES     AGE      VERSION
master.k8s   NotReady    master    2m       v1.8.4
```

See, only the master is listed as a node. And even the master is shown as being Not-Ready. You'll see why later. Now, you'll set up your two nodes.

B.3 *Configuring worker nodes with kubeadm*

When using kubeadm, configuring worker nodes is even easier than configuring the master. In fact, when you ran the kubeadm init command to set up your master, it already told you how to configure your worker nodes (repeated in the next listing).

Listing B.6 Last part of the output of the kubeadm init command

```
You can now join any number of machines by running the following on each node
    as root:

kubeadm join --token eb3877.3585d0423978c549 192.168.64.138:6443
    --discovery-token-ca-cert-hash
        sha256:037d2c5505294af196048a17f184a79411c7b1eac48aaa0ad137075be3d7a847
```

All you need to do is run the kubeadm join command with the specified token and the master's IP address/port on both of your nodes. It then takes less than a minute for the nodes to register themselves with the master. You can confirm they're registered by running the kubectl get node command on the master again:

```
# kubectl get nodes
NAME          STATUS     ROLES     AGE      VERSION
master.k8s    NotReady   master    3m       v1.8.4
node1.k8s     NotReady   <none>    3s       v1.8.4
node2.k8s     NotReady   <none>    5s       v1.8.4
```

Okay, you've made progress. Your Kubernetes cluster now consists of three nodes, but none of them are ready. Let's investigate.

Let's use the kubectl describe command in the following listing to see more information. Somewhere at the top, you'll see a list of Conditions, showing the current conditions on the node. One of them will show the following Reason and Message.

Listing B.7 Kubectl describe shows why the node isn't ready

```
# kubectl describe node node1.k8s
...
KubeletNotReady        runtime network not ready: NetworkReady=false
                       reason:NetworkPluginNotReady message:docker:
                       network plugin is not ready: cni config uninitialized
```

According to this, the Kubelet isn't fully ready, because the container network (CNI) plugin isn't ready, which is expected, because you haven't deployed the CNI plugin yet. You'll deploy one now.

B.3.1 *Setting up the container network*

You'll install the Weave Net container networking plugin, but several alternatives are also available. They're listed among the available Kubernetes add-ons at http://kubernetes.io/docs/admin/addons/.

Deploying the Weave Net plugin (like most other add-ons) is as simple as this:

```
$ kubectl apply -f "https://cloud.weave.works/k8s/net?k8s-version=$(kubectl
    version | base64 | tr -d '\n')
```

This will deploy a DaemonSet and a few security-related resources (refer to chapter 12 for an explanation of the ClusterRole and ClusterRoleBinding, which are deployed alongside the DaemonSet).

Once the DaemonSet controller creates the pods and they're started on all your nodes, the nodes should become ready:

```
# k get node
NAME         STATUS   ROLES    AGE   VERSION
master.k8s   Ready    master   9m    v1.8.4
node1.k8s    Ready    <none>   5m    v1.8.4
node2.k8s    Ready    <none>   5m    v1.8.4
```

And that's it. You now have a fully functioning three-node Kubernetes cluster with an overlay network provided by Weave Net. All the required components, except for the Kubelet itself, are running as pods, managed by the Kubelet, as shown in the following listing.

Listing B.8 System pods in the kube-system namespace after deploying Weave Net

```
# kubectl get po --all-namespaces
NAMESPACE     NAME                                 READY   STATUS    AGE
kube-system   etcd-master.k8s                      1/1     Running   1h
kube-system   kube-apiserver-master.k8s            1/1     Running   1h
kube-system   kube-controller-manager-master.k8s   1/1     Running   1h
kube-system   kube-dns-3913472980-cn6kz            3/3     Running   1h
kube-system   kube-proxy-hcqnx                      1/1     Running   24m
kube-system   kube-proxy-jvdlr                      1/1     Running   24m
kube-system   kube-proxy-qb709                      1/1     Running   1h
kube-system   kube-scheduler-master.k8s            1/1     Running   1h
kube-system   weave-net-58zbk                      2/2     Running   7m
kube-system   weave-net-91kjd                      2/2     Running   7m
kube-system   weave-net-vt279                      2/2     Running   7m
```

B.4 *Using the cluster from your local machine*

Up to this point, you've used `kubectl` on the master node to talk to the cluster. You'll probably want to configure the `kubectl` instance on your local machine, too.

To do that, you need to copy the /etc/kubernetes/admin.conf file from the master to your local machine with the following command:

```
$ scp root@192.168.64.138:/etc/kubernetes/admin.conf ~/.kube/config2
```

Replace the IP with that of your master. Then you point the KUBECONFIG environment variable to the ~/.kube/config2 file like this:

```
$ export KUBECONFIG=~/.kube/config2
```

Kubectl will now use this config file. To switch back to using the previous one, unset the environment variable.

You're now all set to use the cluster from your local machine.

appendix C
Using other container runtimes

C.1 Replacing Docker with rkt

We've mentioned rkt (pronounced rock-it) a few times in this book. Like Docker, it runs applications in isolated containers, using the same Linux technologies as those used by Docker. Let's look at how rkt differs from Docker and how to try it in Minikube.

The first great thing about rkt is that it directly supports the notion of a Pod (running multiple related containers), unlike Docker, which only runs individual containers. Rkt is based on open standards and was built with security in mind from the start (for example, images are signed, so you can be sure they haven't been tampered with). Unlike Docker, which initially had a client-server based architecture that didn't play well with init systems such as systemd, rkt is a CLI tool that runs your container directly, instead of telling a daemon to run it. A nice thing about rkt is that it can run existing Docker-formatted container images, so you don't need to repackage your applications to get started with rkt.

C.1.1 Configuring Kubernetes to use rkt

As you may remember from chapter 11, the Kubelet is the only Kubernetes component that talks to the Container Runtime. To get Kubernetes to use rkt instead of Docker, you need to configure the Kubelet to use it by running it with the `--container-runtime=rkt` command-line option. But be aware that support for rkt isn't as mature as support for Docker.

Please refer to the Kubernetes documentation for more information on how to use rkt and what is or isn't supported. Here, we'll go over a quick example to get you started.

C.1.2 *Trying out rkt with Minikube*

Luckily, to get started with rkt on Kubernetes, all you need is the same Minikube executable you're already using. To use rkt as the container runtime in Minikube, all you need to do is start Minikube with the following two options:

```
$ minikube start --container-runtime=rkt --network-plugin=cni
```

> **NOTE** You may need to run `minikube delete` to delete the existing Minikube VM first.

The `--container-runtime=rkt` option obviously configures the Kubelet to use rkt as the Container Runtime, whereas the `--network-plugin=cni` makes it use the Container Network Interface as the network plugin. Without this option, pods won't run, so it's imperative you use it.

RUNNING A POD

Once the Minikube VM is up, you can interact with Kubernetes exactly like before. You can deploy the kubia app with the `kubectl run` command, for example:

```
$ kubectl run kubia --image=luksa/kubia --port 8080
deployment "kubia" created
```

When the pod starts up, you can see it's running through rkt by inspecting its containers with `kubectl describe`, as shown in the following listing.

> **Listing C.1 Pod running with rkt**

```
$ kubectl describe pods
Name:          kubia-3604679414-l1nn3
...
Status:        Running
IP:            10.1.0.2
Controllers:   ReplicaSet/kubia-3604679414
Containers:
  kubia:
    Container ID:   rkt://87a138ce-...-96e375852997:kubia     ◁─┐  The container
    Image:          luksa/kubia                                  │  and image IDs
    Image ID:       rkt://sha512-5bbc5c7df6148d30d74e0...    ◁─┤  mention rkt
...                                                              │  instead of
                                                                 │  Docker.
```

You can also try hitting the pod's HTTP port to see if it's responding properly to HTTP requests. You can do this by creating a `NodePort` Service or by using `kubectl port-forward`, for example.

INSPECTING THE RUNNING CONTAINERS IN THE MINIKUBE VM

To get more familiar with rkt, you can try logging into the Minikube VM with the following command:

```
$ minikube ssh
```

Then, you can use `rkt list` to see the running pods and containers, as shown in the following listing.

Listing C.2   Listing running containers with rkt list

```
$ rkt list
UUID       APP               IMAGE NAME                        STATE   ...
4900e0a5   k8s-dashboard     gcr.io/google_containers/kun...   running ...
564a6234   nginx ingr ctrlr  gcr.io/google_containers/ngi...   running ...
5dcafffd   dflt-http-backend gcr.io/google_containers/def...   running ...
707a306c   kube-addon-manager gcr.io/google-containers/kub...  running ...
87a138ce   kubia             registry-1.docker.io/luksa/k...   running ...
d97f5c29   kubedns           gcr.io/google_containers/k8s...   running ...
           dnsmasq           gcr.io/google_containers/k8...
           sidecar           gcr.io/google_containers/k8...
```

You can see the `kubia` container, as well as other system containers running (the ones deployed in pods in the `kube-system` namespace). Notice how the bottom two containers don't have anything listed in the UUID or STATE columns? That's because they belong to the same pod as the `kubedns` container listed above them.

Rkt prints containers belonging to the same pod grouped together. Each pod (instead of each container) has its own UUID and state. If you tried doing this when you were using Docker as the Container Runtime, you'll appreciate how much easier it is to see all the pods and their containers with rkt. You'll notice no infrastructure container exists for each pod (we explained them in chapter 11). That's because of rkt's native support for pods.

LISTING CONTAINER IMAGES

If you've played around with Docker CLI commands, you'll get familiar quickly with rkt's commands. Run `rkt` without any arguments and you'll see all the commands you can run. For example, to list container images, you run the command in the following listing.

Listing C.3   Listing images with rkt image list

```
$ rkt image list
ID             NAME                        SIZE     IMPORT TIME   LAST USED
sha512-a9c3    ...addon-manager:v6.4-beta.1 245MiB   24 min ago    24 min ago
sha512-a078    .../rkt/stage1-coreos:1.24.0 224MiB   24 min ago    24 min ago
sha512-5bbc    ...ker.io/luksa/kubia:latest 1.3GiB   23 min ago    23 min ago
sha512-3931    ...es-dashboard-amd64:v1.6.1  257MiB   22 min ago    22 min ago
sha512-2826    ...ainers/defaultbackend:1.0  15MiB    22 min ago    22 min ago
sha512-8b59    ...s-controller:0.9.0-beta.4  233MiB   22 min ago    22 min ago
sha512-7b59    ...dns-kube-dns-amd64:1.14.2   100MiB   21 min ago    21 min ago
sha512-39c6    ...nsmasq-nanny-amd64:1.14.2   86MiB    21 min ago    21 min ago
sha512-89fe    ...-dns-sidecar-amd64:1.14.2   85MiB    21 min ago    21 min ago
```

These are all Docker-formatted container images. You can also try building images in the OCI image format (OCI stands for Open Container Initiative) with the acbuild tool (available at https://github.com/containers/build) and running them with rkt. Doing that is outside the scope of this book, so I'll let you try it on your own.

The information explained in this appendix so far should be enough to get you started using rkt with Kubernetes. Refer to the rkt documentation at https://coreos .com/rkt and Kubernetes documentation at https://kubernetes.io/docs for additional information.

C.2 Using other container runtimes through the CRI

Kubernetes' support for other container runtimes doesn't stop with Docker and rkt. Both of those runtimes were initially integrated directly into Kubernetes, but in Kubernetes version 1.5, the Container Runtime Interface (CRI) was introduced. CRI is a plugin API enabling easy integration of other container runtimes with Kubernetes. People are now free to plug other container runtimes into Kubernetes without having to dig deep into Kubernetes code. All they need to do is implement a few interface methods.

From Kubernetes version 1.6 onward, CRI is the default interface the Kubelet uses. Both Docker and rkt are now used through the CRI (no longer directly).

C.2.1 Introducing the CRI-O Container Runtime

Beside Docker and rkt, a new CRI implementation called CRI-O allows Kubernetes to directly launch and manage OCI-compliant containers, without requiring you to deploy any additional Container Runtime.

You can try CRI-O with Minikube by starting it with `--container-runtime=crio`.

C.2.2 Running apps in virtual machines instead of containers

Kubernetes is a container orchestration system, right? Throughout the book, we explored many features that show that it's much more than an orchestration system, but the bottom line is that when you run an app with Kubernetes, the app always runs inside a container, right? You may find it surprising that's no longer the case.

New CRI implementations are being developed that allow Kubernetes to run apps in virtual machines instead of in containers. One such implementation, called Frakti, allows you to run regular Docker-based container images directly through a hypervisor, which means each container runs its own kernel. This allows much better isolation between containers compared to when they use the same kernel.

And there's more. Another CRI implementation is the Mirantis Virtlet, which makes it possible to run actual VM images (in the QCOW2 image file format, which is one of the formats used by the QEMU virtual machine tool) instead of container images. When you use the Virtlet as the CRI plugin, Kubernetes spins up a VM for each pod. How awesome is that?

appendix D
Cluster Federation

In the section about high availability in chapter 11 we explored how Kubernetes can deal with failures of individual machines and even failures of whole server racks or the supporting infrastructure. But what if the whole datacenter goes dark?

To make sure you're not susceptible to datacenter-wide outages, apps should be deployed in multiple datacenters or cloud availability zones. When one of those datacenters or availability zones becomes unavailable, client requests can be routed to the apps running in the remaining healthy datacenters or zones.

While Kubernetes doesn't require you to run the Control Plane and the nodes in the same datacenter, you'll almost always want to do that to keep network latency between them low and to reduce the possibility of them becoming disconnected from each other. Instead of having a single cluster spread across multiple locations, a better alternative is to have an individual Kubernetes cluster in every location. We'll explore this approach in this appendix.

D.1   Introducing Kubernetes Cluster Federation

Kubernetes allows you to combine multiple clusters into a cluster of clusters through Cluster Federation. It allows users to deploy and manage apps across multiple clusters running in different locations in the world, but also across different cloud providers combined with on-premises clusters (hybrid cloud). The motivation for Cluster Federation isn't only to ensure high availability, but also to combine multiple heterogeneous clusters into a single super-cluster managed through a single management interface.

For example, by combining an on-premises cluster with one running on a cloud provider's infrastructure, you can run privacy-sensitive components of your application system on-premises, while the non-sensitive parts can run in the cloud. Another example is initially running your application only in a small on-premises cluster, but when the application's compute requirements exceed the cluster's capacity, letting the application spill over to a cloud-based cluster, which is automatically provisioned on the cloud provider's infrastructure.

D.2   *Understanding the architecture*

Let's take a quick look at what Kubernetes Cluster Federation is. A cluster of clusters can be compared to a regular cluster where instead of nodes, you have complete clusters. Just as a Kubernetes cluster consists of a Control Plane and multiple worker nodes, a federated cluster consists of a Federated Control Plane and multiple Kubernetes clusters. Similar to how the Kubernetes Control Plane manages applications across a set of worker nodes, the Federated Control Plane does the same thing, but across a set of clusters instead of nodes.

The Federated Control Plane consists of three things:

- etcd for storing the federated API objects
- Federation API server
- Federation Controller Manager

This isn't much different from the regular Kubernetes Control Plane. etcd stores the federated API objects, the API server is the REST endpoint all other components talk to, and the Federation Controller Manager runs the various federation controllers that perform operations based on the API objects you create through the API server.

Users talk to the Federation API server to create federated API objects (or federated resources). The federation controllers watch these objects and then talk to the underlying clusters' API servers to create regular Kubernetes resources. The architecture of a federated cluster is shown in figure D.1.

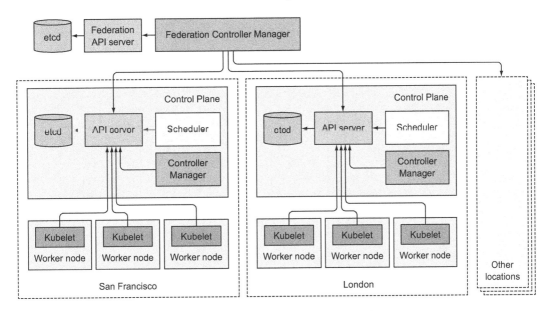

Figure D.1   Cluster Federation with clusters in different geographical locations

D.3   *Understanding federated API objects*

The federated API server allows you to create federated variants of the objects you learned about throughout the book.

D.3.1   *Introducing federated versions of Kubernetes resources*

At the time of writing this, the following federated resources are supported:

- Namespaces
- ConfigMaps and Secrets
- Services and Ingresses
- Deployments, ReplicaSets, Jobs, and Daemonsets
- HorizontalPodAutoscalers

NOTE   Check the Kubernetes Cluster Federation documentation for an up-to-date list of supported federated resources.

In addition to these resources, the Federated API server also supports the Cluster object, which represents an underlying Kubernetes cluster, the same way a Node object represents a worker node in a regular Kubernetes cluster. To help you visualize how federated objects relate to the objects created in the underlying clusters, see figure D.2.

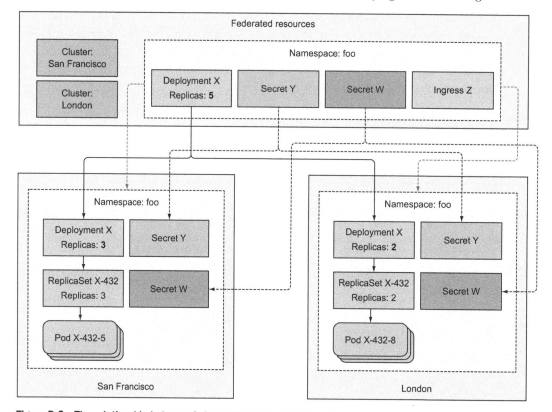

Figure D.2   The relationship between federated resources and regular resources in underlying clusters

D.3.2 *Understanding what federated resources do*

For part of the federated objects, when you create the object in the Federation API server, the controllers running in the Federation Controller Manager will create regular cluster-scoped resources in all underlying Kubernetes clusters and manage them until the federated object is deleted.

For certain federated resource types, the resources created in the underlying clusters are exact replicas of the federated resource; for others, they're slightly modified versions, whereas certain federated resources don't cause anything to be created in the underlying clusters at all. The replicas are kept in sync with the original federated versions. But the synchronization is one-directional only—from the federation server down to the underlying clusters. If you modify the resource in an underlying cluster, the changes will not be synced up to the Federation API server.

For example, if you create a namespace in the federated API server, a namespace with the same name will be created in all underlying clusters. If you then create a federated ConfigMap inside that namespace, a ConfigMap with that exact name and contents will be created in all underlying clusters, in the same namespace. This also applies to Secrets, Services, and DaemonSets.

ReplicaSets and Deployments are different. They aren't blindly copied to the underlying clusters, because that's not what the user usually wants. After all, if you create a Deployment with a desired replica count of 10, you probably don't want 10 pod replicas running in each underlying cluster. You want 10 replicas in total. Because of this, when you specify a desired replica count in a Deployment or ReplicaSet, the Federation controllers create underlying Deployments/ReplicaSets so that the sum of their desired replica counts equals the desired replica count specified in the federated Deployment or ReplicaSet. By default, the replicas are spread evenly across the clusters, but this can be overridden.

> **NOTE** Currently, you need to connect to each cluster's API server individually to get the list of pods running in that cluster. You can't list all the clusters' pods through the Federated API server.

A federated Ingress resource, on the other hand, doesn't result in the creation of any Ingress objects in the underlying clusters. You may remember from chapter 5 that an Ingress represents a single point of entry for external clients to a Service. Because of this, a federated Ingress resource creates a global, multi-cluster-wide entry point to the Services across all underlying clusters.

> **NOTE** As for regular Ingresses, a federated Ingress controller is required for this.

Setting up federated Kubernetes clusters is outside the scope of this book, so you can learn more about the subject by referring to the Cluster Federation sections in the user and administration guides in the Kubernetes online documentation at http:// kubernetes.io/docs/.

index